THE STRENGTH OF THE WOLF

THE STRENGTH OF THE WOLF

The Secret History of America's War on Drugs

◆

DOUGLAS VALENTINE

VERSO

London • New York

First published by Verso 2004
© Douglas Valentine 2004
All rights reserved

The moral rights of the author have been asserted

1 3 5 7 9 10 8 6 4 2

Verso
UK: 6 Meard Street, London W1F 0EG
USA: 180 Varick Street, New York, NY 10014−4606
www.versobooks.com

Verso is the imprint of New Left Books

ISBN 1−85984−568−1

British Library Cataloguing in Publication Data
Valentine, Douglas,
   The strength of the wolf: the secret history of America's war on drugs
   1. United States. Federal Bureau of Narcotics − History
   2. Drug traffic − Investigation − United States − History
   I. Title
   363.4'5'0973
   ISBN 1859845681

Library of Congress Cataloging-in-Publication Data
Valentine, Douglas, 1949−
   The strength of the wolf: the secret history of America's war on
   drugs / Douglas Valentine.
      p. cm.
   Includes bibliographical references and index.
   ISBN 1-85984-568-1 (hardcover: alk. paper)
   1. United States. Bureau of Narcotics − History. 2. Narcotics, Control
   of − United States − History. 3. Drug traffic − United States − History.
   I. Title.
   HV5825.V25 2004
   363.45'0973'0904−dc22
                                                          2003027102

Typeset in Bembo
Printed in the USA by R. R. Donnelley & Sons

to Alice,
with love

CONTENTS

CAST OF MAIN CHARACTERS

Acampora, Colonel Tulius – US Army counterintelligence officer assigned to Rome and Saigon; confidant of Charles Siragusa and Henry Manfredi; friend of Andrew Tartaglino, Michael Picini, Fred Dick and John Cusack.

Amato, Joseph – Joined the FBN before the Second World War; was the original leader of the International Group and its forerunner, the Mafia Squad; was the respected and knowledgeable leader of Enforcement Group Four in New York until his transfer to Boston in 1964.

Angleton, James J. – Worked with George White and Charlie Siragusa in the OSS; was chief of counterintelligence at the CIA, and in that capacity was the CIA's liaison to FBN agents Charlie Siragusa and Hank Manfredi; was also in touch with the Mafia through labor lawyer Mario Brod, and, through his staff, with the Israeli intelligence service, the Mossad.

Anslinger, Harry J. – Employee of the Pennsylvania Railroad Police; joined the State Department in 1918, served at the Hague, in Hamburg, Venezuela and Bermuda; brought by his wife's uncle, Andrew Mellon, into the Treasury Department in 1926 as chief of the Prohibition Unit's Division of Foreign Control; Commissioner of the Federal Bureau of Narcotics, 1930–1962. Shaped the FBN's policies and procedures in his own image.

Attie, James – Honest, dedicated, much decorated undercover agent who worked alone in the Middle East, Europe, and Mexico, as well as Chicago and New York. Adversary of Anslinger and Charlie Siragusa; believed the Mossad was involved in drug trafficking.

Belk, George M. – Joined the FBN in 1948; worked with Howard Chappell on an integrity case in Chicago; became district supervisor in Chicago in 1958; aligned with Henry Giordano against George Gaffney; became district supervisor in New York in 1963; managed the CIA's safehouse in New York, and became embroiled in Andy Tartaglino's anti-corruption investigation, 1967–68.

Benjamin, Mortimer L. – Worked in New York on the French Connection, Castellani–Brown, and Nebbia cases, among others, and was a close friend and partner of Lenny Schrier, perhaps the FBN's most effective case-making agent.

Biase, Patrick – Undercover agent in the Cotroni and Air France cases in Canada and France; member of the Gambling Squad and the Gaffney–Ward–Dolce clique that competed with Lenny Schrier in New York.

Bransky, Joseph – Arrested Lucky Luciano in 1923 as a member of the Prohibition Unit's Narcotics Division; known as the dean of the FBN's district supervisors; served most of his career in Philadelphia.

Chappell, Howard W. – A decorated OSS veteran; met Garland Williams at the OSS training school and was hired by Williams into the FBN in 1947; befriended by George White; served as an agent in Cleveland, New York, Houston, and Toledo, and as agent in charge in Los Angeles; made many undercover cases in Mexico; resigned rather than accept a transfer to New York in 1961.

Coursey, John T. – Very successful undercover agent in New York for many years; responsible with Jack Peterson for the "panic" of 1962.

Cunningham, George W. – Agent in the 1920s in many locations, and in the FBN served as district supervisor in New Orleans and New York; would finance undercover agents out of his own pocket; friend of vice president Alben Barkley; respected Deputy Commissioner of the FBN from 1949 until his death in 1958; Anslinger's liaison to the Democrats on Capitol Hill.

Cusack, John T. – Accompanied Charlie Siragusa to Rome in 1951; leader of the Court House Squad in New York; district supervisor in Atlanta, Rome, and Kansas City; later chief of foreign operations at FBN headquarters.

Davis, William B. – Outstanding undercover agent in New York, Detroit, and Europe; resigned from the FBN in 1959 over Anslinger's policies toward Black agents and addicts; joined the United States Information Agency.

DeFauw, Robert J. – Talented agent, started in Chicago; assigned to Marseilles in 1965; participated in many important cases across Europe.

Dick, Fred T. – Agent in New York and Kansas City until 1958, then field inspector investigating agent wrongdoing; participated in Lee Speer's thwarted investigation of agent wrongdoing in New York in 1961; a Giordano loyalist, he replaced Chappell as agent in charge of Los Angeles and later replaced George White as district supervisor in San Francisco.

Dolce, John M. – Always in New York as an agent, as leader of Enforcement Group Three, and as enforcement assistant to George Belk until his transfer to Miami in 1965, after which he quit the FBN; instrumental in the Cotroni case with his mentor, Pat Ward and his friend, Patty Biase; Lenny Schrier's archrival.

Dolce, Frank – Well-liked veteran of the Second World War; John Dolce's brother; a member of the Gambling Squad and Group Three; later joined the Nassau County Sheriff's office and was arrested with his partner Jack Gohde for selling heroin.

Dunagan, Richard J. – Started his career as a Spanish-speaking federal agent in the Border Patrol, then joined the FBN in Miami; in 1964 was the third FBN agent assigned to Mexico.

Durkin, William J. – Joined the FBN in Pennsylvania; agent in charge in Pittsburgh; was George Belk's enforcement assistant in Chicago starting in 1958; did a review of Lee Speer's corruption investigation in New York in late 1961, and exonerated the New York agents; opened the FBN's first office in Mexico City in 1962 and remained there until 1967.

Dyar, Charles B. – Joined the State Department in 1906; met Anslinger at the Hague in 1918; served in the Narcotics Division of the Prohibition Unit; recruited by Anslinger into the Flying Squad of the Division of Foreign Control; recruited by Anslinger into the FBN in 1930 to run European operations; worked briefly for Customs, back into the FBN, then to the OSS, back to the FBN; no records about his service after 1947.

Enright, John R. – Agent in New York; managed the Genovese case at the Court House Squad; district supervisor in Atlanta; consultant to the McClellan Committee; acting district supervisor in New York; the FBN's assistant for enforcement at headquarters under Henry Giordano.

Evans, John G. – Agent and enforcement assistant under district supervisor Ross Ellis in Detroit and a member of Detroit's "Purple Gang"; district supervisor in Atlanta; a member of Andy Tartaglino's Task Force that investigated agent corruption in New York in 1968.

Feldman, Ira – Army counterintelligence officer in Korea; hired into the FBN in 1955 in San Francisco where he managed, under George White's direction, a CIA MKULTRA Program safehouse; later an agent and group leader in New York.

Fitzgerald, Benjamin – Respected agent and group leader in New York; confidant of James C. Ryan; head of the Court House Squad in the mid-1960s.

Fluhr, Arthur J. – Always in New York, as an agent, group leader, and executive assistant to District Supervisor George Belk. Demoted in October 1967 after the "Day of Infamy."

Frias, Ralph – Successful and multilingual undercover agent in Los Angeles, then Europe, especially in Sicily. Resigned in 1958.

Gaffney, George H. – Protégé of Pat Ward; agent, group leader, and first representative to the Court House Squad in New York; district supervisor in Atlanta (1956–57) and New York (1958–62); brought by Bobby Kennedy to Washington as the FBN's enforcement assistant in 1962; in 1964 became Deputy Commissioner under Henry Giordano. Led the New York office from 1958 to 1962 during its most successful case-making era.

Gentry, Ernest M. – An agent in New York right after the war; district supervisor in San Francisco and Dallas; deputy assistant for administration at FBN headquarters, 1965–68.

Giordano, Henry L. – Pharmacist and agent in Seattle; agent in charge in Minneapolis; district supervisor in Kansas City; served as a consultant to the Boggs Committee; field supervisor, enforcement assistant, Deputy Commissioner, and from 1962 to 1968 Commissioner of the FBN.

Gohde, Jack L. – Member of Group Three and the Gambling Squad; quit the FBN to join the Nassau County Sheriff's office; arrested with Frank Dolce for selling heroin.

Gonzalez, Angel L. – Successful and well-liked undercover agent in New York, Miami and New Orleans; caught up in Tartaglino's Task Force investigation in 1968.

Greenfeld, Irwin – Agent in New York before the war; well-liked group leader in New York; acting district supervisor in New York; district supervisor in Baltimore; field supervisor at Washington headquarters investigating agent wrongdoing.

Habib, Albert – Former Tunisian policeman; recruited by Ike Feldman into the FBN in 1955; an agent and manager of a MKULTRA safehouse in San Francisco; an agent in Bangkok and throughout Southeast Asia starting in 1964.

Harney, Malachi L. – In the early 1920s served as a supervisor in the IRS Intelligence Unit; established a reputation as a "gang buster" while overseeing Eliot Ness and the legendary Untouchables in their successful pursuit of Al Capone in Chicago; served in Anslinger's Flying Squad, and as FBN enforcement assistant until the mid-1950s, when he was appointed assistant to the Treasury Secretary for law enforcement.

Hayes, Crofton J. – Agent in New York; agent in charge of the Newark field office; died under mysterious circumstances of a heroin overdose in September 1953.

Knight, Paul E. – Agent in New York; joined Siragusa in Rome in 1952; first agent in charge in Beirut in 1954; helped make the First Ambassador case in 1960, then assigned to Paris; joined the CIA in 1963 and returned to Beirut where he worked undercover as an FBN agent and chief of security for Pan Am.

Manfredi, Henry L. – As an Army CID agent worked with Charlie Siragusa in Italy in 1950; joined the FBN in 1951; was an FBN and CIA agent in Rome until 1967, when he returned to work at FBN headquarters as chief of foreign operations, as well as other capacities.

Mangiaracina, Anthony – Known as "Tony Grapes", did the undercover work for Schrier on the Orlandino case; transferred to Rome in 1959; then back to New York in 1961; jumped to BDAC in 1966.

Maria, Victor G. – Joined the FBN in San Francisco; studied under Howard Chappell in Los Angeles; fluent in Lebanese; replaced Paul Knight in Paris and made many cases across Europe; involved in the controversial Ben Barka Affair of 1965.

Marshall, Eugene J. – Agent in New York; agent in charge of Miami; arrested in Miami in 1965 for taking bribes.

McDonnell, Charles R. – Undercover agent and member of Group Three in New York, then in Los Angeles; jumped to BDAC; was arrested and imprisoned for selling heroin in 1968.

O'Carroll, Patrick P. – Agent in New York; chief of the Treasury Department's training school in Washington.

Oyler, Ralph H. – Top narcotic agent of the 1920s, he made the case through which the Supreme Court found latent police powers in the Harrison Narcotic Act; made the case that led to the Jones–Miller Act of 1922, which standardized licensing and registration practices, and provided for a federal narcotics commission, later chaired by Anslinger, which controlled the importation and exportation of narcotics; district supervisor in New York and Chicago in old Narcotics Division; FBN district supervisor in Detroit until his death in 1947.

Panich, Walter – Joined the FBN in 1942 as a clerk in Detroit and became an agent in 1948; served almost continually in Detroit until Henry Giordano brought him to headquarters in late 1961 as his personal assistant on administrative matters.

Pera, Martin F. – Joined the FBN in Chicago; traveled to Europe with Charlie Siragusa in 1951; worked on a special case with George White in 1952; leader of the International Group in New York; acting district supervisor in Rome in 1961; consultant to the McClellan Committee; resigned and joined the Office of Naval Intelligence in 1963.

Picini, Michael G. – An undercover agent in New York, Washington, DC, and California; then group leader in New York; then district supervisor in Boston; district supervisor in Rome under Commissioner Henry Giordano from 1963 until 1968.

Pohl, Anthony S. – A French-speaking agent recruited into the FBN from the Army CID in 1960; sent to Paris in 1961 and established the FBN's first official office in Marseilles in 1962; transferred to Chicago in 1963.

Salmi, Richard E. – Joined the FBN in Los Angeles, worked undercover there and in Mexico and Las Vegas; involved in the controversial Bobby Baker wiretapping incident; transferred to Turkey in 1966 where he made many important undercover cases.

Schrier, Leonard S. – Considered by many to be the premier case-making agent in New York; competed with the Gaffney–Ward–Dolce clique;

leader of Enforcement Groups One and Two in 1964, and the International Group from 1965 until his resignation in 1967.

Seifer, Matthew – Pharmacist and agent in the FBN before the Second World War; served in New York, Buffalo and Boston.

Selvaggi, Francis J. – Controversial agent married to Charlie Siragusa's niece, made the Joe Valachi case and the Rinaldo–Palmieri case; targeted by the FBI as a result of the Valachi case; accused by Valachi of being a member of the Bronx mob; resigned in 1967 rather than take a transfer to San Francisco; perhaps the greatest case-making agent of his era.

Siragusa, Charles – Joined the FBN before the Second World War; protégé of George White; served in the OSS; group leader in New York; opened the FBN's first overseas office in Rome in 1951; became the FBN's liaison to the CIA in 1959 when he returned to Washington as field supervisor; competed with Giordano to replace Anslinger as Commissioner, served as Deputy Commissioner until his retirement in December 1963.

Speer, Wayland L. – A pharmacist and agent in Texas; served in Japan for four years after the Second World War; field supervisor investigating agent wrongdoing; and a consultant to the Daniel Committee; as enforcement assistant at headquarters, launched a corruption investigation in New York in 1961; his investigation failed and he became district supervisor in Denver.

Tartaglino, Andrew C. – Started as an agent in New York, went to Rome in 1956 and became Charlie Siragusa's protégé; opened the Paris office in 1959 and helped make the First Ambassador case; member of the New York Court House Squad; Gaffney's assistant at headquarters before his transfer to Main Treasury where, in 1965, he organized a corruption investigation focused on the New York agents. The investigation began in earnest in 1967 and climaxed in 1968 with the formation of a four-member Task Force that helped bring about the FBN's abolition in April 1968.

Taylor, Bowman – An agent in Texas until his transfer to Bangkok, where he opened the FBN's first office in the Far East in 1963; while working undercover in Vientiane, arrested General Vang Pao, head of the CIA's secret army in Laos, for selling fifty kilograms of morphine base; expelled from Laos by the CIA as a result; a member of Tartaglino's Task Force that investigated agent corruption in New York in 1968.

Taylor, Thomas P. – Former NYPD detective and IRS inspector, became an FBN agent in 1967 to work for Andy Tartaglino during his corruption investigation in New York.

Tripodi, Thomas C. – First an FBN agent in New York, then an assistant to Charlie Siragusa at headquarters; joined the CIA for five years; returned to the FBN in 1967 to work for Andy Tartaglino during his corruption investigation in New York.

Vizzini, Salvatore – Joined the FBN in Atlanta in 1953; transferred to New York in 1955 and to Miami in 1957; performed lots of undercover work in Cuba; assigned to Rome in 1959, where he made a case on several of Lucky Luciano's associates; opened the FBN's first office in Istanbul in 1961; worked in Bangkok before Bowman Taylor; returned to Miami and went on disability after getting mugged in Puerto Rico; resigned in 1966.

Ward, Charles G. – Joined the FBN in New York as a clerk; leader of Enforcement Group Three and mentor to many of the FBN's finest agents, including George Gaffney and John Dolce; enforcement assistant to New York district supervisors Ryan and Gaffney; head of the Gambling Squad; district supervisor in Chicago starting in 1964.

Waters, Francis E. – The agent most responsible for the 1962 French Connection case, later a group leader; a target of Andy Tartaglino, he resigned in 1967 rather than take a transfer to Texas; tried and acquitted of selling to Charlie McDonnell a small portion of the heroin from the French Connection case that may have gone astray.

White, George H. – Perhaps the FBN's most flamboyant and controversial character, his claim to fame was making the 1937 Hip Sing T'ong case; joined the OSS in 1942 and worked with James Angleton in counter-intelligence; also worked on OSS Truth Drug operations; after the war served as district supervisor in Chicago, Detroit, and San Francisco; in 1951 he hoped to become New York's district supervisor, but the job went to James C. Ryan, so he took a contract with the CIA and managed its MKULTRA safehouse in New York until 1954; became the FBN's supervisor at large; in 1955 became district supervisor in San Francisco, where he ran three CIA safehouses until his retirement in 1965.

Williams, Garland H. – Joined the customs service in 1929, worked for Anslinger in the Flying Squad on some of the Foreign Control Board's most important cases; in 1936 negotiated an anti-smuggling agreement that allowed Treasury agents to operate inside Mexico, and formed the

Southwest Border Patrol in El Paso; in 1937 became the FBN's district supervisor in New York; left the FBN in 1941 to organize the Army's Counterintelligence Corps; joined the OSS in 1942 in a senior position; returned to New York in 1945 as district supervisor; left the FBN in 1951 to organize and command the Army's 525th Military Intelligence Group; in 1952 became assistant Commissioner of the IRS Intelligence Division, fired in late 1953 for some unknown reason, and vanished for two years; surfaced as a narcotic specialist for the State Department's Office of Public Safety, where he remained until retiring in 1964.

Wurms, Ivan – Narcotic detective in Washington, in 1953 assigned to the US Attorney investigating Garland Williams and problems at FBN headquarters; joined the FBN in 1956; worked with Frank Selvaggi on the Valachi investigation; later worked as inspector with Andy Tartaglino investigating agent wrongdoing in New York, 1967–68.

Zirilli, Anthony – Perhaps the greatest FBN undercover agent ever, worked on top Mafiosi in New York and Europe; worked with Howard Chappell on an integrity investigation in the Chicago area in 1956; later targeted himself in New Orleans; said to Jim Attie, "They can't pay me enough to do this job." Then quit the FBN in disgust rather than apologize to Giordano.

INTRODUCTION

A writer's research can take him to unexpected places, and I had little idea of my final destination when I began work on *The Strength of the Wolf.*

Over ten years ago, I started researching a book about the CIA's infiltration and subversion of the Drug Enforcement Administration (DEA). I had just finished writing a book about the CIA's Phoenix Program in Vietnam, and I knew that with the gradual reduction of forces there, many CIA officers had been transferred to other government agencies, and that a few were filtered into the DEA and the DEA's predecessor organization, the Bureau of Narcotics and Dangerous Drugs (BNDD), which existed from April 1968 until the DEA was created in July 1973. I was curious to know how these officers were put to use in the war on drugs and who was really giving them their orders.

A retired colonel, Tully Acampora, was my entrée into the arcane underworld of spies, drug smugglers, and narcotic agents. Tully had worked closely with the CIA's Phoenix Program in South Vietnam, and he told me that he had funneled some junior CIA officers into the BNDD and the DEA through his old friend Andrew Tartaglino. Before going to work for the CIA in Vietnam in 1966, Tully had served for seven years in Italy, and during that time he had come to know Andy Tartaglino, as well as Andy's mentors in the Federal Bureau of Narcotics (FBN), Charlie Siragusa and Hank Manfredi.

The FBN is the main subject of this book. It existed from 1930 until 1968, and it was the federal drug law enforcement agency that preceded the BNDD and DEA. Charlie Siragusa and Hank Manfredi established the FBN's first overseas office in Rome in 1951, and Andy Tartaglino joined them there in 1956.

Tully's insights into the personalities and activities of Siragusa and Manfredi, and several other FBN agents, were invaluable contributions to this book, as was his introduction to Andy Tartaglino. A member of the FBN since 1952, Andy rose steadily through the ranks and reorganizations of federal drug law enforcement until July 1973, when he was named the DEA's first chief inspector. Shortly after his appointment to this critical position, Andy initiated a controversial corruption investigation that culminated in 1975 with sensational hearings before a Senate committee. Among other things, there were allegations that a CIA assassination squad, staffed by former Phoenix personnel, existed inside the DEA's Special Operations Unit. I wanted to know if those allegations were true.

As a favor for Tully, Andy agreed to tell me about his corruption investigation, and the role the CIA played in it. We began by discussing a Justice Department report that enumerated the charges Andy had brought against several of the DEA's senior officials, and about forty DEA agents, most of whom had started in the FBN.

During our interviews, Andy made it clear that in order to understand the DEA's integrity problems, I had to learn how they originated in the FBN. Having been a "shoofly" (Bureau jargon for an inspector who investigates agent wrongdoing) in the FBN, Andy knew almost everything about this subject, and it was through him that I first heard about the fascinating characters who appear in the pages that follow – the "case-making" agents he targeted, and the executive officers he contended with, back in the rough-and-tumble days of the FBN. And that's when I seriously considered writing this book.

Before I could begin work on it, however, I first had to find and interview the old FBN agents, and that was no easy task. But Tully came through once again and introduced me to Fred Dick, the first federal narcotic agent assigned to South Vietnam. Tully and Fred had met and become friends in Saigon, and Fred provided me with a book listing the names and addresses of the members of the Association of Former Federal Narcotics Agents. One thing led to another and, with very few exceptions, the agents I located were agreeable and eagerly discussed everything that contributed to the FBN's successes and failures. It didn't take long to realize that I had a chance to do something truly original: that these FBN agents were a new cast of characters on America's historical stage, and that their collective recollections were a priceless contribution to American history.

The Strength of the Wolf is the first non-fiction book to thoroughly document the history of the FBN, from its birth in 1930 to its wrenching termination in 1968. It is based largely on interviews with agents, but their recollections are set within the context of the full extent of literary sources on the subject of federal drug law enforcement. There were never more than 350 agents in the FBN at any time, and I've refined the book by focusing on the most outstanding agents and their cases.

The moral to their story is simple: in the process of penetrating the Mafia and the French connection, the case-making agents uncovered the Establishment's ties to organized crime; and that was their great undoing. That's also where the CIA comes into the picture. This book shows that federal drug law enforcement is essentially a function of national security, as that term is applied in its broadest sense: that is, not just defending America from its foreign enemies, but preserving its traditional values of class, race, and gender at home, while expanding its economic and military influence abroad. This book documents the evolution of this unstated policy and analyzes its impact on drug law enforcement and American society.

The Strength of the Wolf weaves together the FBN's most significant cases with its political, bureaucratic, and national security-related problems, while progressing through two major integrity investigations. The first integrity investigation began in 1960 and arose from a power struggle among senior FBN executives vying to replace Harry J. Anslinger, the FBN's prestigious Commissioner from 1930 until 1962. The second investigation, which Andy Tartaglino initiated in 1965, reflected a struggle at the highest levels of government for control over the direction of federal drug law enforcement.

Apart from the integrity issue, there are two main themes in the book. The first is the FBN's overseas expansion and subversion by the CIA. The second is its fatal clash with the FBI. Sadly, the CIA and FBI were often protecting the FBN's targets in the Mafia and the French connection. Likewise, the CIA and its Nationalist Chinese allies operated the world's largest drug-trafficking syndicate, but for political and national security reasons, the FBN was prevented from investigating this overarching conspiracy.

The Strength of the Wolf integrates these and several lesser themes and culminates in 1968 when, in the wake of Andy Tartaglino's second corruption investigation, the FBN was merged with another federal agency and renamed the Bureau of Narcotics and Dangerous Drugs.

The tension that binds the book stems from three things: the tempting and often terrifying nature of undercover work; the provocative relationship agents have with their mercenary informants; and the subordination of FBN executives and case-making agents to spies, politicians, and influential drug traffickers. This is very heavy stuff, and the CIA did its best to prevent me from writing this book. It tried to prevent Andy Tartaglino from discussing the role it played in his integrity investigations, and told several other agents not to discuss with me its infiltration and subtle behind-the-scenes control of the FBN.

Luckily, many federal narcotic agents aren't intimidated or even impressed by the CIA. For example, in 1994 I was granted permission to interview Steve Green, the acting administrator of the DEA. Green's public affairs officer met me in the lobby of the DEA building, brought me upstairs to the executive suite, sat me down on a sofa and got me a cup of coffee. There were a few things he wanted to ask me in the ten minutes we had before the interview. He wanted to know what my questions were going to be, and when I told him what they were, he thought they were fine. Next he asked me about the book I'd written about the CIA's Phoenix Program. I answered his questions forthrightly, and he was pleased. Then he sat down on the sofa beside me and said, "I'm going to tell you something, and if you tell anyone, I'll deny I ever said it. Understand?"

"Yes," I said.

His eyes twinkled. "The CIA called yesterday. They knew you were coming and they asked us to cancel the interview. They said you're trying to get at them, through us. Is that true?"

"I'm writing a book about federal drug law enforcement," I said. "But if I find out that the CIA was interfering in any way, you can be sure I'll write about that too."

The public affairs officer stood up and smiled. "That's exactly the answer I wanted to hear," he said, and escorted me into Steve Green's office.

Several other people deserve a tip of the hat. I'd like to thank John Warner for introducing me to Paul Knight and for providing me with a copy of *Project Pilot III*, the DEA's history of the French connection. Thanks also to Professors Alan Block and John C. McWilliams for unveiling the FBN's history as a cover for government intelligence operations. Alan provided me with portions of FBN agent George White's diaries, which record White's role in the CIA's MKULTRA "mind control" Program. And John gave the first few chapters of my book an early editing, which helped me on my way. I'd like to thank Tony "Grapes" Mangiaracina for giving me his copies of the National and International List books of major, mostly Mafia, drug smugglers; and George Gaffney for giving me his annotated copy of a 1964 Senate Report that had an incredible amount of valuable historical information about the FBN and its cases.

Special thanks also to all the FBN agents who openly told me about their hassles with one another, as well as with the CIA and the FBI. I'd like to think that everyone owes them a debt of gratitude. Much of our history is hidden behind a wall of national security, and that sad fact prevents

America from realizing its destiny. By contributing to this book, the FBN agents named in the following pages have given us back a portion of our rightful heritage – the substance of self-knowledge.

1

THE BIRTH OF A BUREAU

"For now we see through a glass, darkly; but then face to face."
1 Corinthians 13, Verse 11

The best way to begin this book is with an account of the Treasury Department's investigation of Arnold Rothstein's worldwide drug-smuggling operation. There can be no better introduction to the kind of people, or the political, national security, and integrity issues that have always defined America's war on drugs.

The son of second generation Orthodox Jews, Arnold Rothstein was the archetypal criminal genius – a man so evil that he fixed the 1919 World Series and got away with it! Rothstein's commandeering of the national pastime, and his ability to avoid prosecution for it, brought him national prominence: sportswriter Damon Runyon nicknamed this devious villain "the Brain," and novelist F. Scott Fitzgerald found him such a fascinating character that he used him as a model for fashionable rumrunner-cum-social climber Jay Gatsby.[1]

Writers Runyon and Fitzgerald understood their era and for them, Rothstein, with his jet-black hair and piercing dark eyes, personified the freewheeling spirit of the American antihero; the desperate man with nothing to lose, relying solely on his wits to beat the system. In this respect Rothstein was not unlike the robber barons of his times. But unlike Morgan, Mellon, and Rockefeller, his stock in trade was human vice. Throughout the 1920s, Rothstein was America's premier labor racketeer, bookmaker, bootlegger, and drug trafficker. He knew that people would drink despite Prohibition, hire prostitutes despite marriage, and gamble despite bad luck. Having been an opium smoker in his youth, he also understood the euphoric hook of narcotic drugs. So, when the federal government outlawed opiated patent medicines in 1915 with the adoption of the Harrison Narcotic Act, he knew that people with no other cure for their ailments, as well as the thrill-seeking sporting and theater crowds, would find a substitute on the black market.

Rothstein, however, always played the odds, and the profit margin in trading illicit narcotics wasn't wide enough until 1921, when the Supreme Court ruled that it was illegal for doctors to prescribe narcotic drugs to addicts. It was at this point, when the legitimate outlets vanished, that Rothstein cornered the wholesale black market. Using a procedure he had developed for smuggling liquor, he sent buyers to Europe and organized front companies for importation and distribution. By the mid-1920s he was in sole control of the lucrative black market in heroin, morphine, opium, and cocaine, and had set up a sophisticated system of political payoffs, extortion, and collusion with the same gangsters who would eventually kill him and divvy up the spoils of his vast underworld empire.

Yes, Rothstein was fatally flawed. Discretion was the cardinal rule of any criminal enterprise, yet in July 1926 he posted bond for two employees who had been arrested for smuggling a substantial quantity of narcotics from Germany. Rothstein likewise posted bail for drug runners arrested in 1927 and 1928. Alas, posting bond for his employees brought the attention of the press upon his business associates, and that indiscretion – plus the fact that his protégés felt it was unfair that one man should control all the rackets – cost him his life.

In the end the evil genius, who preyed upon human weakness, was destroyed by the folly of pride. On the evening of 4 November 1928, Rothstein was shot in the groin while in his room at New York's swank Park Central Hotel. It was a terrible wound, intended to inflict maximum pain, and Rothstein died several days later amid much controversy and mystery. To this day his murder remains officially unsolved. However, many of his secrets were revealed as a result of his bookkeeper's penchant for keeping accurate records.

THE POLITICAL IMPACT OF THE ROTHSTEIN INVESTIGATION

Arnold Rothstein was a legend in his lifetime, worthy of the attention of literary giants – but the impact of his legacy transcended the lofty standards he set as the paragon of criminal etiquette. Indeed, the US Treasury Department's investigation into his drug trafficking and distribution empire triggered a series of developments that in turn fostered national security and law enforcement policies and practices that endure into the twenty-first century.

At the law enforcement level, the Rothstein investigation revealed the staggering extent of illegal drug trafficking in the US. This revelation would lead to the reorganization of the Narcotics Division of the Internal Revenue Service's incredibly corrupt Prohibition Unit (fondly referred to as "the Old PU") and result in the creation of the Bureau of Narcotics in June 1930.

These bureaucratic developments began when certain documents were found at a realty company Rothstein used as a front for his illegal enterprises. The documents confirmed that Rothstein was financing an international drug cartel based in Holland. They also revealed that the cartel had been supplying (primarily through trans-shipment points in Canada) millions of dollars' worth of illicit drugs to American gangsters since 1925, when Rothstein's emissaries first contacted a Chinese gang in Shanghai. Treasury Department narcotic agents, having confiscated the incriminating papers from reluctant police detectives, were certain that his murder was related to an ongoing struggle for control of the burgeoning underworld drug trade. They also felt that his papers would provide additional leads in several major narcotics investigations.

The Treasury agents were right. Although the police would never solve the murder case, Rothstein's financial records did enable Treasury agents – operating independently of the police – to seize several million dollars' worth of narcotics in early December 1928 and to establish a link between Rothstein and the narcotics, which had been legally manufactured in Europe, then diverted onto the black market and smuggled from France.

While the law enforcement developments of the Rothstein investigation were significant, they were eclipsed by the resulting political fallout. The biggest impact was felt in New York, where newspapers printed rumors that Rothstein had financial ties with the city's most prominent public figures, including New York's celebrated mayor, James John "Jimmy" Walker. More importantly, the *New York Times* reported that Rothstein had used a portion of his drug profits to finance communist-sponsored strikes in the city's garment district. This was the first time in American history that politicians and policemen were linked with Bolsheviks and drug traffickers. In conjunction with charges that Democratic Party officials were on Rothstein's payroll, the specter of sedition enabled Republican US

Attorney Charles H. Tuttle to demand the immediate dismissal of all officials associated with Tammany Hall (the Democratic Party's infamous headquarters in New York), including a number of judges.[2]

Two weeks after Tuttle's explosive charges, Representative Stephen G. Porter (R-PA), Chairman of the Foreign Relations Committee, arrived in New York. Porter was the nation's leading anti-narcotics crusader, and accompanying him was Colonel Levi G. Nutt, head of the Treasury Department's Narcotics Division. In the 11 December *New York Times*, Porter was quoted as saying that he and Nutt had been tracking the Rothstein narcotics investigation since its inception several years before. Porter then escalated America's war on drugs to international proportions by declaring that Rothstein's records proved that "some" European companies that legally manufactured narcotic drugs were not abiding by agreements made at the Hague Opium Convention of 1912, "with the result that dope rings existed throughout the world."[3]

Porter was a Prohibitionist and an Isolationist, and believed that America's drug problem was caused by supply, not demand. For years he had wrangled with the colonial powers that ruled the League of Nations' Opium Advisory Committee, and in 1925 he and the American delegation had stormed out of a meeting in protest over the Opium Bloc's refusal to curb overproduction. But Porter was a crass opportunist too, and his interest in narcotic law enforcement, as we are told by historian William O. Walker III, "was not only on the humanitarian side, but also because it was a good subject for publicity in the newspapers."[4]

US Attorney Charles Tuttle had a partisan agenda too, and he and New York State's most powerful Republican power brokers, Jacob Livingstone and Kingsland Macy, took immense pleasure in discrediting Mayor Jimmy Walker, forcing his resignation in September 1932, and paving the way for the election of Republican Fiorello H. LaGuardia in 1934.

The lessons of the Rothstein case were undeniable: first and foremost, politicians had discovered that the war on drugs could be exploited for promotional purposes; and secondly, the immensity of America's drug habit had become a public issue that demanded immediate attention.

ROTHSTEIN'S HEIRS APPARENT

In the weeks following Rothstein's assassination, Treasury narcotic agents questioned material witnesses in the case, one of whom, Sidney Stajer, provided critical information about the organization's international dimensions. Under arrest on another charge and unable to make bail, Stajer, in exchange for his freedom, told investigators that he had gone to Europe in 1927, as Rothstein's purchasing agent, to buy narcotics that had been diverted from pharmaceutical firms in Germany. Stajer also revealed that he had been in China, Formosa, and Hong Hong in 1925, establishing contacts and buying opium for Rothstein on the unregulated Far East market.

Treasury agents also questioned an uncooperative witness identified in the *New York Times* as Charles Luciano. A Sicilian immigrant (real name Salvatore Lucania), Luciano was being held in connection with an armed robbery.[5] The federal agents knew that he had been a dope peddler since 1916, when he was arrested for possession of a small quantity of heroin, and that he and his partners – Frank Costello, Meyer Lansky, and Louis Buchalter – were the self-appointed heirs to Rothstein's drug-trafficking operation. They also knew that Luciano and associates had formed ties with America's major new sources of narcotics: the Ezra brothers in China, and the Eliopoulos ring in Paris. By 1929, these two gangs were the primary exploiters of the economic forces that drove illicit drug manufacturing deeper underground and opened up the Far East as the main source of narcotics in the wake of the Rothstein investigation.

A Greek national and cosmopolitan conman whose father had been a diplomat in Turkey, Elie Eliopoulos launched his drug-smuggling operation in 1927, when he visited China and contacted Greek nationals involved in the opium trade. He arranged to ship raw opium to two complicit manufacturers in France, purchased police protection in Paris, and by May 1928 was selling diverted pharmaceutical grade narcotics to America's major illegal drug distributors. In 1930 he financed a clandestine laboratory in Turkey, and thereafter narcotics from Turkey and China were routed to Paul Ventura (alias Paul Carbone), the Corsican crime boss in Marseilles, and then forwarded by American Express to Parisian restaurateur Louis Lyon for packaging and shipment to America. In 1930 and 1931, on behalf of the Eliopoulos syndicate, Peruvian diplomat Carlos Fernandez Bacula made six trips to New York, each time carrying 250 kilograms of narcotics under the protection of his diplomatic passport.[6]

The Ezra brothers, Judah and Isaac, had a different pedigree and modus operandi. Their father had dominated the legitimate opium business in Shanghai prior to the First World War, and according to scholar Terry Parssinen, "once headed the city's powerful Opium Combine."[7] Unlike the Eliopoulos brothers, the Ezras had a huge stockpile of opium and were making large profits in 1912, when the Hague Convention made it illegal to import opium from India into China.

Left to their own devices, the degenerate Ezra brothers squandered the family fortune and by the mid-1920s had decided to start trafficking in illicit drugs. Judah opened a silk-importing company as a front for smuggling narcotics from Europe to China. Then in 1931 he formed a wood oil-importing company in Shanghai and started shipping opium, cocaine, heroin, and morphine on Japanese freighters into San Francisco, where Isaac had rented a warehouse and had formed relations with Chinese and Italian distributors, including Mafioso "Black Tony" Parmiagni. An agent of Chiang Kai-shek's Kuomintang Party, Ye Ching Ho (alias Paul Yip), was Ezra's chief contact in China. With the blessings of Chiang's Nationalist government, which relied on opium profits for its survival, Yip ran a morphine factory in the wicked, wide-open city of Shanghai.[8]

THE CHINA CONNECTION, CORRUPTION, AND NATIONAL SECURITY

The Ezras had established their contacts prior to the Hague Convention, at a time when the Astors and relatives of the Roosevelts (Russell and Company in Boston) had increased their family fortunes by shipping opium from Turkey, Iran, and India to China. However, while most American shippers complied with the Hague Convention, many of Europe's colonial powers felt no obligation to honor rules set by sanctimonious American moralists, and the Opium Bloc inserted loopholes in the agreement that allowed them to continue to legally trade opium in the Far East, alongside clandestine traffickers like the Ezras.

International drug control policy improved in 1928 with the creation of a Permanent Control Board at the League of Nations. The purpose was to prevent diversions by having licit manufacturers of narcotics report to the Control Board. Further controls were established in 1931 when, with the League's Limitation Agreement, European manufacturers agreed to stop overproducing narcotic drugs. But exceptions in the trade of opium remained. Great Britain in particular had relied on the opium trade to support its colonial empire since the eighteenth century. Under the aegis of preserving free trade, the British fought two Opium Wars in the nineteenth century, thus encouraging the spread of addiction throughout the Far East. So in the 1930s, Shanghai's British, French, and international concessions were still the easiest places in the world to make banking and shipping arrangements for the opium trade. As Professor Parssinen notes, "By 1933, China and Japan had become the major exporters of opiates to the US illicit market, a position which they held throughout the decade."[9]

The Treasury Department was aware of this fact, and in 1926 Narcotics Division agent Ralph H. Oyler, the man in charge of the Rothstein investigation, traveled to China to assess the situation. But in his attempts to deal with this problem, Oyler and his colleagues were thwarted by the War and State Departments, which had an overarching need to accommodate a strategically placed ally, Nationalist China, whose survival depended on profits from drug smuggling. As it was in the beginning, it is now and ever shall be: national security interests superseded those of the drug law enforcement agencies of the US government.[10]

The primacy of China as a source of narcotics had been known to the US government since the turn of the century, when the father of the Harrison Narcotic Act, Dr. Hamilton Wright, having tended to the benighted, opium-addicted masses of the Far East, convinced President Theodore Roosevelt that drug addiction was on the rise in America, thanks to China's opium surplus. The government did not sit idly by, and it eventually sent Foreign Service officer Walter Adams to Changsha, China, specifically to curtail opium smuggling by Chinese and American smugglers. On 8 August 1921, Vice Counsel Adams, with the help of sailors aboard the US Navy gunboat Villa Lobos, seized a ton of opium that was being stored on the premises of an American commercial concern, right next door to the consulate in Changsha.[11]

This initial victory, however, did not bring an end to the problem, and on 3 December 1925 a headline in the *New York Times* declared: "American Directs Far East Opium Ring." The *Times* withheld the man's identity for national security reasons, but it did report that a huge consignment of narcotics had been shipped through Russia to Shanghai, and had resulted in a battle between Chinese warlords and the Chinese Navy at the island arsenal where the drugs were stored.

Another example of US government involvement in the Chinese opium trade was the so-called Opium Scandal of April 1927. At the center of the scandal was Leonard Husar, a former US Attorney in Shanghai. In 1924 Husar (and his lawyer) formed relations with Colonel Hsu, the intelligence officer for General Chang Tsung-chang, a Shangtung warlord contending with Chiang Kai-shek and the Kuomintang Party (KMT) for control of Shanghai. With the knowledge of the State and War Departments, Husar provided Colonel Hsu with 6,500 Mausers he acquired from an Italian arms merchant, in exchange for $500,000 worth of opium.[12]

The middleman in the transaction was State Department special employee A. M. "Tracey" Woodward. No stranger to shady drug deals, Woodward had been caught shipping opium from Iran to Shanghai in 1925. At his trial in a Consular Court in Bushire, Woodward claimed he was in the business in order to spy on foreign drug traffickers. Evidently this was true, and Woodward received only a slap on the wrist and was transferred to Shanghai, where Husar destroyed the transcripts of his trial for a cool $25,000.[13]

The government would never have revealed any of this, but the facts came tumbling out in 1927 when Husar's wife, in the course of suing him for divorce in San Francisco, revealed his dirty little secrets for all the world to see. (A public figure as well as a scoundrel, Husar was then contemplating running for governor of California.) As a result of Mrs. Husar's testimony, federal investigators also learned that Captain William Eisler of the American Chamber of Commerce had been with Husar when the payoffs were made. Eisler's presence suggested official sanction, and profits from the opium-for-arms trade were rumored to be filtering back to US congressmen.

The true extent of the involvement of government officials in the Opium Scandal was never made known, and the affair ended abruptly when Husar was sentenced to two years in federal prison. Soon thereafter, Chiang Kai-shek and his National Revolutionary Army drove Chang out of Shanghai and then turned their wrath on the communists. Armed with 5,000 rifles provided by Sterling Fessenden, the American in charge of Shanghai's International Settlement, members of Du Yue-sheng's Green Gang, headquartered in the French Concession, murdered hundreds of striking dockworkers. The so-called "White Terror" secured the city of Shanghai for the KMT and its capitalist American backers.[14]

Chiang's fascist Kuomintang Party then formed China's Nationalist government and created an opium monopoly that was supposed to end illicit trade in opium, but which in fact ensured that it would be entirely controlled by the Kuomintang Party through crime lord Du Yue-sheng. "In return for services rendered during the White Terror of 1927," researcher John Marshall writes, the officials in charge of France's concession in Shanghai, "Police Captain Etienne Fiori and his superior, Consul General Koechlin, agreed to protect Du's organization and the opium trade."[15]

After consolidating his power, Chiang would name Du Yue-sheng – an opium addict and respected member of Shanghai's Municipal Council – as Chief Communist Suppression Agent for Shanghai and chief of the

Shanghai Opium Suppression Bureau. Bribes paid by Du reached French officials in Paris. When word of the payoffs resulted in a minor scandal, a new contingent of French officials were assigned to Shanghai, but Du simply moved into the suburbs and continued his operations unabated, in league with the Chinese Navy and the Ezra brothers' connection in Shanghai, the aforementioned Mr. Paul Yip.

With Chiang Kai-shek's ascent, and consent, drug smuggling from China became official, albeit unstated policy, and in July 1929, while pursuing leads from the Rothstein case, federal agents arrested Mrs. Yang Kao in San Francisco. In her luggage was a large quantity of opium, heroin, and morphine base. What made the Kao case so unusual, however, was that Mrs. Kao's husband was a top official in the Chinese Consulate in San Francisco. The consulate's chancellor was indicted along with the Kaos, as was the Chinese minister in Washington.[16]

The Kaos and their colleagues claimed diplomatic immunity, and before the case could be brought to trial in the US, Treasury Secretary Andrew W. Mellon referred it to Secretary of State Henry L. Stimson. Placing national security interests above those of drug law enforcement, Stimson decided that the Kaos must be returned to China for trial. In December 1929 they set sail for Shanghai and freedom. And in the process American drug law enforcement suffered yet another irreversible setback.[17]

THE DEMISE OF THE NARCOTICS DIVISION

While Secretary Stimson was covering for the Kaos, a team of Narcotics Division agents under Ralph Oyler's command was wrapping up the Rothstein investigation. They had arrested fourteen drug dealers operating three major rings: one out of a Harlem nightclub; another from an East Coast mail order company that sent most of its product to Hollywood; and a third in Atlantic City. In Washington, the assistant secretary of the Treasury Department's Narcotic Control Board announced a series of related arrests, including one in distant Davenport, Iowa.[18]

Like Elie Eliopoulos in Paris, and Du Yue-sheng in Shanghai, the manager of the Harlem nightclub had paid for police protection – and the local magistrate was on his payroll too.

But there were more startling revelations to come, and the final twist in the precedent-setting Rothstein investigation was when a federal grand jury reported evidence of collusion between narcotic agents and drug dealers in New York. Agents were using and selling drugs, stealing government funds, padding reports, and falsely reporting city investigations as federal cases. The investigation into Rothstein's drug-smuggling empire had led narcotic agents through a maze of corruption to their own doorstep, and on 13 January 1930, US Attorney Tuttle began interrogating federal narcotic agents named by the grand jury as having engaged in corrupt activities. Each agent was questioned about his or her role in the drug rings established by Rothstein, and after the interrogations, leaks to the press indicated that prominent attorneys, politicians, and private citizens were also involved.

Then a truly amazing thing happened. On 14 January 1930 the son of Narcotics Division chief Colonel Levi Nutt appeared before the Grand Jury. Employed as a tax attorney in the nation's capital, Roland Nutt was accused of filing false income tax statements for none other than Arnold Rothstein! There was even a suggestion that Roland was involved in drug trafficking. Stung by the allegations, Roland declared his innocence. Yes, he had examined Rothstein's tax returns in 1926 – but only as a favor for his brother-in-law![19]

The scandal simmered and in late February, amid charges that the Narcotics Division office in New York was guilty of "misconduct, incompetence and dereliction of duty," the grand jury released its final report. It revealed that the Narcotic Division's Deputy Commissioner, William C. Blanchard, had instructed George W. Cunningham (Oyler's replacement as agent in charge of the Narcotics Division's New York office) to "pad" reports. Blanchard in turn pointed the finger at Colonel Nutt, who, he said, had become obsessed with "showing success."[20]

The affair ended with Colonel Nutt's demotion and exile to an Internal Revenue office in upstate New York. Congressman Hamilton C. Fish (D-NY) then presented Congress with a plan to reorganize the Narcotics Division. No further investigations into official corruption were conducted, and any relationships that might have existed between federal narcotic agents and congressmen receded into the shadows of history.

THE BIRTH OF A BUREAU

On 30 June 1930 the Bureau of Narcotics was formed from the remnants of the Narcotics Division and the Treasury Department's Foreign Control Board. As part of the reorganization, President Herbert C. Hoover, on the recommendation of Representative Porter and William Randolph Hearst, appointed Harry Jacob Anslinger as acting Commissioner.

Anslinger was not the only contender for the job, but he was uniquely qualified. As a former captain in the Pennsylvania Railroad's police force, he understood the security needs of private industry, and was able to manage rough-and-tumble detectives. Having served as a Foreign Service officer from 1918 to 1926 in Germany, Venezuela, and the Bahamas, he also had the diplomatic experience that was necessary to represent America abroad. This latter qualification was especially important in view of a mandate, imposed by Congress upon the Commissioner of narcotics, to go to the foreign source of America's narcotics problem, without upsetting the State Department's apple cart.[21]

Furthermore, Anslinger was familiar with the modus operandi of international smugglers. In 1926 he was transferred from the State Department to the Treasury Department, where he served until 1929 as chief of the Prohibition Unit's Division of Foreign Control. In this position he honed his bureaucratic skills working with the senior administrators of several government agencies to halt the flow of illegal liquor and narcotics into US ports. In 1929 he was appointed assistant Commissioner of prohibition, and for over a year directed the Old PU's elite Flying Squad, composed of the Treasury Department's top agents, against interstate and international drug and alcohol smuggling rings. But it was his marriage to Andrew Mellon's niece, Martha Denniston Leet, that secured for Anslinger the highly sought-after job as Commissioner of narcotics. This Establishment family connection, and the financial security it entailed, meant that Anslinger, unlike his ill-fated predecessor Colonel Nutt, could not be bought and would not use his position to enrich himself. In addition, it helped him garner the support of the industries, business associations, and social organizations that were investing in drug law enforcement. Among Anslinger's supporters (later referred to as "Anslinger's Army") were the blue chip drug manufacturing and pharmaceutical lobbies, several conservative newspaper publishers, the law enforcement community, the Southern-based evangelical movement, and the powerful China Lobby. Anslinger's in-law connection with the Mellon family also reinforced his ideological association with other Roosevelt Republican scions of America's Establishment.[22]

Anslinger took charge of the Bureau of Narcotics in September 1930, at the age of thirty-eight. He was given a broad international mandate to pursue, at their sources, the drug smuggling rings that had proliferated in the 1920s. He was also told to work with state and local narcotic bureaus to disrupt interstate trafficking and eliminate corruption. As the record shows, Anslinger performed his job with flair. For thirty-two years, until his retirement in 1962, his personality, policies, and appointments defined both the Narcotics Bureau and the nation's war on drugs.

2

THE COMMISSIONER
AND HIS CLIQUE

"In all that the Law leaveth open, the word of the Head Wolf is Law."
Rudyard Kipling, "The Law of the Jungle"

In the course of its obscure existence, the Bureau of Narcotics embarked on the most successful federal law enforcement endeavor in American history. On a per capita basis, it put more hardened criminals behind bars and penetrated more deeply into the underworld than its rival, the FBI. The magnitude of this accomplishment is even more astounding when one considers that the Bureau of Narcotics rarely employed more than 300 agents at any time, and that those 300 in turn relied upon a small percentage of "case-makers" to perform the dangerous undercover work and handle the duplicitous informants required to get the job done.

The story of these case-making agents is at the heart of the tragedy of the Bureau of Narcotics – and America's fatally flawed war on drugs. For in the course of bringing down one predatory drug trafficker after another, these superlative agents were perpetually on the verge of uncovering the underworld's clandestine relationship with America's Establishment, that "exclusive group of powerful people who rule a government or society by means of private agreements and decisions."[1]

As demonstrated by the Rothstein, Husar, and Kao cases, the Establishment preferred to dismantle the Narcotics Division rather than endure the consequences of thorough investigations that would have revealed the corruption within the system and the fact that the government was protecting the Nationalist Chinese drug-smuggling syndicate. As a result, the case-makers walked a very thin line. And the one thing that kept them from crossing that line – and bringing down the Bureau of Narcotics – was Harry J. Anslinger, the organization's inimitable Commissioner from 1930 until 1962.

Harry Anslinger was an imposing figure, husky and nearly six feet tall, with an intimidating stare, an imperious air, and a flair for self-promotion. But first and foremost he was a patriot with a deep and abiding commitment to the security of America's ruling elite. As an apparatchik of corporate America, he faithfully subordinated federal drug law enforcement to the Establishment's national security interests and, when necessary, concealed the government's involvement with foreign nations that profited from trafficking in illegal narcotics.

On the domestic political front, Anslinger kept Congress satisfied through an unwavering law-and-order approach to drug addiction policy, and he kept state and local officials happy by making politically astute appointments at the Bureau's fourteen district offices, which he staffed with supervisors he chose as much for their contacts as their management skills. Supervisors were expected to adhere to Anslinger's orthodoxy and to solve problems of agent misbehavior on the spot and without fanfare. Younger agents, other than "Special Hire" appointments (agents hired for a unique qualification, such as the ability to speak a Sicilian dialect) were college graduates with degrees most often in pharmacy or law, while senior agents were usually veterans of the First World War, former private detectives, or former Prohibition agents.

Whatever their backgrounds, federal narcotic agents were unique in the field of law enforcement. Upon joining the Bureau they were given a gun and a badge and taught how to make arrests, gather evidence for presentation in court, test and handle seized narcotics, tail a suspect without being seen, and rule their informants with an iron fist. They learned how to use disguises, marked bills, and opium-sniffing dogs, and were taught how to raid opium dens and "shooting galleries" where addicts gathered to smoke or inject drugs. They were also pioneers in the use of wiretaps and hidden microphones: and when court orders for electronic surveillance were not forthcoming, "gypsy wire" men emerged from the ranks and the practice continued *sub rosa* as a means of developing leads.

In their role as provocateurs, case-making agents "created a crime" by posing as buyers and setting up drug deals. At great personal risk they lived within the criminal milieu and, by necessity, developed extra-legal tactics. They knew how to hold "sidewalk court" and administer "street justice." They knew how to use a blackjack or brass knuckles instead of their fists, how to pick a lock and search a room without leaving a trace, and how to check their scruples at the door; for their work began on skid row, searching the lining of a pocket, or in a sock, or a body cavity of some sniveling, sniffing, lice-infested junky.

Creating a crime required agents to fool addicts and smugglers into making mistakes, and conservative judges and prosecutors often admired such proactive tactics. As a result Narcotics Bureau agents acquired a reputation as the most daring and productive, albeit unscrupulous, of all federal lawmen. In stretching the limits of the law, case-making agents also developed an abiding and self-destructive antipathy for liberal lawyers and lenient judges. Frustrated by what they perceived as a rigged judicial system, they viewed the Bill of Rights as an obstacle and, instead of acting in strict compliance with a suspect's rights under the law, they formed an unwritten code of silence to protect themselves.

The sacred rite of passage for case-makers was undercover work. When delving into the deadly recesses of the underworld, they assumed a criminal persona and worked alone and incommunicado. Though beaten and tossed in jail by policemen who were unaware (or resentful) of their true identity, or when tested to the limits of their endurance (or conscience) by the felons they deceived, undercover agents did what was necessary to preserve their cover and honor their creed.

The result was unrivaled success, and as America's silent law enforcement agency, the Bureau of Narcotics charted the hierarchy of crime in America, as it was organized by the Mafia's boss of bosses, Charles Luciano, and his Polish-born Jewish partner, Meyer (real name Suchowljansky) Lansky. Their strength and determination won Anslinger the trust of America's law enforcement community. But it was Anslinger, not his agents, who single-handedly earned the trust of America's drug-manufacturing and pharmaceutical industries by forcefully backing a proposal at the League of Nations for an open, competitive drug market. Restricted by Prohibition-era laws, the American drug industry was disadvantaged on the unregulated world market, and Anslinger's prominent role in the passage of the 1931 Limitation Agreement did much to level the playing field. After it was ratified in 1933, and America officially joined the League's Opium Advisory Committee, Anslinger arguably became the most influential member in the global drug community.

He was certainly its most aggressive member, and on the diplomatic front his chief rivals were the elegant gentlemen of the Opium Bloc – the venerable colonial powers that had the largest financial stake in the licit opium trade. Using his considerable intelligence and security-related talents,

Anslinger co-opted this powerful clique in 1931 by forming the Committee of One Hundred, a secret group consisting of the chief narcotics officers from Canada, Great Britain, Germany, Holland, France, Switzerland, and some two dozen other nations that would be required by the Limitation Agreement to establish narcotics bureaus like the one Anslinger managed.

In addition to setting up this global law enforcement and intelligence network (which helped crack the Eliopoulos case), Anslinger worked closely with the Foreign Policy Association and drug industry lobbyists to square foreign and domestic drug policy to the advantage of the industrial elite. The support of the private sector and its adjunct, the espionage Establishment, as well as the Committee of One Hundred, provided Anslinger with a unique unofficial apparatus that facilitated the Bureau's clandestine operations.

Apart from being an international operator, Anslinger was a bureaucrat and was required to show success in a cost-effective manner, and he achieved this feat during the Great Depression by having his agents seize a quantity of narcotics that exceeded, in dollar amount, his annual budget of about $3 million. A tight-fisted manager, he kept his agents' expenses to a bare minimum too.

Anslinger also exploited the controversy over national drug policy to bolster his standing with Washington's conservative Establishment. His primary weapon in this endeavor was a talent for generating the type of sensational publicity that elevated his status in the tabloid press and enabled him to upstage social scientists and other liberals who advocated legalization and a reduction in the price of prescription medicines as the most cost-effective ways of putting drug traffickers out of business. Defusing such progressive notions was the major public relations issue Anslinger faced, and he cleverly stalemated his critics by emphasizing the evils of the Mafia and its phantom communist allies, rather than focusing attention on misguided pharmacists and family physicians dispensing narcotic drugs to middle-class, mostly female, addicts. In this way the Commissioner moved the debate over national drug policy away from the ambiguous issue of demand, which he could not control, to the issue of supply – the grist of his guerrilla warfare organization's mill.

To convince congressional appropriations committees that his outfit was performing effectively and efficiently, and to obtain scarce resources during the Depression, Anslinger presented politically correct but dubious statistics about the number and nature of drug addicts, thus enabling Congressmen to wage the popular "tough on crime" campaigns that consistently ensured their re-election. As each new crop of Congressmen demanded stronger medicine to cure the nation's drug plague, Anslinger promoted mandatory sentencing and longer prison terms. Convinced that Anslinger's agents were all that stood between America's impressionable youth and the irresistible temptations of narcotic drugs, Congress in turn expanded the Bureau's search and seizure powers, enhancing its ability to make cases and improving agent morale.

Blessed with a knack for hype, Anslinger in the mid-1930s christened his organization the Federal Bureau of Narcotics (FBN), to liken it in the public's mind with the fabled FBI. In similar fashion he created a pseudo-crisis that helped justify the FBN's existence during the Depression, when the federal budget was being drastically trimmed, and bureaucrats who were not showing success were being sent to the gallows. At the time, Anslinger's job was in jeopardy too, so borrowing from Madison Avenue and creating a need that could never be fulfilled, he launched his infamous "Reefer Madness" crusade to rid America of marijuana.

Relying on his contacts in the press, the drug industry, and the evangelical movement, Anslinger conjured up a rogue's gallery of undesirable minorities that appealed to traditional race and class prejudices. According to Anslinger's Army, those pushing the Killer Weed were lazy Mexicans on the southwest border, sex-crazed Negroes and Puerto Rican seamen, inscrutable Chinese pagans who turned weak-willed white women into prostitutes, and lewd Lost Generation atheists preaching free love and Bolshevism in Greenwich Village cafes. Anslinger cynically linked crimes of passion and wanton violence, sexually transmitted diseases, insanity, and even eternal damnation to that fatal first puff of pot.

In 1937, with the support of some of America's most prominent citizens, federal legislation was enacted making the sale and possession of marijuana illegal. A new class of criminal was created, as was the "stepping-stone" myth that smoking marijuana led to heroin addiction. Making cases on pot smokers became a rite of passage for FBN agents, and, as the war in Europe and Asia increasingly hampered international smuggling routes and thus reduced the number of heroin cases that could be made, it became a surefire way for mediocre agents to meet their case initiation and arrest quotas.

ANSLINGER'S INNER CIRCLE

As a Roosevelt Republican, Anslinger shared an uneasy alliance with Treasury Secretary Henry Morgenthau, Jr. A keen advocate of his Department's law enforcement branches, Morgenthau in 1934 created an

Enforcement Board consisting of the heads of the Secret Service, the Bureau of Alcohol Tobacco & Tax, the Internal Revenue Service's Intelligence Unit, the Coast Guard, the customs service, and the Bureau of Narcotics. The goal was to improve efficiency through closer coordination, and the Board's chief coordinator became Anslinger's boss.

Harold Graves was the first chief coordinator, and after his promotion to assistant secretary of Treasury in 1936, Graves was succeeded by IRS Inspector Elmer Irey. Having arrested several Narcotics Division agents in Chicago on corruption charges in 1925, Irey fully understood the challenges facing Anslinger. Moreover, he and Anslinger had formed a close personal relationship in 1931, when they quietly quashed an extortion scheme aimed at implicating President Herbert Hoover and Andrew Mellon in a bootlegging conspiracy worth millions of dollars. A pioneer in crafting conspiracy cases, Irey established the Treasury Department's Law Enforcement Training School in 1937. Greatly admired by Morgenthau, he was the last chief coordinator to wield more power than Anslinger.[2]

Starting in 1932, Stuart J. Fuller was Anslinger's counterpart at the State Department. Fuller's appointment as chief of the East Asian Division underscored the importance of protecting Nationalist China, and represented a shift away from the isolationist policies of Congress toward the expansionist policy advocated by the Foreign Policy Association and other Establishment front organizations. As the government's representative to the Opium Advisory Committee, Fuller, until his death in 1941, assumed the lead role in formulating foreign narcotics policy, while working hand in glove with Anslinger.

Anslinger's most trusted staff assistant was attorney Malachi L. Harney. In the early 1920s Harney served as a supervisor in Irey's IRS Intelligence Unit, and in the late 1920s he established a reputation as a "gang buster" while overseeing Eliot Ness and the legendary Untouchables in their successful pursuit of Al Capone in Chicago. Tall, dignified, and tough as nails, Harney served in Anslinger's Flying Squad, and then joined the FBN. As Anslinger's enforcement assistant, Harney shaped the FBN's operating procedures and methods of managing informants, and built conspiracy cases against the most notorious drug traffickers of the 1930s and 1940s. His career culminated with his appointment as Treasury's assistant secretary for law enforcement in the mid-1950s.

Anslinger's top overseas agent in the 1930s was case-maker Charles B. Dyar. Fluent in French, German, Dutch, and Italian, Dyar joined the State Department in 1906 and served with the American Embassy in Berlin through the First World War, reporting on political, economic, and military

matters. After Dyar was reassigned to The Hague in 1918, he met and formed a fast friendship with Anslinger, who also spoke German and Dutch, had recently joined the State Department, and was performing security- and intelligence-related tasks for the Embassy. Anslinger looked up to Charlie "the Sphinx" Dyar (famous for his grace under pressure), and after he became chief of the Division of Foreign Control, Anslinger hired Dyar as a Prohibition Investigator. Dyar worked with the Flying Squad in Canada until 1927, when assistant secretary of State Seymour Lowman personally assigned him to Berlin, where he served until 1930, at which point Anslinger brought him into the FBN.[3]

Like many of Anslinger's top agents, Dyar was hired as a special employee on the basis of his linguistic abilities, his experience as an intelligence operator, and the overarching fact that although he was suave and sophisticated, he was tough enough to handle the dangerous informants who made their living entrapping violent drug smugglers. Anslinger in 1931 put Dyar in charge of all FBN narcotics investigations in Europe, and in this capacity he was responsible for uncovering the ties between Eliopoulos and his array of American customers.

Dyar and Anslinger became intimately linked in 1934, when there was a sharp drop in the number of narcotics seizures in America, and Morgenthau put the blame squarely on their shoulders. The problem began in late 1933, when the last of the world's licit heroin-manufacturing facilities in Bulgaria was shut down, and international drug traffickers switched to clandestine factories and smaller shipments to evade detection. Morgenthau unintentionally made it harder for the FBN to adjust to this change in the underworld's modus operandi when, in 1934, he gave the customs service jurisdiction for drug investigations in Asia, Latin America, and Mexico. The FBN had jurisdiction everywhere else, but conflicts arose, and the flashpoint in the FBN's feud with Customs was in February 1937, when Morgenthau put Customs agent Alvin F. Scharff in control of anti-narcotics operations in Europe. Ambitious and domineering, Scharff tried to convince Morgenthau that Customs, not the FBN, should manage any investigation that had to do with drug smuggling, anywhere.

If an adversary can be included in Anslinger's inner circle, then Al Scharff, along with FBI director J. Edgar Hoover, deserves the honor. Based in Texas, Scharff's area of expertise was Mexico, where in the First World War, while operating as a special employee of the War and Justice Departments, he assassinated two German spies. After that the customs service hired him, and over the ensuing years he made many alcohol- and drug-smuggling cases. But it was not until 1936, when he smashed a drug-smuggling ring that stretched from Shanghai through Havana to Mexico City, that Scharff's competition with Anslinger, Dyar, and the FBN began. The drug ring, which was depicted in the 1948 movie *To The Ends of the Earth*, included a Eurasian femme fatale, a Prussian count-cum-Nazi spy, the Paris-based playboy brother of the mistress of Rumania's King, and the Istanbul-based son-in-law of Mexico City's police chief. All were associates of Elie Eliopoulos.[4]

The problem for Anslinger was that, although the case had been made in Mexico, Scharff had generated leads and developed informants in Europe, which he was not about to share with the FBN. As noted, Morgenthau had lost faith in Anslinger and had instructed Scharff (as we are told in his biography, *The Coin of Contraband*) to assist the American Embassy in Paris "in organizing a system to combat the flow of narcotic drugs from the Far East through Europe to the United States." In addition, the chief of Naval Intelligence wanted Scharff to obtain "certain information from Europe on matters not being investigated by its other agents." Obviously, in this latter respect, Scharff's narcotics investigation was merely a cover for espionage activities.[5]

In Europe, Scharff used an "unlimited expense account" to hire forty-six men in key European cities and, based on this vast informant network, found that narcotics from the Far East were smuggled through the Suez Canal into Italy and Turkey, then to Corsica and Marseilles, and that French Corsicans, financed by Greek racketeers, controlled the traffic. Scharff also discovered that the overland narcotics route included the Trans-Siberian Railroad and the Vienna Express from Istanbul to Paris. He located poppy fields in Yugoslavia, and learned how narcotics were moved to Trieste, Rome, and Naples, where he "saw American tankers pumping gasoline into German submarines and barges, and into tank cars bound for Berlin."[6]

In Paris, as part of his espionage mission, Scharff worked with Ambassador William C. Bullitt in an effort to penetrate a faction of the Sûreté that protected Louis Lyon. Through the family connections of his wife, Ida Nussbaum, whose cousin was related to French Premier Léon Blum, Scharff was eventually able to initiate action against Lyon. It is a case worth examining.

As mentioned in chapter 1, Lyon had worked with Eliopoulos smuggling narcotics to various American gangsters. Lyon, however, played a double game and information he provided to French officials resulted in Eliopoulos being expelled from France. In exchange, Lyon was allowed to operate a heroin factory in Paris, directly across the street from the French Ministry of Foreign Affairs. From his factories in Turkey and China, tons of opium

was moved to his accomplice, Corsican Paul Carbone in Marseilles. The Sûreté even protected Lyon after an explosion in his Paris factory in 1935. Everyone knew Lyon was the factory's owner, but he was not tried until 1938, and then received only a light sentence. Why? Because high government officials, including Max Dormoy, the former Socialist minister of interior, employed Lyon as a spy against fascist French with ties to Nazi Germany.[7]

By 1940, the French were deeply divided along ideological lines, and while his former partners Elie Eliopoulos and Paul Carbone became Nazi collaborators, Lyon played a precarious triple game, posing as a Nazi sympathizer in order to expose Gestapo agents trying to infiltrate the Resistance. As Anslinger grudgingly observed, "Following the war, the French government awarded ex-gambler, ex-bookmaker, ex-dope dealer Lyon the Legion of Honor."[8]

Throughout his tour in Europe, Scharff had a huge ego battle with Charlie Dyar, whom he started supervising in 1937. In a July 1940 letter to his supervisor in El Paso, Scharff disparagingly and unfairly said of Dyar, "so far as I knew he had not done anything up to the time I left Paris."[9]

One can imagine refined, taciturn Charlie Dyar suffering sidewinder Al Scharff, with his cowboy boots and grating Texas drawl that so irritated the French officials he was trying to outwit. And of course Dyar was anything but unproductive. After the First World War, he had helped French counter-intelligence identify some 13,000 German spies, and thereafter Dyar relied on his friends in the Sûreté for the successes he achieved in his European narcotics investigations. So when Scharff tried to penetrate the Sûreté, the two men clashed immediately, and Scharff had Dyar summarily transferred to Customs in June 1937. But as soon as Scharff left Paris to return to Texas, the Treasury Attaché summoned Dyar back to resume control. Dyar remained in France until his investigations were interrupted by the Second World War, at which point he was reassigned, to his eternal dismay, to Scharff in El Paso, where the feud between Customs and the FBN simmered in the sweltering Texas heat.

At home, Anslinger's top gun was fearless Ralph Oyler, the premier narcotic agent of the 1920s. In 1916, having transferred to the Narcotics Division as a special employee, Oyler made the seminal Jim Fuey Moy case in Pittsburgh. Moy, an addict, was arrested because his doctor had prescribed him narcotics, and the Narcotics Division wanted to challenge the legality and wisdom of the practice, because narcotics were being diverted from many of the treatment clinics that existed at the time. A milestone in drug law enforcement, the Moy case went to the Supreme Court, which ruled against Moy and found, in effect, latent police powers in the Harrison Act, which had been enacted as a revenue-gathering measure.[10]

In 1921 Oyler initiated another landmark case against several major American drug manufacturers and wholesalers. An estimated 300,000 ounces of heroin was being produced every month in New York, much more than was needed by area hospitals. Licenses were easy to obtain, and huge amounts of narcotics were being diverted onto the black market. At Oyler's direction, an agent was placed in each manufacturing and importing house, and for the first-time purchasers, as well as manufacturers and wholesalers, were investigated. The result was the Jones–Miller Act of 1922, which standardized licensing and registration practices, and made the mere possession of narcotics a crime. Jones–Miller also provided for a federal narcotics commission, later chaired by Anslinger, which controlled the importation and exportation of narcotics.[11]

Oyler was also the brawling undercover hero of the Battle of the King Alexander – the King Alexander being a Greek ship whose crew was smuggling a million dollars' worth of opium and cocaine to the Mafia. Oyler, leading seventeen fellow agents, raided the ship on 9 September 1921. As the *New York Times* reported, "Oyler and his companions used their revolvers freely and with effect."[12] Two crew members were killed, four hospitalized, twenty-eight arrested, and eleven convicted.

Not only was Oyler a skilled investigator, he had high-ranking contacts in the military. Most important was an association he formed in 1923 with Assistant US Attorney William J. Donovan. Together they cracked an international drug ring based in Buffalo, New York, and a huge seizure they made in Canada became a hot topic at the 1924 Geneva Opium Conference, and provided Representative Porter with the evidence he needed to trace the source of the narcotics to British and French Opium Bloc colonies. It is very likely that Oyler introduced Donovan to Harry Anslinger. Along with Donovan, future Central Intelligence Agency (CIA) chief Allen W. Dulles, and Andrew Mellon's son-in-law David K. Bruce (later ambassador to France, Germany, and Great Britain), Anslinger would become one of the founding fathers of the Office of Strategic Services (OSS) in the Second World War and the CIA in 1947.

The turning point in Oyler's career, however, was the Rothstein investigation, and his reward for smashing the world's biggest narcotics ring and

for uncovering corruption within the Narcotics Division was a summary transfer to Chicago. But Anslinger recognized Oyler's talents and in 1934 resurrected his career by appointing him district supervisor in Detroit. Oyler served in this position until his death in 1947, making numerous newsworthy (but local) cases against mostly Chinese and Afro-American gangs dealing in opium and marijuana.

While Oyler's tenure in Detroit was marked by mostly small and safe investigations, other case-making agents were actively pursuing heroin traffickers and establishing the basis for the FBN's great post-war Mafia hunting expedition. Bespectacled, demure, and small in stature, Benedict "Benny" Pocoroba was one of the few undercover FBN agents ever to slip unnoticed inside the upper echelons of the Mafia. A man of immense courage, Pocoroba worked from 1918 to 1928 for a private detective agency that had launched its own investigation of the Mafia. Through this experience he had acquired insights into the secret organization that had taken over drug trafficking from the original Chinese and Jewish gangs. Pocoroba was recruited by Anslinger in 1930 and assigned the task of infiltrating Mafia chapters in California, Virginia, Pennsylvania, Ohio, and New York.[13]

The exact opposite of flashy Ralph Oyler, Benny Pocoroba was unglamorous and eminently un-newsworthy, but he and a few Italian, Chinese, and Jewish undercover agents are said to have "made the Bureau," which by the late 1930s was accurately mapping out the Mafia's hierarchy.

By 1937 the FBN's rising star was George Hunter White, the organization's most flamboyant and controversial character. White's claim to fame was the 1937 undercover case he made against the Hip Sing T'ong, the infamous drug-smuggling Chinese–American trade association. Posing as John Wilson, a nephew of his "Uncle Sam" (a hitherto unknown gangster forming a new drug syndicate), White initiated the case in Seattle, then crossed the country contracting with Hip Sing T'ong members for huge purchases of opium. According to legend, White was initiated into the T'ong, swearing to accept "death by fire" should he ever break its sacred oath of secrecy.[14] The investigation climaxed in November 1937 with a series of spectacular mass arrests, one of which implicated Charles Luciano through the arrest of the wife and brother of one of his top aides. The Hip Sing T'ong case earned White his well-deserved status as one of the FBN's top case-making agents.

At five feet seven inches tall and 200 pounds, White, with his head shaved bald, was the picture of the mythical detective who made bad guys tip their hats and speak politely to cops. A native of California, White was ebullient and exceedingly confident, and as a former crime reporter for the *San Francisco Call Bulletin*, he had a nose for sniffing out trouble – and trouble was what he enjoyed more than anything else. It didn't matter that he collected confiscated opium pipes or drank to excess, because White was the roughest and the toughest, and he fought with the troops on the front lines. More importantly, his newspaper contacts were always available to his publicity-hungry boss – and after he helped to extricate Anslinger's stepson, Joseph, from an undisclosed legal problem, White became Anslinger's favorite and most trusted agent.

Anslinger's top field manager was Garland H. Williams from Prentiss, Mississippi. After earning a degree in civil engineering, Williams served in the Louisiana National Guard until 1929, when he entered the customs service. An intrepid investigator, Williams worked for Anslinger in the Flying Squad on some of the Foreign Control Board's most important and wide-ranging cases. Utterly dependable, Williams in 1936 was chosen to negotiate, with Mexican president Lazaro Cardenas, an anti-smuggling agreement that allowed Treasury agents to operate inside Mexico. That same year Williams organized the customs service's southwest Border Patrol in El Paso, Texas, to monitor the entire US–Mexican border.[15]

Williams was transferred to the FBN in November 1936, after Manhattan US Attorney Lamar Hardy complained to Secretary Morgenthau about the FBN's failure to make any significant drug cases in New York in the previous two years. Morgenthau, without notifying Anslinger, sent a team of IRS agents to New York to find out why. What the IRS agents found was an office paralyzed by corruption and a lack of leadership. Morgenthau, having lost confidence in Anslinger (who nearly lost his job, and did lose all of his hair as a result of the stress), assigned Williams the job of cleaning up the mess in New York.[16]

As New York district supervisor, Williams whipped the office's maverick case-making agents (aka the Forty Thieves) into line, and then tied Yasha Katzenberg's gang of Jewish narcotics smugglers to Japan through their source in Tientsin, China, at the same time that Anslinger, in March 1937, was accusing the Japanese of dispensing opium in Manchuria as a weapon of war.

The Katzenberg case marked a pivotal point in the history of international drug smuggling. To sum it up, Yasha Katzenberg managed an elaborate drug ring that, with the help of corrupt Customs officials, smuggled huge amounts of narcotics on luxury liners from China to Mafia and Jewish distributors in New York. After Katzenberg was indicted in 1937, Garland Williams tracked him across Europe and caught him in Greece. Brought back to New York to stand trial, Katzenberg "flipped" and became the main witness against his fellow conspirators. But of his many revelations, the most important was that Giuseppe "Joe Adonis" Doto had stolen his last drug shipment, and had effectively taken control of narcotics importation. The significance of Katzenberg's revelations about Adonis cannot be overstated: it confirmed that the Mafia had always obtained narcotics from the Far East, and that it had taken over international drug trafficking from the Jewish gangs; but it also meant that the FBN had identified a top member of the conspiracy – as well as his political protector, Brooklyn District Attorney William O'Dwyer.[17]

THE POLITICS OF ASSASSINATION IN NEW YORK

A member of Mafia boss Vincent Mangano's crime family in Brooklyn, Joe Adonis rose to power in the underworld by providing the Ford Motor Company with the muscle it needed to smash an autoworkers strike outside Detroit in 1932. He was rewarded with a lucrative franchise, and until 1951 his Automotive Conveying Company freely moved sedans and drugs between Detroit and New Jersey, and thence throughout New England and the East Coast. "In the eight years from 1932 to 1940," investigative journalist Fred Cook wrote, "Ford paid this Adonis-controlled company a cool $8 million."[18]

The FBN's headquarters staff knew this about Adonis, but Katzenberg provided an astounding new insight into the relationship between Adonis, his Mafia and Jewish associates, and politicians in New York. According to Katzenberg, Adonis had used his political influence to ensure that Brooklyn policeman William O'Dwyer first became a magistrate, and then Brooklyn's District Attorney. By 1941, O'Dwyer was a powerhouse in his own right and would successfully run as the Democratic candidate for mayor of New York, presumably with Mafia backing.

Anslinger and Harney knew that O'Dwyer, while serving as DA, had investigated the murder of labor leader Joe Rosen. They knew that O'Dwyer's informant in the case, Abe Reles, a professional hit man for Murder Incorporated (the joint Jewish–Mafia operation that sanctioned underworld murders nationwide) had named Katzenberg's financier, Louis

"Lepke" Buchalter, as having ordered Rosen's murder. O'Dwyer indicted Buchalter for murder, of course, but what troubled Anslinger and Harney was that Reles had also named Joe Adonis, Willie Moretti, Meyer Lansky, Benjamin Siegel, Frank Costello, and Albert Anastasia as Buchalter's co-conspirators – and yet they were not indicted. In fact, when prosecutors in California sought Reles's testimony in order to indict Siegel on murder charges, O'Dwyer declined to send him.[19]

Then on 12 November 1941, Reles ("the canary who couldn't fly") took a fatal fall from the sixth floor window of the Half Moon Hotel in Coney Island while under the protection of six policemen – all of whom had fallen asleep simultaneously. With no material witness to testify against Adonis and the other members of Murder Inc., the case against them evaporated.[20]

Bigger problems, however, were looming for the FBN, and two weeks after Reles was silenced, the Japanese attack on Pearl Harbor forced the wholesale reorganization of American society and ushered in a more complicated phase in the FBN's history. The exigencies of world war would turn Anslinger's enemies into unwanted allies and would pervert the nature of drug law enforcement for a long time to come.

ANSLINGER'S ANTAGONISTS

In 1930 the Mafia's boss of bosses, Charles Luciano, and his Polish-born Jewish partner, Meyer Lansky, incorporated crime in America. As the organization's financial manager and executive producer of vice, Lansky located and shielded investors in its various rackets and channeled mob profits into an assortment of legitimate business ventures, including Florida land deals, Mexican racetracks, and casinos in Cuba. A financial wizard and a government informant when it suited his purposes, Lansky was a seeker of the respectable façade. But he could never expunge from his lengthy rap sheet a Public Health Act charge for violating drug laws that he incurred in January 1929 with his partner since childhood, Benjamin "Bugsy" Siegel.[21]

Lansky's other boyhood friend, Charles Luciano, was born in Sicily in 1897 and arrived in New York in 1904. A fifth-grade dropout and compulsive gambler, his first arrest for heroin possession was in 1916. His second occurred in 1923, and this time he cooperated with New York Narcotics Division agent Joe Bransky and set up a rival gang member rather than face charges. Six years later, on a chilly October night, Luciano earned his famous nickname. As related in *The Luciano Story*, a drug shipment from the Eliopoulos gang was headed for New York on a Greek ocean liner. Unaware that rivals had betrayed him, Luciano went to the pier to receive the load, but was tailed by Narcotics Division agents. He recognized the agents before the exchange was made and backed away, but the agents wanted to know where the drugs were hidden, so they took Luciano to a secluded spot on Staten Island where a brutal interrogation ensued.[22]

Luciano was cut so badly he acquired a permanent droop to his right eyelid; but he remained true to the Mafia code of omerta (a word derived either from the Sicilian *umirta*, for humility, or the Spanish *hombre*, to be a man) and revealed nothing. By the time the story got around town, he had also acquired the nickname "Lucky" and the abiding respect of the upper underworld. He also acquired a seething Sicilian hatred for federal narcotic agents in general, and for Anslinger in particular, whom he mockingly referred to as "Asslicker." It was the start of a very bitter rivalry that would help define the course of FBN history.

Shortly after his run–in with the federal narcotic agents, Luciano retired the old Mafia dons, established New York's five crime families, made peace overtures to his rival crime lords in Chicago, and formed a national commission of Mafia bosses, with himself as chief executive officer, Lansky as chief financial officer and liaison to a worldwide network of Jewish gangsters, and respectable Frank Costello as prime minister and liaison to the Establishment. The Commission settled disputes and regulated four industrial-sized rackets: labor racketeering, gambling, prostitution, and a drug importation and distribution syndicate which, according to Anslinger, had its own legal staff and sales force. Under general manager Nicola "Nick" Gentile (a member of the Mangano family), this Mafia drug syndicate would secure a monopoly (originally established by Jewish gangs) over interstate distribution, and by the late 1930s was the focus of the FBN's attention.[23]

Incredibly, Luciano's reign as the *capo di tutti capi* (boss of bosses) did not end in 1936, when New York State's special prosecutor Thomas E. Dewey – using wiretaps placed in Luciano's bordellos, the perjured testimony of three addict prostitutes, and the testimony of Mafia turncoat Joe Basile, an informant for FBN agent J. Ray Olivera – convicted Luciano on sixty-two counts of compulsory prostitution. Luciano received a thirty-to-fifty-year prison sentence, but maintained his status as boss of bosses even behind bars. Lansky eluded the long arm of the law altogether, and the Mafia's drug syndicate survived, as did the Luciano family under the leadership of politically astute Frank Costello. With its managers still in place, the Mafia would ironically in 1942 become one of America's most undesirable allies.

This development was a terrible blow to Harry Anslinger. He hadn't been to the right schools, and he didn't speak with the right accent, but he did understand the meaning of power, privilege, and place. Standing erect with his head held high, he was the image of strength and sobriety. He owned a home in Hollidaysburg, Pennsylvania, and he resided at the exclusive Shoreham Hotel in Washington, DC. His circle of friends included judges, bankers, diplomats, and affluent executives who liked to hunt bear and elk in Canada, or deer and pheasant on their country estates. He was not the type of man to suffer underlings, let alone mobsters.

Indeed, few FBN agents ever met the Commissioner; and if they did, it was while serving as his chauffeur when he was in town courting police chiefs or politicians. Anslinger only discussed Bureau matters with his deputies, never with agents. When he did receive an agent, he was reserved and soft-spoken, but direct and to the point. "If you got a 'well done' from him," Agent Howard Chappell recalls, "it was like getting a citation from someone else." There were only a few agents Anslinger considered equals. Charlie Dyar was a close friend, as was Ralph Oyler. Both, like Anslinger, were married to money and when necessary, flamboyant enough to bring the Bureau favorable reviews.

Most everyone in Anslinger's inner circle came from the Old PU, and when he became Commissioner he took these men into the FBN and made them district supervisors. He had a soft spot for old-timers like George Cunningham, his deputy from 1949 until 1958, and Joe Bransky, the dean of district supervisors, stationed in Philadelphia. No one in the FBN after the Second World War ever got as close to him as they did, with the exception of Ross B. Ellis in Detroit and George White.

With the advent of the Cold War, no agent had the courage to publicly question Anslinger's policies either. His control over the FBN and its agents was absolute and served to magnify his mistakes, the biggest of which was having agents initiate two cases a month, thus forcing them to arrest as many addicts as possible. This "two buys and a bust" format enabled him to compile the statistics he needed to impress the congressional appropriations committees, and ensure that conspiracy cases were managed by a cadre of trusted friends, but it also focused attention on addicts rather than distributors, and it fostered a cut-throat environment that pitted case-making agents against one another, with dire consequences for the FBN.

Anslinger was the prototype of what modern agents facetiously call "a suit." His battles were waged in boardrooms, the halls of Congress, and the press. His angst was over the fate of the nation's ruling elite, not its average citizens, and yet that class consciousness served only to enhance his exquisite mystique – his carefully crafted image as a man serving a higher purpose in which his agents could believe. And they believed. They looked at Anslinger with nostalgic awe, as a symbol of the higher authority from which their powers derived. His presence looms.

3

ANSLINGER'S ANGST

"Y'see, we're doing somebody else's dirty work."

Lepke Buchalter to Lucky Luciano

Despite Harry Anslinger's penchant for self-promotion, much of the FBN's pre-war activities on behalf of the national security Establishment remain unrecorded. The only detailed account is Maurice Helbrant's frank and colorful autobiography, *Narcotic Agent.*[1]

Born in Rumania and raised in Brooklyn, Helbrant spied for the British in Palestine during the First World War. His work involved him in the region's drug trade, and when he returned to America he joined the Old PU's Narcotics Division. Personable, attentive, and physically unthreatening, Helbrant was the ideal undercover agent, able to pose as a crazed cocaine addict when working the streets or as a wealthy underworld financier when pursuing wholesale distributors. Among his many accomplishments, Helbrant made the case on Jacob Polakiewitz, the primary purchaser from the Eliopoulos syndicate for one of the largest Jewish–American drug-smuggling syndicates prior to the Second World War.

As Helbrant explains in his book, agents in the early days of the FBN received little guidance from headquarters. They had a procedures manual, yes, but Prohibition had blurred the line between right and wrong, and case-makers learned to be wary of ambitious bosses who, in their quest to show success, asked them to do little things – like setting up illegal wiretaps or breaking into a drug dealer's apartment to plant evidence – that could get them in trouble. They were also suspicious of bosses who asked them to look the other way.

A story from Helbrant's life neatly captures this predicament. Through an informant he acquired in New Orleans in the fall of 1934, he learned that two oystermen were trying to sell a shipment of heroin to a distribution syndicate managed by Sylvestro "Sam" Carolla, head of the Mafia in New Orleans, and Carolla's *consigliere*, Onifio "Nofie" Pecoraro. Helbrant subsequently tailed the oystermen to a meeting with their supplier, Eugene Coindet Aguilar, whom he arrested. During a routine body search, Helbrant found a slip of paper with Coindet's address, and the ensuing search of his apartment led to the seizure of $100,000 worth of heroin. It also turned up a list of firearms Coindet intended to purchase with the money he would have made from selling the heroin to the oystermen. However – and this is where he was asked to look the other way – Helbrant soon discovered that Coindet was planning to use his drug-smuggling profits to help Honduran opposition leader Jose Maria Guillen Velez finance a rebellion in Honduras, where the collapse of the banana economy had prompted President Tiburcino Carias Andino (the man Guillen hoped to topple) to resort to drug smuggling too.

Worse news was yet to come, for Helbrant had inadvertently opened a window onto the activities of Raymond J. Kennett, traffic manager in late 1934 for the cargo airline Transportes Aereos Centro-Americanos (TACA). Kennett had been arrested for selling drugs in New Orleans in the early 1930s, but New Orleans police chief Guy R. Maloney had reduced his sentence and then quit his job to become the arsenal inspector for the Honduran government. Also involved with Kennett were arms smuggler Edwin E. Huber, head of the Huber-Honduras Company, a link in a narcotic pipeline from Germany to North America; Isodore Slobotsky, owner of the Star Furniture Company and the TACA agent in New Orleans; and Lowell Yerex, owner of TACA.

Helbrant noted that the Honduran Drugs For Guns case sparked "an international incident with strange detectives from Washington making mysterious appearances and disappearances and rumblings like small earthquakes upsetting the New Orleans underworld."[2] What he was implying was that the "strange" detectives from Washington were there to shield Kennett and his TACA associates. And they were: elections were to be held in Honduras in October 1936, and Kennett and associates, by supporting the US-backed candidate, Tiburcino Carias Andino, required protection. So the State Department "ordered all surveillance of the TACA group curtailed," and the detectives concluded their investigation in March

1936 without uncovering any hint of TACA's involvement in drug smuggling.[3] Carias went on to win the election, and though the FBN knew he was smuggling drugs into Panama on TACA planes in 1937, top US officials, including Stuart Fuller and Harry Anslinger, looked away, because Carias provided the US government and its corporate backers with a valuable ally in Latin America as war loomed on the horizon and America's enemies maneuvered for influence in the region.

As historians Kinder and Walker said about the case, "the defense of the Western hemisphere against the Axis powers ... reduced to insignificance clandestine attempts to link the managerial personnel of a major cargo airline to smuggling."[4]

Author Peter Dale Scott, an expert on the "deep political" aspects of drug smuggling, is blunter and notes that Anslinger "cracked down on the Liberal opposition's New Orleans heroin connection, but let the government's connection [Carias] continue unhindered."[5]

The government's pseudo-investigation of TACA was terminated in 1938 with the Treasury Department promising "to halt all surveillance of Yerex's activities whenever he came to the United States." By March 1939, TACA held cargo service concessions in Costa Rica, Nicaragua, Guatemala, El Salvador, and Honduras and continued to engage in smuggling activities "virtually untouched by government action." William K. Jackson, vice president of United Fruit, put the situation in economic perspective: "The greater the development of our trade relations with Latin America, the lesser will be their dependence and ours upon the whims of some European dictatorial ruler."[6]

Along with the Opium Scandal of 1927 and the Kao case of 1929, the TACA case proves that the government protected drug smugglers to ensure national security, as well as to protect corporate profits. It also highlights the sad fact that case-making agents like Helbrant were aware of such machinations, but were unable to stop them. Anslinger went along with this unstated policy for two reasons: he needed drug addicts to justify his Bureau's existence and, by allowing certain politically acceptable drug rings to exist, he became a key player in the espionage Establishment.

GUNS AND DRUGS AND NATIONALIST CHINA

Anslinger was a seasoned bureaucrat with secret police powers that enabled him to decide, in consultation with other top officials, which drug-smuggling rings were to be targeted and which were to remain intact. This applied especially to the Nationalist Chinese government, which, since its inception in 1927, relied heavily on drug-smuggling revenues.

Reports submitted by Foreign Service officers, military Attachés, informants, and Treasury Attaché M. R. Nicholson in Shanghai left no doubt that China and Japan were the major exporters of opiates to the US illicit market throughout the 1930s.[7] As historians Kinder and Walker explain, "Fuller and Anslinger clearly knew about the ties between Chiang and opium dealers."[8]

Anslinger knew that Shanghai was "the prime producer and exporter to the illicit world drug markets," through a syndicate controlled by Du Yue-sheng, the crime lord who facilitated Chiang's bloody ascent to power in 1927.[9] As early as 1932, Anslinger knew that Du's political protectors were Chiang and his finance minister, T. V. Soong. He also had evidence that American t'ongs were receiving narcotics from Du and his KMT associates and then distributing them to the Mafia. For example, after their arrest by FBN agents in 1933, the Ezras revealed that Paul Yip was their contact in Shanghai. Yip worked with Du, the Japanese occupation forces in Manchuria, and Dr. Lansing Ling, who "supplied narcotics to Chinese officials traveling abroad."[10] In 1938 Chiang Kai-shek would name Dr. Ling head of his Narcotic Control Department!

The evidence continued to mount and in October 1934 Treasury Attaché Nicholson submitted reports implicating Chiang Kai-shek and possibly T. V. Soong in the heroin trade to North America.[11] And in 1935 he reported that Soong's protégé, the superintendent of Maritime Customs in Shanghai, was "acting as agent for Chiang Kai-shek in arranging for the preparation and shipment of the stuff to the United States."[12] Nicholson's reports reached Anslinger's desk, so the Commissioner knew which KMT officials and trade missions were delivering dope to American t'ongs, which American drug rings were buying it, and that the t'ongs were kicking back a percentage of the profits to finance Chiang's regime – none of which he could ever reveal.[13]

After Japanese forces seized Shanghai in August 1937, Anslinger was less willing than ever to deal honestly with the situation. He knew that Du had sat on Shanghai's Municipal Board with William J. Keswick – a director of the Jardine Matheson Shipping Company – and that through Keswick, Du had found sanctuary in Hong Kong, where he was welcomed by a cabal of free-trading Brits whose shipping and banking companies earned huge revenues by allowing Du to push his drugs on the hapless Chinese. The revenues were truly immense: according to Colonel Joseph Stilwell, the US military Attaché in China, in 1935 there were an estimated "eight million Chinese heroin and morphine addicts and another 72 million Chinese opium addicts."[14]

Corporate profits were as important as national security and by 1938, Du was collaborating with the Japanese while his Green Gang was spying on them for Chiang's intelligence service. From the national security perspective, to which Anslinger adhered, information provided by Du's agents to Chiang's intelligence chief, General Tai Li, offset the human damage done by the shiploads of Persian opium Tai Li and Du sold to the Japanese, for distribution in China. But Du's massive payoffs enabled the KMT to purchase $31 million worth of fighter planes from arms dealer William Pawley, and that national security exigency, as Anslinger knew, trumped any moral dilemmas about trading with the enemy.

His resolve stiffened as war with Japan became imminent. He put his stamp of approval on a Foreign Policy Association report exonerating the Nationalists and blaming Japan for the narcotics problem in China. And, after a dozen of Lucky Luciano's associates were nabbed during the Hip Sing T'ong roundup in November 1937, he even sought information from his most hated rival; in the summer of 1938 he sent George White (the FBN agent who had made the Hip Sing T'ong case) and Secret Service Agent John Hanly to interview Luciano at Dannemora Prison in upper New York State. Though Hanly reported that Luciano was unhelpful, the Navy would soon form relations with the Mafia – and the Kuomintang-connected Hip Sing T'ong would continue to receive opium from the Far East with apparent impunity.[15]

DRUG SMUGGLING, NATIONAL SECURITY, AND THE MAFIA

Anslinger not only cooperated with America's espionage Establishment by protecting Nationalist China's drug-smuggling operations, he also turned a blind eye to the TACA operation and thus provided the Mafia with a steady source of supply into Louisiana at the same time Frank Costello and Meyer Lansky were opening a slot machine franchise in New Orleans and entrusting it to Mafia chieftain Sam Carolla. Though convicted of murdering a federal narcotic officer in 1932, Carolla had used his drug-smuggling profits to buy political protection and, after receiving a pardon from Louisiana Governor O. K. Allen, served only two years in prison for his crime.[16]

Anslinger bitterly complained about this incident in his book *The Protectors*, telling how Carolla "gunned down Agent Moore," and throughout his career Anslinger would place much of the blame for America's drug problem on the Mafia's corrupting influence on local officials.[17] But Anslinger, again, was being less than honest; he knew that Carolla had been released in the TACA case and that the espionage Establishment protected Carolla's source of supply.

To put it kindly, Anslinger liked to eat his cake and have it too. In public he was a staunch law enforcement crusader; behind the scenes he was complicit. But he felt justified in maintaining this double standard, because drug smugglers provided a vital counterintelligence resource for the government's security services. In 1940, for example, a special group of Treasury agents under assistant secretary Harold Graves discovered that Japan's top narcotic agent, Shinji Taniguchi, was using a West Coast drug ring to spy on the American military. In that instance, as in others, the security services could not have succeeded without the help of confidential informants they inserted within a foreign intelligence service's drug-smuggling operation.[18]

So Anslinger proceeded on two tracks: if it were in the national interest, Mafiosi were allowed to receive and distribute drugs; but if not, Anslinger's agents were free to energetically pursue them, and with the arrest of Nick Gentile in 1937, the FBN made its first breakthrough into the Mafia's national drug-trafficking syndicate. A close associate of Lucky Luciano, Gentile was general manager of distribution and, when arrested, had in his possession two address books naming his contacts across the country.

The next breakthrough came in April 1941, when FBN agents arrested Carl Caramussa in Kansas City. Through Caramussa – the first Mafia drug trafficker to turn informer – and Gentile's address books, the FBN was able to chart the flow of drugs from Europe and the Far East, through Mexico and Cuba to Florida, and thence to Kansas City for distribution nationwide. But concerns about the security of American ports and shipping negated these important achievements, and with America's entry into the Second World War the FBN found itself at the center of one of America's darkest scandals – the so-called Luciano Project, or Operation Underworld.

The government's secret policy of seconding drug law enforcement to national security geared up in February 1942 when a French ocean liner was sunk in its berth in New York Harbor. In response, the Navy, which was responsible for securing all US ports, assigned officers to work with federal, state, and local law enforcement officials across America. FBN agents in Seattle and San Francisco helped intern Japanese suspects, while in Texas Al Scharff asked Galveston's Mafia boss, Sam Maceo, to have his underlings watch for German submarines along the Gulf Coast. Maceo, as Scharff and Anslinger knew, reported to Sam Carolla, and had been arrested in 1937 with Nick Gentile and eighty-seven other defendants in the FBN's

Special Endeavor case 131. But Maceo, like Carolla, was powerful enough to escape justice.

The government's Faustian pact with the Mafia was largely developed in New York, where District Attorney Frank S. Hogan gave Navy officers access to his Racket Bureau files so they could hire low-level Mafiosi to spy on potential saboteurs along the waterfront. But the hoods refused to cooperate without the consent of their bosses, at which point Assistant DA Murray J. Gurfein introduced the Naval officers to Meyer Lansky's attorney, Moses Polakoff. A former Assistant US Attorney, Polakoff assured Lansky that the Navy was not interested in mob affairs, but that for security reasons the deal had to be made on a handshake. That being the case, Lansky said he needed a sign of good faith – and the approval of Lucky Luciano in Dannemora Prison.

In a move that satisfied the first condition, Luciano was transferred to Great Meadows Prison near Albany in May 1942. Now accessible, the boss of bosses was soon being visited by a steady stream of Navy officers and mobsters including Lansky, Frank Costello, and Bugsy Siegel. In exchange for a promise to reconsider his lengthy prison sentence, Luciano gave his assent, thus satisfying Lansky's second condition, and Mafia bosses began providing Navy officers with union books and undercover jobs on fishing boats from Maine to Florida. In at least one instance they helped nab Nazi spies; but more importantly there were no crippling labor strikes by longshoremen during the war.

The officer in charge of the Luciano Project, Navy Commander Charles R. Haffenden, worked closely with Mafiosi with great success. But the deal had its downside too, for it allowed the criminals to insinuate themselves within mainstream America. In return for services rendered, ruthless hoods were protected from prosecution for dozens of murders that went unsolved during the war, including the 11 January 1943 assassination of *Il Martello* publisher Carlo Tresca in New York. A staunch anti-fascist and socialist, Tresca in the early 1930s had prevented Luciano's top lieutenant, Vito Genovese, from starting a social club for Italian seamen, knowing that it was going to serve as a front for drug smuggling, and he had threatened to expose the Mafia's connection to pro-fascist publisher Generoso Pope. By ordering Tresca's murder, and getting away with it, Genovese used the Mafia's *modus vivendi* with the government to exact his revenge.

Tresca's murder, however, put a dent in the Mafia's armor. Tresca was a respected publisher and his murder could not be ignored, so District Attorney Frank Hogan launched an investigation and, through a wiretap on Frank Costello, unintentionally learned that Costello had gotten

Magistrate Thomas A. Aurelio a seat on the New York State Supreme Court. Someone – most likely George White, as we shall see later in this chapter – leaked portions of Costello's conversations with Aurelio and, as reported in the 29 August 1943 *New York Times*, Aurelio was overheard pledging his "undying loyalty" to Costello.

The phrase "undying loyalty" graphically expressed the Mafia's power inside Tammany Hall, but it was unrelated to the Tresca murder case, and could not legally be used against Costello. And due to the government's secret pact with the Mafia, which Costello had helped to broker, action against him would have to wait until after the war. But when the time finally came to exact revenge, the man the Establishment turned to, as we shall see, was Harry Anslinger.

THE POLITICS OF HEROIN IN NEW YORK
IN THE SECOND WORLD WAR

After Lucky Luciano was imprisoned in 1936, he entrusted his family to Vito Genovese. But Genovese was indicted for murder and fled to Italy in 1939, and the position passed to Frank Costello, who served admirably in the job; unlike most hoods, he was never seen at nightclubs with his girlfriends or in public with underworld contacts. But serving directly under Costello were some of the most vicious gangsters in the country, including *caporegimes* Thomas Eboli and Gerardo Catena, *consigliere* Michel Miranda, and crew chiefs Vincent Alo, Michael Coppola, and Anthony "Tony Bender" Strollo. Nationwide, Costello managed gambling operations and casinos with Meyer Lansky and bookmaker Frank Erickson. He managed a casino in Louisiana with Tunisian-born Carlos Marcello (real name Calogero Minacora) and Lansky's brother, Jake. He had joint gambling ventures in California with Bugsy Siegel and in New Jersey with Joe Adonis. As the Mafia's prime minister his political contacts included congressmen and Tammany bosses, and individuals within Mayor William O'Dwyer's administration. He was even said to have been a bootlegging partner of Joseph Kennedy's, the wealthy Boston patriarch, US ambassador to Great Britain, and father of JFK.

When the Aurelio "undying loyalty" scandal hit the papers, Anslinger was fully aware of Costello's immunity through the Luciano Project, but looking to the future, he directed the FBN's New York office to link Costello to drug smuggling through East Harlem's 107th Street Gang. Under District Supervisor Robert W. Artiss, the New York office had been monitoring the Gang since 1939. It knew that the Gang's narcotics manager, Joe Gagliano, organized opium smuggling from Mexico through Texas to New York, where it was processed into heroin in clandestine labs, and in 1942 the investigation resulted in the conviction of several of the Gang's top members – excluding, however, their family boss, Thomas Lucchese.

In 1942, Lucchese appointed John Ormento as his new narcotics manager, and the Gang continued to operate until Agent J. Ray Olivera uncovered its new connections in the Caribbean. Designated Special Endeavor case 204, Olivera's investigation culminated in 1943 with the arrest of 106 smugglers in Mexico, including several Germans, and the conviction of seventeen Mafia smugglers in the US. Though implicated and certainly the financial backers of the conspiracy, Thomas Lucchese, Meyer Lansky, and Frank Costello were not indicted.

The reason was simple enough: the triumvirate of organized crime – Luciano, Costello, and Lansky – was providing the military with an invaluable service. They were doing someone else's dirty work, and for that reason they would enjoy political protection, for a while.

THE OSS SUPPORTS THE MAFIA IN ITALY

In January 1943 the Allies decided to invade Sicily, and soon thereafter Navy officers from the Luciano Project joined the Seventh Army in Algeria. On 10 July 1943, Project member Paul A. Alfieri entered Sicily with the invasion fleet and was led to his Sicilian Mafiosi contacts by members of Brooklyn's Vincent Mangano's family.[19] Amazingly, as revealed by Rodney Campbell in *The Luciano Project*, Naval Intelligence acquired hundreds of informants from Mangano and his *caporegime* Joe Adonis in Italy.[20] With the help of these Mafia contacts, Alfieri slipped through enemy lines and was guided to a villa housing the Italian Naval Command. There he cracked open the safe and found invaluable codebooks and documents on the disposition of Italian and German Naval forces in the Mediterranean.

The Mafia was proving very helpful – according to historian Richard Smith, "A very few OSS men had indeed been recruited directly from the ranks of Murder, Inc., and the Detroit 'Purple Gang'" – and after Sicily fell to the Allies, control over Mafia affairs passed from the Navy to several OSS officers.[21] One of them, Vincent J. Scamporino, in a report dated 13 August 1943, described the depth of the OSS's dependence on the Mafia in Sicily: "Only the MAFIA is able to bring about the suppression of the black market practices and influence the 'contadini' who constitute the majority of the population," he said. "We have had conferences with their leaders," Scamporino added, "and a bargain has been struck that they will be doing as we direct." Through them, "We will have an intelligence network established throughout the island."[22]

Working with the Army's Civil Affairs Branch, the OSS proceeded to install Mafiosi in top political positions in Sicily. Don Calogero Vizzini, Mafia boss of bosses in Sicily, was appointed mayor of Villaba, and his successor in 1954, Genco Russo, was named mayor of Mussumeli. As the FBN would soon learn, Vizzini and Russo masterminded Sicilian Mafia narcotics operations before, during, and after the war. Next, highly placed Mafiosi were used to extend US influence into mainland Italy, with the assistance of Lieutenant Colonel Charles Poletti, chief of the American Military Government of the Occupied Territories (AMGOT) in Rome, and Vatican cleric Giovanni Battista Montini (later Pope Paul VI), whose intelligence network of Apostolic Delegates proved helpful in nations around the world.[23]

Here it is crucial to note that the secret pact between America's spy-masters and the Mafia was made before the war, when, according to historian Richard Smith, Earl Brennan, a young Foreign Service officer in Canada, "made the acquaintance of the chiefs of the Italian mafia, sent into exile by Mussolini."[24] Based on these contacts, OSS officer David K. Bruce (Anslinger's friend and in-law through Andrew Mellon, whose daughter Bruce had married) recruited Brennan as chief of OSS Special Intelligence. One can safely assume that Anslinger was deeply involved as a security specialist in this matter, and indeed Smith claims that Brennan "remained aloof, partly at the insistence of Major George White, director of Donovan's counterespionage training and a veteran of the federal Narcotics Bureau who refused to trust the syndicate."[25]

Brennan may well have remained aloof, but as we know from Scamporino, the OSS had intimate relations with the Mafia, and as we shall see, White was less than reluctant to work with them.

THE FBN AND THE LUCIANO PROJECT

George White and Garland Williams were two of a select group of FBN agents to serve with the OSS and get involved in the most arcane aspects of drug-related espionage intrigues.

Garland Williams was well versed in intelligence matters. In June 1941 he took command of the Army's Corps of Intelligence Police, which he reorganized into its first Counterintelligence Corps. Williams next served as an instructor at the Chemical Warfare School, then in June 1942 joined the OSS and was sent, with M. Preston Goodfellow, a former Hearst executive and publisher of the *Brooklyn Eagle*, to London to confer with the chief of the British Special Operations Executive (SOE), William Keswick – the same William Keswick who had sat on Shanghai's Municipal Board with Du Yue-sheng. Meanwhile, William's brother John, with Chiang Kai-shek's spy chief, General Tai Li, was directing SOE operations in Chungking, where Du had relocated in 1941.

After meeting British spymaster Keswick, Williams returned to Washington with the SOE's training manuals and helped establish OSS training schools in Maryland and Virginia. He was the OSS's chief of sabotage training; a member of the Army's Strategic Logistics Committee; helped form OSS Detachment 101 in Burma under Customs Agent Carl Eiffler, whom he knew from his stint with the southwest Border Patrol; and in 1944 served in some undisclosed capacity with the OSS's secret Y Force in Kunming, base of the famous contrabandista airline, the Flying Tigers.

George White also slipped into top-secret operations. In late 1941 he was assigned to the Office of the Coordinator of Information (OCI) and in February and March 1942 received training in the fine arts (as he described them) of "murder and mayhem" at the OSS counterintelligence school in Toronto. In the summer of 1942 he became a member of the X-2 counterespionage training division and, according to reporter Al Ostrow, "established America's first school for spies and counter-spies." The idea, White avowed, "was that a cop should be able to teach others how to escape being caught by cops." And, he might have added, how to teach spies to elude FBN agents. Accompanied by an interpreter, White then moved throughout North Africa before the Allied landings, organizing resistance groups among the Arabs.[26]

White slipped into Cairo in early November 1942, then visited Lebanon, Syria, Iraq, and Iran, where he surveyed opium stockpiles. By early 1943 he was in Jerusalem with Colonel Harold Hoskins, the OSS officer in charge of Mideast operations, and Ulius Amoss, a Greek–American importer, and executive officer of the OSS's Mideast detachment. Notably, White and Amoss had met in February 1942 while working on the Eliopoulos case with White's protégé, Agent Charlie Siragusa, and Charlie Dyar (both of whom, along with J. Ray Olivera and several other FBN agents, would also join the OSS). Through March 1943, White and Amoss investigated "the frequent tie-up"[27] between smuggling and spying, until Amoss was fired for importing "an ex-convict from the United States for the purposes of expert assassination."[28] If anyone knew assassins it was White, not Amoss, but OSS security officer Robert Delaney cleared White of wrongdoing. Apparently Amoss was expendable, but White's underworld connections were not, and in April he met again with Delaney to discuss what in his diary he termed the "Mafia Plan."[29]

In 1943 the Mafia Plan was what historian Rodney Campbell dubbed the Luciano Project, otherwise known as Operation Underworld. Whatever it was called, White was at the heart of it, though not as a foil as historian Richard Smith claims, but as security chief and fixer. In the summer and fall of 1943, as described in his diary, White attended several Mafia Plan meetings, including an August excursion into Chinatown with James J. Angleton, who was soon to become chief of OSS X-2 operations in Rome and later chief of the CIA's Counterintelligence Division. One month later White escorted Angleton into Chinatown again, this time with his boss from the Mideast, Colonel Hoskins. Considering that the OSS was passing X-2 personnel through the FBN's New York office at the time, the purpose of these trips undoubtedly concerned the Mafia Plan – which translated into drug smuggling, espionage, and assassination.

While serving as chief of Mafia Plan security, White shared an apartment with John Hanly, the Secret Service agent with whom he'd visited Lucky Luciano in 1938. Then serving as a Navy officer in the Luciano Project, Hanly kept White up to date on the frequent chats his boss, Charles Haffenden, was having with Frank Costello – chats that DA Frank Hogan was secretly recording! In this way White covered all the bases; through Hanly he was able to keep Anslinger abreast of Haffenden's deep political machinations and, as Mafia Plan security chief, with access to Hogan's tapes, he could apply pressure on Mafioso Frank Costello, for example, by leaking Magistrate Aurelio's aforementioned "undying loyalty" pledge to the *New York Times*.

As if that wasn't enough, George White was just getting started.

TRUTH DRUGS, NARCOTICS AND COUNTERESPIONAGE

In early 1942 OSS chief William Donovan decided that extracting the truth from enemy soldiers and spies was essential to winning the war and he directed his staff of research scientists to produce a Truth Drug. The scientists worked under the supervision of a committee that included Anslinger and Mal Harney, and after experimenting with the most powerful drugs the FBN could produce, the scientists settled on tetrahydrocannabinol acetate, the active chemical compound in marijuana. The scientists, however, were not equipped to handle street work, so Donovan and Anslinger chose George White to test the Truth Drug on unsuspecting hoods, spies, and assassins.[30]

In May 1943 the OSS Truth Drug team assembled in Anslinger's office with a beaker full of liquid marijuana extract and an eyedropper and began lacing loose-leaf tobacco, which they rolled into a joint that was potent enough to knock White on his ass. High as a Rastafarian, and probably laughing at the irony of Anslinger's Killer Weed campaign, he embarked on his mission.

White's mission was to discover how enemy spies were exploiting drug smuggling routes worldwide. Like its progeny the CIA, the OSS wanted to use secret drug smuggling routes to insert agents behind enemy lines and recruit foreign national drug smugglers in the cause for freedom and democracy. Liberating occupied France was a major goal and the OSS was aware that some drug smugglers were collaborating with the Gestapo, while others were in the Resistance. One of the leading experts in this matter was Lucky Luciano's associate, August Del Grazio, who'd been the Mafia's representative to Elie Eliopoulos and had managed a heroin factory in Istanbul on their behalf – until the US consul in Turkey saw Del Grazio's face on the Committee of One Hundred's blacklist. Anslinger informed the Gestapo and Del Grazio was arrested in Berlin in late 1931 and served a brief stint in prison. To avoid a similar fate, Eliopoulos initiated a meeting with Charlie Dyar in Athens where he ratted out his rival, and partner, Louis Lyon. Ten years later, Nazi sympathizer Eliopoulos and his brother George were arrested in New York by George White, Charlie Dyar, and Charlie Siragusa; but to no avail – the statute of limitations had expired on the 1931 case, and the Eliopoulos brothers were set free. Lyon, meanwhile, would arrange the assassination of his and Eliopoulos's former partner, Gestapo agent Paul Carbone, in December 1943, forcing Carbone's protégé, François Spirito, to flee to Madrid.[31]

White's Truth Drug experiments were related to these intrigues, which is why he traveled to New York in May 1943 to test his superpot on Del Grazio, whose connections to Corsican and Mafia drug smugglers were well known. According to author John Marks, what Del Grazio revealed about "the ins and outs of the drug trade" was "so sensitive that the CIA deleted it from OSS documents it released thirty-four years later."[32]

Obviously, White's session with Del Grazio was a smashing success, and subsequent Truth Drug experiments included the interrogation of German prisoners of war and American soldiers suspected of harboring communist sympathies. On 25 September 1943, White visited Manhattan Project security officer John Lansdale in San Francisco to administer the Truth Drug to scientists developing America's atomic bomb.

Having completed this assignment, White in April 1944 was assigned as OSS X-2 chief in the India–Burma–China theater. One of his tasks was to investigate rumors that Detachment 101, which had been organized by Garland Williams under former Customs Border Patrol Agent Carl Eifler, was providing opium to Burmese guerrillas fighting the Japanese. The rumors were true and on Anslinger's behalf, White asked Eifler to stop. But the OSS officer refused.[33]

As Eifler's replacement William Peers succinctly stated, "If opium could be useful in achieving victory, the pattern was clear. We would use opium."[34]

America's spymasters would never sever the drug-smuggling connections they established during the war, nor could the FBN exert any influence over the situation. On the contrary, the FBN assumed a collateral role in narcotics-related espionage activities that was antithetical to its mandate. The Luciano Project and Truth Drug programs are examples, as was the formation of the Sino-American Cooperative Organization (SACO) by Navy Secretary Frank Knox, OSS chief William Donovan, and Chiang Kai-shek's intelligence chief, General Tai Li. SACO would effectively put an end to any drug control over Nationalist China.

SACO went into action in 1943, when a team of Americans under Treasury Agent Charles Johnston was sent to Chungking to train Chiang Kai-shek's secret police force. Milton Miles, the Navy officer who commanded SACO with General Tai Li, describes Johnston as having spent fifteen years "in the narcotics game."[35]

When Johnston and his team, which included FBN agents, arrived in China, Tai Li was working closely with drug smuggler Du Yue-sheng in Chungking. It was an open secret that Tai Li's agents escorted opium caravans from Yunnan to Saigon and used Red Cross operations as a front for selling opium to the Japanese. His drug-smuggling operation undoubtedly reached American shores, but once he was appointed co-director of SACO, he received the same immunity afforded Detachment 101.

VITO GENOVESE BRINGS IT ALL BACK HOME

In July 1944, the Army's Criminal Investigations Division (CID) learned that the former lieutenant governor of New York State, Colonel Charles Poletti, then running AMGOT in Italy, had authorized the appointment of Vito Genovese as an interpreter, first in Sicily then Naples, for a succession of Army Civil Affairs and Judge Advocate General officers. Amazingly, one of the most violent and corrupt Mafia chieftains had become a special employee of the US Army. But spymasters as well as politicians rely on the underworld, and Genovese had developed extensive contacts in Europe in 1933 when, while setting up narcotics connections in Italy, he befriended the secretary of Mussolini's Fascist Party. Six years later Genovese was named as a suspect in the 1934 murder of gangster Ferdinand Boccia, and fled to Italy, where his friendship with Mussolini's top aides proved beneficial, as did a $250,000 donation to the Party. In return for his generosity, Genovese was allowed to purchase a power plant near Naples and manage a chain of banks controlled by the Fascist government. For ordering the murder of anti-fascist publisher Carlo Tresca in New York in 1943 he was awarded Italy's highest civilian title, presented personally by Mussolini.

Genovese's narcotics connections reportedly enabled Mussolini's son-in-law to fly opium out of Turkey to refiners in Milan. The heroin was then flown to Mediterranean ports on Italian Air Force planes and routed by Genovese to Nicolo Impostato, an assassin from Kansas City who had replaced Nick Gentile, then in Italy assisting Genovese and Poletti, as general manager of the American Mafia's national drug syndicate.[36]

As the war came to a close, Genovese used his privileged position as Poletti's liaison to the Italian Mafia to establish black-market routes between Germany, Yugoslavia, and Sicily. But the happy arrangement ended in June 1944 when CID Agent Orange Dickey arrested two Canadian deserters for having stolen two US Army trucks. The Canadians fingered Genovese as their boss, and Dickey tracked him down and arrested him on 27 August 1944. Forewarned, Genovese had in his possession letters of recommendation from three Army officers, praising him for having exposed several cases of bribery and black marketeering. The letters, and the fact that Genovese had been forewarned, sparked Dickey's curiosity, so he contacted the FBI and was told that Genovese had been indicted and was wanted for Boccia's murder.

After searching Genovese's apartment and finding a powerful radio receiver, Dickey sought entry to his bank vault. But the Italian authorities refused, and by the time he did get in, the vault was empty. Frustrated, Dickey wrote a report in which he named several high-ranking Army officers as being involved in a conspiracy to protect Genovese; at which point the US consul told Dickey that Genovese was an Italian citizen and could not be held in an American jail.

Unaware of just how well-connected Genovese was, Dickey went to Rome to seek Poletti's advice; and there, by coincidence, he encountered

William O'Dwyer, former Brooklyn DA, friend of Joe Adonis and Frank Costello, then serving as the Judge Advocate General in Italy. When Dickey described the Genovese investigation, O'Dwyer said it was of no concern to the Army and he suggested that Dickey contact the current Brooklyn DA, which Dickey did. The DA put the machinery in motion and in November 1944 the State Department issued Genovese a passport, allowing him to be returned to New York to stand trial for the Boccia murder. But a general's name had become involved in the case, and in December the Provost Marshal told Dickey to transfer Genovese to a civilian prison in Bari, where OSS officer Charlie Siragusa, having transferred from the FBN, questioned him. As Siragusa recalled, "being a civilian cop I couldn't resist pushing the hood on his New York City rackets. It was known that he still pulled the strings back there." [37]

By Siragusa's account, the interview was a waste of time – possibly because he had been instructed to give Genovese a free pass. In any case, Dickey's efforts to achieve justice met yet another obstacle when, in January 1945, the principal witness against Genovese died of an overdose of barbiturates while sequestered in a Brooklyn jail. Shortly after the murder of the only material witness against him, Genovese's extradition was processed, and Dickey single-handedly brought him to New York in May 1945. But there was one last surprise to come: as Dickey arrived at the DA's office, General O'Dwyer came walking out. For what it was worth – and it certainly wasn't worth all his efforts, including threats on his life and his family's – Dickey dutifully transferred Genovese to the authorities and then faded into obscurity. O'Dwyer was elected mayor of New York, and the case against Genovese was dismissed. As Brigadier General Carter W. Clarke remarked in a memo dated 30 June 1945, the Genovese file was so "hot" that it should "be filed and no action taken." [38]

Criminology professor Alan Block asserts that the Genovese case "marks an important point in American political history" in which professional criminals continued to ply their trade, but "for new patrons." [39]

No doubt these "new patrons" were America's master spies.

4

INSIDE THE FBN

"What's past is prologue."
Shakespeare, *The Tempest*, act II, scene 1

At the end of the Second World War, momentous changes were taking place in US foreign and domestic policies that would radically affect the FBN's organizational consciousness and direction. Within the FBN the issues were corruption and competition among agents, race relations, closer collaboration with government security and intelligence agencies, the fallout from the Luciano Project, and bureaucratic conflicts with the FBI and customs service. In this transitional period dynamics were set in motion that would determine the course of drug law enforcement during the second half of the twentieth century and set the stage for the FBN's demise in 1968.

The FBN's primary image-maker and consciousness-shaper was Harry Anslinger. Unlike many of his bureaucratic peers, Anslinger had seen the war coming and had taken steps to ensure that a five-year supply of opium would be available to America's military and civilian populations. In 1939 he had "arranged with drug manufacturers to stockpile a sufficient quantity of opium to carry the US and her allies through a conflict."[1] He did this without congressional appropriations, by having private funds made available directly to opium manufacturers in Turkey, Iran, and India. To ensure security he convinced the League of Nations to move its narcotics files and experts to the US, and in early 1942 he instructed the Defense Supplies Corporation to "acquire all available stocks of opium in preparation for a long war."[2] He personally determined the amount of opium that was brought from Turkey and Iran to the manufacturing companies and he stationed inspectors at their facilities.

"He would send surrendered drugs down to Fort Knox by American Express," recalls Agent Matt Seifer. "Ten trucks loaded with opium, guarded by FBN agents armed with Tommy guns. From Fort Knox it went to the pharmaceutical companies where the morphine was extracted; places like Ligits, New York Quinine, and Mallinchrodt and Merck. Anslinger had a control committee and every manufacturer had a quota."

As a result of Anslinger's foresight, the Allies by 1943 were relying on America for most of their opium derivatives, and Anslinger was serving as the guardian of the free world's drug supply. When he learned that Peru had built a cocaine factory, he and the Board of Economic Warfare confiscated its product before it could be sold to Germany or Japan. In another instance Anslinger and George A. Morlock (who had replaced Stuart Fuller as his counterpart at the State Department) prevented a Hoffman La Roche subsidiary in Argentina from selling drugs to Germany. At the same time, Anslinger met his security and counterespionage responsibilities by permitting "an American company to ship drugs to Southeast Asia despite receiving intelligence reports that French authorities were permitting opiate smuggling into China and collaborating with Japanese drug traffickers."[3]

Reconciling the FBN's incompatible espionage and drug law enforcement functions would become one of Anslinger's primary public relations goals throughout the remainder of his tenure as Commissioner of Narcotics.

PROMOTING THE BUREAU

As a result of his wartime services, Anslinger's prestige and power increased dramatically within the national security Establishment. But there had been no sensational narcotics cases, and drug law enforcement was of little concern to the war-weary public. Many of his agents had been conscripted into the military, and his agent force had dwindled to a bare minimum, to as few as 150 agents. So Anslinger launched a major publicity campaign to create an urgent need for his organization.

The campaign kicked off in 1945 in Washington, DC, when he accused Judge Bolitha Laws of being soft on drug offenders. When, in response to the provocation, Judge Laws suggested that Anslinger's agents might be inept, the Commissioner was ready and waiting: noting to his friends in the press that the Washington field office had only three agents, he summoned fifty more from around the nation and divided them into two teams.[4] With the aid of local policemen and Deputy US Marshals, the teams led spectacular raids on several narcotics rings. One team under Agent LeRoy W. Morrison arrested 200 Blacks in the capital's ghetto and seized a quantity of heroin that was traced to Harlem. The other team, under the direction of Agent Gon Sam Mue, arrested 123 Chinese suspects in fourteen downtown opium dens. The raids brought home the immediacy of the drug problem, proved the FBN was not inept, and scored Anslinger points with the Washington press corps, which appreciated the well-staged publicity stunt.[5]

Sustaining the public's perception of an urgent need, however, required a steady diet of sensational publicity, so Anslinger aimed his agents at celebrities like Robert Mitchum (busted for marijuana possession) and Errol Flynn (vilified for his cocaine habit). FBN agents paid particular attention to Black jazz musicians like Billie Holiday, arrested by Agent Joe Bransky in 1947 in Philadelphia, and saxophonist Charlie Parker, arrested by Agent John T. Cusack in June 1948 in New York City.

Putting a famous face on the drug problem highlighted the increasing availability of heroin and, as a bonus, by linking marijuana to surges in juvenile delinquency, homosexuality, interracial sex, and other signs of social decay brought about by liberalism, Anslinger bolstered the need for a punitive approach to drug abuse, thus satisfying his conservative core of supporters in Congress while, at the same time, reinforcing the urgent need for his organization.

Another aspect of Anslinger's publicity campaign began in January 1946, when Governor Thomas Dewey approved the commutation of Lucky Luciano's lengthy prison term in return for his wartime services. Luciano was deported to Italy and freedom on 9 February 1946, bringing joy to his Mafia associates. Anslinger, however, was livid with rage, and within a year, allegations that the Mafia had purchased Luciano's freedom were traced to FBN agents, prompting Dewey to engage Anslinger in a bitter feud that would last for years and ultimately damage the FBN's credibility. But Anslinger served the espionage Establishment, which had a vested interest in denying that the Luciano Project ever took place; and in the long run Luciano's deportation benefited Anslinger by providing the FBN with a durable scapegoat and the basis for a sustainable PR campaign. Luciano contributed to the FBN's cause by immediately conferring, upon arriving in Italy, with the Sicilian boss of bosses, Don Calogero Vizzini, and by surrounding himself with fellow deportees.

Anslinger would also suggest that Luciano was part of a communist plot to subvert America with narcotic drugs. This unproven allegation would also damage the FBN's credibility; but the fiction was accepted at the time and helped Anslinger to persuade Congress that stopping drugs overseas, before they reached America's shores, was a matter of national security – a prescient notion that fitted neatly with the Cold War imperative for foreign intervention and helped to establish the need for a larger, more powerful federal Narcotics Bureau.

THE ASCENT OF THE MAFIA

While Anslinger was exploiting America's prejudices and fears to advance the interests of the FBN, the underworld was reorganizing its drug smuggling and distribution industry. Central to this reorganization was Vito Genovese's release from jail on 24 June 1946. Having worked for the US Army in Italy, Genovese enjoyed a degree of political protection in Manhattan, where he took over the multimillion-dollar Italian lottery. Once the money started rolling in, he began scheming to seize control of the Luciano family from Frank Costello and claim the title of *capo di tutti capi* of the American Mafia.

During this violent transitional stage, gangster veterans of the Luciano Project began to play a more important role in the deep politics of American society. A quick examination of the background characters in the 1943 murder of *Il Martello* publisher Carlo Tresca provides a graphic example of organized crime's deep political association with members of the Establishment.

Tresca was an avowed socialist, and his political adversary was Generoso Pope, publisher of the pro-fascist *Il Progresso Italo-Americano*. It has always been easy for fascists to acquire political patrons in America, but once it became clear that America was going to war with Italy, Pope enlisted the help of New York Congressman Samuel Dickstein, co-founder of the House Un-American Activities Committee (HUAC). In 1941 Dickstein defended Pope before Congress, a fact that contributed immensely to Pope's successful attempt to achieve respectability. [6]

With Dickstein in his corner, Pope emerged as a wedge between the Establishment and the Mafia and, with the support of influential friends like columnist Drew Pearson (a former employee of *Il Progresso*), and Assistant US Attorney Roy Cohn, he was able to provide political cover for his gangster cronies. Frank Costello, for example, was godfather to his children. But Pope's closest underworld ally was Joseph Bonanno, whose narcotics manager, Carmine Galante, though never convicted, was universally recognized as Tresca's assassin.[7]

All the Mafia families were investing in labor racketeering, and Pope had aligned with International Ladies Garment Workers Union leader Luigi Antonini through a sweetheart deal arranged by Joe Bonanno's *consigliere*, Frank Garofalo. A vicious killer, Garofalo had been Pope's "factotum" since 1934, when, as Professor Alan Block asserts, Pope had used him to intimidate "other Italian-language newspapers which were anti-fascist and anti-Pope."[8] Tresca threatened to expose Garofalo's connection with Pope, and as a result of that (and because he had blocked Genovese's attempt to establish a social club as a front for drug trafficking), Genovese ordered his execution. Tresca was shot and killed on 11 January 1943. Galante was arrested and held for eight months, but was never indicted, and the FBI failed to connect any Mafiosi with the crime – despite the fact that contributions to Galante's defense fund were funneled through Lucchese family member Joseph DiPalermo and the Teamsters' Union.

Aware that the Mafia was serving new patrons in the wake of the Luciano Project, Pope threw his weight behind the CIA-supported Christian Democrats and became a key player in shaping US foreign policy in Italy. His relations with the espionage Establishment were reportedly cemented when his son, having served briefly in the CIA, purchased the *New York Enquirer* and turned it into the public opinion-shaping, Mafia-friendly tabloid the *National Enquirer*.[9]

In these ways the Mafia began the post-war era on a firm political, economic, and national security footing. The same, however, could not be said for the understaffed, fragmented FBN.

A PERIOD OF READJUSTMENT

In 1945 the FBN was composed of approximately 150 agents and inspectors. The agents had passed the Treasury exam and spent two weeks at the Law Enforcement School, or as Special Hires they were exempt from the standard Civil Service rules, based on some unique qualification such as the ability to speak a Sicilian dialect. FBN inspectors were licensed pharmacists who worked compliance cases, which involved checking the records of pharmacies and physicians. Some inspectors were agents as well.

Within this small group, a smaller group of case-making agents began to emerge as the organization's leaders. Chief among them was George

White, whose wartime activities and involvement with the Luciano Project placed him squarely in the middle of the FBN's alliance with America's security and intelligence apparatus.

In July 1945 White returned to the US and, after conferring with William Donovan, visited Garland Williams (back from the war and serving again as FBN district supervisor in New York) to study the office files and meet with Mafia expert Arthur Giuliani. In early August, White and Anslinger's trusted enforcement assistant, Malachi Harney, traveled to Kansas City to interview Mafia boss Charles Binaggio, and review the watershed Impostato–DeLuca case of 1942.[10]

As mentioned briefly in the previous chapter, Kansas City since the mid-1930s had served as the way station in the Mafia's national distribution system, under the auspices of Mafia boss Joseph DeLuca. Based in Kansas City, Nick Gentile managed distribution until his arrest in 1937 in FBN Special Endeavor case 131, at which point Nick Impostato took over, traveling the country to make sure that drugs flowed freely from Florida, through Kansas City, to Denver, Dallas, Los Angeles, and other western cities. But the success of the nationwide operation relied on political security in Kansas City, and in that respect Joe DeLuca was the key until his downfall in 1942. As Ed Reid notes in *Mafia*, the FBN's 1942 case "shook Kansas City's Mafiosi to the bone."[11] But by 1945 James Balestrere, manager of the Chicago-based racing wire service in Kansas City, and Charlie Binaggio, the Mafia's liaison to Kansas City's Pendergast machine, were back in control.

Apart from its central role in the Mafia's drug syndicate, two things made Kansas City of special importance to the FBN in August 1945. The first issue was personal: Carl Caramussa – a member of the syndicate and the main witness against Impostato and DeLuca in the 1942 case – had been killed by a shotgun blast to the head two months earlier in Chicago, where he was living under an assumed identity. That was bad enough, but the Mafia assassins had hung a wreath in the local FBN agent's garage as an unsubtle warning, and Anslinger, Harney, and White were enraged and determined to put the arrogant hoods back in their pre-Luciano Project place.

The second matter was political, and concerned President Truman's relationship with Kansas City's infamous Pendergast machine. A compulsive gambler, successful businessman, and astute political kingmaker, Thomas Pendergast had handpicked Harry Truman for the Senate in 1934 and had supported Truman throughout his political career. But Pendergast had earned the wrath of the FBN when, in an effort to help Kansas City survive the Depression, he opened up the city to gambling, Black jazz musicians, and by extension, the Mafia's drug syndicate.

As the FBN's Mafia experts knew, the Kansas City Mafia had recovered from the 1942 catastrophe and was functioning as usual under new bosses James Balestrere and Charlie Binaggio. Anslinger's enforcement assistant Mal Harney, a staunch Republican, knew that the Pendergast machine relied on Binaggio and Balestrere to bring out North Side voters on election day. And while it may not have mattered to Harney that the votes invariably went to Democrats, his personal involvement in the Kansas City investigation earned him Truman's eternal enmity and prevented his promotion until the Eisenhower administration.

Though a self-professed Democrat, White was Harney's protégé, and after raiding Binaggio's gambling joint he dutifully and delightedly punched Binaggio in the nose when the hood "tried to get tough."[12] At Harney's direction, White next met with John Larocca, the Mafia boss in western Pennsylvania. In quick succession White visited major Mafiosi in Chicago, Nevada, New Orleans (where he met Sam Carolla), and New York and on 3 September he met with Santo Trafficante in Tampa. White did not disclose in his diary the purpose of their meeting, but he knew the Kansas City syndicate was supplied "by Mafia agents in Tampa, Florida, who received the smuggled drugs from Marseilles, via Havana."[13]

White undoubtedly let Trafficante know that the FBN was aware of his activities, but he *may* have done something more significant than that. Trafficante, Larocca, and several of the other Teamster-connected Mafiosi whom White visited in the summer of 1945 would eventually become involved in CIA intrigues in Cuba — and if anyone was in a position to help the Mafia reorganize its narcotics activities after the war, on behalf of its new patrons in the espionage Establishment, it was White. While it is only circumstantial evidence, immediately after White's meeting with Santo Trafficante, the patron "saint" of drug "trafficking" fought and won a war with his Mafia competitors in Florida and went on with Luciano Project veteran Meyer Lansky to acquire total control of the Cuba-to-Tampa drug connection.

On 12 September, having touched base with many of America's most powerful Mafiosi, White traveled to Chicago to replace James Biggins as supervisor of District 9, covering Illinois, Indiana, and Wisconsin. White would remain there until June 1947 when he would replace Ralph Oyler as district supervisor in Detroit.

Meanwhile, Garland Williams in 1945 had resumed his post as New York district supervisor, and under his direction the office was focusing its attention on the 107th Street Gang and its Mexican connection; on polished Frank Costello, the FBN's most wanted man in New York since the Aurelio scandal of 1943; and on Joe Adonis, the Mafia's handsome field marshal, now headquartered in New Jersey.

The FBN's propaganda campaign against Costello began with a front page article in the 19 December 1946 *New York Times* detailing the arrest of six men from the "East Harlem Narcotics Syndicate." Among the six were Vito Genovese's *caporegime* Mike Coppola and Tom Lucchese's narcotics manager Joseph Gagliano. Williams branded them "the young Mafia of Harlem" and claimed that Costello was their "mastermind and absolute ruler."[14] In a 21 December 1946 article in the *Times* Costello vehemently denied the charge.

There was a ring of truth to Williams's allegation, but the FBN was in fact concentrating on Brooklyn Mafioso Joe Adonis, who was far more deeply involved in drug trafficking than Costello. Prior to his transfer to the OSS, White had spearheaded the FBN's investigation into Adonis's drug-smuggling activities. In March 1941, White and Agent William J. Craig had tracked Adonis to Duke's Clam Bar in Fort Lee, New Jersey, where Adonis regularly met with Willie Moretti, Tom Lucchese, and other Mafia leaders to discuss business.[15]

Under the direction of Garland Williams, Agent Ross B. Ellis picked up the trail in 1945 and through a wiretap placed in the phone booth at Duke's he discovered exciting new information about Adonis's drug and gambling connections in Saratoga Springs, New York, Miami, and Detroit. All involved Meyer Lansky's Jewish associates in the Purple Gang, with whom Adonis co-owned gambling houses in Florida, in partnership with Frank Coppola and other major Mafiosi from Detroit. Ellis also learned that Adonis was in contact with Lucky Luciano, Vito Genovese's *caporegime* Tony Bender, and Vincent Mangano's *caporegime* Albert Anastasia. By December 1945 Garland Williams had joined forces with DA Frank Hogan and, through Ellis, had inserted an informant (Dr. H. L. Hsieh, a wealthy Chinese merchant and gambler) inside Duke's – and the hammer was about to fall on the Adonis operation.[16]

FBN FACTIONS AND HEADQUARTERS AFTER THE WAR

Having completed his wartime tour with the OSS in Italy, Charlie Siragusa returned to New York and was assigned by Garland Williams as a group leader, and emerged as the titular leader of New York's Italian agents. In

New York in 1946, Charlie Siragusa, Joe Amato, Arthur Giuliani, and Angelo Zurlo formed the original Italian Squad, which focused exclusively on penetrating the Mafia and formed the basis of what would later become the International Group, the critical point of contact with the Bureau's expanding overseas operations.

Also arriving in New York was tall, handsome Howard Chappell, who had met and formed a friendship with Garland Williams while serving as a parachute instructor at the Army Airborne Ranger Training School in Fort Benning. OSS chief Donovan had, at the time, appointed Williams commanding officer of the Airborne Training School, and it was there that Williams recognized Chappell's exceptional courage, composure, and combative spirit, and recruited him into the OSS.

As an OSS officer, Chappell led Italian partisans in daring sabotage missions behind enemy lines, and after the war his exploits were chronicled in a *Reader's Digest* article commissioned by "Wild Bill" Donovan, who needed good press to maintain the OSS over the objections of FBI director J. Edgar Hoover and the joint chiefs of staff. But Donovan's effort failed, the OSS was disbanded, and after the fanfare died down Chappell found himself looking for work.

"In 1947 I decided to stop at the FBN office at 90 Church Street and see Garland Williams," Chappell recalls, "and he suggested I come into the Bureau, which I did. I was hired in Cleveland, my hometown, and in 1947 I began working cases under Joe Bell in Detroit."

Chappell goes on to describe the core group that was managing the FBN when he joined it: "Anslinger was the Commissioner, and Mal Harney and George Cunningham were his assistants. Harney was straight-laced and aloof, but a tireless worker, while Cunningham was laid-back and liked by all the agents. Cunningham was a friend of Kentucky Senator Alben Barkley, and after Barkley became Truman's vice president, Cunningham became Anslinger's deputy in 1949. Cunningham had the lobbying power on the Hill on the Democratic side, while Anslinger and Harney had the influence on the Republican side, along with several powerful supporters outside of government.

"Baxter 'B. T.' Mitchell from Tupelo, Mississippi was chief counsel and an assistant to Cunningham. His rabbi was Senator Theodore G. Bilbo [D–MS]. Mitchell died at a fairly young age and was replaced by Carl DiBaggio. Betsy Mack handled all financial operations, including final approval of expense vouchers. Betsy was about fifty years old: a big, attractive, good-natured woman as long as you leveled with her, but hell on wheels if anyone tried to flimflam her. Betsy had an assistant, and Anslinger had a driver named Tommie Andrews. Andrews doubled as agent in charge of the Washington field office, which was separate from Bureau headquarters. Headquarters itself occupied two floors in the Coast Guard building on 290 Pennsylvania Avenue.

"Garland ran the New York office with the help of Group Leader Irwin Greenfeld. Greeny was known for his imagination and intelligence, and Garland held him in such high esteem that he always named him as acting supervisor in his absence, much to the dismay of the Irish and Italian agents in the office.

"Incidentally," Chappell adds, "if you think there was a small number of people running the Bureau in the late 1940s, remember, we only had 160 agents and a $2 million budget. We had one-man offices in important places like Cincinnati, Buffalo, Miami, and New Orleans."

CORRUPTION AND COMPETITION WITHIN THE FBN

While FBN headquarters was staffed by an elite group of veteran insiders, its fourteen district supervisory positions were up for grabs, and the competition was fierce; factions were forming and Anslinger's assistant, Mal Harney, was looking for reasons to put the old bulls out to pasture. Corruption, which most commonly meant taking bribes from drug dealers or providing drugs to addict informants, had emerged as the FBN's biggest internal problem, with Chicago as the focus.

Chicago had earned its dubious reputation in 1925 when Elmer Irey arrested Narcotic Division Supervisor William Beech and three agents for selling seized drugs to gangsters. Upon arriving in Chicago in 1927, Maurice Helbrant was told by the new district supervisor, "There is no dope in Chicago." There was "no moral regeneration, either," Helbrant quipped, noting that the price of dope was very affordable and that business was flourishing. [17]

The situation hadn't improved by 1948, when Agent Martin F. Pera was assigned to the Windy City. One of a new breed of earnest young agents (including Frank Sojat, Paul Gross, and George Emrich) to join the FBN in Chicago after the war, Pera was born in France and was fluent in German, French, and Assyrian. As a soldier in the Army Signal Corps during the Second World War, he had developed a passion for electronics and after graduating from Northwestern University he joined the FBN.

Pera describes Chicago as a "hell hole" with two types of agents: "Old-timers who were a legacy of Prohibition and told great stories about how they'd raid a speakeasy then commandeer it like pirates raiding a ship. And young kids fresh out of college with a totally different perspective. They knew that local corruption was a fact of life, but they saw a higher role for federal law enforcement, one that focused on interstate distribution, and could not be handled by 150 agents."

Pera and the new breed in Chicago were fortunate to come under the tutelage of Vince Newman, "the only older agent with his head above water." As Pera explains, "Newman had worked on the Hip Sing T'ong case with George White, and he showed us the importance of Special Endeavor cases. He made us read the files to see how they worked, and in doing that I learned three things: that nothing changes; that I had to get out of Chicago; and that in order to get to the top in the Bureau you had to have the respect of your peers, *and* a rabbi, someone like Wilbur Mills at Appropriations. Most of the old-timers knew that and had grown jaundiced. They were just plodding along, serving out their time as administrators. The only active old-timer was Benny Pocoroba, who did special projects for Anslinger. Benny had enormous patience: he'd feed pigeons on a stakeout, then trap, cook, and eat them.

"There were twenty-five agents in Chicago when I got there," Pera continues, "and it was fascinating to learn how the system worked. My first group leader gave me fifty dollars and said, 'Go buy pot. You have a week.' So I ventured into Chicago alone and started buying pot and less often heroin. I'd make two or three buys, then we'd hit the pad. I was getting pretty good at it and eventually made what I thought was the perfect case: three buys, marked bills, no defense. Well, the judge throws it out. 'It's too pat,' he says."

Pera rolls his eyes. "Chicago was an incredibly corrupt place, so I wasn't too surprised when one of my cases led to a sergeant on the vice squad. I followed him on his route, and everywhere he went he collected money and/or junk. So I went to our district supervisor, R. W. Artiss, but he told me to shut up. So I learned there are limits set by big-city vice squads — which are usually run by some paunchy disreputable guy working with whores, degenerate gamblers, and drug dealers — and that kickbacks are funneled to the top through them. In big cities like New York, Chicago, and Los Angeles, in the days before the Kennedys, certain neighborhoods were controlled by political machines working with the vice squad and the Mafia. There wasn't a drug deal on the South Side of Chicago that didn't pass through the police to the politicians."

Pera was determined to find a better way, and his solution was the Special Endeavor conspiracy case, in which agents followed cases across district lines and used all the investigative tools available to them, including undercover agents, wiretaps, and informers. Serving as a model was George White's case on the Hip Sing T'ong.

But Pera became disillusioned with undercover work. "Only four or five agents in the whole organization were any good at it. Most were corrupted by the lure of the underworld. They thought they could check their morality at the door – go out and lie, cheat, and steal – then come back and retrieve it. But you can't. In fact, if you're successful because you can lie, cheat, and steal, those things become tools you use in the bureaucracy. You're talking about guys whose lives depended on their ability to be devious and who become very good at it. So these people became the bosses, and undercover work became the credo – and a source of boundless, profitable hype. Meanwhile the agents were losing their simplicity in subtle ways."

The profane nature of undercover work spilled over into competition for the fourteen district supervisory jobs, and only four districts were large enough to have group leader positions. Competition for these jobs was fierce. At the same time, budgetary restraints made promotions hard to come by, especially for the aging, tainted agents from the Old PU. In addition to that a battle royal was being waged by the drugstore inspectors and the street agents. At the time the inspectors had the advantage, because most of the dope that hit the streets during the war had been diverted by crooked doctors and pharmacists. As a result, registrant and compliance work had become more important than undercover work, and pharmacist/ agents like Joseph Bransky and Henry Giordano had emerged from the rank and file to get supervisory positions.

Bransky in particular was one of Anslinger's favorite agents. Not only had he arrested Lucky Luciano in 1923; more importantly, Bransky had made the 1941 case on the Direct Sales Company, which was selling morphine tablets through the mail to doctors in South Carolina. More than 1,350 wholesalers were providing doctors with narcotics, and the Direct Sales case put a stop to the practice. As Anslinger proudly proclaimed in *The Protectors*, Bransky was "the instrument through which the Supreme Court hammered home the responsibility of the drug trade and medical profession alike for alert narcotics supervision and control."[18]

But the most successful of the drugstore men would be Henry L. Giordano. A pharmacist from Seattle, Giordano became a full-fledged agent working on an important undercover case in Canada. More remains to be said about him, but for now it's enough to know that in 1962 Giordano would replace Anslinger as Commissioner of Narcotics.

RACE RELATIONS WITHIN THE FBN

After the war, with the resurgence of the Mafia and international drug smuggling, the emphasis shifted from compliance work to undercover work and conspiracy cases, and street agents became more important than the inspectors. Likewise the war brought about desegregation, a mass migration of Southern Blacks to Northern cities, and a rise in drug addiction, much of it among former soldiers and much of it in Black communities. Congress, ever vigilant, declared a heroin epidemic and pushed for results, which Anslinger was happy to deliver. But in order to achieve those results, Anslinger had to increasingly rely upon Black undercover agents, a development that put his personal prejudices on a collision course with his organization's vital needs.

Anslinger boasted of having more Black employees than any other federal agency, and in *The Protectors* he claimed that his anti-narcotics crusade against Black musicians had nothing to do with prejudice. He had worked nights as a piano player in a silent movie theater, he liked jazz, and he had compassion for people who ruined their careers with dope. He could even relate to poor folk: "For some," he acknowledged, "narcotics block out the sights and sounds of poverty." [19] But throughout his tenure as Commissioner of the FBN, Anslinger's unstated policy was blatantly segregationist, and he instructed his supervisors to keep Black agents on what they privately and snidely called "the merry-go-round," which meant sending Black undercover agents from district to district so they could never stay in one place long enough to exert any individual or concerted influence. The result, of course, was that tensions began to build between White and Black agents.

"Undercover agents were used against their own ethnic groups," Matt Seifer says in defense of Anslinger and the FBN. "Italians went after Italians; Jews went after Jews; Blacks went after Blacks. There was a lot of teasing to ease the tension, so you couldn't be thin-skinned about your heritage. People even teased Benny Pocoroba because he spoke broken English and urinated in a bottle on stakeouts."

But Irish, Italian, and Jewish agents *were* promoted to management positions, while Blacks, though performing an increasingly larger percentage of the undercover work, were not. (The one Hispanic agent to be put in charge of an office, J. Ray Olivera, was fortunate to have Congressman B. Carroll Reece as his rabbi.) Yet in order to keep faith with the White agents who *sometimes* covered their backs, the Black agents were expected to honor the FBN's sacred code of silence.

The predicament of Black agents is best expressed by William B. Davis. After graduating from Rutgers University, Davis, while visiting New York City, heard singer Kate Smith praising Agent Bill Jackson on a radio show. "She described him as a Black lawyer who was doing a fine job as a federal narcotic agent, and that was my inspiration. I applied to the Narcotics Bureau and was hired right away, but I soon found out there was an unwritten rule that Black agents could not hold positions of respect: they could not become group leaders, or manage or give direction to Whites. The few Black agents we had at any one time," he says bitterly, "maybe eight in the whole country, had indignities heaped upon us."[20]

Davis tells how Wade McCree, while working as an FBN agent in the 1930s, created a patent medicine called Mother McCree's Goose Grease. But McCree made the mistake of writing to Eleanor Roosevelt to complain that federal prosecutors in the South were calling Black agents "niggers." As a result, Anslinger had his legal staff charge McCree with using FBN facilities to create his patent medicine. McCree was fired and his dismissal had the intended ripple effect: it sent a clear message that complaints from Black agents would not be tolerated.

Clarence Giarusso, a veteran New Orleans narcotic agent and its chief of police in the 1970s, explains the situation from local law enforcement's point of view: "We made cases in Black neighborhoods because it was easy. We didn't need a search warrant, it allowed us to meet our quotas, and it was ongoing. If we found dope on a Black man we could put him in jail for a few days and no one cared. He has no money for a lawyer, and the courts are ready to convict; there's no expectation on the jury's part that we even have to make a case. So rather than go cold turkey he becomes an informant, which means we can make more cases in his neighborhood, which is all we're interested in. We don't care about Carlos Marcello or the Mafia. City cops have no interest in who brings the dope in. That's the job of federal agents."

Alas, under Anslinger's bigoted guidance, his agent force often seemed more intent on perpetuating addiction in America's ghettos than in eradicating it.

ANSLINGER'S DOUBLE STANDARD AND ITS IMPACT

The FBN was a political animal and political patronage was one of its traits. Matt Seifer recalls the time Eleanor Roosevelt was unhappy with Anslinger and wanted to replace him. So he appointed one of the First Lady's classmates as district supervisor in Denver. "She [Elizabeth Bass] always went about in the company of two male agents," Seifer says, "and she always carried two semi-automatics in her handbag. She'd get to a hotel and plop that bag down on the counter and you could hear the guns clanking inside. She was quite a character!"

But the fish rots from the head down, and Anslinger's penchant for patronage, and for asking agents to perform petty favors, created a venal environment that fostered corruption. Charges that Anslinger was abusing his power began in 1939, after Professor Alfred Lindesmith questioned his punitive approach toward addicts and charged that Anslinger's policy only added a profit motive to trafficking. In retaliation, Anslinger sent Chicago District Supervisor James Biggins to Indiana University to warn the authorities that Lindesmith's Narcotic Research Foundation, which advocated the treatment of addicts, was sponsored by "a criminal organization," which it was not.[21]

To justify his punitive stance, Anslinger also (at the expense of making conspiracy cases) focused his agent force on bringing in all known addicts, fingerprinting them, and counting them for statistical purposes. But behind the scenes, some of his agents were handing out dope to the addicts, feeding their habits in order to make cases and inflate the statistics, thus fostering corruption throughout the organization.

"Anslinger got away with murder," Matt Seifer says. "He catered to the wealthy and instead of prosecuting their kids, he sent them to Lexington [where the Public Health Service drug addiction treatment center was located]. He played politics, but he was smart. Our jurisdiction in Boston covered all of New England into Canada, and some of the houses that were used as depots were half in and half out, and one time one of our men killed a Canadian. But Anslinger wouldn't let them extradite the agent. He was very protective."

Despite the discontent of some Black agents, and despite policies that, by fostering corruption, disturbed both Black and White agents, Anslinger maintained his exquisite mystique – and the loyalty of the vast majority of his agent force.

"FBN agents were dedicated," Seifer says proudly. "None of this nine-to-five crap. We worked a hundred hours a week and kept a change of clothes in the office. Back in the old days the agents used their own money too. Earl Teets used money from his own pockets to feed his dogs, which he had trained to sniff out opium. Greeny used to say, 'You get bit by the bug.'"

With Anslinger and his agents it was tit for tat. In order to make cases, agents had to start with addicts on the street and work their way up the food chain to the Mafia kingpins. To pave the way for his men, Anslinger promoted the myth that potheads and junkies were as guilty as the drug lords who managed the trade. Stigmatizing and criminalizing users did nothing to reduce demand, but it did make it easier for agents to turn minor offenders and addicts into informants. Ironically, in this consciously misconstrued way, myths about pot smokers and heroin addicts advanced the short-term interests of the FBN and laid the groundwork for its epic Mafia hunt.

5

GOD'S WORK

"When you look long into an abyss, the abyss also looks into you."
Friedrich Nietzsche, *Beyond Good And Evil*

By mid-1946, Lucky Luciano was settled in Rome with his trusted cadre of deported American Mafiosi and had formed working relations with the Sicilian Mafia. Then in October 1946, in a bold attempt to reorganize the American rackets under his command, the droopy-eyed villain traveled to Havana and, after establishing contacts, summoned his former paisanos in December. Among those paying homage (some grudgingly) to the resurrected boss of bosses were Vito Genovese, Meyer Lansky, Frank Costello, Joe Adonis, Santo Trafficante, Carlos Marcello, and Chicago's Charlie Fischetti. At this infamous Cuban crime summit, the Mafia's top priorities were reorganizing its drug syndicate and settling a dispute between two competing racing wire services. At the center of both issues was tempestuous Bugsy Siegel.

In order to appreciate this situation it is necessary to know some of the details of the Mafia's sordid history. In 1937 Lansky and Costello sent Siegel to Los Angeles so that, together with the reigning Mafia boss of California, Jack Dragna, he could seize control of the various West Coast gambling and labor rackets. Pleased at the prospect of ruling his own fiefdom, Siegel energetically pushed his way into independently owned racetracks and gambling houses, and set about replacing James Ragen's Continental Press Service out of Chicago with Trans-America, a racing wire service he and Dragna eventually formed in 1945. The Chicago mob, which had joined with Lansky and Costello in the West Coast venture, had a stake in reaching a settlement with Ragen, and made him an offer he should not have refused. But the feisty newspaperman sought protection from the FBI instead, and that was a big mistake. On 24 June 1946, Ragen was shot in traditional gangland style as he stood on a street corner. He died a few weeks later in a Chicago hospital, allegedly from a lethal injection of mercury.

With Ragen out of the way, the Mafia's takeover of the West Coast racing wire business seemed a sure bet. But Siegel, suffering from delusions of grandeur, refused to fold Trans-America into Continental. The ensuing "wire service war" raged for a year and was bad business for everyone except Bugsy, who controlled both services and profited doubly by forcing bookmakers to buy from both. Siegel further aggravated his patrons by spending huge amounts of their money building the Flamingo Hotel in Las Vegas and trying to grab control of the Mexican drug trade.

Meanwhile, on 11 February 1947, radio host Walter Winchell announced to the world that Lucky Luciano was consorting with known criminals in Cuba, at which point Garland Williams sent veteran Agent J. Ray Olivera to Havana to investigate. Working with Treasury representative Joseph A. Fortier and Cuban secret police chief Renito Herrera, Olivera uncovered Luciano's involvement with a slew of crooked Cuban generals and politicians, including Senator Eduardo Suarez Rivas and Congressman Indelicio Pertierra, the "axle," as Olivera called him, between the Cuban and American gangsters.[1] One of their joint ventures was a small airline that landed at Key West, without passing through US Customs, and undoubtedly served to smuggle narcotics.

Eager to do business with the Mafia, Senator Suarez Rivas had endorsed Luciano's entry visa and was proud to be his political protector, though Lucky was cutting deals with everyone of importance in Cuba including First Lady Paulina Aleina Ida de Grau; her nephew by marriage, Manuel Arias, operator of the National Casino; and Senator Paco Prio Socarras, a drug addict and brother of Premier (and future president) Carlos Prio Socarras.[2]

Through an informant and a microphone hidden in Suarez Rivas's office, Olivera discovered that the Senator was in business with Lansky, that Costello owned the Hotel Presidente, and that Luciano was negotiating to buy a piece of the National Casino. He also reported that a Peruvian woman brought cocaine to Suarez Rivas and Paco Prio Socarras and, more importantly, that Luciano was allegedly planning to divert narcotic medicines, exported to Cuba by American pharmaceutical firms, onto the black market.

Outraged that Luciano was conspiring to traffic in black-market narcotics only ninety miles off the Florida coast, Anslinger threatened to cut off *all* medical supplies to Cuba unless Luciano was immediately expelled. He didn't have the authority to impose an embargo, but Attorney General Thomas C. Clark and the State Department supported him, and as a result, Cuban president Ramon Grau San Martin acceded to Anslinger's ultimatum. Luciano was arrested on 23 February, and in early March was forcibly returned to Italy, in steerage, aboard a Turkish tramp steamer. The mortified mobster arrived in Genoa on 11 April 1947, having failed in his audacious attempt to restructure the Mafia drug syndicate, and Anslinger savored his victory.

ANSLINGER'S ASCENT AND THE CHINA LOBBY

Anslinger was formidable in 1947. His wartime service, his law and order stance, and his efforts on behalf of the increasingly profitable pharmaceutical and drug manufacturing industries had earned him numerous supporters in Congress, while on the international scene he had brought global drug policy firmly under American control. With State Department official George A. Morlock and drug industry lobbyist Herbert May, Anslinger organized the UN's Commission on Narcotic Drugs and located its lab in New York. He exercised greater influence than ever before, by monitoring drug production and trade around the world, and by linking favored nation status and International Monetary Fund loans to nations that abided by the tenets of American drug policy.

The Far East was of special concern to Anslinger, and in November 1945 he sent Ralph Oyler on a "confidential mission" of "an exceptional nature" to survey stockpiles of opium and narcotics that had been confiscated from the Japanese.[3] After meeting in Tokyo with General Douglas MacArthur, Oyler inspected an opium factory three miles outside Seoul. He reported that the factory was guarded by US Army military policemen, and was strewn everywhere with morphine and opium. Upon opening the factory's vault, Oyler found fifty tons of opium – enough, in his opinion, to supply the underworld for two and half years.[4]

Next he traveled to Tientsin, China, where the Communists had closed all of the opium dens the Japanese had operated during the occupation. A few days later in Peking, Oyler witnessed the burning of thirty tons of opium the Communists had confiscated from the Japanese.

As Oyler's reports clearly indicate, the Communists, not the Nationalists, were the ones conducting anti-narcotic activities in China. In fact the Nationalists were still deeply involved in the drug trade. But Anslinger was unwilling to acknowledge that reality, so he buried Oyler's reports, and thereafter drug law enforcement in the Far East proceeded in sync with national security concerns. Anslinger sent Customs Agent Melvin Hanks to Manila to prove that the Communist Chinese were smuggling narcotics to the Philippines, and he sent FBN Agents William F. Tollenger and Wayland L. Speer to Japan for basically the same political purpose.[5] After authoring Japan's anti-narcotics laws and organizing its narcotics squads, Tollenger and Speer traveled throughout the Far East with Army CID agents, seeking evidence that would link the Communist Chinese to drug rings in Japan, Korea, and China.[6]

These developments marked an important turning-point in FBN history, for by suppressing Oyler's reports about Communist Chinese anti-narcotics activities, while publicizing all allegations of communist wrongdoing, Anslinger made the FBN an integral part of America's propaganda machine. And by swearing his undying loyalty to China Lobby Senators Patrick A. McCarran (Chairman of the Judiciary Committee), James O. Eastland (Chairman of the Internal Security Subcommittee), and Richard B. Russell (Chairman of the Appropriations Committee), Anslinger assured the FBN's bureaucratic survival at a time when the Truman administration was thinking about transferring the Bureau to the Justice Department.

Anslinger's devotion to the China Lobby had something to do with self-preservation too. Having witnessed the Lobby's destruction of John S. Service, a Foreign Service officer who had reported on the Kuomintang's narcotics dealings, the Commissioner was keenly aware of its power over the fate of government employees. For this reason the Service case is worth reviewing.

While serving as General Joseph Stilwel's liaison to the Communist Chinese in 1944, Service reported that the whole lifestyle of Kunming, the city where the Flying Tigers and OSS were headquartered, "was tied to opium smoking."[7] He said the Nationalists were decadent, totally dependent on opium, and "incapable of solving China's problems."[8]

Service was a senior officer with years of experience in China, and his reports contributed to the Truman administration's decision not to come to Chiang Kai-shek's rescue. In retaliation, General Tai Li's agents in America accused Service of leaking the Kuomintang's battle plans to a leftist newsletter.[9] He was arrested in June 1945 and, though cleared of any wrongdoing, the China Lobby persisted in attacking his character for the next six years. He was subjected to eight loyalty hearings and dismissed from the State Department in 1951.

Service's persecution was a clear signal that anyone linking the Nationalist Chinese to drug smuggling would, at a minimum, be branded a communist sympathizer and have his reputation ruined. It was a warning Anslinger heeded.

THE MEXICAN CONNECTION

Mid-1947 marked a turning point in the FBN's collaboration with the espionage Establishment. With only token support from the Truman administration, the Nationalists' war with the Communists was faltering, and in Thailand a war had erupted between the police and army over the opium trade. Then a registered foreign agent for the Thai government, former OSS chief William Donovan traveled to Bangkok to unite the squabbling factions in a strategic alliance against the Communists. The Nationalist Chinese who served as middlemen in the production and transportation of narcotics from Thailand to Hong Kong, Macao, and other Asian markets, benefited greatly from Donovan's intervention.

Concurrently, a delicate, drug-related national security situation had developed in Vietnam. During the war, Iran, with the knowledge of its American financial advisors, had shipped tons of opium to the Vichy French in Saigon. Pressed by Anslinger, France in June 1946 pledged to disengage – but after the Viet Minh launched their insurgency a few months later, France, with America's tacit approval, continued to trade opium to help finance its counterinsurgency.

Helping to manage public perceptions in this regard was former ambassador to France and Russia William C. Bullitt. One of several diplomats linked to smuggling in the post-war era, Bullitt journeyed to the Far East as a reporter for China Lobby activist Henry Luce.[10] A feature article Bullitt subsequently wrote for *Life Magazine* slammed Truman for not supporting the Nationalists and provided the Republicans with the enduring "Truman lost China" theme which they used to bash the Democrats. Bullitt, meanwhile, was dining regularly in Paris with Vietnam's playboy Emperor Bao Dai, an opium smoker who relied on opium profits to finance his decadent regime.

In secret the government rationalized its protection of the drug-smuggling Nationalists by insisting that any consequent health problems were confined to the Far East. But by mid-1947, Kuomintang narcotics were reaching America through Mexico. The Mafia was involved, as was Bugsy Siegel through his ill-fated love affair with curvaceous mob courier and courtesan Virginia Hill. Described by Anslinger as a "prominent narcotics figure," Siegel in 1947 was the subject of an FBN conspiracy case that included all the usual suspects: Lucky Luciano, Joe Adonis, Frank Costello, Meyer Lansky, and Chicago's Charlie Fischetti.[11]

The Siegel drug conspiracy had its inception in 1939 when, at Meyer Lansky's request, Virginia Hill moved to Mexico and seduced a number of Mexico's "top politicians, army officers, diplomats, and police officials."[12]

Hill soon came to own a nightclub in Nuevo Laredo, and started making frequent trips to Mexico City with Dr. Margaret Chung, an honorary member of the Hip Sing T'ong and the attending physician to the Flying Tigers – the private airline formed under China Lobby luminary General Claire Chennault to fly supplies to the Nationalists in Kunming, the city John Service described as infused with OSS agents and opium. More to the point, as investigative journalist Ed Reid reported in *The Mistress and the Mafia*, the FBN knew that Dr. Chung was "in the narcotic traffic in San Francisco."[13]

Chung took large cash payments from Siegel and Hill and delivered packages to Hill in New Orleans, Las Vegas, New York, and Chicago. These deals involved Kuomintang narcotics, and yet, despite the fact that the FBN agents "kept her under constant surveillance for years," they "were never able to make a case against her."[14]

Why not? Because she was protected, of course. Admiral Chester A. Nimitz was just one of her many influential friends in Washington. And unlike Bugsy Siegel, she wasn't making waves; although where, exactly, Siegel went wrong is open to debate. By most accounts he was murdered by the Mafia for squandering mob money on the Flamingo Hotel. But FBN Agent Joe Bell – George White's replacement as district supervisor in Chicago – advanced a more plausible theory: that Siegel's murder "paved the way to complete control of illegal narcotics distribution in California by the Mafia."[15]

Bell was alluding to a drug smuggling operation Lansky had initiated in Mexico in 1944 under Harold "Happy" Meltzer. Described as "the man who most feared Bugsy's grab at Mexico," Meltzer based his operation in Laredo, directly across the border from Hill's nightclub, and moved drugs to the Dragna organization in California. Meltzer was an associate of John Ormento, the Lucchese family's link to Mafia boss Joe Civello in Dallas, and he worked with the Mexican consul in Washington, who located suppliers and bribed border guards. Bankrolled by Lansky and Harry Stromberg in Philadelphia, Meltzer traveled regularly between Mexico City, Cuba, Hong Kong, and Japan. He was also a professional hit man, and in December 1960 the CIA would ask him to join an assassination team – a sinister overture that suggests that his connection to the espionage Establishment dated back to the Luciano Project, along with Lansky's and Siegel's.[16]

Meltzer's proximity to Virginia Hill in Laredo also strongly suggests that he was a recipient of Dr. Chung's Kuomintang narcotics. And if that was the case, Siegel may not have been murdered by the Mafia, but by agents of the US government, because his grab for control of the Mexican connection threatened to expose Dr. Chung's protected Kuomintang operation. Even the way Siegel was murdered – by two rifle shots to the head – has been characterized as very "ungangsterlike."[17]

Protecting the Mexican connection was business as usual for the espionage Establishment, and when Siegel was killed in her house on 15 June 1947, Virginia Hill was already in France setting up an import agency that would exploit this most important gateway for moving narcotics to the Mafia in America. Again, there is convincing evidence that the secret government was aiding and protecting Hill in this endeavor: her passport was stolen while she was in France, and yet despite her ties to organized crime, the State Department quickly provided her with a new one.

In August, Hill traveled to Miami to deposit a large sum of cash in the National Bank of Mexico and then retreated with Dr. Chung to Mexico City, where in early 1949 she re-established her contacts. Hill then traveled to Europe to confer with Lucky Luciano – Lansky's partner in a new operation that relied on French Corsicans (many with intelligence connections) and clandestine labs producing high quality heroin in France and Sicily.

Why would the government protect notorious drug traffickers in this manner? Peter Dale Scott theorizes that it preferred "organized crime to disorganized crime or radicalism."[18] And by mid-1947 there was more at stake than the fate of the Nationalist Chinese; there was the fate of Israel too, and several gangsters from the Luciano Project, including Lansky, were actively involved in arms and drug smuggling in the Middle East. As the *New York Times* reported on 28 November 1948, the new state of Israel was combating "widespread narcotic smuggling" by "a small number of hardened criminals" who had slipped in and still practiced the black-market arts that had kept them alive during the war.

As John Service had reported three years earlier, and as Anslinger knew was still the case, the Nationalist regime was totally dependent on illicit narcotics. According to a 14 July 1947 State Department report, Nationalist forces were, at that moment, "selling opium in a desperate attempt to pay troops still fighting the Communists."[19] He also knew that Kuomintang opium and narcotics were reaching Mexico. In a 15 November 1946 report to Anslinger, New Orleans District Supervisor Terry A. Talent reported that, "Many Chinese of authority and substance gain their means from this illicit trade," and that, "In a recent Kuomintang Convention in Mexico City a wide solicitation of funds for the future operation of the opium trade was noted." Talent listed the major Chinese traffickers by name.[20]

However, reports emanating from Mexico avoided any mention of the Mafia–Kuomintang connection. For example, in February 1947, Treasury Attaché Dolor DeLagrave, a former OSS officer, reported from Mexico City that three major drug rings existed, but he made no mention of Virginia Hill's connections, Albert Spitzer and Alfred C. Blumenthal.[21] Though these connections were revealed to Senator Estes Kefauver, and even though Anslinger knew that Spitzer and Blumenthal were Lansky's associates, and that large opium shipments were coming out of Mexico "under police escort," there was no follow-up by the FBN.[22] In 1948 the FBN would declare that Mexico was the source of half the illicit drugs in America – but nothing was done about it.

Nothing was done, because the drug trade enabled the Central Intelligence Agency (CIA), which was created in 1947, to destabilize the Mexican government by pitting officials of the central government in Mexico City against warlords in the northern border region. Just as the CIA was pleased to see drug-addicted officials compromise the Cuban government, it was also glad when Captain Rafael Chavarri, founder of Mexico's version of the CIA, the Federal Security Directorate (DFS), formed relations with Mexican drug smuggler Jorge Moreno Chauvet. According to Professor Scott, at this point the CIA "became enmeshed in the drug intrigues and protection of the DFS."[23] By 1950, Chauvet was receiving narcotics from the new Lansky–Luciano French connection;* and the mob-connected, former mayor of New York, William O'Dwyer, was the US ambassador to Mexico.

CONFLUENCE: DETROIT, THE CIA, AND THE ITALIAN MAFIA

While the FBN focused on corrupt officials in Mexico, the Mafia was moving high-grade heroin through Canada to Detroit, where George

---

* The term "French connection" applies generally to a narcotics source originating in France or with French or Corsican smugglers operating anywhere; it also applies specifically to the French Connection case of January 1962.

White arrived in June 1947 as district supervisor following Ralph Oyler's death in March. Oyler's fatal heart attack came just a few weeks after Detroit was identified in the 25 February 1947 *Detroit Times* as a "key city" in a new dope ring established by Lucky Luciano. Anslinger was quoted as saying that after Luciano's arrival in Havana the FBN had discovered a Mafia scheme to make Tampa and New Orleans "the new main ports of entry for a gargantuan flood of illicit dope." Anslinger added that the Mafia had "obtained a vast dope hoard through looters in the last chaotic weeks of the European and Asiatic wars." [24]

Anslinger's revelations, and the situation in Detroit, are two more examples of the FBN's inability to neutralize the Mafia in the late 1940s. One reason was the FBN's reduced strength – but there was a more sinister reason as well. According to Paul Newey, an FBN agent in Detroit from 1943 until 1948, "We were restricted from taking cases that concerned the Mafia before the US grand jury unless the US Attorney cleared it with the Attorney General in Washington, DC. This, to me, was a method of putting the 'fix' *sub rosa* for political purposes."

From the ports of Marseilles and Hong Kong, to the streets of America's cities, political considerations shaped the drug trade, and during Oyler's twelve-year tenure as district supervisor in Detroit, the agents under his command were focused on making politically correct cases against pot smokers, Black heroin addicts, and Chinese opium dens. The Mafia, which controlled importation and distribution, was not a concern, and George White's arrival as acting district supervisor failed to signal a shift in policy. Characteristically, White's primary function in Detroit was to bring the FBN good press. "The FBI had hired a Public Relations man," Newey explains, "but Anslinger didn't have enough money to do likewise, so he relied on White to get the Bureau publicity."

White, as ever, was glad to oblige, and posed, a mere month after his arrival in town, with a Tommy gun in one hand and an opium pipe in the other for the 27 July 1947 *Detroit Free Press.* Throughout 1946 and 1947, White also continued to experiment with "a speech inducement drug that could be administered orally in alcohol or by insertion in crystal form into a cigarette." [25] Thus his pursuit of publicity, and his activities on behalf of the espionage Establishment, occupied more of his time than investigating the Mafia in Detroit at a critical point following the war.

Meanwhile, as Anslinger had revealed, Detroit drug smugglers were receiving narcotics from Santo Trafficante in Tampa, via New Orleans. The connection was established in December 1945 when Costello and Lansky opened the Beverley Club in New Orleans under the supervision of Sam

Carolla and Frank Coppola. Originally a member of the Luciano family, Coppola moved to Detroit in the late 1930s and enjoyed political protection there after he joined forces with Jimmy Hoffa and the Teamsters to kick the Congress of Industrial Organizations out of town in 1941. Coppola was godfather to Hoffa's foster son, and Hoffa protected Coppola's narcotics receivers in Detroit, John Priziola and Raffaele Quasarano, "by assigning them to Teamsters Local 985."[26]

From Hoffa's headquarters in Detroit, the Teamsters facilitated the Mafia's national drug distribution system. After being received from overseas sources, Frank Coppola's narcotics were transported to Joe Civello in Dallas and Frank Livorsi in New York by John Ormento's trucking company. Family ties were the key to success; Livorsi's in-laws included Ormento and brothers John and Frank Dioguardia, who controlled Teamsters locals in New York and Florida with their uncle, James Plumeri, a ranking member of the Lucchese family.

Another advantage was political control at the local level, through which the Mafia was able to seamlessly maintain its national drug distribution network even though the federal government deported dozens of Mafiosi in the post-war years. Case in point: New Orleans boss Sam Carolla was deported to Sicily in May 1947, and Frank Coppola was deported to Italy in January 1948, at which point the New Orleans operation passed to Tunisian-born Carlos Marcello. But drug operations proceeded apace, for like his predecessors, Marcello was protected at home; although FBN agents had arrested him in 1938 for possession of 23 pounds of pot, while he was known to be running one of the "major narcotics rings in the New Orleans area," Louisiana Governor O. K. Allen arbitrarily reduced his sentence, and within nine short months Marcello was back on the streets.[27]

Deportation didn't cramp Carolla's or Coppola's style, either. For many years Coppola had made frequent trips to Europe to purchase narcotics, and he and Carolla merely re-established their base of operations in Sicily, where they continued working with the ranking Sicilian narcotic traffickers, the Badalamentis and the Grecos. It is even likely that Carolla and Coppola, as a result of their Luciano Project and anti-communist activities, were part of what Professor Scott describes as "a post-war intelligence-mafia collaboration" that exploited "international drug traffickers for covert purposes."[28]

The foundation for this symbiotic relationship was laid by the OSS during the war, when it placed Mafiosi in positions of political importance in Sicily and Italy and helped forge their alliance with the Christian Democrats. Involved in this criminal conspiracy were remnants of Mussolini's secret police force (the OVRA); the Italian Masonic Order,

P-2; the Vatican's intelligence service; and the CIA, through William Donovan's World Commerce Corporation (WCC). Formed in 1947 with the financial backing of the Rockefellers, WCC was a private sector version of the Marshall Plan, investing primarily in munitions and strategic materials. Based in Panama and composed largely of former OSS officers, WCC has been described as a cross between "an import-export combine and a commercially oriented espionage network." [29]

One covert and commercial use to which international drug traffickers were put was as a tool in the suppression of communists and labor organizers. In May 1947, for example, Mafioso Salvatore Giuliano and his gang killed eight people and wounded thirty-three in a Sicilian village that had voted for the Communist Party's candidates in elections held four days before. Frank Coppola, from his base in nearby Partinico, reportedly provided Giuliano with the bombs and guns, and was himself "allegedly financed by former OSS chief William Donovan." [30]

"Coppola was the controller behind the scenes, the maker of Sicilian and Roman deputies," author Gaia Servadio says in *Mafiosi*, and "the deus ex machina of the Salvatore Giuliano saga." [31]

By 1948, the CIA was so influential in Italy that the leader of its Communist Party, Palmiro Togliatti, charged the US with subverting Italy's national elections. He also charged that reporter Michael Stern (who had glorified Giuliano in a series of articles for *True Magazine* in 1947) was a spy for William Donovan and China Lobby Senator Carl Mundt, one of Anslinger's strongest backers. That implies that Anslinger knew everything about the alleged "post-war intelligence-mafia collaboration" that exploited "international drug traffickers for covert purposes." [32]

THE PEOPLE'S REPUBLIC VS. TAIWAN

US government support for drug smugglers as a function of national security moved with the Kuomintang to Taiwan in October 1949, when the People's Republic of China (PRC) was established. At American insistence, the Nationalists were recognized by the UN as China's legitimate government. Meanwhile, under the direction of the CIA, drug smuggler General Li Mi and the Nationalists' 93rd Division crossed into Burma and, with the assistance of CIA assets in Vietnam, Laos, and Thailand, began launching covert paramilitary operations against mainland China. To bolster the CIA's covert actions, China Lobby Senator Pat McCarran in February 1949 requested $1.5 million in aid to the Kuomintang, and in April Senator Knowland began attacking KMT critics in the State Department. Determined to prevent the UN from admitting the PRC, the China Lobby launched a massive propaganda campaign based largely on Anslinger's allegations that the PRC was the source of *all* the illicit dope that reached Japan, the Philippines, and Hong Kong – despite the 23 July 1949 seizure reported by the *New York Times* at Hong Kong's Kaituk airfield of 22 pounds of heroin that had emanated from a CIA-supplied Kuomintang outpost in Kunming.

Anslinger pulled his weight in many ways: in 1950, when the PRC announced its desire to sell 500 tons of opium on the open market, he refused to allow New York Quinine and Chemical Works to import samples. His stated reason was to prevent the PRC from acquiring the staggering sum of foreign currency the sale would have generated. Anslinger said that he was afraid the PRC would use the money to buy weapons to support communist insurgencies worldwide. But the refusal served an insidious ulterior purpose as well, for by forcing the PRC to sell its opium on the black market – or by creating the impression that it was doing so – Anslinger was able to sustain a black propaganda campaign against the emerging communist nation.

To protect Taiwan from the PRC, the China Lobby raised nearly $5 million of private money, which the CIA used to purchase General Chennault's fleet of planes and convert them into the CIA's first proprietary air force, Civil Air Transport (CAT). Working with Chennault were William Peers, the CIA station chief in Taipei (a former commander of the OSS's opium-dispensing Detachment 101), and Desmond Fitzgerald, the CIA's deputy for Asian affairs. Like Peers, Fitzgerald was no stranger to opium: as a liaison officer to Nationalist troops fighting the Japanese during the war, he had "enjoyed the exotic life of the bush, smoking opium with Burmese chieftains."[33]

Wall Street lawyer Fitzgerald, a figure of some importance in the FBN's clandestine history, had also dabbled in the dirty partisan politics of New York. In February 1949 he had joined with Clendenin J. Ryan and several Republican reformers to create the ostentatiously named Committee of Five Million, whose mission was to expose Mayor O'Dwyer's ties with Frank Costello and torpedo the Democrats in the upcoming mayoral election. But according to his biographer, Evan Thomas, Fitzgerald "was embarrassed" in March when two of the Committee's private investigators were caught wiretapping the home of a Tammany Hall leader. Fitzgerald had attended the wiretap planning sessions and, while not named in the indictment, the experience "soured his enthusiasm for public politics."[34] But it did propel him into the highest echelons of the

CIA, where his madcap adventures on behalf of the Republican Party continued apace.

Joining Fitzgerald and Peers in 1950 was General Richard Stilwell. As special military advisor to the US ambassador to Italy from 1947 to 1949, Stilwell had helped the Christian Democrats and the Mafia solidify their positions. As CIA logistics chief in Asia from 1949 to 1952, he arranged for CAT to support General Li Mi's incursions from Burma into Yunnan, and thus enable the renegade general to bring to market "a third of the world's illicit opium supply."[35]

The plan to save Taiwan advanced on 7 November 1949, when privateer William S. Pawley received permission from Secretary of State Dean Acheson to lead a group of retired military officers, headed by Admiral Charles Cooke, to Taiwan to advise the KMT on security affairs. No stranger to political intrigues or the underworld, Pawley owned sugar plantations, an airline and a bus system in Cuba, and was linked to Mafia leaders who had investments there too. He was well connected to the espionage Establishment as well: Bill Donovan met with Chiang Kai-shek's defense minister and secret police chief to grease the skids on Pawley's behalf, and William Bullitt in December began raising funds for the so-called Pawley–Cooke Advisory Mission – the lion's share of which was provided by a group of Texas oilmen led by right-wing fanatic H. L. Hunt, a one time professional gambler who, in his younger days, helped finance his empire by running a private racing wire.[36]

Also involved in the Pawley–Cooke escapade was M. Preston Goodfellow, former publisher of the *Brooklyn Eagle* and Donovan's liaison, with Garland Williams, to William Keswick and the British SOE in 1942. Later in the war Goodfellow managed sensitive OSS operations in Burma and China, and formed close ties to General Tai Li and drug smuggler Du Yue-sheng. According to Korean War historian Bruce Cumings, Goodfellow made a fortune by combining business ties with "right wing regimes in Asia, with interests in Central America."[37]

Pawley's collusion with Cooke, Donovan, Goodfellow, Bullitt, and Hunt is a textbook example of how Establishment privateers run the secret government. And naturally the mission dovetailed with federal narcotics activities. In January 1950 Goodfellow traveled to Taipei with Cooke, and in April Bullitt's bagman arrived. Soon thereafter, a "Colonel Williams" introduced the bagman to Satiris Fassoulis, "who gave him $500,000 for a PR campaign on Taiwan."[38]

Was this our Garland Williams? Probably. Williams had experience at both ends of the Iran–China connection. In 1948 and 1949 he had conducted surveys of Iranian opium production and had reported to Anslinger that Iran's most influential families had amassed fortunes through the opium trade, and that they intended to keep anti-drug laws weak. [39] He knew that Iran shipped tons of opium to Indochina through Greek and Armenian brokers like Fassoulis. But Williams was also a security chief for the secret government, and at the same time that CIA officer Allen Dulles was meeting with KMT officials to seal the Pawley–Cooke deal, he was recalled to active duty and took command of the Army's 525th Military Intelligence Group. Among its functions, the 525th MIG prepared intelligence officers for duty in Korea, and as chief of the Group, Williams was in a position to provide covert support to the Pawley–Cooke Advisory Mission, or to Satiris Fassoulis.

For his part, Fassoulis denies ever having met Williams, or that Hunt provided money, or that Pawley was involved. He denies everything. However, he had been an American pilot in China during the war, where he may have met Garland Williams, and in 1950 he was vice president of Commerce International China (CIC), a subsidiary of Donovan's WCC. CIC was exempt from the Foreign Agents Registration Act and supplied the Pawley–Cooke mission with everything from gas masks to airplanes. It was also accused of smuggling contraband to America. [40]

FROM COVER-UPS TO DECEPTIONS

CIC was accused, but not investigated. On the contrary, FBI and Army counterintelligence agents began investigating critics who might expose the secret government's drug-related operations. In October 1951, none other than Admiral Charles "Savvy" Cooke testified that John Service, the State Department officer who'd reported on the Kuomintang's narcotics dealings, was a communist sympathizer. In a similar instance, State Department officer Oliver E. Clubb objected in one of his reports to Chiang's use of the opium traffic to further his designs for a "Nazi"-style dictatorship. [41] Soon thereafter, *Time* editor and former communist Wittaker Chambers told the Internal Security Subcommittee that Clubb had gotten Professor Owen Lattimore (coiner of the pejorative phrase "the China Lobby") a phony passport. Clubb was suspended from the State Department in July 1951.

More and more reports, some generated by the FBN, appeared linking liberals with drug-dealing communists. Following Agent J. Ray Olivera's investigation of Lucky Luciano in Cuba, for example, someone at FBN headquarters told muckrakers Jack Lait and Lee Mortimer that the Peruvian communists had built seventeen cocaine factories in Lima, but that the "New Deal State refused to intervene;" the reporters called this "criminal negligence." [42]

Meanwhile, Anslinger was nursing a Congressman through a morphine addiction. "Anslinger would have preferred to treat the Congressman as any other addict," one journalist reported, but he continued to fill the man's prescriptions because, "the national interest was involved." [43]

By June 1950 and the start of the Korean War, everything was over-shadowed by the national interest. In terms of drug law enforcement, this meant promoting the myths that America was being poisoned by dope that originated "behind the Iron Curtain," and that Russia used drug profits to pay its secret agents in America; that "the titular head of the Cuban Communist Party offered [Luciano] 'sanctuary,' and that 'a pink lawyer' represented the Mafia's drug syndicate in the East Harlem district of 'left wing Congressman Vito Marcantonio.'" During Marcantonio's ascendancy, Lait and Mortimer said, "Labor Party district leaders were able to supply police protection [to drug dealers] through alliances with both Tammany Hall and anti–Tammany Hall Mayor LaGuardia." [44]

They said that Anslinger had been "handcuffed" for eighteen years by liberal judges who were sure to keep junk peddlers "out of jail because of a fix or muddle headedness." [45]

Lait and Mortimer weren't scholars, but their books were popular, and the public perceptions they created, amid the mass hysteria of the McCarthy era, help to explain why Anslinger's campaign to link Lucky Luciano and the Mafia to a mythical communist drug-smuggling conspiracy was conceived and believed.

Few public officials dared dispute Anslinger's assertion that the PRC was using opium profits to finance wars in Korea, Vietnam, and Malaysia, even if that assertion was contradicted by the facts. But considering the poisonous atmosphere of the McCarthy era, evidence was not all that important. It didn't matter, for example, that Huang Chao-chin, who "narrowly escaped conviction while he was Consul General in San Francisco in 1937 on charges of smuggling narcotics in the United States," sat on the Kuomintang's Central Committee, or that the KMT had massacred thousands of opponents in Taiwan, or that the goal of its CIA-advised secret police was the creation of a police state under Chiang's son and dynastic successor, Chiang Ching-kuo. [46]

It didn't matter that the CIA was protecting America's drug-dealing allies or that Anslinger, whose broad shoulders had attained Herculean proportions, was running interference. In the Cold War climate, that was how the Great Game was played.

6

CREATING A CRIME

"People are mobs that make six percent more on the dollar."
"Crazy Willie" Moretti, as quoted in *The Secret Rulers*

The FBN's Mafia hunt began on the ground with addict informers, the grimy grist for their mill; but junkies didn't volunteer their services, so case-makers had to create a crime.

According to former drug addict and best-selling author William S. Burroughs,

> The usual routine is to grab someone with junk on him, and let him stew in jail until he is good and sick. Then comes the spiel: "We can get you five years for possession. On the other hand you can walk out of here right now. The decision is up to you. If you work with us, we can give you a good deal. For one thing, you'll have plenty of junk and pocket money. That is, if you deliver. Take a few minutes to think it over."

Burroughs goes on to say that while the junky is pondering his decision, the agent puts a few caps of heroin on the table. "This is like pouring a glass of water in front of a man dying of thirst," Burroughs observes, "and the junky starts spewing names."[1]

The agent's goal was to move up the food chain: to force junkies to set up pushers, pushers to set up retailers, and retailers to set up wholesalers with sizable amounts of heroin. Anyone arrested for selling a kilogram of junk could receive a ten-year prison term, and mounting the head of a

Mafia wholesaler on his mantle was every case-maker's dream. But it was impossible for an undercover agent to buy heroin from a Mafia don, and informers in the upper echelons of the Mafia were rare, and their fate certain, as Carl Caramussa learned the hard way. The FBN never had more than five informers inside the Mafia, which in New York numbered around 2000 "made" (meaning officially inducted) members, all of whom were willing "to do the time" in prison to protect their revered and ruthless bosses.

Complicating matters was the fact that most informers were acquired through the plodding process of "two buys and a bust"; two buys being required by law to transcend entrapment and prove intent. So FBN agents scoured the city's seedy hotels, rooftops, and back alleys, searching for the rare addict or street pusher who could entrap a disgruntled Mafioso, who in turn would lead them into the dark heart of the international drug conspiracy.

Though arduous, the two-buys-and-a-bust routine paid dividends by enabling the FBN to record and compile biographical data on almost every major drug trafficker in a two-volume leather-bound blacklist. Domestic violators were listed alphabetically in the dark brown *National List*, while the foreign varieties were listed in the burgundy International List. Both books were published by the Treasury Department and made available to FBN agents. A separate Mafia Book, specific to that genre, was also compiled in an eight and a half by eleven-inch book that was about two and a half inches thick.

The books featured approximately 800 traffickers, plus their aliases, associates, and *modi operandi*. In the days before computers, this composite rogues' gallery was more than just an encyclopedia of dope dealers; it was the first organizational chart of the underworld. It showed relationships that revealed corporate veils, and offshore businesses and bank accounts. And by enabling federal agents to check the passenger lists of ocean liners and merchant vessels for known smugglers, it sometimes allowed them to anticipate deliveries and make significant seizures. But best of all, the books impressed politicians.

Using its blacklists, stable of informers, guerrilla warfare tactics, and contacts in local, state, and foreign law enforcement groups, the FBN by 1950 was putting more bodies in prison than any other federal agency and often provided the evidence the other agencies needed to make gambling, tax, weapons, or counterfeiting cases. As respected investigative reporter Fred Cook gushed, the FBN always seemed to know what was happening "as soon as it happened."[2]

THE GANGS OF NEW YORK

In the early 1950s, New York was the major port of entry for most of America's illicit narcotics. Demand was rising, and huge profits awaited the highest concentration of Mafiosi in the nation, represented by the fabled Five Families of scrap-metal czar Vito Genovese, olive oil importer Joe Profaci, cheese importer Joe Bonanno, tomato importer Vincent Mangano, and clothing manufacturer Thomas Lucchese.

In those days the FBN's primary target was the resilient 107th Street Gang, which distributed heroin to Jewish, Italian, Black, and Puerto Rican gangs in and around the city. Observing the Gang's operation was easy: FBN agents would sit outside its depots, watch its customers make purchases, then follow them to their packaging plants, where New York City narcotic squad detectives could, in their jargon, "kick in doors" on suspicion and make busts.

But putting the Gang out of business was impossible, according to Lait and Mortimer (based on tips they received from FBN executives), because Labor Party district leaders loyal to Congressman Marcantonio assured police protection through their allies in Tammany Hall. This accommodation allegedly allowed Marcantonio's political operatives to import Puerto Rican immigrants into the neighborhood for the purpose of selling Mafia narcotics, and to encourage their countrymen to vote for Mafia-approved candidates. The effect of these allegations was to stigmatize Democratic Party officials by linking them to a drug-smuggling conspiracy with Blacks, Puerto Ricans, the left-wing labor movement, the Mafia, and communists.[3]

The FBN considered Thomas Lucchese as the mastermind of this conspiracy for two reasons: because John Ormento, a ranking member of his family, managed the Gang's narcotics operations; and because Vito Marcantonio was Lucchese's political patron. Marcantonio had even gotten Lucchese's son into West Point. But Lucchese's circle of influential friends transcended partisan politics and included Republicans and the local US Attorney, Myles J. Lane, one of whose top aides paid for rooms used by Lucchese at the Hotel Astor in March 1948. Thus, by 1950, Lucchese ranked with Joe Adonis as the FBN's most wanted drug kingpin, although Frank Costello was still, politically speaking, its most wanted man.[4]

PRELUDE TO A KANGAROO COURT

Tom Lucchese represented everything the Establishment despised about immigrants, the working class, and organized labor. He was born in Palermo in 1899 and his criminal record dated to 1921. Ten years later, Lucky Luciano awarded him one of the Five Families, and by 1939, having formed relations with Tammany Hall, the pint-sized godfather replaced Louis Buchalter as the underworld boss in New York's garment district. Through extortion, drug trafficking (he was No. 139 on the International List) and labor racketeering, he came to own legitimate garment and trucking businesses that extended throughout New England and New Jersey. However, as a family boss, he sat above the drug syndicate managers on his family's organizational chart. He never actually handled narcotics, and only through a well-orchestrated conspiracy case could the FBN possibly convict him. But that was impossible, because such a complex conspiracy case would necessarily implicate the Establishment judges, prosecutors, and politicians who protected him.

The only alternative was to expose the system itself – the alliance between gangsters, policemen, and politicians that the Establishment secretly maintained. Anslinger and his inner circle understood this, and their relentless PR campaigns acted as bait for the national press corps: reporter Ed Montgomery won a Pulitzer Prize for a series of articles on organized crime in the *San Francisco Examiner*; Don Petit gained fame for exposing the mob in Florida; and Ed Reid won acclaim for revealing that New York's top bookmaker paid members of the NYPD $1 million a year for protection, and that Mayor O'Dwyer's clerk had done favors for "waterfront characters who were close to Albert Anastasia and his mob of killers."[5]

In March 1950, the avalanche of press reports had the desired effect, and New York State Representative Kingsland Macy – a Taft Republican veteran of the Rothstein scandal and true believer in the theory that all crime emanated from Tammany Hall – demanded a congressional investigation. Taking up the gauntlet was Estes Kefauver, a Democratic Senator from Tennessee whose goal was to run for president in 1952, and whose strategy was to achieve favorable national attention by exposing the role of organized crime in political corruption, illegal gambling, and labor racketeering. In order to embark on such a perilous mission, the ambitious Senator needed only – and this was no easy task – the approval of President Truman and Judiciary Committee Chairman Pat McCarran.[6]

A conservative ideologue with a grudge against Big City Democrats, McCarran recognized the merit in Kefauver's idea; however, having legalized gambling in 1931, Nevada was dominated by organized crime figures, to the extent that McCarran was facetiously referred to as "the Gambler's Senator." This fact put McCarran in a compromising position, so he initially decided to run the investigation himself. But after Senator

Joseph R. McCarthy gained instant notoriety in February 1950, by claiming that he had a list of 205 people in the State Department who were "known members" of the American Communist Party, McCarran turned his attention to the more politically promising anti-communist witch-hunt, and established the Senate's Internal Security Subcommittee. Unable to manage both projects simultaneously, he came to terms with Kefauver.

Truman, of course, was concerned that the investigation would reveal his ties to the Pendergast machine in Kansas City. But his fears were allayed when McCarran agreed to allow vice president Barkley (a close friend of Anslinger's deputy, George Cunningham) to name the other four members of the Committee. McCarran and Barkley then announced the formation of the Special Committee to Investigate Organized Crime in Interstate Commerce. Chaired by Estes Kefauver, its purpose was to expose the system that bound policemen, criminals, politicians, and businessmen to the detriment of American society.

Kefauver, however, immediately ran into opposition from FBI director, and avid racetrack better, J. Edgar Hoover. By investigating the gambling syndicate, Kefauver was destined to expose the underworld's ties to several of Hoover's Establishment patrons, so the FBI director refused to allow his agents to serve as investigators for the Committee. Hoover claimed that he was too busy saving the country from communists, and that it would be counterproductive for him to devote his Bureau's resources to investigating what he deemed to be consensual crimes. Though ostensibly his superior, Attorney General J. Howard McGrath was unwilling to anger Hoover and backed his decision.

Without the support of the FBI, the Kefauver Committee had little chance of proving interstate criminal conspiracies; but it was already formed, and several senior politicians were deeply involved with the project. For a moment it appeared that Kefauver had committed political suicide, and then Harry Anslinger stepped out of the shadows with a solution that saved the day. At a 6 June 1950 executive session of the Kefauver Committee, Anslinger presented each member with a copy of the Mafia Book. And when the Senators saw that most of the people in its pages were of Italian extraction (or belonged to some other undesirable minority), often with union affiliations, they heaved a collective sigh of relief. Their Establishment benefactors did not drive trucks, unload ships, or wait on tables, and that overarching class distinction made it possible for them to agree to try to sell Anslinger's proposition that the Mafia controlled crime in America, through the interstate distribution of drugs with the help of the Teamsters, and through international drug smuggling with the help of certain longshoremen.[7]

Anslinger further advanced his position by offering to make FBN agents available as expert witnesses in every city the Committee intended to visit as a way of compensating for the lack of FBI support. And he volunteered the services of his top gun, George White, who had given up his post as district supervisor in San Francisco in June and taken up residence in New York in anticipation of acquiring the district supervisor's job Garland Williams had left that very same month. Awaiting what he felt was a certain appointment, White joined the Kefauver Committee's staff as a full-time consultant, and proceeded to Kansas City to guide its investigators through the matrix of drug trafficking to the inner recesses of organized crime.

With FBN superagent George White setting the tone of the investigation, the Committee began to examine evidence (provided by the FBN and the IRS Intelligence Unit) of joint financial ventures involving drug traffickers, gamblers, and labor racketeers. As suggested by Anslinger, the Committee had only to present the evidence to the public to prove a conclusion it had already reached – that the Mafia was at the center of an international conspiracy (linked to communism) that controlled crime in America's major cities. But there were unexpected consequences for Anslinger, and by trying to make that elaborate conspiracy case the Committee put the FBN on a collision course with the FBI and the CIA and changed the nature of the war on drugs forever.

THE KEFAUVER HEARINGS

At the start of the Kefauver Hearings in the summer of 1950, journalist Drew Pearson, quoting Anslinger, defined the Mafia as fifty men under Lucky Luciano, all but one (presumably Meyer Lansky) Italians. When critics said this was absurd, Anslinger provided a list of people he knew would prove his point. Topping the list, and billed as the Committee's prime target at a public hearing to be held in New York City in early 1951, was Frank Costello, and by default – as the Committee's chief counsel, Rudolph Halley, intended – Anslinger's old foe from the Luciano Project, former Mayor William O'Dwyer.[8]

From start to finish, Anslinger and White set the tone of the Kefauver Hearings, and FBN agents were essential to the Committee's ability to package and sell its product. At public hearings across the country, FBN agents explained how the Mafia was organized, how it laundered money, infiltrated legitimate businesses, and funded narcotics ventures through gambling profits. In July in Kansas City, FBN Agent Claude Follmer described Charles

Binaggio – whom the Committee had scheduled as a witness, but who had been murdered three months earlier – as the city's political boss and a certified Mafioso. Follmer tracked the Italian arm of the Pendergast machine through the drug syndicate's erstwhile general manager, Nick Impostato, to New York's Mangano and Profaci families. He explained how Kansas City received French heroin from Tampa, via Havana, and to dramatize the seriousness of the situation, he described Carl Caramussa's murder.

White bolstered Follmer's case for the existence of a Mafia by tying Mangano warlord Joe Adonis to Frank Costello. White also produced documents linking gambling czar Frank Erickson to the Democratic Party, legal gambling establishments, and politicians in Florida, thus paving the way for the Committee's hearings in the Sunshine State. There, Adonis, Erickson, and Lansky were shown to have invested mob money in hotels, real estate ventures, and illegal bookmaking enterprises. Santo Trafficante in Tampa was linked to fourteen murders over twenty years, including the June 1950 murder of James Lumia, another potential witness the Committee intended to hear from. Tampa's police chief told the Committee that the Mafia had a standard operating procedure for murder, which included the importation of hired killers from out of town, and setting up patsies to take the fall.

Hearings in New Orleans identified drug trafficker Carlos Marcello as the main cog in southern interstate crime. FBN Agent Thomas E. McGuire (a veteran of the Rothstein investigation, known for his glen-plaid suits and Kelly green handkerchiefs), linked Marcello to Trafficante and Costello, as well as to the political opponents of Louisiana Congressman Hale Boggs.

But the most sensational revelation came from White when he claimed to have a "pipe line" to the "inner circle" of four Mafia bosses (in New York, Los Angeles, Kansas City, and Chicago), "who passed on murder requests from the underworld and occasionally commissioned a Mafia enforcement ring to do the killing."[9] The murders of Binaggio and Lumia, both of whom were scheduled to testify before the Committee, were interpreted by the Committee as proof positive of the Mafia hit team's existence, and of the Mafia itself.

Then, in late September 1950, as the Committee approached Chicago, the hit team struck closer to home, assassinating former Chicago police captain William Drury just days before he was scheduled to give public testimony before the Committee. Drury's testimony would surely have been explosive. In 1947 he had arrested three suspects in the murder of James Ragen and had publicly linked them to Mafia chief Tony Accardo, manager of Chicago's narcotics and prostitution rackets. George White had been the FBN's district supervisor in Chicago during the Ragen investigation and while serving in that position had established a link between Cook County Sheriff Dan Gilbert (known locally as "the richest sheriff in America"), the Mafia, and Democratic politicians. White was certain that Drury was murdered precisely because he was going to expose this link. Impulsively, in a reckless attempt to trump Drury's assassins, White leaked Drury's preliminary testimony, which had been taken at a secret hearing, to the press. The result, Lait and Mortimer commented, served only to rub "Democratic dirt on the record."[10]

White had achieved his goal of exposing the underworld's accommodation with Chicago's Establishment, but at a high price. The ensuing scandal cost Illinois's Democratic Senator Scott Lucas the November 1950 elections, and out of spite, while serving out his term as a lame-duck Senator, Lucas would deny Kefauver's request for arrest warrants for Chicago Mafiosi Tony Accardo and Charlie Fischetti. In addition, White was forced off the Committee and, to everyone's disappointment, the Kefauver Committee's final report contained none of his promised revelations about the Mafia's inner circle.

Last but not least, Kefauver asked the FBI to investigate Drury's murder, but "Hoover found no jurisdiction for his agency in the case."[11]

These setbacks, however, were forgotten in January, when Kefauver held hearings in New Jersey and successfully issued indictments against Joe Adonis and Willie Moretti. Adonis, pleading "no defense" in May 1951, received a two-year prison sentence and, after a long legal battle, was deported to Italy in January 1956. As a direct result of the Kefauver Hearings, some two dozen Mafia aliens and naturalized citizens were likewise deported.

"Crazy Willie" Moretti was less fortunate. At a public hearing held on 13 December 1950, he told the Committee, "Yeah, sure, I know George White for a long time. George is a swell fellow."[12] While not exactly admitting he was White's pipeline, Moretti had confessed to having a big mouth, and was summarily murdered on 4 October 1951 at Joe's Elbow Room in Palisades, New Jersey.

THE GRAND FINALE

By early 1951, the Kefauver Committee had determined that "the vice squad" pattern "gave control of vice payments to a few officials and demoralized law enforcement in general."[13] It concluded that local law enforcement managed local crime – "that local law enforcement officials, as the brokers between the law and reality, were more important in setting policy than the gamblers"[14] – and that the federal government could not stop it. As a result a campaign to discredit Kefauver was quickly mounted, and up popped allegations that he had skimmed over Mafia activities in Texas on behalf of oilman H. L. Hunt, and in Louisiana on behalf of Congressman Boggs.[15] Drew Pearson even claimed that Chicago mobster Tony Accardo exerted influence in the White House through Truman's aide, General Harry Vaughan.[16]

By the time the Kefauver circus pulled into Grand Central Station in March 1951, the nation's nascent television audience was glued to its seats, waiting for the next bombshell. The New York hearings did not disappoint, and featured an appearance by Virginia Hill, the curvaceous mob courier and former mistress of Joe Adonis and Bugsy Siegel. Hill's contemptuous testimony was followed by a stern lecture by Rudolph Halley, the Committee's chief counsel, on the links between former New York Mayor William O'Dwyer and Frank Costello.

Next to appear before the Committee was the eminent O'Dwyer himself. In 1949 he'd won a second mayoral term, but resigned in June 1950 to accept an appointment as ambassador to Mexico. Summoned by Kefauver to explain his past associations, O'Dwyer, in a thinly veiled reference to the Luciano Project, told the Committee that Costello had helped him in his investigations for the Army during the war. Unapologetic and in ill health, he said that he favored legalized gambling and, referring to charges that Park Davis and Eli Lilly monopolized the gelatin capsule market to the detriment of the working class, he suggested that the Committee examine inside trading on Wall Street rather than people who enjoyed betting on popular sports, like horse racing.[17]

O'Dwyer's unrepentant attitude didn't help the Committee's next witness, Frank Costello. While Halley systematically linked him to Luciano in Italy, Lansky in Las Vegas, Adonis in Florida, Fischetti in Chicago, dubious Texas oil deals, gambling joints in New Orleans, Tammany intrigues, and bookies everywhere, Costello fidgeted nervously, projecting consciousness of guilt before the TV cameras. As his *coup de grâce*, Halley played a tape in which the loquacious Willie Moretti referred to Costello as "chief."[18]

Capping an FBN publicity campaign that had started in December 1946 – when Garland Williams branded him as the "absolute ruler" of the Mafia and its drug syndicate – Costello was jailed for contempt. While he was stewing in jail, IRS agents amassed enough evidence to convict Frank

Costello of tax fraud, and the Mafia's elegant prime minister was summarily incarcerated in the Atlanta Penitentiary.

TRUTH OR CONSEQUENCES

The Kefauver Hearings were a boon for the FBN and enabled Anslinger to declare in May 1951 that heroin smuggling was America's "greatest narcotics problem."[19] Deputy Commissioner George Cunningham pleaded in June that the FBN needed more agents to handle the problem, and the next day Congressman Charles Kersten introduced a bill authorizing 132 more agents. Riding on the momentum, Cunningham equated the rise in addiction with liberal judges, and Congressman Boggs immediately introduced legislation mandating longer sentences for drug offenders. The Senate approved the legislation in July, expanding the FBN's powers, and authorizing money for scores of new agents. A wave of public support followed: the Women's Federation called for a quarantine of all addicts; Senator Everett Dirksen (R–IL) called for the death penalty for peddlers who sold drugs to kids; and New York's chief rabbi, W. F. Rosenblum, challenged the FBN to "go to the source," meaning Israel's foes, Egypt and Lebanon.[20]

The Hearings also put immense pressure on organized crime. Apart from the convictions of Costello and Adonis, indictments were issued for Lansky and several of his associates. Lucchese was forced into hiding. Vincent Mangano's brother Phil was murdered in April 1951, and in what Lait and Mortimer called "an unrealistic coincidence,"[21] Sam Maceo and Charlie Fischetti died within a week of one another in the summer of 1951, prior to their scheduled appearances before the Committee – which was chaired from May through July by Senator Herbert R. O'Conor (D–MD), with FBN Agent Charlie Siragusa as his chief investigator.

Not everyone, however, attributed the timely deaths of Charles Fischetti and Sam Maceo, and the murders of James Lumia, Charles Binaggio, William Drury, Phil Mangano, and Willie Moretti – all prior to their testimony before the Kefauver Committee – to some mythical Mafia hit team conjured up by George White. Willie Moretti's murder in October 1951 was especially troubling and prompted eccentric New Jersey millionaire Clendenin Ryan, the financier of Desmond Fitzgerald's Committee of Five Million, to call it "a clear-cut case of murder to prevent testimony concerning gambling and corruption."[22]

Perhaps Ryan doubted that Moretti's murder was a Mafia hit. If not, was it committed by law enforcement officials, the people referred to by the Kefauver Committee as "the brokers between the law and reality," those who had so much to lose by Moretti's confessions? Or were organized crime's new patrons in the US intelligence and security agencies weeding out troublesome Mafiosi? The master spies certainly had the capability; they even had their own hit team under Colonel Boris Pash, former counterintelligence chief of the Manhattan Project and George White's colleague in the OSS Truth Drug program. As revealed in Senate hearings in 1976, Colonel Pash had joined the Office of Policy Coordination in March 1949, to manage a five-person unit that conducted assassinations for the State Department and the CIA.[23]

Is it possible that Pash's hit team murdered Moretti, and perhaps other alumni of the Luciano Project, to prevent the Kefauver Committee from uncovering the Mafia's ties to the espionage Establishment – to people like Kefauver's close friend William Donovan, whose law firm provided the Committee with several staff members? Though not widely disseminated, this theory has a lot to recommend it: as Salvatore Vizzini – an FBN agent with solid CIA connections – says so succinctly, "Starting around 1947, a lot of Mafia hits weren't."

Be that as it may, the Mafia did some serious house cleaning after the Kefauver Hearings. After his brother Phil was murdered, and his biggest money-maker Joe Adonis was imprisoned, Vincent Mangano chose to retire and pass control of his family to Albert Anastasia. With Costello out of the picture, and Lucchese hounded by the FBN, Vito Genovese became more powerful than ever, and his *caporegimes*, Joey Rao and Mike Coppola, seized control of narcotics distribution in Harlem and the Bronx.

The Kefauver Hearings had negative consequences for everyone involved, not just the Mafia. Kefauver's call for a National Crime Commission was squelched by J. Edgar Hoover, and while Kefauver was nominated as his party's vice presidential candidate in 1952, the Democrats had become synonymous with crime and corruption, and the Hearings contributed mightily to their loss of the Senate and the presidency in the 1952 elections. After the Committee was disbanded, its files were transferred to the Commerce Department, where they gathered dust.

The Hearings did some damage to the FBN as well. Increased public attention to drug addiction engendered a perceived need for more governmental oversight, and in November 1951, Truman formed the Inter-departmental Narcotic Committee (INC) to coordinate all federal agencies in the new war on drugs. Though Anslinger chaired the INC, its representative from the Federal Security Agency, Oscar Ewing, publicly defined drug addiction as a health issue related to public access to doctors and medicine. Ewing admitted Black doctors, for the first time in history, to Washington, DC hospitals, and noting that Black children were not getting medicine, he called for comprehensive prepaid health coverage financed through social security. The AMA opposed him in this effort, as did his segregationist foes, with significant success.[24]

Ewing publicly advocated treatment as an alternative to Anslinger's punitive approach, and although opposed by powerful forces, he was supported in this effort by Rufus King, the Chairman of the American Bar Association's Commission on Organized Crime. King and the ABA opposed mandatory sentencing and launched a campaign opposing the Boggs Bill, stressing that the legislation was flawed because it failed to distinguish between addicts, first-time pot smokers, and Mafia distributors.

Personal animosities that would haunt the FBN were also bred by the Hearings. In March 1951, Charlie Siragusa returned to New York, after having established the FBN's first overseas office in Rome, to testify before the Committee. Touted as "the" expert on the Mafia, Siragusa claimed that Luciano was the Mafia's exiled king and referred to rumors that his commutation may have been the result of a bribe. Shocked, Kingsland Macy called for an investigation of Governor Dewey, reigniting Dewey's simmering feud with Anslinger. In desperation, Dewey "summoned FBI director J. Edgar Hoover ... and strongly urged that Anslinger be replaced as narcotics Commissioner." But Anslinger's "ardent Republican backers (especially in the pharmaceutical industry that the FBN monitored) and their plaudits" came to his defense and prevailed.[25] When that effort failed, Dewey in 1954 would direct William B. Herlands, the New York State Commissioner of Investigations, to conduct an inquiry that would finally clear his name.

NEW YORK: THE CENTER OF FBN OPERATIONS AND INTRIGUES

In addition to having made powerful bureaucratic and political enemies during the Kefauver Hearings, the FBN was damaged by internecine warfare within the all-important New York office. The problem climaxed when Garland Williams was recalled to active duty in June 1950. Certain he would be chosen to replace Williams as district supervisor, George White, as Agent George H. Gaffney recalls, "hung all his prize photos up on the wall, including the one of the Jap he'd killed with his bare hands in New Delhi. The photos were there for about two weeks, then for some reason George was sent to Boston."

One reason was Truman's unhappiness with White's attempts to link him to Kansas City's Pendergast machine. Another was Hoover's anxiety over White's increasingly cozy relationship with the CIA. But the ultimate veto came from Dewey, who blamed White for the ongoing Luciano commutation scandal. But White was too important to be slighted, so Anslinger avoided a confrontation with his rivals, and assuaged White, by appointing him as the district supervisor in Boston. According to agents on the scene, White was rarely there. Instead he kept his apartment in New York and went to work for Newbold Morris, a Labor Party functionary who served as a special assistant to the Attorney General on organized crime from February to April 1951, when Hoover summarily derailed his investigation. A great opportunity arose at this point, and White signed a contract with the CIA and began a secret LSD-testing project, which will be discussed at length later. The CIA arrangement allowed White to run operations in New York, to the dismay of James Clement Ryan, the FBN agent who was appointed to the New York district supervisor's job.

A former Marine Corps officer, Ryan was a veteran agent with a wide range of experience, including investigations in Latin America. But he'd spent most of his career in New York, where he was plugged into the Irish Establishment through his rabbi, Cardinal Spellman, and his many friends in the senior ranks of the NYPD. One of his colleagues, George H. Gaffney, describes him as a "superb agent, honest and fair, and blessed with a pleasing personality," and says that Ryan was genuinely admired by his colleagues. Another agent compares him to John Wayne in style and appearance, and says that he was the last popular supervisor in the highly visible New York office.

When Ryan took command, there were approximately sixty agents working in the New York office, accounting for one-third of the FBN's entire field force. Within the office there were four enforcement groups, a compliance squad, and three Special Endeavor groups, one each under agents LeRoy Morrison, Price Spivey, and J. Ray Olivera. Another select group under Joe Amato focused exclusively on the Mafia and its international connections. One agent was assigned to satellite offices in Buffalo, Newark, and Patterson, New Jersey, the latter having been established by Anslinger as a personal favor for Representative Gordon C. Canfield (R-NJ), Chairman of the House Appropriations Committee.

The most significant members of Ryan's Celtic clique were Charles G. "Pat" Ward (leader of Enforcement Group Three), Patrick P. O'Carroll, Benjamin Fitzgerald, George H. Gaffney, John T. "Jack" Cusack, Thomas "Old Tom" Dugan, and LeRoy "Roy" Morrison, the only non-Chinese agent to work the t'ongs independently of George White in New York. Fitzgerald was said to be Ryan's closest confidant. Known for his horn-rimmed glasses and florid face, "Fitz" was often seen huddled with Ryan at a local saloon, where they spent their time talking in whispers and playing dollar poker. A tough Welshman from Hell's Kitchen, Pat Ward was Ryan's chief lieutenant; he knew all of the city's narcotic detectives and drug dealers by sight and name, and managed the office's most important investigations. Maxie Roder, a German-American agent who had been in New York continually since his days in Colonel Nutt's Narcotic Division, was Ryan's liaison to the NYPD precinct captains and, based on his seniority, ran the office's Irish sweepstakes.

Crucial to Ryan's success was his relationship with the NYPD's narcotic squad, which had the power to conduct warrantless searches and shared with Ryan its numerous informers, as well as its contacts at the telephone company and the District Attorney's office. In return, Ryan provided the City's narcotic squad with the latest wiretap and bugging technology, as well as intelligence on the national and international activities and associates of New York-based drug traffickers.

The problem was that Ryan's Celtic clique was insensitive to the feelings of other ethnic groups, and there was resentment over assignments and perceived insults. As Howard Chappell notes, "It was the Irish Catholic agents against everybody else. They especially resented Garland Williams for always assigning Irwin Greenfeld as acting district supervisor in his absence."

Chappell – who arrived in New York in 1949 and served in Sam Levine's enforcement group through 1951 – cites as an example the case his group made on Ellsworth R. "Bumpy" Johnson, Harlem's biggest heroin distributor. With Meyer Lansky as his advisor, Johnson had taken over the numbers racket in the 1930s, but in order to prevent his rivals from amassing enough power to challenge him, he became a drug distributor for the Mafia. Genovese's *caporegime*, Joey Rao, was his heroin supplier. In 1950, Black Agent Bill Jackson made two undercover buys from Bumpy, with Chappell covering his back, under the direction of Sam Levine. But Ryan allowed Pat Ward and George Gaffney to make the arrest and take credit for the bust.

Complaints of favoritism were annoying, but Ryan's biggest headache was George White. White had an extensive network of informers in New York, and his private investigations undercut and often upstaged Ryan. Worse, White sent poison-pen letters to Anslinger, relaying rumors about Ryan and members of his inner circle being involved in corruption. White's source of gossip was his own clique of agents, including several who lurked in Chinatown and Little Italy as part of Joe Amato's wide-ranging Mafia Squad.

A major member of White's clique was Price Spivey. A heavy-set Southerner, Spivey had worked closely with White in New York before the war and during the war had served in the US Army CID tracking black marketeers in France, before returning to the FBN. Spivey's Special Endeavor case (SE 226) focused on Harold Meltzer's drug-smuggling operation out of Mexico. In October 1950, while putting the finishing touches on the case, Spivey suffered a broken leg and seven broken ribs when a mob hit team ran him off a road outside Atlantic City. Despite three months on the critical list, he returned to action and in March 1951 wrapped up the case. Meltzer received a stiff sentence in California, although his New York connection, John Ormento, was sentenced to only two years. Unindicted co-conspirators included Meyer Lansky and Mickey Cohen in California.

One of the items of business for the New York office was tracking down fugitives from the Meltzer case. High on the list was Frank Tornello, a major drug dealer whose arrest would break open an important aspect of the post-war French connection and set Agent George Gaffney on the fast track to success.

A Naval Academy graduate, Gaffney had served as a navigator on the USS Missouri during the war. But his real interest was in intelligence work, so he resigned his commission in 1949 and, based on a brief association with Admiral Roscoe Hillenkoetter, the CIA's first director, sought work with the CIA. Hillenkoetter, however, had disappointed Truman and was on the way out when Gaffney applied, and after the CIA rejected his application, he turned to the FBN and was hired in 1949 by Garland Williams. Charlie Siragusa was his first group leader, and Pat Ward was his first partner in Group Three. In 1950 he attended the CID's School of Investigations at Camp Gordon, and upon his return he joined Group One under Irwin Greenfeld and began tracking Frank Tornello.

Gaffney's partner on the Tornello case, Mike Picini, was slightly senior and had already made his mark as the undercover agent who made buys in Los Angeles from Waxey Gordon (real name Irving Wexler), a notorious drug trafficker since 1917!

Picini's induction into the FBN is worth describing, for it illustrates how freewheeling the organization was in the 1940s. Following a tour in the Army CID, Picini enrolled in Rutgers University's Law School, then went to work as a clerk for a judge in Camden, New Jersey. One day, while filling a prescription for the judge in a local drug store, Picini was spied by

Joe Bransky, the FBN's district supervisor in Philadelphia. Branksy was conducting a compliance inspection, and Picini so closely resembled a typical Mafia hood that Bransky offered him a job on the spot.

Picini accepted the offer and, after a brief period of familiarization, was assigned to the Washington field office where, under the direction of Mal Harney, he was sent to Los Angeles to work on the Waxey Gordon case with San Francisco District Supervisor Ernie Gentry. Pretending to be an East Coast gangster on the lam, Picini and special employee John Pitta, a former Mafia drug dealer, worked eighteen months on the case. Picini says with pride, "There only were about twelve of us doing undercover work then; three Italians – me, Tony Zirilli, and Benny Pocoroba – and the rest were Blacks."

After the Gordon bust, Picini tracked Frank Tornello to New York. District Supervisor Ryan, however, was not inclined to let his turf be worked independently by Picini out of Washington, so he relieved Gaffney of his other duties and ordered him to help Picini locate and arrest Tornello. As Gaffney recalls, "Tornello was a used-car salesman who was last seen driving a 1946 Cadillac Sedan. I knew the plate number and I followed leads in seven states and Canada until finally, alone, I found him in the cocktail lounge at a bar in Eastchester, New York, in January 1952."

"What?" says Picini in mock disbelief when told of Gaffney's apocryphal account of the Tornello case. "The truth," he says, "is that some guy who went to this club in Eastchester saw Tornello's face in *True Detective* magazine. There was a reward for any information leading to his arrest, so the guy went to the editor, Rene Buse, to collect. Well, George was a friend of Buse's, and on a Friday she tells him that Tornello goes to this club. Gaffney tells me, and we agree to wait till Monday before we pick him up. So what happens?" By now Picini is convulsing with laughter, "That little shit arrests him while I'm home in New Jersey visiting my wife over the weekend."

Picini, like Gaffney, would enjoy a successful career in the FBN, and having already made a name for himself in the Gordon case, he didn't care that Gaffney claimed credit for making the Tornello case – although the episode does underscore the virtue of corroborating what any FBN agent says about his prowess and achievements. In any event, the Tornello case was more than a stepping-stone in Gaffney's career. After his capture, Tornello would provide significant new leads to an important avenue of the French connection.

Meanwhile, Agent Henry Giordano was working on a related French connection case in Canada and had made undercover buys from George Mallock, a big-league trafficker working with Mafia and French traffickers in Canada. Although George and his brother John Mallock fled before the Mounties closed in, Anslinger was impressed by Giordano's style, and took a personal interest in his career (some say because Giordano's mother was a bigwig in the Republican Party), appointing him agent in charge in Minneapolis in 1952, then district supervisor in Kansas City in 1954.

Two years later came the twist of fate that opened the door to a headquarters position. In 1956, Irwin Greenfeld was serving as district supervisor in Baltimore, and was in line to become Anslinger's field supervisor. But a beloved younger brother had a sudden, fatal heart attack. Greeny was so devastated that he was placed on sick leave, and in his absence, Giordano got the job. He would remain at headquarters for the rest of his career, and would stay in Anslinger's good graces by adopting his Spartan management style and militant crusade against marijuana. Giordano's pharmacological background further endeared him to Anslinger, for it enabled him to provide Congressmen with credible explanations as to why methadone should not be considered a treatment for addiction.

After he became Commissioner in 1962, Giordano would try to perpetuate Anslinger's policies. But the policies were obsolete by then, and he lacked charisma, let alone Anslinger's exquisite mystique; and in less than six years, the FBN under Giordano would descend into oblivion.

But those developments were far off in the future, and in 1951 the FBN's greatest days lay ahead, thanks largely to Giordano's chief rival, the inimitable Charlie Siragusa.

7

CONTINENTAL CAPERS

"It's a small underworld after all."

Maurice Helbrant, *Narcotic Agent*

While the FBN focused its feeble post-war international powers on the Mafia's smuggling operations out of Mexico, Frank Coppola and his associate Sam Carolla were setting up operations in Sicily and branching out through Europe, just as Lucky Luciano and his entourage of deported Mafiosi were doing in Rome. Meyer Lansky, meanwhile, was discreetly forming prostitution, gambling, and narcotics enterprises in the Middle East with two Corsican crime lords – Marcel Francisci in Marseilles and Joe Renucci in Tangiers – whose lieutenants controlled Mediterranean smuggling routes and had connections in East Asia as well. As a result of these developments, by 1950 pure white French connection heroin was appearing in volume on America's streets, available through Mafia distributors to an ever-increasing number of consumers.

The timing of this resurgence in international drug trafficking corresponded neatly with Anslinger's desire to increase the FBN's influence at home and abroad. Political developments were favorable everywhere, but most importantly in Italy. Threatened by communist movements in Yugoslavia, Albania, and Greece, the Vatican prayed for help, and America's Roman Catholic bishops responded by forming the Save Europe Committee, and the State Department delivered a multimillion-dollar emergency loan to the Christian Democrats in Rome. When the communists began to organize the Italian peasantry in preparation for the 1948 general elections, Secretary of Defense John Forrestal authorized the CIA to route US weapons to the Italian Army and the Royal Counterespionage Service, the Carabinieri. There were allegations by the Italian left that former OSS chief William Donovan was also moving guns and propaganda materials to goon squads composed of Fascists and Mafiosi, including Salvatore Giuliano and Frank Coppola, operating under the protection of local police forces.

To roll back Soviet expansion and protect American investments in Europe, Congress approved the Marshall Plan, which provided billions of dollars to avowed anti-communist nations. To protect this huge capital investment, the National Security Council (NSC), at its first meeting on 19 December 1947, directed the CIA to launch an all-out, covert campaign of economic, political, and psychological warfare against the Soviets. In June 1948 the Soviets replied with the Berlin blockade, and the Cold War escalated in deadly earnest. The Asiatic strain of the Cold War virus erupted in October 1949 with the establishment of the People's Republic of China and turned sizzling hot with the Korean War in June 1950.

As America's commitments grew overseas, so did the FBN's opportunity to establish a permanent base abroad. Anslinger had only to suggest that communist agents and drug smugglers were conspiring to subvert America's security by subsidizing addiction. In his bid to expand the Bureau's influence worldwide, he followed one path in Europe and another in Asia.

THE EUROPEAN PLAN

As Anslinger told Ray Richards of the *Detroit Times* on 25 February 1947, the Mafia had "obtained a vast dope hoard through looters in the last chaotic weeks of the European and Asiatic wars."[1] And it was true. The black market was booming in post-war Europe, and narcotics were one of the more precious commodities being traded. Germany was at the center of the trade, in part because the German Medical Corps had abandoned a huge stash of cocaine in Garmisch, a city south of Munich in an area occupied by the US Army. A group of enterprising former Polish prisoners of war found the stash and sold it in Italy and France in 1946. Other smugglers naturally gravitated toward the Polish operation, and for the next two years Garmisch was home for three major drug rings. A German and a Chinese man called Leo ran one, and moved heroin into Bolzano, Italy. Lucky Luciano was involved in a second ring based at the White Horse

Inn, Garmisch's underworld and espionage hangout, through his representative, Rino San Galli. And the Polish smugglers, still percolating, moved cocaine through Bari, Italy, to Cairo.[2]

The CID investigated the drug trade in Garmisch, after receiving evidence that the business was financed with $3 million that US Army officers had stolen from the Reichsbank. But senior Army officers impeded the CID's investigation and destroyed the evidence in order to preserve the Army's good-guy image. To this day the CID claims to have "no papers" regarding its narcotics investigations between 1945 and 1948.[3]

The Army's image problem, notably, reached critical mass in December 1947 when Guenther Reinhardt, a special employee of the Army's Counter-Intelligence Corps (CIC), revealed that CIC officers were participating in drug smuggling operations that involved Hubert von Blucher, a wealthy, influential Bavarian. A former German intelligence officer, von Blucher, with the help of two US Army colonels, had buried $15 million in Reichsbank gold near his home in Garmisch in April 1945. It was a profitable venture and von Blucher, after relocating to Argentina in 1948, would move to California in 1951, become a chief shareholder in Pan American Airways and a successful Hollywood screenwriter.

An idealist at the time, Reinhardt took his charges of corruption and drug smuggling directly to the assistant secretary of the Army, Gordon Gray. But Gray, a profound realist, was in no mood for a scandal involving the CIC and von Blucher. One of the most powerful men in the espionage Establishment, Gray undoubtedly feared that an investigation into the drug smuggling indiscretions of US Army and ex-Nazi officers would expose Operation Bloodstone, the US intelligence operation in which Nazi scientists and spies were being relocated to the US, Canada, and South America. So Reinhardt was discredited and sent away. General Lucius D. Clay, commander of the military government in West Germany, summarily closed the Garmisch investigation on 1 March 1948, although, to the dismay of the Americans, the story was picked up in the East European communist press.

Anslinger was aware of these developments and immediately sent Charlie Dyar to Germany to straighten things out. Assigned to General Clay's office as a Narcotic Control officer, Dyar traveled to Garmisch in March 1948 – right after General Clay closed the case – and on 3 April reported to Anslinger that the communist press was expanding on a January 1948 article in the *New York Herald Tribune*, in which reporter Ed Hartrich identified "a wealthy Bavarian" as "director of the narcotics ring."[4] The communists had dug a little deeper and discovered that the drug ring was financed with stolen Reichsbank money, that it included former Gestapo chief Ernst Kaltenbrunner, and that it was selling indigent German girls to brothels in South America.

Dyar reported that von Blucher had, in fact, been the director of the drug ring. Unfortunately, the Nazi had already obtained a phony Swiss passport and would escape to Argentina in October 1948. Dyar also reported that although the Polish and Chinese rings were still operating in Garmisch, Hamburg had become the new center of narcotics activity in Germany. Finally, he tried to make a case on the Polish cocaine ring, but the US Army CID would not provide the front money. His informant blamed this on the CID's fears that Dyar would discover its past indiscretions, and that's where the matter ended.[5]

Well, almost: seeking redemption, Reinhardt in 1953 wrote a book alleging that ex-Gestapo agent Irmgard Bidder was the Soviet agent in control of a Communist Chinese dope ring launched in Europe after the war. He totally ignored Garmisch, and instead said that Bidder smuggled tons of raw opium from China to an East German pharmaceutical firm for refinement into heroin. He said the Soviet operation supplied Luciano in Italy, and that Frau Bidder had 4,000 agents doing her bidding, including former Nazis working for the Soviets in Argentina. And in this way history was rewritten.[6]

Anslinger knew that the Garmisch drug operation had been managed for three years by US counterintelligence officers, in league with a group of prominent Nazis, and that some of the profits went to finance Operation Bloodstone, through which von Blucher made his way to Argentina. But it would have been bureaucratic suicide to reveal any of this, so he propagated the myth that Luciano was managing the drug trade with Soviet and Chinese Communists.

The situation in Asia required an even less sophisticated approach.

DEFENSIVE AVOIDANCE IN THE FAR EAST

Anslinger knew the Nationalist Chinese were smuggling opium to Hong Kong, but he didn't want to suffer the same fate as John Service or Guenther Reinhardt, so whenever he was faced with overwhelming evidence of Kuomintang drug smuggling, he adopted, according to historian William O. Walker III, "a strategy of defensive avoidance."[7]

Avoidance meant feeding lies to the news media to shift the blame, and after the People's Republic of China (PRC) banned the cultivation of

opium in November 1950 and began to impose severe penalties on violators, Anslinger initiated a campaign of disinformation, much of which
he acquired from Taiwan's representative to the UN, Hsia Chin-lin. In
1952 Hsia would tell the UN that Communist military authorities had set
up a narcotics-refining factory in China and were producing three hundred
pounds of morphine base a day, which was then smuggled across China's
southeastern border. Having served as General Tai Li's representative to the
Chinese Embassy in Washington, DC, Hsia was well acquainted with
narcotics trafficking.

This dubious Kuomintang evidence was supported by reports filed by
FBN agents Bill Tollenger and Wayland "Lee" Speer, in accordance with
Anslinger's policy objectives. Initially sent to Japan to organize narcotics
squads within the Japanese police force, Tollenger and Speer found that
their mission had changed in 1949 when the Nationalists lost the war.
That year, with the help of the CID, the FBN agents first heard about a
communist heroin lab in Tientsin; and in 1950, with the help of the CIA,
they linked drug-dealing communists in Japan and China. Allegedly
managed by the Soviets, as Reinhardt would claim in 1953, the ring relied
on Japanese prisoners of war. During their incarceration in North Korea
and China, the Japanese were allegedly brainwashed by the wicked Soviets
and, when repatriated to Japan, they formed a prostitution ring that pushed
Communist Chinese narcotics on unsuspecting American soldiers, specifically to finance Communist Party activities.

Jack Pruitt, a CID agent on the scene, recalls how the smugglers oper-
ated: "We first learned about [the ring] from Japanese soldiers on leave in
Shanghai, when we still had reasonable relations with mainland China.
Taiwanese ships that were bringing supplies to help rebuild Japan –
everything from sugar and grain, to lumber and steel – were stopping in
Shanghai, and that's where the drugs were smuggled aboard the ships."

At the same time, as Anslinger knew, opium from Iran, Thailand, Laos,
and Burma was flooding the East Asian market, and not only the
Nationalists were profiting from it. After a visit to Saigon in early 1948,
Agent Bill Tollenger reported that opium was "the greatest single source
of revenue" for the French.[8]

This politically incorrect but honest assessment reinforced Anslinger's
strategy of defensive avoidance, and with the start of the Korean War and
covert CIA assaults on mainland China from Taiwan, Speer and Tollenger
were withdrawn from the region. No news being good news, ten years
would elapse before an FBN agent would return on a permanent tour of
duty.

GEORGE WHITE'S BIG ADVENTURE

With Iran and the Far East having been declared off limits by the espionage Establishment, the FBN turned its attention to an operation, allegedly controlled by Lucky Luciano in Rome, in which Turkish morphine base and opium were smuggled through Yugoslavia to Italy, and through Lebanon to France. To gather information about this operation and to see what could be done about it, Anslinger decided to send George White and Garland Williams to several nations in Europe and the Middle East. His unstated motive was to turn the probe into a pretext for establishing a permanent office in Europe by showing that an FBN agent (White) could make undercover cases in Europe, and that an FBN agent (Williams) could convince Public Health officials and the police forces of opium-producing nations to crack down on smugglers and not supply Russia. In March 1948, the House Appropriations Committee authorized the necessary funds, and Anslinger sent White and, a few months later, Williams on their missions.

White's continental caper began in New York, where, posing as a merchant seaman, he paid opium smugglers Ivan and Catina Dodig to connect him with their Turkish supplier, Sev Dalgarkiran. White then set sail for Istanbul.

The flaw in White's plan was revealed to Howard Chappell a few years later by Jesse Johnson, a professional pickpocket and FBN informant. Jesse had been White's contact with the Dodigs. She didn't know that White was an undercover agent, but after he got drunk and passed out on her floor, she rifled through his pockets and found his badge. Jesse alerted the Dodigs, and just for the fun of it, they decided to set White up. They made the usual arrangements, but told Dalgarkiran that White was a federal agent, and at a prearranged meeting in Istanbul, Dalgarkiran stole White's flash roll and took him hostage. But White magically escaped, returned with a squad of Istanbul policemen, captured the villains and seized their narcotics. At least, that's how the caper was described, based on White's account, in the *New York Times*.[9] He then traveled to Bahrain "to get the facts" about the emerging Middle East conspiracy, then to Marseilles where, according to reporter Al Ostrow of the *St. Louis Post Dispatch*, "he hobnobbed about the waterfront dives until he learned some sources of dope being smuggled into America. He told the French police of his finds, and they made the requested arrests."[10]

In a telegram to Anslinger dated 22 June 1948, White, in clipped phrases, said that he was working with French Narcotic Agent Robert Pasquier, and that he had purchased a "quarter kilo [of] heroin from three Indo-chinese and [a] white woman and [had] apprehended them." White said the situation was "opening up," and that the Indochinese in Marseilles were handling a "large quantity [of] Turkish opium [and] selling [it through] Chinese seamen."[11]

A few days later in Trieste, White conferred with CID Agent Henry L. Manfredi about Lucky Luciano's drug operation in Italy. Manfredi subsequently launched his own investigation and in October 1948 he located a cache of opium, morphine, and cocaine near Bad Ischl, Austria. In all likelihood this cache had originated in Garmisch. Fascinated by the intelligence angle of international narcotics trafficking, Manfredi would soon join the FBN and (if he hadn't already) the CIA.[12]

From Trieste, White traveled to Rome where he met William Donovan. His mission was to gather intelligence on Luciano's drug smuggling activities, and through Donovan's contacts at the local CIA station, White penetrated Luciano's entourage and negotiated a twenty-kilogram heroin deal with Nick DiMarzo, a Genovese family member with connections in Texas, Chicago, and California.[13] Through DiMarzo, White also learned that Paul Gambino was Luciano's source in Palermo, and he made plans to go to Sicily to investigate. But DiMarzo knew that White was an FBN agent and blew his cover. So White traveled instead with an Italian police informant to Genoa, carrying a pistol he'd borrowed from a "CIA man."[14]

According to journalist Michael Stern (a friend of William Donovan's), White and the informant tailed the Italian representative of "a Wall Street trading firm" from a meeting with Luciano in Rome to Genoa, where narcotics were being smuggled from China "as goods in transit."[15] Although White was unable to make a case on anyone, the Italian mission was a propaganda success: Stern reported that the Luciano ring was receiving narcotics from Chinese communists, and leads from the case enabled White to implicate sailors in the leftist National Maritime Union in drug smuggling.

Upon arriving back home in San Francisco, White bought $600 worth of opium from some drug smugglers, then spent a week with their associates in Los Angeles, where he contracted to buy a quantity of opium from Francisco Lavat, "an important official of the Mexican Civil Aeronautics Administration."[16] White entered Mexico to help make the arrest, and then settled into a cushy job as San Francisco's district supervisor.

White's antics in Turkey, France, Italy, and Mexico generated favorable publicity for him and the FBN, and for his efforts, he received the Exceptional Civilian Service Award from Treasury Secretary John W. Snyder in late 1948. But much of the publicity was based on fabrications, and though reporter Al Ostrow portrayed him as a "lone wolf," White in reality had relied upon foreign policemen, or the CIA, in every case. This essential need for external assistance factored heavily in Anslinger's decision to send Garland Williams* on his survey of Europe and the Near East as a prelude to establishing a permanent office in Italy.

THE WILLIAMS SURVEY

In the autumn of 1948 and in early 1949, Williams toured Iran, Iraq, Syria, Lebanon, Egypt, Turkey, Greece, Yugoslavia, Italy, and France, to identify sources and drug-smuggling routes, and to establish relations with each nation's narcotic law enforcement officials. This was not an easy task. In Italy, Williams informed Anslinger, "Narcotic law enforcement is actually non-existent."[17] In Egypt he met with Arab League representatives regarding the illicit trade in hashish, and in Syria and Lebanon he conferred with officials about hashish production. His most urgent business was conducted in Iran, however, which was flooding French Indochina with opium, despite US appeals made through diplomatic channels.[18]

Williams's reports about Iran painted a bleak picture. The country's great families had made fortunes from opium, they deliberately kept the anti-drug laws weak, and there were more than a million addicts. But the espionage Establishment was more concerned with keeping the Shah in power than in reforming its narcotic policies, and in April 1949, following on Garland Williams's heels, a small delegation of American economic and engineering experts, and its legal spokesman, Allen W. Dulles, advised the Shah to ignore "uninformed political or public clamor."[19] The Shah followed Dulles's advice, but the Iranian people did not, and in 1951 a coalition led by Prime Minister Mohammed Mossadegh, a European-educated lawyer hoping to reform Iran's narcotic laws, toppled the Shah and began to nationalize the Anglo-Iranian Oil Company's holdings.

To say the least, it was not the sort of anti-narcotic action that Anslinger appreciated, and in 1953, Mossadegh would himself be ousted in a bloody coup engineered by the British and the CIA.

ANSLINGER SENDS SIRAGUSA TO ITALY

Italy by 1950 had emerged as the logical choice for locating the FBN's first overseas office, not only because it was Luciano's base of operations, but

---

* Snyder awarded Williams the Exceptional Civilian Service Award in October 1949.

for political reasons as well. Unlike the French, the Italians were solicitous of US intervention. Anxious industrialists in Milan petitioned Wall Street for economic assistance, and the Vatican beseeched its friends in America for protection from encroaching communists in Yugoslavia, Greece, and Albania.

Another reason for opening an FBN office in Italy was the Bureau's ability to facilitate the CIA's covert activities. Occupied by American and British forces, Trieste was both a transit point in drug traffic and a base for CIA spies using refugee relief programs and proprietary trading companies to filter agents through the Iron Curtain. Ever in need of cutouts and deniability, CIA officers suborned American businessmen and government employees who had legitimate reasons for being in foreign countries. At the same time, international criminals and enemy spies were diverting massive amounts of Marshall Plan largesse to the Soviet Bloc, so Congress, in an effort to protect its investment, allowed the FBN to establish an office in Italy as a front for military and CIA counterintelligence operations. The one condition was that they did not embarrass the State Department.

To help avoid the State Department, Anslinger relied on friends in industry, especially Pan Am executive Sam Pryor. In 1940 and 1941, Pryor had built fifty air bases in South America as a deterrent to a rumored Axis invasion, and during the war he managed the Pan Am subsidiary that flew Lend-Lease supplies from India to Nationalist forces in Chungking. In 1949, he helped the Nationalists relocate to Taiwan, and in return for his patriotic endeavors, he obtained government-awarded franchises for Pan Am in Turkey, Lebanon, Iran, Africa, Italy, and France. Thereafter Pryor provided logistical support and cover for FBN and CIA agents overseas.[20]

Pryor was only one of the Establishment scions Anslinger relied upon, and the FBN was fortunate to have a Commissioner so intimately connected to the espionage Establishment – people like Bill Donovan and David Bruce – who conspired with their British cousins to create tax-exempt foundations to fund surveys abroad and to promulgate unstated policy through journalists, academics, and businessmen attached to the Council on Foreign Relations and the Foreign Policy Association.

Keeping big business and the CIA content were key to Anslinger's success, as was his decision to send Charlie Siragusa to open the FBN's first overseas office in Rome. With his black-rimmed glasses and large Sicilian features, chain-smoking, restless Charlie Siragusa resembled a frenetic Groucho Marx, and for that reason may have seemed an unlikely choice to represent the US government overseas. But Siragusa was a man of substance, charisma, and deep commitment to national security as well as drug law enforcement. His fervor was deeply personal. One of his relatives had returned to Sicily as a result of anti-Italian prejudice, and another had been killed by a Mafia shotgun blast. Consequently, his avowed, sacred mission was to eradicate the Mafia and restore the tarnished Italian image to its Classical brilliance.

A college graduate from a middle-class family in the Bronx, Siragusa had worked as a stenographer for the Immigration Service from 1934 until 1939. Bored with mundane clerical duties, he joined the FBN and began making cases in Chinatown and Little Italy with his group leader and mentor George White. As White's protégé, Siragusa learned how to spot drug addicts, exploit informers, pose undercover as a seaman, and raid opium dens. He learned quickly and was rewarded with special assignments. He traveled to Canada and worked undercover cases with the Mounties, and then toured the Southern states with an informer named Kenny, arresting marijuana farmers. When Kenny stole a necklace in Dallas, Siragusa, as he explained in his autobiography, chose to look the other way. He was fervent, yes, but as a disciple of George White he knew that an agent never let a minor transgression jeopardize a major investigation.

Siragusa's aptitude and friendship with White brought him to the attention of the espionage Establishment, and in 1944 he was recruited into the counterintelligence branch of the OSS. As a cover for his spy work he was commissioned as a Navy ensign, then assigned to Italy where he worked with White's friend James Angleton. In late 1944, his spy and narcotics missions dovetailed when he interrogated Vito Genovese at Bari Prison at the request of Andrew Berding, the OSS counterintelligence chief in Italy. Siragusa recalled that "being a civilian cop I couldn't resist pushing the hood on his New York City rackets. It was known that he still pulled the strings back there." [21]

By Siragusa's account the interview was a waste of time, but shortly after his chat with Genovese, he found himself on the trail of Annabella Von Hodenburg, a director of Nazi stay-behind agents in Italy. Siragusa caught the baroness ten miles from the Brenner Pass, and in March 1946 returned to New York an authentic war hero.

Under the tutelage of Garland Williams, Siragusa was promoted to group leader and joined the crusade to link the American Mafia's drug syndicate with Lucky Luciano in Italy, communists in general, and the labor movement in New York. Williams also instructed Siragusa in the fine art of disinformation. During a press conference in 1948, Williams announced the FBN's successful investigation of Puerto Rican seamen smuggling heroin to New York. Naming Luciano as their source, Williams called it "the most important" case ever.[22] When Customs inspectors found heroin on seamen in January and May 1949, Williams blamed Luciano; and when a New York taxi driver was arrested in Italy with nine pounds of heroin in June, Williams again claimed that Luciano was responsible. As Siragusa learned, it didn't matter that there was never enough evidence to indict Luciano, the idea was to feed sensational headlines to the press – headlines that Anslinger could use to pressure the Italians at the UN.

In another instance Williams sent agents John Hanly (George White's best friend in the FBN) and Crofton Hayes to contact Meyer Lansky at New York's Plaza Hotel, to find out why the mob's chief financial officer was traveling to Italy. On 28 June 1949, Lansky, describing himself as a "common gambler," told the agents that yes, he was planning to visit Lucky, but no, the visit had nothing to do with drug smuggling.[23] But Hanly and Hayes didn't care what he said, and when Lansky arrived at his ship the next day, they were waiting with a reporter and photographer from the *New York Sun*. The following day the newspaper headlines blared, "Lansky Sails In Luxury To Italy Expected To Confer With Luciano." The agents never expected Lansky to incriminate himself, but they had generated some very good publicity.

Siragusa's next task was to prove he could work effectively with foreign police forces, so Anslinger sent him to Puerto Rico to organize a police narcotic squad. He successfully performed that task, and next was sent to Greece to harass aging Elie Eliopoulos, who had applied for Marshall Plan funds to develop a gold mine in northern Greece, in an area where poppies were cultivated. Arriving in Athens in the summer of 1950, Siragusa visited CIA station chief Tom Karamessines, with whom he would form a life-long friendship. Siragusa provided the history, Karamessines provided the contacts, and through their collaboration, details of Elie's scandalous past appeared in the Greek press. The Marshall Plan loan was blocked, at which point intrepid Elie turned to stock swindles and arms smuggling to Israel.

Siragusa's next stop was Trieste where, with undercover Agent Benny Pocoroba, he set a trap for Matteo Carpinetti, a major supplier of heroin to the California Mafia. Needing cash to make the buy, Siragusa called on his old friend Hank Manfredi, the Army's CID man in Trieste. Throughout his tenure as supervisor of District 17 in Rome, Siragusa would rely heavily on Manfredi; as in the Carpinetti case, the FBN's successes in Europe were based largely on Manfredi's long-standing contacts in the Italian police and security services.

To finance the Carpinetti case, Manfredi introduced Siragusa to the US Army's counterintelligence chief in Trieste, through whom a $10,000 flash roll was given to Pocoroba, enabling him to make a buy from Carpinetti. Manfredi had arrest powers in occupied Trieste, and personally put the cuffs on Carpinetti. In an effort to obtain leniency, Carpinetti named his supplier, Dr. Ricardo Morganti of RAMSA, a wholesale drug company in Trieste. Morganti in turn revealed that he received mail-order heroin from the Schiaparelli pharmaceutical firm in Turin and opium that was diverted from the Yugoslavian government's supply. Morganti named the smugglers he worked with in Belgrade and the manufacturers in Italy who produced surplus heroin for sale on the black market.

In solving this groundbreaking case, which would lead to even bigger fish, Siragusa formed relations with the Yugoslavian police, from whom he acquired informants inside Yugoslavia's anti-Soviet faction, further endearing him to Tom Karamessines and the CIA. And by bringing Siragusa into contact with Army counterintelligence, the Morganti case led to an investigation of US Army personnel smuggling heroin to America. Siragusa exposed the sergeant at the center of the ring and identified the supplier, Greek black marketer Marinos Bouyoukas.

As soon as Siragusa stumbled upon the Bouyoukas operation, CIA officer Karamessines again offered his assistance, only this time there was a catch. Karamessines believed that Bouyoukas was using communist spies to smuggle heroin through Egypt to America, and Siragusa was sympathetic. But when Karamessines suggested that the CIA and FBN stage a controlled delivery into the US as a way of identifying everyone in the Bouyoukas organization, Siragusa objected. Allowing Kenny to steal a necklace was one thing, but as Siragusa emphatically stated in his autobiography, "The FBN could never knowingly allow two pounds of heroin to be delivered into the United States and be pushed to Mafia customers in the New York City area, even if in the long run we could seize a bigger haul." [24]

Siragusa drew the line at facilitating drug trafficking, but he helped the CIA in other ways. For example, he reportedly helped black-bag CIA money to Italian politicians for James Angleton, the CIA's aggressive counterintelligence chief. Although he maintained many assets within the military, especially the Italian Navy, Angleton relied almost exclusively on Siragusa and Manfredi for access to their contacts within the underworld and the Italian police, whose files contained crucial background information about individuals that was essential for penetrating foreign intelligence services and conducting political espionage operations. [25]

Siragusa was especially helpful to the CIA in regard to investigating diversions of Marshall Plan aid. In one case he learned through an informer that the commercial Attaché at the Romanian Embassy in Berne was diverting American-made ball-bearings to the Soviet Union, which the Soviets used to build tanks for North Korea. According to Siragusa, the Attaché traded the ball-bearings for heroin as part of a sinister scheme to steal strategic materials with the one hand from the West, while the other poisoned it with addictive drugs.[26]

As a result of the Berne case, a CIA team was sent to Rome under military cover to stop diversions, and with Siragusa's help, it intercepted all manner of strategic items, including uranium for the Soviet atomic energy program. Numerous foreign officials were involved in a variety of schemes, including a Middle Eastern king, a Swiss millionaire, a high-ranking cleric, a Polish spy, and a Turkish drug and arms merchant in Geneva. Siragusa exposed them all by leaking stories of their misdeeds to the press, thus proving that FBN drug investigations complemented US national security interests and the interests of American businessmen abroad.

In October 1950, Siragusa returned to New York to peruse the Mafia Squad's files and to report to Anslinger in Washington. Three months later he returned to Europe with Mafia Squad leader Joe Amato and Martin Pera, and established the FBN's first permanent overseas office in Rome. He also carried a promise from Anslinger that he would succeed him as Commissioner if all went well. With his right-hand man, Hank Manfredi, Siragusa settled down among the urbane Italians, developed informers and cases, and dreamed of expanding his empire.

THE FRENCH CONNECTION EXPOSED

In April 1951, the FBN initiated a significant case on Joseph Orsini, a Corsican and former Nazi collaborator illegally residing and trafficking narcotics in the US since 1946. Orsini used French seamen to smuggle heroin to Lucchese family member Sal Shillitani and his Mafia associates. The ring included Giovanni Mauceri in Italy, Nazi collaborator Antoine D'Agostino in Canada, Angel Abadelejo (believed to be Nazi collaborator Auguste Ricord) in Buenos Aires, Free French hero Marcel Francisci in Marseilles, chemist Dominique Reissent in Marseilles, Lucien Ignaro in Tunisia, middleman Jean "Laget" David, and former Gestapo agent François Spirito. A protégé of Paul Carbone, Spirito delivered Yugoslavian opium to Marseilles, where it was processed into heroin in clandestine labs belonging to wine broker Marius Ansaldi.[27]

Alas, the arrest of drug smugglers Orsini and Shillitani came at the climax of the Kefauver Hearings, and the case lacked any connection to Luciano, so it failed to generate any spectacular publicity. But it was the first post-war crack in the French connection, and its importance cannot be overstated. Agent Anthony Zirilli, posing as a West Coast buyer, did the undercover work with the help of special employee Pierre Lafitte, a former narcotic trafficker who had become a successful restaurateur in New Orleans. While awaiting deportation on Ellis Island, Lafitte had contacted FBN Agent Irwin Greenfeld, and had offered to set up his cellmate, Joe Orsini. Lafitte and Orsini had known one another for twenty-five years, but Lafitte wanted to remain in America with his wife and children, and after his release from Ellis Island in May 1951, he began systematically setting up his former drug-smuggling associates, most of who were arrested in July. Orsini was sentenced to ten years in the Atlanta Penitentiary in December.[28]

The Orsini case was the FBN's first look at the new dimensions of the French connection as it had been re-established in 1949 and 1950. It paved the way for closer relations with the French police and led to the arrest of wine broker Ansaldi in France in 1952. But it also hinted at espionage intrigues. Spirito was extradited to France to face charges of being a Nazi collaborator, but was never tried, and like other former Gestapo agents, returned to drug smuggling with apparent impunity. And while the case revealed that Marcel Francisci was Lansky's connection in Beirut, no information was revealed about Francisci's source in Indochina, and the French took no action against him either.

SIRAGUSA'S EMPIRE

While case-making agents in Irwin Greenfeld's enforcement group were exposing the French connection, Siragusa and a squad of Italian police were arresting deported mobster Frank Callace in Naples with six kilos of heroin. The ensuing investigation led to a licensed narcotics distributor in Milan, and through him to the Schiaparelli firm's top chemist, Carlo Migliardi, who was charged with diverting over 300 kilograms of heroin and morphine between 1948 and 1951! The case was the brightest jewel in Siragusa's crown and eventually led to the revelation that an estimated 800 kilograms of heroin had been diverted to Mafiosi between 1946 and 1953. As a result, US Ambassador Clare Booth Luce threatened to cut off all foreign aid to the Italian government unless it prohibited the manufacturing of heroin, which it did.

With the dismantling of Italy's heroin industry, the Mafia lost a major source of supply. But the traffic continued to expand and, despite evidence to the contrary, Anslinger continued to blame Communist China. He named "Po I-po" as the supervisor of the PRC's heroin factory in Tientsin, and charged that Po managed 4,000 secret agents (the same number Reinhardt credited to Frau Bidder), whose job was to get American GIs in Korea hooked on heroin.[29] And yet, at the same time, FBN counsel Baxter Mitchell was describing Frank Coppola, the deported Mafioso who allegedly served as Donovan's contact in Sicily, as the "top man."[30]

Siragusa knew that Mitchell was right, and while Anslinger publicly bashed the People's Republic, Siragusa secretly concentrated on Coppola. The investigation began in San Diego with the September 1951 arrest of Sal Vitale, who flipped and gave information that led to the arrest of a dozen big league Detroit drug traffickers in February 1952. More leads followed and in April 1952, Siragusa and the Italian police raided Coppola's house outside Palermo, Sicily, and arrested deported drug trafficker Serafino Mancuso and several accomplices with six kilograms of heroin. The famous Green Trunk of Alcamo case even led to the arrest of Frank Coppola's receivers, John Priziola and Ralph Quasarano, in Detroit. But Luciano and his lieutenants, Joe Pici and Nick Gentile, eluded the authorities, and Coppola, who had brokered the deal, would not be arrested until December 1953 – and was eventually acquitted.

Siragusa had finally smashed the Mafia's venerable Detroit connection, but he had failed to make a case against his nemesis, Lucky Luciano. Siragusa did get some satisfaction when Luciano was banished from Rome to Naples as a result of the case, but that did little to reduce the heroin trade. As author Peter Dale Scott notes, the busts in Detroit and Alcamo "happened after Priziola and Quasarano had already become marginalized to the main Operation X [by which he means French connection in Southeast Asia] drug connection."[31]

Other outlets had opened as well and by 1952, Turkish, Iranian, and Asian narcotics were flowing through Beirut to Marseilles and being converted into heroin by the Francisci and Guérini Gangs, with protection from the CIA and French intelligence services. French author Alain Jaubert notes that in Bordeaux, in 1952, Corsican gangster Antoine Guérini took part in a "mysterious meeting" with Irving Brown (the American Federation of Labor's representative in Europe), Guérini's chemist Jo Cesari, and two other traffickers.[32] Jaubert reported that Corsican crime lord Guérini next brought CIA Agent Brown into contact with the Mafia in Italy.

The insinuation is that the CIA was managing a facet of the international drug conspiracy, and in the pages that follow a considerable amount of evidence will be presented in support of that contention. In the meantime, while CIA Agent Irving Brown was meeting with Corsican and Mafia drug traffickers, Meyer Lansky was purchasing a share in the Cabaret Montmartre gambling casino in Havana and entering into a partnership with Cuban dictator Fulgencio Batista. Lansky's gambling clubs in Florida had been closed in the wake of the Kefauver hearings, and the deal with Batista allowed the mob to control Cuba's hotel and tourist unions and convert Havana into the acknowledged whorehouse of the western hemisphere. The deal also enabled Santo Trafficante to move narcotics from the Middle and Far East through Cuba to Miami, where wholesalers from around the nation bid on the product. Lansky's partner John Pullman formed the Exchange and Investment Bank of Geneva specifically to launder money for the senior managers of this most powerful drug syndicate.

For national security-related reasons, drug-dealing anti-communist allies like Batista in Cuba and anti-communist factions within the Mafia and the French connection existed beyond Charlie Siragusa's grasp. It was a hard pill for Siragusa to swallow, but his *bête noire*, Lucky Luciano, having personally signed-off on the deal during the war, also benefited from the espionage establishment's *modus vivendi* with the underworld. The dance with the devil lasted for a decade. During that period, Siragusa and Manfredi, through the Italian police, routinely monitored Luciano's telephone calls and photographed his visitors. Luciano in turn publicly complained that Siragusa's harassments kept him from going legit and privately he cautioned his family to open his casket and check his pockets for the heroin he was sure Siragusa would plant on his corpse when he died. But it was all an act. Luciano kept his freedom and, in return, his case officer, Hank Manfredi, working for both the CIA and FBN, was able to monitor his underworld and official contacts. The CIA was then able to blackmail or bribe these people into performing illicit acts in its covert war against communism. As ever, national security trumped drug law enforcement, and Charlie Siragusa had no choice but to protect Lucky Luciano, despite their epic animosity.

The Kefauver Committee had determined that local law enforcement officers used the vice squad pattern to allow politicians in America to control the rackets. Simply stated, Siragusa and Manfredi performed a similar function, internationally, for the CIA.

And yet no other FBN agent knew the Mafia as well or preyed on its members as ruthlessly as Charlie Siragusa. He knew how to torment the hoods, and would do anything to make a case. But some of his colleagues felt he refused to share the limelight with anyone else. George White in particular resented Siragusa for not giving him the credit he deserved as a mentor, and everyone knew that Siragusa was dependent on Manfredi's contacts in the Italian police forces. Some say that undercover ace Benny Pocoroba took all the risks in Italy, while Siragusa wrote the reports and got the credit. His most ardent critics argue that Agent Jim Attie stole Charlie's thunder and, as will be made clear in later chapters, paid a dear price for doing so. An Arab linguist and the FBN's most highly decorated agent, Attie worked alone from Beirut to Mexico City, negotiating with bandits while buying tons of opium. Attie was also fiercely independent – a trait Siragusa could not tolerate in subordinates.

Siragusa had devotees as well: agents who looked up to him and formed a faction around him. To this day, many believe that if he had replaced Anslinger as Commissioner, he could have saved the Bureau of Narcotics from the terrible fate that befell it.

"Charlie was the best," one of the old-timers says. "He had a neurological condition that caused him terrible pain in the muscles in his face. Sometimes the pain got so bad he had to wear a patch over one eye." The old-timer smiles: "I can still picture him standing in a doorway in Little Italy in the middle of winter, late at night, wearing that eye patch, his Borsalino hat, and a black overcoat, waiting for his snitch. Yeah, Charlie was the best. Charlie didn't need anybody."

Charlie Siragusa's contribution to the FBN was incomparable. By proving that an FBN agent could forge relations with foreign policemen and still make cases, he made the FBN's overseas expansion possible. In addition, his agents and informers provided the intelligence that led to a string of domestic conspiracy cases that helped define the FBN's Golden Age.

8

THE BEIRUT OFFICE

*"You couldn't throw a tomato into a crowd of Lebanese
and not hit a hashish trafficker."*

Agent Paul Knight

Paul Emerson Knight is a refined, handsome man with interests in poetry, philosophy, and espionage. A graduate of Exeter Academy, he enlisted in the Army at seventeen and was hardened by months of fierce combat following the Normandy invasion. After the war, he remained in France, attending Grenoble University for a year. In 1950 he graduated from Harvard and returned to New Hampshire with "a burning desire to get back abroad," so he could use the languages he had acquired and learn more. Through acquaintances he applied for work with the FBN and CIA.

The FBN called first and, after meeting with Anslinger and Deputy Commissioner George Cunningham, Knight was hired in the fall of 1950 and assigned to the New York office. He was trained in elementary investigative techniques at the Army CID and Treasury Law Enforcement schools, and then returned to New York where he learned the realities of street work on the Lower East Side under the tutelage of veteran Agent Benjamin "Benny" Groff, and with the help of a Black informant named Hubbard in Harlem.

But Knight wanted only to work on the international scene, so he attached himself to Price Spivey's Special Endeavor Group, which was focusing on the French connection, and to Joe Amato's Italian Squad, which was charting the Mafia's organizational hierarchy. By studying the files of these groups, Knight became familiar with the shadowy individuals and loose-knit groups involved in international drug trafficking.

According to Knight, the FBN already knew which nations produced opium and processed morphine base into heroin, but it was primarily through Spivey and Amato's investigations that the FBN learned which French and Italian traffickers were purchasing opium and morphine base from sources in Lebanon. At the same time, however, there was an institutional reluctance to focus on any international conspiracy.

"Spivey and Amato were right," Knight says, "but the idea of a conspiracy was something they had to sell, because it was very difficult to get anyone to cooperate as an informant. The activity that upper echelon people engage in is illegal, but you can never find them doing anything wrong – you would never hear a Mafia don say, 'Please buy three kilos of heroin.' So in the early 1950s the policy of making conspiracy cases was hard to implement. Policy from headquarters in Washington was only applicable to work on the street, and old-timers like Benny Groff did mostly low-level work by default."

Aware that Charlie Siragusa had opened an office in Rome, and anxious to pursue the international conspiracy aspects of drug law enforcement, Knight requested an overseas transfer. His timing was perfect. Posing as a Mafia buyer, Siragusa had done some undercover work in Marseilles in May 1951, with limited success. Marseilles was teeming with French and Indo-Chinese drug smugglers, and the prospects of making cases there were excellent, but the Marseilles narcotic squad consisted of only two men. The one active member, Inspector Robert Pasquier, lived in a two-room flat reminiscent of a New York tenement and was limited in his efforts by a paltry budget and weak laws. Defendants in possession of fifteen kilos of heroin, arrested the previous year by Pasquier and George White, had received one-month sentences![1]

Pasquier, however, was well informed, and he notified Siragusa that French Customs had seized 300 kilograms of opium aboard a French ship that had arrived from Beirut and that the shipment was destined for Antoine Cordoliani, an important trafficker in Marseilles. Cordoliani had a conversion lab outside Paris and sold pure heroin to Italians in Rome and Milan, as well as to French-Americans under investigation by the Italian Squad. Pasquier also provided Siragusa with contacts in Egypt and Beirut, the soft spot in a smuggling route that originated in Turkey.

In desperate need of a French-speaking agent to help develop these cases, Siragusa asked Knight to join him in Rome in August 1952. Upon arriving there, Knight found himself living in hotels, out of a suitcase, on a per diem basis. But the freewheeling lifestyle suited him, and he formed an immediate rapport with urbane Hank Manfredi. With Manfredi's help he began to learn Italian, and he began working undercover cases all over Europe with chunky, prematurely balding Jack Cusack. The first agent to join Siragusa in Europe on a permanent basis, Cusack tried in 1951 to make an undercover buy from chemist Marius Ansaldi in Paris. He failed, but French undercover agents, under the direction of Commissaire A. Edmund Bailleul, made the case soon thereafter. Having participated in the case, Cusack was able to claim a share of the credit, and he remained in Rome on permanent assignment, as New York District Supervisor Jim Ryan's eyes and ears – for at the time, Rome was a sub-office of District 2, and Ryan and Siragusa were competing to make big cases.

Unable to master French, Cusack was relegated to writing reports and backing up Knight and a series of temporary duty agents – including George Lendrihas, Mike Picini, Gregory Poulos, and Anthony Zirilli – who were spreading out from Rome on undercover assignments. Knight worked mostly in France and Germany; Lendrihas and Poulos in Greece and the Middle East; and Zirilli and Picini in Italy and Sicily. For all of them, imagination and innovation were crucial to their successes.

Knight, for example, knew that the foreign traffickers were aware that American agents, alone among the world's police forces, were pursuing them. So he devised a plausible cover that would enable him to make undercover buys and set up deliveries. Through a friend who operated a travel agency in New York, he printed business cards with a picture of a man astride the globe and presented himself as Robert Martel, a Canadian employed by the travel agency. Other times he posed as a US Air Force pilot, a Danish seaman, or as a Pan Am pilot or crew member.

Knight's undercover abilities were tested in Paris in the spring of 1953. Since 1951, the FBN had been receiving reports that Mahmoud Pahlevi, younger brother of the Shah of Iran, was trafficking in narcotics between Tehran, Paris, New York, and Detroit.[2] In February 1949, Garland Williams had reported that Iran's great families had been made rich by opium, and deliberately kept the anti-drug laws weak. Evidently, he was referring to members of Iran's ruling Pahlevi family, whose holdings included vast opium fields.

The first documented report of Pahlevi's involvement was in February 1951. Siragusa and Joe Amato were in Hamburg when Siragusa's special employee, Prince Vittorio San Martino, saw the young Persian prince getting into a purple Cadillac with two beautiful women. Martino told the agents that Pahlevi was "a notorious playboy and bon vivant," and was smuggling narcotics.[3]

When Jim Ryan received Siragusa's report, he said he couldn't believe that the Shah's younger brother, because of his position and wealth, would be smuggling. Siragusa calmly replied that, only a few months earlier, he had arrested Prince Alessandro Ruspoli in possession of ten pounds of opium and that Ruspoli was royalty and a millionaire too. Prince Ruspoli was also an addict, Siragusa added, hinting that Pahlevi may have had a drug habit too, and that he was supplying his jet-set friends so they could all enjoy the same exclusive kick.

More information came that winter when French trafficker Louis Carlicchi, "an intimate associate of the notorious Joe Renucci, a Corsican gangster living in Tangiers," introduced one of Siragusa's informers to Mahmoud Pahlevi in Paris.[4] The prince's family owned huge opium farms, and the Corsican asked him to supply raw opium and build a heroin conversion factory in Tehran. The prince had agreed to be the supplier and build the factory, and the informer had agreed to be the chemist, but Carlicchi was arrested in another case before the Pahlevi operation could begin.

Despite this failed venture, Pahlevi continued to traffic in narcotics, and in March 1953 Knight discovered that the prince, using the alias Marmoud Kawa, was smuggling heroin between Iran, Paris, New York, and Detroit. Based on the information Knight had gathered, Agent George Lendrihas tried to make an undercover buy from the prince at the Imperial Court Hotel in New York. Lendrihas was unsuccessful, but information he gained in the course of his investigation led Knight, through the Riviera glitterati, to Ingebord Griffell, a beautiful young German nightclub singer selling morphine and heroin to a small group of wealthy Americans in Europe.

Knight informed Commissaire Michel Hugues, head of the Sûreté's narcotic squad in Paris, and together they set a trap. Ingebord Griffell was part of a gang of traffickers, and in June, after winning her affections, Knight was able to meet with her boss, Armen Nercessian. At the meeting, Knight bought a sample of heroin from Nercessian and arranged to buy two kilograms more. A time and place were set, but during their meeting in the designated cafe, Nercessian told Knight that he had changed the plan, and that they would have to drive to the place where the heroin was located. Knight agreed and, to the surprise of the French agents covering him, calmly walked outside and got into Nercessian's car. The French policemen waited a moment, then ran to their Citroen. They did their best to catch up without being seen, but as Nercessian drove through Paris, he saw them in his rearview mirror and began to panic. Showing great presence of mind, Knight said he had a hideout nearby, and directed Nercessian into the Sûreté's garage, where he pulled his gun and arrested him.

The arrest caused quite a stir in celebrity-conscious Paris: Knight, the hero, was blond and handsome; Ingebord, the femme fatale, was dark and beautiful; one member of the gang had been Iran's counsel in Brussels and Cairo; and Nercessian's wife was the daughter of South Africa's minister to France. But the CIA was plotting to overthrow the government in Iran, and reinstall the Shah, so FBN headquarters never revealed that Pahlevi's address was found on Nercessian. In a 22 February 1954 letter to Anslinger, Siragusa merely said there was enough surplus opium in Iran to make what had happened "a trend."[5] In August, after the CIA's successful coup, the oil fields that Iran had nationalized were returned to their former British and American corporate owners.

CHARLIE'S ANGELS

Impressed with Knight's finesse and composure, Siragusa brought him into collateral operations with the CIA and military intelligence. "In the early days," Knight explains, "we did a lot of odd jobs for the government. Most were investigations regarding the Export Control Act of 1949 – making sure that strategic materials weren't going to the wrong end-users behind the Iron Curtain. We did quite a bit of that in Milano using sources in the East European refugee community. The Treasury Department was asking the military, 'Is this a real company?' We'd be asked to find out who was who.

"It wasn't case-making," Knight stresses, "it was helping people. It was Charlie passing information to an American colonel in Rome."

Their involvement in the shadowy realm of spies was a valuable experience for Knight and his fellow overseas agents, and helped the FBN establish good relations with the CIA and military intelligence. But this commitment absorbed half of their time, and as a result, FBN operations in Europe in the early 1950s were slow getting off the ground. Under Siragusa's direction, these early operations were catch as catch can. Siragusa's top priority was accessibility, Knight explains – a matter of "Do you have a chance of getting him?"

"We were trying to make cases to demonstrate we could stop heroin from going to America, so they were small cases at first, only three or four kilograms. But in the process we learned about Corsicans like Dom Albertini, who managed heroin labs in Marseilles, and about Mafiosi out of Sicily doing business in Milan and Rome. We learned about Black servicemen moving heroin into Harlem, and about Air France crew members. But the most attractive leads were those that had to do with the supply of raw materials from Iran and Turkey to Lebanon."

Crucial to FBN operations in Europe were special employees Orlando Portale, a deported Mafioso, and Carlo Dondola, a Lebanese-Greek smuggler and member of the Lebanese Christian Phalange. Dondola moved all manner of contraband between Italy, Greece, Israel, Lebanon, and Africa, and like Portale, often made the necessary arrangements for FBN agents. Portale and Dondola would elicit and authenticate potential leads, and then FBN undercover agents would approach the traffickers. In this way the agents came into contact with the Corsican and Italian smugglers they were seeking.

Complicating matters was the fact that in most European countries, FBN agents were prohibited by law from conducting unilateral operations, or making arrests, or even initiating contact with informers without permission from the local constabulary. In almost every case, success depended on forming good liaison relationships with the local police forces. Entrapment was a crime in France, so agents also had to learn how to make cases without provoking a suspect into buying or selling narcotics. Confidence-building buys, in which there were no witnesses, were allowed on occasion, according to Knight, but only with the tacit approval of a judicial official beforehand. Some foreign policemen were helpful, others were not, but over time, Siragusa, Knight, Cusack (who returned to New York in 1953), and Manfredi were at least recognized in police stations across Europe. By 1954 their presence was firmly established, and under the direction of Charlie Siragusa, the FBN was ready to expand its operations into the Middle East.

OPENING THE BEIRUT OFFICE

In 1954, Charlie Siragusa decided to open an office in Beirut. There were several reasons for this decision. To begin with, the Italian government's crackdown on diversions had forced the Mafia to seek new sources, and after the exposure in 1954 of a heroin lab owned by Don Calogero Vizzini in Palermo, it was determined that most of the illicit traffic in heroin had been rerouted to Beirut, where Corsicans were working with Meyer Lansky's associate Samil Khoury, a notorious Syrian smuggler and counterfeiter. Married to a French singer, Khoury had "influence and solid support among top ranking policemen and politicians."[6]

Khoury's drug-smuggling operation was facilitated by Mounir Alaouie, an official in the criminal investigations branch of Lebanon's Sûreté. Their *modus operandi* was simple: Alaouie and Khoury would drive to Damascus, Syria, to purchase morphine base, then bring it back across the border, with the help of accomplices in Lebanese Customs, to Beirut's Casino de Liban, where they made arrangements, through Corsican associates of Marcel Francisci, to transport it to secret labs in and around Marseilles.

Siragusa had known about Khoury's operation since 1950, but at that time there were too many political complications to allow the FBN to establish a presence in the region. The Arab nations were angry at the creation of Israel, and in 1951 Egypt complained to the UN that Israeli and Lebanese drug lords were deliberately subverting its economy. According to news reports, Lebanese hashish was being smuggled through Israel to Egypt's huge addict population. The profits represented a major source of unaccounted foreign exchange for both Israel and Lebanon, but the black-market traffic caused a serious financial drain on Egypt.[7]

In an attempt to assuage the Egyptians and slow Soviet expansion in the region, the State Department offered financial aid to Lebanon, and in exchange the Lebanese premier pledged to clamp down on trafficking. But, as the *New York Times* reported on 2 July 1951, when Lebanese Premier Abdullah Yafi sent army troops to destroy hashish crops in the northeast, "men who had occupied high office went livid with rage."[8]

Most of these livid officials were members of the Maronite Christian minority and its paramilitary action arm, the Phalange. For decades the Maronites served as middlemen between the Turks and French along the Syrian border, and though dedicated fascists during the Second World War, the Maronites secretly supported Israel in exchange for US political and financial support against rival Muslim factions in Lebanon.

Siragusa's hands were tied by the CIA, while the Maronites and Israelis established their domains in the early 1950s. By 1954, however, both were firmly entrenched, and Siragusa was authorized to open an office in Beirut, which by then was the acknowledged gateway of illicit drugs from Greece, Turkey, and Syria to Western Europe. Opening the office was a job that required an exceptional individual with fluency in foreign languages and that ability, rare among Americans, to make foreign officials feel comfortable. Paul Knight got the job.

Opening an office in Beirut also required the permission of the Lebanese government, so a trial investigation was mounted to prove that drug arrests would not be embarrassing to Maronite officials. The investigation was aimed at a Lebanese–Israeli drug ring managed by Cafe Palestine proprietor Mahmoud Abou Suleiman. The ring smuggled hash to Egypt, had a heroin conversion lab in Tel Aviv, and moved narcotics to Italy.[9] Siragusa mounted the operation from Rome, and in July 1954, based on intelligence supplied by Knight and Orlando Portale, the Lebanese Sûreté arrested Suleiman along with a corrupt Lebanese Customs Agent who had helped smuggle three kilos of morphine base aboard a ship that sailed to Naples, where Lucky Luciano was located.[10]

Having opened the door, Knight moved on to bigger and better things, and his next case relied on international confidence man Carlo Dondola. Described by Siragusa as an agent "for the Greek intelligence service as well as the Arabs and Israelis," Dondola, at one point in his illustrious career, had "sold some horses to the Israelis, arranged to have them stolen, then resold them to the Arabs ... and never got caught."[11]

"When I first met Carlo in 1953," Knight recalls, "he was working for Charlie in Bulgaria, posing as a trafficker. Carlo had made a fortune smuggling gold out of Africa through Lebanon into Egypt."

Knight's case with Carlo began when Beirut moneychanger Abou Sayia cheated Dondola in a financial transaction, and Dondola, seeking revenge, volunteered to show the FBN just how easy it was to make narcotics cases in the Middle East. He began by initiating a drug deal with Sayia, and then brought in Knight, undercover of course, as the buyer. Next he convinced Sayia's source in Syria, Mr. Tifankji, to reveal his source of opium in Turkey, Mr. Mehmet Ozsayar. As the case expanded, Dondola introduced Siragusa (posing as Cal Salerno, a corrupt US Air Force pilot) to Ozsayar. Siragusa assigned Agent George Abraham to work on Tifankji, and then arranged to buy a quantity of opium himself from Ozsayar in Adana, Turkey.

With Dondola having already lined up the ducks, Siragusa was able to persuade the chiefs of the Lebanese, Greek, Turkish, and Syrian police forces to support his investigation. Accompanied by Greek and Turkish officials, Siragusa arrested Ozsayar in early April 1955. The Syrian police, assisted by George Abraham, arrested Tifankji in Aleppo two days later, while the chief of Lebanon's Sûreté, Emir Faoud Chehab, raided a clandestine lab in Beirut with Lebanese Customs chief Edmond Azizi and Paul Knight. In total, twenty-seven traffickers were arrested, ringleader Omar Makkouk was identified (though he remained at large), and 800 pounds of opium and forty-four pounds of morphine base were seized.[12]

As Siragusa said with pride: "We got the Greeks to work with the Turks and, as you know, they're dedicated enemies. We also got the Syrians to work with the Turks at a time when there was no love lost between them either."[13]

Soon thereafter, Paul Knight cautiously opened the FBN's second overseas office in Beirut. At the time, Lebanon was a bubbling cauldron of political intrigues. Having been carved out of their country by the French, the Syrians considered Lebanon to be stolen property, and Syrian agents enthusiastically smuggled weapons to the Lebanese Muslim factions that were fighting the Maronites. Lebanon was also flooded with Palestinian refugees; the Egyptians were unleashing the Fedayeen on Israel; and Israel was raiding Syria, Egypt, and Jordan. As the British withdrew from their commitments in the region, America stepped gingerly into the breach. To keep the Soviets at bay and protect the Arab–American Oil Company (ARAMCO) pipeline that stretched from Saudi Arabia to Lebanon's coast, the CIA began secretly arming its Christian and Israeli allies, buying politicians, and backing Stravos Niarchos in his competition with Aristole Onassis for the lucrative Saudi oil-shipping contract.

When Knight arrived in Beirut, he was given a room in the American Embassy, in the Agency for International Development's Office of Public Safety, which provided material aid to the Lebanese police forces. But Lebanese security officials were aware that CIA officers were operating undercover of the Public Safety program, so Knight had to keep his distance from the Embassy. He also had trouble forming relations with Lebanese police officials. He had a personal, not a diplomatic, passport, and he lived at the St. George Hotel, posing as a travel agent, in order to make undercover cases. As a result of his multiple identities, some Lebanese officials were suspicious. "They weren't quite sure why I was there," Knight recalls. "Was I an Israeli spy?"

Knight's initial contact was Lebanon's national security chief Emir Faoud Chehab, but the influential Chehab family had been involved in corruption under the French mandate, which ended in 1945. As a result, Knight says, "for political, economic and cultural reasons" there wasn't much Chehab could do to help him make narcotics cases. It was not until Captain Azizi of the customs service introduced him to Hannah Yazbek, a Maronite strongman, that Knight was able to begin recruiting informers and gathering intelligence on local drug traffickers.

As Knight explains, "They had a system in Beirut not unlike that in Chicago, in which the city was divided into ethnic and religious neighborhoods. Each neighborhood had a strongman, the *abada*, from whom criminals and businessmen alike bought protection. Hannah Yazbek, otherwise known as Abu George [meaning father of George], was the Maronite *abada*. He was a hashish smuggler connected to the Gemayel family, which controlled the Fascist Phalange and had collaborated with the Vichy French, so he was not beloved of the British or Israelis. But he was essential to getting the job done."

At first Knight would meet Abu George at his house, where the *abada* would introduce him to the right people. Soon informants were visiting Knight's office. But some were "dragging their coats," intending to deceive him, so Knight would tell Abu George who they were and what they said. Like Orlando Portale in Rome, Abu George would authenticate the informants' stories – if doing so did not conflict with his own prosperous hashish business. "He would confirm," Knight explains, "if it helped make a case against Sami Khoury or the Druze."

The Maronites were deeply involved in financial crime and hashish smuggling. It was a part of Lebanese culture Knight did not like, but he came to regard Abu George as indispensable. After it became known that they were friends, however, they were no longer able to meet, so Abu George introduced Knight to his nephew, Elie, a concierge at the Capitol Hotel, and thereafter Elie served as Knight's indispensable link to Beirut's teeming underworld.

Through Abu George, Elie, and his own unilateral contacts, Knight began to collect intelligence on drug smuggling operations in Beirut and the nearby Bekka Valley, the ancient Biblical land between Syria and Lebanon where hashish was grown and narcotics were smuggled. In concert with Customs officer Azizi, Knight provided the intelligence to undercover Agent Jim Attie, the initiator of a string of significant cases.

JIM ATTIE, UNDERCOVER ACE

Jim Attie was uniquely qualified for undercover work in the Middle East. His father had led a band of Assyrian rebels that protected Christian settlements from the Ottoman Turks. Slated for a hangman's noose in Istanbul, Attie senior fled to Detroit, where Jim was raised in abject poverty. During the war he served with the US Navy and fought his way to the welterweight championship of the Pacific Fleet. After the war he earned a college degree and took a job as a therapist with the Veteran's Administration. Proud, restless, and adventurous, Attie joined the FBN in Detroit in 1950. In 1954, under the direction of District Supervisor Ross Ellis, he made a major case on a hapless Lebanese baker. The case brought him to Anslinger's attention and launched his career as an undercover agent in the Middle East, where he came into serious conflict with Paul Knight and Charlie Siragusa.

"It all started with the case I made in Detroit," Attie says ruefully. "I still pity the poor guy [Hussine Hider] to this day. He was merely *thinking* about getting into the business, and I talked him into it. Eventually he gave me a number, and they sent me to Beirut to meet a politician and rug merchant named Amir Ghoriab. I persuaded Ghoriab to deliver two kilograms of morphine base to me in Beirut, where Lebanese Customs agents arrested him in May 1955.

"After he was arrested, Ghoriab told me, 'You'll never leave here alive.' And he was almost right. I was staying at a hotel we suspected of being a depot for dope dealers and, a few days after the Ghoriab bust, I walked into the lobby and was arrested. I was taken to Sûreté headquarters and brought before Haj Touma, director of the Sûreté's security branch. Touma was a big dope dealer himself, and at his direction the interrogator asked me who I was. I said I was a tourist and I demanded to know why I'd been arrested. At which point they handcuffed me. Then Touma reached over and punched me in the face.

"Well," Attie says coolly, "I'd been cuffed in front, so I dove at him. But before I could grab his throat, the others jumped on me. They cuffed my hands behind my back and worked me over pretty good. Luckily the Customs chief, Edmond Azizi [Paul Knight's contact] came in and saw my face was smeared with blood. Azizi, who was a big dope dealer too, took me to Customs headquarters and tried to smooth everything over."

Attie held no grudge against Touma, but he did harbor tremendous resentment for Knight over the incident – a personal animosity that was inflamed after Knight's mother-in-law referred to Attie's son as "a dirty little Arab." Attie also came to hate Charlie Siragusa. He felt that Siragusa was more concerned with feathering his own nest, through investment opportunities at the Merrill Lynch brokerage house in Rome, than in making cases. There was another reason, too, which happened later on. But his first adversary was Paul Knight.

As Attie recalls, "Knight was always partying with Elie Yazbek. Elie's uncle was the gangster over gambling and smuggling in Beirut. He worked with the Gemayels, who controlled the waterfront and got a fee from all the ships that docked there. President Chehab was involved too. And everything Knight said, whether he knew it or not, went directly from Yazbek and Azizi to Sami Khoury, who sold 50,000 submachine guns to the Israelis while I was there."

According to Attie, the Israelis spent millions of CIA dollars bribing officials in Europe and the Middle East for information and protection. He claims that Khoury relied on Customs chief Edmond Azizi for protection in Lebanon, and that the Israelis provided the contacts and money that enabled Khoury to move narcotics across Europe. With protection guaranteed by the Mossad, Khoury packed his car full of morphine base and drove to France, where he stayed at an Israeli safehouse. Attie also claims that the Israelis prevented the FBN from conducting investigations against drug-dealing Israeli agents in Aleppo, Syria, the major transit point in the region.

THE FOUR HORSEMEN

Despite political impediments and a minuscule budget, operations in the Middle East generated tremendous publicity for the FBN. In November 1955, Attie single-handedly stole a significant quantity of heroin from drug lord Mohammed Oz Yurik in Turkey. And in May 1956 (a year after the League of Arab States named Israel as the major source of illicit drugs in Lebanon), FBN agents and Lebanese Customs official Edmond Azizi arrested Omar Makkouk, the biggest laboratory operator in Beirut. The case was widely reported in the press, as was a shoot-out Paul Knight had, around that time, with drug smugglers in the Syrian desert.

Each of Knight's and Attie's adventures helped Siragusa to better understand how illicit drugs were moved to America, with the result that cases made in the Middle East led to arrests in America, where it mattered most. For example, a tip given to undercover Agent Tony Zirilli in Italy allowed the FBN to arrest fugitive George Mallock in New York, and force his brother John to flee to Mexico. The Mallock brothers case led to bigger cases in Hollywood and Chicago, and to members of the French connection in Mexico, Canada, and New York.

FBN successes in the Middle East were also beneficial to Harry Anslinger. In June 1955, the Commissioner proudly told a Judiciary Subcommittee that the Army, Navy, Coast Guard, and FBI combined could not stop heroin smuggling into New York. But four men – Charlie Siragusa, Paul Knight, Hank Manfredi, and Jim Attie – by themselves stopped 40 percent.

"These four men," Anslinger said, "are worth one hundred men here."[14]

9

THE SECRET POLICEMAN

*"A. J.'s cover story? An international playboy and harmless
practical joker. It was A. J. who dosed the punch with a mixture
of Yage, Hashish and Yohimbine during a Fourth of July
reception at the US Embassy, precipitating an orgy."*
William S. Burroughs, *The Naked Lunch*

While Charlie Siragusa was establishing his overseas empire and envisioning himself as Harry Anslinger's successor, his erstwhile mentor, George White, was embarking on a secret mission that would forever pervert American drug law enforcement.

The process began during the Second World War, when the OSS concocted a Truth Drug derived from marijuana, and White was chosen to test it on human subjects. White's marijuana experiments continued at least through 1947, but failed to produce the desired results. Then in 1950, several US soldiers were captured in North Korea and publicly claimed they were members of a secret bacterial warfare unit. This changed everything. On the assumption that the POWs had been brainwashed – and that America, like it or not, must now enter a race against the communists to perfect methods of mind control – the CIA established covert research programs in several major psychiatric hospitals, universities, and pharmaceutical companies, in an effort to find a drug more powerful than marijuana that it could use to manipulate thoughts and behavior. By February 1951, Harry Anslinger and his deputy, George Cunningham, were providing the CIA with every drug imaginable, and the CIA was performing potentially lethal experiments on scores of unwitting American citizens.[1]

It wasn't long before the CIA decided that lysergic acid diethylamide (LSD) was the most effective drug for identifying double agents, eliciting information from prisoners of war, and for "implanting suggestions and other forms of mental control."[2] LSD could also be used to discredit the opposition's politicians. In one case, according to author Michael McClintock, CIA agents in 1953 drugged President Elpidio Quirino of the Philippines before he gave a speech, "so that he would appear incoherent."[3]

LSD also had the potential to expose and disable the enemy within, especially labor leaders and citizens suspected of spying for the Soviets. A clause in the National Security Act was interpreted as sanctioning CIA participation in domestic Internal Security programs, and by 1952 the CIA had hired George White to test LSD on unwitting American citizens in New York. Earnest and experienced in such matters, White's status as a federal agent provided him with carte blanche to conduct experiments on anyone anywhere. His references included CIA counterintelligence expert James Angleton, and former OSS chief William Donovan. But White's major qualification was a wicked mean streak.

After Paul Newey left the FBN and joined the CIA in 1951, he met with the CIA security officer who had conducted White's background check. The CIA security officer told Newey that White's sadomasochism was a way of overcompensating for a poor body image he'd developed in 1945, when his second wife Ruth deserted him, calling him "a big fat slob." The words hurt, so the five-foot-seven 200-pounder tried to overcome his hang-up by inflicting pain on others. Several pertinent cases will be discussed.

White's operational relationship with the CIA began in April 1952, when he was introduced to Dr. Sidney Gottlieb, the club-footed, stuttering research scientist selected to manage the CIA's LSD-testing program. A native New Yorker, Gottlieb headed the Chemical Branch of the CIA's Technical Services Staff. Gottlieb and White formed an instant rapport, and together they would manage the LSD testing program in New York until 1955; then in San Francisco until 1957, when Gottlieb was reassigned; and again from 1961 until White's retirement in 1965. It could safely be said that these two eccentrics ushered America into its psychedelic age.[4]

To assist him in finding unwitting subjects for his LSD experiments in New York, White recruited Gilbert Fox, a softcore pornographer he met in October 1952.

"I knew George well," Fox says. "Extremely well, in a strange sort of way. We met through John Wiley, an artist who was putting out a little magazine called *Bizarre* that featured scantily-clad women wearing high heels. George liked it. As a child he'd been infatuated with an aunt who wore high heels. So George's fetish was spiked high-heeled shoes and leather boots. He liked my books too, and he asked me to write about high heels.

"George was an interesting guy with a sensitive side," Fox explains. "He loved little birds, like canaries. But he was a gin drunk. He drank morning, noon and night. He was playing out his sexual fantasies too. One time my wife Pat and I went with George to see a hooker at a hotel. She tied him up and strapped him to the bed and whipped his ass. She had on high heels.

"George's wife, Albertine [whom he married on 18 August 1951] knew George was playing around," Fox continues, "but she was a social climber, and she pushed him to succeed. At the time George was big into the New York mayoral election. The man he was backing, Rudolph Halley, had been chief counsel on the Kefauver Committee, and was running for mayor on the Fusion Party ticket. If Halley won the election, he was going to make George Commissioner of the New York City Police Department."

It's rumored that White put LSD in the drinking water of one of Halley's opponents at a political debate, much as the CIA drugged Philippine president Elpidio Quirino.[5] But while that is just a rumor about White, in his own diary he told how, on 28 November 1952, he dosed Gil and Pat Fox, and their friends Kai and Jo Jurgenson, with LSD.

As Fox recalls, "We were all boozing and smoking pot in those days, and one night George gave us LSD. He slipped it to us secretly. Kai and Jo were visiting us, and we had gone to the Whites' for dinner. Afterwards we went slumming around the Lower Village. It was snowing. We stopped the car on Cornelius Street and the snow was red and green and blue – a thousand beautiful colors – and we were dancing in the street. Jo thought she had on lace gloves up to her elbows. Then we went into a lesbian bar and Pat freaked out. Pat had trouble coming off the trip. Kai's wife Jo later went wacko, like Eliot Smithe's wife.

"I was angry at George for that," Fox says. But he and his wife remained good friends with the Whites, as if nothing unusual had happened. And considering their proclivities, that was true. Indeed, Gil Fox introduced White to his next unwitting victim only a few days later.

Eliot Smithe knew Gil Fox from the swinging Greenwich Village sex scene, and in mid-December 1952, Eliot and his nineteen-year-old wife, Barbara, joined the Foxes for dinner and drinks at the Whites' apartment on West 12th Street. In an attempt to entice the Smithes into an orgy,

White proudly displayed his pretty wife's closet full of stiletto heels. Eliot found George way too repulsive, however, so White's orgy didn't happen. But everyone remained friends and while Eliot was out of town, his young wife Barbara accepted an invitation to join the Whites for dinner and drinks. Barbara was so naive that she brought along her twenty-month-old baby daughter, Valerie.

Also present on the evening of 11 January 1954, and also surreptitiously dosed with LSD, was Clarice Stein, Albertine's friend and colleague at the Abraham & Strauss department store in Brooklyn. For Clarice it was an experiment that ended in trauma.

According to Clarice, the evening started out happily enough. White served Martinis, and about half an hour later, Clarice, Barbara, and Albertine embarked on a "laughing jag." But the fun ended when Clarice got home and she began to see multicolored images whenever she closed her eyes. She got frightened and called White for help, but he was totally unsympathetic; his response was to mock her and then hang up the phone. Her fear grew into abject terror as the trip intensified, and she promised herself that if she never fell asleep again, which seemed a distinct possibility at the time, she would kill herself. But her symptoms subsided later the next day, and she elected to remain friends with Albertine.[6]

Barbara Smithe was less fortunate. Shortly after George White dosed her with LSD, she began a steady descent into paranoia, and in 1958 she was admitted to a mental hospital in New York. She developed cancer (as did Clarice) and died in 1978. No one knows what happened to Barbara or her baby that night; she never told Eliot she was there. And for that reason Eliot suspects that George White, the CIA's rampaging secret policeman, may have molested her.

DRUGS, AND AMERICA'S UNSTATED FOREIGN POLICY

While he gleefully engaged in the CIA's nefarious LSD testing program, George White continued to serve as an FBN agent, and in January 1953 he traveled to Cuba at Anslinger's request to gauge the degree of newly elected president Fulgencio Batista's commitment to drug law enforcement. It is hard to believe that Anslinger had any illusions in this regard, for White must have learned through his underworld informants what everyone else knew: that the Cuban dictator had renewed the illicit contracts Meyer Lansky had entered into with his predecessors, and that narcotics were pouring through Cuba, into America, as never before. But the US customs service had jurisdiction in Cuba, and FBN agents were not supposed to operate there unless the Treasury Attaché asked for their help – and for this purely bureaucratic reason, Anslinger was passively able to suppress the truth. This situation left Batista in charge of drug law enforcement in Cuba, and as a result the only drug smugglers the FBN was allowed to pursue were those who hadn't paid Batista his required tariff. According to Sal Vizzini, an FBN agent who regularly worked undercover cases in Cuba during the mid- to late 1950s, the tariff was a hefty 50 percent of the profits.

Behind the scenes, national security was the real reason Anslinger kept his hands off Cuba. In April 1952, Batista's customs service detained two Soviet diplomats who had arrived from Mexico with two suitcases weighing 154 pounds. Whatever was inside the suitcases was so valuable that the Soviets chose to break relations with Cuba "rather than have them inspected."[7] Cuba was only ninety miles away from Florida, and by keeping the Soviets at bay, Batista provided a security service that trumped drug law enforcement. In return the CIA supported him and, by default, or design, the Mafia's drug syndicate.

Anslinger would later excuse himself by writing:

Our agents made more than fifty cases against Cuban pushers and dealers in the Batista era. The Batista government did nothing about putting these men in jail in spite of our cooperation in working with their own people to get the evidence, so I sent word to our agents, 'Cease cooperating and come on home.'[8]

George White, meanwhile, completed his Cuban survey and then mounted investigations in Ecuador and Peru that brought the FBN favorable publicity. He returned to New York in the throes of alcoholism, and resumed his LSD duties in April 1953. The Eisenhower administration had given the program a shot in the arm with the appointment of Allen W. Dulles as director of Central Intelligence and Richard C. Helms as chief of the CIA's clandestine services. Both were willing to use any weapon to fight communism and, with Dulles's support, Helms on 3 April 1953 proposed funding for a biochemical warfare program named MKULTRA, whose purpose was to develop drugs that would enable the CIA to discredit friends and foes alike, and that could be delivered clandestinely and kill without a trace. White's inside knowledge of the Mafia's committee on assassinations and its murder techniques – such as hiring foreigners, and setting up dupes to take the fall – made him uniquely qualified for this lethal aspect of the job. Dulles approved MKULTRA operations on 13 April 1953, and the CIA's quest to create better killers through chemistry commenced in earnest.[9]

Next, White moved the MKULTRA operation out of his apartment and into a safehouse at 81 Bedford Street in Greenwich Village. Using the alias Morgan Hall, he began drawing rent money from a CIA bank account. Pat Fox decorated the apartment, and White's closest special employee, Pierre Lafitte (the agent provocateur in the Orsini case), installed an air conditioner, a telephone, and a cabinet full of gin. After CIA technicians had installed a two-way mirror and hidden microphones, and had supplied White with the latest photographic equipment, Lafitte hired call girls to lure spies, diplomats, gangsters, politicians, and even average citizens to their doom. The victims were dosed with aphrodisiacs and/or LSD while White, his FBN cohorts, and assorted CIA scientists watched through the two-way mirror and filmed and tape-recorded the action.

White's first MKULTRA briefing at the Bedford pad occurred on 23 June 1953 and included James Angleton, Dr. James Hamilton, and Gregory Bateson, a former OSS officer with radical ideas about political and psychological warfare. Hamilton had been White's partner in the OSS Truth Drug program, had conducted opium surveys in Burma during the war, and in 1953 was involved in psychologically assessing White's MKULTRA subjects.[10] Angleton, the counter-spy, was curious to know how LSD might help him uncover enemy agents within the CIA and penetrate foreign intelligence services. And Bateson was there to explain how LSD and narcotics could be used to reconstruct American society. In a memo he sent to William Donovan nine days after the US dropped an atomic bomb on Hiroshima, Bateson predicted an era in which propaganda, subversion, and "social and ethnic manipulation" would be more critical to national security than guided missiles.[11]

The expertise these men brought to the June meeting at the Bedford apartment highlights the two new tactics the CIA was about to employ in its quest to conquer the world: 1) using LSD as a weapon of psychological warfare; and 2) turning drug smuggling routes into fifth columns that undermined the ability of foreign nations, and undesirable minorities in America, to organize themselves economically, politically, or militarily.

OPERATION X AND THE CIA'S DRUG-SMUGGLING ENTERPRISES

The only hitch in the plan concocted by Angleton, Hamilton, Bateson, and White was the occasional, unpredictable security breach, such as occurred in March 1953, when Burma charged Kuomintang General Li Mi with opium smuggling. Knowing the charge was true, the CIA requested "a rapid evacuation in order to prevent the leakage of information about the KMT's opium business," and in November the State Department announced that Li Mi's troops were being airlifted by the CIA's proprietary airline, Civil Air Transport, to Taiwan.[12] In reality, most of the troops were left behind in Burma or dropped in northern Thailand with the consent of General Phao, Thailand's top policeman and drug lord. Even Ambassador William J. Sebald wasn't fooled by this chicanery, and asked if the CIA had deliberately left the KMT troops behind in Burma to continue "the opium smuggling racket."[13] Which they had.

Anslinger's job was to deflect attention away from the CIA, and in June 1953 – while in New York to sign a UN Protocol limiting opium production to Bulgaria, Greece, India, Turkey, Iran, the USSR, and Yugoslavia – he bludgeoned the People's Republic of China with allegations of drug smuggling. He claimed that the PRC's Opium Prevention Bureau was running opium caravans from Yunnan Province into Burma and that its agents delivered narcotics to unnamed Mafiosi in Hong Kong. In remarks delivered to the UN's Commission on Narcotic Drugs in April 1953, Anslinger cited reports, including those issued by the Supreme Command for the Allied Powers (SCAP) in Japan, showing that all heroin seized in Japan "came from Communist China."[14]

Not even the US Treasury Attaché in Hong Kong, however, could offer evidence to support these wild allegations about the PRC and, as historian William O. Walker III notes, Anslinger's claims about SCAP were disingenuous too. What SCAP had really said was that the heroin "was of Asian origin, but from an indeterminate source."[15]

Anslinger knew full well that indeterminate source was the fabled Golden Triangle, the opium-rich area encompassing portions of Laos, Burma, and Thailand. He also knew, as Agent Bill Tollenger had reported to him in 1948, that opium was "the greatest single source of revenue" for the French in Indochina. In *The Politics of Heroin*, Professor Alfred W. McCoy describes how the French obtained that revenue through what they called Operation X. Starting in 1950, the French foreign intelligence agency, Service de Documentations Extérieure et de Contre-Espionage (SDECE), flew opium from Laos to a French Special Forces camp at Cap St. Jacques in South Vietnam. From Cap St. Jacques the opium was sold to a consortium of Vietnamese gangsters, Kuomintang brokers, and Corsicans in Saigon. The Corsicans moved their share to Marseilles, the KMT distributed theirs in Hong Kong, and the Vietnamese sold their opium locally. That was Operation X.[16]

According to McCoy, as America displaced France in Vietnam in 1953 and 1954, the CIA inherited many of SDECE's drug-smuggling contacts in Laos and Vietnam. Anslinger knew about this development, and that the Southeast Asian French connection ran through Batista, Lansky, and Santo Trafficante in Cuba, directly to America's ghettos. But he chose to use his position as the world's leading authority on narcotics to fool the American public. He also misused his formidable powers to protect his beloved Bureau from a series of MKULTRA and corruption-related mishaps.

CLOSE CALLS, COMPLICATIONS, AND COVER-UPS

The first potential disaster occurred in New York on 12 September 1953, when aspiring actress Linda King was admitted to Lenox Hill Hospital, ranting and raving, and accusing George White and FBN Agent Paul Gross of having drugged her. As White noted in his diary, he had indeed given Linda King a surreptitious dose of LSD, and Gross was there when he did it. But CIA security officers had anticipated that someday some MKULTRA guinea pig would figure out what was going on and lodge a complaint, so White maintained "close working relations with local police authorities which could be utilized to protect the activity in critical situations."[17] The arrangement existed with area hospitals too, and the doctors at Lenox Hill simply ignored King's charges. After she came down from her trip, King, like Clarice Stein, decided to drop the matter in order to remain part of White's exciting social circle. Had King pursued it, however, the incident could have exposed the FBN's role in the MKULTRA Program; but instead it proved that the security system worked and that White was invincible.

The next close call was the death by heroin overdose of FBN Agent Crofton Hayes in late September. A Fordham graduate and charter member of the Jim Ryan Celtic clique, Hayes was serving as the agent in charge of the FBN's office in Newark, New Jersey. As Agent John L. "Jack" Kelly Jr. recalled in his autobiography, *On The Street*, the day before Hayes died, a group leader offered Kelly seized heroin as bait for his informers. Kelly declined the offer; but the next morning, after being told that Hayes had died of an overdose, he "knew immediately" that the overdose was from "the heroin that the group leader had offered" him.[18]

If Kelly knew, then Anslinger knew. But launching an investigation into Hayes's death was something the Commissioner dared not do, for it would have revealed that there were other addicts in the New York office and that agents tempted informers with seized heroin. There was another more sinister reason for looking away, too. There was a rumor that Hayes was about to confess his sins and implicate other agents in illicit activities, and that, as a result, he was murdered – given a hot shot – by a colleague. There was a MKULTRA angle as well. Several agents knew about White's LSD experiments, and in 1979 Agent Pat Ward told CIA investigators that an office clerk had gone "berserk" around the time of Hayes's death and that he suspected that White had dosed the clerk, and perhaps Hayes, with LSD.[19] For all these reasons, Crofton Hayes's death was officially attributed to liver failure, again with the apparent complicity of hospital authorities.

Another potential problem arose a few days later, when the chief of the US Attorney's Racket Squad in Washington, DC, Thomas A. Wadden, made two startling charges in a feature article in the 3 October 1953 issue of the *Saturday Evening Post*. According to Wadden, an FBN agent was moving seized narcotics from the drug disposal room at the Treasury Annex to "Big Jim" Roberts, "the Negro crime king in Washington." Even more sensational was Wadden's accusation that his investigation had been subverted by Anslinger. The Commissioner eventually admitted that there had been pilferage, but he blamed the theft of the narcotics on a Black janitor, and Wadden, who resigned shortly after his investigation, was never able to identify the FBN agent he believed was involved. And he never discovered that Anslinger and George Cunningham were passing drugs from the drug disposal room to the CIA for its MKULTRA Program experiments.

The next complication occurred a few weeks later, in late November 1953, when Garland Williams unexpectedly announced his retirement from the Treasury Department. The chain of events that led to this surprising development began in September 1952, when Williams finished his tour as commander of the 525th Military Intelligence Group. He wanted to return to his former position as district supervisor in New York, but, as Howard Chappell recalls, "There was no room at the inn. Jim Ryan was firmly entrenched, so Garland was made assistant Commissioner of the IRS Intelligence Division, where he was not well received."

Unfortunately for Williams, he had intruded on IRS turf at the wrong time. The IRS had recently created an Inspections Unit and, just after Williams arrived on the scene, this Inspections Unit investigated the upper echelons of the IRS and uncovered wrongdoings by several bureaucrats and political appointees, including Williams, who had failed to pay taxes on some bonds he owned. Williams was allowed to cite ill health as the official reason for his resignation, but his reputation was tarnished. Some FBN agents believe that he must have committed a far greater crime, or perhaps taken a fall for Anslinger, or the CIA. In any event, Williams sought solace in what was most familiar to him: secrecy. After his formal retirement in March 1954, he embarked on a two-year odyssey that took him from Washington, DC, through undisclosed activities in San Francisco (where George White set up another MKULTRA safehouse in 1955), and back to Washington, where he organized a special unit in the Army Chemical Corps.[20]

Then came the suicide of Frank Olson on 28 November 1953. A CIA scientist specializing in the airborne delivery of diseases like anthrax, Olson was attached to the MKULTRA Program under cover of the Department of Defense. His bizarre tale began on the night of 19 November 1953, when, at a secluded country lodge outside Washington that served as a retreat for MKULTRA researchers, one of Dr. Gottlieb's equally deranged colleagues dropped LSD in Olson's Cointreau. Unaware that he'd been drugged, Olson embarked on a bad trip that triggered a nervous breakdown and, a week later, a compulsory visit to Dr. Harold Abramson in New York. An allergist with a MKULTRA contract, Abramson treated Olson with a combination of goof balls and bourbon. The effect was hardly therapeutic, and after spending Thanksgiving Day with Abramson on Long Island, Olson returned to his room at the Statler Hotel in Manhattan and, in the presence of CIA psychiatrist Robert Lashbrook, allegedly dashed across the room, dove through the window, and plummeted to his death.[21]

New York detectives first called it a "homocide" because Lashbrook was in the room, then backed away and allowed CIA Inspector General Lyman B. Kirkpatrick Jr. to close the case without further ado. Olson's death is still officially recorded as a suicide. However, Eric Olson had his father's body exhumed in 1994 and, based on a belated autopsy, he contends that Frank Olson was hit on the head with a blunt object and then pushed out the window, to prevent him from revealing MKULTRA secrets, like the CIA's use of biochemical weapons in North Korea.

Even if Eric's theory is correct, George White (according to his diary) was in California when Frank Olson died and could not be considered a suspect in his murder. That was fortunate for the FBN because White's soft-porn helper, Gil Fox, was aware of the implications of Olson's death at the time it occurred – which suggests that Olson may have visited the Bedford Street safehouse while he was in New York. But the connection between the FBN and the MKULTRA Program was never made, and like the Linda King incident, the Olson mishap was contained.

But integrity issues continued to plague the FBN, and a few months later the NYPD revealed to Anslinger that, through a wiretap, it had overheard an FBN agent discussing cases with a drug trafficker nicknamed Tony Iodine (real name Daidone). The police couldn't prove that the agent had taken a bribe from Iodine; but the agent had been involved in a case against major drug trafficker Sol Gelb (who allegedly had a source in the PRC), and the case against Gelb evaporated as a result – as did $10,000 Jim Ryan had given the agent to buy half a kilogram of heroin from Gelb. In 1954, $10,000 was the New York office's budget for an entire month.[22]

Minimizing the impact and implications of the above incident, Anslinger in 1961 referred to it as "the type of shock that comes occasionally in our kind of job." Then, as if to put this shock in perspective, he told of an agent who had been "a spy for the underworld" and had killed several drug traffickers for his Mafia employers. Anslinger claims this agent-cum-assassin committed suicide outside his office, after Anslinger confronted him with his crimes.[23]

An FBN assassin for hire; an agent caught selling out cases; agents addicted to heroin, and one dead from an overdose; allegations of agents handing out seized narcotics from the drug disposal vault at headquarters: all of this was business as usual for Anslinger, and he simply applied to the FBN's integrity problems the same policy of "defensive avoidance" that he adopted when dealing with drug smuggling allies like Batista and the Nationalist Chinese. Anslinger looked the other way, for acknowledging the extent of corruption within the FBN would have brought the organization to its knees, and perhaps would have revealed that George White was dosing unwitting people with LSD on behalf of the CIA. Anslinger looked the other way, and as a result the problems just got worse.

Such was the web of deceit Anslinger had woven around the FBN when, in January 1954, Governor Dewey asked the chief of the New York State Commission of Investigations, William B. Herlands, to investigate the oft-repeated rumor that Dewey had commuted Lucky Luciano's prison sentence in exchange for a bribe. Because it was out of his hands, and because several FBN agents had played a role in spreading the rumor, this investigation was one of the greatest threats Anslinger had ever faced.

Lucky Luciano and other Mafiosi did help the government's intelligence services during the Second World War; this fact was uncovered during the Herlands investigation. And yet, while the details were not released to the public for twenty years, Anslinger, Garland Williams, George White, and Charlie Siragusa knew the truth at the time. Their problem began in 1947, when Walter Winchell suggested that Luciano might be awarded the Congressional Medal of Honor for his wartime services. Aware that they could not sustain their crowd-pleasing, anti-Luciano propaganda campaign if the *bête noire* was portrayed as a hero, they scrambled to preserve the government's dirty little secret. Garland Williams obtained denials from William Donovan and Charles Haffenden, and repeated their denials in a 22 February 1947 article in the *New York Times*.[24]

As a way of further concealing the truth, Anslinger fueled rumors that Dewey had taken a bribe in exchange for commuting Luciano's sentence. His loudest mouthpiece in this regard was Michael Stern. In several articles he wrote for *True: The Man's Magazine*, Stern asserted that Luciano's commutation "had cost him $75,000 in favor of the Republican electoral campaign," and that "experts in this field estimated that he had to spend $200,000."[25] Stern even suggested that Dewey, having freed Luciano, was personally to blame for America's drug problem. Based on Stern's allegations, Senator Kefauver raised the issue in 1951, and a Democratic State Senator charged that Luciano had bribed Dewey with $300,000.[26]

Dewey endured the smears until 1954, when he directed Herlands to bury the rumors once and for all. The records of the Commission remained secret for twenty years, but it is now known that Luciano and the Mafia served the government, and that George White and Charlie Siragusa gave perjured testimony about it during the Kefauver Hearings. When called before the Herlands Commission, Siragusa "grudgingly admitted editing parts" of Stern's article. He denied, however, editing the parts that had to do with the bribe. This was a lie, too. Siragusa, in a 1952 letter to Anslinger, indicated that Stern had based his false allegations on a memo written by Mafia Squad leader Joe Amato. Sent by Amato to Jim Ryan on 16 August 1951, the memo said that $500,000 had been paid to the "right" people for Luciano's parole, in exchange for Mafia help in the 1948 presidential election. The memo referred to Stern's article in *True Magazine*.[27]

Siragusa's testimony, along with that of Navy intelligence officers, led Herlands and other powerful Establishment insiders to speculate that the CIA and military intelligence, through the FBN, were still employing drug lords like Luciano. Were the hoods, or even FBN agents, serving as CIA assassins? A Pandora's Box was about to be opened, and that's when Anslinger asked his masters to intervene: on 7 July 1954, the CIA sent Herlands a telex indicating that his investigation jeopardized national security. He was forced to back off, and George White continued his extra-legal MKULTRA activities apace.[28]

As a postscript to this shameful episode in FBN history, it should be noted during the Herlands Commission investigation, Senator Joe McCarthy crowned his disreputable career by claiming there were subversives within the US Army and the CIA. McCarthy directed his assault at CIA officer Cord Meyer. As chief of the CIA's International Operations Division, Meyer was responsible for infiltrating domestic and foreign labor unions and preventing them from being controlled by communists. His search for the so-called "compatible Left" was steeped in underworld intrigues, and dovetailed with operations conducted by CIA counter-intelligence chief James Angleton and his assets in the FBN, Charlie Siragusa and George White. In other words, McCarthy, through his investigation of Meyer, was getting close to the CIA's international drug-smuggling conspiracy.

The Senate launched an investigation of McCarthy shortly after he began to attack the espionage Establishment, and for reasons that were never made public, he was censored and stripped of power by his colleagues in December 1954. The reason may have been connected to narcotics. In 1962, Anslinger confessed in his book *The Murderers* that he had nursed an important Congressman through a drug addiction. Perhaps that Congressman was McCarthy? If so, did Anslinger's CIA masters encourage him to engage in this illicit activity? What better way to compromise a political hack? Anslinger kept McCarthy high, while the CIA fed him an enemies list; and when he became a liability, they pulled the plug. If true, it was the perfect MKULTRA operation.

THE BEASTLY NATURE OF THE BUSINESS

MKULTRA operations were coordinated with political operations that impacted the CIA's protected drug routes. As noted, one such operation was reportedly conducted by George White on behalf of Rudolph Halley. In 1953, as the Fusion Party's candidate for Mayor, Halley was working with two of the CIA's primary International Operations Division assets; Fusion Party Co-Chairman David Dubinsky of the International Ladies Garment Workers Union, and the AFL's Irving Brown.[29] Seafarers' Union president Paul Hall was certainly involved too, in working to discredit left-leaning waterfront and maritime unions, and union officials, by tying them to drug traffickers. George White dropping LSD in the drinking water of one of Halley's opponents was another surefire way of discrediting someone.

FBN agents also helped to provide security for the CIA's drug smuggling operation by keeping certain longshoremen under surveillance, because they were "working with ... smugglers."[30] Those longshoremen were invariably with the left-leaning National Maritime Union, or the Mafia-tainted International Longshoreman's Association. Topping the list of drug-dealing longshoremen was Rosario "Saro" Mogavero, former vice president of ILA Local 856, a post he left in 1953 after being charged with extortion. Mogavero's son was married to Rocco Pellegrino's daughter, and Pellegrino controlled all the rackets in Westchester County, New York. Pellegrino supplied heroin to Joe Civello in Dallas through Mogavero, his contact man with John Ormento, manager of the Mafia's drug distribution syndicate.[31]

The ILA, notably, was in competition with the CIA-connected International Brotherhood of Longshoremen. The situation was fraught with political intrigues, and White addressed the problem with his old friend Price Spivey – who had quit the FBN and gone to work for the Seafarers' Union as a security specialist after gangsters planted heroin in the car of the Seafarers' president, Paul Hall.[32]

On 2 October 1954, White met with another old friend from the FBN, John Hanly, then with the Secret Service, to discuss what he called in his diary the "CIA Avenue." This was a reference to the CIA's protected drug route from the Far East, through Cuba, to the Mafia in New York. Two days after White and Hanly met, Saro Mogavero went to trial for harboring drug lord John Ormento, a fugitive in the Happy Meltzer case, which Price Spivey had managed in 1952. A made member of the Genovese family, Mogavero pled guilty and received a short prison sentence. This enabled Ormento to walk away – or, more precisely, to be driven home to Manhattan by George White. According to White they went out for drinks, Ormento promised to be a good boy from then on, and White, defying logic, believed him.

There are several disturbing aspects to this sequence of events. In September 1954, an informant for Agent Ben Fitzgerald arranged to buy kilogram amounts of heroin from Chicago mobster Jacob Klein, and Klein agreed to introduce the informant to Mogavero. But someone tipped Klein off and, at the very last minute, he refused to meet with undercover Agent Angelo Zurlo. The case, as a result, fell apart in October, and Klein continued to deal narcotics in Chicago with apparent immunity. To wit, in January 1958, Agent Jack Love spotted Klein with Saro Mogavero at the Sheridan Bar in Chicago; but Love was transferred to Los Angeles and the Klein case was passed to another agent. In 1960 the Klein investigation collapsed, once and for all, when the new agent's informant was murdered.[33]

What is especially disturbing is that the failure to make the New York case on Klein enabled Mogavero to take the fall for Ormento, and for Ormento to open the heroin gateway from Cuba, evidently with George White's tacit approval – unless White actually believed Ormento's pledge to give up drug smuggling, which he did not do. Instead, Ormento formed an alliance with Joe Bonanno's drug manager, Carmine Galante, and they began moving massive amounts of narcotics from Cuba and Montreal to New York, Chicago, and Dallas. It's an unbelievable coincidence that White met with Ormento at the exact moment the New York agents had a chance to kill the biggest Mafia drug-smuggling operation (the CIA Avenue) in its cradle. It's as if White on behalf of the CIA, and Ormento on behalf of the Mafia, were conspiring together.

There is one more unsettling aspect to this story. In early 1955, through a police wiretap, agents Greg Poulos and Louis Pagani learned where and when a drug delivery was to be made. They waited patiently, and when John Ormento and his bagman Sal LoProto pulled up to make the drop, the agents descended and searched the car. In a trap under the front right seat they found not drugs, but $5,000 in cash and a silenced .22 automatic, the type of gun typically used in CIA assassinations.[34]

Having arrested John Ormento, and having stopped a murder in progress, Poulos and Pagani vaulted into the big leagues. Then things got weird. Within weeks, both agents were transferred (like the aforementioned Jack Love in Chicago) and the Ormento case was given to more deserving agents in New York. LoProto, like Mogavero before him, took a fall for John Ormento, and Agent Gregory Poulos, who had come to hate "the beastly nature" of the business, quit the FBN in disgust.

What was most bestial about this line of work was articulated in a bizarre letter White wrote to his MKULTRA partner Sid Gottlieb. In it White said: "I was a very minor missionary, actually a heretic, but I toiled wholeheartedly in the vineyards because it was fun, fun, fun. Where else could a red-blooded American boy lie, kill, cheat, steal, rape and pillage with the sanction and blessing of the All-Highest?"[35]

Where else indeed?

Granted, George White was an aberration; and it's important to remember that only a few FBN agents worked with him in illegal CIA operations. But White was the CIA's secret policeman and was always protected, and in the wake of the Herlands "quiz" (as Dr. Gottlieb sarcastically referred to it), arrangements were made to close the Bedford Street pad. On 6 December 1954, Gottlieb visited White and Pierre Lafitte one last time in New York. He arrived with a fountain pen air-gun and an instruction manual on the use of drugs and prostitutes in sexual seduction blackmail schemes, as part of the new MKULTRA Leather Project to be conducted by White in San Francisco, where he had been safely ensconced as the FBN's new district supervisor.

10

TRUE DETECTIVES

"A dog with a full belly won't hunt."
Deputy Commissioner George Cunningham

George Gaffney arrested fugitive Frank Tornello in January 1952, and a few weeks later tracked Tornello's co-defendant in the Orsini case, Ray DeMartino, to the Hotel New Yorker. It wasn't possible to snap a photograph of DeMartino without alerting him to the fact that he was being watched, so Gaffney drew a sketch of the fugitive drug trafficker from memory and then distributed it to other FBN agents on the scene. Thanks to Gaffney's quick thinking and artistic aptitude, DeMartino was easily arrested later that day in the hotel lobby.

Having played a major role in the capture of Tornello and DeMartino, and having proven his abilities in a number of other ways, Gaffney by 1953 was ready for his next special assignment, as the FBN's original representative to the newly formed Court House Squad. Partially in response to the Kefauver Hearings, Congress had enacted statutes in which anyone committing any act, no matter how small, in the *furtherance* of a crime was guilty of conspiracy. This new law was a potent weapon that required closer coordination between federal law enforcement agencies and prosecutors, so the Justice Department formed a special unit in New York to implement the new statutes. Located in the Federal Court House under Assistant US Attorney Robert Patterson Jr., the Court House Squad consisted of representatives from the customs service, the IRS Intelligence Unit, the IRS Alcohol Tobacco Tax Division, the FBN, and the Secret Service. But as Gaffney caustically observes, "The FBI didn't join, because it didn't want to share information."

Tornello, meanwhile, had become an FBN informant, and under the guidance of Group Three Leader Pat Ward, had introduced undercover Agent Angelo Zurlo to a prominent French narcotics smuggler, Jean "the Silver Fox" David, co-owner of a fashionable restaurant in Midtown Manhattan. Zurlo made kilogram purchases of heroin from David, and the suave Frenchman was arrested in April 1953.

Although David refused to cooperate, the case advanced when Zurlo found a letter from Mexico in David's Midtown apartment inquiring about the price of linen in New York. At Pat Ward's direction, a French-speaking agent, pretending to be David, wrote a reply in December. It was a simple response, saying that the price was good. And though the letter was considered a long shot, the ploy worked, and a most unexpected response was soon forthcoming.

At the time, veteran Agent Angelo Zurlo was sharing an apartment in Brooklyn with a promising new agent named Andrew Tartaglino. According to Andy, he came home from work one day to find his elderly Italian landlady waiting for him excitedly at the front door. "There's a man upstairs in your room," she whispered, "and he wants to talk to Angelo."

Tartaglino realized that the man upstairs was there in response to the contrived letter, but he was concerned because there were several items in the apartment, including his FBN credentials, that revealed the true nature of his and Zurlo's employment. But the French smuggler, Roger Coudert, didn't notice any of the incriminating signs. Overcome by greed and impatience, he fully accepted Tartaglino's assertion that he was Zurlo's protégé in the drug smuggling business.

Zurlo arrived at the apartment a few hours later and, after haggling with the Frenchman over price and quantity, he agreed to buy five kilograms of heroin, contingent on Coudert delivering a sample so he could ascertain its quality. Exuding confidence, Coudert assured Zurlo that it was 99 percent pure. Heroin of that high a quality was rare, but Zurlo calmly replied that if it was 99 percent pure, he was willing to pay $7,000 per kilogram. Hearing that, Coudert instantly lost his composure and dashed out of the apartment in an effort to retrieve a consignment he'd just sold to Anthony Farina, his usual Mafia connection, for a mere $4,500 per kilogram. But Farina, to Coudert's dismay, refused to return it.

Several days later, Coudert delivered a sample to Zurlo – one ounce of pure heroin from a lab in Marseilles. "But because Farina had refused to part with his heroin," Gaffney explains, "Coudert told Zurlo that he'd have to get the five kilograms he promised from Mexico. We monitored the call that Coudert made to his connection in Mexico, then notified Customs Agent Ben White in Mexico City. White traced the number to the home of the commanding general of the federal district. We also learned from White that Zurlo's letter had been delivered to a cafe a block from the American Embassy, and that the cafe was owned by the mistress of the Mexican president.

"Coudert told Zurlo not to worry," Gaffney continues, "that he would go to Mexico and get the heroin himself, right away. Then he asked Andy if he knew anyone who could repair suitcases. Andy didn't know anyone who could do that, but he said he did, of course, at which point Coudert gave him the key to a footlocker at Penn Station. We went there and retrieved the suitcases and when we examined them we found traces of heroin inside a hidden compartment. So now we had Coudert on possession, as well as the transfer of the sample to Zurlo. I arrested Coudert," Gaffney says with pride, "and Pat Ward arrested Farina.

"Farina had been a soldier with the Italian Army in Ethiopia," Gaffney continues. "He was a tough guy and he didn't say a word. But Coudert gave chapter and verse on the Corsican connection, and how it was run in Mexico by Antoine D'Agostino, Paul Mondoloni, and Jean Croce. He said that Mondoloni had been a policeman in Saigon, and that he'd been arrested for the Aga Khan robbery on the French Riviera. None of us knew any of this before, and it was all very exciting."[1]

THE GEORGE WHITE SCANDALS

While the New York office was unraveling the reorganized French connection, Anslinger in January 1954 assigned George White as the FBN's one and only supervisor at large (a position Anslinger created just for him), and in May 1954, after testifying before the Herlands Commission, White traveled to Texas to challenge the customs service over its use of convoys, and to investigate allegations that Customs Agent Alvin Scharff was sending informants into Mexico to buy narcotics, with the aim of setting up local suspects for arrest in Texas.

A convoy was an investigative technique devised by Customs agents in the early 1950s, and it began when a Customs inspector seized narcotics at a port of entry, often through a routine search. Other times, through informants, the inspector knew when and where a drug shipment was coming across the border. In either case, after he made the seizure, the inspector would call in Customs agents, who could move around the country following cases. The agents would turn the person delivering the drugs (the mule) into an informant in exchange for a reduced sentence. Next they would replace most of the narcotics with flour, then one of the Customs agents would climb into the trunk of the car and, with the informant driving, would ride with the substitute shipment to its destination – a warehouse in Chicago perhaps – where an arrest would be made. Customs agents felt that convoys, by eliminating the intermediary steps and taking them directly to the receiver, were quicker and more effective than the FBN's protracted two buys and a bust technique.

The FBN's district supervisor in Houston, Piney Williams, didn't care that Customs agents were mounting convoys. The objection came from Anslinger. By 1954, Customs agents in the southwest were making so many narcotics seizures and arrests, that they were upstaging the FBN. Through their informant network in Mexico, they were also interfering in FBN undercover operations. So Anslinger went to court and challenged the legality of convoys and the right of Customs agents to hire informants in Mexico. He was especially angry at his old nemesis Al Scharff. The reader will recall that Scharff, as a Justice Department special employee, had assassinated two German spies in Mexico during the First World War and, after joining the customs service, had briefly managed Treasury Department narcotics operations in Europe before the Second World War, causing Anslinger and Charlie Dyar an immense amount of grief. But Scharff's unforgivable sin was preaching that all drugs smuggled into America should come under Customs jurisdiction.

The conflict between Anslinger and Scharff climaxed in the spring of 1954, when several detectives on the Houston narcotic squad were accused of mishandling seized narcotics. Initially it seemed like any other big city corruption case, and in March the Treasury Department's law enforcement coordinator, James Maloney, sent Agent Fred Douglas to Houston to investigate the charges. A few weeks later, Douglas discovered that Scharff was involved in the case through one of his informants – and that's when Anslinger sent George White to Texas. His mission: to rid Anslinger of aggravating Al Scharff, once and for all.

Described by Scharff as "domineering and ruthless," White began by questioning the main suspects about Scharff's alleged role in the movement of seized drugs to a local trafficker.[2] One of the people White interrogated was an unfortunate Houston detective named Billnitzer - and that's when the trouble began. An hour after his final session with White, Billnitzer was found dead in the Houston police department's narcotic squad room.

Exactly what happened is unclear: FBN Agent Jack Kelly said that Billnitzer "had either blown out his brains or someone had done it for him."[3] By another account, Billnitzer shot himself twice in the heart. Twenty-five years after the incident, when questioned by a CIA officer investigating the MKULTRA Program, George Gaffney suggested that Billnitzer's suicide might have been provoked by a dose of LSD administered by George White.[4]

In any event, Scharff blamed White for having pushed Billnitzer over the edge. Bent on revenge, he holstered his pistol and headed to the William Penn Hotel for a reckoning. When he arrived, Fred Douglas and Henry Giordano were seated at a table in the coffee shop. They invited Scharff to join them.

"Billnitzer just shot himself," Scharff said, as rotund George White, dressed entirely in black, stepped up to the table. Looking at Scharff in a manner laden with "premeditated scorn and action," White asked Scharff, "What in hell are you so nervous about?"[5]

The "urge of violence" fell upon Scharff. "Look here," he said to White, "If you don't like what I just said, you've got a six-shooter on your hip. Reach for it."

According to Scharff's biographer, only "the timely interference of Douglas and Giordano brought the heated situation under control."

Angrier than ever at Scharff, White resumed his investigation with renewed vigor, with the result that the head of the Houston vice squad was indicted, and that ten charges were brought against Scharff. But the trial of the vice squad captain resulted in a hung jury, and though his reputation was sullied, Scharff escaped punishment. The FBN paid a higher price than anyone. Reeling from the negative national publicity White had visited upon them, Houston's town fathers forced Anslinger to remove the FBN's district office from Houston. Eventually it was relocated to Dallas. Supervisor Piney Williams (a veteran of the old Narcotics Division) was reassigned as the deputy district supervisor in Atlanta, and Howard Chappell was named acting agent in charge in Houston.

Having satisfied Anslinger by publicizing Scharff's dubious tactics, White was rewarded with an appointment as district supervisor in San Francisco, displacing veteran FBN Agent Ernest M. Gentry. Gentry in turn was reassigned as district supervisor in Dallas, where he became embroiled in the FBN's holy war against Scharff and the customs service, and nurtured his abiding resentment for George White.

White settled in the San Francisco Bay area in March 1955, where his MKULTRA experiments would continue for the next ten years. In June, he conscripted Agent Ira "Ike" Feldman into the program. Fluent in several

Chinese dialects, Feldman had served as an Army intelligence officer in the Korean War, and may have known Garland Williams, who might have brought him into the FBN. One of the most colorful agents in FBN history, Feldman stood five feet two inches tall, wore a full-length Chesterfield overcoat with velvet collars, a black fedora, and smoked humungous Winston Churchill cigars. Gruff and tough, he posed as a pimp when working undercover cases, and allowed the prostitutes in his employ to indulge their heroin habits; in return the ladies of the night lured their unwitting victims to White's MKULTRA pad at 225 Chestnut Street for an evening of sex, drugs, and observation. To ensure that the illegal CIA program would not be exposed, White used a coded chit system to alert the San Francisco police whenever one of Feldman's girls was arrested on narcotics or prostitution charges.[6]

For the next five years, White and Feldman, with the assistance of the CIA officers Sid Gottlieb and Dr. Raymond Treichler, would open two more MKULTRA safehouses in the San Francisco Bay area, birthplace in the early 1960s of America's psychedelic subculture.

THE EMERGENCE OF MARTY PERA

While the turf war between Customs and the FBN broiled in the southwest, and White moved his little shop of MKULTRA horrors to San Francisco, Jack Cusack returned from Europe and replaced George Gaffney at the Court House Squad in New York. Gaffney replaced Pat Ward as the leader of Group Three, and Ward became Jim Ryan's enforcement assistant. Because it was so large and so critical to FBN operations, New York was the first office to have an enforcement assistant position. Then in 1956, true detective George Gaffney was named district supervisor in Atlanta and, in his absence, Martin F. Pera emerged as the New York office's new shining star.

How Pera achieved prominence within the FBN is interesting and important. Following a four-month assignment in Europe in 1951, he had joined George White and Pierre Lafitte in an investigation of corrupt policemen and drug smugglers in the southwest. "We were successful," Pera recalls, "but the bender ended in controversy, because we were going into districts without the knowledge of the supervisors. Gentry in San Francisco was especially livid. After that, I went back to Chicago where the synthetic narcotic amadone was appearing on streets and causing a lot of overdoses. No one had a handle on it, so I took a look, and because of my background in chemistry I found out how the dealers were making it. Two manufacturers in the New York area were the source of the precursors, so I was sent there in 1953 to follow up. I was assigned to Joe Amato's International Group [formerly the Mafia Squad], along with Andy Tartaglino, Don Miller, and Arthur Giuliani, who soon left to join the Air Force's Office of Special Investigations in Italy."

When Amato was made leader of Group Four in 1956, Pera took over the International Group. As he explains, the job was to respond to queries from Charlie Siragusa in Rome; gather information and originate leads in the US regarding the traffic overseas; recover fugitives; and conduct special projects. Under its uniquely qualified leader, the International Group would expand from four to twelve members, and become one of the most powerful weapons in the FBN's arsenal.

Central to the International Group's success was Pera's friendship with George White. A high tech enthusiast himself, White knew that Pera was developing useful gadgets in an electronics shop he'd set up in his office. To help Pera in his research work, White introduced him to Al Stern at the engineering firm Devenco, a CIA-connected company that developed and supplied the intelligence community with spy gadgetry. With Devenco's help, Pera built several devices that enhanced the FBN's case-making ability, including a tiny transmitter for tapping telephones, a microphone that could be slipped into a room without opening the door, and a radio wave direction finder that could be hidden in a car. For his technical innovations, Pera earned the (rarely employed) nickname Captain Video and the unwarranted suspicions of some of his colleagues, who were undergoing a spate of integrity investigations initiated in Washington by controversial Lee Speer.

CHICAGO AND THE RESURRECTION OF HOWARD CHAPPELL

In Houston, in the wake of what the local newspapers dubbed "The George White Scandals," straightforward Howard Chappell restored relations with the prosecutors and police. But Chappell was unhappy serving under Ernie Gentry in Dallas. A raw-boned Alabaman, Gentry was rabid at having been pushed out of San Francisco by Chappell's friend George White. Gentry directed his anger at Chappell, and after Chappell refused to curb an investigation into John Ormento's narcotics connections in Texas, Gentry reprimanded him for insubordination. Bill Tollenger — having spent two years as an inspector checking on agent misdeeds, and two years as agent in charge in St. Louis – was assigned to replace Chappell in Houston. Reluctantly, Deputy Commissioner George Cunningham sent Chappell into internal exile at the one-man office in Toledo, Ohio.

There were few cases to be made in Toledo, and immediately upon arriving there, Chappell was ordered by Anslinger to conduct an integrity investigation in the Chicago area with Tony Zirilli. Then about thirty years old, Zirilli was courageous and smart, a natural undercover agent with all the mannerisms and the dialects of an old-country Italian. He knew how the top hoods thought and behaved, and he knew that in order to gain their confidence, he could not act, in FBN jargon, like "a boot-and-shoe bum." So Zirilli affected the persona of a high-stakes gambler.

"Tony was so goddamned authentic," Chappell sighs. "But he was impetuous. We were working in the Chicago area without the knowledge of Al Aman, the district supervisor. Aman was suspected of having relations with local gangsters, but he was tight with one of Anslinger's most ardent supporters, Senator Paul Douglas, so we had to be careful. Tony and I were posing as gamblers – I was his money-man and bodyguard – and that way we gathered intelligence and made a lot of buys. Chicago Agent George Belk was picking up the evidence and taking it to Detroit for analysis. Belk was the only person, other than three or four in Washington, and Ross Ellis in Detroit, who knew we were there. It had to be kept quiet because we were getting information on a Chicago police lieutenant who was a source of information for the syndicate. There was politics involved, too.

"Tony *was* a gambler," Chappell stresses. "It wasn't just a role he played. When he was in New York, he was one of the agents who stayed late on payday to shoot craps with Angie Zurlo. Some agents would lose two weeks' pay on Friday night, then go home empty-handed to their wives. So it got to be a problem. Tony was like that, and while we were working this case around Chicago, he lost $10,000 in cash he'd been fronted by headquarters. Then he got into a game going head to head with a local hood called Johnny C. Tony wound up winning back the ten grand, but Johnny didn't have the cash. First he offered us the title to his Cadillac, and when we refused that, he came back with a tray of diamonds. 'That's the best I can do,' he said.

"I called Washington," Chappell continues, "and I asked Anslinger to stall B. T. Mitchell, who wanted to round everyone up the next day. Anslinger didn't want to know any of the details, but he did give me twenty-four hours to unload the stones. So I had an idea. Tony and I got in my car and drove to see Johnny C's boss in Calumet City. He agreed to see us, and I told him the score. I said 'Johnny C's your man, so our problem's your problem.' He agreed, and asked what I wanted him to do. I gave him the stones and told him to wire a $10,000 money order to Anthony Zirilli at 90 Church Street in New York. Which he did."

The quiet Chicago integrity investigation uncovered the ties between the local policemen and Mafiosi, and resulted in Al Aman's retirement and replacement by George Belk. Chappell's quick thinking also enabled Tony Zirilli to return $10,000 in front money to FBN headquarters, saving his career. As a reward, Chappell was restored to the good graces of his bosses and in April 1956 he replaced George Davis (an ally of Ernie Gentry) as the agent in charge of the increasingly important Los Angeles office. His boss was his friend George White in San Francisco. Chappell quickly improved relations with the sheriff's office and built the office up from twelve to thirty-three agents. He equipped his agents with the best weapons and the latest technology, formed a friendly and reciprocal working relationship with Customs Agent Ben White in Mexico City, and focused his personal attention on making cases in northwest Mexico.

ANGLETON, LABOR, AND THE INTERNATIONAL NARCOTICS CONSPIRACY

From his post in San Francisco, China expert George White concentrated on slowing the surge of East Asian heroin that was flooding the West Coast. The political context of the problem had changed after the Vietnamese defeated the French at Dien Bien Phu in May 1954, and the US had assumed responsibility for the defense of Southeast Asia from communism. By default the US had also assumed responsibility for drug control in South Vietnam, where President Ngo Dinh Diem's brother, Nhu, was deeply involved in the regional opium trade through his secret service. For that reason, drug control in Southeast Asia became a task for diplomats, spies, and generals.

It was a fact that only a handful of the American soldiers in the Far East were becoming addicted, and on that basis the officials in charge of the counterinsurgency refused to allow an FBN agent to be assigned on a permanent basis in South Vietnam. For propaganda purposes, however, Anslinger was permitted to send Lee Speer to Saigon in January 1954, and in May, based on Speer's reports, he told a Foreign Relations Subcommittee that the People's Republic of China was the "major source of illicit traffic for the entire world."[7] Anslinger knew the allegation was untenable and that the Southeast Asian narcotics trade was in the hands of Vietnamese politicians, generals, and gangsters working with Corsicans in the Golden

Triangle, as well as CIA-protected Kuomintang brokers in Bangkok, Hong Kong, and Saigon. Nevertheless, he repeated his charges in 1955 before the Senate Internal Security Committee, claiming that 95 percent of the heroin that reached San Francisco came from the PRC.

Helping to spread Anslinger's disinformation was the Committee of One Million, a lobby composed of establishment scions and prominent senators, including Anslinger's admirer, the aforementioned Paul Douglas in Illinois. Formed in 1953, the Committee's *raison d'être* was to keep the PRC out of the UN, and to that end it consistently charged the PRC with operating a worldwide drug network to finance communist subversion in Asia.

Also backing Anslinger was Richard L. G. Deverall, the AFL's Free Trade Union Committee representative in India and Japan. In a 1954 book titled *Red China's Dirty Dope War*, Deverall thanked Anslinger and repeated his claim that 4,000 communist agents were pushing drugs on American soldiers in Japan. Deverall was a close friend of several prominent trade union officials working with the CIA's International Operations Division, especially the AFL's Jay Lovestone and Irving Brown, and in this respect, his support for Anslinger against the PRC was understandable. However, organized labor lobbied for national health insurance in America, which Anslinger opposed. Deverall's book, though an obscure footnote in history, is significant because it shows how America's top labor leaders betrayed their own union members by spreading CIA disinformation, and otherwise serving its anti-labor activities. The relevance, in regard to drug law enforcement, of this pact between labor leaders and the CIA became evident in 1955 when the AFL and CIO merged, and CIA counterintelligence chief James Angleton became Jay Lovestone's case officer. A former communist, Lovestone had founded the Free Trade Union Committee, which, with CIA black-bag money, financed compatible left labor unions outside of the US. Organized crime was involved in this certified CIA covert action. According to author Tom Mangold, "Lovestone's payments and logistics were handled in New York by Mario Brod," a labor lawyer from Connecticut and New York who, as an Army counterintelligence officer, had worked with OSS officers James Angleton, Vincent Scamporino, and Charlie Siragusa in Italy during the Second World War. He was also a wedge. Mangold quotes Sam Papich, the FBI's liaison to the CIA, as saying: "Mario had contacts with the mafia."[8]

Mario Brod was Angleton's contact to the Mafia, and through Siragusa and Hank Manfredi, he knew exactly where the Mafia was receiving its narcotics. Through assets in the labor movement, like Lovestone, Brown, and Deverall, he could also learn about and contact drug traffickers all over the world. And there was more. As the CIA's chief of counterintelligence, he was in liaison with all US law enforcement agencies and many foreign police agencies, and he alone possessed the coveted Israeli account. Angleton and his inner circle alone were in liaison with the Mossad – which according to FBN Agent Jim Attie was backing Sami Khoury's narcotics operation in the Middle East. If anything put Angleton at the center of the CIA's international narcotics conspiracy – which is where he was – it was the fact that it was his job to penetrate the intelligence services of the French, as well as the Communist and Kuomintang Chinese.

THE DANIEL ACT

In 1955, few people dreamed that the CIA was involved in international drug smuggling. But the gap between the government's stated and secret policies was widening, in direct proportion with the public's growing demand for drugs. More and more people were starting to question Anslinger's policies towards drug addicts. Rufus King said that year: "All the billions our society has spent enforcing criminal measures against the addict has had the sole result of protecting the peddler's market, artificially inflating his prices and keeping his prices fantastically high. No other nation hounds its addicts as we do, and no other nation faces anything remotely resembling our problem." [9]

Having said that, King challenged Congress to re-evaluate its position. Picking up the gauntlet was Senator Price Daniel (D-TX), a member of the Internal Security Subcommittee and a participant in Senate Hearings held in 1955 on Communist China's involvement in the illicit narcotics traffic. At those hearings, Anslinger convinced Senator Daniel that the PRC was responsible for drug addiction throughout the world, and Daniel deduced that by linking drugs to communism, he could justify a punitive approach toward drug addiction in America – and that by running as a law and order candidate, he could achieve his life's ambition, to be elected governor of Texas.

Daniel jumped in with both feet, and from June through December 1955, his Criminal Code Subcommittee, with Lee Speer as its chief investigator, heard FBN agents Jim Ryan and Ernie Gentry link the PRC to drug smuggling. Gentry went so far as to claim that the PRC was using drugs as a weapon of psychological warfare, "to try to demoralize any of our people who get in touch with it." [10] Anslinger, on 1 August 1955, called the PRC "the greatest purveyor of drugs in history." [11]

As a direct result of the Daniel Hearings, the Senate passed legislation sharply increasing the penalties for drug trafficking. The Senate legislation, which was based largely on charges brought against the PRC by Anslinger and his FBN experts, was pushed through the House by one of the FBN's greatest supporters, Congressman Hale Boggs, whose subcommittee on the Control of Narcotics, Barbiturates, and Amphetamines met from October through December 1955. And again, one of Anslinger's top field agents was available; George White testified to the Boggs Committee that the PRC packed every President Line ship full of drugs in exchange for gold, with which it bought strategic materials to arm North Vietnam.

The Daniel Act was the most important piece of legislation in the FBN's history. By providing for mandatory sentencing, it enabled the FBN to more easily acquire informers and thus achieve greater success in the burgeoning war on drugs. However, under the new laws, a teenager caught with a joint was treated as severely as a Mafia don, so many judges resisted the Act, as did many of Anslinger's critics. Alfred Lindesmith stated in 1956 that "the disastrous consequences of turning over to the police what is an essentially medical problem are steadily becoming more apparent as narcotic arrests rise each year." [12]

But the disastrous consequences of a mainly Black urban problem were not yet apparent to the general public. The majority was unaffected, and almost everyone believed Anslinger's propaganda, so Congress implemented his hard-line approach, thinking it was the best way to curb drug addiction – and it blamed the PRC for international drug trafficking. The problem was that Anslinger was wrong on both counts.

THE FIRST SOLID EVIDENCE OF CIA COMPLICITY

The flaw in Anslinger's theory of a communist drug conspiracy was revealed in August 1955. In testimony before the Daniel Committee, Anslinger had said that Kuomintang troops were not growing opium in Burma, and that Thailand was likewise uninvolved in the drug trade. But one week later, Thailand's prime minister fired police chief Phao Sriyanond for awarding himself (in his dual role as finance minister) a $1 million reward for having seized twenty tons of opium on the Thai–Burma border. Shocked that an official would do such a thing, US Ambassador John Peurifoy criticized Phao and urged the Thai military to take over drug law enforcement. Seeking vindication, Phao revealed that the seized opium belonged to the Kuomintang. [13]

One month later, in October 1955, the *Nation* reported claims by UN officials that the PRC's role in the drug trade was diminishing, if not gone. It also reported a claim, made by a Russian delegate to the UN, that fabricated files about the drug trade had been planted in the UN's Secretariat. The article quoted British Customs officials in Hong Kong calling Anslinger's reports "political exaggerations," and noted that Hong Kong's biggest bust in 1955 occurred when an American soldier was jailed for importing and possessing drugs.[14] The article's author, John O'Kearney, reported that Interpol had arrested twenty-seven Chinese in 1954, but none were communists. He cited India, Lebanon, and Iran as bigger sources, and noted that the FBN had no agents assigned to the Far East, but depended on foreign sources, most in Kuomintang-controlled Taiwan.

Reporter Darrell Berrigan expanded on O'Kearney's observations in an extraordinary article in the May 1956 *Saturday Evening Post*. Flying in the face of Anslinger's propaganda, Berrigan reported that Taiwanese businessmen financed the drug trade in Bangkok in league with South Vietnamese generals. He traced the $70 million-a-year business to the 1947 truce between Thailand's police chief and General Sarit Thanarat. "By accident of history," Berrigan wrote, "the middlemen between Yunnan and Thailand are ... 3,000 KMT troops who turned over the famous 20 tons in the summer of 1955."[15] Berrigan tied the KMT to an international ring, with ships and planes, as well as secret airfields in Laos, and the CIA.

Anslinger was quoted in Berrigan's article as saying that the PRC was smuggling half-ton loads of opium to South Vietnam. But Anslinger had studiously ignored the fact that Thailand had an opium monopoly, an opium processing plant, and fifty tons of opium in its larder. He also ignored the fact that the CIA was facilitating Thailand's drug business through the Sea Supply Corporation, a Miami-based CIA proprietary formed, with the legal assistance of former OSS officer Paul Helliwell, to advise the Thai police and clandestinely provide arms to KMT troops spread along the Thai–Burma border.

Paul Helliwell is the personification of the CIA's respectable, financial aspect of international drug trafficking. While serving as an Army intelligence officer in the Middle East in the Second World War, he was drafted by William Donovan to manage OSS Special Intelligence operations in China. In that sensitive position, Helliwell worked with Chiang Kai-shek's intelligence chief, General Tai Li, and through him the drug smuggling Green Gang in Shanghai. Under his direction, OSS officers also employed opium as a weapon of political warfare. As historian Richard H. Smith informs us, "Through his agent, Le Xuan, [OSS officer] Roberts bribed an old Vietnamese nationalist with a pouch of opium and thus secured a full dossier on Ho's revolutionary background, including the record of his years in Moscow." [16]

This was no small event. The discovery of that dossier convinced the Americans not to back the Vietnamese nationalists against the French in Indochina, and turned the tide of history.

After serving as chief of a Strategic Services Unit in the Far East, Helliwell joined a Miami law firm in 1947. A specialist in private financing, he helped set up the CIA proprietary companies Civil Air Transport (later renamed Air America) and Sea Supply in Thailand, and in 1952 became general counsel to Sea Supply and the Thai Consulate in Miami. A mover and shaker in the Florida Republican Party, Helliwell reportedly helped Thai officials invest their drug profits in Florida land deals through Miami's National Bank and Lou Chesler's General Development Corporation, and at the same time Meyer Lansky and the Kuomintang were doing likewise. [17]

Anslinger knew this; however, in order to get Congress to pass tougher drug laws, he propagated myths that not only obstructed any long-term solution to the problem – they had a deleterious effect on the morale of his own agents. None of this was widely known in 1956, and making matters worse, no one within the FBN dared to contradict Anslinger's self-serving pronouncements.

CLIQUES WITHIN THE FBN

In 1956, Anslinger still firmly controlled FBN policy. But by then it was evident that he would never resign, a realization that had prompted Mal Harney, who had long aspired to Anslinger's job, to accept an appointment as the Treasury Department's assistant to the secretary for law enforcement – in theory, if not practice, becoming Anslinger's boss. Legal counsel B. T. Mitchell temporarily filled the enforcement assistant position after Harney's departure and, with Deputy Commissioner George Cunningham, managed the Bureau's daily operations. Meanwhile the agents knew that Anslinger's days were numbered, and as he approached mandatory retirement in 1962, they were quietly forming factions in anticipation of the battle to succeed him. The main contenders were Charlie Siragusa, Henry Giordano, and Lee Speer.

After serving as district supervisor in Kansas City, Giordano in July 1956 became the FBN's field supervisor, and in September its deputy assistant for administration. A year later he replaced Mitchell as enforcement assistant, the number three job at headquarters. He was assertive, and the aspirant in the best position to promote his backers, a strength he demonstrated by creating a fifth Enforcement Group in New York so that his disciple, Mike Picini, could gain management experience as a group leader. And as Anslinger's valued liaison to prominent Congressmen on technical matters, Giordano was, overall, the strongest candidate.

A better-qualified candidate, according to many agents, was Charlie Siragusa, whose worldwide operations had generated the intelligence that had resulted in so many domestic arrests and seizures. But his chances were based on Anslinger's promise to back him for the job, and that promise was based on the condition that he return to Washington to assume a headquarters position. Thus Siragusa faced the dilemma of having to abandon his overseas power base, to placate Anslinger.

Speer was the odd man out. Upon returning from Japan, he became one of the FBN's two inspectors, along with Bill Tollenger. Keeping track of agent infractions gave management the leverage it needed to dismiss troublemakers, and for doing that unenviable job, shooflies were rewarded with a measure of influence at headquarters, where they were assigned. Plus Speer had Texas Senator Price Daniel in his corner. As Daniel's chief investigator, Speer had played a major role in the passage of the Daniel Act, and partially on the basis of that triumph, Daniel was elected governor of Texas. In return, Daniel entrusted Speer's career to fellow Texas Democrat and Speaker of the House, Sam Rayburn. Although he mistrusted Speer, Anslinger was in Daniel's debt and had no choice but to abide when Rayburn insisted that Speer fill the enforcement assistant position that opened up in November 1958, when Giordano became Deputy Commissioner. At this important turning point, Speer became a powerhouse, and launched his own campaign to succeed Anslinger.

With Harney's promotion to assistant secretary, the FBN gained greater influence within the Treasury Department, the Bureau of the Budget, and the Appropriations Committee. But his promotion was an ominous development, for it pit Giordano against Siragusa, and both of them against Speer, who had little support among the agent population. Indeed, Speer's biggest mistake was his forthcoming war on corruption and, as the antagonist of George Gaffney and the case-making agents in New York, he would bring about his own undoing.

While the FBN was bracing for the battle to succeed Anslinger, the Mafia was gearing up for a bloodletting of its own. Santo Trafficante Sr, the patron saint of traffickers, died in 1954, and his namesake son inherited his rackets in Cuba and Florida, as well as his father's partnership with

Meyer Lansky. Having taken over the Mangano family after spending ten months in prison on a tax evasion charge, vicious Albert Anastasia decided that Lansky and Trafficante Jr. (hereafter referred to simply as Trafficante) were being greedy, and thinking they were weak, he made a grab for the Havana action. The resulting mob war would begin in 1956 and intersect with the FBN's own increasing internecine strife.

11

ST. MICHAEL'S
SERGEANT AT ARMS

"There is a great outer world ... in which telegrams and anger count."
E. M. Forster, *Howard's End*

The FBN's ability to pursue international drug traffickers was enhanced in late 1954 when, at the urging of the Treasury Department's assistant secretary for law enforcement, the US government decided to become a dues-paying member of Interpol. At this point, Charlie Siragusa, as supervisor over the newly created District 17 in Rome, started attending Interpol's annual General Assembly meetings and getting together regularly with top policemen from around the world. Through these official Interpol connections, Siragusa gathered support for his investigations and increased his own and the FBN's stature abroad.[1]

As the government's premier law enforcement agency, the FBI was the logical choice to work with Interpol, but J. Edgar Hoover considered the Paris-based organization a security risk and refused to participate. The CIA, however, wanted to penetrate Interpol precisely because it was based in Paris. But the spy agency needed a surrogate to provide it with deniability, so at the insistence of the White House, Treasury Agent Fred Douglas was allowed to serve as the government's official representative to Interpol. Douglas functioned as a back channel to the CIA on Interpol affairs, as did Siragusa – and in this way, and several others, the CIA grew ever closer to the Treasury Department and the FBN. Specifically, the CIA began using the Treasury Department's Attaché slots and its customs service and FBN positions overseas as cover for its agents. Plus which it used six national coordinator positions, which the Treasury Department's Enforcement Board had created and spread evenly across the country under the supervision of the chief coordinator, as cover positions for CIA officers operating domestically within the US.[2]

Interpol now provided significant information on important narcotics traffickers to the four FBN agents assigned on a permanent basis in Rome: Charlie Siragusa, Paul Knight, Hank Manfredi, and Jim Attie. For these four men, and the temporary duty agents who assisted them, the ability to claim they were working with, or at times for Interpol contributed largely to their successes. But the challenges of undercover narcotics operations were enormous, and the agents suffered failures too, as illustrated by the Dominick Albertini case. Perhaps the largest producer of illicit heroin in 1955, Albertini managed several clandestine labs in France and dealt with Sami Khoury in Beirut and Mafiosi in Italy and America.

The Albertini case began in 1954 when Giovanni Mauceri, an Italian fugitive in the Orsini case, offered to sell Paul Knight ten kilograms of heroin. Though he never actually sold the drugs to Knight, Mauceri faced a charge of attempted sale, and in October 1955 he agreed to help the FBN entrap his source, Dom Albertini. By coincidence, Albertini's chemist had recently been arrested, and Albertini was looking for a replacement to manage his labs in France. Seizing the opportunity, Siragusa devised a bold scheme with the French authorities in which Jim Attie was taught how to convert morphine base into heroin. Six weeks later, Mauceri introduced Attie to Albertini as an underworld chemist from Beirut, and trusting Mauceri's word on the matter, Albertini hired him. But someone, either Mauceri or a corrupt French official, betrayed the daring, isolated undercover agent. Attie barely managed to escape with his life, months of costly preparation were wasted, and it would be fifteen years before Albertini's heroin conversion labs were located in and around Marseilles.

Devious informants and corrupt officials were not the only problems disrupting District 17 in Rome. Stress was taking a toll, too.

"Jim had been an amateur boxer," Paul Knight explains, "and all the fights may have contributed to the problem. But after the beating he got by Haj Touma [as described in chapter 8], Jim seemed narcoleptic: one minute he was wide awake, the next he was falling asleep at his desk. His speech was impaired, and when he spoke he'd say funny things. He thought Israeli intelligence was after him. I was concerned for his health, so I told Charlie, and Charlie insisted that Jim be admitted to a hospital in Rome. And that's when we found out that he had encephalitis. Jim was sent to a veterans' hospital in Detroit, and Charlie, mistaking encephalitis for syphilis, wrote a terrible letter saying that Jim didn't deserve health benefits, because he had contracted a venereal disease."

Confused about the nature of Attie's illness, Siragusa accused him of being a malingerer and tried to have him fired. Luckily, headquarters realized that a mistake had been made, and after Attie was released from the hospital, he was allowed to return to duty in Chicago under District Supervisor Al Aman. He was bitter, however, and still showing signs of weakness, and his bosses doubted his ability to function. Aman wouldn't even let him drive a company car. But they did let him work dangerous undercover cases against the Chicago Mafia, and deep inside Mexico, and despite his health problems, brave Jim Attie remained one of the FBN's premier case-making agents.

THE EMERGENCE OF ANDY TARTAGLINO

Andy Tartaglino, one of the most significant and controversial characters among the FBN's dramatis personae, replaced Jim Attie in Rome in the autumn of 1956. Said to have the mind of a mathematician and the soul of a Dominican monk, Tartaglino graduated from Georgetown University in 1949. A year later, while serving in the Naval Reserve aboard a ship in the Mediterranean Sea, he met a navigator who had been in the Treasury Department's old Alcohol Tobacco Tax unit. Standing on the bridge at night, charting a course by the stars, the navigator regaled Tartaglino with tall tales of true crime. Eager to live the exciting life of an undercover narcotic agent, Tartaglino approached Charlie Siragusa while on shore leave in Naples and applied for a job with the FBN.

"The Bureau had six Special Hires coming to it each year," Tartaglino recalls, "and my special quality was that I spoke an Italian dialect. I was told to go to Washington and was hired in 1951 while still in the Naval Reserve."

Fresh from the spic and span Navy, Tartaglino was taken aback upon arriving at the New York office in 1952. "The Bureau was badly under-manned," he explains, "and there were forces at work that prohibited the necessary countermeasures. Some of those forces were bureaucratic, but some were the result of the agents' own weaknesses. In New York," he says ruefully, "some of the agents were junkies.[3]

"Anslinger never asked for sufficient resources to investigate corruption within the Bureau," Tartaglino continues, "and even though addiction was skyrocketing, he harassed the doctors who were researching methadone, which was hard to regulate and was finding its way onto the streets. This negative attitude out of headquarters obstructed any non-enforcement solution to the problem."

Despite the obstacles, Tartaglino was intrigued with international drug smuggling, and under the tutelage of Angelo Zurlo, he began working as an undercover agent. He bought narcotics from Joseph Armone, an underboss in the Anastasia family, and he laid the groundwork for the Anthony Vellucci–Nathan Behrman case, the largest Italian–Jewish–French connection operation at the time. Recognized by his bosses as honest and possessing leadership abilities, Tartaglino was assigned to the International Group, where he learned about overseas operations from Joe Amato, and formed a fast friendship with Marty Pera. One of the new breed of younger agents seeking to overcome the inertia and corruption of the past, Tartaglino heeded Pera's advice concerning the realities of working overseas.

As Marty Pera recalls: "In 1951, I was chosen to go to Europe with Charlie Siragusa and Joe Amato on a ninety-day temporary duty assignment. Siragusa went to Italy, Amato to Germany, and I went to Turkey, where a pro-American government had been established and was allowing the US to open military bases. It was the start of a large US presence there.

"As you know, George White had been to Turkey in 1948 and Hollywood made a movie about his adventures called *To The Ends Of The Earth* [starring Dick Powell] in which the Turkish police were portrayed as bumbling fools, which they are not. So when I met Kamal Aygun, the head of the Turkish Sûreté in Istanbul, the first thing he told me was that, contrary to press reports and the movie, White had bungled the operation. He'd never made a raid or an arrest, and in fact, the Turkish police had someone deliver five kilograms of heroin to White, in order to placate Anslinger, who was giving the Turks grief at the UN about diversions. They'd done Anslinger this tremendous favor, so he could save face, but as a result of all the negative publicity White had generated, Turkey became a pariah.

"After we talked for a while, Aygun asked me, 'What are you going to do here?' I said I was there to make undercover cases, to which he replied: 'We cooperated fully last time, and it was turned against us. So no help this time.' Then he wished me good luck."

Pera sighs. "From Istanbul I ventured into the countryside, where I found that opium reporting by farmers was a total sham. They sold what was required to the government and the rest to the highest bidder. I learned that we had to solve the problem here," he stresses, "before we went overseas. And I learned that without Hank Manfredi, Charlie Siragusa would have been nothing."

Starting in 1956, in his position as chief of the International Group, Pera's primary task was tracking heroin from its overseas sources to the American Mafia. "Some leads came from Frank Sojat," he says, "after Sojat was sent to Turkey to straighten out their reporting. Other leads came from Paul Knight in Beirut. But most came from Manfredi in Rome; and that's when I realized how incredibly strong Hank's ties were with the Italian police. In the early days after the war he brought them food and clothing, and when they rose through the ranks, they remembered. Hank was honest and hardworking, and the Italians loved him."

TARTAGLINO GOES TO ROME

Tartaglino's dream of an overseas assignment came true when Jack Cusack, his supervisor at the Court House Squad, wrote a letter to Siragusa recommending him. Within weeks, Tartaglino was on his way to Rome to replace Jim Attie. It was a tough act to follow, but the most important relationship in FBN history was about to be formed. Speaking with devotion about his mentor, Tartaglino says, "If Charlie Siragusa were alive today, we wouldn't have the drug problem we have in America. Charlie was a workaholic who traveled by train with a typewriter on his lap, and he expected the same from his agents. If he sent you to Beirut, you sent him a telegram saying when, exactly, you arrived – then you unpacked your bags and went to work. And you wrote reports on Sunday, on your own time. But Charlie was gold, a nuts–and–bolts person who showed you the basics; how to set up an office, what questions to ask your counterparts, and how to act in their presence. I remember when the mob was shaking down the famous opera singer Mario Lanza in Italy. We were going to meet him, and I was nervous. Charlie looked at me with disapproval and said: 'He's awed by us.'

"Charlie was on top with everybody," Tartaglino beams. And under Siragusa's tutelage, Tartaglino found, as one colleague puts it, "the *consigliere* within."

According to Tartaglino, the FBN's focus in 1956 was to find "the Conspiracy" between communists and international drug smugglers. "In the process of doing that," he says, "we made buys in Italy from American seamen and followed leads to Turkey and France. Charlie had developed a good rapport abroad, and that allowed us to do some unilateral operations too. Anslinger's only rule was, 'stay away from State,' meaning ambassadors Clare Luce and her replacement, James Zellerbach.

"When Charlie wasn't there," Tartaglino continues, "I stepped in as acting supervisor and representative to the other agencies at the Embassy. Francis Coleman, the CIA station chief, was very helpful. We borrowed flash money from him. Lots of it. 'If you hear anything about East–West trade, let us know,' he'd say, and that's all he wanted. The other helpful person was Treasury Attaché Francis DiLucia, although Francis was more concerned with the price of merchandise for tax purposes. Our thing was drugs, and that's what we did." [4]

In doing that thing, Tartaglino worked closely with Hank Manfredi and Paul Knight, as well as CIA officers Joe Salm and Fred Cornetta, who had been assigned to the FBN after the Hungarian uprising in 1956. Also arriving at the FBN's Rome office in late 1956 was Agent Ralph Frias.

INTRODUCING RALPH FRIAS

A native of Prescott, Arizona, and a veteran of the Second World War, Frias spoke fluent Spanish and for that reason was hired by the FBN in Los Angeles in 1951. Blessed with a knack for undercover work, Frias learned the tricks of the trade from the agent in charge of Los Angeles, George Davis. A craggy old-timer, Davis relied on Frias to produce almost all of the office's cases against Hispanic violators. But by the time Howard Chappell replaced Davis in 1956, case-maker Frias was ready for a change of scene, and greater challenges.

Able to speak French and Italian as well as Spanish, Frias was accepted by Siragusa in Rome, and began sharing office space with Manfredi, Tartaglino, and Cornetta. At the time, Knight and Joe Salm were in Beirut, where, according to Frias, "they had lots of dubious information in big files," but were accomplishing little in the absence of undercover ace Jim Attie.

Frias, like Attie, disliked Siragusa, whom he considered a publicity hound. But he did form a friendship with Tartaglino. "Andy was serving as Siragusa's administrative aide," Frias recalls, "and eventually Andy became so well-informed and so influential that he actually began to guide Siragusa. But Andy did very little undercover work."

Tartaglino's exit from undercover work, notably, was the result of a harrowing experience in Monte Carlo in October 1956. His informer had set up a deal with two Corsican traffickers. But instead of delivering six kilograms of heroin, as agreed, the traffickers arrived with sugar and put a gun to Tartaglino's head. Some agents say the Corsicans knew that they'd encountered an FBN agent, and that they made Andy beg for his life. Meanwhile, Siragusa and the French police were next door, but their hidden microphone malfunctioned, and the Corsicans got away with $16,000 in buy money.

"They were quickly captured," Tartaglino explains, "but Charlie took a beating in the press, because the French police had taken the $16,000 dollars from their Treasury without authorization." The *Saturday Evening Post* described the incident as "the first big defeat for Siragusa."[5]

Siragusa's first big failure also marked the end of Tartaglino's undercover days. But fortunately for District 17, Ralph Frias was there to pick up the slack. Fashioning a persona as Johnny Rizzo, the son of a made man from San Bernardino who was willing to smuggle anything, Frias quickly acquired a number of informants and began to make a string of significant cases. The first climaxed on 18 June 1957, when he made a buy in Beirut from Sami Khoury's associate Youseff el-Etir. Covering Frias were Lebanese Customs chief Edmond Azizi and Joe Salm. To everyone's surprise, el-Etir arrived at the meeting with Omar Makkouk, the most wanted chemist in Lebanon. The ensuing bust resulted in the seizure of three kilograms of heroin and twenty-five kilograms of morphine base. Makkouk's lab in Syria was located, and leads were developed into German, Swiss, and Iranian smuggling rings. The case contributed to the indictment of sixty-two traffickers in New York as well. This worldwide ring, managed since 1950 by Meyer Lansky's associate in Philadelphia, Harry Stromberg, moved fifty kilograms of heroin a month from Macao and Turkey, through Lebanon and France, to major Mafiosi in America.[6]

Next Frias was introduced through a special employee to Giuseppe Badalamenti, a top Mafia source of heroin in Sicily. Linked closely to deported American Mafiosi Frank Coppola and Sam Carolla, Giuseppe took Frias into his confidence, and after Giuseppe died of the Asiatic flu in December 1957, Frias made a buy from his brother Vito in January 1958. Despite the fact that a vicious war was underway between the Badalamenti and the Greco clans in Sicily, Frias, backed up by Hank Manfredi, made a second buy from Vito in March. Vito Badalamenti and his two closest associates were arrested in June, and the Grecos temporarily took over the Sicilian heroin business.

Until Frias came along, no FBN agent had generated so much intelligence on the Sicilians or their Corsican partners in Mexico, Cuba, and Canada. For example, it was through a case made by Frias that the FBN learned that after the Mexican federal police had arrested Antoine D'Agostino in March 1955, Paul Mondoloni and Jean Croce had escaped to Cuba, where they re-established their drug-smuggling business under Batista's protection. And it was through Frias that the FBN learned, in August 1958, that a French diplomat was carrying heroin to Vincent Todaro, a member of the Trafficante organization in New York. Frias's successes also helped the FBN to smash the Stromberg and Badalamenti rings – although, within a month, Corsican Antoine Cordoliani had set up a new operation with the Grecos, on behalf of Dom Albertini, the Guérini brothers, and Robert Blemant in Marseilles. This major reorganization had begun, notably, a year earlier, in June 1957, when Lucky Luciano arrived in Palermo to attend an historical and soon-to-be discussed summit meeting between senior representatives of the American and Sicilian Mafias.

ST. MICHAEL'S SERGEANT AT ARMS

More on the ramifications of the Palermo summit remains to be said, but for now we must turn our attention to Henry L. Manfredi, the extraordinary agent who made the fateful decision that kept Charlie Siragusa from replacing Harry Anslinger as Commissioner of Narcotics.

Manfredi's first job was as a textile cutter in Brooklyn. But he longed to be a policeman and shortly before the war he obtained part-time work fingerprinting Civil Service personnel for the NYPD. Through that job he met FBN Agent Irwin Greenfeld, and in 1942, Greenfeld got Manfredi a job with Lieutenant Rudy Caputo, chief of security for the Brooklyn Navy Yard. Caputo's office was collocated with the FBN at 90 Church Street, and under Caputo's direction, Manfredi set up an Identification Bureau at the Naval Yard. He also began tracking subversives as part of the Luciano Project. In 1943, Manfredi joined the Army CID and served in North Africa, Italy, and Austria. After the war he returned to Italy as a security specialist and, in 1948, he caught Anslinger's eye when he found a huge stash of narcotics in Austria. After helping Siragusa identify the Italian companies that were diverting heroin onto the American market, he joined the FBN and began to investigate the money-laundering activities of the Mafia.[7]

The CIA also employed Manfredi. "One time he asked me to cover him while he met an East German at a cafe on the Via Parioli," Ralph Frias recalls. "He wanted to know if anyone was watching. He described the guy and told me to be there an hour early to see if he came alone. Which he did. Hank arrived later, sat down, got something to drink, lit one of his short, black cigars, and started talking with this guy. I walked around behind to see if anyone else was covering the meet. There wasn't, and afterwards I followed the guy Hank had met and I watched him get in a taxicab. I never told Charlie," Frias confesses, then adds that Manfredi returned the favor. "No one else was willing to cover me when I went to meet Vito Badalamenti in Sicily," he says. "But Hank wasn't afraid. He said, 'Okay, kid. I'll go with you.' And he did.

"The CIA guy in Rome, John Riordan, also asked me to drop off things and eyeball people," Frias adds. "Riordan's area of interest was in the Middle East, and he asked me who I knew there. I knew a Maronite in the Bekka Valley who'd been a priest in East Los Angeles, so Riordon recruited him as an asset. Riordan ran his operation out of the Merrill Lynch Brokerage House in Rome, and the money he paid to his assets in the Middle East was funneled through it. Hank and Charlie knew about Riordan's operation, and they used the Brokerage House to make money on the side for themselves and to pay for things for the office. I had an account there as well, which I used when I set up a deal with Dom Albertini."

The Merrill Lynch Brokerage House not only funded CIA operations in Beirut, Italy, and Greece, the CIA also used it to launder money for P2, Italy's ultra-right-wing Masonic Lodge. Hank Manfredi was at the center of these espionage intrigues, and by 1957 his contacts in the Vatican and Italian security services had earned him a reputation as "the fount." According to Colonel Tulius Acampora, an Army counterintelligence officer detached to the CIA and assigned as an advisor to the Italian Carabinieri, "Hank had more contacts across the board than Charlie. The problem was that he went to work full time for Bob Driscoll and the CIA.

"The CIA succeeded in putting the Christian Democrats in Italy," Acampora explains, "but the communists made gains anyway, so the Pentagon's counterintelligence staff drew up plans to change the political climate of Italy through counter-subversion. Jack Kennedy was a key player in Congress, as was Fig Coleman in Rome. The Dulles complex made it a unified thing: State, CIA, military, the Church. And that's where Hank comes in. The Dulleses knew what Hank was doing and they were covetous of his friendship with Paul Marcinkus. Marcinkus was right-hand man of Giovanni Montini, the Vatican's Secretary of State, and the real power behind the Pope."

A native of Chicago and a protégé of Cardinal Cody, Marcinkus initially went to work for Montini in 1952, serving as his emissary in Canada and then Bolivia. Montini had worked with the OSS in the war and had relationships with the Mafia, the P2 Masonic Lodge, and neo-fascist ultras within the Italian security services. Montini's link to the Mafia was Massimo Spado, a financier he later hired to invest the Vatican's money. Spado in turn hired tax attorney Michele Sindona. Now famous for his role in the collapse of the Franklin National Bank in 1979, Sindona had formed relations with the Mafia in 1943 when, as a budding black marketeer, he was granted permission by Vito Genovese to provide produce to certain cities in Sicily. Sindona prospered and with his profits he opened an accounting office in Milan, where Montini was serving as Archbishop. In November 1954, at Montini's request, and certainly with Hank Manfredi's knowledge, Sindona channeled the CIA funds that enabled the Italian security forces to hire goon squads to suppress striking communist workers in Milan. In 1960 Sindona purchased the Banca Privata Italiana, into which the Vatican began making deposits. Sindona came to occupy a pivotal position in Italian politics, as the wedge between the Vatican, the Mafia, and the P2 Masonic Lodge.[8]

"After Montini became Pope Paul VI in 1963," Acampora continues, "Marcinkus became his personal secretary and later boss of the Vatican Bank. And that's when Marcinkus got into all sorts of mischief with Sindona." Acampora winks. "Hank was so close to Marcinkus that on a moment's notice he could get Anslinger's friends an audience with the Pope.

"Back in Washington," Acampora continues, "CIA director Allen Dulles decided to send Bob Driscoll to Rome under commercial cover. Driscoll was a Navy commander with a low key style. A few years earlier he'd snatched the British contacts in the Greek police, so Dulles gave him a charge to create the same sort of alternative in Italy. But in order to do that, Driscoll needed to get away from Angleton's commitments in the military. The police are the crucial element in countering subversion, and what Driscoll wanted were Hank's contacts in the Carabinieri in Trieste. Driscoll wanted to hire them as the nucleus of a special operations unit he could use to reshape the political climate in Italy. From his years in Trieste, Hank knew all the Carabinieri, as well as all the top policemen in Rome.

"I remember the night that Hank made his decision to go with Driscoll," Acampora says softly. "Charlie, Hank, and I were having dinner at a Chinese restaurant in Washington. Charlie kept saying, 'Hank, don't go. Stick with me.' Charlie was in a race with Giordano to succeed Anslinger, and if Hank went with Driscoll, then Charlie wouldn't be able to contend with Giordano. But Hank thought he'd find more personal fulfillment with the CIA. And once Hank went with the CIA, Charlie, who was heading back to Washington, lost a lot of influence over foreign operations."

Hank Manfredi was a father figure and raconteur, admired by all the agents and their wives. Yet he was secretly infatuated with Jackie Kennedy, whom he adoringly called "the lady." They'd met while she was visiting her sister in Ravello, and thereafter he served as her advance man and bodyguard whenever she was in Europe. His dream was to become the caretaker of her estate when he retired. But none of his or Siragusa's dreams would ever come true, thanks to the CIA.

"Charlie used to say that Hank wasn't good at reporting," Andy Tartaglino recalls. "But he was just too busy giving information to the CIA. There was a segment of the Mafia he was interested in, an intelligence angle dating back to World War Two, Sicily. He knew organized crime, but he was interested in intelligence. And that's where he went."

"THE CONSPIRACY"

Hank Manfredi's obsession with the intelligence angle of drug smuggling ultimately led him to "the Conspiracy" Harry Anslinger had been seeking all his life. Manfredi began to assemble the evidence in late June 1957, when the Carabinieri informed him of Luciano's presence in Palermo. Manfredi alerted his Italian police contacts and, in October 1957, a series of Mafia summit meetings at the Delle Palme Hotel were carefully monitored, and verified Anslinger's theory that an International Grand Council of Mafiosi existed. Among the Americans at the summit were Joe Bonanno and Santo Sorge, the Mafia's financial advisor. According to Marty Pera, Sorge desperately tried to convince the bosses to get out of the drug business.

"Bonanno was polished," Pera explains. "Lucchese and Lansky had sent their sons to West Point. They were rich and they didn't need the hassle."

Representing the Sicilians, among others, were Vito Badalamenti and Leonard Greco, the most powerful Mafiosi in Sicily. Leonard's brother Salvatore had a fleet of ships that sailed under the Honduran flag and, through Frank Coppola, moved narcotics to Cuba in food shipments. But the Sicilians were not as diversified as their American counterparts and could not afford to pull out of the drug trafficking business, despite Sorge's admonitions. [9]

"The Sicilians gave the Americans an ultimatum at Palermo," Pera explains. "They knew there were a number of rebellious young hoods in America, so they told the bosses, 'If you don't deal with us, we'll deal with them.' Not having control over narcotics would have put all their other rackets at risk, so the Americans had no choice but to go along."

Once the ultimatum was accepted, arranging political protection became the main order of business. Coppola and Greco were the principal negotiators and they authorized Michele Sindona to move drug-generated protection money through the Italian Secret Service to ultra powerbrokers in the Italian government. This was the intelligence angle that fascinated Manfredi – though it was fascist, not communist in nature – which meant he was nearly powerless to stop it in Italy. However, he was able to track Palermo summit-attendee Philip Buccola to Boston, and by wiretapping Buccola in Boston, FBN agents were able to learn of a follow-up American Mafia summit to be held in Apalachin, New York, the overarching significance of which will be discussed in the next chapter.

THE IRAN CONNECTION

Another narcotics route with an intelligence angle was uncovered in Iran in 1956, when Charlie Siragusa and Paul Knight, working with Iranian police chief General Alavi Moghaddam, raided a lab in Tehran that was producing 100 pounds of heroin a week! It was a huge bust, but the operation persisted, so in February 1957, Knight escorted Garland Williams to Tehran to solve, at President Eisenhower's personal request, Iran's drug problem. With Williams was CIA officer Byron Engle, chief of the Agency for International Development's Office of Public Safety (OPS) Program. Two years after his forced retirement from the Treasury Department, Williams had resurfaced as an employee of the OPS. His job was to create a narcotic squad in Tehran, at the same time that Engle and the CIA were forming, with the Mossad, Iran's brutal secret police force, SAVAK.[10]

The Williams expedition was nothing new. America had been enmeshed in Iran's opium business since 1943, when the Third Millspaugh Mission arrived in Tehran to take control of Iran's economy, in return for the granting of oil, air transport, and various other commercial rights to American industrialists. As part of its job, the Millspaugh Mission also collected opium revenues, managed the Pharmaceutical Institute, and directed the Royal opium factory, prompting critics to call the Millspaugh team "drug sellers."[11]

In his defense, team leader Arthur Millspaugh pointed out that the US Army, which provided Iranian narcotics to Kachin soldiers in Burma during the Second World War, operated beyond his control through its "wild-cat" Bank Sepah. "Our long term program looked to the eventual elimination of the opium business," he wrote, but "a large part of Persia's production went into the illicit trade" anyway.[12]

As Garland Williams had reported to Anslinger in 1949, and as the Prince Pahlevi case had proven in 1954, the Iranian royal families never stopped overproducing or selling black-market opium. Perched perennially atop the UN's list of nations that violated international drug laws, Iran was aware of its addiction problem, and in 1953, newly elected president Mohammed Mossadegh banned opium production. But he also nationalized American and British oil firms, so the British Secret Service called upon Kim Roosevelt and the CIA. Roosevelt in turn concocted a *coup d'état* with Lebanon's security chief, Faroud Nashashibi, a CIA asset employed as Pan American airlines' chief of security in Beirut.[13]

After the successful completion of the bloody takeover, the American and British oil companies regained their properties in Iran, and Roosevelt became a vice president at Gulf Oil. The CIA moved in and from Iran launched penetration operations inside the Soviet Union. In so far as Iran, along with Turkey, was one of only four allied nations that bordered the USSR, supporting the Shah was a matter of national security that eclipsed local issues of drug law enforcement.

Through the Office of Public Safety, CIA officers would also organize and support repressive security forces in Lebanon and South Vietnam, which were both protecting narcotics traffickers. In exchange for their silence, and the type of favors described by Ralph Frias, FBN agents in return received tips on politically incorrect drug smugglers from CIA officers working under OPS cover. And through OPS's chief, CIA officer Byron Engle, the FBN would form a relationship with TWA like the one it enjoyed, through Sam Pryor, with Pan Am.[14]

THE BEIRUT CONNECTION

While national security interests were served by making allowances for foreign leaders involved in drug trafficking, these accommodations caused difficulties for overseas FBN agents. In Lebanon, as we know, the major hash growers were legislators and officials of cabinet rank, which is why Customs Captain Edmond Azizi and Sûreté officer Haj Touma were able to protect Sami Khoury and Mounir Alaouie, and profit from their drug smuggling operation. In addition, the Middle East faced an explosive political situation. After the Israelis seized the Suez Canal, the Sinai Desert, and the Gaza Strip in 1956, the US government – in order to maintain good relations with the oil producing Arab nations – agreed to provide Israel with billions of dollars of financial aid so that some of these stolen territories would be returned to their rightful owners. But the extent of Israel's military power terrorized the Arab world and widened the gulf between the Christian and Muslim sects in Lebanon. As a result, arms smuggling proliferated between Beirut and Damascus, making drug law enforcement all the more difficult.

Arriving in Beirut in 1956 to help Paul Knight manage the situation was Joe Salm. Born in Egypt and raised in America by Benedictine monks, Salm was the most improbable FBN agent imaginable. He met his father (who owned 3,000 acres of land at the mouth of the Nile) once a year, and he met his mother, a French poetess, for the first time in 1939, when at age eighteen he went to work for the Ford Motor Company in Cairo. During the war, Salm served with the Royal Air Force and then the US Army CID. He joined the CIA after graduating from Harvard, serving undercover in the State Department's Refugee Program in Genoa. In 1954 he transferred to Beirut, where he processed visa applications for Palestinian and Armenian refugees wishing to emigrate to America.

Birds of a feather, Joe Salm and Paul Knight became fast friends in Beirut. Relying on Frias to do most of the undercover work, Salm and group leader Knight made whatever cases were politically permissible, such as the June 1957 case against Youseff el-Etir and Syrian chemist Omar Makkouk. But their ability to operate in Beirut diminished in 1958 when Muslim nationalists and communists revealed that the CIA had rigged Lebanon's presidential elections in favor of the Christian Maronite candidate, Camille Chamoun. In August, communists and outlawed Syrians bombed the American Embassy, and Ambassador Donald Heath ordered the evacuation of American women and children to Athens and Cyprus.

Tensions increased when Egypt and Syria formed the United Arab Republic. In response, the CIA, with the consent of Iraq's King Faisal, armed the Kurds in Northern Iraq and encouraged them to attack Syria, which the US considered a Soviet pawn. Within weeks, however, Iraqi forces loyal to Colonel Abdul Karim el-Kassem overthrew King Faisal and restored relations with the USSR. This coup incited Arab nationalists in Lebanon and, in May, armed revolt erupted in Beirut. The US Information Agency building was burned and sacked, and the ARAMCO pipeline from Saudi Arabia to Tripoli was severed – at which point Joe Salm was reassigned by the CIA as a consultant to Tapline, the company that provided security for ARAMCO.

Fearing that the Syrians would attack Lebanon, and that Muslim rebels would assist them, President Chamoun asked for US help in sealing Lebanon's borders. To protect the region's oil reserves, Eisenhower agreed:

the Sixth Fleet put Marines ashore at Tripoli, and US jets flew over Beirut in a show of force. But Chamoun's government collapsed in October when the Marines left, and General Faroud Chehab, promising neutrality, was elected president. At America's urging, Muslim leaders were granted seats in his new government.

Events in Lebanon in 1958 left America more deeply entrenched in the region than ever before. To placate King Hussein, America began selling arms to Jordan and mounting covert operations against Iraq, including a MKULTRA operation in which Dr. Gottlieb sent, from New Delhi, India, a handkerchief laced with a deadly poison to Colonel Kassem.[15] (Gottlieb's assassination attempt failed, but Kassem was overthrown in 1963 by the CIA-supported Ba-ath Party, which included Saddam Hussein.[16]) Gottlieb's assassination attempt evidently involved Anslinger through Ulius Amoss, the nutty private investigator fired from his OSS post in Cairo for using official funds to hire, with George White's assistance, an ex-con for assassinations. In a 1958 letter to Anslinger, Amoss expressed concern about "our men" in Iraq being able "to evacuate in time."[17]

Were Paul Knight and Joe Salm "our" men? They certainly were in the midst of the fireworks. One illuminating episode began when Knight received a tip about a warehouse full of hashish. After arranging to rent space at the warehouse, Knight visited friends in the Royal Navy on Cyprus, from whom he acquired an incendiary bomb and a timer, which he sealed inside a bail of hash then stored in the warehouse – which exploded and burned the warehouse to the ground.

By 1958, FBN agents were setting off bombs and making loud noises in numerous places of strategic interest to the CIA.

12

GANGBUSTERS

"In those days, New York City was narcotic law enforcement."

Agent Arthur J. Fluhr

The political dynamics of domestic drug law enforcement varied from city to city, but were governed by similar forces in each instance. In New York, for example, the Mafia had a monolithic organization presiding over an immense importation and distribution system that straddled the nation. In battling this behemoth, FBN agents worked closely with NYPD narcotic detectives – not just because they could kick in doors on suspicion, but also because they had a handful of fixers who maintained the balance of power between the underworld and the Establishment.

But Los Angeles, like Miami, was an open city. The Mafia had a control-ling interest in several rackets, and supplied a portion of the narcotics that reached LA, but Blacks and Hispanics were independently involved in the action too. There had been only one Mafia turf war, in the late 1940s, when Tom Dragna and Johnny Roselli, with the help of LA police chief William "Whiskey Bill" Parker, forcefully settled their differences with Bugsy Siegel and Mickey Cohen.[1] After Siegel was killed and Cohen went to prison, Roselli shifted his attention to more profitable Mafia ventures in Las Vegas. According to Howard Chappell, Dragna's successor in 1957, Frank DeSimone, was a weak boss, and the Mafia actually had a stronger presence in San Diego.

There were demographic differences as well. While pure China white heroin arrived in the San Francisco Bay area from the Far East, Los Angeles was infused with marijuana and opium from Mexico. As the FBN agent in charge in LA, Howard Chappell's jurisdiction covered the California and Arizona borders, and extended into Mexico's northwestern states. But unlike the NYPD, the LAPD narcotic squad refused to help the FBN in its international effort, and was content to focus its efforts on the city's disenfranchised Hispanic and Black communities.

Chief Parker's refusal to share informants or work with the FBN led to a bitter feud. "He turned the cops loose," Chappell says, noting that Parker allowed his narcotic detectives to stretch search and seizure laws to the limit. "They'd find five or six joints and tear the place apart. But worse than that, they were intentionally screwing up our federal cases."

The District Attorney ignored the problem, and as a result the California courts dismissed several important cases. Out of frustration, a few disgruntled LAPD narcotic detectives brought their cases to Chappell, and Chappell, working with the Sheriff's department, took the cases to federal court. Tensions intensified and at a press conference, Chief Parker charged that Chappell's agents were illegally using prostitute addicts as informants. Chappell, through reporter George Putnam, in turn leaked information about several LAPD narcotic detectives who were taking money from drug dealers. He had photos of the detectives in $500 suits, placing extravagant bets at the racetrack, and he secretly taped incriminating conversations the detectives had with the District Attorney.

Soon thereafter several FBN informants were murdered with a type of revolver used by the LAPD – at which point Chappell grabbed a Tommy gun and made a personal call on Whiskey Bill. Fearing for his life, Parker complained to the governor and demanded that the Treasury Department replace Chappell. Never one to avoid trouble or publicity, District Supervisor George White called a press conference in San Francisco and declared that Whiskey Bill was covering up for the bad cops on his narcotic squad and interfering in federal cases in Mexico.

After several failed attempts at mediation by state and federal officials, the impasse ended when Harry Anslinger refused to transfer Chappell, and LA Mayor William Paulson forced Chief Parker to accept a shaky truce. It was a victory for Chappell, but there was a downside too, for by demonstrating his bureaucratic courage and leadership abilities, Chappell had frightened Anslinger's heir apparent, Henry Giordano, at FBN headquarters. In addition, Los Angeles had begun to rival New York as the nation's premier city – all of which meant that Chappell had become a contender in the race to succeed Anslinger and thus a threat to Giordano and his new ally, George Gaffney, who in January 1958 became New York's district supervisor, the most important job in the Bureau.

THE ASCENT OF GEORGE GAFFNEY

Propelled by his successes as an investigator and his membership in the Jim Ryan clique in New York, Gaffney in 1956 was named district supervisor in Atlanta, with jurisdiction over Miami and the Caribbean. Although he was the youngest district supervisor in the FBN, Gaffney did well in Atlanta, and won the admiration of Mal Harney. A native of Minnesota, Harney, who had no children of his own, took a fatherly interest in Michigan-born Gaffney, with whom he felt a certain affinity. They shared the same conservative Republican politics, and Harney admired Gaffney's toughness; he once remarked to him that "you must have some iron ore in your veins." So when Jim Ryan retired from the FBN in 1957, due to serious injuries suffered in a car accident, Harney recommended Gaffney as Ryan's replacement as district supervisor in New York. Also fond of Gaffney – he referred to him as "Gaffioni" in private correspondences – Anslinger agreed, and in doing so, ushered in the FBN's most successful and controversial era.

Howard Chappell describes high-strung, diminutive George Gaffney as "energetic, opportunistic, and not overly modest," all of which is true. But giving the devil his due, Gaffney had reason to be proud. He was street-smart, a strong manager, and able to make complex conspiracy cases. As to being energetic, that's a vast understatement: driven is a much better word. During his four and a half years as district supervisor in New York, Gaffney set the highest standard of performance for his agents, and under his leadership the FBN would make landmark cases on four of the Mafia's five fallen families, as well as two spectacular French connection cases.

One factor in Gaffney's success was his policy of maintaining good relations with the NYPD's narcotic squad, whose detectives (unlike FBN agents) could legally install wiretaps without court approval and kick in doors on mere suspicion of wrongdoing. He also credits the Daniel Act as contributing to his success. "Until mandatory sentencing came along," he explains, "it was impossible to get an informant inside the upper echelons of the Mafia. But once the judges started handing out forty-year prison sentences, we got the leverage we needed. No one wanted to do that much time."

Three other timely developments helped Gaffney and the New York office wage the FBN's most successful campaign ever. The first was Albert Anastasia's suicidal attempt to muscle in on the Cuban rackets. As boss of the old Mangano family, Anastasia controlled various labor union, gambling, and narcotics rackets in Brooklyn, New Jersey, and Las Vegas. He was powerful, yes, but he was a vicious megalomaniac too, and he not only took on Meyer Lansky and Santo Trafficante in Cuba, he mistakenly challenged the Commission itself, which was dominated by Vito Genovese and the closely allied Bonanno, Profaci, and Magaddino families.

Anastasia's downfall began in April 1957, when Italian drug smuggler and part-time FBN informant Giovanni Mauceri told Charlie Siragusa that a heroin shipment was being delivered to Frank Scalici in New York aboard a merchant ship from Marseilles. Something of a mystery – his fingerprints and criminal records have been removed from the files of all US government agencies – Scalici managed a Mafia narcotics syndicate based in the Bronx that dealt directly with French and Corsican wholesalers in Europe and Montreal.[2] Unfortunately for Scalici, Siragusa was able to seize his heroin, as well as the Mafia money he'd fronted to Mauceri, which left Scalici holding a big empty bag. Anastasia, having kicked in some of the money for the purchase, concluded that Scalici had betrayed him, and on 17 June 1957, at Anastasia's behest, Vincent Squillante shot and killed Scalici in front of a grocery store in the Bronx, as portrayed in the movie *The Godfather*.

Anastasia, however, was not the only person who had invested in Scalici. Vito Genovese, Carlo Gambino, and Meyer Lansky had fronted money too, and murdering Scalici without their consent was a serious mistake – as was Anastasia's unauthorized sale of Mafia memberships, which he was doing to increase the size of his private army. But his fatal mistake was trying to muscle in on Lansky and Trafficante's lucrative Cuban connection. Lansky and Trafficante brought their problem to Vito Genovese, their closest associate in New York, and Genovese in turn persuaded Anastasia's *caporegime*, Carlo Gambino, to betray his boss. A few days later, on 25 October 1957, Trafficante arrived in New York with Genovese's *consigliere*, Mike Miranda, and they made Anastasia an offer he should not have refused. An hour later, Anastasia was shot and killed, while getting a shave, by Profaci family gunmen Larry and Joey Gallo.

Anastasia's assassination sent shockwaves through the underworld and prompted the Mafia Commission to schedule a Palermo-style summit that November in Apalachin, New York, at the estate of Joseph Barbara, a wealthy member of the Stefano Magaddino family in Buffalo. Insiders say this college of blood-soaked cardinals was being convened to anoint Vito Genovese as the Mafia's new boss of bosses and Carlo Gambino as the new boss of the Mangano family. Two other items reportedly on the agenda were 1) how much support to give to Fidel Castro in Cuba, and 2) whether or not to target certain FBN agents for death. But all that is speculation and the summit, as we shall see, never occurred.

The second timely development in Gaffney's ascent was Robert Kennedy's appointment as chief counsel for the Senate's Permanent Subcommittee on Investigations. While serving in that position, Bobby and his staff assistant, retired FBI financial investigator Carmine Bellino, launched an investigation of Teamster boss Dave Beck. In 1957 the investigation was transferred to Senator John McClellan's Select Committee on Improper Activities in Labor and Management, and Bobby's nascent war on crime gathered steam. He became the McClellan Committee's chief counsel and, with Bellino's help, acquired the evidence that enabled a court to convict Beck of embezzling $320,000 in Teamster funds. Tenacious Bobby Kennedy then took aim at Beck's swaggering successor, James R. Hoffa.[3]

In his quest to learn as much as possible about Hoffa and the Teamster's link to organized crime, Bobby Kennedy came to rely on the FBN – and in particular, George Gaffney. Through the Irish Catholic network, Bobby was persuaded to ask Anslinger for copies of the Mafia Book and FBN case files, and after reading them and talking to Gaffney, Bobby came to realize that the FBN knew more about the Mafia than the FBI. The FBN had solid evidence that Hoffa was beholden to the mob, and that certain Teamster "paper locals" (with no membership), like the one run by Johnny Dioguardia in New York, were providing logistical support to the Mafia's national drug-distribution syndicate.[4]

With Bobby Kennedy as his new rabbi, Gaffney would acquire powerful new contacts at the highest levels of government and, in 1962, would be promoted, as a direct result, to the number three enforcement assistant position at FBN headquarters.

The third timely development in Gaffney's ascent happened on 14 November 1957, when State Trooper Edgar Croswell spied an armada of black limousines – all packed with mean-looking men wearing wide-brimmed black hats – berthing at Joseph Barbara's estate in rural Apalachin, New York. By most accounts, Croswell recognized Carmine Galante in one of the cars and instantly realized that he had stumbled upon a Mafia convention. In fact, he'd been alerted by the FBN agents who had Palermo summit attendee Philip Buccola under surveillance. Fully aware of what was afoot, Croswell and his fellow Troopers set up roadblocks around Barbara's estate and began stopping and searching cars. Taken by surprise, some fifty immaculately dressed Mafiosi panicked and, stepping out of character, tried to escape by scampering through the surrounding forests. Almost all were quickly captured. A trooper on the scene, Robert Furey, vividly recalls the bosses of the five New York families – Thomas Lucchese, Joseph Profaci, Carlo Gambino, Joseph Bonanno, and Vito Genovese, as well as Santo Trafficante and dozens of other delegates arrested that day – sitting on the floor of the Vestal substation in mud-caked overcoats covered with brambles, with their manicured hands on their neatly trimmed heads, and scowls on their sullen faces.

The indignity of the Apalachin debacle was so deep that many young hoods lost all respect for their Mafia bosses. Equally important, the Apalachin debacle provided Robert Kennedy with the pretext he needed to wage a national war on crime. And it provided the FBN with its biggest coup since the Kefauver Hearings. In the months following Apalachin, several agents would address the Senate about the relationship between drug smugglers and organized crime. International Group Leader Marty Pera told how opium was moved from Turkey to Syria, where it was processed into morphine base, then shipped to France and converted into heroin, and then smuggled through Mexico, Cuba and Canada to America. Veteran Agent Joe Amato explained how Vincent Squillante and Joe Mancuso were the kingpins of a secret society "specifically" organized for smuggling narcotics.[5] And Jack Cusack, then serving as Gaffney's replacement as district supervisor in Atlanta, described the link, through John Ormento, between the Civello family in Dallas and the Magaddino family in Buffalo. Cusack linked the Civellos with Carlos Marcello in New Orleans, Santo Trafficante in Tampa, and, remarkably, with Jimmy Hoffa and gunrunning to Cuba.[6] There was evidence backing the charges, and in January 1958 the FBN conducted raids on Mafia drug rings in New York, Pennsylvania, and Virginia. The Virginia raid alone netted ten kilograms of heroin and led to the arrest of Frank Coppola in Italy.

Could the Mafia's patrons in the espionage Establishment have played a role in setting the stage for these events? Perhaps. Only the CIA had the power to remove Scalici's records from every government file, and providing the Commission with a reason to eliminate Anastasia served to strengthen the position of the drug smugglers the CIA relied upon most – Lansky and Trafficante in Cuba. The FBN raids in January 1958 were a temporary setback, and Lansky and Trafficante knew that better days lay ahead in Cuba. That scenario, of course, is speculation, although the CIA, through Hank Manfredi, certainly knew about the Apalachin summit before it happened; and sabotaging the summit would have served the CIA, perhaps most importantly, by providing it with a means of severing its contract with Vito Genovese, its major Luciano Project liability.

DECONSTRUCTING GENOVESE

Bolstered by Apalachin and Bobby Kennedy's ascent, George Gaffney arrived in New York in January 1958 with a simple strategy. "We didn't have specific targets," he explains. "There was no purpose following Joe Profaci around town. What we did was develop the informants we had in place. We picked targets based on the best information, and that's where we began."

Gaffney's first target of opportunity was Vito Genovese, former special employee of Army Intelligence, now Mafia boss of bosses. The case against Genovese began serendipitously when Agent Anthony Consoli arrested an ordinary drug addict, and the addict revealed that his supplier was Nelson Cantellops, a Puerto Rican and, curiously, an erstwhile Communist. Agent Steve Giorgio made two buys off Cantellops, who, with very little arm-twisting, flipped and turned out to be anything but ordinary. By his own account, Cantellops since 1954 had been running heroin and cocaine from Cuba to Las Vegas, Miami, and El Paso for Joey DiPalermo of the Lucchese family. He was so successful in this venture that in 1956, in an extraordinary breach of Mafia protocol, DiPalermo introduced him to John Ormento and Carmine Galante, co-managers of the Mafia's national drug syndicate, and they asked him to start an operation out of Puerto Rico. According to Cantellops, Vito Genovese personally blessed the deal. Knowing he was on to something big, Gaffney assigned the case to John R. Enright, a veteran agent who had replaced Jack Cusack as head of the Court House Squad. Married to a girl friend of George Gaffney's sister, Enright worked under the direction of William "Tendy" Tendesky, the Assistant US Attorney in charge of the narcotics "Junk Squad" in the Southern District of New York.

"We were determined to prepare an airtight case," Enright says, "and I remember the excitement I felt when Tendy came out of his interview with Cantellops and said, 'We're going to indict Vito Genovese!' Right away I called headquarters, and they said, 'Challenge Cantellops!' Which we did. But we couldn't shake him. So Genovese was indicted on July 8, 1959. John Ormento and Carmine Galante too."

According to Agent Tom Tripodi, it wasn't quite that simple. Tendy wanted corroboration, so Cantellops agreed to meet with Genovese under FBN surveillance. In another extraordinary breach of Mafia protocol, the syphilitic Puerto Rican was brought before the Mafia boss of bosses in a German restaurant, where Genovese allegedly acknowledged that Cantellops was "all right."[7] Tripodi also claims that FBN agents Francis E. Waters and James Hunt overheard his words while seated at the bar, and that the Genovese indictment was based on their corroborating testimony.

When approached by the author, Hunt was unavailable for comment, and Waters claimed not to recall the incident. Not exactly, that is. Waters did say, "I was a rookie agent at the time, and I probably would have said it, if asked to."

Genovese was arrested on 7 July 1958, and – along with Carmine Galante, John Ormento, and thirty-four major Mafia drug traffickers – was charged with trafficking in more than 160 kilograms of heroin since 1954. One day later US Attorney Paul Williams announced his candidacy for governor of New York. The arrest was that big.[8]

MYLES AMBROSE AND THE SPECIAL GROUP

Vito Genovese's problems were compounded by two related developments that occurred outside the FBN. The first was the appointment of Myles J. Ambrose as the Treasury Department's law enforcement coordinator. The son of a prominent Republican Wall Street broker, Ambrose had served as Devenco's personnel director from 1948 to 1953. If the reader will recall, Devenco was the CIA firm that helped Marty Pera build several electronic devices that enhanced the FBN's case-making ability, and possibly outfitted George White's MKULTRA pad in Greenwich Village.

After receiving his law degree, Ambrose served as an Assistant US Attorney in New York's Southern District, often prosecuting drug cases made by FBN agents. This hands-on experience, plus his charismatic personality and his CIA-related work at Devenco, had prepared him, though he was only thirty-one years old, for one of the most important jobs in federal law enforcement.

Ambrose replaced John Lathem as chief coordinator in July 1957. His boss was assistant secretary of Treasury David Kendall. "While I was preparing for the job," Ambrose recalls, "I met with Mal Harney, who gave the history of the job, with an emphasis on the importance of IRS Intelligence. Lathem was helpful too. John had come from IRS Intelligence, and during his tenure as acting chief coordinator he had expanded the Law Enforcement Officer Training School under director Pat O'Carroll, an FBN agent I'd known in New York. Fred Douglas, incidentally, continued to serve admirably as my assistant and liaison to Interpol.

"My job," Ambrose continues, "was to coordinate the investigative activities, oversee the budgets, and referee disputes between the Bureau of Alcohol Tobacco Tax, the Coast Guard, the customs service, the Secret Service, the IRS Intelligence and Inspections Units, and the Bureau of Narcotics. I also tried to establish a local coordinator in each of the six districts around the country, and explain to these guys that their enemy was the FBI, not each other."

Ambrose cites, as an example of his intimate involvement with FBN affairs, a dispute in Texas in which District Supervisor Ernie Gentry accused Customs Agent Dave Ellis of obstructing FBN cases through the use of convoys. Ambrose went to Texas, reviewed the case, and advised that Gentry be reassigned. But Anslinger, ever protective of his agents, interceded on Gentry's behalf, and Ellis was transferred to New York instead.

"Anslinger was like the Pope," Ambrose says with awe. "When he spoke, it was *ex cathedra*. Everyone knew he was a tough in-fighter who had outfoxed Hoover for years, and I wasn't about to tangle with him. The biggest hassle I had was with Fred Scribner, the under secretary over the IRS. IRS Intelligence had about 1,400 agents, and Scribner only wanted to use them to pursue tax evasion cases, not for organized crime law enforcement.

"Well," Ambrose states matter-of-factly, "Apalachin changed that. The ATT and FBN were already involved, but I wanted IRS Intelligence in it too. So I went to Scribner and he agreed to open a file on every Apalachin attendee. After that, IRS agents started furnishing monthly reports to me and the evidence started piling up. Then William Rogers became Attorney General and in April 1958 he assigned anti-trust lawyer Milton Wessel to start a Special Group with several sub-groups around the country. And I became Treasury's liaison to Wessel at the Justice Department."

The formation of the Special Group to prosecute the Apalachin alumni was the second development that put pressure on Vito Genovese. But there was a hitch: the Apalachin scandal had forced the FBI to join the investigation, and that spelled trouble for the FBN. As Gaffney recalls, "No less than a dozen FBI agents rummaged through our files at 90 Church Street trying to find out who the arrestees were, and two were still there when I took over the New York office on the first working day in 1958."

Gaffney assigned Thomas J. Dugan as his representative to Wessel's Group. A veteran agent, "Old Tom" brought a vast knowledge of the Mafia to the investigation. Also assigned were agents William Rowan, Jack Gohde, Armando Muglia, Norman Matuozzi, and Norris "Norey" Durham; John Enright at the Court House Squad; overseas Mafia experts Hank Manfredi and Charlie Siragusa; and FBN informants Orlando Portale and Roger Coudert.[9]

The Special Group's purpose was to build a conspiracy case against 387 Mafiosi nationwide, but for budgetary reasons the investigation focused on the seventy-two Apalachin alumni, of whom only twenty-seven were indicted. On a single day in May 1959, FBN agents in Dallas, Cleveland,

Tucson, Los Angeles, Miami, Boston, and New York arrested twenty-one of the suspects. Two later surrendered, four remained at large, and in October 1959, twenty-three Mafia bosses, including Vito Genovese, were brought to trial in New York. All were found guilty of conspiracy in November.

Although an Appellate Court overturned the verdict, the Apalachin conspiracy case kept Genovese scrambling while Gaffney's case-makers groomed Nelson Cantellops for his courtroom appearance; and based on his testimony, Genovese and fourteen accomplices were convicted in April 1959 of conspiring to smuggle heroin from Cuba, Mexico, and Puerto Rico. Charged and convicted, but not present for the trial, were fugitives Carmine Galante and John Ormento.

Not since Lucky Luciano's downfall in 1936 had a gangster of Vito Genovese's status been convicted of such a serious crime – but there was more to come. In March 1959, Marty Pera and Jim Hunt captured John Ormento at gunpoint in his apartment; and in June 1959, Pera and Agent Bill Rowan, with the help of the New Jersey State Police, captured Carmine Galante after he was betrayed by Sal Giglio, his trusted representative to the Corsicans in Cuba.

Exactly why Giglio betrayed Galante is a story worth telling, as it reveals how intimately involved FBN agents often were with drug smuggling Mafiosi. Through NYPD detective Tommy O'Brien, Marty Pera placed a wiretap on Galante's *consigliere*, Joe Notaro, and through the wire Pera located Giglio. Meanwhile, agents Anthony Mangiaracina and Bill Rowan found, in a Canadian newspaper, a photograph of Giglio getting married to Florence Anderson, a waitress at the El Morocco Casino in Cuba, on 22 March 1957. A few weeks later, Pera appeared at Giglio's house in Queens, and while the gangster's original wife, Mary, was in the kitchen cooking pasta, Pera sat in the living room and presented Giglio with the incriminating photo. In exchange for a pledge that Mary would not be told about Florence, Giglio revealed Galante's location, before returning to Cuba to resume his drug-smuggling enterprises.

AGENT LENNY SCHRIER AND THE ORLANDINO CASE

Within two years of taking on what Anslinger called "the toughest job in the Bureau," Gaffney had done the incredible; he'd made cases on Genovese, Ormento, Galante, and other ranking members of the five families. This was an achievement upon which a typical district supervisor would have coasted for the rest of his career. But not Gangbuster Gaffney. He forged ahead like a man possessed and, in 1959, under the guidance of his mentor Pat Ward, he artfully orchestrated the sensational Giuseppe "Pepe" Cotroni Conspiracy case in Montreal.

The younger brother of Vincent and Frank, Pepe managed the family's narcotics business in league with Carmine Galante, his American Mafia contact in New York, and Lucian Rivard, his French connection in Montreal. In 1956, at Galante's insistence, Rivard relocated to Havana, where he joined Paul Mondoloni and Jean Croce in the operation of several nightclubs, through which they moved narcotics at a cost of approximately $20,000 a week to Batista. The Corsicans in Cuba had a steady source of supply and, at a meeting with Croce in Paris in 1957, Pepe agreed to buy heroin from Mondoloni's associates in France, Jean and Dominick Venturi. By the year's end, Pepe and Galante, whose trucking company did business in Montreal, were supplying the five biggest Italian wholesalers in New York (including Angelo Tuminaro and Anthony DiPasqua, about whom much more remains to be said) with fifty kilograms of heroin a month.[10]

New York District Supervisor George Gaffney was aware of Pepe's operation, but making a case against him in Canada depended on the co-operation of the Royal Canadian Mounted Police (RCMP) and the ability of courageous undercover Agent Patrick Biase to make a buy directly from him. That challenge was hard enough, but Gaffney was ambitious and wanted to expand the case into a conspiracy that enveloped Pepe's Mafia customers in New York as well. How that was done was complicated, and requires the introduction of a number of individuals in a very short space. It also requires a profile of Lenny Schrier, one of the most significant agents in FBN history. And it needs an examination of the Orlandino case, which Schrier made in New York in 1959.

Two aspects of the Orlandino case have special significance. To begin with, it did not rely upon the testimony of a dubious informer like Nelson Cantellops, but upon seized heroin that was placed on a courtroom table for a jury to see. Secondly, Gaffney's management of the case contributed to the internecine strife that brought the FBN to its knees. At the center of this tragic tale is Lenny Schrier. Tall, intelligent, and engaging, Schrier was born in Brooklyn, trained as an accountant, and seeking excitement, joined the FBN in 1951. Considered the best case-maker ever by many of his colleagues, he began to shine in the summer of 1956. Schrier remembers it well, because The Platters had just released their fabulous song, *The Great Pretender*. That summer, Schrier and undercover Agent Marshall Latta arrested Tony and Rocky Flamio for delivering heroin to Schrier's best informant, Cleveland Lockwood.

"We took them down to 90 Church," Schrier explains, "and split them up. Rocky was a furniture stripper with a couple of kids and a nice wife. This was a one-time favor for his brother Tony, and he was feeling suicidal. So he flipped. And to work off the bust, Rocky started making introductions to Tony's customers, and that's when things really start to pop. We got Rocky a second-hand car and brought in Tony Grapes [Anthony Mangiaracina] to do the undercover work. And we made cases for two years! We were making so many cases we needed help, so they gave us Steve Giorgio, a very smooth guy who made two buys from Sammy 'the Jew' Manis. That's Sam Monastersky, who took us to Marcantonio Orlandino – one of Pepe Cotroni's customers.

"This," Schrier says, "is the big time. Unfortunately, Grapes had been making cases for two years straight and he wanted a transfer to Rome. But as the undercover agent who'd made the buys, he had to testify in court before he could go. So Gaffney ordered me to wrap things up. He said to me, 'Schrier, I want these cases wrapped up, or your ass is mud.' Then he walked away."

Schrier repeats the word mud, then continues. "I sat at my desk until I calmed down, then I went to the front office and asked Gaffney for a little more time to make this last part of the case on Sammy the Jew. I told him that Rocky was essential to the case, and that I needed time to make arrangements for him. He wouldn't have to testify because he'd only made the introductions, but we were going to have to pay him something so he could move his family out of New York. I had to argue for everything, but finally Gaffney said I could have the money for Rocky's expenses, and the time I needed to make Sammy Manis and Richie McGovern – which is the key to Orlandino.

"So Rocky takes Giorgio to Sammy Manis. Sammy didn't have his hands on the junk, but he did the negotiating at a bar where he and Richie McGovern hung out. And when it was time for the delivery, Manis took Giorgio to an apartment in Midtown where they met Richie, who, by the way, was a real maverick. His body was covered with tattoos. Richie told Giorgio that the junk wasn't there, but that it was being delivered. Meanwhile, Grapes was waiting downstairs with the buy money, and me and Jimmy Doyle were watching from a car outside. Another car pulls up and we see William Struzzeri get out and take the junk up to the apartment. The guy driving the car is looking around, so I pull alongside. Doyle rolls down the window and asks, 'You pulling out?' That way we get a good look at the driver. It's Marcantonio Orlandino. He's out on parole, and he doesn't know McGovern, and he doesn't trust Struzzeri, so he went along to protect his money.

"That first buy was two half-kilogram packages from Manis and McGovern. We saw the people bring it in, we followed them to Orlandino's house in Levittown, and then we set up another buy for three more kilograms. After the second buy, we followed Struzzeri back to the plant at Phil Orlandino's place in Flushing. Phil was Marcantonio's brother. Of course we wanted to know where Orlandino got his junk, so we put a tap on Phil's phone.

"Gaffney, meanwhile, is huddling with Marty Pera. It's all very *hush hush*," Schrier says facetiously. "The junk is coming out of Canada from the Cotronis, and the guys behind Orlandino are Angelo Tuminaro and Anthony DiPasqua. But somehow Bayonne Joe Zicarelli in New Jersey is involved too. Johnny Dolce and Patty Biase are working the Cotroni case, and Pera's got three or four guys on Bayonne Joe – they got radar in the sky following his car. I'm not supposed to know that, or that Dolce and Biase have an informant, Eddie Smith, into Cotroni, or that they're going to use *my junk* to tie everyone else into him. They're going to use Eddie Smith for information, but without *my narcotics* they haven't got a conspiracy in New York.

"Now it's time for the roundup," Schrier says, "and the whole office is involved. We had buys on thirty Italians in East Harlem, plus Ralph Wagner and Herbie Sperling – both of whom delivered junk for Joe Valachi. It was a Saturday night [14 February 1959]. We had a combat photographer with us from one of the newspapers. All the dignitaries from City Hall were at the St. George Hotel, waiting with Gaffney. So we round up all these kids, then finish up at Phil Orlandino's house. There's ten kilograms of pure heroin at the plant in Flushing, and we find a gym bag with $50,000, which nobody claimed."[11]

Schrier smiles, then gets serious. "Orlandino blamed Richie McGovern, who fled to Mexico with Ralph Wagner. McGovern wasn't an informant, but in April they found his body in a ditch outside Acapulco. His face was so badly mutilated, the only way they knew it was him was by the tattoos."

To Lenny Schrier's credit, the Orlandino case enabled federal prosecutors to make a conspiracy case in New York on Canadian Pepe Cotroni and twenty-eight American co-defendants. As noted, Cotroni supplied five major wholesalers in New York, including Angelo Tuminaro and Anthony DiPasqua. But the Cotroni case was so spectacular that it eclipsed Schrier's accomplishment. Adding insult to injury, the Cotroni case was made by

Gaffney's mentor and enforcement assistant Pat Ward, and Ward's protégés in Group Three, agents John M. Dolce and Patrick J. Biase. Smart and sophisticated, Dolce lived in Bethpage, as did Ward and Biase. Biase, a former CID agent who had investigated drug cases in Korea, was a ladies' man and racetrack gambler who broke all the rules and exasperated his bosses.

After the Cotroni and Orlandino cases, the New York office would fracture along a fault line, with the supporters of Schrier on one side, and those of Ward, Dolce, and Biase on the other.

THE COTRONI CASE

The case on Pepe Cotroni began in April 1958, when one of Pat Ward's informers revealed that the aforementioned Eddie Smith was Cotroni's courier. After several months of observing Smith's activities, Ward and the agents he assigned to the case – Johnny Dolce and Patty Biase – planted a homing device in Smith's car (a black Lincoln with a white top and a blue and pink interior) with the intention of catching him red-handed with a load of heroin at the tollbooths on the Tappan Zee Bridge. But when they stopped and searched the car, the person they found inside was diamond merchant Ben Sachs. As the FBN agents soon learned, handsome Eddie Smith was engaged to Sachs's daughter. Sachs, of course, was aghast to discover his future son-in-law's occupation, and he prevailed upon him to become an FBN informant. And under Ward's guidance, Eddie Smith 'cut' (in FBN jargon) daring undercover Agent Patty Biase, posing as Jack Farraco (the fictitious brother of Mafioso George Farraco), into Pepe Cotroni.[12]

Covered by his close friends Pat Ward and John Dolce, as well as a contingent from the RCMP's narcotic squad, Biase in June 1959 twice purchased two kilograms of heroin from Pepe in Montreal. Those buys led to Pepe's arrest on 8 July on the charge of conspiracy to sell $8 million worth of narcotics. Pepe was tried and convicted in Montreal that October. Subsequently, federal prosecutors charged twenty-eight co-defendants in the Southern District of New York, including Angelo Tuminaro, Anthony DiPasqua, Carmine Galante, Sal Giglio, John Ormento, and the Mafia's courier to Texas, Benny Indiviglio. Alas, the trial turned into a three-ring circus: the defense attorneys objected to every witness statement; there were charges of jury tampering; the jury foreman was hurt in a freak accident; and Pepe's mistress recanted her testimony. And even though everyone was convicted, Giglio, Tuminaro, DiPasqua, and Indiviglio were released on bond and became fugitives. All of which, in conjunction with the collapse of the Apalachin case, underscored how much more federal prosecutors had to learn about making major drug conspiracy cases.[13]

Nor did the drug trafficking out of Montreal abate with Pepe's demise; his former contact Lucien Rivard returned from Cuba and, with Paul Mondoloni, revived the Canadian facet of the French connection. Rivard was well placed in this regard: he and Mondoloni were co-owners of the El Morocco club in Cuba with Norman Rothman, a close associate of Meyer Lansky and Santo Trafficante.[14]

As Paul Knight in Beirut and other FBN agents were aware, Mondoloni's Corsican partners, Jean Croce and Dominique Nicoli, were in Cuba in early 1958, waiting while their chemist, Dom Albertini, negotiated a morphine base deal with Sami Khoury. Knight wanted to let the Corsicans move freely in Cuba to see which American mobsters they contacted, but Batista's Secret Police – perhaps at the request of a foreign intelligence service – arrested Croce and Nicoli on 13 March 1958 and deported them to France, nipping the FBN investigation in the bud.[15]

Not much had changed eight months later. In a 24 November 1958 memo to Anslinger, Atlanta District Supervisor Jack Cusack, the agent with jurisdiction over Cuba, reported that every three to six months, Mondoloni sold between 50 to 150 kilograms of heroin to Rothman and "almost all important Italian–American suspects visiting Havana." Cusack said that Mondoloni's operation in Cuba, which had begun in 1955 with Norman Rothman and Trafficante, "poses a most serious threat to the suppression of the illicit heroin traffic at the present time."[16]

While Mondoloni's operation proceeded apace, Rothman and former Cuban president Carlos Prio Socarras were indicted for arms trafficking to Castro.[17] And Rothman and Salvatore Mannarino, a Pittsburgh Mafia boss (and co-owner with Trafficante of the Sans Souci club in Cuba), were indicted with Pepe Cotroni for receiving stolen bonds from a 1958 bank robbery in Canada.[18] But the bonds were being used to pay for Castro's guns, so the CIA had the gangsters set free. According to historian Peter Dale Scott, "In 1978, Rothman told a CBS television interviewer that he had avoided conviction because of the CIA's interest in his gunrunning activities."[19]

FALLOUT

By early 1959, with Castro in power and Cuba no longer a friendly base for American drug lords, French and Corsican suppliers began to make deliveries directly to New York. This development would bring the FBN's New York office into the next and most famous French connection phase of its four-year winning streak under George Gaffney.

This development occurred simultaneously with a decision, resulting from the Genovese and Apalachin cases, by the Mafia Commission to protect itself by prohibiting its made members from directly trafficking in narcotics; at which point a new legion of unfamiliar faces from Sicily appeared on the scene, adding new complications to the arcane narcotics trafficking situation.

For Gaffney, the FBN's winning streak was a mixed blessing. It would secure forever his reputation as the FBN's greatest district supervisor; but his successes engendered a sense of infallibility which hampered his judgment.

In utter exasperation Lenny Schrier says, "For two years, Lee Bennett and I made 50 percent of the cases, and 50 percent of the seizures in New York, by ourselves. So when Angelo Zurlo was transferred to Washington in June 1959, everyone knew I should get Group Three. But Dolce got it instead." Schrier scowls. "Dolce didn't deserve the promotion, and the only reason he got it was because he was *in* with Ward and Gaffney."

As the New York office descended into bitter internecine warfare, Henry Giordano further subverted agent morale by initiating an integrity case against revered undercover Agent Tony Zirilli.

"They'd sent him to Baltimore to work a gypsy wire, and he came back tired and disgusted," Tony Mangiaracina recalls. "Then they sent him down to New Orleans. An agent down there supposedly had an informant who was willing to tie him into a dealer. So Tony goes down and meets the agent, Jack Frost, the informant, and Tom Dean, another agent from Texas. Frost and Dean introduce Tony to a third agent from New Orleans, Fred Young, who was posing as a bartender. The three of them kept track of Tony's drinks, and when he wrote up his report, they nailed him. Tony's unforgivable sin was having spent ten bucks on booze one night, then reporting that he'd spent five dollars two nights in a row, so as not to appear to be a boozer."

Mangiaracina sighs. "The Bureau was so small. There were only five groups in New York, so you had to knock the other guy out of the box to get a promotion. But what goes around comes around. Frost left under a cloud a few years later, Dean was forced to take a job with Customs, and Young, the agent in charge in New Orleans, was arrested by the police on a morals charge, then fired.

"Giordano set the whole Zirilli thing up," he adds bitterly. "Then Giordano had the nerve to tell Tony that he'd forget the whole thing if he'd apologize. Tony had a wife and a couple of kids, but he didn't take crap from anybody, least of all a punk like Giordano. Tony had worked inside the Bonanno family and had made some of the biggest cases overseas. So he quit. He told me he'd lost the wanderlust."

According to Howard Chappell, Zirilli was set up because he had gotten close to Carlos Marcello in New Orleans, through Marcello's girlfriend. Chappell claims that Gentry, the district supervisor over New Orleans, "set him up on purpose to protect Marcello."

Whatever the cause of Zirilli's fall from grace, it had a ripple effect, and by 1959 the FBN's premier case-making agents were looking over their shoulders for shooflies, as the power struggle to replace Harry Anslinger turned lethal.

13

ANGLOPHILES AND FRANCOPHOBES

"You could always count on the French to be difficult."

Agent Paul Knight

With the death of Deputy Commissioner George Cunningham in October 1958, the political positioning to replace Harry Anslinger took a new twist. Henry Giordano was named Deputy Commissioner as a way of rewarding Congressman Hale Boggs for his years of support, and Lee Speer was appointed enforcement assistant as a way of appeasing both Sam Rayburn, the powerful Speaker of the House, and former Senator Price Daniel. Summoned back from the far reaches of the globe to find the number two and three headquarters positions already filled, Charlie Siragusa got what was left; a quick fling as field supervisor, then the number four post as deputy assistant for administration.

Finding himself low man on the totem pole was a big blow for proud Charlie Siragusa. He had made over one hundred cases in over a dozen nations since 1950, and had accomplished far more than Giordano and Speer combined. But now, as field supervisor, and in other non-enforcement roles, such as updating the Mafia Book, he was taking orders from his inferiors. According to agents on the scene, the tension between Siragusa, Speer, and Giordano was visceral, and negatively affected how the FBN was managed.

The reorganization spelled trouble in District 17 too, where Ralph Frias had come to despise Paul Knight. He blamed Knight for the beating Jim Attie received from Lebanese security chief Haj Touma, and he resented

Knight for giving him the majority of the dangerous undercover assignments, while, in his opinion, Knight sat in his office, writing reports and taking all the credit. "At a meeting in Rome, Paul said he was too well known to do undercover work," Andy Tartaglino recalls. "To which Ralph sarcastically replied: 'Well, Paul, you *do* let everybody know.'"

Another personality clash had developed as well. While inspecting the Beirut office, Tartaglino had opened the safe and found "gossipy" letters from Siragusa. Some belittled him and Frias, others advised Knight to keep them away from the press "if," Siragusa had written, "we're going to get anywhere." Each letter closed with the words "Burn this letter." Angry at the content of the letters, and the fact that Knight hadn't burned them, Tartaglino confronted Siragusa in Rome. When faced with his own duplicity, Siragusa chose to blame Knight rather than himself. He forced Knight to destroy the letters in his presence and, upon his return to Washington in 1958, he named Tartaglino, not Knight, as the acting district supervisor in Rome. Tartaglino held the position until Giordano's nominee, Jack Cusack, arrived in early 1959. Having been unfairly upbraided and passed over for a position he deserved, Knight decided to seek employment with the CIA.[1]

A CHANGING OF THE GUARD

Tensions in Rome were further heightened by the arrival of Sal Vizzini. Audacious and smooth as silk, Vizzini had served as an Air Force investigator prior to joining the FBN in Atlanta in 1953. Two years later he was transferred to New York and inducted into the ruling Ward–Gaffney–Dolce clique. Vizzini made several important undercover cases and in 1956 was sent to Miami to work in Cuba under the direction of Atlanta District Supervisor George Gaffney, and later under Gaffney's replacement, Jack Cusack.

Vizzini's exceptional undercover skills were highly prized by Anslinger, Cusack, and Gaffney, but his arrival in Rome was not universally welcomed. Tall, dark, and handsome – and a swashbuckling ladies' man – Vizzini stood in stark contrast to diminutive Andy Tartaglino, his temperamental nemesis. Tartaglino had formed an abiding animosity for Vizzini in 1955, when Vizzini stole the important Vellucci–Berhman case from him. Tartaglino had done all of the thankless preliminary work, but Vizzini had made the arrest and gotten credit for the bust. For freewheeling Sal it was part of the game, but for high-strung Andy it was an unforgivable sin. It didn't help that Vizzini was part of a clique that was contending with his mentor,

Charlie Siragusa, or that Cusack had brought Vizzini to Rome specifically to replace Tartaglino's close friend Ralph Frias. Frias had performed the lion's share of District 17's undercover work for the past two years, but had lost his enthusiasm for the job when his son died at birth in Rome; and rather than accept a transfer to unfamiliar and, by reputation, unhealthy New York, Frias resigned from the FBN in December 1958 and, broken-hearted, returned to California.

Eager to set the world on fire, Vizzini began to do what no agent had done before: penetrate a faction of Lucky Luciano's inner circle which was managing a clandestine heroin conversion laboratory in Sicily. The FBN wanted to smash the operation, so an introduction was arranged and, posing as a corrupt Air Force pilot, Vizzini used his considerable charms to seduce the FBN's *bête noire*. He tells how he did this in his autobiography, but omits three important details that he wasn't permitted to tell at the time: 1) that he was introduced to Luciano by one of Hank Manfredi's CIA assets; 2) that he reported to Manfredi, not District Supervisor Jack Cusack, on the case; and 3) that copies of his reports about Luciano went to Bobby Kennedy.

Despite Vizzini's threadbare cover, Luciano accepted him on the word of Manfredi's asset. As improbable as it may seem, Luciano's skeptical associates also came to accept Vizzini, and they eventually got him a job as an assistant to Mafia chemist Joe Mancuso in a heroin conversion lab in Sicily. Over the course of a few harrowing weeks, Vizzini worked closely with a backup squad of Italian police to engineer Mancuso's arrest. The case led to the arrest of Luciano lieutenant Joe Pici, and several Corsicans in Marseilles. Although he wasn't able to implicate Luciano in the conspiracy, Vizzini's success in smashing the Sicilian heroin ring so enhanced his reputation that, in late 1959, Anslinger gave him the honor of opening the FBN's first office in Istanbul.[2]

Meanwhile, having finished testifying in the Orlandino case in New York, Tony Mangiaracina was rewarded with the transfer he desired, and arrived in Rome. Affable and easy-going, but resolute, his primary mission was to work on Italians wherever they were – Germany, Sicily, France, Beirut – but he did special jobs as well. His big problem was adjusting to Jack Cusack's hypercritical, micro-management style, which often reduced the four office secretaries to tears.[3] Consequently, Mangiaracina had little success making cases overseas. He describes Cusack as "an okay conspiracy maker," but is careful to note that Cusack couldn't speak Italian, and Hank Manfredi was much better equipped to head the Rome office. "The Italian police," Mangiaracina says, "always used to ask me: 'Why isn't Mr. Manfredi the boss? He's been here ten years!'"

The reason, of course, was that Hank Manfredi was mired in the murky depths of espionage. As the lynchpin in CIA officer Bob Driscoll's initiative, Manfredi had formed a cadre of Italian policemen from Trieste into a secret operations unit designed to neutralize the Communist Party in Rome and infiltrate its Soviet link. But Driscoll hadn't consulted with James Angleton, the CIA's tyrannical counterintelligence chief, and when Angleton (who was running a parallel operation through the Italian military) found out what Driscoll was doing, he notified General Giovanni De Lorenzo, the Sicilian-born chief of Italy's secret service. Word of Driscoll's secret unit hit the papers, scandal ensued, the initiative fizzled, and Driscoll was sent to Tangiers to await his next assignment. The call would come in June 1960, when the Belgian Congo declared its independence, and by posing as a doctor and recruiting Joseph Mobuto, the chief of staff of the Congolese Army, Driscoll would resurrect his CIA career.[4]

But redemption would elude Manfredi. He wasn't exposed in the scandal, thanks to his FBN cover and friends in the Italian police forces – and he did manage to maintain good relations with Angleton – but his faith in the ideal that all Americans were working together, for God and country, was shattered by Angleton's betrayal. He'd also blown his chance to achieve stardom in the CIA. But worst of all, he had to go back to work for Jack Cusack, for whom he had no love or respect. Insecure by nature, and a hypochondriac, father figure Hank Manfredi fell into a black depression that disturbed everyone in District 17.

Back at FBN headquarters, the CIA was casting its wicked spell on Charlie Siragusa too. Wrapped in red tape by Giordano and Speer, he longed for an investigation he could sink his teeth into. Instead, Anslinger made him the FBN's liaison to the CIA, and Siragusa became inextricably entwined in the MKULTRA Program and the CIA's disastrous plots to assassinate Fidel Castro. Like Hank Manfredi before him, Siragusa's career was compromised as a result.

Siragusa's walk down the primrose path began in January 1959, when Anslinger, expecting more cooperation from Castro than he'd gotten from Batista, sent Charlie to Cuba with a list of fifty drug traffickers he wanted arrested and expelled. Topping the list was Santo Trafficante, who had been subpoenaed in the Anastasia murder case. But the fledgling Cuban government couldn't find the Batista regime's dossiers on the gangsters Anslinger wanted expelled. Then the case against Trafficante was mysteriously dismissed in the US, probably at the behest of the CIA, and the patron saint of drug traffickers was released from a Cuban detention facility and returned to Tampa a free man.[5]

Meyer Lansky, meanwhile, had ransomed his brother Jake from the same detention facility and was relocating his offshore banking and gambling operation to the Bahamas, where he teamed up with a motley crew of dissolute British barristers and bankers. Lansky financed the operation with laundered drug and gambling money, his business friends provided the respectable façade, and together they created a formidable criminal empire. Making the whole thing possible was the CIA, which had hired a slew of gangsters, including Trafficante, in its mad attempt to murder Castro. In return for their services, the hoods were protected from criminal prosecution, and in this way and others, the CIA would subvert the FBN's efforts against the American Mafia. It was also the beginning of what Andy Tartaglino referred to as "The Age of Anglophiles and Francophobes."[6]

THE ANGLOPHILES

In 1953, Siragusa had reported that Corsicans smuggled morphine and heroin from Indochina.[7] What he didn't know at the time was that the Corsicans relied on CIA assets in the Kuomintang as their source of supply. Garland Williams, however, clarified the situation once and for all in a 25 July 1959 report titled "The Narcotics Situation in South Asia and the Far East." As Williams noted, 10,000 Kuomintang soldiers living illegally in Burma had "almost exclusive responsibility for moving opium shipments out of the area." This Kuomintang operation, Williams said, supplied, "the persistent major violators of French nationality who operate in New York City."[8]

Williams wasn't whistling in the wind, and in May 1959 – a month after he recommended that the Kuomintang–French operation be destroyed – the Burmese attacked a KMT camp where they discovered 6,000 CIA-supplied KMT soldiers and "three morphine base refineries operating near a usable airstrip."[9]

According to Williams, American mercenaries working for the CIA flew refined heroin out of the Golden Triangle to contacts in Hong Kong and Saigon. All of this was known to Anslinger and his chief executives, and in one instance, according to Andy Tartaglino, FBN agents arrested two CIA agents carrying twelve kilograms of morphine base from Thailand to Hong Kong. But the CIA said they were low-level rogues, and the incident was swept under the carpet.

Taking his cue from the CIA, Anslinger did nothing to embarrass the Kuomintang or the French, and he continued to claim that all heroin reaching Hong Kong came from the People's Republic of China. "The Los Angeles area alone probably received forty percent of the smuggled contraband from China's heroin and morphine plants," he said in 1961.[10]

However, behind the veil of political propaganda, Anslinger was being pressured to post an agent in Hong Kong, as Williams had recommended. But the British colonialists in control of Hong Kong were not sending out engraved invitations. On the contrary, they'd seen America snatch South Vietnam away from the French and, fearing that America had similar designs on Hong Kong, they put up as many barriers as possible. For example, when the British learned that George White had slipped an agent into the Crown Colony in 1959, Hong Kong's customs service, in retaliation, searched a Pan Am passenger plane and miraculously discovered four pounds of morphine base in an unnamed person's luggage. The airline was fined a mere $2,700, but the message was clear: the center of the Far Eastern drug trade was off-limits to the FBN. To get around this No Hunting ban, Anslinger sent Bill Tollenger to Hong Kong as Pan Am's security chief. Operating under CIA control, Tollenger's job was to snoop around the Far East without upsetting the status quo, while keeping Sam Pryor's airline out of trouble.

The Hong Kong No Hunting ban also gave Anslinger a convenient excuse: if FBN agents weren't there, they couldn't prove that the CIA, Kuomintang, and French Corsicans were involved in a drug smuggling conspiracy. Thus, when twenty-one Chinese-Americans were arrested in San Francisco in 1959 with heroin obtained in Hong Kong, Anslinger and George White could say without blushing that it had come from mainland China, because the conspirators referred to themselves "in customary Communist terms."[11] They made this claim despite the fact that a former president of the Hip Sing T'ong was the mastermind of the conspiracy, and that the president of the Bing King T'ong in Portland was the middleman in the transactions. And that wasn't the worst of it; according to Peter Dale Scott, "The arrests were delayed until after the ringleader, Chung Wing Fong, a former Hip Sing president and official of the San Francisco Anti-Communist League (a KMT front) had been ordered by the US Consulate in Hong Kong to travel to Taiwan. In this way ... the KMT disappeared from view."[12]

Such was the paradoxical beauty of the special relationship with Great Britain. More than any other nation in history, Britain had profited from opium. By distributing narcotics to addicts in the United Kingdom, British public health officials repudiated Anslinger's punitive approach to drug addiction. British businessmen dealt with the PRC on the Hong Kong Exchange through British banks and shipping companies like Jardine

Matheson. And, as Williams implied in his 25 July 1959 report, the British actually protected Kuomintang drug traffickers. The British, he said, seized "eight or ten heroin factories each year," and "many more" were in operation. But they punished the Kuomintang traffickers merely by "deporting them to Macao." US Customs agents working with the Brits tried to stop this awful practice; but, due to CIA intervention, they did not have "effective support from the State Department in this endeavor." [13]

The Brits, however, weren't doing seditious things like France. The British intelligence service wasn't supplying heroin conversion labs outside London, like SDECE was by facilitating the supply of morphine base to labs outside Paris. Nor were they courting the Soviets and contending with the CIA at every coordinate on the drug smuggling map, from Laos and Beirut, to Algeria and Marseilles. The Brits and Americans were cousins, and the French were ridiculous, after all.

THE FRANCOPHOBES

Until May 1954, America and France had a *modus vivendi*: French colonies were allowed to absorb opium revenues in return for waging the First Indochina War. But the accommodation collapsed at Dien Bien Phu, and soon the two nations were struggling for hegemony in the region. Five years later, on 19 November 1959, the role of the illicit drug trade in this *salle guerre* was publicly revealed when a Corsican with SDECE credentials, Renaud Desclerts, was arrested in Ban Me Thuot, Vietnam, with 293 kilograms of Laotian opium. [14]

As Marty Pera told the McClellan Committee that year, "When French Indochina existed … quantities of opium were shipped to the labs around Marseilles … then transshipped to the US." Since then, Pera added, the US had become "preoccupied" with France itself. [15]

Preoccupied, indeed. By 1960, France had replaced Italy as the focus of federal drug law enforcement, but with a national security twist. According to Agent Tom Tripodi, "An investigation undertaken in 1960 by American General E. G. Lansdale … concluded that elements of the French government were engaged in the heroin traffic." [16]

As we shall see, it wasn't long before the FBN got dragged into the dirty underground war – the *sale guerre* – that the CIA and SDECE were waging within the arcane world of international drug trafficking.

Laos was the source of the opium that the French converted into heroin, and so the CIA, which was anxious to deprive SDECE of this untraceable source of income, staged a coup that brought its man, General Phoumi Nosavan, to power in November 1960. French advisors to the Laotian military departed in protest, and CIA paramilitary officers took control of the opium-growing hill tribes the French had formed into its anti-communist Armée Clandestine.[17] In 1963 Laos would withdraw from the UN's 1961 Single Convention and, under the guidance of the CIA, start mass-producing narcotics to support the CIA's own secret army of Laotian hill tribesmen.[18]

But Laos was remote and primitive, and the axis of the CIA's *salle guerre* with SDECE was between Marseilles and urbane Beirut, where, with the failure of the United Arab Kingdom, the Christian Maronites had emerged as the CIA's only viable allies in the struggle against Arab nationalism and communism in the Middle East. Suffering the Francophiles in order to make cases posed enormous challenges for FBN agents in the region. Paul Knight's primary informer was a Maronite, and thus loyal to the French, and the Lebanese police were of little help, when they weren't actually protecting drug smugglers like Sami Khoury – who by 1959 had, ironically, become Knight's best informant.

Small attempts at cooperation were made. In November 1956, the French arrested Khoury in Paris and connected him with Paul Mondoloni. And in January 1959, Khoury, with the approval of the French, enabled Knight to make a case in Paris against Khoury's partners – Antoine Araman, Antoine Harrouk, and Agop Kevorkian – none of who were French citizens. But the French, as Knight notes, could be *"très difficile,"* and cooperation was not forthcoming in December 1959, when Khoury presented Knight with a plan to entrap several of his French customers. The idea, Knight told Cusack in Rome, was to create an international conspiracy case, the likes of which had never been seen before. But the French objected and the plan never got past the drawing board – because Knight wanted to include Frenchman Robert Blemant in the trap. Described by Knight as an "ex-French cop and major if unpublicized trafficker," Blemant was the founder of Les Trois Canards gang and an employee of SDECE.[19]

Without French aid, there could be no proof of "the Conspiracy." There was, according to Knight, only a loose confederation of gangsters, some of whom, like Joe Orsini (who'd settled in Spain and returned to drug smuggling upon his release from the Atlanta Penitentiary in 1958) and François Spirito, had been Nazi collaborators, while the Francisci and Guérini gangs had fought with the Resistance. All had political protectors, and all suspended their vendettas in order to make money through drug smuggling. As Knight explains, "They weren't emotional over long-term issues. After all was said and done, they were still Corsicans."

Complicating the situation was the fact that SDECE was divided into contending factions that, Knight explains, "spent most of their time mounting operations against each other. Each of these factions kept Corsicans in its stable [of non-official agents], and one faction employed drug traffickers who had been of service to de Gaulle during the war. Afterwards they couldn't go into legitimate businesses, so they became his SAC (Service d'Action Civique) people."

Formed in 1958 by Jacques Foccart, President de Gaulle's deputy for secret foreign affairs, SAC was a parallel service to SDECE, designed specifically to ensure political stability in France's colonies. SAC employed Corsican gangsters to fight the Algerian Liberation Movement, and when a band of French Army officers (aligned with US and British interests in North Africa) formed the Organization de l'Armée Secrète (OAS) to maintain French rule in Algeria against de Gaulle's wishes, Foccart again called upon the Corsicans. Seeking *laissez-passer* to smuggle all sorts of commodities in return for their mercenary services, Free French and Nazi-collaborator Corsicans joined forces and defeated the OAS in Algeria, adding yet another deep political subtext to international drug trafficking.

THE FBN'S FIRST OFFICE IN FRANCE

Having returned to the FBN after a stint with Tapline, Joe Salm recalls how difficult it was to make cases in Marseilles. While working undercover in 1960, he arranged to meet with a Corsican chemist at a cafe in the Vieux-Port. Police officers under the direction of French narcotic detective Robert Pasquier were there to cover and film the meet. "We met, shook hands, and arranged to meet again," Salm says, "but our liaison *forgot* to put film in the camera.

"The problem," Salm explains, "was that [Inspector Robert] Pasquier was in the pay of these people."

Political intrigues and police corruption would confound FBN agents in France for the next decade, and in many instances their unintentional insults to French sensibilities only made things worse. According to Salm, "Many agents projected their prejudices onto the situation, misunderstood what was being said, and were summarily dismissed. It was an anti-intellectual pattern established by Siragusa and made worse by Cusack. Whatever success we had against the Corsicans was made possible by the absence of Siragusa and Cusack, and by the arrival in Paris of Andy Tartaglino."

At enforcement assistant Lee Speer's direction, Andy Tartaglino opened the FBN's first office in Paris in March 1959. Having worked all over Europe since 1956, Tartaglino knew the top French policemen, and was smart enough to avoid the Francophobes at the American Embassy. His big problem was that FBN credentials were being provided to CIA agents, and that Cusack was sending undercover agents into France on unilateral operations. The French were aware of these shenanigans and had come to mistrust anyone working for the Bureau. Knowing that he was under constant scrutiny, Tartaglino compensated for Cusack's misadventures by keeping a low profile. He left his family in Rome and formed good relations with Customs Attaché Andrew Agathangelou and the US Army CID. It was a delicate situation that also required extreme demonstrations of good faith.

As Tony Mangiaracina recalls, "Cusack sent me to Le Havre to see a dealer alone, and while I was on my way, Tartaglino heard about it and told the French police. They chased me down and said, 'France is not a colony! You can't operate here alone!'"

The same willingness to appease the French by exposing unilateral FBN operations also brought Tartaglino into conflict with Paul Knight. As Tartaglino recalls, Knight sent an informant from Beirut to Paris without any warning, as part of a CIA operation designed to uncover KGB agents in France. Tartaglino learned about the informer only after he was caught by the French security services – at which point the informant falsely claimed, on Knight's instructions, that he was working for Tartaglino on a drug case. Outraged that Knight had deceived him and had taken his cooperation for granted, Tartaglino refused to go along with the charade. He told the French everything and had the agent blacklisted.

Tartaglino's personal and professional relationship with Knight disintegrated as a result, but he gained the trust of Charles Guillard, chief of the Sûreté's Central Narcotics Office. Having done that, Tartaglino started conducting his own unilateral operations against the French officials who, as General Lansdale noted in his 1960 report, "were involved in the heroin trade."

One case in point began in 1955, when the Bureau developed information that Charles Valle, chief of the Central Pharmacy Service in the French Ministry of Public Health, was diverting heroin onto the black market.[20] The French refused to investigate Valle, so in December 1959, Lee Speer sent Agent Bill Davis from Detroit to Paris. Working undercover, Davis pretended to be following leads on American soldiers; but, as he recalls, the real object "was to make a case on [Valle]. French merchant seamen would throw waterproof bags full of heroin into Long Island Sound, and motorboats would pick them up. We had to lie to the Sûreté to make the case, but in April [1960] we got enough evidence to present to Guillard. The French apologized and in return, nothing was said publicly."

Privately, Tartaglino and Guillard came to terms, and despite Tartaglino's undercover operation against Valle, they formed a joint task force to target Paul Damien Mondoloni, the most influential and most wanted narcotics trafficker of his era. Often described as a captain in the Francisci crime family, Mondoloni spoke excellent French, Spanish, Italian, and English, and had more narcotics connections worldwide than anyone else. Handsome, soft-spoken, and well-mannered, he was married to Juana Carlotta Maria Flores Escobar, a Nicaraguan living in Cuba, and kept a mistress, Marcelle Senesi, in Mexico. Mondoloni was cunning, and dangerous when backed into a corner. A former policeman in Saigon, and a SAC veteran of the OAS war in Algeria, he had solid intelligence connections; indeed, until his murder in Marseilles on 29 July 1985, Mondoloni operated with almost total impunity.

The main weapon in tracking down Mondoloni was Gabriel Graziani, an international drug smuggler arrested in Switzerland in April 1958 for selling stolen securities to Third World nations as short-term loans. According to Tartaglino, Charles Guillard gave him Graziani as an informant as a reward for having exposed Knight's unilateral CIA operation – in which Graziani was the agent provocateur.

Tartaglino describes Graziani as "a Corsican gentleman who said we were wasting our time on small cases. He was very helpful regarding cases in New York, where there were more people involved than we ever dreamed."

Having served as Mondoloni's operations manager, Graziani was able to explain how the Corsicans worked with Mafiosi in Canada, Mexico, Cuba, Miami, and New York, and he identified the Mafia's two main couriers, Ernesto Barese and Giuseppe DiGiorgio. He had considerable information about his Corsican associates in Lebanon, and he revealed that Sami Khoury had hired a new Syrian chemist, Mahmoud Badawi. He also identified the French restaurants and hotels in New York that served as depots for drug smugglers. In effect, Gabriel Graziani opened the door to the next phase of the ongoing French connection.

THE MEXICAN CONNECTION

As a result of Graziani's information, the FBN was able to track Paul Mondoloni from Havana, through Madrid (where he conferred with Joe Orsini), Marseilles, and Palermo to Acapulco, where in March 1960 he was seen in the company of Lucien Rivard, Rosario Mancino, and Marius Cau.[21] Rivard, of course, was Montreal's reigning drug lord in the absence of Pepe Cotroni. Mancino, a Sicilian, was suspected of shipping heroin (manufactured in a clandestine lab he owned in Lebanon) in tomato cans to Vito and Albert Agueci in Toronto. Cau was a Corsican drug smuggler and former associate of Gabriel Graziani operating mostly in Canada. These smugglers were organizing a major new drug ring in league with Mondoloni's contact in Mexico since 1954, Jorge Asaf y Bala, a Mexican of Arabian descent living in Mexico City.

Seeking to disrupt this conspiracy before it could start moving narcotics through Texas, Customs Agent Ben White convinced the Mexican Federal Police to arrest Mondoloni on 8 April 1960. But the clever Corsican was protected and fled to Havana six weeks later. The FBN had more luck with Canadian officials and, when Mancino arrived in Montreal on 14 April, the Mounties persuaded him to return to Italy that same day.[22] But the conspiracy that Mondoloni organized in Mexico in the spring of 1960 would unfold nevertheless, and persist for years, for the FBN had been rendered virtually powerless in Mexico as a result of a case Jim Attie and Ray Maduro made on the aforementioned Jorge Asaf y Bala in November 1959. For that reason it is a case worth reviewing.

One of the first Puerto Ricans hired by the FBN, Ray Maduro, in mid-1959, was introduced to a Cuban drug dealer named Escabi in New York. Working undercover, Maduro met with Escabi and placed an order for cocaine, with the delivery to be made in Mexico City. The New York office provided Maduro with documentation and booked him into a hotel in Mexico City where Jim Attie, on a separate case out of Chicago, was also staying. This proved to be very fortunate, for Escabi came to his meeting with Maduro not with cocaine, as agreed, but with heroin he'd obtained from Asaf y Bala. Rookie Agent Maduro was nonplused by this unexpected turn of events, and was exceedingly grateful when veteran agent Attie entered the negotiations "cold" (meaning without any preparation in FBN jargon), posing as Maduro's rich Arab money-man.

After Attie arranged a second meeting to make the buy, Anslinger personally asked Mexico's representative to the United Nations, Dr. Oscar Robasso, for assistance. Robasso called for police backup, and Attie – after a good deal of macho posturing that nearly resulted in a shootout – purchased the heroin. On 11 November 1959, Mexican Federal policemen arrested Asaf y Bala with three kilograms of heroin. But the Mexican Supreme Court overturned the conviction and Asaf was set free to conspire for the next five years with Mondoloni, Rivard, and Mancino.[23]

In Mexico, as in France, Cuba, Lebanon, and Hong Kong, unilateral FBN operations were not often rewarded with prosecutions or convictions. Issues of national sovereignty and corruption trumped drug law enforcement, and after the Asaf y Bala case was overturned by the Mexican Supreme Court, Mexican Attorney General Fernando Lopez Arias met with US Assistant Treasury Secretary A. Gilmore Flues in Washington in early 1961. Arias told Flues three things: 1) that no more buy cases would be allowed in Mexico; 2) that FBN agents would not be allowed to testify in Mexican courts; and 3) that traffickers had to be arrested in possession of narcotics before the delivery was made.[24] Clearly, these legal regulations hindered the FBN's efforts against Mondoloni and the French connection, which as a result had found safe haven in Mexico.

THE FIRST AMBASSADOR CASE

Although the French connection had settled safely in Mexico, its operations in Lebanon suffered a temporary setback when Paul Knight initiated two important cases there in 1960. The first began when Gabriel Graziani revealed the activities and whereabouts of his erstwhile partner, Antranik Paroutian. A financial manager in the Mondoloni organization, Paroutian handled bank accounts in Switzerland for Corsican and Lebanese drug smugglers. Paroutian, however, was under indictment in New York, so Knight (based on information provided by Graziani) arranged for his arrest in Beirut in early March 1960, on trumped up charges related to the seizure of two shipments of morphine base. International Group Leader Marty Pera immediately flew to Beirut, only to find that Paroutian had been acquitted, but that Knight, through his friends in the Lebanese police force, had arranged for the drug trafficker to be held without charges until his arrival. Upon arriving at the airport, Pera forcefully took Paroutian – a martial arts expert who put up a fight – into custody and brought him in shackles back to New York where, with the assistance of Swiss banking officials, he was tried and convicted. The Paroutian case was a major breakthrough for the FBN in regard to investigating the money-laundering activities of international drug smugglers. And, thanks to Marty Pera's painstaking research, it set an important precedent. At first the Swiss refused to release information about Paroutian's account, and did so only after Pera reminded them that their government had signed an agreement with the League of Nations that required them to do so, if the account holder was laundering drug money.

The second case began a few weeks later, in June 1960, when Maronite underworld boss Abu George personally gave Paul Knight a tip about one of the most important drug rings operating between Beirut and Paris. Knight passed the information along to Lee Speer in Washington, and he, acting on what he'd been told, asked Customs to check its files for diplomats named Maurice. Only about one hundred diplomats routinely arrived and departed from Eastern ports, so it didn't take long to identify Mauricio Rosal Bron, Guatemala's ambassador to Belgium and Holland, as the main suspect. A dapper dresser with a fatal fondness for young boys, Rosal had been making bimonthly trips to New York for a year. As Customs discovered, his baggage always weighed less when he departed than when he arrived, and he often traveled with a Corsican named Etienne Tarditi.

Next, at Andy Tartaglino's request, the French placed a wiretap on Tarditi, and overheard Tarditi and Rosal making plans to visit New York in August. Taking charge of the case in New York, George Gaffney arranged surveillance, and FBN agents watched while Tarditi met with Charles Bourbonnais, a TWA purser, and Nick Calamaris, a longshoreman in the Gambino family. Gaffney informed senior State Department officials of what was happening, and they persuaded Guatemala to revoke Rosal's diplomatic immunity, without his knowledge, paving the way for his arrest when he returned to New York in October.

On 2 October 1960, having returned to New York with another load of heroin, Rosal and Tarditi left their hotel to meet Calamaris and Bourbonnais. They climbed into a cab driven by FBN Agent Francis E. Waters, and were tailed by Gaffney and Ray Maduro. As Maduro recalls, "They were in the cab, and Rosal's luggage was in the trunk, and we had probable cause. But it was a hot day, and Gaffney was wearing a heavy wool suit, and he got itchy. So we arrested them before the exchange. Agent Tony Falanga was stopped at a red light in front of Calamaris's station wagon, and Gaffney called him on the radio and said, 'Box him in! We're right behind you!'"

FBN agents found fifty kilograms of heroin inside Rosal's luggage, and nearly $70,000 cash on the floor of Calamaris's car. Further investigation led to the discovery of another fifty kilos at a safehouse in Long Island. Altogether it was one of the biggest heroin seizures ever, and a fantastic public relations coup for the FBN. The intelligence take was phenomenal too. Tarditi named Robert LeCoat and Felix Barnier as his sources, and they were arrested in France in February 1961. He fingered Gilbert Coscia as the man handling transactions in Canada, and Coscia surrendered in

April 1961. Tarditi identified the four major trafficking groups in France, the three major labs, and the manager of his organization's Swiss bank accounts. He also revealed that a "bigger" diplomat than Rosal, someone accredited with the British Commonwealth, was smuggling for the Charles Marignani Group.[25] And before he clammed up, Tarditi made the provocative statement that he "was involved in intelligence work beneficial to American interests."[26]

Was Tarditi a CIA spy, reporting to the CIA about KGB agents within SDECE? Perhaps. The French did have legitimate complaints against the United States, and they were using the drug issue as leverage. Indeed, after "L'affaire Rosal," Secretary of State Dean Rusk raised the narcotics issue with Paris, "but was told that no extra men could be assigned until the problem in Algeria (where the CIA was meddling) was settled."[27]

In any case, the FBN would soon come to regard Tarditi and Rosal not as CIA agents, but as members of a SDECE drug-smuggling operation formed by SAC chief Jacques Foccart. This SDECE operation was different than other drug-smuggling rings in that it blackmailed French diplomats (like the pedophile Rosal) into becoming couriers. Its existence contributed to James Angleton's theory – which was planted in his mind by KGB defector Anatoly Golitsyn in 1962 – that the KGB had infiltrated SDECE. However, considering that Golitsyn's attorney, Mario Brod, was Angleton's liaison to the Mafia, the allegations against SDECE and Foccart (separate from the drug-smuggling issue) are just as likely to have been disinformation designed by Angleton to throw the FBN off the trail of certain drug-smuggling Mafiosi in the CIA's employ.

Tarditi's affiliations and Angleton's intentions remain impenetrable mysteries; what is known is that Rosal's accomplice, Charles Bourbonnais, did provide the FBN with information that led to Gambino family members Joseph Biondo, Arnold Romano, and Joseph Cahill. Documents seized at Cahill's home incriminated Profaci family member Frank Dioguardia in Miami, and Pepe Cotroni's lieutenant Frank Dasti in Montreal. All of which was very helpful.[28]

L'affaire Rosal was one of the FBN's most spectacular successes, and Andy Tartaglino and Paul Knight shared the credit, though their rewards were hardly commensurate with their achievement. In March 1961, Lee Speer brought Tartaglino back to New York and reassigned him to the Court House Squad, as a sort of demotion. As Gaffney explains, "Andy was Siragusa's protégé, and Siragusa and Speer hated each other. And rather than give Andy a commendation, Speer wanted to fire him on the pretext that he was always telling the French everything, and because he hadn't found any labs. So I offered to put him in the Court House Squad to follow up leads from Tarditi."

Knight replaced Tartaglino in Paris, and went to work for the CIA on an unofficial basis. Former FBN inspector Fred Wilson replaced Knight in Beirut. Wilson was an ally of Speer, and Speer was capitalizing on his role as enforcement assistant to place his slim supply of supporters in positions of importance, to improve his chances of succeeding Anslinger.

FBN OPERATIONS IN MEXICO AND LATIN AMERICA

The Rosal and Asaf y Bala cases underscored the fact that the FBN needed to expand its operations in Latin America and Mexico, but Congress would not authorize the funds, primarily because South America was not a major opium producing region, and cocaine had yet to eclipse heroin in popularity. Little would be done during the FBN's existence. George White conducted perfunctory investigations in Peru and Ecuador in 1954, and George Gaffney, as district supervisor in Atlanta in 1957, worked with the Colombian Security Service and CIA officer Robert Service (son of John Service, mentioned in chapter 5) to make a case on Tomas and Rafael Herran Olozaga in Medellin, Colombia, on the heels of related cases in Cuba and Ecuador. "The brothers had been in business since 1948," Gaffney explains, "selling heroin and cocaine in Cuba. They had a lab on their estate, and we identified the chemicals there as the same ones from the Quito bust." [29]

In response to the increasing frequency of Customs seizures along the border, FBN forays into Mexico did increase in number throughout the 1950s, although most were conducted close to home by agents out of California and Texas. As Howard Chappell recalls, "I worked Mexico fairly regularly, and from 1956 to 1961, I made around two dozen cases down there. I usually had an agent from the office with me and sometimes someone from Customs. But no one else was aware of the cases during development, other than Mexican officials, which in my cases was usually the district attorney in Vera Cruz, Toca Canges. Customs Agent Ben White in Mexico City would send Toca up to Tijuana to help me knock off labs. The Bureau certainly knew nothing about these manipulations, because it frowned on agents working with Customs. The Bureau also thought that all Mexican officials were crooks, which in the main was true.

"Here's an example of how a Mexican case worked," Chappell continues. "I got a call from the Buena Park Police in August 1960: a fellow named Wilson was being held on suspicion of auto theft. He asked for me and when I got there, he said that he and his partner Webster, and another guy named Goldheimer, had a plan to lease Burt Lancaster's yacht and use it to haul a ton of marijuana and some opium up from Mexico. After Lancaster agreed to let us use his yacht, I went to Guadalajara with Wilson to meet Webster, who had the Mexican connection. Goldheimer stayed in the States to bring the boat down to Ylapa when they were ready.

"Wilson went to Ylapa, a popular hippy tent village on the coast, to locate Webster, and they returned together to meet me, the money-man. Webster said the connection was in the Guadalajara Prison, so I went there next – hoping not to meet anybody I'd put inside – and from the prison connection I got the names of the people who were going to make the delivery in the mountain village of Urapan. The connection, while in prison, made all the arrangements as to the place and date of the meet.

"Next I went to Mexico City where I met Ben White, Colonel Manuel Dominguez Suarez (Director of the Mexican Federal Judicial Police, 1959–61) and Colonel Hector Tello.[30] White put up the money for the Federales to fly over to Guadalajara. At Chapala we rented a VW bus from a couple of hippies, then drove to Urapan, where I met the connections and got a sample of the opium. After making sure it was not synthetic, I gave the signal and the deliverymen and I were arrested. In Mexico there is no charge for sale, only possession, so the Federales took the evidence away from me and gave it back to the peddlers. Then by forceful inter-rogation they located the balance of opium and marijuana, and several more defendants, all of whom went to jail.

"Incidentally, I had no advance funds for purchases or flash on that trip," Chappell adds. "Giordano thought it was too risky and suggested I use a bogus letter of credit." Rolling his eyes, Chappell asks, "Can you imagine Mexican wholesalers accepting a letter of credit?

"Otherwise it was the same procedure in all cases," Chappell concludes, "and as long as everything turned out okay, Anslinger left me alone, used the information when it could be used to his advantage, and acted like it hadn't happened otherwise."

JIM ATTIE IN CHICAGO, MEXICO, AND LATIN AMERICA

Upon his transfer there in 1957, Jim Attie learned that Chicago was still the unsavory place described by Maurice Helbrant and Marty Pera. "I'd been diagnosed at the VA hospital as having encephalitis," Attie says.

"They'd done a spinal tap and found a high degree of infection, and they said my days of undercover activity were over. But I wanted to keep working, so they sent me to Chicago, where I continued to have physical problems and where [District Supervisor Al] Aman wouldn't let me drive a company car. When I complained to Giordano, the only thing he said was: 'If you don't like it, quit.'

"That just made me more determined. I had this parochial belief that diligent work would lead to success. So I used my own car."

Attie established a false identity and, while covering himself from the Mafia – as well as from FBN agents on its payroll – infiltrated the inner circle of Chicago's notorious Mafia boss Sam Giancana. Giancana hired Attie as his chauffeur, a position that enabled him to purchase half a kilogram of heroin from a vicious killer, Carlo Fiorito, and to identify Giancana's sources of supply in Canada, Mexico, and Latin America.

Meanwhile, Al Aman had retired and been replaced by George M. Belk, one of the FBN's most respected agents and managers. At Belk's direction, in coordination with Belk's enforcement assistant William J. Durkin, Attie prepared for his first ventures into Mexico – forays he describes as "deadly" because "there was always shooting."

"Howard Chappell came to me one day while I was working a case out of California into Mexico, and said, 'I hear you think you made some big cases in the Mideast.'

"'No,' I said. 'I don't think that.'

"'Well,' he said, 'Don't. Not until you work the Yacqui Indians down in Mexico.'

"Chappell was feared in Mexico," Attie says with awe. "He shot and killed Puerto Vallarta's biggest dealer, who was also the sheriff, in a gunfight at high noon in a hotel lobby." [31]

Attie's fake ID and travel documents were prepared in the San Antonio office with the help of the agent in charge, John Frost. Colonel Hector Tello, a drug trafficking policeman who readily informed on his competitors, provided many of Attie's leads in Mexico. Tello's help, however, did not make it any easier to operate. Attie rarely worked with an informant or backup agent, and eventually ended up with a reward on his head for illegal provocation. His main targets were Sicilians working with Chicago and New York hoods, but he also made cases on Asaf y Bala, Jose Garcia Aiza, Chinese restaurateur Simon Hom, and Alfred Trevino, a Mexican out of Monterey. He also developed leads into Bolivia and Peru. "When I got to La Paz," he recalls, "the US ambassador summoned me to his office and said: 'We know about you from the Middle East. Mess things up here, and I'll get you fired.'" [32]

Attie didn't mess up, and the case led to the arrest of Blanca y Ibanez de Sanchez and Ebar Franco, who dealt in New York through Cuba. But, as heroic Jim Attie confesses, "By then the job was making *me* feel like a criminal."

14

A SHOOFLY IN THE OINTMENT

"If we hide the truth, we become part of the conspiracy."
Agent Bill Davis

J. Edgar Hoover liked to remind Harry Anslinger that agent corruption was an inherent part of drug law enforcement. And it was true, every few years a scandal rocked federal drug law enforcement, one of the biggest having occurred in 1929, when the son of Anslinger's predecessor, Colonel Nutt, was accused of filing false income tax statements for drug trafficker Arnold Rothstein, and the Narcotics Division office in New York was charged with "misconduct, incompetence and dereliction of duty."[1]

While Anslinger was Commisioner, the corruption that crippled the FBN was fostered by his unrealistic policies and sloppy management style. He had only one field supervisor on his staff (although sometimes there were two – one for offices east of the Mississippi, one covering those west) and discipline was left to supervisors whose priority was making cases, and who gave agents the leeway they needed to show success. Standard procedure was to warn new agents about "the three Bs" – booze, broads, and bread – then hand them over to the veterans and say a prayer.

Anslinger didn't set the best example either.

"He tried to do what Hoover did," Matt Seifer observes. "There was a New York case involving a drug lab, and we had information in our Boston file about it. A letter came to us with Anslinger's stamp, requesting the file. We sent it down, but it never came back, and the main file in DC was never seen again." Seifer shakes his head. "There was a letter in the Boston file from a politician, asking for consideration."

And while Anslinger coddled the drug-addicted offspring of the Establishment elite, his agents were pretending to be New York City detectives and kicking down doors in Harlem without search warrants.[2] This double standard was not lost on the Black agents, and while the CIA prevented the FBN from properly fulfilling its mission overseas, this pervasive racism undermined its integrity at home.

"We went through hell," Bill Davis says. "We wanted to be accepted as full-fledged agents, not just Blacks doing the bidding of Whites. But even though in many cases we could write better and testify better, we weren't allowed to supervise Whites. They'd come by and say, 'I want to *use* him today.' They'd have us make buys and try to cover us, and then they'd take the evidence so they could mark it up and get credit. If we complained, we got harassed.

"We had to survive the heaviest stress," Davis asserts. "We had to watch our backs, not just from the crooks, but from the White agents who didn't want us moving 'out of our place.' And we were held to a higher standard." Davis notes that Black agents were not allowed to physically intimidate White informers, although White agents routinely roughed up Blacks.

"We had an interrogation room with a two-way mirror in New York. One day I was standing outside, looking in. An agent I'll call Mr. Tex had a man stripped naked and was verbally abusing him, calling him 'nigger.' I went in and asked Mr. Tex to come out, and then I asked him why he was abusing the man. He said, 'If they won't come up to my level, I have to go down to theirs.' I told him not to use the word nigger again, and that if he used it around me, I wouldn't let it drop. So he wouldn't speak to me again. Same with Pat Ward, who always called the Italian agents 'dagos' and 'guineas.' When I called him on it, he said I was too 'thin-skinned.'

"We also knew about the shenanigans – that White agents were stealing drugs." Davis refers to the wall of silence around Crofton Hayes's heroin overdose. "But we couldn't say anything, or they'd nitpick us to death."

Granted, Anslinger didn't create racism, but the organization he fashioned in his image, like the criminal justice system it served, fully accepted White superiority as gospel; and belief in that fiction made it easier to propagate other myths, like the Communist Chinese drug conspiracy, or that pot was as dangerous as heroin. These fallacies supported the double standards that elevated Anslinger above the law, and gave George White the license to poison people with LSD.

The subordination of its ethical standards to issues of national security caused tremendous damage to the FBN. If agents were expected to fabricate evidence about the People's Republic of China, as in the George Yee case, or suppress evidence about CIA drug smuggling, as happened with increasing frequency after 1959, how could they be expected to inform on corrupt colleagues? Either they had a code of silence, or they obeyed the law. It couldn't work both ways. But the biggest lie of all was that agents weren't involved in the crimes they investigated.

"You can't make a case without informants," an agent explains, "and you can't get information unless you pay for it. So you give them three dollars, and they use it to buy dope. There's no way around it: paying addict informants perpetuates the business. The rationale is that we're not 'creating a crime' because it would have happened anyway. But you *are* creating a crime, and that's why you need two busts – to transcend entrapment. Giving addicts dope is probably a better idea, because it doesn't put money into the system and doesn't send them running to the man. But if you do that, then you can't ever make a case, and you've put yourself out of business."

Anslinger's way of reconciling this contradiction was through a standardized reporting system that required agents to explain exactly how they interacted with informants, gathered evidence, and made arrests. In practice, however, agents revised their reports to disguise the tactics they actually used. For example, it was customary for a case-making agent to give his informant money, and for the informant to show the agent where his source was by going there and buying heroin. That trick of the trade was called taking a "free look." But no agent ever wrote in a report that he took a free look to find out where the dealer and his dope were located. No one ever said that he learned where and when a delivery was being made through a "gypsy wire" (FBN jargon for an illegal wiretap). And no agent ever said that he "spooned out," which meant siphoning off a small amount of heroin from a bust.

"Even Charlie Siragusa spooned out," one agent claims. "He told me not to do it – but he said they all did it back in the old days before the war, when the New York agents were called the Forty Thieves. Because, when you bust a guy, no one sees. So a lot of agents decide to protect themselves. If someone sells them turkey, or if they get ripped off at gunpoint, they're out the official funds. So they keep a few ounces tucked away in a bag in their pocket. Agents carried a drop gun for the same reason."

"We didn't get paid very much," another agent explains. "The office furniture was crud. The typewriters didn't work. We worked with city detectives going late at night to tenements in Harlem and kicking in doors until we dropped. It was exhausting work, because the dope dealers put iron bars across their windows and doors. But that's how cases began. We kicked in doors until we found a stash of dope, or some stolen TVs, or a weapon; whatever we could use to turn someone into an informant."

By rewarding those who initiated the most cases, Anslinger's tightfisted management style and flawed reporting format compelled agents to make as many small cases as possible, at the expense of pursuing drug kingpins through complex, time-consuming conspiracy cases. But of all the FBN's problems, none was as dangerous as an agent's relationship with his informants. So rules were put in place. Agents were required to frisk an informant before and after a buy, to make sure the snitch didn't buy five ounces for the agent, and one for himself. Payments to informants were authorized only when fingerprints and a mug shot were obtained. But those safeguards were impractical in some situations, such as when an agent met a heroin-addicted prostitute in an alley in Harlem, in the middle of the night in February. "How the hell are you going to fingerprint her there?" an agent exclaims in frustration.

All the case-makers worked alone, and became friends with their best informants. But it was a double-edged sword, as one agent explains: "She calls you at two a.m. to get her out of jail. Your wife answers the phone, now you got to explain. But it's impossible not to become friends. You meet, you socialize, you drink together in bars. The really good agents knew that you had to get people to like you. Any of the bosses who'd been street agents understood."

So case-making agents kept their best informants secret, to prevent other agents from arresting them, or even killing them. The result was a cut-throat system in which informants began to manipulate their case agents, and the organization slowly came apart at the seams.

THE O'KEEFE INCIDENT

Sadly, at the end of his career, the cumulative effects of Anslinger's secret practices and double standards eclipsed the brilliance of his mystique. The process began in February 1959 in New York, when an agent named O'Keefe was found unconscious in his car. An FBN inspector's report written in 1968 claims that O'Keefe was shaking down drug dealers who were protected by corrupt agents in Group Three. The bad agents allegedly turned him in, but after O'Keefe complained to his Congressman, Anslinger let him off the hook. Next, according to the report, the corrupt agents gave O'Keefe a beer laced with pure heroin; but he survived the hot shot because he was a user and had built up a tolerance to the powerful drug.[3]

One Group Three agent agrees that O'Keefe was using drugs in order to win the trust of dope dealers, but denies that he was given a hot shot. The agent also questions why the inspector's report misconstrued the incident. It is absurd, he suggests, to think that corrupt agents would inform on another corrupt agent, or that Anslinger would forgive a blatant wrongdoer.

George Gaffney gives his version of what happened. "I interviewed and hired O'Keefe when I was the supervisor in Atlanta. He'd been a lieutenant in the Army and I thought he had the right stuff. Then he came up to New York and decided to become a loner, and that's when he got into trouble. He went into a bar in Little Italy, thinking he could blend in. Well, the hoods fingered him in a second and the next thing you know, they take his gun and badge.

"By then I was the supervisor in New York, and I referred the problem to headquarters. Meanwhile O'Keefe contacted his Congressman, which he had every right to do. Siragusa was the field supervisor, so Charlie, the Congressman and Anslinger met with O'Keefe. Anslinger asked him, 'How could you possibly lose your gun?' Quick as a flash, O'Keefe reaches over and snatches Charlie's gun. Charlie's standing there flabbergasted, and that's that.

"O'Keefe was sent back to work, and not long after that he was found passed-out in a car. The police reported it, and when we went to investigate, we found a matchbox folded in a V shape under the seat. It was the kind of thing addicts use to sniff dope, and there was heroin residue in it. So I asked for his resignation."

THE INSTITUTE OF CORRUPTION

"You start learning about these things," an agent says, "when you get a corrupt partner. He 'accidentally' busts another guy's informant, and then things get serious.

"It was tough to begin with," the agent continues. "You had to feed your informants two or three dollars every time you'd see them, but you had to wait until the case went down before you got reimbursed. That's when you filled out a voucher. But if your informant didn't produce, or if you bought turkey or got ripped off, then you had to put the money back from your own pocket. You'd say to your boss, 'I want to get reimbursed.' He'd say, 'You know how to make it up.'

"He doesn't explain. You just know.

"Remember, you can't make a bust based on one buy: that's entrapment. You have to make two. So the first time you make a buy, you sign a receipt saying you handed over $300. But you only hand over two-fifty. Second buy, same thing. Third buy you bust him. That's how it worked. The guy you busted doesn't know what you told your boss, and the extra hundred covers your out-of-pocket expenses, like buying people drinks so they think you've got a lot of money.

"An agent meets his connection in a bar. He buys a round of drinks and adds that to the price of the buy. And that simple act is how you get sucked in. The bigger the case, the bigger the pad. Then after awhile it becomes a way to make an extra grand, so you can buy your wife something nice. Other agents would angel off [another way of saying that they "spooned out"] a little dope from every bust, and keep it in their pocket just in case they bought turkey."

Agent Tom Tripodi – a towering, muscular man of conscience – claims that corruption was "institutionalized" in the New York office.[4] In his autobiography he tells how, in January 1960, as a rookie agent in Group Four, he followed five senior agents into a tenement. The older agents told him to wait outside an apartment and, a few minutes later, they signaled for him to come in. Tripodi grew suspicious when they sent him into a room alone and told him to search it; and when he found a package inside a dresser, he wisely decided to leave it there. Later that day the older agents angrily explained that the package contained heroin they had saved from a previous seizure. They'd been unable to make a case on the drug dealer living in the apartment, so they snuck in when he wasn't there and planted the heroin where Tripodi could find it. Not having been part of the frame, he could, theoretically, testify against the dealer without perjuring himself.

Thirty years later George Gaffney seethes when told of the incident. "How come Tripodi didn't report it then?" he demands. "If everybody keeps quiet, how can I do anything?"

BREAKING THE CODE OF SILENCE

Enter Edward Coyne, the agent who did bring the integrity issue to Gaffney's attention. Described as "straight" by his colleagues, Coyne joined the FBN in 1951 as a clerk and became an agent in 1953. For six years he worked on cases without making waves, but he began to have misgivings after the O'Keefe incident. Like Tripodi, he began to see signs of institutionalized corruption.

"One of the clerks told me that a group of agents were ripping off apartments and selling confiscated drugs and guns," he recalls, "so I went to Gaffney. I explained that I knew nothing first hand, but that I felt he should be aware."

Coyne told Gaffney that the corrupt agents would raid an apartment where they knew there were drugs and cash. The agents would keep the money and sell, plant, or give the drugs to their informants, who could then entrap other drug dealers. After the targeted drug dealer was arrested, the agents would cut the recycled junk with sugar and return half to the informant, so he could set up more arrests. The agents turned in some of the money and what was left of the diluted heroin, which was tested for purity only after it was submitted.

"Gaffney called the group leaders while I was in his office," Coyne recalls angrily, "and told them to stand by. Then he turned to me and said, 'Eddie, you're a good friend, and no one will ever hurt you while I'm here.'"

A few days later an agent approached Coyne and said he was fed up with the corruption too. "I told him to tell it to the people up front, but he never did. No one backed me up. Not even the *honest* guys." Coyne's body tenses. "I went in with sincere belief it was the right thing to do."

Meanwhile the group leaders had alerted the accused agents, and Coyne found himself being threatened. "One agent made a remark on the elevator," he recalls, "so I asked him if he thought the office should be corrupt. By his response, I knew that was a serious mistake."

A week later Gaffney summoned Coyne to his office and asked him if he'd been parked in a car behind the Court House with a female secretary. Coyne denied the allegation, and Gaffney said he didn't believe it either – but that once an allegation was made (he imparted with a wink) he had to check it out.

"Maybe he was sending a message?" Coyne muses. He conjures the image of O'Keefe passed-out in his car with a bag of heroin in the glove compartment. Then he tells how, on the morning of 31 August 1960, Agent Charles Thompson's wife found her husband in the living room, sitting in his favorite easy chair, dead from a heroin overdose.

"The rumor was that he'd been given a hot shot," Coyne explains, "and there was a big meeting with Treasury people from Washington. But they swept it under the carpet. And that's when I started thinking, 'I'd better get out of here. They're going to set me up for sure. Maybe not a hot shot, but someone's going to put something in my car, at least.'"

In late 1960, Eddie Coyne asked for and received a transfer to the customs service office in New York. "By 1961," he says, "the guys who are under suspicion are making big cases, and the guys who didn't back me up all get promoted. There were never any confrontations, but you have to ask the question: Can you have widespread corruption without management being part of it?"

George Gaffney has a different recollection of events. "Eddie was conscientious," he admits. "He came in and he told me. But he didn't come to *me* right away. He called Washington first. I know because Charlie McDonnell came to me, and said that Eddie had tried to recruit five agents to go to Washington with him. But no one else would go. *Then* he came to me, and at that point I called Anslinger and told him what was going on.

"Anslinger sent up District Supervisor Sam Levine from Philadelphia. Sam was in my office when Eddie made his allegations, and Sam asked him to come up with one single fact. But it was all rumors, and a week or two later Eddie came in and expressed regret. He said a Bureau guy had called him at home and told him to meet him in a motel room in New Jersey. The Bureau guy swore Eddie to secrecy, and got him to make a commitment that if he came across any wrongdoing, Eddie would contact him in DC. Not Anslinger. Not me. Just him."

Gaffney composes himself. "A few months later, this same Bureau official came up to the New York office with Fred Dick to conduct an inquiry."

The Bureau official was Wayland L. "Lee" Speer, a stocky man with thinning blond hair and a burning, all-consuming desire to put an end to corruption within the FBN.

THE SHOOFLY IN THE OINTMENT

According to Howard Chappell, "Lee Speer was probably the finest investigator in the history of the Bureau. For much of his career he was a traveling supervisor, checking the offices for misuse of funds and equipment, and for efficiency. He was death on any signs of lack of integrity, but he was compassionate and helpful in correcting honest mistakes, and in training agents to improve their operations. He was highly moral himself, and perhaps for that reason he scared the hell out of most of the people in the Bureau, including the other executives. But the truth of the matter was that Lee Speer was an asset to any office he visited – if you wanted help, and if you weren't doing anything wrong from a legal standpoint."

Speer's detractors insist that he put his ambitions above the organization's well-being at a time when Anslinger's wife was dying, and he was pre-occupied with weighty matters before the UN and Congress. Speer wanted to be Commissioner, they say, and his probe was a pretext to smear Anslinger, while upstaging Siragusa and Giordano.

Andy Tartaglino, a Speer supporter, claims that Anslinger had sent Speer to New York specifically to investigate a group of Black agents backing Harlem Congressman Adam Clayton Powell, but that Speer, on his own, expanded the investigation to include agents loyal to Gaffney and former District Supervisor Jim Ryan. Speer had heard rumors for years, and not just about gambling in the office. Among other things, it was said that the district supervisor would dress up in a judge's robes and hold mock court sessions, in which unwitting addicts were coerced into becoming informants.

So after Coyne's complaints of theft, and worse crimes committed by certain agents, Speer began a systematic check of vouchers and informant contact reports, and in June 1961, after a year of preparation, he traveled to New York to investigate the agents he believed were corrupt. But Speer did not have the authority to conduct the investigation on his own, and Deputy Commissioner Giordano sent his loyal ally, Fred T. Dick, then serving as the FBN's field supervisor, to accompany Speer.

One of the FBN's most infamous agents, Dick joined the FBN in 1951 following a stint with the New York State Police. Meticulous, tough, and street-smart – although characterized as sarcastic and arrogant by one of the agents he rubbed the wrong way – he worked in New York for three years before transferring, "for health reasons," to Kansas City, where he formed close relations with District Supervisor Henry Giordano. After Giordano became the FBN's field supervisor in 1956, Dick returned to New York, where he remained until 1959, when Giordano, having become Deputy Commissioner, brought him to headquarters as his dependable field supervisor. This was a very good decision on Giordano's part, because Fred Dick, it is safe to say, knew where all the bodies were buried.

"Giordano said that Speer had identified receipted payments to informants which had not been made," Dick says, "so Speer and I went up to New York, and he called the agents over to his hotel room at all hours of the night. He grilled them without informing them of their rights, while I'm there cringing in the corner. It took six weeks, during which time the case turned to pumpkin pie."

Several agents complained to their Congressman that they were being harassed. One said that Speer had indecently exposed himself (it was late at night, he was changing his clothes, and was wearing only his boxer underpants during part of the interview), and another said that he made racist remarks. But worst of all, Speer waited until Gaffney was on leave, then rifled through the district supervisor's desk.

"Anslinger called me down to Washington," Gaffney recalls, "and when I stepped into his office he pulled some glassine bags out of his desk. 'I understand the agents use these to steal heroin from seizures,' he said."

Gaffney speaks very calmly and carefully. "I told him that all the agents had glassine bags, because Speer had complained that our chemists were reporting different weights, other than what was recorded as having been submitted. What Anslinger didn't know was that the chemists were shaking the heroin out of the bags onto their scales, while we were weighing it *in* the bags. The difference was in the weight of the bags, so we kept the bags to compensate. In other cases the heroin was transferred to containers so we could raise fingerprints from the bags it had come in. So there were good reasons for this, and Anslinger was satisfied with my explanation."

As Fred Dick explains: "Speer and I returned to headquarters, where the stink of this mess was hanging in the air, and Henry called me into his office and asked what had happened. I told him, and he sent me to explain the situation to Gilmore Flues, the assistant secretary over law enforcement at Treasury. And Flues came down hard on Speer."

"Speer chose to walk away from the number three job after this," Gaffney says. "He became the district supervisor in Denver, and Siragusa became the enforcement assistant."

In his final report, Fred Dick said that nine agents had improperly given money to informants, and he recommended they be demoted or suspended. They were not. He said that Group Three, then under John Dolce, led the office "in the exaggerated reporting of seizures," and he criticized Gaffney for not insisting that regulations be followed.[5] Anslinger then assigned Chicago's enforcement assistant, William J. Durkin (one of Anslinger's favorite agents, and John Dolce's former partner in New York) to conduct an independent analysis of the Speer inquiry. Durkin wrote a "bland" report in December 1961, exonerating the case-makers for their "zeal" and recommending that the investigation be concluded in order to remove the "aura of suspicion" that was hanging over their heads. And that was the end of that corruption scandal.[6]

FALLOUT FROM SPEER'S FAILED INVESTIGATION

After Gaffney promoted some of the agents that Lee Speer had investigated, several New York agents resigned in despair. One was Robert J. Furey. A former state trooper, Furey had investigated Black Muslims, Cuban gunrunners, and political subversives, and he was no *ingénu* when he entered the FBN in 1959. "I went into the Third Group under John Dolce," he recalls, "and in less than a year it was clear that what was going on in New York was beyond the comprehension of the bosses in Washington." Seeking sanctuary, Furey requested a transfer to the Court House Squad. Like many of his colleagues, he viewed the Court House Squad and the International Group as the only honest ways of conducting federal drug law enforcement. "Marty Pera and Andy Tartaglino had more smarts and integrity than all other bosses in the FBN put together," he asserts. "They were looking at various elements of the French connection that didn't fit together, and they were making progress; but at the same time, things were getting worse."

For Furey, the last straw was the murder of informant Shorty Holmes on 8 August 1961. Holmes was a key witness in an important case on several major Mafiosi. He was found mutilated and stuffed in a garbage can. "The world was collapsing around my head," Furey recalls, "so I and a few other agents transferred out. People went to the State Department, or to ATF, or to Customs. Everyone was afraid of seeing or hearing the wrong thing."

Tony Mangiaracina sums the situation up: "Everything in the FBN was rush rush rush. But you can't buy a dealer a beer then ask him for a kilogram of heroin." He blames Anslinger for a nickel-and-dime management system that forced agents to bend the rules. "Once I wanted to get close to a woman in Beirut. She expects me to buy her champagne. I got eleven dollars per diem! Another time I buy cocaine in Milan, but the FBN didn't have a lab to test it in, so I had to take it to a drugstore!"

"Why were there only two inspectors while Anslinger was Commissioner?" another agent asks rhetorically. "Because he didn't want to find anything wrong. He wanted Congress to believe we could handle the problem with 300 agents. But that only made it harder for agents to cooperate with one another. There was nowhere to go, and we ended up eating our own!"

Marty Pera blamed the corruption problem on the intrinsically profane nature of undercover work. "If you're successful because you can lie, cheat, and steal, those things become tools you use in the bureaucracy," he said.

But it was more than that, it was Anslinger's reactionary policies. In a March 1962 article for *Harper's Magazine*, Benjamin DeMott said that Anslinger's "cop mentality" was responsible for the FBN's "carelessness about the Constitutional rights of its opposition." DeMott astutely observed that, "The handmaid of the cop mentality in the Narcotics Bureau is a whole complex of attitudes associated with Bible-Beltism."[7]

In 1961, Bill Davis went directly to Anslinger to protest against the cop mentality, and argue for a more humane approach toward addicts. "Mr. Commissioner," Davis said, "I'd like to talk to you about the high rate of recidivism."

"Mr. Davis," Anslinger replied, "we're law enforcers, not social workers."

Thoroughly disenchanted, Davis resigned and took a job with the US Information Service.

Agent Tony Johnson also resigned in 1961, for reasons associated with that complex of attitudes known euphemistically as Bible-Beltism. "I'd made thirty cases in six weeks in Gary, Indiana," Johnson says, "and I requested a transfer to Indianapolis. Instead I was sent to Houston, where Jack Kelly was the agent in charge. Kelly was cooperating with Mexican officials, and I was going to be sent into Mexico with an informant. As part of the deal I was told to go to Dallas to get a truck. I left Houston and along the way I stopped at a place to get a cup of coffee. The people behind the counter tell me to, 'Get your head out of that door, nigger.'

"Well, I didn't, and the next thing I know, here come the cops. They didn't believe my credentials and they held me in jail for two hours. When I finally got to Dallas, the agents there weren't expecting me. They hadn't been told I was coming. But the stool, a White guy, had been told a week ahead of time! That was the last straw, so I decided to quit. I went to the New Jersey Crime Commission."

THE CHANGING OF THE GUARD

Harry Anslinger spent much of 1961 pouring the little energy he had left into modifying a plan that was designed to combine all prior UN narcotics agreements under one charter. Known as the Single Convention, one of its provisions allowed several African nations to raise revenue by growing opium for export. Anslinger opposed this aspect of the treaty, but he signed it anyway, at the request of newly elected president John F. Kennedy. In recognition of that gesture, President Kennedy reappointed Anslinger Commissioner of Narcotics. It was a politically smart move by a president whose ambitious brother, Attorney General Robert Kennedy, was planning an assault on organized crime that depended largely on the FBN.

When his wife died in September 1961, Anslinger was physically strong for a seventy-year-old man, and still politically sharp. Nearing mandatory retirement in May 1962, and grieving for his wife, he described himself in March to Benjamin DeMott as "burned out" and spending no more than "an hour a month at his desk."[8] Hopelessly stuck in a bygone era, he coasted through his last months with the FBN. But he had an ulterior motive. If he had wanted to, he could have brought order to FBN headquarters, which was still reeling from Speer's fated integrity investigation. Instead, so as not to sully his reputation, he kept his distance and cynically allowed his subordinates to fight amongst themselves. And he ended his career in Geneva in characteristic fashion, by blasting Red China one last time at the UN's seventeenth Narcotics Convention. Having fired his last volley, Anslinger reluctantly passed his mantle to Henry Giordano and then retired to Hollidaysburg.

Unfortunately for the FBN, Henry Giordano was less intent on bringing a new, ethical sense of purpose to the FBN than he was in making appointments that reinforced his position. One beneficiary was Walter Panich, a savvy agent who had joined the FBN in Detroit as a clerk in 1942. George White, while serving as Detroit's district supervisor in 1947, had introduced Panich to Giordano (then a member of White's inner circle), and they had been friends ever since. On the recommendation of Baltimore District Supervisor Irwin Greenfeld, who had done a review of headquarters procedures, Deputy Commissioner Giordano brought Panich to Washington in late 1961 as his assistant on administrative matters.

"Headquarters had a lot of administrative problems," Panich explains. "There was a general accounting office staffed by one accountant, and the personnel office consisted of four female clerks. It was a complete disaster, so Henry asked me to straighten things out. He was more progressive than Anslinger. He got more money from Congress, hired a personnel manager, and got promotions for the staff, which slowly started to grow."

But Giordano did not tackle the issue of corruption by expanding the inspections staff as well as the accounting and personnel staffs. He also made the mistake of adopting Anslinger's cop mentality, despite the overwhelming evidence that methadone was beneficial in treating drug addicts. Worst of all, from an organizational point of view, he advanced Anslinger's essentially suicidal policy of accommodating the CIA.

15

THE MAGIC BUTTON

"And all are suspects and involved
Until the mystery is solved."

W. H. Auden, "The Double Man"

While the case-making agents were dodging enforcement assistant Lee Speer's corruption investigation in the conflicted New York office, the CIA was adding to the organization's mounting ethical woes by employing FBN agents and informants, as well as major drug traffickers, in an official assassination program codenamed ZR/RIFLE. Charlie Siragusa was the main player, through the CIA's MKULTRA Program.

George White, of course, had set up the first MKULTRA pad in New York in 1953, and in 1955 had moved his operation to Chestnut Street in San Francisco, where Ike Feldman joined him. Siragusa got involved in 1959 in his capacity as the FBN's field supervisor, when he inspected White's second MKULTRA facility (the Chestnut Street pad having been closed in 1958) at 261 Green Street in Mill Valley, across the Bay from San Francisco in Marin County. There White (increasingly debilitated by alcoholism), Feldman, and sundry CIA scientists tested stink bombs, itching powders, diarrhea inducers, and other "harassment substances." Also tested was "a fine hypodermic needle to inject drugs through the cork in a wine bottle."[1] The needle was so fine it could pierce a person's skin without being felt, and had potentially lethal applications.

The Mill Valley safehouse proved unsuitable, for a number of reasons, and in February 1960 the CIA opened a new one in San Francisco. Used until 1965, the so-called Plantation Inn was a favorite watering hole for San Francisco's inner circle of FBN agents. Siragusa described it as "one large room and a small kitchen and bath." He said that "White had the place wired up, and there was a two-way mirror. When White wanted to use the mirror, he would rent the adjoining apartment." Ike Feldman had the key to the safehouse and any agent who wanted to use it had to clear it with him. "Feldman was a wise little guy, a fast talker, and overly aggressive," Siragusa said.[2]

Feldman operated the Bay Area safehouses with Dr. Ray Treichler, a reclusive and timid, yet effective spook. Treichler had been assigned as the CIA's liaison to the major American pharmaceutical companies, and had acquired the MKULTRA account in 1957, when Sid Gottlieb embarked on an overseas assignment. White, Feldman, Treichler, and various CIA scientists conducted an array of experiments at the MKULTRA pads and at nightclubs in the Bay Area. One exotic weapon they tested was a gas cartridge, calibrated to fit certain types of guns, and designed to spray an incapacitating chemical more disabling than tear gas.

Despite being aware of these MKULTRA operations and facilities, Siragusa was prohibited from reading White and Feldman's reports, or listening to their tape recordings. All that changed, however, in January 1961, when Treichler asked Siragusa to open a safehouse in New York City, at 105 West 13th Street, at which point he too, perhaps unwittingly, became a part of the MKULTRA Program. By Siragusa's account, Treichler did not tell him why the CIA was opening the 13th Street pad; but in 1977, he told a Senate Subcommittee that he assumed it was because the CIA wanted "to uncover defectors in their own organization."[3] The New York pad had hidden tape recorders, bugs in the telephone, spike mikes (microphones that looked like nails) in the molding along the floor, and a two-way mirror behind a sofa bed, in the wall between the adjoining apartments.

Treichler gave Siragusa cash, which he deposited in an account under the alias Cal Salerno, for furniture and rent. Andy Tartaglino, having just returned from Europe and joined the Court House Squad, helped his mentor furnish the pad. The FBN's firearms instructor, veteran Agent John Tagley, was assigned as its caretaker.

Siragusa then introduced George Gaffney to Treichler at a restaurant in New York. Gaffney recalls that Treichler spoke with a British accent, wore a derby hat, carried an umbrella, and gave him two very specific instructions. He said the CIA had priority over the safehouse, that Siragusa would call him when the CIA wanted to use it, and that he should keep the FBN agents away when that happened. Gaffney was also told to make the apartment look "lived in." In compliance with this second instruction, the 13th Street pad became a convenient place for FBN agents to make cases, quiz informants, and have parties. It was also a place where out-of-town agents, family members, old friends, and dignitaries could stay while in New York.

Few agents knew that the mysterious apartment was funded by the CIA, and its existence fueled rumors that headquarters was involved in corruption – that the bosses, perhaps, were receiving "things," if not money, from Establishment benefactors like Pan Am executive Sam Pryor. In this way the 13th Street pad further undermined the integrity of the stressed-out New York office. But bigger CIA-related problems were looming.

THE PATRON SAINT OF ASSASSINATIONS

Through MKULTRA, the FBN factored in the CIA's plots to murder Fidel Castro. One of these plots was launched in March 1960 at the direction of President Eisenhower, and relied on what the CIA euphemistically called "the gambling syndicate" for help in recruiting assassins inside Cuba. To implement the plan, CIA security chief Sheffield Edwards recruited Robert Maheu, a private investigator whose firm had been subsidized by the Agency since 1955, when it helped Stavros Niarchos wrestle a lucrative Saudi Arabian oil-shipping contract from Aristotle Onassis. Maheu in turn enlisted Johnny Roselli, a Mafioso he'd met through criminal defense attorney Edward Bennett Williams. Then managing a vending machine concession on the Vegas Strip, Roselli (born Francesco Sacco) had been arrested for peddling heroin in 1921, and had served three years in prison (1941–44) for his role in a Hollywood union extortion scam. A very well known and influential gangster, he traveled to New York in September 1960 to meet his CIA case officer, James O'Connell. One month later in Miami, Edwards, O'Connell, and Maheu (all former FBI agents) brought Sam Giancana and Santo Trafficante, the patron saint of drug traffickers, into the murder plot.[4]

Santo Trafficante was the indispensable man in the Castro assassination plot, even though he was listed as No. 234 in the FBN's International List book, and even though there were serious doubts about his loyalty. The CIA knew, for example, that during the four months he'd been detained in Cuba, Trafficante had lived in relative luxury while he negotiated the return of seized Mafia assets with Fidel Castro's brother Raoul. The CIA also knew that after his release, Trafficante traveled freely to and from Havana. But the doubts were set aside because he was intimately connected to leaders in the anti-Castro Cuban exile community and could contact their secret agents in Cuba. One of the purported secret agents, Juan Orta Cordova, was the director of Fidel Castro's ministerial office in Havana. On the assumption that Orta was willing and able to kill Castro, CIA security chief Edwards had Trafficante arrange the delivery of MKULTRA poison pills to him. The plan was that Orta would drop the pills in Castro's coffee. But Cuban security officials discovered that Orta was a counter-revolutionary, and a Mafia flunky, and he was fired on 26 January 1961. By the time the pills arrived in February, he was unavailable to do the job.

Immediately after this plan failed, Trafficante − not the CIA − allegedly devised a second assassination plot in which one of Castro's mistresses, Marita Lorenz, was (like Orta) to administer a lethal dose of MKULTRA poison to the prime minister. This hit, for which Trafficante was to be paid $150,000, was contingent on his business partner, Dr. Manuel Antonio de Varona. Linked with former Cuban president Carlos Prio Socarras, Tony Varona in 1961 headed the Meyer Lansky-financed, CIA-created, avidly anti-Castro political front, the Frente Revolucionario Democratico, in Miami.[5]

After Trafficante had introduced the various conspirators to one another, CIA officer Jim O'Connell passed a handful of poison pills to mobster Johnny Roselli. On 13 March 1961, Roselli, in the Boom Boom room in Miami's Fontainebleau Hotel, passed them to Varona's son-in-law for delivery to the femme fatale, Marita Lorenz. But the Bay of Pigs invasion disrupted that particular scheme and, three months later, in July 1961, Siragusa denounced Trafficante as a double agent. He insisted that Castro had jailed the Mafioso as a ruse, and that Trafficante was in fact working with Castro's agents in the lucrative bolita gambling business in Miami. [6] The implication was that he had sabotaged the CIA's first assassination attempt on Castro, and had probably betrayed the CIA in other ways as well. But Trafficante − like Dr. Chung before him − was never arrested for treason or drug trafficking, and though closely monitored, continued to manage his bolita and narcotics trafficking businesses with impunity.

How could this be, one might ask? The answer is quite simple: so that Trafficante, and other international drug smugglers and degenerate hoods like Johnny Roselli, could arrange assassinations for the CIA.

THE CENTRAL INSTITUTE OF ASSASSINS

In 1960, the CIA derived its authority to conduct assassinations from President Eisenhower, through the National Security Council's Special

Group. The members of the Special Group were Allen W. Dulles, National Security Advisor Gordon Gray, Undersecretary of State Livingston Merchant, and Assistant Secretary of Defense John N. Irwin. Gray, it should be recalled, had buried Guenther Reinhardt's exposé on drug dealing by US military officers in Germany after the Second World War.[7]

After the Special Group decided to create an assassination program, Dulles passed along the president's wishes to Richard Bissell, the CIA's deputy director of plans. Bissell in turn activated a super-secret assassination unit under William K. Harvey, chief of Division D of the CIA's Foreign Intelligence Branch. Harvey's "executive action" (a euphemism for assassinations) unit was hidden within a larger program, codenamed ZR/RIFLE, which was designed to obtain foreign ciphers and codes through burglaries and safecrackings, and by kidnapping couriers and spies who sometimes doubled as narcotics smugglers, and stealing the contents of their diplomatic pouches.[8]

Harvey was, in some ways, George White's doppelganger in the CIA. An overweight, pear-shaped, belligerent drunk and womanizer with a close association with James Angleton, he had resigned from the FBI in 1947 to become chief of counterintelligence in the Office of Special Operations. In 1948, he joined the CIA and achieved instant fame by discovering that Kim Philby, the British liaison officer to the CIA, was a Soviet spy. In 1953, he was assigned as chief of the Berlin station, where he served for several years until returning to headquarters to take charge of Division D.[9]

Division D was cloistered in the most secluded chamber in the CIA's enchanted mansion, and most of Harvey's minions remain unknown. The little that is known about them is contained in Harvey's handwritten notes, outlining his search in the fall of 1960 for a principal agent, codenamed QJ/WIN, whose task was to recruit underworld assassins and burglars. In his notes, Harvey displays an intimate knowledge of the underworld's drug smuggling milieu, and in considering candidates for the QJ/WIN position, he suggested using "former resistance personnel" from OSS days. "Corsicans were recommended," Harvey wrote, "as Sicilians could lead to the Mafia."[10]

So we have it from the horse's mouth that the CIA hired Corsican drug smugglers as assassins, in order to protect certain Mafiosi in its employ. If only we knew who they were!

Harvey considered nine candidates for the QJ/WIN position, though in the documents the CIA released to the public it deleted the names of eight, as well as the name of the CIA station chief who recommended them. The anonymous station chief said very little about each candidate.

Candidate One thought the matter was being handled by the FBN! Two was fully informed, and had identified a possible assassin. Four was an American in Rome, experienced with criminals, and may have been Jack Cusack, Hank Manfredi, or Paul Knight. Five was in Milan, which "offered good possibilities." Six was a multilingual bar owner in Florence, acquainted with Belgium's criminal milieu, and thus suitable for work in the Congo, where the CIA was planning on assassinating Premier Patrice Lumumba. Seven had introduced Jack Cusack to two expert safecrackers on 19 July 1960 in Barcelona. Eight was a Russian living in Antwerp, and was reachable through the Army CID in Frankfurt. Nine was a Frenchman involved in the commercial film industry.

And Three was Charlie Siragusa. The station chief who proposed the list to Harvey described Siragusa as a "source on Corsicans and Sicilians," and suggested that Harvey "query him whether District 2 [New York] has any West Indian colored contacts usable for our purposes." [11]

Harvey was so dependent on the FBN and its underworld contacts that he scribbled the words "the Magic Button" beside a reference to the Bureau in his notes. But the need to exclude Mafiosi and Americans from the operation prevailed, and another individual was selected in November 1960 – although, even then, Harvey wondered, "How much does Siragusa know?" [12]

He knew a lot. Sometime between the summer of 1960 and the spring of 1961, CIA officer Vincent Thill, a veteran of the Berlin station, where he had served under Bill Harvey, asked Siragusa "to recruit an assassination squad." [13] In making this request, Thill referred to Siragusa's many contacts in the underworld and said the CIA was prepared to pay $1 million per hit. He also asked Siragusa to set up a detective agency as a front for illegal CIA operations in America. [14] Siragusa said he refused on moral grounds, and his acknowledgment of Thill's overture seems to clear him of any involvement in Harvey's ZR/RIFLE Program. However, at least one expert, according to Professor Alan Block, believed that Siragusa was dissembling, and that he was, in fact, QJ/WIN. [15]

QJ/WIN's nationality itself is uncertain. His background file (called a "201-file" by the CIA) contains twenty-seven documents, spanning the period from February 1955, when he was caught smuggling nickel behind the Iron Curtain, until his termination as an agent in 1964. None of the documents reveals his name. Not that it matters. Harvey in his notes insisted on a "phony 201" that was thoroughly "back-stopped" and looked like a counterespionage file. So even the extant evidence on QJ/WIN is dubious at best.

The best evidence suggests that this mysterious operative was Jose Marie Andre Mankel, as Mason Cargill (a staff member of vice president Rockefeller's Commission to Investigate CIA Activities within the United States) reported in a 1 May 1975 memo. [16]   Harvey in his notes refers to QJ/WIN as "FNU Mankel," which seems to corroborate Cargill's claim. But author Richard Mahoney claims that QJ/WIN was Mozes Maschkivitzan, a Russian émigré living in Luxembourg. Mahoney is the son of a CIA officer who served in Africa at the time, and he may have inside knowledge. Without citing sources, he also claims that among the assassins on Harvey's payroll were two Corsicans, "Santelli and Garioni," holding Italian passports, as well as "Italians from the Trieste area [Manfredi's area of expertise] who were ready to use the gun." [17]

What is known, and what is most important, is that Harvey wanted to recruit Corsicans to spy on the Soviets, and the man he selected for the QJ/WIN position was hired in Frankfurt on 1 November 1960 for the Lumumba assassination operation in the Congo. He was told that the "Soviets were operating in Africa among nationality groups, *specifically Corsicans* [italics added], and that he was being asked to spot, assess, and recommend some dependable, quick-witted persons for our use." [18]

THE TIE-IN BETWEEN DRUG SMUGGLING AND ESPIONAGE

According to documents contained in his 201-file, QJ/WIN was tall and thin, married (although homosexual), with many friends in well-to-do Parisian circles. He was a conman *extraordinaire*! He'd been a double agent during the war and had testified at the trial of Marshall Pétain. After the war he got involved in smuggling, and one of four or five FBN agents in Europe at the time recruited him and set him up in a business in Luxembourg. Through this FBN agent, the CIA's Luxembourg station chief, Arnold Silver, contacted QJ/WIN in the autumn of 1958 "in connection with an illegal narcotic operation into the United States … in behalf of the Bureau of Narcotics." [19]

QJ/WIN worked for the FBN and CIA over the next eighteen months, during which time Silver came to view him as a potential agent provocateur against the Soviets.

Curiously, and perhaps not by coincidence, the CIA hired QJ/WIN shortly after Henry J. Taylor, the US ambassador to Switzerland, was quoted in the 18 July 1958 *New York Times* as saying that the Communist Chinese, in league with the Soviets, were using Bern as the center of a huge narcotics enterprise, and were using the profits to finance spy operations, as well as Colonel Abdul Karim el-Kassem's revolution in Iraq. (If the reader will recall, Sid Gottlieb sent Kassem a MKULTRA "Black Valentine" shortly thereafter.) A week later Taylor retracted his claim, but the stage was set for Silver's provocateur, QJ/WIN, and his master, Bill Harvey at Division D, to exploit the situation.[20]

The machinery was set in motion and in April 1959, QJ/WIN told Silver that he had been approached by a French national and asked to join a narcotics ring that was receiving huge amounts of opium from the Chinese Communists. The Frenchman had brown hair and brown eyes, and was a heavy smoker. Born in Basque country, he'd smuggled narcotics before and after the war from North Africa, and had been convicted three times on criminal charges, most recently in December 1958. The French-man told QJ/WIN that two Sicilians living in Paris were already engaged in this traffic (perhaps the aforementioned Santelli and Garioni), and that one had received fifty kilograms of free opium in Hong Kong and had delivered it to the US through Canada. The Frenchman said that the Chinese provided the narcotics free of charge, on condition that they were delivered to the US.[21]

QJ/WIN stated his willingness to infiltrate the Chinese Communist drug ring, but the CIA had doubts about his reliability – and Silver felt the Frenchman was involved in some shady side deal, and had offered his services simply because he wanted free passage to smuggle drugs as a special employee of the FBN – so on 29 April 1959, Allen Dulles directed that "the nearest narcotics bureau officer" be summoned to interrogate QJ/WIN and the Frenchman, assess their stories, and decide what action, if any, was warranted.[22] Dulles's personal involvement underscores how important the potential operation was, precisely because it "tied in" with another report by a CIA agent who claimed to be in a similar (if not the same) drug ring managed by the Chinese Communist Embassy in Bern.

Richard Bissell, the CIA's deputy director for plans, summarized the details of this tie-in case in a 5 May 1959 letter to Harry Anslinger. As Bissell told the Commissioner, a CIA agent had a contact in the Chinese Communist Embassy in Bern. In February 1959, the agent was informed by his contact that he would be handling the narcotics business in Hamburg. In March, the contact said he would also be managing Chinese Communist drug rings in France, Italy, and Spain. The contact was to be the liaison between the ringleaders and the Bern Embassy, and would have a car and a diplomatic passport at his disposal. He had seen at least ten boxes of opium in the cellar of the Chinese Embassy in Bern. Each box contained about fifty kilograms of opium, and in the agent's opinion, the boxes would be transported by car from the Embassy to a prearranged location and from there to America.[23]

In preparation for the sale of the opium, he was introduced to the two men managing the French ring, and to Gabrielli, who handled the Italian ring and paid cash for 100 kilograms of the drug. Three nights later the contact met two Spaniards (perhaps in the nascent Orsini ring), but they didn't need anything because they still had a supply on hand.

Bissell told Anslinger that while the CIA agent was handling his contact in the Chinese Embassy, another person (later known as QJ/WIN) had been asked to join a ring that got large amounts of opium from the Chinese Communists. Bissell asked Anslinger to send an FBN agent to work with "the Luxembourger" (which implies Maschkivitzan rather than Mankel) to find out if the two operations were linked. Portions of the letter are deleted, but Bissell expressed serious doubts about this linkage being a possibility.

Knowing Anslinger's penchant for pillorying the PRC, one can imagine how passionately he would have exposed this Chinese Communist narcotics activity – if it existed. But the FBN agent sent to debrief QJ/WIN saw no need for action, and the CIA concurred. Silver and his assistant, John Stein, continued to work with QJ/WIN on the Soviet matter, and Silver said that FBN files indicated an "excellent" performance by QJ/WIN during this eighteen-month period leading up to November 1960; and on that basis Harvey decided to employ QJ/WIN as a principal agent in his ZR/RIFLE assassination program.[24]

What this means is that for eighteen months, under the guidance of FBN agents, QJ/WIN dealt narcotics as a cover for CIA double agent recruitment and provocation activities aimed at the Soviets. He was fully protected in this endeavor – and in others afterwards. The Church Committee Report notes that in 1962, QJ/WIN "was about to go on trial in Europe on smuggling charges," but the CIA wished to "quash charges or arrange somehow to salvage QJ/WIN for our purposes."[25]

Obviously, the importance of FBN agents, and their drug smuggling employees, in providing cover for CIA operations cannot be overstated – and should never be forgotten when analyzing FBN statements and operations. For example, Charlie Siragusa was in Miami in March 1962, when FBN agents arrested five Cubans with a half-pound of opium they had allegedly obtained from China. Siragusa said that with that particular arrest, "the international drug conspiracy had assumed communist overtones."[26]

Although the Chinese Communist–Cuban drug connection was based largely on dubious information, some of which the CIA itself discarded as implausible, Siragusa's charges prompted Senator Charles Keating (D-NY) to initiate a congressional study into the problem, and added steam to the CIA's churning propaganda war against Castro's Cuba.[27]

NIMBLE JACK CUSACK AND THE PHANTOM CHINA CONNECTION

Siragusa was not the only FBN agent involved in Harvey's ZR/RIFLE Program. As Luxembourg station chief Arnold Silver noted in an 11 October 1960 memo to Harvey, candidate Number Seven had two expert safecrackers at his service "who were introduced to Cusack on July 19, 1960, in Barcelona."[28]

Arturo Ureta Gallardo, a Spanish policeman, was candidate Number Seven, and as a way of proving his bona fides for the QJ/WIN position, he introduced Cusack to a pair of expert safecrackers, while Cusack and Anthony Mangiaracina were in Barcelona on a multipurpose narcotics investigation. The pretext for the Spanish investigation was the elusive Communist Chinese narcotics connection. As Cusack explained in a 29 July 1960 report to Anslinger, he and Mangiaracina had met ten days earlier with Luis Pozo, chief of Spain's Central Narcotics Bureau, and falsely claimed that an American seaman in Naples had told Mangiaracina that he could obtain Communist Chinese heroin from a Mr. Sung Hon Yung in Barcelona. Cusack unabashedly told his Commissioner that "it was necessary to fabricate this background to give us a concrete reason for our visit to Spain."[29]

Though he knew Cusack was lying, Pozo provided him with an introduction to Arturo Ureta Gallardo, the Spanish policeman Bill Harvey was thinking of recruiting for the QJ/WIN position. Apparently, Ureta Gallardo was auditioning for the part, and when Cusack and Mangiaracina arrived in Barcelona, he graciously offered to produce his file on Sung – although it was locked in a rusty old combination-style safe, which had recently gotten jammed. Not to worry; there just happened to be two professional safecrackers in the local jail, and Ureta Gallardo had them released, and they opened the safe.

This sequence of staged events would have appeared highly providential under normal circumstances. But Cusack, of course, was expecting a demonstration and he never told Mangiaracina what was going on. And while it's unclear if Cusack actually made a pass at Ureta Gallardo in Barcelona, he could have done so very easily. As Mangiaracina recalls, Cusack was staying in a separate hotel room and could have interviewed Ureta Gallardo later that night. When approached by the author, Cusack declined to address the subject of using an expensive federal narcotics investigation for nefarious CIA purposes.

Next, after reading the file on Sung Hon Yung, Cusack and Mangiaracina engaged in their undercover narcotics assignment and approached the suspected Chinese drug trafficker at his apartment. They initially presented themselves as businessmen who sold appliances to American soldiers and sailors, but after dinner Cusack disingenuously confessed that he and Mangiaracina were really after heroin. Sung and his compatriots recoiled in horror and responded with unsolicited denunciations of Communist China. But wiley Jack Cusack didn't believe them, and he reported to Anslinger that he was sure they were part "of a ChiCom espionage organization and that their tailoring business [was] merely a vehicle to carry out their mission [which, along with drug smuggling, included spying on the Sixth Fleet] and give them cover."[30] Finally, he alleged that the Spanish police officials were in cahoots with the Chinese.

On this last detail, Mangiaracina is in total agreement with Cusack. "I'd developed the lead," he says, "and it was supposed to be my investigation, but Cusack decided that he had to handle it, because the Chinese were part of a spy ring. They were with the Thin Blade Gang out of Macao and Hong Kong. But the Spanish police told them we were narcotic agents, so they amused us and sent us on our way."

As the Sung Hon Yung case illustrates, it was standard procedure for the CIA to hide its espionage operations inside FBN investigations. It also shows how an FBN agent could advance his career by accommodating the CIA. Cusack knew this, and he carefully cultivated his relationship with CIA officer Raymond Rocca, whom he had reportedly met in Rome in 1952. By 1960, Rocca was Angleton's chief of research and was in close liaison with Bill Harvey; which is how Harvey knew to approach Cusack for the mission in Barcelona. And that is why ambitious Jack Cusack began to envision himself as Siragusa's successor, under the forthcoming Giordano regime, as the FBN's chief of foreign operations and its primary liaison to the CIA.

THE RE-EMERGENCE OF GARLAND WILLIAMS AND OTHER MKULTRA DEVELOPMENTS

One of the people QJ/WIN sought to recruit in the Congo was Joseph Brahim, also known as Joe Attia.[31] A hero of the Resistance, Attia had worked for SDECE in Morocco and Tunisia in the 1950s. Then in 1960, he purchased the Refuge Nightclub in Abidjan, the capital city of the Ivory Coast. The Refuge was the unofficial hangout of Jacques Foccart's SAC spy ring, as well as various spies and smugglers operating across Africa.[32]

As one might expect, the CIA was on top of the situation, and its freelance expert on such matters, Garland Williams, arrived in Abidjan in September 1961 undercover as a narcotic specialist for the Agency for International Development's Public Safety Program.[33] His cover job was to develop security programs throughout the Entente states, at a time when the Belgian consul in Syria was accused of running guns to the Congo, and Liberia (with its liberal banking and shipping laws) had become a banking center for drug smugglers. It was also, according to Ike Feldman, a period when the CIA was using the Dark Continent to test its germ warfare capabilities.[34]

While Garland Williams established a spy network to monitor Corsican drug smugglers in Africa, Feldman was transferred to New York and began working in Chinatown. Siragusa was the Deputy Commissioner by then and would not allow Feldman to use the 13th Street pad. So, behind Siragusa's back, Feldman procured apartment 1B at 212 East 18th Street. He did this with the help of Treichler and money provided by George White. He also brought along all the erotic literature and technological devices from the Plantation Inn in San Francisco and, true to form, established himself as a pimp.[35]

Taking over Feldman's responsibility for the Plantation Inn in San Francisco was Albert Habib. Born in Tunisia, where he had served as a policeman until 1955, Habib worked closely with White and Gottlieb, and they provided him with an undercover box at the San Francisco Post Office for secret MKULTRA correspondences. On one occasion, he accompanied White and Gottlieb to an air force base in Nevada where MKULTRA experiments were being conducted. According to Habib, White was as powerful as ever in the early 1960s and could get anything he wanted from the mayor, the governor, the police chief, or FBN headquarters. He was still influential enough to prevent West Coast inspector Lee Speer from looking into his MKULTRA records and facilities.

White was the CIA's original MKULTRA contact in the FBN, and its ranking expert on Mafia murder techniques, and on 21 November 1960, just three weeks after Harvey had recruited QJ/WIN, Siragusa and Gottlieb visited White in hopes of recruiting Harold Meltzer into Harvey's ZR/RIFLE hit team. One of the premier drug smugglers of all time, and a contract killer to boot, Meltzer was recently out of prison and operating a sportswear company in Los Angeles. White, of course, knew all the top hoods on the West Coast, including CIA Agent Johnny Roselli, and thus it is not surprising that on 19 December 1960, one month after Siragusa and Gottlieb's visit to San Francisco, Roselli introduced Meltzer to Harvey. There can be no doubt about who brought about this meeting. As Feldman confessed in 1994, "On more than one occasion White sent me to the airport to pick up Roselli and bring him to the office." [36]

The existence of CIA-connected FBN agents working with CIA-connected Mafiosi was not, in a word, conducive to effective federal drug law enforcement. It was impossible for such relationships – in all their manifestations – not to compromise agents in the US who were attempting to make cases on the same CIA-connected Mafiosi and their associates. It was wrong, in so many ways. For example, the Agency, as Charlie Siragusa feared, was providing Bureau credentials to its operatives. One FBN report stated that a man named Harry Martin was traveling through Europe in the late 1950s posing as an FBN agent. According to Ralph Frias, "There were two or three cases like that." [37]

The CIA probably was providing FBN credentials to its ZR/RIFLE assassins-cum-drug smugglers. It could have provided them to anyone, including drug smuggling Mafiosi in its employ. According to Jill Jonnes, when FBN agents were closing in on Guatemalan Ambassador Mauricio Rosal and Corsican drug smuggler Etienne Tarditi in October 1960, "a corrupt New York agent was seen running full tilt up Lexington Avenue to the stakeout site to warn off Nick Calamaris. The agent working with Calamaris's underworld boss arrived too late." [38]

Dismissing Jonnes's assertion as preposterous, George Gaffney exclaims: "How could anybody rush to warn Calamaris when we didn't even know he was involved? And if the bad agent did know he was involved, why didn't he just call him up on the phone?"

But there's a possibility Gaffney hadn't considered. Perhaps the CIA had planted one of its agents in the New York office, and maybe he was working with Calamaris's boss in the Gambino family – someone, perhaps, from back in the Luciano Project days. There are so many possibilities. As noted earlier, Tarditi claimed he was involved in intelligence work beneficial to American interests. Maybe he was one of the Corsicans working for Bill Harvey. As a hero of the Resistance, he certainly fit the bill. Maybe some deeply sequestered CIA faction, like Bill Harvey's, decided to pull the plug on one of the Agency's own operations. Or maybe it *was* just a corrupt agent working for the Mafia.

What is perfectly clear is that Jonnes's unsubstantiated and unattributed allegation, against nobody in particular, casts suspicion on every FBN agent in New York in October 1960. Someone in the FBN, the person who made the allegation to Jonnes, knew about it at the time; and what better way to discredit an entire organization and justify its destruction, eight years later, when the FBN had finally become a liability to both the CIA and FBI.

In any event, as the Kennedys burst upon the scene, the CIA had turned the FBN completely upside down. CIA agents were blackmailing spies, diplomats, and politicians at three Bureau safehouses. With the support of complicit FBN agents, the CIA was hiring Corsican drug smugglers as assassins and using Mafiosi to smuggle MKULTRA poisons into Cuba in an attempt to assassinate Fidel Castro. On behalf of the Agency, FBN headquarters focused public attention on the phantom Chinese Communist–Cuban connection – even going so far, as explained in the previous chapter, as to allow top members of a Kuomintang drug smuggling ring in San Francisco to escape punishment, while George White covered for them by telling the press that their heroin had come from Communist China. Meanwhile, the CIA's anti-Castro terrorists were smuggling spies and assassins into Cuba, and returning with shiploads of narcotics for sale in America. And the United States had conceded defeat in its war on drugs.

16

MAKING THE MAFIA

"He who laughs last, never really got the joke."

Anonymous

On 21 October 1960, FBN agents and detectives from the Westchester County Sheriff's office arrested Salvatore Rinaldo and Matteo Palmieri for possession of ten kilograms of high-grade heroin. While the case did not receive the same sensational headlines as L'affaire Rosal – which involved the seizure of 100 kilograms of heroin and the arrest of an ambassador – the ramifications of the Rinaldo-Palmieri case were equally important, leading to the arrest of dozens of drug traffickers in Italy and America, and indirectly to the death of Lucky Luciano.

The Rinaldo–Palmieri case also brought Agent Frank Selvaggi into the limelight. Tall, edgy, and tragically hip, Selvaggi rivaled Lenny Schrier as the premier case-making agent of their era. During the course of his nine-year career, Selvaggi took into custody dozens of the most dangerous drug traffickers in America, many of whom he bruised and bullied while managing their passage from predator to prisoner. Belligerent when necessary, always astute, he knew how to be charitable, pleasant, and cool. Very cool. When he walks, with one hand in his blazer pocket and the other holding a cigarette, it's as if he were shuffling to a Tony Bennett tune. Frank Selvaggi was not someone to trifle with, but to his friends he was a reliable and eminently likeable man.

"Frank was a great raconteur," George Gaffney says with unabashed affection. "He spoke in the authentic idiom of the Mafia, and he could tell a fabulous story. Sitting for hours on a stakeout with Frank passed by in a minute. Customs agents would come to the office and sit around him like little kids while he told stories about the Mafia hoods he knew. He was a true hero," Gaffney adds with emotion, "the greatest agent the Bureau ever had. No man made a greater contribution. I wanted to give him the Treasury medal, but instead he got the rawest deal of any man I've ever known."

Tragically hip, indeed. A perpetual worrier, at times manic, Selvaggi grew up in the same Pelham Bay section of the Bronx as Charlie Siragusa's younger brother. "I went to high school with Charlie's niece," Selvaggi explains, "and after I graduated from the Maritime Academy, I asked her to marry me. But the Siragusas were old-fashioned Sicilians, and you know what that means?" He gives a quizzical look. "I had to have $25,000 in the bank to get permission, and it took two and a half years to scrape it together."

The marriage was fine, but Frank's wife was lonely, and the kids needed to see their seafaring father more often, so Charlie Siragusa, as a favor for his brother, offered Frank a job with the FBN. "I'd done Charlie a favor a few years earlier," Selvaggi explains. "I was on an American Export Line ship, and he asked me to keep an eye out on a particular voyage. When we put into port in Marseilles, I saw the third mate toss a package overboard. I told the captain and he had the package retrieved, and it turned out to contain ten kilograms of heroin. I'd done that favor for Charlie, and my wife wanted me at home, so in 1958 I became a Special Hire."[1]

Giving up his maritime job wasn't easy: as a seaman Selvaggi made three times as much money as a basic FBN agent. Being married to Siragusa's niece didn't afford him any special privileges either. On the contrary, his fellow agents assumed that Siragusa was helping him behind the scenes, and so they held him to a higher standard. Yet Frank Selvaggi surpassed everyone's expectations, and among his many achievements, he made the historically important case on notorious Joe Valachi, and pressured the old hood into exposing the Mafia's history and hierarchical organization. Sadly, this amazing accomplishment went unacknowledged outside the FBN. More to the point, the FBI deliberately ruined Selvaggi's career because of it, as will be explained in a subsequent chapter.

"My first group leader," Selvaggi recalls, "was Angelo Zurlo in Group Three. The members of that group were all respected street agents who knew what was going on. Art Mendelsohn was my first partner. Art had been around for years, and he treated me like a kid, but I learned a lot from him – as well as from Angie Zurlo, who made me read all the files. Ben Fitzgerald had Group One. Ben had a reputation as the most intelligent agent in the office, although he'd been Fred Dick's partner, and even though he'd walk off a surveillance at dinnertime. But Group One did okay because of Lenny

Schrier. George O'Connor had Group Two. Joey Amato had Group Four. Pat Ward was the enforcement assistant, and Jack Cusack had the Court House Squad. Cusack," Selvaggi says candidly, "was a clerk who wrote stories, and John Enright was his disciple. Enright was a nine-to-fiver who ran the Court House Squad after Cusack and later moved to Washington headquarters.

"When I arrived, Lenny Schrier was making a lot of cases with an informant he'd inherited from Fred Dick. Then Lenny made the Orlandino case, and when Angie Zurlo retired, Lenny thought he'd get Group Three. And he should have. But Gaffney gave it to John Dolce instead, and that's when the animosity began.

"Gaffney was a good district supervisor," Selvaggi continues, "but he was a square, and he was duped by Pat Ward, just like John Dolce was poisoned by Patty Biase. My own problems with them began during the Cotroni case. I was in the hotel room with Dolce, Biase, and Jack Brady while they were guarding Cotroni's girlfriend. It was the night that Pat Ward's informer, Eddie Smith, was going to make John Ormento, and because I was a new guy, they wanted me out of their hair." Frank frowns. "First they told me to stand in a corner, then they told me to go up to Harlem and toss junkies. They weren't supposed to do that, but I didn't know any better, so I went up there alone and got slashed in the leg by a Puerto Rican whore. I wrapped my handkerchief around the gash, went back to the hotel, and asked them what I should do next? They told me to forget about it, and avoid the hassle of trying to explain to the bosses what had happened up in Harlem."

Selvaggi was trying to fit in, so he did what he was told. But his wife saw the bloody bandage when he got home and she told her father, and he told Charlie Siragusa, and Siragusa blasted John Dolce for sending Selvaggi into Harlem alone.

"Dolce had a nice wife," Selvaggi says, "and we all felt bad when she lost a child at birth. I grew up in the same neighborhood with Patty Biase, and went to school with his younger sister, Angelica. Jack Brady had been in the New York narcotic squad, and Gaffney was so impressed with his performance that he hired him. They were all good agents; but after Charlie gave them hell, Dolce, Biase, and Brady spent the rest of their lives trying to get even."

INROADS INTO THE MAFIA

As a rookie agent in late 1958, Frank Selvaggi, along with his senior partner Art Mendelsohn and veteran NYPD narcotic squad detective Harold

Kunin, arrested Helen Streat, a heroin addict and prostitute in Harlem. They found ten ounces of heroin on her during a routine shakedown, and rather than go to jail, she flipped. And based on information Helen provided, Selvaggi and his colleagues made a series of street-level cases that led to John Freeman, a powerful drug trafficker from Louisiana. From his flower shop in Harlem, Freeman supplied drug dealers in Chicago, Detroit, and Los Angeles. Freeman stood six feet four and weighed 350 pounds, and he was known in the underworld as "Mr. Big." As Selvaggi recalls, "When he was arrested, he looked around the room and said: 'Anyone talks to the cops has his tongue cut out.'

"Although we didn't know it at the time," Selvaggi adds matter-of-factly, "Freeman was supplied by Valachi, and Valachi copped from Sal Rinaldo."

The Valachi case developed when Helen Streat set up her supplier, Hank Townes, and he flipped and took undercover Agent Charles "Charlie Mac" McDonnell to Freeman's runner, a one-eyed gangster from Brooklyn called Slim. Freeman never handled narcotics himself, but instead he had Slim receive the heroin from Joe Valachi's deliveryman, and then Slim in turn delivered it to Freeman's customers, including Hank Townes. Freeman had five customers, and all five were hand-picked because they were ex-cons with records for armed robbery or other gun-related charges.

Charlie McDonnell made two undercover buys from Slim, each for 100 ounces of heroin. Then, showing tremendous composure, he met alone with Freeman in his flower shop. On this critical occasion, which assured Freeman's conviction, McDonnell persuaded Mr. Big to supply him directly, and Freeman unwisely had his son, John Jr., personally deliver 100 ounces of heroin to McDonnell.

Surveillance conducted during the buys revealed that Ralph Wagner was Valachi's delivery man to Slim. And during a forceful interrogation, in which Selvaggi and Jack Brady placed him under extreme duress, Slim revealed that the "Italian boss" lived in an apartment building with unusual gates in a neighborhood Selvaggi was familiar with in the Bronx. Selvaggi drove around the neighborhood for several days until he found the apartment building, and then he and Agent Ivan "Ike" Wurms staked it out. Eventually they saw Joe Valachi enter the building, and they discovered that Michael Monica was the "plant-man" holding the heroin for Valachi in his apartment. But Valachi, Wagner, and Monica realized they were being watched, and after Freeman was arrested in May 1959, they tried to slip out of sight.

"Valachi hid out in New Rochelle for awhile," Selvaggi says, "then moved to a trailer camp in Connecticut. Ralph fled to Mexico then Texas, where he was arrested. Ralph was returned to New York, and while he was out on bail, we started meeting."

Ralph Wagner, a one-time professional boxer with a bad temper when he got drunk, became Selvaggi's informant, and in November 1959 he provided Selvaggi with the vital information that led to Valachi's arrest. While Valachi was on the lam in the Freeman case, he turned his jukebox concession over to a young hood named Paulie. Paulie would make the rounds, collect the coins, count them up, and then call Valachi and tell him how much money he'd made that week. Wagner knew the number that Paulie called every Friday night around eleven o'clock. He knew it was a pay phone off a two-lane highway near Thomaston, Connecticut, but he didn't know the exact location. So Selvaggi, Art Mendelsohn, and Ralph Wagner drove to Thomaston one Friday night. It was a shot in the dark, yes, but they didn't expect to find themselves in the middle of nowhere, driving up and down an unlit road in rural Thomaston, looking for a pay phone booth.

"We'd made two swipes," Selvaggi recalls, "then by sheer coincidence Valachi lights a cigarette in the phone booth just as we're passing by. The whole thing lit up, and we could see his white hair. We stopped the car and Ralph jumped out. To this day I have no idea how he got back to New York. We didn't have time to do anything about Ralph running away, so we went to grab Valachi, and as Mendelsohn and I approached the phone booth, he saw us coming. It was a very spooky night and he thought we were mob guys come to kill him. 'Don't shoot! Don't shoot!' he said, as he came out of the booth.

"Valachi was mine ten minutes after we grabbed him," Selvaggi says with satisfaction. "We'd been driving all over, up and down the highway, and we were about to run out of gas. So we pulled into a fire station, identified ourselves as federal agents, and while Mendelsohn filled up the car, Valachi and I went inside to take a piss. He was a diabetic, and I agreed to drive back to the trailer park so he could get his pills. After I agreed to do that, he said he wanted to make a deal. But only with me, because I was an Italian, and because he thought that Mendelsohn was Jewish. So," Selvaggi shrugs, "between him thinking that Mendelsohn was Jewish, and me agreeing to drive him back for his pills, that's how I became Valachi's case agent."

In January 1960, Joe Valachi pled guilty in the Eastern District Court in New York, and was let out of jail with the agreement that, prior to sentencing, he'd secure information for the initiation of a major federal narcotics case. "After that we started going for drives late at night," Selvaggi says, "talking in bars around Westchester County. One night we're having a beer at Foley's in Pleasantville. Valachi's hinky. He's a tough guy, a buttonman in the Genovese family, so he doesn't want to give anyone up. He tries to put a $100 bill in my pocket." Selvaggi scowls. "I told him: 'I give *you* money.' Then I reminded him that he was due in court for sentencing in February, and that time was running out. I said I'd delay the proceedings, but only if he gave up Michael Monica as a sign of good faith. So Valachi made an appointment to meet Monica on a street corner in East Harlem at two o'clock in the morning. And when Monica climbed out of the cab, I arrested him. He was the last fugitive we picked up in the Freeman case."

REBELLION IN THE GENOVESE FAMILY

With Monica's arrest, Valachi's crew chief, Tony Bender (real name Anthony Strollo), sent him and Ralph Wagner to Stefano Magaddino in Buffalo. Bender assured the fugitives that Magaddino, the Mafia boss of upper New York State, was going to smuggle them into Canada. But Wagner had a gut feeling that Bender had actually paid Magaddino to kill them, so he fled to Texas, where he pulled two armed robberies and was arrested in March 1960. He was tried, convicted, and sentenced to twelve years at the Atlanta Penitentiary. Valachi, meanwhile, remained in Buffalo until Bender summoned him back to New York City. "Bender told him the fix was in," Selvaggi explains. "He said he'd only get five years, so Valachi turned himself in to John Enright at the Court House Squad.

"To understand all this," Selvaggi says, "you have to go back to Vito Genovese. Genovese was a classy guy. He'd been convicted on a narcotics rap in 1959, and I met him in Tompkins Square late one night while he was out on bond. I asked him why he didn't skip town. 'Generals don't run,' he said. Then he told me to get a haircut. Joe Adonis was a classy guy too. When they were in charge, there was no crime in their neighborhoods. But they had a strict code. If you were a made guy like Valachi, you had to adhere to the rules. If you adhere to the rules, no one can slap you, no one can bother your business, no one can mess with your wife. But you have to follow orders. You have to follow the rules that the smart old Mustache Petes put in place to keep buttonmen like Valachi in line. The old bosses knew they couldn't trust the buttonmen, but they needed money-makers, so they made the rules.

"Then Genovese decided that Anastasia had gone too far, after he had Scalici killed. That's when Genovese made the rule, 'No drugs.' But the younger guys didn't want to give up the drugs because it was a good way to make money. So the bosses said, 'OK, long as you keep it in Harlem. It's not in our neighborhood, who cares?'"

Despite his own rule, Vito Genovese was convicted (some say falsely) on drug charges, and that's what set the stage for Joe Valachi's great betrayal. While Genovese was out on appeal, Tony Bender started plotting to take over the family with his two top lieutenants, Vinnie Mauro and Frank Caruso. Mauro and Caruso were vicious hoods, and Valachi was working for them. But he was a disgruntled employee. His godfather was Joe Bonanno, and he was married to the daughter of a powerful Mafia don, Giacomo Reina – so Valachi thought he should have been a boss, not a buttonman. But Genovese put him in Tony Bender's crew, and then Bender made Vinnie Mauro, not Valachi, his top lieutenant. That hurt, because Mauro had been Valachi's protégé. And once Bender and Mauro were in charge, they never let Valachi make any real money. They gave him about twenty-five jukeboxes, that's all, and that's how they kept him down. And that's why he dealt narcotics on the side.

"Ralph told me about Valachi's hassles with Bender and Mauro," Selvaggi explains, "and that's how I learned he was a disgruntled employee. Been one for years. Then Genovese lost his appeal [in February 1960] and was sent to the Atlanta Penitentiary. But he still wanted to run the show. But he knew he couldn't trust Bender, so he sent Tom Eboli to Detroit, where Eboli was inducted into the Mafia. After Eboli was made, Genovese named him head of the family; at which point Bender decided he was going to overthrow Eboli. But Bender needed cash to finance the revolution, so his money-makers, Frank Caruso and Vinnie Mauro, took $500,000 in drug money to the track and lost it all in two weeks. And that's when everyone started getting desperate."[2]

THE RIPPLE EFFECT

Like every made man, Joe Valachi paid a percentage of his business profits to his bosses, and they in return were obligated to support his family if he was imprisoned. But Tom Eboli had no prior relationship with or commitment to Valachi, and when the aging hood surrendered and was no longer productive, Eboli gave his jukebox concession to someone else, leaving Valachi without any means of supporting his family. When Selvaggi heard about this development from Ralph Wagner, he started visiting the vengeful hood at the Federal House of Detention – what FBN agents called West Street – with the intention of exploiting him.

"He told me he'd run out of time before," Selvaggi explains, "but he still wanted to make a deal. But he's nervous. The meetings we're having at West Street don't look good. A young hood from the Bronx made a remark: 'Why you talk to Selvaggi?' So he calls me up during the Army-Navy [college football] game. The guards bring him down, and he puts on the act: he storms out of the holding cell yelling how I'd set him up. But just before he does that, he whispers a telephone number to me. 'It's the biggest operation in the city,' he says. It's Sal Rinaldo's number, and he thinks it'll help reduce his time. But I already had Rinaldo from another source." Selvaggi shrugs indifferently. "What he gave was confirmation, that's all. So in June 1960, Valachi got fifteen years in the Freeman case. He was fifty-seven, and there was no consideration."

Valachi's confirmation, however, was one of the factors that allowed the deputy sheriff in Westchester to put a wiretap on Rinaldo's home phone in New Rochelle. Detectives and FBN agents listened in constantly for the next few months, until they overheard Matteo Palmieri telling Rinaldo that something "big" was coming in on a particular ship. "He gave the date and location," Selvaggi says, "so Charlie Mac and I followed Rinaldo up to Pier 84, and that's when Customs Agent Mario Couzzi sees us. He asks me what we're doing there." Selvaggi smiles. "There's a war going on with Customs, so I tell him, 'I'm waiting for my aunt.' Then Palmieri shows up and pays off the Customs inspector. We watched Palmieri meet Rinaldo, and we saw them load the trunk with the heroin in the back of a bakery van. Gaffney and Ward were with us, and they let Sheriff Hoy and his people bust them up in Yonkers with ten kilograms of pure heroin that had been transported from Italy aboard the Saturnia.

"Right after the bust we went back to the machine in New Rochelle," Selvaggi continues. "Frank Caruso's calling. He's asking, 'Where's Rinaldo?' He's calling Mrs. Rinaldo so she can warn Sal. He was calling to tip him off, but it was too late.

"Next we searched Rinaldo's house, and Agent Dave Costa found a trap. Inside it was twenty grand and two half-kilogram packages of heroin, which meant that Rinaldo had been stealing from his bosses. And once we announced to the press that we'd found the junk at his house, Rinaldo knew he was dead, so he flipped and told us how tons of dope from Turkey passed through labs in France to Sicily, where Mafia travel agents got unwitting immigrants to agree to bring along a trunk. The immigrants were on a waiting list, and they would agree to carry the trunk to speed up their paperwork. The trunks had false bottoms and each one was packed with ten kilograms of heroin in long thin packages. They moved over $150 million over ten years that way."

Thanks to Frank Selvaggi, the Rinaldo–Palmieri case exposed the Mafia's biggest drug smuggling operation in Italy and America. His main informant, Sal Rinaldo, was the plant-man, and through Rinaldo the case led to many of New York's major drug dealers, including Saro Mogavero. As recounted in chapter 9, Mogavero was a former vice president of ILA Local 856, and the protégé of Rocco Pellegrino, the Mafia boss in Westchester. Pellegrino supplied heroin to Joe Civello in Dallas through Mogavero, his contact-man to John Ormento. Mogavero, in 1954, had taken a small fall for Ormento, which allowed the latter to initiate the drug smuggling operation through Cuba that led to Vito Genovese's downfall.

A hit man at the age of fifteen, Saro Mogavero was such a ruthless predator that he forced his childhood friend, Salvatore "Billy Boy" Rinaldo, to become his plant-man. How he did this is worth recounting, for it's a perfect, graphic example of the cruel methods gangsters used to build their drug trafficking empires. Mogavero knew that Rinaldo loved to gamble, so he persuaded him to borrow money from loan shark Frank Caruso. Mogavero and Caruso knew that Rinaldo would lose the dough, which he did, at which point they made him borrow even more money and then use it to invest in drug shipments with Willie Locascio and Sam Accardi. In order to protect his investment, Rinaldo had no choice but to take the job as plant-man.[3]

Selvaggi's other major informant, Matteo Palmieri, was a baker by trade, and the contact man with the Italians. Whenever a shipment arrived, Palmieri would notify Albert Agueci in Buffalo, and Vinnie Mauro and Frank Caruso in New York. Palmieri was also responsible for making sure the shipments were safely delivered to Rinaldo. These were things he had done correctly many times before, but it was the smallest mistake on 21 October 1960 that led to his becoming Selvaggi's reluctant informant.

As Selvaggi explains, "On the day we arrested them, Palmieri showed up late at the pier. Palmieri spoke broken English, and because the Customs guy couldn't understand him, he wouldn't release the trunk at first. So Palmieri panicked and called Vinnie Mauro, which was something he shouldn't have done. That put Mauro in the case, and Mauro, who was the most vicious of them all, swore he was going to kill Palmieri; and that's why Palmieri flipped and started talking about forty-three Italians. Together, he and Rinaldo testified against dozens of people in the US and Italy. They named Mauro, Caruso, and Sal Maneri – a big money-man who ran a crap game and had his own sources in Italy; Albert and Vito Agueci;

Sam Accardi; the Caneba brothers in Sicily; and," Selvaggi shrugs, "Valachi. From their testimony we developed one conspiracy in Italy, and two [including the Frank Borelli case] in New York.

"Rinaldo," Selvaggi stresses, "was a death sentence for everyone. Right away, Eboli puts out a contract on all of these guys. Each one's got a price on his head, but $1 million dollars for anyone who kills Rinaldo. That's when things get rough. A witness in the case, Shorty Holmes, is found stuffed in a garbage can in August. Then in September, Judge Dimmock reduces bond on Mauro, Caruso, and Maneri, and they flee; which means that Valachi, who's in jail and can't go anywhere, becomes the main target of the State prosecutor. So now, more than ever, he wants assistance. He's hoping to do the Rinaldo time on top of the Freeman time, but I told him that I already had Rinaldo's number. 'Cop a plea,' I said, 'or come up with something new.'

"Valachi became incensed," Selvaggi says. "'You double-banged me!' he yelled. Then he tells me that Mauro, Caruso, and Maneri fled to South America, thinking that might help. But we knew that too. So tough. Then Albert Agueci gets pissed off at Magaddino. Magaddino got two grand for every kilogram Albert brought in, but he wouldn't bail him out of jail. Albert had to mortgage his house. Well, Albert's a badass, so he goes to Magaddino and confronts him. A few days later [23 November 1961], they find Albert's body near the Canadian border. He'd been burned with a blowtorch and chunks of flesh had been carved out of legs. It was grue-some. At which point his brother Vito wants revenge and starts cooperating. So now we have Rinaldo, Palmieri, and Vito Agueci. And that's when Matteo Palmieri and I go up to Buffalo to make a case on Magaddino."[4]

THE ISOLATION OF FRANK SELVAGGI

As mentioned earlier, Charlie Siragusa had chewed out John Dolce for sending Frank Selvaggi alone into Harlem. For that reason, and because he was Siragusa's in-law, one of the Group Three agents christened Frank with the nickname, "Selagusa." That didn't bother him, as it was part of the ribbing that went back and forth in the New York office. What troubled him was that the Group Three clique was starting to interfere in his cases.

"Sal Rinaldo had two other connections," Selvaggi explains, "a guy named Shears, whom we hadn't heard about before, and a super-connec-tion named Mickey Blair. You couldn't go to Blair [real name Dominick Castiglia] for less than five kilos. He'd been in the Army during the war, and when he was arrested in the Borelli case, he said that General Mark Clark would vouch for him." Selvaggi arches his eyebrows.

"Anyway, Brady found out that Shears was Sal Maneri, the contact-man between the Italians and the French. So we arrested Maneri one night on the street, and during the arrest I treated his wife with respect – which is why Maneri called me when he got out on bail. Like everyone else in the Rinaldo case, he was on Eboli's hit list and wanted help. So we started meeting in Times Square on Sunday afternoons. Maneri tells me things. He says he'll give me 'a house,' meaning a plant, if I can help him. 'They'll make you a general,' he says.

"Well, Dolce is my group leader, and he knew I was meeting with Maneri. He also knew that Maneri was running a crap game down on the Lower East Side with a Czechoslovakian guy, Jan Simack. The next thing I know, Dolce decides he's going to hit Maneri's crap game. Everyone in the group gets an envelope. The way it works, you open the envelope at a prearranged time, and inside is a piece of paper telling you where to meet everyone. But there's no envelope for me." Frank pauses reflectively.[5]

"Later on I heard what happened. They're outside Maneri's crap game and they see him handing something to someone on the street. They think it's a pass, so they hit them right then and there. But it's cash, not drugs. Maneri hands ten grand to Simack. Not long after that, Maneri flees the country with Mauro and Caruso."

Selvaggi lights a cigarette. "After that I requested a transfer to the Court House Squad. An agent could avoid trouble by joining the Court House Squad," he explains. "Same with the International Group. Those groups could subpoena their suspects under the Thirty-Five Hundred Rule. They didn't need dope on the table, and they didn't have to testify in court." And testifying in court was risky business, because slick criminal defense attorneys invariably claimed that the arresting agent had stolen money from, or planted evidence on, the defendant. But even at the Court House Squad, Selvaggi was on the frontlines, eyeball to eyeball with hoods, even if he wasn't turning them into informants anymore.

"I talked to everyone," Selvaggi says with pride. "I talked to Genovese. I talked to John Ormento too. I was in the courtroom when he was sentenced. He was fifty-three years old and he got forty years. I was sitting behind him and he turned to me and said, 'It's nothing, kid. I can do it standing up.'"

As any FBN agent will attest, no one had the Mafia sources Frank Selvaggi had. But what made him strong also made him vulnerable. "I was doing pretty good," Selvaggi says. "I'd made Valachi, and Rinaldo, and an eleven-kilogram case on Frank Frederico. But then I made the mistake of telling Assistant US Attorney John Rosner that I didn't believe that Nelson Cantellops ever met Vito Genovese. I said that Genovese was the smartest of all the bosses, that he'd made more judges than anyone could ever know, and that there was no way a little nine-plus syphilitic Puerto Rican like Nelson Cantellops could ever get near him.

"Well, Rosner tells Bill Tendy at the Junk Squad. Tendy is tight with Ward and Dolce, and Tendy tells Dolce that I called Genovese 'the frame of the century.' Tendy tells Dolce, and Dolce tells John Enright, who's my boss at the Court House Squad. And now Enright and Dolce both want me out!"

LUCIANO'S LUCK RUNS OUT

While tensions were mounting among the case-making agents in the New York office, the Italian police were doing their part to find three of the fugitives in the Rinaldo–Palmieri case. They had seen an American couple, Henry and Theresa Rubino, visiting Lucky Luciano in Naples. Something about the Rubinos aroused their suspicions, so they told Hank Manfredi and, at his request, they tailed the couple to the border of Spain. Spanish officials picked up the trail and followed them to a meeting with Vinnie Mauro and Frank Caruso. On 14 January 1962, FBI agents arrested Mauro and Caruso in Barcelona, and Sal Maneri in Majorca.[6]

The next day, in an attempt to curry favor with the FBI, Mauro called Luciano, and over Lucky's futile protestations, he explicitly mentioned drugs. The FBI was listening in, of course, and one week later the Italian police summoned Luciano for questioning about his conversation with Mauro. During the interrogation, Hank Manfredi taunted the once powerful boss of bosses. Complaining of heart palpitations, Luciano was released and proceeded under police escort to the Naples airport to meet Martin Gosch, a writer with whom he was co-authoring an exposé. As Gosch stepped off the plane, Luciano reached to shake his hand, and then collapsed on the tarmac and died of a massive heart attack.

Thirty minutes later, Deputy Commissioner Henry Giordano "revealed that [the FBN] had been on the point of arresting the powerful Mafioso for having introduced $150 million worth of heroin to American territory over the previous ten years."[7]

It's unbelievable that the FBN had decided to label Luciano as the mastermind of the Rinaldo–Palmieri ring on the basis of a phone call from

Vinnie Mauro. And it's incredibly uncanny that Luciano died half an hour before his arrest. It is an unlikely sequence of events that suggests that this was not death by natural causes. But the FBN would not have killed him. For over a decade he'd been a source on numerous drug traffickers, and during that time Harry Anslinger had shamelessly exploited him for publicity purposes. But Anslinger was on the verge of retirement, and perhaps Giordano felt that the *bête noire* had outlived his purpose. Or perhaps, as Sal Vizzini claims, the CIA was afraid of what Luciano might say if he was put on trial. The CIA knew that Luciano was concerned about his heart condition, and that American mobsters routinely sent vitamins to him in Naples. According to Vizzini, the CIA simply intercepted a delivery and substituted identical pills laced with an untraceable poison.

That particular conspiracy theory will never be proven, but two things are perfectly clear: despite the myth that Lucky Luciano controlled international drug trafficking, the illegal movement of narcotics did not abate with his death; and once Anslinger had handed over the organizational reigns to hapless Henry Giordano, the FBN could no longer defend itself from its arch bureaucratic rival, J. Edgar Hoover. The FBI director moved in for the kill, and Lucky had the last laugh in hell.

17

AGGRAVATING EDGAR: BOBBY KENNEDY AND THE FBN

"What to ourselves in passion we propose,
The passion ending, doth the purpose lose."

Shakespeare, *Hamlet*, act III, scene 3

For thirty-two years, Harry Anslinger suffered J. Edgar Hoover's insults and interference and did nothing in response. Anslinger submissively accepted the fact that Hoover was a more powerful bureaucrat, with ten times as many agents, a vastly bigger budget, a broader mandate, and secret files he'd been compiling since his salad days as a special assistant on subversive matters to Attorney General Mitchell Palmer. It is said that Hoover brought along these files when he became the FBI's assistant director in 1921, that he continually expanded them after he became FBI director in 1924, and that he used them to compile dossiers full of dirty little secrets on America's top politicians during a reign of intimidation that lasted forty-six years, and spanned the incumbency of eight presidents.

Knowing he was outgunned, Anslinger refrained from directly challenging Hoover; but a rivalry simmered between them, and for years, Hoover kept Anslinger on the defensive by making snide comments about the corrupting influences of undercover narcotics work. Plus which the publicity-conscious FBI director grabbed all of the glory by having his agents chase celebrity public enemies like John Dillinger, at the expense of mounting arduous investigations of organized crime. Anslinger, however, had Andrew Mellon and several other Establishment heavyweights in his corner, and he could not be dismissed. He wasn't intimidated by Hoover's bluster and prominence, and he continued about his business. In public he behaved properly, as if he respected the despicable little man.

Behind the scenes, the personal animosity between the two bureaucratic warlords began in 1932, during the Charles Lindbergh kidnapping case. Anslinger's mentor and friend, Elmer Irey, chief of the IRS Intelligence Unit, played a decisive role in the investigation by having marked bills passed to Richard Hauptmann, the alleged kidnapper. That measure, which was standard operating procedure for FBN agents, led to Hauptmann's capture and conviction. Lindbergh was grateful, but Hoover was incensed. Fearing that Irey would solve the case, Hoover initially tried to have him removed from it; but Lindbergh objected and prevailed. So Hoover put Irey under FBI surveillance in a brazen attempt to steal his investigative leads. Despite Hoover's juvenile attempts to preempt him, Irey single-handedly solved the case, and Lindbergh publicly credited him for doing so. But the indignity of having been upstaged prompted Hoover to open one of his secret files on Irey and, for years afterwards, Irey routinely checked his telephone for FBI taps. This episode taught Anslinger a valuable lesson about the petty FBI director's unforgiving and abusive nature, and the advantages of staying out of his line of fire. [1]

Hoover's fad for chasing down "Most Wanted" criminals subsided with the Depression, and Anslinger's prestige grew during the Second World War. But Hoover's power grew even greater. While many of Anslinger's agents joined the Armed Services, and his workforce diminished, President Roosevelt increased the number of FBI agents fivefold, and gave Hoover carte blanche to bug and wiretap anyone in the name of national security. The FBI was also made responsible for intelligence operations in the western hemisphere, and Hoover spread 150 Special Intelligence Service agents throughout Latin America and Canada. The FBI director also entered into an exclusive liaison relationship with William Stephenson, chief of Great Britain's intelligence operations in the western hemisphere.

Hoover savored his exclusive relationship with Stephenson while it lasted, but then in 1942, President Roosevelt put William Donovan in charge of the OSS. The British welcomed Donovan and his OSS forces, which started fighting behind enemy lines in Europe, and "Wild Bill" cheerfully crashed what J. Edgar thought was going to be a private party with Bill Stephenson. That hurt, socially and professionally. But when Donovan's OSS agents started mounting counterintelligence operations in the US – in one instance breaking into the Spanish Embassy – Hoover retaliated in every way possible.[2] Having formed a fast personal friendship with Donovan, and having sent several of his best men into the OSS, Anslinger again found himself allied with one of Hoover's most hated rivals.

Still steaming after the war, Hoover opposed Donovan's efforts to form the Central Intelligence Agency. He repeated a claim he had made about the OSS, and said that the CIA was hiring communists. But the Agency was created over Hoover's protests, and when President Truman decided that the new spy agency should absorb the FBI's operations in the western hemisphere, Hoover vindictively ordered his agents not to share their files or sources with the CIA, with whom Anslinger had also aligned.[3]

The new wave of anti-communist witch-hunts instigated in 1950 by Senator Joe McCarthy restored Hoover's confidence and sense of purpose, and during the ensuing Cold War his powers peaked: FBI agents were exempted from Civil Service rules and, under the aegis of national security, were allowed to conduct burglaries and all types of illegal surveillance. With eyes and ears in bedrooms all over Washington, Hoover packed his files full of sexy secrets that he traded to beholden politicians for power. Then in 1956, he unveiled his most awesome weapon ever, the notorious Counter-intelligence Program (COINTELPRO), which allowed FBI agents to commit any crime imaginable in order to suppress civil rights and leftist groups that threatened national security. COINTELPRO enabled him to shape the political climate in America, and his bulging secret files prompted Senator Estes Kefauver to declare that Hoover had "more power than the president."[4]

That may have been true, but Anslinger wasn't afraid, and he eventually forced a showdown with Hoover over the Mafia. As we know, Hoover denied its existence, and his disingenuous position on this issue had a cumulative, negative effect on federal drug law enforcement. So, in his last year as Commissioner of the Bureau of Narcotics, Anslinger unleashed his frustration and fury. In a 1962 interview, he said that he had refused to give a copy of the Mafia Book to Hoover because he "just wouldn't risk it."[5]

Anslinger insinuated that Hoover had been corrupted by organized crime, and it was true; Hoover's friend, columnist Walter Winchell, socialized with Meyer Lansky and Frank Costello, and served as an intermediary between the famous, influential gangsters and the star-struck FBI director. Hoover and Costello actually met on occasion, and investigative journalist Anthony Summers, citing several sources, reports that Lansky acquired, from Donovan and the OSS, photographs of Hoover engaged in a homosexual act, and that those pictures put him in the mob's pocket forever.[6]

Not only was Hoover a closet queen, he was a degenerate gambler too. He liked to bet on the ponies and, in exchange for free passes and hot tips, he repaid his underworld patrons by insisting that racetrack gambling was not a federal crime. He pretended not to know that Lansky and Costello controlled the off-track bookie business, or that it was one of organized crime's biggest sources of revenue.

Anslinger's standing with Hoover did not improve during the Kefauver Hearings, which, with the FBN's expert assistance, forced Costello into early retirement and Lansky into exile. But Hoover quickly found a new patron in Texas oil tycoon Clint Murchison, and starting in 1953, Hoover and his housemate, FBI executive Clyde Tolson, became Murchison's annual guests at the Del Mar Racetrack in California. The oilman's ties to organized crime were not as close as Costello's, but they were there. According to Summers,

> "20 percent of the Murchison oil lease company was owned by the Vito Genovese crime family. Handridge Oil, a Murchison owned outfit, was the subject of a deal with Las Vegas gamblers involving massive security violations. There were also to be deals with Jimmy Hoffa, the crooked boss of the Teamsters Union, and Clint, Jr., established financial ties with Mafia boss [Carlos] Marcello." [7]

Hoover's defenders say he had bigger fish to fry, and that he let Anslinger and the IRS chase the gangsters, while his G-men pursued communists, civil rights leaders, and other menaces to national security. But the man had a secret agenda, and, as the Establishment's private police force, the FBI served its patrons by allowing organized crime to subvert the labor and civil rights movements from within. If the hoods moved drugs in their spare time, who cared (like the Mafia bosses said), as long as the poison ended up in ghettos, and not in good neighborhoods?

Anslinger and Hoover obviously agreed on the racial issue, but the FBI director's protection of organized crime undermined Anslinger's mission and his legacy. So he waited and in a veiled attack on Hoover, he said in 1964, "Sometimes our strongest foes can be found in the chambers of justice, the state houses and even higher." [8]

ENTER BOBBY KENNEDY

Anslinger waited until he was on the verge of retirement to attack his old foe, but he never would have had the opportunity if not for the November 1960 election of John F. Kennedy as president, and his appointment of his brother Bobby as Attorney General. Ambitious, ruthless, and cunning, Bobby wasn't content to behave in the traditional role as the president's *consigliere*, and he used his authority as Attorney General to sidestep Hoover. Declaring war against organized crime, he increased the number of attorneys in the Justice Department's Criminal Division from fifteen to sixty and directed them against the nation's leading racketeers. Bobby had a mean streak, too; in order to make his presence felt, he openly inquired how a behemoth like organized crime could escape the attention of the FBI's director. He further bruised Hoover's gigantic ego by praising the FBN for putting more Mafia bosses behind bars than the FBI, and, according to George Gaffney, by dubbing it "the Marine Corps of federal law enforcement."

Figuratively speaking, this insolent behavior was a death sentence for both Bobby Kennedy and the FBN. Hoover was so angry that he sent a letter to Anslinger calling the Genovese case a "frame-up" and a "travesty of justice."[9]

Heedless of having made an enemy of J. Edna (as he privately referred to the lavender-scented FBI director), Bobby formed a special group in the Justice Department to pursue Jimmy Hoffa and Hoffa's closest Mafia associates – Santo Trafficante, Sam Giancana, and Carlos Marcello – all of whom shared Hoover's hatred of the overly aggressive AG. But Bobby was looking for a fight, and his first reckless act as Attorney General was to deport Marcello to Guatemala in April 1961. As a pretext, Bobby claimed that Marcello was an undesirable alien, based on the fact that the FBN had busted him in 1938 for selling twenty-three pounds of marijuana. With this fateful action, Kennedy pushed his criminal and government enemies into an alliance and, six weeks after the Bay of Pigs fiasco, Marcello slipped back into America and, with equally furious anti-Kennedy factions in the FBI, CIA, Mafia, and Cuban exile community, began plotting revenge.

MILLION-DOLLAR MEN

While serving as chief counsel on Senator John McClellan's Select Committee on Improper Activities in Labor and Management, Bobby Kennedy learned how drug smuggling factored into the Mafia's relationship with the Teamsters. He was present in July 1959 when FBN Agent Ike Wurms explained to the Committee how Teamsters official Abe Gordon laundered drug profits through a union welfare fund. Bobby learned that Carlo Gambino was involved with the Teamsters through his labor-consulting firm in Manhattan, and that Jimmy Hoffa had protected

Detroit's major drug traffickers, John Priziola and Raffaele Quasarano, by assigning them to Teamsters Local 985. He knew that Trafficante and Marcello were associated with Hoffa; that Marcello influenced the Teamsters and Longshoreman's unions in Louisiana; and that Trafficante had an office at a Teamsters Local in Miami, which had been established by Mafia drug traffickers James Plumeri and Frank Dioguardia.

Kennedy knew that Marcello's representative in Dallas, Joe Civello, had attended the Apalachin conference on Marcello's behalf, and he suspected that Marcello, through Trafficante in Florida, and Sam Carolla and Frank Coppola in Sicily, played a dominant role in international drug trafficking. As Bobby was certainly aware, the FBN office in New Orleans believed that Marcello received narcotics from Trafficante in Florida on Teamsters trucks, and that his Pelican Tomato Company, which supplied Naval bases in Louisiana, smuggled drugs from Mexico "without interference from customs."[10]

Kennedy wanted to nail Trafficante and Marcello, but the FBN had only four agents in its Miami and New Orleans offices, and the FBI – though it had the manpower – chose not to place wiretaps on them. These two were the only Mafiosi to receive such privileged treatment from J. Edgar Hoover. The FBI agent in charge in New Orleans, Regis Kennedy, even made the outrageous claim that Marcello was not involved in crime – so Bobby took matters in hand. INS officials arrested Marcello on a street in New Orleans, placed him in handcuffs, drove him to an airport, put him on a plane, and whisked him off to Guatemala – which he had identified on a falsified birth certificate as the land of his birth – without so much as a toothbrush.[11]

Marcello, however, had friends in high places in Central America and, in addition to receiving a free pass from the FBI, he probably enjoyed CIA protection. They certainly shared the same unsavory business partners. Marcello ran a counterfeiting scam in Nicaragua that required kickbacks to Anastasio Somoza, the brutal dictator who, on behalf of the CIA, harbored anti-Castro terrorists on one of his private estates. As we know for a fact, the CIA sometimes employed gangsters for its nefarious purposes, and the Agency probably arranged for Marcello's flight to Miami aboard a Dominican Air Force jet, "without either customs or immigration officials noting his arrival."[12] Considering that his re-entry occurred prior to Trafficante's exposure as a double agent, it's also likely that, in return for the favor, Marcello joined William Harvey's ZR/RIFLE project as a recruiter of assassins.

By 1960, the CIA was protecting Joe Bonanno for the same murderous reason. Having moved to sunny Tucson, Arizona, and started a legitimate real estate company, he also formed a profitable regional alliance with his fellow racketeers, Santo Trafficante and Carlos Marcello. Like his newfound friends, he bought protection from the CIA too. According to investigative reporter Seymour Hersh, during the winter of 1960 to 1961, Bonanno was "always calling" William Harvey's boss, Richard Bissell, on an outside line. He even wrote a letter offering to do what Bissell "wanted him to do" – in other words, having people killed.[13]

Bissell accepted the offer, and Bonanno's *caporegime* in New Jersey, Joseph Zicarelli, provided the services. With the assistance of CIA asset Robert Maheu, Zicarelli sold guns to Rafael Trujillo, the dictator of the Dominican Republic, and Zicarelli's goon squad reportedly murdered one of Trujillo's political opponents in New York. Zicarelli's henchmen may even have switched alliances and served as the intermediaries in the 30 May 1961 assassination of Trujillo, which relied on guns that were provided to the victim's political opponents by the CIA, as part of Harvey's ZR/RIFLE Program.[14]

Zicarelli enjoyed political protection locally through his Congressman, Cornelius E. Gallagher; but it was his dirty work for the CIA that made him a million-dollar man – as mobsters with CIA or FBI protection are called – and granted him temporary immunity from prosecution on federal narcotics charges.[15] This was an unfortunate development for the FBN, in so far as Zicarelli had replaced the recently incarcerated Carmine Galante as the Bonanno family's narcotics manager. Zicarelli was a suspect in the Cotroni and Rinaldo cases and, through a wiretap on a gun-store owner in New Jersey, the FBN knew that he had attempted to purchase 1,000 rifles for anti-Castro exiles in the CIA's employ.[16] But Zicarelli, like Marcello and Trafficante, was light-years beyond the FBN's reach.

BOBBY KENNEDY'S MORTAL FOES

Bobby Kennedy, like Harry Anslinger, could not be bought. He was a rich man bent on destroying organized crime's corrupting influence on American society. And yet, just a few months after he had taunted Sam Giancana during televised hearings before the McClellan Committee (he said that Giancana "giggled like a girl"), his father, on 29 February 1960, met with Giancana at a restaurant in New York. Joseph Kennedy was there, with Giancana, Johnny Roselli, and Mario Brod (James Angleton's liaison to the Mafia) to negotiate the terms by which the Mafia's constituents in Illinois would vote for JFK in the upcoming presidential election. The hoods were trying to decide whether to support JFK or Texas Senator Lyndon B. Johnson, who was backed by Carlos Marcello, through Joe Civello, in his bid for the Democratic Party's presidential nomination. Family patriarch Joe Kennedy argued that Giancana's organization would fare better under a Kennedy administration, which had many financial holdings in Chicago, and he asked the hoods to contribute $500,000 to JFK's campaign. For practical business reasons the money was forthcoming, despite Giancana's hatred of Bobby. [17]

Then the inexplicable happened. Sometime in October 1960, while plotting with the CIA to murder Castro, Giancana came to suspect that comedian Dan Rowan was putting the moves on his girlfriend, Phyllis McGuire. Rather than use his considerable muscle to resolve the matter privately, Giancana asked CIA asset Robert Maheu for help, and Maheu, breaching CIA security, sent an employee to spy on Rowan in Las Vegas. In another departure from standard security practices, Maheu's private detective left his listening post in the room next to Rowan's, ostensibly to watch a Vegas floorshow, and while he was gone a chambermaid found his tape recorder running. She called the hotel manager, who called the police; they called the FBI, the FBI eventually called the CIA, and the case was buried eighteen months later, on 7 April 1962, when CIA General Counsel Lawrence Houston explained to Herbert J. Miller, the Assistant Attorney General in charge of the Justice Department's Criminal Division, that the Agency had employed Giancana in its assassination plots, and that prosecuting him would harm national security. [18]

What's important about this botched bugging incident – assuming that it wasn't intentional, and that Bobby Kennedy had no knowledge of his father's meeting with the mob – is that Bobby didn't know that Giancana was a million-dollar man until April 1962, when Hoover finally told him about Giancana's role in the CIA's assassination plots. Hoover had known, since October 1960, about the role the Chicago hood played in the CIA's plans to kill Fidel Castro, and his long delay in notifying Kennedy was a clear indication of his hostile intentions, as well as his partisan political support for Richard Nixon. [19] Giancana had exposed his CIA connection simply as an insurance policy – but Maheu, like Hoover, had assisted him on behalf of Nixon. The future president had been party to the Castro assassination plots from their inception during the Eisenhower administration, and Maheu, at the time of the Vegas bugging blunder, was handling public relations for billionaire Howard Hughes, one of Nixon's biggest financial backers. [20]

The CIA and FBI had one thing in common – neither was anxious to help Bobby Kennedy, and it wasn't until 7 May 1962 that the CIA finally told Bobby about its Cuban escapades. And even then, CIA security chief Sheffield Edwards and General Counsel Laurence Houston lied; they said that their assassination attempts had ended with Trafficante's exposure as a double agent, and they promised to warn Bobby if they ever dealt with gangsters again. The smirking CIA officers then slinked away, knowing full well that Maheu had introduced Johnny Roselli to CIA assassination chief Bill Harvey on 8 April 1962, without the Attorney General's knowledge, and that Harvey had delivered poison pills and weapons to Manuel Varona, the anti-Castro politician Trafficante had brought in to assist in the conspiracy. "The Attorney General was not told that the gambling syndicate operation had already been reactivated, nor, as far as we know, was he ever told," the CIA casually admitted in an inspector general's report dated 1967.[21]

In yet another telling sin of omission, James Angleton, who deeply resented Bobby's interference in CIA counterintelligence operations, would neglect to tell Bobby about Mario Brod, his liaison to Sam Giancana and Johnny Roselli, until 1963.[22]

Yet another million-dollar man, Roselli was assisting Hoover as well as the CIA in the conspiracy to sabotage Bobby Kennedy. Through an FBI wiretap on Roselli, Hoover was aware of some seventy phone calls between Jack Kennedy and pretty Judith Campbell, a mob courier in the mold of Virginia Hill, but without Hill's stature. Roselli had introduced Kennedy and Campbell at a swinging Frank Sinatra campaign party in Vegas, while Campbell was romantically involved with Sam Giancana (who experienced no irrational fits of jealousy this time). Suffering from terminal satyriasis, Kennedy continued to see Campbell until 22 March 1962, when Hoover confronted him with his indiscretion.[23] At this meeting, he also let the president know that he was aware of the deal that Mario Brod, on behalf of James Angleton, had brokered between Giancana and Joe Kennedy.

Hoover tried to blackmail him, but Jack Kennedy wasn't intimidated; and after the revelation that top CIA officers had encouraged ultra generals in Algeria to mutiny against French president Charles de Gaulle, he stunned the Establishment by firing the popular and much admired Allen Dulles – at which point the most powerful people in the CIA and the military started skirting the White House, leaving Jack and Bobby to defend themselves.

BOBBY KENNEDY'S ASSASSINATION PLOTS

While CIA assassinations were flourishing under Bill Harvey's ZR/RIFLE Program, Bobby Kennedy launched three of his own Mafia-related plots to kill Fidel Castro. The first, incredibly, involved drug smuggler Norman Rothman. As Rothman reported to his FBI masters on 26 June 1961, Bobby's aides had invited him to the White House a few days earlier, and had offered him leniency in a gunrunning case (in which he was caught smuggling arms to Castro with former Cuban president Carlos Prio Socarras) if he would arrange to kill Castro. Rothman said he refused, and maybe he did; but the point is that his information certainly made a beeline to Hoover, supplying the devious FBI director with yet another dirty little secret to use against his nemesis.[24]

Putting Hoover's petty intrigues to one side, we should ask when, if ever, the FBN learned that the Attorney General was offering a major drug smuggler immunity to commit a political assassination, and how much the Bureau might have known. If anyone was in a position to know, it was Charlie Siragusa. Bobby's approach to Rothman occurred five days after Siragusa had denounced Santo Trafficante as a double agent. That vital piece of information undoubtedly reached Bobby immediately, in view of his deep personal involvement in Cuban affairs. Siragusa may have delivered the message himself. At the time, July 1961, he was working closely with Bobby in an effort to ransom David Christ, a CIA officer who'd been captured in Cuba while trying to bug the Chinese News Agency. He was also managing the MKULTRA pad in New York, and he'd been asked to help the CIA recruit gangsters for its political assassination plots. Charlie was involved in almost every important counterintelligence activity, so it's very likely that Kennedy, or one of his aides, consulted him about Rothman.

The nature of Siragusa's relationship with Bobby Kennedy raises several questions about the thrust of federal drug enforcement. Specifically, is it conceivable that Siragusa did not tell Bobby about Rothman's long-standing association with Meyer Lansky, financier of international drug smuggling? Or that Rothman co-owned the El Morocco club in Havana with Corsican drug lord Paul Mondoloni, or that Mondoloni had been selling 50 to 150 kilograms of heroin every few months to Rothman and Trafficante since 1955? Or that Rothman had invested with Genovese family member Charles Tourine in Havana's Capri Casino, and that Giuseppe DiGiorgio, a card dealer at the Capri, was one of Trafficante's two major narcotics couriers, and an associate of Sal Maneri from the Rinaldo–Palmieri case? How could Siragusa not make these connections known to the Attorney General – especially when Bobby had, at the time, aimed his first drug strike force at the defendants in the Rinaldo–Palmieri case.

In the year since Rinaldo and Palmieri were busted, Siragusa had been closely tracking Lansky, Trafficante, Mondoloni, and Rothman – four men at the top of the international drug trafficking conspiracy. He knew that Mondoloni had been in Havana in January 1960, and had met in Acapulco in April 1960 with drug smugglers Lucien Rivard, Marius Cau, and Rosario Mancino. He was aware that Mancino was the Sicilian supplier of ill-fated Albert Agueci in Canada. Did he tell Bobby about this aspect of the Rinaldo–Palmieri case? Did he seize the opportunity to pump Rothman for information about these interrelationships?

Or was Rothman the ultimate million-dollar man? Remember, he would avoid imprisonment with Pepe Cotroni and Pittsburgh Mafioso Sal Mannarino (whose brother Gabriel was Trafficante's partner in Havana's Sans Souci casino) for attempting to sell $8.5 million worth of stolen securities. The reason, as explained in chapter 12, was that Rothman had used the money to ship guns to Cuba, in what was obviously a CIA-sponsored criminal conspiracy.

Rothman was never investigated for drug smuggling, either. By the summer of 1961, Castro had closed the last of Cuba's casinos, and the international drug lords were making new political arrangements in Mexico, Canada, and elsewhere. Rothman was privy to their plans and could have explained their intentions. If Siragusa did not corner Rothman in this regard, so that Bobby Kennedy could proceed in his assassination plots, then he had abandoned his personal commitment to drug law enforcement and had condemned the FBN to failure, at the exact same time Lee Speer was conducting his integrity investigation in New York.

On the other hand, if – given the chance – Siragusa did tell Bobby the facts, then it was the Attorney General who chose to abandon his war on crime, simply for a chance to kill Castro. This seems to be the case, in so far as Bobby launched a second assassination project in early 1962, using CIA officer Charles Ford (a veteran of the Far East Asia Division) to contact Mafia bosses in America and Canada for the sole purpose of finding someone to kill the Cuban prime minister.[25]

Bobby's third Mafia-related assassination plot, Operation Mongoose, was activated in March 1962. Managed by the National Security Council's Special Group under the direction of General Edward Lansdale, Mongoose included William Harvey's ZR/RIFLE unit, now dubbed Task Force W. In league with Harvey, Lansdale conjured up thirty-three often bizarre ways of destabilizing the Castro regime, including the introduction of cheap marijuana into Cuba and falsely accusing Cuba of drug trafficking.[26] There were plans to assassinate Castro too, and in one remarkably explicit memo to his staff, Lansdale suggested that, "Gangster elements might prove the best recruitment potential for actions [murders] against police G-2 [intelligence] officials." Lansdale added that, "CW [Chemical Warfare] agents should be fully considered." [27]

One can only imagine which Mafia hit men Charles Ford recruited, and the crimes they, Lansdale, and the CIA committed in Cuba, with the blessings of Bobby Kennedy – all to the detriment of the FBN and the American public.

THE INTELLIGENCE ANGLE

While Bobby Kennedy was using Mafia drug smugglers in murder plots against Castro, and thus neutralizing the FBN, the CIA was relocating its Havana station and anti-Castro terror activities to Miami. Known as JM/WAVE, the station was managed by Theodore Shackley, a protégé of Bill Harvey from Germany. It included Lansdale's Mongoose unit, and some 400 CIA case officers. Already the preferred habitat of America's mobsters, Miami was soon packed with dozens of CIA front companies, thousands of CIA informers and assets, and several drug smuggling terror teams financed by wacky privateers like William Pawley, mentioned in chapter 5 as having engineered the Pawley–Cooke Advisory Mission to Taiwan in 1950.

To cover a fraction of the cost of this massive enterprise, former OSS spymaster Paul L. E. Helliwell established and directed a string of drug money-laundering banks for the CIA. At the time, Helliwell was general counsel for the Thai Consulate in Miami, an active leader in Florida's Republican Party, and a friend of Nixon's cohort Bebe Rebozo. Among his drug smuggling credentials, Helliwell had worked with Chiang Kai-shek's intelligence chief, General Tai Li, and had set up the CIA's drug smuggling air force, CAT (later Air America), as well as the Bangkok trading company Sea Supply, which provided cover for CIA officers advising the drug-smuggling Thai border police. [28]

Functioning in a similar capacity in Panama was the ubiquitous World Commerce Corporation, the "commercially oriented espionage net" formed by ardent Republican William Donovan and British spymaster William Stephenson. In Honduras, Richard Greenlee, a member of Donovan's law firm and a former OSS officer in Bangkok, set up Vanguard Services in 1962 as a front for yet another batch of CIA-financed, drug-related anti-Castro operations. [29]

There were dozens of CIA proprietary companies operating worldwide in similar fashion, and Anslinger in 1964 alluded to the power of this interlocking cabal of gangsters and spies, when he referred to "higher authorities" (meaning the CIA, or Hoover, or both) subverting a grand jury that had been convened in Miami to probe the financial affairs of dozens of top mobsters. The excuse was that "delicate investigations conducted by another government agency were under way," but, Anslinger added angrily, this was "a dodge to call us off, and it succeeded."[30]

All of which brings us back to Meyer Lansky, the ultimate sleeping partner whose drug money-laundering enterprises stretched from Beirut, to Las Vegas, to the Bahamas, where, following the loss of his concessions in Cuba, he re-established his gambling business with, among others, Louis A. Chesler and Wallace Groves. A Canadian millionaire and former rumrunner, Chesler made a fortune in Florida land deals, then moved to Freeport and formed the Grand Bahama Development Company in 1961 with Groves.[31] With the help of Helliwell, Donovan, and other CIA assets, mountains of Thai, Nationalist Chinese, and Vietnamese drug money were allegedly invested in Castle Bank and Florida real estate deals through Chesler's General Development Company.[32]

Groves had fronted for Lansky since 1951, when he sold valuable Key Biscayne property to Elena Santiero Aleman, mother of Santo Trafficante's Cuban business partner, Jose Aleman.[33] Eventually the CIA hired Groves, Tex McCrary (Lansky's public relations consultant, whom George White had visited in Mexico in 1954), and Michael McLaney, manager of Lansky's Miami Beach dinner club, to suborn the top governing officials in the Bahamas, the tropical paradise that quickly became a major, and luxurious, transit point for Latin American drug smugglers.[34]

Meanwhile, Lansky's financial aide, John Pullman, incorporated the Bank of World Commerce in the Bahamas to handle the skim from several Las Vegas casinos. Pullman then merged his Atlas Bank "in some shadowy way" with Intrabank in Beirut.[35] Formed by Palestinian Youseff Beidas, and financed by several Arab nations under the direction of a Saudi Arabian arms trader, Intrabank owned the Casino du Liban in Beirut. This world-famous casino was managed by Lansky's drug smuggling Corsican contact, Marcel Francisci. Like the banks cited above, Intrabank's Bahamian branch laundered Mafia gambling and drug money, with the full knowledge of the CIA.[36]

Despite the FBN's spotlight on Lucky Luciano, Meyer Lansky was the lynchpin in the intelligence aspect of international drug smuggling that fascinated Hank Manfredi. Charlie Siragusa watched him closely, and he knew that Lansky sent Joseph F. Nesline and Charles Tourine around the world in 1962 to set up nightclubs and arrange drug deals. FBN agents followed Nesline (a hit man from Ohio who ran a sexual blackmail ring in Washington) to a meeting in Germany with Daviad Dargahi, "an Iranian ... with a background in drug smuggling."[37] FBN agents also followed Tourine, a mob killer in the Genovese family, to Bermuda. And yet, despite the surveillance, neither Lansky, Tourine, nor Nesline would ever be convicted on drug charges.

"Lansky was a chameleon who compartmented his operations, bought political protection, and established fronts," George Gaffney explains. "Not even the McClellan Committee and Department of Justice under Bobby Kennedy could get to him."

Tom Tripodi is blunter. "Siragusa was neutralized," he says with regard to the CIA and FBI's million-dollar men – among them, Meyer Lansky – and their seething hatred of the Kennedy administration.

Here's one example of how this animosity was inspired. JFK wanted to expel Air America, the CIA's drug smuggling proprietary airline, from Laos. And in 1962, in another attempt to curb the CIA's drug smuggling activities in East Asia, Bobby indicted Sea Supply manager Willis Bird (the original OSS liaison officer to General Tai Li) for having bribed a US official in Laos.[38] The president also fired ultra General Edwin Walker for attempting to indoctrinate US troops on behalf of the Christian Crusade.[39] These were dangerous moves, but not as perilous as Kennedy's plans to desegregate the South and eliminate the oil depletion allowances that enriched Texas oilmen – like Hoover's patron, Clint Murchison, the emerging Bush dynasty, and right-wing zealot, H. L. Hunt – and allowed them to seize control of oil reserves in the Middle and Far East. So Kennedy's enemies ensured that the Bird prosecution was blocked, and that Air America kept its contract in Laos, and continued to fly drugs.[40] Meanwhile, General Walker, the far-right American Security Council (including General Lansdale and Air America Chairman Admiral Felix Stump), and the Texas ultras started plotting their *coup d'état* in Dallas.

Such was the new frontier the FBN's wolf pack entered as the Kennedy brothers burst upon the scene; it was a wild country populated by an angry FBI director, CIA assassins and drug smugglers, and – starting in March 1962 with the creation in the Pentagon of the Special Assistant for Counter-Insurgency and Special Activities – members of the US Army Special Forces, assigned by the CIA to monitor the drug trade in areas under communist control. In view of these developments, the new frontier was an inhospitable place for the FBN, which continued its descent into knavish spookery and internecine warfare.

18

THE FRENCH CONNECTION

"You can't hide your true feelings."
Dick Powell in *To the Ends of the Earth*

As they mature, Americans have a tendency to revise their history, and in this tradition author Robin Moore offers two different explanations for how the famous French Connection case began. In his first book, *The French Connection* (published in 1969), Moore claims the case began on 7 October 1961, when NYPD detectives Eddie Egan and Sonny Grosso came to suspect that Pasquale "Patsy" Fuca was dealing narcotics from his lunch-eonette. Their suspicions were confirmed two days later when an agent in the FBI's fugitive squad told Grosso that Patsy was Angelo Tuminaro's nephew. A member of the Lucchese family and a major narcotics trafficker since 1937, five-foot-two "Little Angie" Tuminaro was married to Bella Stein, the daughter of a powerful Jewish racketeer, and was sought after by the FBN as a fugitive in the Cotroni case.[1]

Eight years later in *Mafia Wife* (a biography of Patsy Fuca's wife, Barbara), Moore claimed that Egan and Grosso learned about Patsy's relationship with Angie several weeks – rather than days – later, after an FBI agent saw Patsy at Angie's father's funeral. But of all the discrepancies in Moore's books, the biggest concerns Egan and Grosso's integrity. Presented as heroes in *The French Connection*, they are characterized as "sloppy and stupid" if not downright disreputable in *Mafia Wife*.[2]

Moore's change of heart is easy to explain: after the heroin that was seized in the French Connection case was found to have gone missing from the NYPD property clerk's storeroom in 1972, he decided to distance himself from any possible suspects in the dope's disappearance.[3]

He is consistent in one respect. In both books Egan and Grosso eventually realize that Patsy is handling heroin from Angie's French connection; and at this point – when the case assumes international proportions – they notify Edward Carey, head of the NYPD's narcotic squad. Carey in turn notifies George Gaffney, and Gaffney assigns Agent Francis E. Waters to work with Egan and Grosso. Tough as nails and a relentless investigator, Waters did far more to make the French Connection case than either Egan or Grosso, and he is eager to explain what really happened.

"Somebody pulled Angie's coat," Waters says, "by which I mean there were twenty-six defendants in the Cotroni case, but only five or six were actually caught with heroin. Angie was only loosely tied in to the case, and if he could hide until the trial was over, he'd be home free, because the government could never assemble the same lawyers and get the same witnesses together to make the same conspiracy case.

"Angie was on the lam in the Cotroni case, but he was still running the show. His brother Frank was his delivery man, but after Frank was arrested for a burglary, Angie had Patsy fill in. FBI Agent Bill Terry, meanwhile, had an informer who identified Patsy as part of a hijacking ring. Terry was on the FBI's fugitive squad and one day he showed a photograph of Angie to this informer. The informer said he'd seen him at Patsy's luncheonette, so Terry gave the photo to NYPD Sergeant Bill McLaughlin, and McLaughlin gave it to Grosso, and Grosso forgot about it. He wasn't about to do Terry's job for him, and he didn't place any significance on Patsy being Angie's nephew. He didn't have any idea that Angie had a French connection. But I did. I was trying to find Angie, and about two weeks later, while I was at Grosso's office, I happened to see Angie's photo on his desk. Right away I got excited. I had a hunch that Patsy might lead us to Angie, who was a far bigger fish.

"Now Grosso's interested too, and that night Egan and I set ourselves up with binoculars on the roof of a building across the street from Patsy's luncheonette. We see a black car pull up and double park outside. An Italian with a black Borsalino hat gets out, goes inside the luncheonette, comes out, drives away. This happens a few times that night, and we realize what's going down. We even followed Patsy back to his mother's house [Angie's sister Nellie, a major member of the drug ring, was married to Joe Fuca] where the plant was."

Waters put the pieces together, but Moore was able to credit Egan with initiating the case because, from the moment the NYPD put a wiretap in Fuca's luncheonette, the case was destined for a New York State Court. As

Waters puts it, "We had the intelligence on Angie, but Egan had the steady source of information from the wire."

Despite the wiretap, from the moment in November 1961 when Frankie Waters saw Patsy meet an unknown man driving a car with Canadian plates, the French Connection case relied almost entirely on his strength and determination. "I followed Patsy for fifty-four days straight without a break," Waters says with pride. "I slept in the back of my station wagon."

As the case developed, more FBN agents and NYPD detectives were assigned to follow Patsy, his longshoreman brother Tony, and their French accomplices: Jean Jehan, aged sixty-four, the debonair and distinguished-looking mastermind of the ring, with direct links to François Spirito and Joe Orsini; François Scaglia, a Corsican member of Les Trois Canards, and the ring's liaison to the American Mafia; J. Mouren, a mystery man who has never been identified; and courier Jacques Angelvin, the handsome host of a popular French television show. A recent widower, Angelvin had fallen in love with Scaglia's sister, from whom he acquired a cocaine habit. In his addled state of bereavement, infatuation, and intoxication, Angelvin, as a favor for Scaglia, agreed to drive a custom-made Buick on and off an ocean liner bound for New York. He would later claim that he had no idea what was hidden inside it.

The case gathered steam on 5 January 1962, when Angelvin embarked for New York. Two days later Scaglia flew to Montreal to meet Jehan, and the next day Grosso and Waters followed Patsy to a meeting with Jehan at a hotel in midtown Manhattan. Jehan, at the time, was completely unknown to Waters and Grosso. Afterwards, Waters followed Patsy back to Brooklyn, and Grosso tailed Jehan to the Victoria Hotel where the elderly Frenchman met Scaglia, age 35, and using the alias François Barbier. Patsy's meeting with Jehan, and Jehan's contact with Scaglia, allowed the investigators to identify two of the three principal members of Angie Tuminaro's legendary French connection for the first time. At this critical point, a French-speaking agent named Johnson (who'd only been with the FBN a few days and left immediately after the case) bugged their hotel rooms, and members of the International Group began listening to the suspects' conversations.[4]

On 10 January, agents Mortimer L. Benjamin and Norris Durham were assigned to watch Jean Jehan. "We saw him meet Scaglia," Benjamin recalls, "and then followed them to the pier for US Lines, where they stood around freezing – it was about ten degrees – while they watched the cars coming off a ship. Then suddenly they took off."

With the appearance of yet another conspirator (perhaps a courier) and a car, Carey and Gaffney formed a task force, consisting of scores of FBN agents and NYPD detectives, to follow the five suspects in the investigation. Angelvin, as yet unidentified, had checked into the Waldorf Hotel and began to tour New York's fashionable nightclubs with a demure secretary named Lilli DeBecque, provided gratis by Scaglia. Patsy was tailed to the lobby of the Roosevelt Hotel, where he met Jehan and a sixth suspect registered at the Abbey Hotel under the name J. Mouren. Patsy, Jehan, and Mouren drove away in Patsy's car, on what was undoubtedly a drug-trafficking mission. Jehan exited the car on 47th Street, and then Patsy and Mouren drove to an underground parking garage managed by suspected drug trafficker Sol Feinberg at 45 East End Avenue.

THE BLUE VALISE

On 13 January, Frankie Waters tailed slippery Jean Jehan to the subway. The insouciant Frenchman jumped on and off the train, then hopped on and waved goodbye to his pursuer, who was left behind on the platform, confounded and amazed, just like Gene Hackman (portraying Egan) would be in the movie. Never one to be nonplused, Waters happily waved back. But the tight surveillance had unnerved Jehan. Playing it cool, he called his accomplices, and over the next few days they quietly checked out of their separate hotel rooms by phone, using money orders to pay their bills. The main suspects in what was certainly a major narcotics case had suddenly vanished, and a moment of panic gripped the task force.

Exactly what happened next is unclear. According to Moore in *The French Connection*, Scaglia called Angelvin and told him to bring the Buick to Sol Feinberg's underground parking garage at 45 East End Avenue. Patsy's brother Tony met them there, then drove the Buick to another garage in the Bronx where he, Patsy, and mystery man Mouren allegedly removed a quantity of heroin from hidden compartments in the car's undercarriage. Patsy gave Mouren $225,000 for eighty-eight one-pound bags of heroin, which Patsy put on the backseat of his car. Mouren kept twenty-three bags and some smaller ounce-sized packets in a blue valise for safekeeping, until Patsy could pay him the balance due. Tony drove the Buick to his house in the Bronx, unloaded the eighty-eight packages, and then took the car to Feola's Auto Body Shop for reconstructive surgery.

As noted, none of what happened above was witnessed by anyone in law enforcement. And what happened next, on 18 January 1962, is also debatable. Depending on who tells the story, either Eddie Egan, while driving aimlessly around Manhattan, stumbled on Patsy and tailed him to

Feinberg's garage; or Frankie Waters drove to Feinberg's on a hunch and arrived just in time to see Patsy going in. Either way, FBN agents and NYPD narcotic detectives surrounded the garage and eventually saw Mouren emerge with the blue valise and climb into Patsy's Oldsmobile. Jehan joined them further down the street. A few minutes later, Angelvin exited the garage in the Buick, which had been returned intact from Feola's chop shop. The French TV host picked up François Scaglia a few blocks down the street. There were now two cars to follow, and that made the hastily assembled surveillance that much more difficult. Mouren got out of the Olds on 79th St, without the blue valise, and a few blocks later Jehan left the car with it — just as the radio system between the NYPD patrol cars and the FBN cars mysteriously malfunctioned. For some unknown reason, Egan elected to follow Patsy rather than Jehan — the man with the blue valise, which undoubtedly contained valuable evidence — and, as anyone who has seen the movie knows, Jehan casually walked away with the cash.

"We had the fish on the hook," Waters recalls, "but we toyed with it too long."

ALLEGATIONS OF CORRUPTION ARISE

While Egan followed Patsy — and Mouren and Jehan slipped away — Frankie Waters and Sonny Grosso stopped Scaglia and Angelvin for running a red light. They did not resist arrest. After dropping their catch at a nearby police station, Waters and Grosso joined in the frantic pursuit of Patsy Fuca, who had picked up his wife, Barbara, at their house in Brooklyn, and was intending to drive as far away as fast as possible.

"I was sitting on the base station radio," Morty Benjamin recalls, "monitoring calls from the field agents with Artie Fluhr. We knew the warrants had been issued and that Waters was about to make the arrest. We're listening. We know that Fuca and Barbara got in the car, and then we hear that Waters lost them. Well, this is Frankie's case. There's fifty feds on the case, and fifty cops; but everybody knows it's Frankie's case, and everyone wants him to make the bust. I'd only been an agent for ten months and I wasn't about to interfere. But Artie'd been around as long as anyone, and when he heard they'd lost Fuca, he said, 'Let's give them a hand.'

"So off we go. We drive across the Brooklyn Bridge and, just like magic, Fuca zips by. Now Artie's a great driver — he's running lights, driving on the sidewalk, doesn't get a scratch. I'm on the radio to Frankie; I tell him what's happening, and he says, 'Follow them, but don't bust them!'

Then he starts worrying and changes his mind. 'Bust them at the next light!' he says."

Benjamin's expression turns serious. "Patsy had a reputation for fighting cops, and he'd killed someone, which is why guys like Frankie Waters carried a blackjack. That's why you want a guy like Waters to bust a guy like Patsy Fuca. Plus which it was Frankie's case, and he had every right to bust him. But I'm the one who actually did it. And by the time we stopped them at the light, I wanted to do it.

"Fuca's driving. His pretty young wife's in a negligee. They're running, but they're stopped at a light in downtown Brooklyn, and Artie drives right in front of them. There's no place they can go. I'm on the passenger side, my adrenalin pumping. I'd made a promise to myself that if Fuca went for his gun, I wouldn't stop to think about it, I'd just shoot him. So I jumped out of the car, stuck my gun in his ear and said, 'Keep your hands on the wheel or I'll blow your fucking brains out.'" Benjamin's voice is trembling.

"Fuca could tell I wasn't kidding. He kept saying, 'Don't worry, kid. Don't worry.' But I was glad when Artie got around to the other side where Patsy's wife was sitting. We got them out of the car just as Waters arrived.

"You know," Benjamin says, "that was the first time I'd ever cocked my gun. But those other guys, Waters and Fluhr, they liked doing that stuff. They'd do anything to make a case.

"So we take Fuca to the precinct. We're at the booking desk when the reporters show up and the flashbulbs start popping. Egan's there with a warrant, and we go to Papa Joe Fuca's house to find the junk. We start in the basement, and that's when Artie sees stains on the floor. We look up and see a hole in the ceiling. Artie pulls a chair over, sticks his hand in the hole, and pulls out a half-kilogram bag of heroin. I'm about ten feet away and I do the same thing. Then Egan comes down, and everyone starts pulling out dope. But Artie and I found it, and Moore didn't get that right either!

"Then Gaffney shows up. He's pissed off, as usual. He thinks we're screwing with the junk because the account we're giving keeps changing as we find more and more packages, all of which goes south anyway. Six months before the French Connection dope was supposed to be destroyed, the NYPD Property Clerk saw beetles coming out of the bags. The heroin had been replaced with flour somewhere along the line. So as it turns out, I was lucky not to get credit for the bust, because I never got blamed for the missing dope, either.

"There're lots of things you don't hear about that French Connection case," Benjamin adds. "You don't hear about the short sentences, or that

Jehan got away with the money, or that Mouren was never identified, or that the heroin we found at Papa Joe's and Tony's house may not have come off the ship. All we found in the Buick was traces. Maybe."

Here it's important to reiterate that some FBN agents believe the Buick that Angelvin was driving was a decoy, and that the heroin at Joe's basement came from a previous shipment.[5]

Adding to the intrigue, Moore claims in *Mafia Wife* that somebody "got to" Angie and told him that if he paid $50,000, "he would know in advance when the arrest was to be made" and could protect himself.[6] This somebody, of course, could only have been a detective or a government agent.

There is another allegation of official complicity in the famous French Connection case. According to Frankie Waters, when he and Grosso searched Apartment 15C at 45 East End Avenue, they found a photo – taken six days before at La Cloche d'Or restaurant on Third Avenue – of the apartment's occupant with Jean Jehan. But the photo was lost and the occupant, having relocated to Mexico, was never pursued.

"That case taught me a lot," Benjamin says solemnly. "It taught me that as a young agent you don't claim credit. You don't testify either, and you avoid writing reports. Artie Fluhr spent seven days on the stand trying to explain to the judge why Egan wasn't lying. And Waters had a hard time explaining why running a red light gave him probable cause to search the Buick."

THE CIA'S FRENCH CONNECTION

Acclaimed as a smashing success, the French Connection case, with its missing money and vanishing Frenchmen, in fact reflected the FBN's increasing incapacity to deal with the espionage aspects of international drug trafficking. The trend started on 22 March 1961, when New York Customs agents arrested thirty-five-year-old Air France stewardess Simone Christmann for concealing four and a half pounds of heroin in her ample brassiere. Christmann said she thought the powder was perfume base, and that a "Mr. Mueller" in Paris had given it to her. In June 1961, she was sentenced to four years in prison, but was soon released on bond.[7]

According to an FBN agent on the case, Christmann was released because she was a spy for the Organization de l'Armée Secrète (OAS), a cabal of French Army officers violently opposed to French president Charles de Gaulle's decision to grant Algeria independence. Because the Soviets were courting the Algerians, the US and Israeli intelligence services secretly supported the OAS. It's a fact that CIA officers Richard Bissell and Richard Helms met in December 1960 with OAS political chief Jacques Soustelle to assure him of their support for a putsch.[8] And it's alleged that CIA officer John Philipsborn met with OAS leader General Raoul Salan in Paris just before the OAS mutiny (a month after Christmann's arrest) in Algeria in April 1961.[9]

The FBN agent cited above claims that Christmann, being a good soldier, took "a small fall to protect her bosses," in the CIA-supported faction within the OAS, so the mutiny could go forward. By not doing anything, the FBN was complicit. Paul Knight, the FBN agent in charge in Paris, then secretly working for the CIA, did not investigate Mueller because, he said, "It was a Customs case." And technically it was. But the Customs agent in Paris at the time, Jacques L. Changeux (a former FBN agent), was also secretly working for the CIA, and he didn't investigate the case either.

Shortly thereafter, Knight quit the FBN and returned to America in February 1962, for training and official enrollment in the CIA, and was replaced in Paris by Agent Victor G. Maria. According to Maria, his job was limited to investigating American citizens involved in drug trafficking, and he was specifically told not to investigate French citizens. So he didn't pursue Mueller either.

And yet, despite the best efforts of the CIA, Mueller's identity was revealed in April 1962, when Etienne Tarditi named Irving Brown in connection with L'affaire Rosal. Through a routine background check, FBN agents learned that Brown, the International Confederation of Free Trade Unions' representative to the UN, often traveled from New York to Paris, where he frequented a restaurant owned by Georges Bayon. A SDECE agent who recruited diplomats as drug couriers, Bayon used the alias Mueller. Further investigation showed that labor leader Irving Brown was a CIA agent, that he had port privileges in New York (meaning his baggage was never checked by Customs), and that his wife Lilly (perhaps Lilli DeBecque from the French Connection case) was a secretary for Carmel Offie, a former CIA agent then managing an import-export business in Manhattan.[10]

Excited by this information, Andy Tartaglino launched a Court House Squad investigation of Brown in June 1962 – but was quickly told to drop it. "Joe Amato told me that someone else was handling it," Tartaglino explains, with a glint in his eye.

That unnamed party was the CIA, of course, which begs the question: Who were Irving Brown and Carmel Offie, and how were they involved with CIA counterintelligence chief James Angleton in the French Connection?

Harry J. Anslinger. (*Chappell Family Collection*)

George H. White. (*Chappell Family Collection*)

Henry L. Manfredi (left) and Charles Siragusa in Italy, celebrating the 1950 Morganti case. (*Manfredi Family Collection*)

Charles Siragusa with Turkish police officers, circa 1954. (*Siragusa Family Collection*)

Howard W. Chappell (left) and Kenneth M. Goven. (*Chappell Family Collection*)

Paul E. Knight. (*Knight Family Collection*)

George H. Gaffney, NYC, circa 1951. (*Gaffney Family Collection*)

Bottom row, left to right: unidentified NYPD detective, Gabriel Dukas, Alfred C. Benza, Max H. Roder; top row, left to right: NYPD detective Thomas O'Brien, and Anthony Zirilli celebrating Sol Gelb seizure, circa 1954. (*Mangiaracina Family Collection*)

Merchant Mariner's identification card used by Anthony Pohl while operating undercover in France, circa 1961. (*Pohl Family Collection*)

Left to right, bottom row: George J. Ward, Daniel D. Moynihan, Angelo Zurlo, James P. Murray, and John M. Dolce; left to right, top row: Lee Bennett, Gabriel Dukas, Edward T. Coyne, Arthur J. Fluhr, Benjamin Fitzgerald, Leonard S. Schrier, and Charles G. Ward, circa 1959. (*Benjamin Family Collection*)

Charles Siragusa and Martin F. Pera, about to board ship in January 1951, on voyage to confer with officials in Europe. (*Pera Family Collection*)

Henry L. Manfredi and his wife Dorothy in Trieste, moments after Manfredi received the Exceptional Civilian Service award from Major General William Bradford in July 1952. (*Manfredi Family Collection*)

Left to right: Charles G. Ward, Walter J. Smith, Jr, Edward R. Dower, unidentified agent, Frank L. Dolce, John. M. Dolce, Charles R. McDonnell, and Frank J. Selvaggi (kneeling), celebrating the seizure of ten kilograms of heroin concealed in a sea trunk, October 1960. (*Mangiaracina Family Collection*)

Left to right: Arthur J. Fluhr, Guatemalan Ambassador Mauricio Rosal, and James M. Burke, October 1960. (*Fluhr Family Collection*)

Lucky Luciano (left) and Sal Vizzini in Naples, 1959. (*Vizzini Family Collection*)

Colonel Orlando Piedra congratulating Sal Vizzini on a seizure in Cuba in 1957. (*Vizzini Family Collection*)

William B. Davis. (*Davis Family Collection*)

Left to right: William A. Carroza, John Ripa, James S. Bailey, Robert Manning (kneeling), Francis E. Waters, and Benjamin Fitzgerald, celebrating the 1962 French Connection case. (*Waters Family Collection*)

Left to right: James Attie, Joseph Gabrys, Martin F. Pera, George M. Belk, Anthony Mangiaracina, Walter S. Fialkewicz, and Louis V. Diveglio, circa 1963. (*Mangiaracina Family Collection*)

Left to right: Irvin C. Swank, John G. Evans, and Allan R. Pringle, displaying a seizure of drugs, guns and money. (*Evans Family Collection*) Note: This photograph was taken by M. Leon Lopez and appeared on the front page of the 24 February 1971 *Chicago Daily News*; though the picture was taken after the FBN had been abolished, Swank, Evans and Pringle were veterans of the FBN.

Victor G. Maria. (*Maria Family Collection*)

Left to right: Michael G. Picini, Captain Wahib Abdul Samad, Henry L. Giordano, and Dennis Dayle in Lebanon. (*Dayle Family Collection*)

George H. White (left, wearing beret) after his illness, Albert Habib beside him, and two unidentified individuals, circa 1964. (*Habib Family Collection*)

Left to right: French narcotic detectives Claude Chaminadas and Andre Andrieux and FBN Agent Robert DeFauw in Marseilles, May 1966, celebrating the seizure of 196 kilograms of morphine base found aboard the SS Karadeniz. (*DeFauw Family Collection*)

Richard E. Salmi (center, with pistol in hand) with Turkish police officials and huge opium seizure, circa 1966. (*Salmi Family Collection*)

Fred T. Dick. (*Dick Family Collection*)

Frank J. Selvaggi. (*Selvaggi Family Collection*)

Left to right: Detective Frank McGuffey, Frank J. Selvaggi, Francis E. Waters, Gerald L. Latimer, Norman R. Matuozzi, Customs Agent George C. Corcoran, CID Agent Arthur W. Gehrig, Customs Inspector William L. Rogers, Customs Supervisor Jesse L. Hatcher, Officer Herman Boone, and FBN Agent Russell Jessup, celebrating the seizure of 95 kilograms of heroin in Columbus, Georgia, on 20 December 1965. (*Gehrig Family Collection*)

Left to right: Mortimer L. Benjamin, Leonard S. Schrier, George M. Belk, Jacques I. Kiere, and Michael A. Antonelli, receiving commendations. (*Schrier Family Collection*)

Left to right: Arthur J. Fluhr, Angel L. Gonzalez, John Ripa, Leonard S. Schrier, James S. Bailey, William A. Carroza, and Ernest Haridopolous, celebrating a 1962 heroin seizure. (*Schrier Family Collection*)

Harry J. Anslinger presents Henry L. Giordano with an award, 1962. (*Picini Family Collection*)

Richard E. Salmi (second from right), arrested while working undercover in Turkey, circa 1967. (*Salmi Family Collection*)

LABOR'S LOVE LOST

Irving Brown was a protégé of Jay Lovestone, leader of the American Communist Party in the 1920s. But after he quarreled with Joseph Stalin, Lovestone was expelled from the Party and by 1936 had joined the United Auto Workers Union. He soon abandoned Marxism altogether and, with Brown, began rooting communists out of the American labor movement. In 1945, with the support of the AFL, Lovestone became executive secretary of the Free Trade Union Committee and sent Brown to Europe to help the CIA subvert communist trade unions.

James Angleton became Lovestone's CIA case officer in 1947 and, according to his biographer, Tom Mangold, after Angleton became chief of counterintelligence in 1955, he contacted Lovestone through Stephen Millet, "the counterintelligence officer who headed the Israeli Desk at Langley. Lovestone's payments and logistics were handled in New York by Mario Brod, Angleton's lawyer friend." [11]

What Mangold is saying is profoundly important, and requires further explanation. First, Angleton contacted Irving Brown's boss, Jay Lovestone, through his liaison to Israeli Intelligence. This is a fact that lends credence to Jim Attie's allegation that the Mossad was involved in international drug smuggling – most likely in support of Angleton and Brown. Next, Angleton paid Lovestone, and thus Brown, through labor lawyer Mario Brod, his liaison to the Mafia. This arrangement put Brod in position to broker drug deals, on Angleton's behalf, between the Mafia, the Mossad, and Brown's soon-to-be-revealed French connection. This explains why Joe Amato told Andy Tartaglino that someone else was handling the Brown investigation of 1962. But could that someone else have been Charlie Siragusa? If the reader will recall, Siragusa knew Angleton and had worked with Brod in Italy during the war; and according to Colonel Tulius Acampora, Angleton was so dependent on Siragusa for his Mafia contacts that he "kissed Siragusa's ass in Macy's window at noon." All of this, even without Siragusa's personal involvement, puts Angleton, Israeli intelligence, Brown, his Corsican contacts, the FBN, and the Mafia at the heart of the CIA's emerging drug-trafficking conspiracy.

Irving Brown has an interesting background. In return for his double agent work in the 1930s, he was named the AFL's representative to the War Production Board, where he befriended Tracy Barnes. (Barnes in 1962 was chief of the CIA's Domestic Operations Division. In that capacity, he managed Cuban exile and Mafia operations, as well as proprietary companies in America, and the dissemination of disinformation through

American academia, publishing houses, and mainstream press outlets.) [12] After the war, Brown worked for the AFL in Europe and in 1949, with CIA money, he established a compatible left, anti-communist union in Marseilles. When the communists called for strikes in Marseilles, Brown enlisted Corsican gangster Pierre Ferri-Pisani, and Pisani in turn recruited Corsican and Sicilian thugs to toss the strikers into the Mediterranean Sea. [13]

In 1952, either Pisani or, more likely, French-spy-turned-gangster Robert Blemant, introduced Brown to drug lords Antoine Guérini and Jo Cesari in Bordeaux, after which Brown met with unidentified Mafiosi in Italy, the scene of his next CIA machinations. [14] According to his secretary, Naomi Spatz, Brown also met Maurice Castellani in Marseilles at this time. Strikingly handsome, and known either as "Le Petit Maurice" or "Tête Cassée" (meaning "Broken Head" – a reference to his talent as an extortionist), Castellani was one of the most enigmatic and successful drug traffickers of his time. As a very young boy, he had served bravely with the Resistance in Marseilles, and was well respected within the Corsican underworld. More importantly, Castellani was one of Robert Blemant's lieutenants in Les Trois Canards gang in Paris, along with François Scaglia of French Connection case fame. Notably, the three ducks often met for fish soup and snails at Georges Bayon's restaurant – Bayon being the aforementioned Mr. Mueller who supplied OAS Agent Simone Christmann with heroin.

During the mid-1950s, Brown came under the tutelage of the aforementioned Carmel Offie, a former Foreign Service officer who had served in Honduras in the mid-1930s during the TACA affair and, following that, as an aide to Ambassador William Bullitt in Russia. (Bullitt, as we know from chapter 5, was one of several diplomats linked to smuggling in the post-war era, and played an instrumental role in establishing the Pawley-Cooke Mission in Taiwan in 1950.) After the war, Offie became a CIA contract agent. He formed refugee groups in Germany and ran agents posing as black marketeers behind the Iron Curtain. He also smuggled Nazis to South America, with James Angleton, as part of Operation Bloodstone. [15]

As a political advisor to the AFL's Information Service and the CIA's bagman to the Free Trade Union Committee, Offie guided Brown in Europe until 1954, when, amid rumors of pouch abuse, gunrunning, and White slavery, he returned to the United States and became a consultant to a Washington law firm whose senior partners included Alben Barkley's son-in-law. (Barkley, of course, was close to George Cunningham, the FBN's deputy director from 1949 until 1958.) Offie's New York-based import-export company did business in France, Germany, South Vietnam, and Italy. In 1957, he acquired part-ownership of a mining company in North Africa, at the same time Brown was in Tunis recruiting Algerian student leaders, through the National Student Association, and sending them into France to infiltrate communist-controlled front groups.[16]

The French intelligence services uncovered Brown's espionage activities and in 1960, having been declared *persona non grata* in Europe and North Africa, he returned to New York and set up shop near the UN. His wife Lilly took a secretarial job at Carmel Offie's import-export firm. As head of the AFL's American African Labor Institute, Brown worked with numerous African leaders in various CIA intrigues, including, evidently, the smuggling of narcotics on behalf of the OAS and Israel.

THE FRENCH CONNECTION'S CIA FACET

On 1 June 1962, Harry Anslinger was quoted in the *New York Times* as saying that heroin was being moved from the PRC on horse caravans to Burma, and from there through Cuba to the US. But he knew that wasn't true. In his July 1959 report, "The Narcotics Situation in South Asia and the Far East," Garland Williams had identified the Kuomintang as the region's primary narcotics producer and Bangkok as "the most important single source of illicit opium in the world today. It is also the locale for the least amount of corrective effort by responsible American agencies," he said, placing the blame squarely on the CIA. Thai Army personnel moved massive amounts of drugs to the seaport and, Williams said, "many Thai officials, some of great prominence in both civil and military echelons of the government, are involved in the drug traffic, but are forbidden to carry on similar activities in the area of enforcement." But, Williams reported, the CIA and State Department "never mentioned the subject to the police chief or any other Thai official. Avoidance is policy," he said, even though the director of the US Mission "knew all about it in detail, names, methods of movement, where it goes." The US counsel in Chiang Mai (an undercover CIA officer) had "uncalled for sympathy with opium producers in his district."[17]

Not only were Thai, CIA, and Kuomintang officials involved in the drug trade in the Golden Triangle; according to Williams there was also, in Bangkok, "an old, experienced, well-equipped, and financially strong" French organization that supplied "the group which supplies the persistent major violators of French nationality who operate in New York City." Alas, Williams did not name the members of this group in his report, but he did say "a trained narcotic investigator could soon develop the facts for use by those who he would find to take action."

What Williams knew, and told Anslinger in 1959, was becoming public knowledge by 1962, and that year author Andrew Tully provided further insights into the central role of the CIA and Kuomintang in international drug trafficking. In his book, *CIA: The Inside Story*, Tully told of a CIA officer arriving in Burma from Taiwan. He saw no soldiers, only a vast plantation. "You see," said the Kuomintang colonel in charge, "it takes money to run an operation like this and so ... we're growing opium." As Tully noted, the treacherous Kuomintang "supplemented" their drug-smuggling income "by selling their arms to the Chinese Communists." [18]

"In 1962, we thought the source was Turkey," Tom Tripodi explains. "But the French were taking drugs out of Southeast Asia. French Intelligence was running the show. Thirty to forty people were involved, including [Ambassador Mauricio] Rosal. Rosal was being blackmailed by Tarditi, and Tarditi was part of the Brown–Lovestone–Angleton net."

Brown's friend, Maurice "Le Petit" Castellani, was the likely operations manager of this CIA facet of the French connection, the group Williams referred to in 1959 – the year Castellani was connected with the seizure of seven kilos of cocaine in Milan. Castellani would also be linked to SDECE front groups, and may have been the mysterious J. Mouren of the January 1962 French Connection case. [19] He was a close friend of fellow Canard, François Scaglia, and, according to Frankie Waters, "Patsy Fuca talked about 'Le Petit Maurice' with great deference."

Waters also stumbled on the Far East and Israeli connections when he discovered that Patsy was connected to Toots Schoenfeld and that Toots was connected to Angie's father-in-law, an important Jewish gangster named Stein. Stein was linked to the Frenchman at Apartment 15C, who in turn was bankrolling Jehan's operation. "We'd found the same address in the possession of a smuggler tied to Marcel Francisci," Waters says, "so Grosso and I got a search warrant and went to the apartment. It was a beautiful place, but it was owned by an executive of the Michelin Tire Company, so we had to back out."

Waters shrugs. "Think about it. Mouren was never identified; Scaglia was trained by the OSS; and Special Forces people were involved in the French Connection case." [20]

Think about this, too: Patsy and J. Mouren allegedly removed about fifty kilograms of heroin from the Buick, though some FBN agents claim the car was a decoy and that someone from the FBN flaked traces of heroin in it. According to Tripodi, the eleven kilograms found at Joe Fuca's house may not have come from the same shipment as the thirty-three kilograms found at Tony's. The car supposedly contained fifty kilograms of heroin, so, Tripodi says, "we started to think that as much as seventeen kilograms had never made it to the evidence room."[21]

How could that happen? Moore in *Mafia Wife* claims that Egan and Grosso knew about the heroin at Tony's house for a month before they seized it, and then waited for two days before they turned it in. For this reason inspectors came to suspect that corrupt cops and/or FBN agents stole the missing heroin: seventeen kilograms of it according to FBN Agent Tom Tripodi; sixteen pounds in Moore's estimation. For now it is enough to know that Frankie Waters was charged and acquitted of selling to Charlie McDonnell a portion of the heroin that went astray.[22]

FALLOUT FROM THE FRENCH CONNECTION

More than ever, after the botched French Connection case, the infighting at FBN headquarters negatively affected investigations of international drug law enforcement. The problem had started festering the year before, when Lee Speer sent Agent Tony Pohl to Paris to work with Paul Knight and conduct undercover operations in Marseilles. A tall, intimidating man, Pohl had served as the Army CID liaison to the Secret Service in Europe in the 1950s, and eventually his connections in the higher ranks of the French and German police forces brought him to Charlie Siragusa's attention. In September 1960, Siragusa recruited Pohl into the FBN, specifically to work on the French connection. Pohl proved his abilities during the interrogation of Etienne Tarditi. Everyone in the office was yelling at the Frenchman, trying to get him to open up. Finally Pohl, who had grown up in France and served in the Resistance, walked over to Tarditi, who was proudly wearing his Legion of Honor ribbon outside his coat. Pohl pointed at it and said, in his booming baritone voice, words to the effect of, "Your activities have brought only disgrace to this." At which point Tarditi cracked.

In March 1961, Pohl arrived in Paris, and was immediately shunned by Knight, and mistrusted by Cusack. As Pohl recalls, "I hadn't been officially transferred, and they couldn't understand why a mere GS-7 had been sent on a special assignment to Paris." He explained that his job was to quietly open an unofficial office in Marseilles (which he did in June 1961 at the US Consulate), and make some undercover cases; but his primary task was to locate heroin conversion labs using Marty Pera's innovative precursor tracking technique. Unfortunately, after years of wrapping himself in the

FBN's devious undercover ethos, Cusack could not prevent himself from believing that Pohl, a wiretap expert, was there as an emissary of Lee Speer, to spy on him! So Knight and Cusack froze Pohl out.

Marty Pera was a victim of the same paranoia that was devouring the FBN. Right after Pohl opened the office in Marseilles, Cusack was summoned back to FBN headquarters for some inexplicable reason, which probably had to do with Speer's integrity investigation. Perhaps Giordano had called Cusack back to help sabotage the crusading enforcement assistant? In any event, Pera was relieved of his duties as chief of the International Group and sent to Rome as acting district supervisor from July until November 1961. As Pohl noted, Pera had developed a precursor tracking system that enabled the FBN to include the operators of illicit labs in France in international conspiracy cases by matching the heroin they produced in France to heroin seized in the US. Pera's International Group had also been narrowing its focus on three major Mafiosi involved in the French connection – Santo Sorge (Joe Bonanno's financial advisor), Carlos Marcello, and Santo Trafficante. Pera was making progress, but he slipped up on two counts: he'd uncovered the CIA's guiding hand, and he'd sided with doomed enforcement assistant Lee Speer.

"Speer was good to me," Pera acknowledges, "but he was hated by the New York agents, especially Gaffney, and I got caught in the crossfire. I tried to avoid trouble, but Gaffney was using Group Three for secret operations, and I was just getting in the way." In addition, Pera says, "Speer was concerned about the CIA. It was obvious that Far East Asian dope was coming to the US, and everyone knew it couldn't happen without SDECE. But it was to the CIA's advantage to have these sources left intact, and Speer was a fool to think otherwise."[23]

Taking on the CIA was hard enough, but Speer was fighting the French too. "SDECE split our people," Pera says. "Cusack wanted to join the CIA [which may be the reason he returned to the US], so he went with the Paris police squad, which the CIA had co-opted. Tartaglino went with the Central Narcotics Office. So Speer calls Cusack back from Rome and sends me over as acting supervisor. Before I go, Gaffney says, 'Relax while you're there. Enjoy yourself. Keep a low profile. Do anything for Speer and you're dead.'

"Those four months in Rome *were* deadly," Pera sighs. "I was reporting back to Washington where Fred Dick, Siragusa, and Cusack were all second-guessing me, because I was 'Speer's man.' Same thing happened to Tony Pohl, a French-speaking agent Speer sent to Marseilles to find the labs that Andy couldn't find."

There were problems in Rome, too. Pera had a skeleton crew that consisted of two agents; Hank Manfredi – helpful, but a part-time employee due to his CIA obligations; and Agent Joe Vullo. Knight, like Manfredi, spent as much time working for the CIA as he did the FBN, and was in and out of Paris. Vizzini would be recalled to the US in late 1961, and Pohl was struggling. There were the usual CIA intrigues too. According to Pera, the Police Judiciare had put a wiretap on an OAS general [perhaps General Salan, although Pohl adamantly denies it] who had served in Indochina. "He was an opium smoker," Pera says, "and we were trying to find his supplier. But SDECE turned us away.

"When I got back," he continues, "the International Group was gone. Gaffney said I'd get an enforcement group, but by then I'd had it. I hung around in New York for a while, then went to the McClellan Committee in Washington with John Enright and Gene Marshall. Then I quit in October 1963 to join the Office of Naval Investigations."

The International Group was splintered by then. Its intelligence function, upon which the FBN relied so heavily, went to Group Three, and its technical responsibilities went to Norey Durham at a small unit dubbed the Radio Shack. A separate fugitive squad was created, and by 1961 strange people started popping up – like Johnson, the wiretap man in the French Connection case. Tony Mangiaracina recalls the arrival in New York of an agent who studied the files, then wound up running Pan Am security in Bremerhaven, Germany. "Another time they sent a kid to us from Chicago. He spoke perfect French and was going to Rome, but all he did was sit around reading the files. Then they sent him to Washington to learn Arabic. Very spooky people."

Lenny Schrier got involved with the spies when he busted a Brazilian lawyer, Luis Almeada, with five ounces of coke. "His brother was a Brazilian congressman, and Luis got the coke from a German priest who managed a lab in Bolivia," Schrier says with a wry smile. "Then Marty Pera brought Antranik Paroutian back from Beirut, and we put Paroutian in the same cell with Luis. They became friends, and Paroutian offered to introduce Luis to his brother, a police official in Lebanon with a morphine base operation in Syria. We got Luis out of jail, to make it look like he was free to travel around, and then Paroutian wrote to his brother, telling him that Luis was coming over with money to buy heroin. We sent undercover Agent Bob Gaudette instead. Gaudette was a French Canadian who looked like Luis. But," Lenny shrugs, "the CIA grabbed Gaudette in Beirut, and nothing happened."

Jim Attie in Chicago had pulled off yet another investigation that led to Sami Khoury and some Lebanese politicians. Attie's cousin was in a Syrian paramilitary organization and was willing to cover him in the interior of Lebanon, Syria, and Iraq. Attie had his suitcase packed, but Chicago District Supervisor George Belk cancelled the operation. No explanation was proffered, nor was one needed – the CIA and Mossad wanted their prize informer, Sami Khoury, left intact for the time being. Plus Attie, like Pera, was a Speer man, and Henry Giordano wasn't about to let him put a feather in Speer's cap.

Even high-strung George Gaffney was getting jumpier than usual. "Charlie Siragusa let us make the Victor Stadter case at the CIA pad on 13th Street, and that's when it occurred to me that we were asking for trouble. 'Suppose the defense wants to know where Stadter [a Texas bush pilot and drug smuggler] was interviewed?' I asked Charlie. 'What are we going to say then?'"

While more and more US-based case-making agents were experiencing CIA complications, it was business as usual for agents overseas. But *unlike* everyone else working abroad, Sal Vizzini knew how to use nitroglycerine. He was also an expert lock-pick and had once cracked the New York office safe in less than five minutes, on a bet. Along with his undercover abilities, these arcane skills made Vizzini attractive to the CIA and, while he was opening the FBN's first office in Istanbul, he was recruited by Harold Fiedler, a CIA advisor to the Turkish secret police.

"Sal," according to Fiedler, "was a wild man whom the Turks loved, because he was as tough and brave as they were. But he was doing more than he should have, taking risks beyond belief. There were gunfights. It was complex, but what he did improved my position."

As Vizzini tells it, "I was there in 1960 during the revolution [when CIA-backed General Cemel Gursel deposed Premier Adnan Menderes] and Hal wanted me to find out how people near the Russian border were feeling, which I was able to do, because I brought along cigarettes and booze. Hal's people were following the Russians, and after I shot two of them, the Turks wanted to hang me. So Cusack calls up Hal and says, 'We'll make it a junk deal gone bad.' Which they did.

"Then in late 1961, I was called back to Washington, so I cleaned out a '57 Chevy Siragusa had given me in Rome. I was looking under the seat to make sure there wasn't anything there that shouldn't be there, and I found a fully automatic, silenced .22. It's a CIA hit gun." Vizzini grins. "I didn't tell Charlie, but when I got back I traded it to Gaffney for a pair of binoculars he said came off the bridge of the USS Missouri. Well, the binoculars didn't come off the ship, and taking the gun from Siragusa and trading it to Gaffney turned out to be a big mistake.

"Nothing happens right away. Anslinger was grateful for what I'd done in Turkey and Italy, and he lets me go to Miami. Then he asks me to go to Thailand on a ninety-day TDY, to open an office in Bangkok. As Charlie puts me on the plane he says, 'We need to convince Customs that they need our help, so glom onto their cases. Be there for the arrest, and send back the photos. But take it away from Customs.

"'Keep your Sicilian up,' Charlie said. 'We need you.'

"Turns out the Thailand job had another purpose. Customs was in Vietnam, but only under the aegis of helping the soldiers. Apart from that, no one's making cases in Vietnam because the CIA is escorting dope to its warlords. Then through the CIA I hear about a processing plant in Burma. It's their idea. I swim across the Mekong and, using CIA explosives, I blow it up. The State Department's pissed, but the CIA's happy, and I'm doing what I'm supposed to do.

"When I come back, the pharmacist [Henry Giordano] is the Commissioner, Siragusa's the deputy, and Gaffney's the enforcement assistant. Anslinger puts me in Miami again, and the CIA puts me with Philippe de Vosjoli. Philippe was SDECE's liaison to Angleton, and Angleton gave him wiretap equipment that we passed to his agents inside Cuba. We took photographs and did some other things that were instrumental in defusing the Missile Crisis of October 1962.[24]

"Next they want me to go back to Thailand, only this time with Bowman Taylor, an agent from Dallas. Taylor was going over to run the Bangkok office that I'd opened. So I introduce him to my informer, an Army intelligence captain with the Thai narcotic police, and Taylor digs up the fact that I'd bought the guy a Lambretta with official funds. By then Siragusa had bugged the DC office, and he'd overheard Gaffney talking about the .22. Charlie had gotten in trouble with the CIA for losing the gun, and when he found out that I'd taken it, he turned against me. He was pissed off because Cusack had gone behind his back to cover me in Turkey too, so he used Taylor's report to destroy me."[25]

The CIA gave and the CIA took cases away; that was the golden rule every case-making agent and FBN executive understood by mid-1962, when James Angleton assigned James Ludlum, a member of his counter-intelligence staff, as the Agency's first official liaison to the FBN. And with that move, Angleton asserted his control. Already compromised by institutionalized corruption and Anslinger's apathy, the case-makers started to walk a high-tension wire the CIA had strung between fantasy and reality, and with the help of the FBI, the effect began to take its toll.

19

VALACHI

"The bravura of revolvers in vogue now,
and the cult of death,
are quite at home inside the City."

W. H. Auden, "The Age of Anxiety"

With Harry Anslinger's retirement in May 1962, the Kennedy administration had a chance to modernize the Bureau of Narcotics, but too many lawmakers had invested too much political capital in promoting the hard line to accept any drastic changes. So the administration formed an Advisory Commission on Narcotics and Drug Abuse in January 1963. Named for chairman E. Barrett Prettyman, a retired federal judge, the Prettyman Commission was to review current drug law enforcement policies and propose alternative policies to those previously pursued.

Prior to this, the search for Anslinger's replacement had turned inward, and in view of Bobby Kennedy's ethnically charged war on the Mafia, a political decision was made that an Italian American would get the job. The choice was between Charlie Siragusa and Henry Giordano, and the key decision maker was Bobby Kennedy's *consigliere*, Carmine Bellino. This should have been to Siragusa's advantage, because he knew Bellino well; Bellino was the Kennedy family's link to his close friend Hank Manfredi, and Manfredi was serving as Jackie Kennedy's personal bodyguard during her occasional visits to Europe. But these personal relationships were not meaningful enough to win Siragusa the Commissioner's job – nor was the support he received from his "rabbi" on Capitol Hill, Rhode Island Senator Claiborne Pell.

"Charlie wasn't a battler," explains Fred Dick, his colleague at head-quarters. "He knew that Giordano and Gaffney were going to screw it up. But he also knew they were going to win."

Siragusa facetiously told a friend, "The trick is to get off the stage before the audience starts throwing tomatoes at you."

After decades of being the alpha wolf, Anslinger, however, wasn't ready to leave the pack, even after his retirement, so despite his promise to Siragusa, he threw his weight behind Giordano. He knew that Giordano was incapable of making decisions without his advice, and that by backing Giordano, and accepting a sinecure position at the United Nations, he would be able to keep his hand in the game.

To assuage Senator Pell and ensure Siragusa a heftier retirement plan, Treasury's assistant secretary for law enforcement, James Reed, on Bellino's advice, persuaded Giordano to accept Siragusa as his deputy for a year, on the condition that Siragusa would then step aside and allow George Gaffney – who had ingratiated himself with Bobby Kennedy – to take his place.

The object was to guarantee political stability at a critical point in Bobby's war on crime. A rebellion by young Mafiosi had erupted after Apalachin, and had never subsided. After Joe Profaci died in June 1962, his ineffectual successor, Giuseppe Magliocco, watched helplessly while Joseph Colombo battled "Crazy Joe" Gallo for control of the family. Having moved to Arizona, Joe Bonanno was fighting an insurgent faction in his family in New York. Stefano Magaddino was under investigation in the Rinaldo–Palmieri case. Carlo Gambino, Tom Lucchese, and Carlos Marcello were in danger of being deported. Sam Giancana was dodging subpoenas. Tony Bender – leader of the mutiny against Genovese family boss Tom Eboli – went for a ride in April 1962 and never returned. And Jimmy Hoffa had been indicted in Tennessee and was set to go to trial in October.

Aware of all this turmoil, Bobby was looking for a knockout punch, the potential for which would emerge in the person of Joe Valachi, the disgruntled Mafia buttonman Frank Selvaggi had squeezed into ratting out Sal Maneri, Sal Rinaldo, and several other hoods. As Kennedy knew, the Rinaldo–Palmieri case had led to the arrest of dozens of major drug traffickers in Italy and America, and had generated two major conspiracy cases. The Attorney General was grateful and in return would reward George Gaffney with a promotion in August 1962 to enforcement assistant, the number three position at FBN headquarters.

Meanwhile, Valachi was convicted in the Rinaldo–Palmieri case in December 1961, and in February 1962, he was sentenced to twenty years in the Atlanta Penitentiary. To his immense disappointment, that time was to be served in addition to the fifteen years he'd received in the Freeman case. But the FBN wasn't through with him, and Gaffney, while still serving as district supervisor in New York, had him returned to the Federal Detention Center on West Street, for questioning in several new and ongoing investigations. Gaffney's plan was to turn up the pressure on the aging hood by making it appear to his criminal associates as if he was already cooperating. To that end, Gaffney, Pat Ward, and Frank Selvaggi began periodically, and visibly, visiting him at West Street.

As Gaffney recalls, "We'd just gotten Mauro, Caruso, and Maneri in Spain, and we had the US Marshals take them to lock-up at West Street where, by cruel coincidence, Vinnie Mauro sees Valachi. Mauro asks him, 'What you doing upstairs with the feds for three hours?'"

Despite the veiled threat from his murderous associate, Valachi felt that Selvaggi had framed him in the Rinaldo case. Angry and obstinate, he refused to cooperate. So US Attorney Robert Morgenthau had him returned to the Atlanta Penitentiary and put in the same cell as Vito Genovese, as a way of softening him up. It was well known that Genovese believed that Valachi was an informer, and in their cell, in full view of everyone, the boss of bosses gave Valachi the "kiss of death," the traditional Mafia gesture of friendship before a fatal betrayal.

Although increasingly apprehensive, Valachi still feigned innocence. But a few days later he heard through the prison grapevine that Joey DiPalermo had accepted a contract to kill him, and that's when he cracked. Valachi wrote a plaintive letter to Gaffney, promising to tell all in exchange for protection. But his probation officer sat on the letter and on 22 June 1962, thinking that DiPalermo was about to attack him in the prison yard, Valachi clubbed to death an ill-fated check forger in a sad case of mistaken identity. Later that day a US marshal at the prison notified Gaffney about the murder, and Gaffney immediately sent Frank Selvaggi to Atlanta. Valachi told Selvaggi that he was afraid for his life, and wanted to make a deal. Informed of the situation, Morgenthau in mid-July had Selvaggi escort Valachi to the Westchester County jail, where he was admitted under an alias. "This action," Gaffney emphasizes, "tipped the scales and assured Valachi's cooperation."

At the Westchester County jail, Selvaggi, Gaffney, and Pat Ward began a slow and steady interrogation of Valachi. "I asked him when he joined the Mafia," Gaffney recalls. "'Right after the war,' he said. 'Which war?' I replied: 'World War One or World War Two?'

"'You don't understand,' he said. 'Right after the war with Chicago.'"

Intelligence of a more significant nature would soon start flowing from Valachi's pliable memory banks, including a flowchart of the Mafia's organizational structure, details of unsolved murders and ongoing dope deals, and the names of public officials on the Mafia's payroll. "He offered to make up names," Selvaggi says with contempt. "With Valachi, the mob lost its honor."

THE POLITICS OF VALACHI

While Joe Valachi was revealing the Mafia's innermost secrets, political developments were negating what should have been a major coup for the FBN. The problem began when George Gaffney became the FBN's enforcement assistant in August 1962 – at the same time Giordano was appointed Commissioner and Siragusa became his deputy. The promotion was based on Gaffney's substantial achievements in New York, but it was also a result of his friendship with NYPD narcotic detective Tommy O'Brien, who had served as an investigator for Bobby Kennedy at the McClellan Committee. "Tommy and I worked as a team for six years," Gaffney recalls, "and when Bobby wanted information on the mob Tommy would tell him to check with me."

At Gaffney's invitation, Bobby went along on an FBN drug bust. Ethel Kennedy in turn invited Gaffney and his wife to dinner, and it wasn't long before the two Irish American pit bulls formed a friendship. Thus, Gaffney says, he had "no choice" but to take the job when Kennedy arranged his promotion. And once he had accepted the job, he felt obligated to present the FBN in the very best light, so he voluntarily briefed Bobby about Valachi's potential. Unfortunately for the FBN, Bobby told Organized Crime chief William Hundley. Eager to reap the political profits that would come from putting Valachi on the witness stand in public during televised congressional hearings, Hundley went to FBN Commissioner Henry Giordano and asked for written reports of Valachi's interrogations at the Westchester County jail. And that's when Valachi began to slip out of George Gaffney's hands.

As Frank Selvaggi recalls, "Gaffney called me at home and said, 'Giordano wants it on paper.'" Selvaggi cringes. "So I did it. I sat there while Valachi rambled on, and I typed up a bunch of bullshit, including the possibility that he could make some more cases, including one against Harry Tantillo, who worked with Frank Borelli and Carmine Locascio."

Here it's only fair to acknowledge that Gaffney had landed in Washington just as the Cuban Missile Crisis took America to the brink of nuclear war. The nation's survival was thought to be at stake, and Jack and Bobby Kennedy were scrambling to prevent Armageddon. When the crisis passed, Bobby sought revenge against Castro through Operation Mongoose, the covert action program under General Edward Lansdale, with its CIA assassination component under William Harvey, and the "criminal elements" it used to murder and maim Cuban intelligence officials.[1]

Corrupted by power and vengeance, Bobby lost his effectiveness as the country's chief law enforcement official. He even sacrificed his personal integrity, succumbing to the charms of actress Marilyn Monroe, whose suspicious death by a drug overdose shocked the nation in August 1962.[2]

Bobby knew that he was playing with fire, but what he hadn't been told by his mortal foe, J. Edgar Hoover, was that Carlos Marcello and Santo Trafficante were plotting bloody treason. In late summer 1962, Marcello told Edward Becker, a businessman from California, that President Kennedy was going to be assassinated, and that a 'nut' was going to be hired to handle the job.[3] Two weeks later in Miami, Trafficante told Jose Aleman, a wealthy Cuban exile and underworld financier, that JFK was "going to be hit" before the 1964 elections.[4] Though Becker and Aleman informed the FBI of their allegations, Hoover found no reason to alert the Attorney General, or the president, or to take any preventative action.[5]

Kennedy's aides were, however, aware that Jimmy Hoffa was boasting about his plans to kill Bobby. In September 1962 they had been told that a Louisiana Teamster official, Edward Partin, had overheard Hoffa discuss "two separate murder plans aimed at Robert Kennedy."[6] Partin's claims were taken seriously after he passed a polygraph test, but Bobby may have dismissed Hoffa's threats as the ranting of a wild man who'd been backed into a corner.[7]

Gaffney, of course, had no knowledge of the deadly intrigues swirling around the Kennedys, nor could he have anticipated the consequences of suggesting that Valachi might make cases against more hoods – perhaps even some million-dollar men working for the FBI and CIA.

"Bobby asked if the Justice Department could build an all-encompassing conspiracy case out of Valachi's testimony," Gaffney recalls, "and I said, 'Yes.' But I added that Valachi was seeking a presidential pardon, and that we couldn't actually convict anyone on his testimony." Gaffney pauses. "Bobby was satisfied, and was content to let the FBN handle it. But Hundley went straight to the FBI, and they asked him for Valachi. Hundley asked Bobby's permission to do so and," Gaffney says forlornly, "Bobby asked me if they could have a chat with him."

On 10 September 1962, FBI Agent James Flynn was introduced to Joe Valachi at the Westchester County jail. "The next thing we knew," Gaffney complains, "the FBI was saying that Valachi's knowledge of the Mafia transcended narcotics, and they began to petition the Justice Department to have him taken away from Selvaggi, into their safekeeping."

"The next thing *I* know," Selvaggi recalls, "Flynn is telling Valachi not to tell *me* anything." He shrugs. "Valachi knew the FBI could do more for him, so he started bad-mouthing me and the FBN, and backing off the cases he promised to make. Finally I came back one day and found that he'd been moved to a prison at Fort Monmouth in New Jersey. Flynn never even told me."

After February 1963, the FBN was no longer allowed to see Valachi. "Anything we wanted after that," Gaffney explains, "we had to get through the FBI. Then Flynn and Agent Moynihan start debriefing Valachi – two Irish guys who didn't speak Italian and couldn't possibly understand, the way Frank understood, the subtle meanings of what he said." Chuckling, Gaffney says, "We used to say you had to take the handcuffs off an Italian before you could interrogate him.

"So Flynn and Moynihan come up with La Causa Nostra, 'The Our Cause,' which they later switched to La Cosa Nostra, 'The Our Thing.' What Valachi was referring to was an activity that his faction was engaged in at the time: drug dealing was 'our thing' at the time. But the FBI felt they needed a different name, because we'd been calling it the Mafia for years, and they didn't want to appear to be stealing our thunder. Which they were."

"First they nullified me," Selvaggi says, "then they handed my reports to [author] Peter Maas [who wrote the FBI-approved biography of Joe Valachi]." Very seriously he says, "Valachi was not the guy Maas describes in his book. Valachi was a treacherous opportunist who killed two dozen people. Then the Senate wines and dines him, and he tells them, 'Selagusa hung me.'"

The FBN agent who did more damage to the Mafia than anyone else stares off into the distance. "Valachi tells the senators I'm connected to the Bronx mob."

JOE VALACHI'S REVENGE

In June 1963, Joe Valachi began his nationally televised testimony to Congress, on behalf of William Hundley, J. Edgar Hoover, and the FBI, about the existence of a second underworld government, "The Our Thing," run by the usual Italian suspects.

"The Valachi Hearings were beginning," Frank Selvaggi says, "and Gaffney calls me down to DC. As I step off the plane, I'm met by two New York detectives who are working for the McClellan Committee. They act like they're going to put the cuffs on me. I ask them what's going on. Well, it's a big joke, and they won't say, but a few hours later I see Pat O'Carroll at the Treasury Department's training school. Pat says, 'I hear you're in trouble.'"

As Selvaggi soon discovered, Joe Valachi had told Senator John McClellan that he was a made member of the Bronx mob. And McClellan believed him.

As George Gaffney recalls, "I was summoned to Senator McClellan's office early in the afternoon. Senators Mundt and Brewster were there too, and McClellan told me about Valachi's accusation. I don't recall if he'd made the accusation directly to the Committee, or if they'd been told by one of Valachi's FBI handlers. In any case, I responded by elaborating on Frank's background, with every detail I could recall. I made them aware, for the first time, that Valachi had been Frank's informant since 1958. I told them that Frank had initiated the case that resulted in Valachi's conviction, that he had captured Valachi after he jumped bail, and that Valachi, in typical Italian fashion, was trying to get even with his long-time adversary.

"When I left the Senator's office I found Charlie Siragusa seated in a chair in the outer office. I briefed him on what had transpired. He was mad as hell, and directed his anger at an individual in the Organized Crime group.

"Later that afternoon, I received a telephone call from Senator McClellan. He told me that he had contacted the appropriate Justice Department official [William Hundley], and had told him that his Committee attached no credence to Valachi's attack on Frank's integrity. The Senator expressed his appreciation for the insights into Valachi, and said that Frank should be commended. As Giordano was out of town, Siragusa and I agreed that the incident should not be made a matter of record in Frank's file. We also agreed not to tell him."

Selvaggi's curt laugh reflects his surprise and exasperation when told of Gaffney's account. "I stayed with Charlie while I was in Washington," Selvaggi says, with a trace of indignation, "and he told me that Valachi had said I was with the Bronx mob. Charlie said to me, 'Frank, they're coming after you.' And that's when he asked me to go with him to the Illinois

Crime Commission as his chief investigator. But my wife didn't want to leave her family in New York, and I loved my job."

THE GAMBLING SQUAD

It's hard to believe that a man of George Gaffney's ambition and drive did not want to go to Washington to become the FBN's enforcement assistant. But the only reason he took the job, he says, was because Jim Reed, the Treasury Department's assistant secretary for law enforcement, told him that Bobby Kennedy insisted. "So I went," he says dejectedly, "but all the love I had for the job evaporated when I moved my family to Washington. The challenges were all behind. It was just shuffling papers and calming down congressmen, and I almost resigned."

Likewise, it's hard to believe that a man of Gaffney's extraordinary willpower couldn't say no to Bobby Kennedy, or anybody else for that matter. One gets the feeling that his regrets might have arisen afterwards, upon reflection – for it is a fact that his decision to go to Washington was a big mistake, in several ways. To begin with, his transfer left a temporary leadership void in New York, where the FBN's ability to conduct narcotics investigations was further impaired by the formation of the notorious Gambling Squad.

As Gaffney recalls: "The Justice Department wasn't happy with the way IRS was investigating gambling, numbers, and off-track betting, so new federal laws were enacted that gave Justice control over interstate gambling and racketeering. Then Morgenthau came up with the idea of a Gambling Squad, and he asked us to contribute a squad of agents in New York. I opposed it on the grounds that we'd alienate the IRS Intelligence Unit, and I was also concerned about problems with the NYPD vice squad people, who would certainly resent us for intruding on their turf. But again I was overruled, and a special squad was set up in New York under Pat Ward."

"The underlying idea for the Gambling Squad," Frank Selvaggi explains, "is that there's a connection between gambling and junk. Gambling's an addiction, and some gamblers deal drugs so they can lose money in crap games, or at the racetrack, or betting on the numbers. And some gamblers – whether they deal narcotics or not – make good informants. I had one," Selvaggi says. "He's sitting in a room, hedging bets. He's an illegal alien and doesn't know anything about junk, but he knows who the dealers are, because they're in the same room. He hears things."

In order to exploit this connection between drug dealing and gambling, especially the bookmaking industry in New York, US Attorney Robert Morgenthau authorized the formation of the Gambling Squad in the autumn of 1962. He asked Bill Tendy, the US Attorney in charge of the "Junk Squad," to put it together. Tendy in turn picked his friend, Pat Ward, to run the Gambling Squad, and he gave Ward the job of selecting the ten best FBN agents to flesh it out.

Regarded by many as the most knowledgeable agent in the office, Ward was a dapper dresser who talked out of the side of his mouth and, according to one agent, resembled a character from a Damon Runyon story. He'd led Group Three before becoming Jim Ryan's enforcement assistant, and he'd mentored many of New York's finest agents, including George Gaffney and John Dolce. And with Dolce's help, Ward drafted the ten best case-making agents into the Gambling Squad, most from Group Three. This quintessential wolf pack included Lenny Schrier as Ward's second in command, Patty Biase, Jack Brady, Jack Griffen (a former NYPD narcotics detective known as "the red-headed lieutenant"), Frank Dolce (John's brother), Jack L. Gohde, Edward "Russ" Dower, Walter J. Smith (a former NYPD narcotics detective and schoolmate of John Dolce's), John Gallagher (a former NYPD narcotics detective who went to the Chicago Crime Commission with Charlie Siragusa), Frank Selvaggi, and Frankie Waters.

Waters half-jokingly describes the group as "the renegades – the semi-legal, ultra-effective ones who no one wanted to work with, and no one wanted to boss."

"Busting crap games tended to be dangerous work," another New York agent explains, "and the IRS wasn't getting the job done. So Tendy put the Gambling Squad under Ward, who ran it over at the Court House with IRS Intelligence, while Gaffney went to Washington and John Enright stepped in as acting district supervisor."

Expanding on the subject, Lenny Schrier says, "Ward was going to be transferred as part of the house cleaning in New York, but he was tight with Tendy. So to keep Pat around, Tendy made him head of the Gambling Squad, and Pat picked ten guys, including me. I was in line for a group and I didn't want to go, but Enright said I had to. And John Dolce, the new enforcement assistant, promised me that I'd get a group once we were through.

"I was Mr. Clean," Schrier laughs, "so they made me number two to Ward. I remember him coming in that first day, with his hat tilted back on his head, rubbing his hands together. 'What're we gonna do?' he says. I told him I had something. One of my informants, Frank Russo, had a cousin who picked up numbers. 'Mikey' was what they call a controller. So we followed him out of Harlem to a Bronx apartment. The next day I get a call from Russo. 'Lenny!' he says. 'What the fuck! They fired my cousin Mikey. Now he's hot and I gotta get him a job as a [drug] courier.'

"What that meant," Schrier says in mock amazement, "is that someone sold us out after one day! But we made the case anyway, and through Frank Dolce and John Gohde we eventually got information about the Lou Ehrlich numbers outfit: night shift, day shift, a pad with the cops. There were 200 guys in the ring and they had 200 one-dollar bills, consecutively numbered. Each guy had a number. If he got pinched, he gave the bill to the cop, and the bill went up the line.

"We arrested these guys in Times Square with a shopping bag full of numbers and a fortune in cash. One guy gave us a marked bill and said, 'Who you from? You a Borough?' I told him, 'We're Feds, and please don't say any more.' We took him to the IRS, turned in the numbers, and drove over to the US Attorney's office. When we get there, the parking lot's packed with twenty-five cop cars and fifty cops shitting bricks. But there was nothing to worry about, because IRS Intelligence was selling out the cases."

Schrier takes a sip on his Scotch. "We were closing in on Ehrlich, then JFK gets shot. I remember that day: Morgenthau and Tendy had gone to Washington to talk to Bobby Kennedy about setting up a permanent Gambling Squad – a new agency apart from the FBI. That's why Tendy asked Part Ward to take charge of it, so he could get in on the ground floor. But after the assassination they shut it down, and I got the job of filing all our reports, which took about two months." He pauses for effect. "The names in there were as big as Lansky. Dignitaries. But it was all for nothing."

GEORGE BELK AND THE SCANDALS OF 1963

The other great change brought about by Gaffney's promotion was the arrival of George Belk as the new district supervisor in New York. According to Howard Chappell, "Anslinger went to George Belk and asked him to help Giordano, who needed all the help he could get, and wasn't about to get it from Siragusa or Gaffney. So Belk left his job as district supervisor in Chicago to take over New York, and Pat Ward left the Gambling Squad and replaced Belk as the district supervisor in Chicago."

An agent since 1948, Belk was a proven manager. He'd purified Chicago in the wake of Chappell's corruption investigation in 1956, and was well aware of the dangers of his New York assignment, which included replacing group leaders and agents suspected of being corrupt. Aware that Giordano was incapable of helping him, and that Gaffney would resist, Belk took the job on the condition that he could bring along a cadre of trusted agents from Chicago, including George R. Halpin to head Group Five, Theodore "Ted" Heisig to head Group Two, and Clarence Cook as his liaison to the Black agents.

Right away there was trouble. "We're all having drinks one night," Frank Selvaggi says, "and Halpin wants to show everyone how tough he is. So he calls me 'Selagusa.' People used to call me that, because they all thought Charlie was doing for me. But Charlie never did anything for me, even though he could have. Anyway, I say something back to Halpin, and as I'm leaving the bar he comes charging out and jumps on my back. I spin around, carry him over to the curb, and dump him in a trashcan. Some tough guy. He pulls the same sort of stunt with Frankie Black [Frankie Waters's nickname] later on. Frankie was getting a little out of control around then, and he put a round between his legs." A smile spreads across Selvaggi's face. "I watched the bullet skip off down the street, while Halpin just stood there with his mouth hanging open."

George Belk arrived in New York in April 1963, knowing that he was stepping into a hornets' nest. But he didn't expect to find that, at George Gaffney's insistence, John Dolce was his enforcement assistant. The rationalization was that Dolce would provide continuity while Belk settled in. But in reality, Gaffney put Dolce in place so he could influence the direction of major investigations. Complicating the situation was the fact that Dolce, as a former leader of Group Three, was at the top of Belk's hit list of agents he wanted to fire.

"Belk knew that the troops needed somebody other than John Dolce to go to," an agent recalls, "and after conferring with Artie Fluhr, he created an executive assistant job specifically for Art. New York was the first office to have that position. As Belk's executive assistant, Artie started hiring replacement agents. He also helped Belk make case assignments, and he got a salary upgrade for everyone."

One cynical New York agent says, "Belk makes Fluhr his executive assistant, and La Fluhr does for Belk what Mendelsohn did for Gaffney: he carries stories. He tells Belk what the agents are doing: anything that can be used against them, like who their girlfriends are. And from then on it's Belk and Fluhr drinking on the arm at [drug trafficker-cum-informer] Gerry Nagelberg's place on 56th Street, while Harry Masi [the office clerk] did all of Fluhr's work."

Although, as the previous paragraph illustrates, some agents resented his promotion and friendship with Belk, Arthur J. Fluhr was a dedicated and effective agent. He'd quit his accounting job with General Motors in 1954, while married with kids, to take an entry-level position with the FBN. A veteran of the Marine Corps and a graduate of Iona College, he was never part of the Gaffney–Ward–Dolce clique, but he could swim with sharks and could hold his Jack Daniels – in other words, Fluhr was precisely the type of executive assistant Belk needed to circumvent Gaffney and Dolce, in an attempt to reform an office that was spinning out of control, in part as a result of the Gambling Squad.

The Gambling Squad scandals of 1963 occupy a prominent place in the annals of FBN folklore. Even a CIA debriefer, when questioning Charlie Siragusa in 1977 about the MKULTRA Program, inquired if "the scandals of 1963" had anything to do with the CIA pad on 13th Street, or Feldman's pad on 18th Street. Siragusa responded with an equivocal "they might have."[8]

The scandals of 1963 grew out of rumors about Gambling Squad members holding up crap games at gunpoint, or stealing bags of money as they were being delivered to bookies. But they also included stories like the one about the time Frankie Waters was found unconscious in a bar in Brooklyn. He'd left his car parked in front of a fire hydrant and a patrol car stopped to check it out. The cops found wiretap equipment on the front seat, a gun underneath it, and a bundle of cash. When taken to the precinct to explain, Waters said the cash was a loan from his father for a down payment on a house.

In a similar incident in the Bowery, cops found an agent passed out in his car, with the headlights on and the motor running, and wiretap equipment, guns, and a briefcase full of cash in the trunk. The agent had just escorted a Frenchman to the airport.

There were only two inspectors investigating these incidents and allegations in 1963. Having been demoted from enforcement assistant, Lee Speer as district supervisor in Denver handled corruption inquiries west of the Mississippi, while Irwin Greenfeld handled those on the east. But Greeny on his own couldn't manage the problem in New York, and as a result, morale was at an all-time low among the agents, good and bad. Violent factions were forming, a whisper campaign raged, and ill feelings simmered, waiting to explode. Eventually it all got to be too much for veteran undercover Agent Jim Attie, who had been transferred to New York in 1961.

"I was Jim's partner during the Gambling Squad era," Tony Mangiaracina recalls. "I was in Group Four at the time. Art Mendelsohn had inherited the group from Joe Amato, who'd transferred to Boston, then retired after developing neurological problems from stress. We called the office 'The Fish Bowl' back then, because everybody was watching everybody else. It was a convoluted situation, and Jim was definitely paranoid – but we were all paranoid, so I didn't notice right away. Then he does a U-turn on a one-way street near Times Square: he thought a Mossad agent was tailing us. Plus he was bitter, and getting angrier all the time.

"Then one day he shows up in the reception area outside Belk's office. He's sitting there muttering about how Siragusa fucked him and how he's gonna kill him. Well, Belk didn't see him right away, so he just sat there getting madder and madder.

"Some guys say he shot up the office, but that's not true. But some guys from Group Four did talk him into giving up his gun and going with them to the Public Health facility, where the doctor said that Jim had to voluntarily commit himself to get an examination – and that's when he took out a drop gun and gave it up. The agents were a little shook up over that. They didn't like the idea that he was sitting between them in the car with a drop gun.

"Well, Jim stayed at the hospital and never came back."

JIM ATTIE'S EXCRUCIATING EXIT

Thirty-five years later, Jim Attie summarized his experience as an FBN agent as follows: "I'm not proud of what I did. It was a dirty job. It was a form of amorality, and to this day I feel tremendous guilt and have unending nightmares as a result of what I did as a narcotic agent."

Through his daring exploits, Attie had generated as much good press for the FBN as any agent, and he felt that Anslinger should have reciprocated with raises and promotions. But those rewards were not forthcoming. "The Hearst newspapers were doing articles on our undercover work in the Middle East," he explains, "and the reporters couldn't believe what they were being told. So the Bureau had me come to Washington to talk about the cases I'd made. And during the interview Anslinger says, 'We've had some better, some worse.' He also said I was always covered, which wasn't true. I was *always* alone. After he said those things, I thought about how he kept the Bureau small enough to fuel the competition, and how that caused all the trouble. So in front of the reporters I said to him, 'What could you possibly know about it?' I called him a manipulator and a cheapskate, and I said I wasn't impressed. He didn't say a word."

But Anslinger didn't forget, either. In 1961, Attie was transferred to New York and put in Group Four, where he was not received with open arms. Based on his reputation as a Speer man, and a potentially homicidal lone wolf, the nervous New York agents considered him both dangerous and a sleeper for the shooflies — and his problems began to mount.

As Attie recalls, "I came to work with two dollars in my pocket and my lunch in a brown paper bag. Meanwhile, the other guys in the group are eating lunch at an expensive Japanese restaurant. Around me, they were all secretive and apprehensive, and I was never asked to do anything. In New York I made nothing but small cases," he sighs. "Meanwhile, Charlie Mac is in town talking with Lenny Schrier and playing cards with Ike Feldman. When we worked together in Chicago, Charlie Mac set me up with a hit man named Garibaldi. Next thing I know, Garibaldi's in New York, looking for me."

Attie's situation didn't improve when his former boss, George Belk, replaced George Gaffney as district supervisor. "When I was in Chicago, Belk was always bragging about how I made so many big cases, using so little money," Attie explains. "In 1960, he even recommended me for the Treasury Employee of the Year Award. In Chicago he was hard, but fair. But in New York, he was told by Giordano to unload me. He puts me in Durham's unit (the Radio Shack) and says: 'You're a grade twelve, like him; but remember, you're not in charge.'

"I'm there in the electronics unit," Attie continues, "but it's all gypsy wires. One day Durham says, 'We've got to tap a phone tonight, and you've got to do it yourself.' I told him I wouldn't do it without written authorization." Jim tenses. "A few days later, Durham invited me for coffee at the Choc Full O' Nuts, and when I got back to the office, my head was spinning. I remember grabbing the desk and thinking I'd ingested something. I put on my coat and hat and when I got on the elevator, my mouth was dry and my body was trying to vomit. Colors were intense and had sound. I walked to the 33rd Street Station and took a train home. And when I got home, my wife took me to two doctors, and they said it sounded like I'd unwittingly ingested LSD."

Jim is sitting very still. "Two days later, when I went back to the office, Belk called me in. He made me sit outside his office for hours while he talked with Greenfeld. Finally he called me in and said I'd have to go to the hospital. Then he asked me to sign something.

"I said to them, 'You people drugged me.'

"Greenfeld was rigid with fear. 'I want your gun,' he said. But I refused, at which point they called in Hunt, Mendelsohn, Krueger, and Durham.

And while they were taking me outside, I heard Greenfeld talking on the phone with Giordano. 'We'll get him admitted,' he said. 'Don't worry.' So I looked at Belk, put my thumbnail under my tooth, and flicked." Attie shakes his head. "And that was my exit from the FBN. I went to the Public Health Service Hospital where they did a spinal tap, but didn't find any drugs in my system."

Jim smiles bravely. "I brought a lot on myself," he laughs, "by telling off Anslinger and Giordano. I should have listened to Tony Zirilli. Tony was the greatest undercover agent ever. He used to gamble with tens of thousands of Bureau dollars. Tony made me look like an amateur. One time he said to me, 'Why use your own money? They can't pay me enough to do this job.' And he was right."

MORE BAD NEWS

The next shock felt by the faltering FBN came shortly after Joe Valachi described Vito Genovese as the boss of bosses on national TV. The problem started on 27 January 1961, when John Ormento took Nelson Cantellops to a church in the Bronx and – in the presence of a priest, notary public, and three lawyers – Cantellops confessed to having lied about his meeting with Genovese. On that basis, Criminal Defense Attorney Edward B. Williams filed an appeal on Genovese's behalf. But Cantellops re-recanted, and the appeal was denied, and in April 1962, at the age of 62, Genovese began serving a fifteen-year sentence at the Atlanta Penitentiary.[9]

In October 1963, Williams filed another appeal on Genovese's behalf, claiming he should have been given copies of the prosecutor's interview notes with Cantellops. "Then, to everyone's surprise," Gaffney recalls, "Williams introduces Bill Rowan as a witness for the defense.

"A few years earlier," Gaffney continues, "Rowan had worked for the Bureau, but I fired him, and he went to work for Prudential Bache. Then Williams brings him up to New York, and I'm called to testify. Williams asks me to explain why I fired Rowan. I told him that he had cracked up a government car, but didn't report it. So Williams walks over with a letter of recommendation I'd written for Rowan, addressed to officials at Bache. The letter listed his good qualities and Williams made me read it out loud. Then he said, 'Reconcile your firing of Rowan with this letter.'

"'There's nothing sinister about it, counselor,' I said. 'The man's got a wife and a couple of kids. Just because he can't take the pressure of the FBN doesn't mean he should be deprived of a livelihood. It doesn't mean he's not suited for a less stressful job.' At which point the judge leaned over and whispered to me, 'Don't say another word. You've got him by the balls.'"

Gaffney laughs bitterly. "Williams accused the Bureau of destroying crucial documents that should have gone to the US Attorney. But the Genovese appeal was denied, and after that, Williams vowed he'd never handle another narcotic case again."

Rowan's testimony didn't help Genovese, but the fact that a former agent would testify on behalf of the Mafia's boss of bosses contributed to the FBN's downward spiral. So did Paul Knight's transfer to the CIA, and Howard Chappell's resignation in 1961. Chappell quit to become Commissioner of Public Works in Los Angeles after Giordano tried to transfer him to New York. Marty Pera's resignation and transfer in October 1963 to the Office of Naval Intelligence was another blow, as was Charlie Siragusa's retirement in December 1963.

Social forces were conspiring against the FBN too. In 1961, the American Medical and Bar Associations issued a 173-page report titled *Drug Addiction: Crime or Disease?* The report blamed surges in drug smuggling and poverty on Anslinger's policy of regarding addicts as criminals rather than people in need of medical assistance. The report argued that the FBN was driving addicts into the black market by ignoring Supreme Court rulings that allowed doctors to prescribe narcotics to addicts for legitimate medical purposes. It was in response to this report that the Kennedy administration had created the Prettyman Commission and had appointed Dean Markham as its drug policy advisor. And in a 30 May 1963 letter to the *New York Times*, Markham backed a Prettyman Commission recommendation that doctors be allowed to prescribe narcotics to addicts on a "maintenance basis." As a result, experimental "halfway houses" like Synanon and Daytop began to emerge as viable alternatives to imprisonment.

Last but not least, the FBN was hurt by a shift in focus by the Giordano administration from the Sicilian Mafia to the French connection and its sources in Turkey. This change served the Mafia well at a time when it should have been reeling from the Valachi revelations, the Rinaldo–Palmieri case, and the wars within the Profaci and Bonanno families. But America's intelligence and security agencies continued to protect the million-dollar men they had conscripted in the Establishment's secret and ongoing war against labor, liberalism, and desegregation.

The loss of case-making agents to the Gambling Squad, several key retirements and resignations, the dismantling of the International Group, and the FBN's emphasis on the French connection, combined to give the

Mafia the breathing room it needed to reorganize its sputtering drug industry. The process began in Sicily on 30 June 1963 when a booby-trapped Fiat, into which Palermo boss Sal Greco was about to enter, exploded and killed several policemen and bystanders. The Ciaculli Massacre put the Carabinieri on a massive manhunt that scattered Sicilian Mafiosi to the four winds. The most important fugitive was Tomasso Buscetta. A participant at the Palermo summit in 1957, Buscetta would become the indispensable middleman between the Badalamenti family in Sicily and the Gambino family in America. While a fugitive, he would form relations with Corsicans in South America, Mexico, and Montreal. Meanwhile, lacking the necessary funds and personnel, the Italian authorities called off their manhunt, and Buscetta's godfather, Gaetano Badalamenti, began waging a vendetta against the Grecos and La Barberas.[10]

The Badalamenti connection dated back to 1946, when Gaetano immigrated to Detroit and formed relations with Frank Coppola, Sam Carolla, and Carlos Marcello. After his deportation in 1950, Gaetano and his brothers teamed up with Coppola, who, having been deported, settled in their neighborhood, and together they became Sicily's major heroin traffickers. The Sicilian Badalamentis were known to the FBN, as was their cousin Salvatore in the Profaci family. Gaetano, like Buscetta, had attended the 1957 Palermo summit, where the old alliance between Luciano and Joe Valachi's godfather, Joe Bonanno, gave way to the new one between Carlo Gambino and the Badalamentis.[11]

Further impacting the situation was a major change at the Vatican, where Giovanni Montini was named Pope Paul VI in June 1963. Son of the founder of Italy's Christian Democrat Party, with whom the Mafia was allied, Montini named Hank Manfredi's close friend Paul Marcinkus as his personal secretary. Marcinkus started working with Michele Sindona to secure their mutual interests, just as Bill Harvey – having been fired from Operation Mongoose by Bobby Kennedy for sending terror teams into Cuba during the Cuban Missile Crisis without permission – arrived in Rome as the CIA's new station chief. Harvey's main job was to help ultra General Giovanni De Lorenzo, head of Italy's military intelligence and security services, subvert the government of leftist Prime Minister Aldo Moro. Naturally, the CIA's efforts on behalf of De Lorenzo further advanced the interests of the Mafia.

Back in the States, a corresponding shift in the Establishment's power base was reflected in the gradual migration of Americans to the south and west. The alliance between Bonanno in Arizona, Marcello in New Orleans, and Trafficante in Florida reflected the trend, as did the consolidation of mob power in Las Vegas, through Morris "Moe" Dalitz, one of Meyer Lansky's closest associates, and the emergence of Miami as America's new crime capital.

Wherever the Mafia went, the CIA was ready and waiting: in New Orleans, home of Carlos Marcello, where Tony Varona – Trafficante's partner in the CIA's murder plots against Castro, and head of the Miami chapter of the terrorist Cuban Revolutionary Council (CRC) – visited in June 1963, after conferring with Anastasio Somoza in Nicaragua, and acquiring funds for an anti-Castro paramilitary training camp in Louisiana.[12] In Dallas, CIA officer Dave Phillips was establishing the state-sponsored, anti-Castro terrorist organization Alpha 66.[13]

Everywhere they went, CIA agents rubbed shoulders with the lunatic fringe: racist Minutemen in cahoots with Carlos Marcello, mercenary and mob hit men, and crazed anti-Castro Cubans, all pledged to kill a Kennedy, any Kennedy, for Christ.

MIAMI'S RED, WHITE, AND BLUES

Richard J. "Rick" Dunagan joined the FBN in 1962 after a hitch in the Air Force and five years with the Border Patrol. A big rough-and-tumble agent, fluent in Spanish and familiar with all types of firearms, Dunagan was assigned to the four-man Miami office where, as he recalls, "Gene Marshall was the boss, Sal Vizzini was the assistant, and Jack Greene, a former Miami cop, was there too. Just the four of us, and deputy sheriff Anthony DeLeon, who later became a fugitive.

"When I started working for the FBN, I was so green the cows could eat me," Dunagan laughs. "Marshall gave me an informer, the brother of a guy he'd put away a few years before. The office had a nice '58 Chevy, which we take for a drive. When we get where we're going, the informer gives me a deck of cocaine and says, 'I'll be right back.' I toss it under the seat. Meanwhile I'm a White guy hanging around a Black neighborhood looking suspicious, and a cop arrests me. I'm undercover, I've got no ID. He says, 'Get out of the car.' He searches the car, finds the coke, and tosses me in jail.

"After that I stayed in the office, playing water boy to Marshall and Vizzini, until the day Sinbad arrived. Sinbad was a Moorish Muslim who saved my career. He came into the office wearing cut-offs, a beanie, and rubber thongs. He'd been put away before by Vizzini, done seven years, and was out and looking to become a professional informant. First he went to Marshall, then Vizzini, then Greene, and they all threw him out. Finally he sticks his head in my office and says, 'Does you be a narcotic agent?' I said, 'Yeah.' He asks, 'Can you make me a helper?' So I pretended to be a government agent and said, 'Depends on what you have to offer.'

"Sinbad rolls off names of people he can make cases on, all big-time traffickers. I hadn't been to the Academy yet, and in the process of making cases on these people he taught me 95 percent of everything I know. He worked for me for years in Miami, through an awful lot. He wasn't a junky, but he'd shoot up to make a case, and one time the bad guys tried to kill him with poison. The only thing that saved his life was that his Muslim brothers in his clan got him a medic.

"Finally they sent me to the Technical Investigations Aide School, which was run by Agent Johnny Thompson, where they taught us how to pick locks, put on wiretaps, and take surreptitious photographs. When I got back to Miami, I was really in business. I had Sinbad, and I'd been trained, but I was still new. One day a big guy walks in the office wearing a planter's hat, a Harry Truman floral shirt, Bermuda shorts, and thongs. He's smoking a big Cuban cigar. 'Is Gene Marshall in?' he asks. 'Depends,' I say. 'Who wants him?'

"Real slow he says, 'Harry J. Anslinger.'

"Well, I burst out laughing. I stick my head into Marshall's office and say, 'Hey Gene, there's a guy out here say's he's Harry J. Anslinger.'

"'What's he look like?' Marshall asks. I tell him.

"'Yep,' he says. 'That's Mr. Anslinger.'

"I soon found out that Anslinger loved Gene Marshall. He and Gene liked to go out fishing on Sal Vizzini's boat, and I'd listen to the stories he'd tell about how he lost his hair from the stress of so many people shooting for his job before the war. Man, the things I heard."

When not entertaining Anslinger, the Miami agents conducted narcotics investigations, and one target was Tampa resident Santo Trafficante. As part of the on-again, off-again surveillance, Dunagan in 1963 monitored Trafficante's daughter's wedding. But that was as close as any FBN agent ever got to the million-dollar man. There were other CIA intrigues too. As Dunagan explains, "The CIA made weekly visits to our office, but they never helped us make cases. It was a one-way street. We helped them. For example, one time one of our Cuban informants said, 'This weekend, some former Bay of Pigs people are going to steal some vessels and armaments and launch an invasion.' So we told the CIA guy, and they stopped it. Another time a Cuban Army major, who had worked for Castro, and had been my informant since I was in the Border Patrol in Daytona, says to me, 'Rick, you like weapons, right? Big weapons, like fifty-caliber and thirty-caliber machine guns?"

"'Yeah,' I said. So he says, 'Can I buy you a cup of coffee?'

"We're having some of that jazzy Cuban coffee, and he says, 'How'd you like to make $5,000 for one night's work?'

"'Is this a bribe?' I ask. 'No,' he says, 'it's business. We're making a run and we need someone on the bow of the boat to man the machine gun.'

"It didn't seem right, so I went back and asked Marshall, and he said, 'You're crazy! You're a goddamned federal agent. How would it look if you got caught invading Cuba?'

"And Marshall was right. They went out, got caught, and Castro had the major shot."

20

THE FBN AND THE
ASSASSINATION OF JFK

"And thus the essence of all crime is undivulged."
Edgar Allan Poe, "The Man of the Crowd"

In May 1963, director of Central Intelligence John McCone instructed his inspector general, Lyman Kirkpatrick, to conduct a review of the MKULTRA Program. An OSS veteran and founding father of the CIA, Kirkpatrick had been serving as IG for almost ten years and, having covered up Frank Olson's death in 1954 (see chapter 9), would certainly have kept the MKULTRA skeletons in the closet. But he was promoted to executive director in April and the responsibility for inquiring into the program passed to John S. Earman Jr. An erstwhile member of the Bloodstone Committee that smuggled Nazis out of Europe, Earman was a dedicated Cold Warrior; but unlike Kirkpatrick, he knew little about MKULTRA, and what he discovered disturbed him. On 14 August, he reported to McCone that MKULTRA was "unethical" and possibly illegal, that it put "the rights and interests of US citizens in jeopardy," and that subjects often became "ill for hours or days, including hospitalization [a reference to Linda King] in at least one case." But the nature and results of the experiments were buried under so much secrecy he couldn't report comprehensively on what had been tested or what conclusions had been drawn. Only two people knew, and they hadn't kept any records.[1]

Sid Gottlieb and Richard Helms, the creators of MKULTRA, had tried to cover themselves by not keeping records, but to their dismay, the new inspector general had also stumbled across the existence of the FBN safehouses, and he reported what he found out. Earman stated that testing at the safehouses had been performed "on individuals at all social levels," including "informants and members of suspected criminal elements from whom the [FBN] obtained results of operational value." He didn't say what results were obtained by sending hoods on trips to Never-Never Land, but he noted that arrangements were made with "police authorities … to protect the activity in critical situations," as was the case when Linda King complained to hospital authorities about George White having dosed her with LSD in September 1953. To further ensure plausible denial, the CIA made sure that the responsibility for the handling of the test subjects rested "with the narcotics agent working alone."

Gottlieb and Helms had been sure to place responsibility on the few FBN agents involved in MKULTRA, but Earman preferred that they not be involved at all. He reported that "deep cover agents" were "more favorably suited" than FBN agents when there was a need "to perform realistic testing."

"Realistic testing," of course, was a euphemism for field operations, and Earman wanted to exclude FBN agents from that potentially compromising activity. But in his response to Earman, Deputy Director Richard Helms said, "We are virtually obliged to test on unwitting humans." He recommended that the CIA make arrangements with America's principal police departments and prison hospitals, as well as "foreign intelligence or security organizations … with this objective in mind." Making his feelings perfectly clear, Helms said, "Our present arrangements with the Bureau of Narcotics appear to me to be the most practical and secure method available to implement this program." [2]

Helms felt that perfecting MKULTRA's offensive capabilities was worth the risk of relying on FBN agents, knowing that "the chief of the Bureau would disclaim any knowledge of the activity." [3] He also trusted the complicit FBN agents to play along, assuming their proven ability to dissemble would make it impossible to determine exactly what happened in the safehouses. To some extent he was right. When asked about the activities at the safehouses, George Gaffney claimed that the CIA used the 13th Street pad "only once" while he managed it. At his CIA debriefing in 1977, Charlie Siragusa denied knowing anything about Ike Feldman's safehouse at 212 East 18th Street – although he said that Feldman and Ray Treichler ran operations behind his back, and he implied that George Belk knew what they were doing. When called before Congress to testify on the subject in 1977, Belk said that Giordano had briefed him about the safehouses, but that he had no knowledge of what the CIA was doing there, that he had never heard of MKULTRA (which was probably true, as the term MKULTRA was used only by CIA agents), and that any documents linking him to it were false.[4]

Despite the fact that Gaffney, Belk, and Siragusa complied with the non-disclosure statements they had signed with the CIA, it's clear what the pads were used for. Al Habib managed the San Francisco safehouse after Feldman's transfer to New York in 1961, and acknowledges that there were frequent visits from Sid Gottlieb through 1963. In chapter 15, John Marks described the types of tests that Gottlieb and his associates conducted at the safehouses starting in 1955. Gaffney has acknowledged that the 13th Street pad was made available to government officials whom the bosses wanted to impress. Agent John Tagley would pick them up at the airport, buy them tickets to a Broadway show, or provide some other form of entertainment, and clean up after they left. Anslinger and Sam Pryor stayed there, as did Gaffney's relatives when they were in town. The pad was so widely used that Gaffney never suspected foul play – not until former District Supervisor Jim Ryan found a wiretap on the phone in the pad. Ryan's shocking discovery made Gaffney wonder if the CIA was tape recording or filming Senators with their pants down. "If the place was bugged," he muses, conjuring up the specter of political blackmail, "it could have been very embarrassing."

As noted earlier, Siragusa assumed that the safehouses were used to uncover "defectors" within the CIA. According to author Tom Mangold, Angleton bugged at least one Treasury official who entertained important foreign guests and diplomats.[5] And if he did it on one occasion, it's likely that Angleton used the FBN pads to monitor other government officials as well.

Political blackmail was not MKULTRA's sole purpose. Feldman, in a 1994 article for *Spin Magazine*, said that another purpose was "assassinations." And indeed, a stated goal of the program was to find out "if an individual can be trained to perform an act of attempted assassination involuntarily."[6] In others words, the CIA was trying to develop mind-control techniques, including the use of LSD, that could be used to create a push-button assassin who would possess no memory of his deadly deeds.

In summation, the FBN safehouses served as bases for counterintelligence operations, political blackmail schemes, training and recruiting of assassins, and, as will become apparent later on as way stations for CIA drug smugglers.

THE GENIE OUT OF THE BOTTLE

Earman did not mention assassins or drug smuggling, but he did say the CIA had perfected "an interrogation theory employing chemical substances."

Theory was practice by 1962, when an Army Special Purpose Team traveled to the Atsugi Naval Base in Japan to use LSD during interrogations of foreign nationals suspected of drug smuggling and spying.[7] Tests were also conducted on prisoners in Vietnam, where the CIA was concerned about a regional drug smuggling operation managed by President Diem's brother, Nhu, through his intelligence service. Clearly, this "Special Purpose Team" was a cover for CIA officers eager to learn if Nhu's drug smuggling operation had been penetrated by the French – or worse, the KGB or Communist Chinese.

Back in the States, the CIA hired "medical specialists" to test LSD on prisoners at the Atlanta Penitentiary and, through the National Institute of Mental Health, drug addicts at the Public Health Farm in Lexington. In doing this, Earman noted, the CIA "buys a piece" of the specialist. What he didn't say was that some zealous specialists got carried away with their fiendish research. Dr. Harris Isbell, for example, kept seven male heroin addicts at Lexington addled on acid for seventy-seven days. A lawsuit was brought against the Army in a similar case, but the Supreme Court ruled against the plaintiff – a soldier named James Stanley – in effect granting the CIA a license to conduct Dachau-style experiments on unwitting American citizens under the aegis of national security.[8]

LSD, meanwhile, had become a fad among the eccentric elite. Ambassador Clare Luce enjoyed it immensely, but felt it would lose its appeal once it fell into the hands of the hoi polloi.[9] Scientists searching for a cure for alcoholism also looked into the potentially beneficial uses of LSD, and criminal psychologist Timothy Leary felt it might rehabilitate prison inmates – then realized it had far greater potential. Such was the paradox of the psychedelic: it could drive a scientist like Frank Olson to suicide, or make an offbeat hustler like Tim Leary soar angelically. So much depended on the subject's state of mind and the motive of the person administering the drug.

Regrettably, the CIA chose to develop LSD as a weapon of unconventional warfare; and once it was determined that the drug was dangerous, the Food and Drug Administration (FDA) demanded tighter government control over unlicensed distributors. As FDA Investigator Frank Larkworthy recalls, "LSD became a violation of the Food, Drug and Cosmetic Act, and my first LSD case began in 1963 when my supervisor in Los Angeles, Orin McMillan, gave me Al Hubbard as an informant."

Alfred Hubbard was in his sixties in 1963. Always dressed in a suit and tie, he was, according to Larkworthy, a conservative businessman bent on acquiring the sole distribution rights for LSD in America. He also had a checkered past. He'd been imprisoned for smuggling liquor to California during Prohibition, but his record was purged in return for his services as a Treasury Department informant, and undisclosed services for the OSS. After the war, the Kentucky-born conman became a Canadian citizen and a millionaire, through wise investments in airlines and uranium. However, a transcendental trip in England in 1951 inspired him to restructure his portfolio based on a vision of the world's political leaders achieving enlightenment, with the aid of a little acid uplift.[10] By 1955, Hubbard had become the self-appointed Johnny Appleseed of acid in America and, before the drug was outlawed in 1966, had turned on an estimated 6,000 people, including beat gurus Alan Watts, Gerald Heard, Keith Ditman, and Aldous Huxley, author of *The Doors of Perception*. Hubbard's pretext for obtaining LSD was his search for a cure for alcoholism and, in 1958, the FDA granted him an Investigative New Drug Permit, allowing him to distribute the psychedelic in the US. This implies that Hubbard had powerful patrons, most likely in the CIA, who guaranteed him a steady source of supply, first from Sandoz, and then – after he got in trouble with the Swiss authorities for not paying export duty on a gram of pure LSD in a bank vault in Zurich – from Chemapol in Czechoslovakia.[11]

FDA Investigator Frank Larkworthy was unaware of Hubbard's CIA connections – or that he'd been an FBN employee, or that George White was probably his case officer – when he acquired him as an informant.[12] He only knew that Hubbard hated Tim Leary and was willing to lead raids on underground labs. "This was before Augustus Owsley Stanley found a cheap way to manufacture single doses," Larkworthy explains. "An LSD session with a psychiatrist in those days could cost as much as $600, and Hubbard wanted to protect what for him was a lucrative business."

Hubbard began making cases for Larkworthy, as he had for his previous case officer, FDA Investigator Stuart "Stu" Nadler. A former FBN agent and protégé of George White in New York in the early 1950s, Nadler had transferred to Alaska in 1954, then Los Angeles in 1956, and was assigned as an administrative assistant to White in San Francisco in January 1960. "Stu was a nice guy," Larkworthy recalls. "Then something happened between him and White, and he quit the FBN around 1961 and joined the FDA. Not long after that, Stu made the Bernard Roseman case using information provided by Hubbard. That's the first big LSD case."

In his book, *LSD: The Age Of Mind*, Roseman describes the bust, which he thought was a robbery, as follows: "As Mr. Pilson (in reality, the F.D.A. agent) started counting out the money, the kitchen door flew open and a man raving something, holding an automatic rifle, burst in."[13]

Roseman, who had purchased his LSD in Israel, was charged with smuggling and selling an unlabeled drug without a license, and was sentenced on several interstate distribution misdemeanors. He went to prison, and Hubbard continued to sell acid trips at five hundred dollars a whack, while making cases on his competitors, until the drug was outlawed in 1966, at which point he surrendered thirteen grams of pure LSD to Larkworthy.

What this means is that for ten years the CIA's Dr Frankensteins had secretly employed LSD, often in FBN safehouses, for nefarious purposes, but by 1963 it had escaped into the streets. No longer the exclusive property of the CIA, it was now judged to be a dangerous drug, and thus, ironically, a law enforcement issue of concern to the FBN.

THE RETURN OF THE CUBANS

Ever ready to try any innovation in unconventional warfare, the CIA in December 1962 enlarged its mercenary army by trading embargoed drugs for anti-Castro Cubans captured during the Bay of Pigs fiasco. Some members of the brigade were sent to secret training camps in Florida and Louisiana, to plot murder and mayhem against Castro; others were sent to fight Congolese rebels; and yet others to stamp out Cuban-inspired "brush fire" revolutions in Latin America. Wherever they landed, especially in Mexico, these CIA-trained Cuban Contras turned to drug smuggling to finance their operations, and their syndicate would soon join its Kuomintang, French, Italian, and American counterparts as one of the world's premier drug trafficking operations.

Manuel Artime is a perfect example of the CIA's lackadaisical attitude toward the drug smuggling activities of anti-Castro Cubans.[14] After his release from prison in December 1962, Artime's case officer, E. Howard Hunt, placed him in a leadership role in the terrorist Cuban Revolutionary Council (CRC) in Miami.[15] Hunt certainly knew that Artime was using drug money to finance his operations in Miami, as did Hunt's bosses, James Angleton, Richard Helms, and Tracy Barnes. As the CIA's domestic operations chief, Barnes was especially well placed to protect Cuban drug distributors. He was in charge of domestic operations involving anti-Castro Cubans and the Mafia, he controlled sixty-four branch offices across America, and, in conjunction with Angleton's counterintelligence staff, he worked with police forces to provide security for CIA safehouses across America, including any in Dallas, Texas.

And indeed, drug-smuggling Cubans were involved in MKULTRA operations by 1963. CIA execution expert Bill Harvey met with Johnny Roselli in June, at the same time that Trafficante's Cuban associate, assassin Tony Varona, visited Artime's CRC offices in New Orleans and Miami. Harvey stayed in touch with Roselli after his exile to Rome, and thus had an open channel to Trafficante and Varona.[16]

There was another Cuban angle as well. In January 1963, prior to his transfer, Harvey turned his MKULTRA operation (but not agent QJ/WIN) over to Des Fitzgerald, his replacement as chief of Task Force W. And Fitzgerald advanced the Castro assassination plot through a disgruntled Cuban military Attaché, Major Rolando Cubela Secades. The CIA had first asked Cubela to kill Castro in March 1961, at a meeting in Mexico arranged by Cubela's drug trafficking associate, Santo Trafficante. Despite Trafficante's exposure as a double agent later that year, Fitzgerald retained Cubela, probably because he enjoyed diplomatic immunity and could travel without his luggage being checked. Fitzgerald, as chief of the CIA's Far East Asia Division, had long been aware of the Kuomintang's narcotics activities, and during 1963 Cubela traveled between Spain, France, Mexico, Prague, and New York – all major transit points in the illicit drug trade. In August, Cubela returned to Havana, and in September he went to Paris to await instructions.[17]

Cubela, notably, was a confederate of FBI informer Jose Aleman, the mob-connected financier who in September 1962 heard Santo Trafficante say that JFK was "going to be hit." And that means that Fitzgerald, like Harvey, had an open channel to the patron saint of drug smugglers.

THE MKULTRA SHUFFLE

While the CIA's Cuban and Mafia assets plotted bloody treason, a CIA public relations consultant using the name Cal Salerno opened a new safehouse in Chicago in July 1963, as part of MKULTRA Subproject 132. Salerno had recently moved his offices from New York, held a top secret Agency clearance and, as the CIA noted in an internal memorandum, "is completely witting of the aims and goals of the project. He possesses unique facilities and personal abilities which have made him invaluable in this kind of operation."[18]

Charlie Siragusa used the alias Cal Salerno throughout his FBN career, but when asked by Senator Edward Kennedy in 1977 if he had set up the Chicago safehouse, he said, "There has been some poetic license taken with the truth. I only just learned the name of Cal Salerno was adopted by others that succeeded me. I had nothing to do with the CIA during the period of time that I was in Chicago."[19]

Kennedy accepted Siragusa's denial, even though Siragusa had traveled to Chicago in July 1963 to apply for the job of chief of the Illinois Crime Commission, and while there had socialized with his MKULTRA liaison, Ray Treichler, who had taken a job with a chemical manufacturing firm in Chicago after retiring from the CIA. So why didn't Kennedy ask the obvious follow-up question and inquire who had impersonated the interviewee and why? Apparently, the Senator's reticence had to do with the fact that Bobby Kennedy had, concurrently with the establishment of the Chicago safehouse in July 1963, entered into relations with Paulino Sierra Martinez, head of the anti-Castro Junta del Gobierno de Cuba en el Exilio (JGCE) in Chicago. Sierra, on behalf of Bobby Kennedy and with State Department support, funded anti-Castro terrorist groups outside of the US – perhaps through Siragusa or his impersonator at the new Chicago safehouse. He was allegedly tied to Trafficante and Marcello, and if he was, Sierra represented yet a third Cuban channel to CIA-protected drug smugglers and assassins.[20]

Meanwhile, Chicago's besieged Mafia boss, Sam Giancana, had revealed his MKULTRA connections as a way of warding off the FBI. On 16 August, the *Chicago Sun-Times* ran an article titled, "CIA Sought Giancana Help for Cuba Spying." Justice Department sources denied the claim, but that very same day Richard Helms sent a memo to McCone regarding the 7 May 1962 briefing of Bobby Kennedy about the CIA's use of Giancana and Trafficante in its hare-brained scheme to kill Castro. It was the first time McCone had heard "of any aspect of the scheme to assassinate Castro using members of the gambling syndicate."[21]

CIA murder plots abounded. In April 1963, the Agency assassinated Quinim Pholsena, the Laotian foreign minister, and in May it tried to kill China's president Liu Shao-chi in Cambodia.[22] In October, President Kennedy authorized the CIA to assist a cabal of Vietnamese generals in the overthrow of President Diem. The generals murdered Diem and his brother Nhu on 2 November 1963.

In New York, the FBN's Gambling Squad was closing in on various dignitaries, as well as Meyer Lansky and other Mafia members of "the gambling syndicate," all of whom were linked to drug trafficking and CIA assassination plots. In Washington, Bobby Kennedy's star witness in the war on crime, Joe Valachi, was revealing the Mafia's top secrets, while in Miami members of the Mafia's Commission were swearing sacred Italian oaths to murder the entire Kennedy family. The CIA and FBI were also concerned about the uppity AG, whose war on crime was about to expose the skeletons in their respective closets. Time was running out.

On 21 November 1963, CIA assassin Rolando Cubela traveled from Brazil to Paris, where Des Fitzgerald handed him a MKULTRA pen loaded with a deadly poison. The pen had been tested in San Francisco by Ike Feldman and George White, and was rigged with a hypodermic needle designed specifically for assassinations.[23] The CIA had gone to such extraordinary lengths to kill the annoying dictator of a tiny island and yet, according to the Warren Commission, a simple Italian bolt-action rifle was employed the next day to kill the president of the United States.

"I'll never forget that day," Tully Acampora says. "Hank Manfredi turned to me and said, 'They got him.'"

"They," in this case, meaning the right-wing ultras who hated Kennedy for, among other imagined offences, imposing racial desegregation on the sovereign slave state of Texas.

THE EYES OF TEXAS

Enter Lee Harvey Oswald, the misfit marine who'd served as a radio operator at the Atsugi Air Base in Japan, where the CIA used LSD to interrogate spies and drug dealers, and where, most likely, they recruited him to work as a double agent in the Soviet Union, and later, in a world of mystifying intrigues that ended in epic tragedy.

But Oswald was not a drug smuggler or special employee of the FBN, and for the purposes of this book, his role in the assassination is not directly relevant, even if he were the Manchurian Candidate – a magic, push-button assassin – or a MKULTRA patsy, programmed to take the fall for the actual assassin. However, the House Select Committee on Assassinations (HSCA) did say "there is solid evidence" that drug smugglers Carlos Marcello and Santo Trafficante, both CIA million-dollar men, were involved in the murder, and this is an issue that must be explored.[24]

The other issue that will be raised in the remainder of this chapter is the utter absence of references to the FBN in any official investigation of the JFK assassination, despite the fact that Bureau informer Jack Ruby killed Oswald and that, as the HSCA concluded, Ruby had "direct contact" with associates of Marcello and Trafficante.[25] Ruby's stated motive in killing Oswald was to spare Jackie Kennedy the pain of a public trial, and perhaps that's true. But if Ruby killed Oswald to protect the people who had conspired to kill JFK, were his FBN case agents wittingly involved in the cover-up?

The Ruby family had a long history in the illicit drug trade. Jack's older brother Hyman was convicted in 1939 of buying two ounces of heroin from Jacob Klein. As described in chapter 9, Klein slipped away from FBN agents in New York in October 1954, thanks to George White's intervention on behalf of John Ormento, and he again avoided arrest by FBN agents in Chicago after Jim Attie's informant was murdered in January 1960.

Klein was luckier than Ruby's next partner, Paul Roland Jones. In October 1947, Hyman betrayed Jones to FBN agents in Chicago. According to White's diary, Hyman had been his informant since July 1946. Jack followed in big brother's footsteps and served White in 1950, when he briefed the Kefauver Committee about organized crime in Chicago – although his attorney, Louis Kutner, agreed to allow him to testify only "on the condition that the Kefauver Committee stay away from Dallas."[26] That raises the question of whether Committee investigator George White, who undoubtedly brought Ruby to Kefauver's attention, concurred with this request. If so, why would White want to keep the Committee out of Dallas? Was it to deflect attention from the Pawley–Cooke mission in Taiwan, which was funded by ultra Texas oilmen like H. L. Hunt, and which, in 1951, was facilitating the CIA-Kuomintang drug smuggling operation that entered the US by crossing the Mexican border at Laredo, Texas?

There was certainly enough evidence for the Kefauver Committee to take a long look at the Lone Star State. In 1951, Lait and Mortimer had identified Hunt as a professional gambler who ran a private racing wire, which suggests Mafia ties. They had also claimed that the Mafia had "taken over the age-old racket of running guns across the border," under the aegis of Carlos Marcello.[27]

The FBN office in Dallas knew Jack Ruby. Murray A. Brown, the acting district supervisor on 22 November 1963, described him as "a sleazy opportunist who was always trying to get the Dallas cops to patronize his club." But, Brown says, "Ruby was not an FBN informant."

George Gaffney, however, vividly recalls Secret Service chief James Rowley asking him on 25 November 1963 if the FBN had a file on Ruby. It did. "But there wasn't much in it," Gaffney recalls. "Just that he was a source on numerous occasions, on unimportant suspects."

Right after Ruby shot Oswald, Mort Benjamin checked the files in the New York office and found one that indicated that Ruby had been an

FBN informer since the 1940s. But the next time Benjamin looked for it, the New York file had gone missing, and Secret Service chief Rowley never returned the FBN headquarters file to Gaffney – which strongly suggests that someone did not want anyone to know that Ruby had been an FBN informant.

Not only do the FBN agents from Dallas disagree with the rest of the outfit about Ruby's status as an informant, the stated focus of their operations is also at odds with Anslinger's legendary obsession with the Mafia. Murray Brown, an agent in Dallas from 1955 until 1976, insists that the Mafia was not selling heroin there. Long-time Dallas agent Bowman Taylor agrees. "We weren't after the Mafia," he says. "That's gambling more than dope. New Orleans had the Mafia."

The small FBN office in New Orleans, which reported to Dallas, had arrested Marcello on a marijuana rap in 1938, and in 1963 it had reasons to believe he was a major narcotics trafficker. He was cited, for example, in the International List as an associate of Frank Coppola's. Furthermore, as the chief of the New Orleans Narcotics Unit, Clarence Giarusso, said (see chapter 4), it was the FBN's job, not his, to investigate Mafia drug smugglers who imported drugs from overseas. But according to agents in New Orleans, they never had the manpower or resources to make a conspiracy case on Marcello, so instead they worked on Black addicts who traveled to New York and returned with heroin, leaving the million-dollar man left unhindered – perhaps to plot the murder of the president?

IRRECONCILABLE DIFFERENCES

Taylor and Brown's assertions are incredible, considering that Jack Cusack had informed the McClellan Committee in January 1958 that Mafioso Joseph Civello ran the heroin business in Dallas in conjunction with John Ormento and the Magaddino family in Buffalo. Cusack linked Civello with Marcello, Trafficante, and Jimmy Hoffa – the HSCA's three prime suspects in the Kennedy assassination. Civello was Marcello's "deputy in Dallas," had attended the Apalachin convention, and is listed in the 1964 Senate Hearings as receiving heroin from Rocco Pellegrino in New York.[28] Pellegrino, notably, was Saro Mogavero's godfather.

Considering the information available on Civello, how could the Dallas office not know of his narcotics activities, or that Jack Ruby was part of his organization? How could the FBN be unaware that the FBI, in 1956, had identified Ruby as a central figure in John Ormento's operation between Texas, Mexico, and New York?[29] Or that the Mafia's courier from New York, Benjamin Indiviglio, was convicted of heroin trafficking in Houston in 1956?[30] Or that Indiviglio, amazingly, while awaiting his appeal, shared a prison cell with Joe Orsini?[31] And that when Orsini was released from prison in 1958, he and Indiviglio, who was acquitted by the US Supreme Court in the 1956 case, immediately went into business?[32]

It isn't impossible that the police were able to keep the Dallas agents in the dark. The Kefauver Committee concluded that big-city vice squads could limit the ability of federal agents to make cases. Civello was a police informant on narcotics cases: perhaps the racist Dallas judicial system was content to protect his narcotics operation in exchange for information on his Black customers, and perhaps the Dallas FBN agents chose to look the other way. That would be in accordance with a formula that is still uniformly applied across America. Or perhaps Civello and Ruby had more powerful patrons. Civello was convicted in 1931 on a federal narcotics charge, but obtained early parole on the recommendation of Dallas Sheriff Bill Decker, a former bootlegger into whose custody Oswald was being transferred when he was shot by Ruby.[33] Civello was also linked through his protected gambling racket with Hoover's patron, Clint Murchison. That relationship may explain why, in 1962, the FBI found no evidence of illegal activity by Civello, despite the fact that he'd been convicted in 1960 and sentenced to five years for obstructing justice.[34] This may also account for why the Warren Commission, whose conclusions were based largely on the FBI's investigation, was not able to turn up any evidence to establish "a significant link between Ruby and organized crime."[35]

Consider also that Ruby met with the FBI eight times in 1959, the same year he visited his friend Lewis McWillie in Cuba.[36] Then managing Lansky's Tropicana club in Havana, McWillie took Ruby to visit Trafficante at Trescornia prison, shortly before Trafficante was released and hired by the CIA, along with Johnny Roselli, to assassinate Castro using MKULTRA technology in part developed by FBN agents. Add to that the fact that Roselli and Ruby had known each other since the 1930s, and the fact that they both knew George White. As Ike Feldman noted in chapter 15, White often sent him to the airport to pick up Roselli and bring him to the office.

The fact that White had long-standing relations with Ruby and Roselli, and the allegation that Ruby and Roselli (then working for Harvey in the ZR/RIFLE assassination project) met twice in Miami in October 1963, is not enough to indict White in a conspiracy to kill JFK.[37] His diaries offer no clues. There are no entries from mid-1962 through 1963, while he was seriously ill with cirrhosis of the liver, and then they resume in 1964 –

which is very strange. Remember, White was linked through MKULTRA to the sex and drugs blackmail schemes Hoover and the CIA used to keep Jack and Bobby under wraps. And there was a lot of mud waiting to be slung: the Kennedy–Campbell–Giancana intrigue; Jack's affairs with Mariella Novotny (of the Christine Keeler sex-ring scandal, which forced Great Britain's defense minister to resign), and with Ellen Rometsch, known to have bedded Soviet agents; and the affairs Jack and Bobby had with Marilyn Monroe, who died from a drug overdose in August 1962.[38]

THE COVER-UP

Besides having a blind spot for Mafia drug dealers in Dallas and New Orleans – and Jack Ruby's relationship with them – the FBN incriminated itself further by becoming involved in James Angleton's effort to blame Castro for the Kennedy assassination. According to George Gaffney, Mexican officials intercepted a call to Havana from the Cuban Embassy in Mexico City. The Cubans were claiming credit for the assassination; but instead of telling the FBI or the CIA, the Mexicans told the FBN agent in charge in Mexico City, William Durkin, and on Sunday Durkin called Gaffney in Washington. Gaffney rushed the message to Secret Service chief James Rowley, at which point Angleton's theory that Castro arranged the assassination emerged as an alternative to the Lone Nut theory promulgated by Hoover, and later embraced by the Warren Commission.

There are two other FBN-related factors to consider in the official cover-up. On 20 November 1963, Rose Cheramie was found on a Louisiana road, dazed and bruised. She was taken to a private hospital where she told a doctor that JFK was going to be killed during his forthcoming visit to Dallas. Later that day, Cheramie was released into the custody of Louisiana State policeman Francis Fruge, and while Fruge was taking her to a state hospital Cheramie said she'd been traveling from Florida to Dallas with two men who "were Italians or resembled Italians."[39] She didn't know their names, but they'd stopped at a lounge for drinks. An argument ensued, Cheramie was evicted and, as she stood outside the lounge, she was struck a glancing blow by a car. She also repeated to Fruge her claim that President Kennedy was going to be killed. But because she was a prostitute and drug addict, neither Fruge nor the doctor believed her – at least, not until the afternoon of 22 November.

On 27 November, Fruge interviewed Cheramie again, and she expounded on her story. She said the Italians were taking her to Dallas to obtain

$8,000, so they could buy eight kilograms of heroin from a seaman. The seaman was to meet them in Houston after disembarking in Galveston. Cheramie gave Fruge the names of the seaman and the ship. As they were on the way to Houston to check out her story, Cheramie told Fruge that she was a stripper at Jack Ruby's nightclub in Dallas, and that she had seen Ruby and Oswald together. She said she was part of a Mafia operation in which call girls were rotated between cities, and that Ruby had sent her to Miami on 18 November.

When contacted by Fruge, the Customs agent in charge of Galveston verified that the seaman was being investigated for drug smuggling. The Coast Guard likewise confirmed that it was interested in the ship named by Cheramie regarding its role in drug smuggling operations. But the state narcotics bureaus in Texas and Oklahoma found Cheramie's information "erroneous in all respects," and when the HSCA asked Customs to produce the agents she had named, and their reports, Customs officials said that neither the agents nor reports could be found.[40]

The HSCA let this promising lead drop without attempting to talk to Customs agents like William Hughes, who vividly recalls "Nutty Nate" Durham as the feckless agent in charge of Galveston in 1963. Nate may have been alive in 1978, but the CIA did not allow Customs to identify him or provide his reports to Congress. The reason for this subterfuge comes as no surprise: some of Nutty Nate's colleagues on the Galveston case were CIA officers operating under Customs cover, as part of a special unit organized in Houston by Dave Ellis. Members of this unit facilitated the activities of anti-Castro drug smuggling terrorist groups in the US, which is why the FBI also "decided to pursue the case no further."[41]

Neither Customs, nor the Coast Guard, nor the FBI, nor any state narcotics bureau revealed the existence of the Galveston drug ring to the FBN. But Fruge did tell congressional investigators that the Cuban Revolutionary Council's delegate in New Orleans, Sergio Arcacha Smith, may have been one of the men who had accompanied and abused Rose Cheramie. Smith's CRC office was located in the same building as Oswald's notional Fair Play for Cuba office at 544 Camp Street in New Orleans, and Guy Banister, a former FBI agent in Chicago, had gotten Smith his office space. Smith and one of Banister's employees, David Ferrie, "were also believed to have ties with organized crime figure Carlos Marcello."[42]

Here the plot thickens, for Banister was the FBI agent in charge in Chicago while George White was there as the FBN district supervisor in 1945 and 1946. Banister moved on to become deputy chief of police in New Orleans, and then opened a private detective firm that served as a

CIA front. A certified right-wing fanatic, Banister was a member of the Anti-Communist League of the Caribbean (funded in part by Anastasio Somoza), as well as Louisiana coordinator of the racist Minutemen.[43] Working for Banister was David Ferrie, a pilot who knew Oswald and worked for Carlos Marcello. Ferrie claimed that he drove to Houston to ice skate on the day Kennedy was killed, and to Galveston to go duck hunting two days later when Ruby killed Oswald. This put him on the same path Rose Cheramie intended to follow – a bizarre coincidence that suggests that he was involved in transporting and paying conspirators, including Arcacha Smith, in the Kennedy assassination. Adding to this possibility is the fact that Ferrie's boss, Guy Banister, assisted Arcacha Smith in his counter-revolutionary activities, as did Carlos Marcello.[44]

Banister brings us to the other FBN-related piece in the JFK puzzle: the French connection.

JFK'S FRENCH CONNECTION

CIA asset Clay Shaw reportedly joined the Permanent Industrial Exhibition in 1957. Known as Permindex, it was a construction company that built trade centers, hotels, and office centers like the Trade Mart he managed in New Orleans. Ten years later, Shaw would attain notoriety as the person New Orleans District Attorney Jim Garrison charged with conspiring to kill JFK. He was acquitted, and as far as this author is aware, was not involved in drug trafficking. However, his company, Permindex, after moving to Rome in 1961 and reforming itself as the Centro Mondiale Commerciale, was reportedly involved as "a cover for the transfer of CIA … funds in Italy for illegal political-espionage activities."[45]

More to the point, CMC was accused of channeling funds to the drug-smuggling OAS.

> In tracing the money used to finance the [July 1961] de Gaulle assassination plots, French Intelligence discovered that about $200,000 in secret funds had been sent to Permindex accounts in the Banque de la Crédit Internationale. In 1962, Banister had dispatched to Paris a lawyer friend … with a suitcase full of money for the OAS, reportedly around $200,000.[46]

Banister's money allegedly went to Jean René Marie Souetre – or someone impersonating him. A French Army deserter and the OAS representative in southern Algeria, Souetre reportedly met in the spring of 1963 with

E. Howard Hunt in Madrid, ultra General Walker in Dallas, and Guy Banister at 544 Camp Street. In June, he offered the CIA a list of KGB penetrations in the French government. Souetre was also reportedly "on the Paris end of drug traffic," and had been followed for years by an undercover narcotics agent in Marseilles.[47]

In 1977, the CIA released a document, dated 1 April 1964, titled "Jean Souetre's expulsion from the US." In this document, the FBI explains that French security officials wanted to know why Souetre was expelled from "Fort Worth or Dallas 18 hours after the assassination." Souetre had been in Dallas on the afternoon of the assassination, and had been expelled to "Mexico or Canada." The French had some reason to believe that Souetre was plotting to assassinate Charles de Gaulle during his upcoming visit to Mexico, and so naturally they wanted to know about Souetre's movements. But the FBI said it had no information on him and, in yet another case of criminal negligence, it never notified the Warren Commission about Souetre.[48]

There's more to this story. The CIA knew that dentist Lawrence M. Alderson in Houston had contacted Souetre in December 1963. Alderson met Souetre in 1953 while serving as an Army officer in France. They worked together on security issues at a French air base. As he did every year, Alderson sent a Christmas card to Souetre, and somehow that came to the attention of the CIA – and the only way that's possible is if the CIA was monitoring Souetre. People were tailing Alderson within days of the assassination, and FBI agents interviewed him around 1 January 1964, four months *before* the French officials contacted the FBI. The FBI wanted to know if he would act as a go-between if Souetre contacted him again. That never happened, but Alderson told this writer that persons claiming to be agents of the Army CID told him that Souetre had been flown from Dallas to New Orleans on 22 November 1963 on a military transport plane.

No one from the US government ever asked Souetre if he was in Dallas on 22 November. But if wasn't there – and we know a Frenchman was – it may have been SDECE agent Michel Mertz impersonating him.

Mertz, when compared to Souetre, is an equally if not exceedingly enigmatic character. Born in 1920 in Moselle, France, he was drafted into the German Army, but ostensibly defected to the Resistance in 1943. After the war, he joined, or infiltrated (as the case may be) SDECE undercover as a French Army captain. He served a tour in Algeria with Souetre (1958–59) and in April 1961 returned to Algeria as a double, or perhaps triple agent. He presented himself as an OAS sympathizer and either learned of, or provoked, an OAS plot to assassinate de Gaulle in July. In either case the plot was foiled, France rallied around de Gaulle, and Mertz won the eternal gratitude of Interior Minister Roger Frey and his chief aide, Alexandre Sanguinetti – Marcel Francisci's protector in the French government.[49]

In 1947, Mertz married the adopted daughter of Charles Martel, a Paris procurer and drug smuggler with connections to François Spirito. It is unthinkable that such a liaison would escape the notice of Charlie Dyar, the veteran FBN agent who worked in France throughout the 1930s. But Mertz was unknown to the FBN, and in 1960, with the blessings of his SDECE bosses, he established a lucrative heroin network between France, Montreal, and New York under the auspices of Spirito's partner, Joe Orsini. Santo Trafficante and Orsini's former cellmate, Benny Indiviglio, the Mafia's distributor in Dallas, managed the American end of the operation. A significant delivery was made in October 1961, just prior to the French Connection case, when Mertz's courier, diplomat Jean Mounet, accompanied a Citroen packed with 100 pounds of heroin to New York. Mounet may have been posing as J. Mouren, and if so, Mertz may have been the guiding hand behind Jean Jehan, Françoise Scaglia, and Jean Angelvin. Apart from any attention he may have attracted if involved in the famous French Connection case, deliveries from Mertz to Indiviglio, averaging ninety kilograms a month, would continue undetected for the next nine years.[50]

ADDING IT UP

Extrapolating on the fascinating information presented in this chapter, one can hypothesize that an assassin used Paul Mondoloni's protected drug route in Mexico to enter Texas through Laredo, and to exit through Houston or New Orleans. Souetre was probably willing to do the hideous deed for money to support the OAS. Mertz was a professional assassin and may have been acting on behalf of the CIA faction within SDECE. CIA counterintelligence chief James Angleton was capable of moving the assassins through his Brown–Castellani network. His staff had a phony 201 file on Oswald and, through MKULTRA, could have set up Oswald as the patsy. Last but not least, William Harvey, who hated Bobby Kennedy, and Desmond Fitzgerald, the far-right Republican, had access to Corsican assassins and the Marcello–Trafficante–Bonanno Mafia clique that could have maneuvered Jack Ruby and the Dallas police. As outlined in chapter 15, Harvey recommended hiring Corsican drug smugglers as assassins, in order to protect certain Mafiosi in the CIA's employ. He also wanted to turn Corsicans, working for the Soviets, into double agents, which brings us to the final piece in the puzzle.

In an incredible coincidence, Angleton met on 22 November 1963 with SDECE Colonel de Lannurien at Le Rive Gauche restaurant in Georgetown, regarding allegations made by Philippe de Vosjoli (FBN Agent Sal Vizzini's partner in operations into Cuba during the October 1962 Missile Crisis) that Colonel Leonard Houneau, deputy head of SDECE, was a KGB agent. De Vosjoli, however, proved to be a double agent working for Angleton against his own government and, according to Angleton's biographer, Tom Mangold, Houneau was exonerated, the CIA acknowledged that de Vosjoli had given "bad information," and de Gaulle was so upset that he severed relations with the CIA over the incident. "The consequences of this split were serious and benefited only the KGB," Mangold said. Among other things, the animosity created by Angleton cost the CIA valuable French intercepts and intelligence assets in Vietnam.[51]

It's almost as if Angleton was a double agent, and if he was the "mole" he was searching for, it's possible that SDECE agents working for the KGB may have sent an assassin into Dallas through Angleton's Brown–Castellani drug network, or through Paul Mondoloni. If Angleton was a KGB mole, perhaps he used QJ/WIN (who could have been Mertz) to assassinate JFK, and programmed Lee Harvey Oswald as the unwitting patsy through the MKULTRA Program.[52]

Speculation such as this will always surround the unsolved assassination of JFK. Angleton was, like White, debilitated by his alcoholism, and the problems he caused may well have been the result of incompetence rather than malice. So this chapter will close by returning to where it started, to eerie MKULTRA. On 29 November 1963, a week after the president was murdered, Marshall Carter, the deputy director of the CIA, met with Richard Helms, John Earman, James Angleton, Sid Gottlieb, and Lyman Kirkpatrick. What a group. At this meeting the CIA chiefs agreed to continue to test unwitting subjects through MKULTRA using the FBN and its safehouses.[53] To this end they launched MKULTRA Subproject 149 in New York in January 1964, specifically to provide a replacement for Charlie Siragusa. An unnamed individual in the import and export business conducted the project at least until April 1965.[54]

These CIA officers, especially Angleton, had the desire and the ability to mold assassins and patsies. The three main suspects in the assassination – Marcello, Trafficante, and Hoffa – were CIA million-dollar men. And the CIA prevented the FBN from going after these drug traffickers, or investigating CIA agents like Irving Brown – and perhaps even Michel Mertz – in Angleton's French connection. All of which forms an unmistakable trail leading from the CIA, through the FBN, to the assassination of JFK.

21

NO INNOCENTS ABROAD

"Remember the Wolf is a hunter —
go forth and get food of thine own."
Rudyard Kipling, "The Law of the Jungle"

Charlie Siragusa's last year at FBN headquarters was not a happy one. As he said in his CIA debriefing, "I was the number two man. But instead of taking orders from me, Gaffney would go over my head to Giordano."

"Charlie felt uneasy in the company of Gaffney and Giordano," says his protégé, Andy Tartaglino. "He'd had a heart attack while shoveling snow, but they pushed him hard and complained when he didn't keep up. It was vicious. It got to the point," Tartaglino says bitterly, "where he wouldn't even have lunch with them.

"Ambassador Rosal was bringing in fifty kilograms at a time," Tartaglino continues, "so Charlie knew there was a lot more heroin entering America than Anslinger acknowledged; and he knew there was pouch traffic between Lebanon and Paris. The Colombian minister to Russia was involved, as were Corsicans and the Lower East Side mob. We were building a case at the Court House Squad, getting close to 'the bigger' diplomat that Tarditi had alluded to, and Charlie knew all the details. I was on the phone with him daily. Meanwhile, Gaffney's on the phone to Pat Ward every day, trying to find out what *we're* up to. Gaffney finally brought me down to Washington as *his* assistant on the Ambassador case, to report the details to *him* every day." [1]

Gaffney, naturally, has a different recollection. "Giordano and Belk built a high wall around New York to keep me from meddling in Belk's affairs," he says. And just as Siragusa complained that Gaffney went "over his head," Gaffney's beef was that Belk bypassed him in the chain of command, and communicated directly with Giordano. As to his clash with Siragusa, Gaffney says, "Charlie was trying to become the Commissioner, so I applied for deputy. When he found out, he called me in and asked, 'What makes you think you're qualified?' I told him that I'd made more cases and put more Mafiosi in prison than him. 'So, if you're qualified for Commissioner,' I said, 'I'm qualified for deputy.'"

Such was the venomous, negative atmosphere at FBN headquarters in 1963. Anslinger had retired to Hollidaysburg, taking his coalescing mystique with him, and Giordano and Gaffney, after they had joined forces to nullify Siragusa, "went after each other like gladiators battling it out in an arena of politics and power," according to FBN historian John McWilliams. Giordano and Gaffney filed civil service charges against one another, and Giordano won; but it was all for nothing, "since he was too weak to survive the massive reorganization that occurred in 1968." [2]

Too committed to law enforcement to break away entirely, Siragusa took a job as chief of the Illinois Crime Commission in 1964. Highly committed to the FBN, he did one other significant thing as well: he introduced Andy Tartaglino to his contacts at the CIA. And by passing that torch, he provided his protégé with the power to avenge him.

"Charlie was good to me," Tartaglino says reverentially. "He tried to keep me out of the office infighting. But several months before Charlie left, Gaffney took me off the Ambassador case and had me reassigned as an inspector. Fred Dick was my instructor, and we immediately left on an extended tour of the Bureau's overseas offices."

As will become evident, Tartaglino's reassignment as an inspector marked a watershed in the FBN's evolution, and was a major factor in the organization's demise. In the meantime, an overview of his tour with Fred Dick will serve as a convenient introduction to the FBN's overseas situation in the early years of the Giordano administration.

THE FBN IN EUROPE AND THE MIDDLE EAST

In March 1963, Henry Giordano assigned his protégé, Mike Picini, as the new district supervisor in Rome. His job, as Picini explains it, "was to focus the local governments on curbing supply. The strategy was political; to show the police how to do it, supply them with intelligence, and get them to increase their commitment."

Picini departed from FBN tradition and took a forthright, political approach toward drug law enforcement when dealing with his foreign counterparts. But conducting operations was still a challenge. His deputy, Hank Manfredi, was less involved than ever in FBN operations. He had bugged almost every Embassy in Rome and was so busy listening to foreign spies and diplomats, and reporting their conversations to the CIA, that he didn't have time to keep up with his FBN workload. "One night in Rome," Fred Dick recalls, "Hank asked me to pose as a White House representative and give $300 to an Italian cop who was bringing police files to the American Embassy almost every night. This was his great source. This was how Charlie Siragusa got all his information on the Sicilian mob."

"Hank was a great believer in collateral missions," explains Colonel Tully Acampora, then in Rome as a CIA advisor to the Carabinieri. "He was passing information to Bill Harvey, who'd landed in Rome as station chief after Bobby Kennedy tossed him out of Washington. We knew the Mexicans were using the pouch in both directions, so Hank and I sat down and wrote reports to the CIA *and* the FBN. But we couldn't disrupt the diplomatic network without putting our own foreign policy objectives at risk. So we identified the Embassy people involved, photographed them, confronted them, and then used them as informants to broaden the thing. This channel was being watched, but it had to be handled carefully, because Hank did not have an entrée to military counterintelligence in Italy. Harvey was the key player in that regard, with Angleton and the Mossad. Military counterintelligence was Angleton, and that was strictly off-limits to Hank."

The situation was just as delicate in France, where President de Gaulle had severed relations with the CIA over Angleton's false allegations that the deputy chief of SDECE was a KGB agent. French security officials knew that the FBN and CIA were in cahoots, and were angry with the FBN for having accused them of conspiring to dump heroin on America. "Cusack had taken a 'get tough' approach," Tartaglino sighs, "but the French were doing the best they could. What was needed was their cooperation, not their wrath, for only they could provide the informants, intelligence, and manpower we needed to conduct stakeouts and make arrests. France was not a victim country and needed to be persuaded, not pushed."

Victor G. Maria agrees. An agent since 1958, first in San Francisco, then under his mentor Howard Chappell in Los Angeles, Maria was the sole FBN agent stationed in Paris from February 1962 until 1966. His top priority, reflecting Giordano's new policy of accommodation, was to find out how drugs were getting to the US without upsetting the French.

"My parents were Lebanese and I spoke Arabic," Maria says, "and I'd been a croupier in Lake Tahoe and Vegas, so I hung around the Paris casinos where the wealthy Arabs and Corsicans went to gamble. I also went to the American areas, where I met young soldiers and musicians who were sending drugs back home. The only rule was: 'If it's an international case, okay.' But as the French authorities repeatedly made clear, the FBN wasn't there to make cases on French citizens, and if we did, then the local police wouldn't help us develop the international cases. It was that simple.

"Charles Guillard, Marcel Carrere, and Emil Angles at the Central Narcotics Office [CNO] were fabulous," Maria stresses. "They built up dossiers on the people we wanted, and persuaded the riot police and the gendarmes to help us too. We also got help from the vice squad of the Prefecture – that's Louis Souchon and Roger Voitot – who went after small retailers and worked up the Corsican ladder.

"The CNO also had access to SDECE people for wiretaps and files on the people we were targeting," Maria says, "like Paul Mondoloni. But the FBN didn't have access to the files, and we weren't prepared to watch Mondoloni all day to the exclusion of everyone else. By myself, I covered Spain, France, Belgium, and Germany, and made trips into Lebanon, Syria, and Turkey. In Europe," he stresses, "most of my support came from the Army CID in Heidelberg. They provided flash rolls and people to cover me. But even Tony Pohl, who was French and spoke French with the right accent, was frustrated. Before Picini arrived in Rome, we'd get little blue memos from Cusack saying, 'Make undercover cases or else.' But all the good cases were made with the expertise of the French police, within the confines of French law. Not undercover."

Anthony Pohl agrees. As noted in chapter 18, he'd been recruited into the FBN by Siragusa in 1960, and after interrogating Etienne Tarditi, had been sent to France in 1961 to open an office in Marseilles and locate heroin conversion labs using Marty Pera's innovative precursor tracking system. But Paul Knight shunned him in Paris, and Cusack initially suspected him of being a spy for Lee Speer. Having come from the military and served as a CID agent in Europe for many years, Pohl was "horrified" by the FBN's "unprofessional" (call it paranoid) and counterproductive culture. Even after Cusack apologized following his return to Rome as district supervisor in January 1962, and even after Pohl had formed official relations with the French in Marseilles in June 1962, he was still beset by problems.

"There was no tight control of information," Pohl says, "and even though we knew when the acidic anhydride was ordered and purchased, sometimes it would sit for months at the depot. Then Jo Cesari [the premier

Corsican chemist in Marseilles] would disappear for a few weeks. When he returned, his face would be pale and we knew he'd been working, but only once did we actually track the precursor to the lab."

Part of the problem was that Cesari's half-brother, Dom Albertini, was an informer for an investigating judge in Marseilles.[3] Likewise, Marseilles Mayor Gaston Defferre protected the Guérini gang for political purposes, and SAC chief Jacques Foccart, along with Interior Minister Roger Frey and his deputy, Alexandre Sanguinetti, protected Marcel Francisci and thus, by default, Paul Mondoloni.[4]

Pohl's failure to locate heroin conversion labs led to his transfer to Chicago and replacement in Marseilles by Albert Garofalo in March 1963. A skilled and fearless case-making agent, Garofalo had made undercover buys in April 1960 from a Dutch seaman carrying kilogram amounts of heroin from the Aranci brothers (thought to have SDECE protection, and a source in the Far East) in Marseilles to Charles Hedges in New York. Hedges was arrested and provided leads to a ring of Air France stewards and their receivers, including members of the Lower East Side mob that Tartaglino referred to above. The so-called Air France case in Canada overlapped with and developed concurrently with the Second Ambassador case in the US.

Meanwhile, CIA Agent Paul Knight was back in Beirut working undercover as Pan Am's regional security chief. When not guarding the Shah of Iran, or accosting KGB colonels, Knight assisted Fred Wilson, the FBN's new agent in charge in Beirut. Wilson, however, quickly became a target of Inspector Fred Dick and his apprentice torpedo, Andy Tartaglino. Fred Dick recalled that Wilson had overcharged the FBN for a trip he made to Turkey. According to another agent, he had gotten involved in the gold trade with Carlo Dondola, the suave swindler and special employee who, from behind the scenes, ran the Beirut office for Knight. Whatever the exact cause, Wilson's troubles climaxed when inspectors Dick and Tartaglino arrived in Beirut.

"While he was driving us to our hotel," Dick recalls, "Wilson said he was being worked to death, and that made me suspicious. So when I got to the Embassy the next morning, I asked the marine guard what kind of hours Wilson was working. The marine said that after he'd dropped us off at our hotel, Wilson had returned to the Embassy and removed some documents from the office safe. We knew he kept a diary, so I told him, 'Give the diary over, or swim back to America.'" Matter-of-factly, Dick says, "We accepted his resignation on the spot."[5]

Wilson's replacement, Dennis Dayle, arrived soon thereafter. Trained as a concert violinist, Dayle sought more exciting work, and was employed as a Milwaukee policeman when FBN Agent George Emrich recruited him in 1958. Assigned to Chicago, Dayle – a good-looking, aggressive case-making agent – came to the attention of headquarters in typically spectacular style. Posing as mobster Mike Novak, he purchased two kilograms of heroin from Mafia boss Joe Marassa while Chicago District Supervisor George Belk, Assistant Treasury Secretary For Law Enforcement James Reed, and FBN Commissioner Henry Giordano watched from across the street in a car. "Afterwards Belk took me to the Playboy Club," Dayle recalls. "'Dennis,' he said, 'you made me look good, and I'll never forget it.'

"Well," Dayle says with a careless shrug, "Treasury had just given Giordano the money to open offices in Bangkok, Turkey, and Mexico, and a few months later I was given a choice: 'Go to Beirut or else.' My initial reaction was, 'Where's Beirut?' Lebanon wasn't well known to FBN agents, except New York's International Group. So I agreed to do a three-month TDY, to identify traffickers and make cases. That was the job. But there was no Foreign Service or language training. I took a plane to Rome, where Mike Picini was supposed to be waiting to escort me to Beirut. But Mike was in Paris, so I went to Beirut alone. I arrived on a Sunday and when I finally found the Embassy, the FBN office was padlocked. I couldn't get in. I didn't even know about the Wilson fiasco until I got there.

"Well, I soon found out that I was there to repair relations, and in doing that I relied on Paul Knight. Paul had left the FBN, but he provided contacts to informants and law enforcement people in Turkey, Lebanon and Syria – my most important contact being Osman Osman, the chief of criminal investigations in Lebanon. Paul and I became close friends and we often dined with Joe Salm, and relaxed while listening to classical music. Other-wise I was the only person in the region, handling all Treasury functions. My family didn't know where I was for weeks at a time."

A typical case began with Dayle posing as an Air France crewman, and Knight introducing him to an informer. The informer then introduced Dayle to morphine base distributor Saleh Ghazer and Ghazer's supplier in Beirut, Abou Jaoude, an associate of Sami Khoury. Dayle and Ghazer opened a joint account at Intrabank (which had branch offices in Paris and the Bahamas) where Dayle deposited "buy" money for morphine base. Next he met Jaoude's suppliers in Damascus, where he sampled and sealed the product in two-kilogram packages. "I said I had to go back to the hotel to get the money," Dayle recalls, "and while I was gone, I called in the Syrian authorities and everyone was arrested. One of the traffickers was a Syrian Army officer using desert patrol vehicles to transport the base from the lab site. He was summarily executed."

Like Knight before him, Dayle would soon employ Sami Khoury as an informant. Fresh out of prison for cigarette smuggling, and looking for free passage to traffic in narcotics, Khoury identified Corsican traffickers and provided information that led to the seizure of morphine base on Turkish ships. He also provided valuable information about South America, where several nations were emerging as major drug transit points. Unfortunately, as Dayle once noted with dismay, "The major targets of my investigations almost invariably turned out to be working for the CIA."[6]

THE LATIN-AMERICAN CONNECTION

After Jacques Foccart and SAC smashed the OAS, many drug smuggling Corsicans moved to Argentina, Brazil, and Uruguay where, according to Dennis Dayle, they began receiving heroin, often shipped in Arabic sweets, from Sami Khoury and his chemist, Omar Makkouk. Heading the Corsican network in South America was Auguste Joseph Ricord. A Nazi collaborator, Ricord fled to Buenos Aires in 1947 and first appeared on the FBN radar screen in 1951 as Angel "Petit Ze" Abadelejo, a member of the Orsini ring. In 1957, he was known primarily as a procurer, with houses of prostitution in Brazil and Venezuela. After being expelled from Venezuela for white slavery in 1963, Ricord moved to Argentina where, as Rico Cori, he established a major drug trafficking operation with Paul Mondoloni's associate, Ansan Bistoni, and several experienced Corsicans. Ricord bought police protection throughout South America and, from their base at Ricord's El Sol restaurant in Buenos Aires, the "Group France" drug smuggling ring established the infamous Triangle of Death, sending cocaine to Europe in return for heroin that was then smuggled to the US. Ricord often obtained heroin from Paul Mondoloni and Jean-Baptiste Croce, whose sources included the Francisci brothers, and Paul Pajanacci, an associate of Maurice Castellani.[7]

Corrupt officials in Latin America greatly facilitated the Group France and its Triangle of Death. A case in point involved Bolivia's Vice President Juan Lechin Oquendo, who resigned in September 1961 after Argentine official Joseph Guzman accused him of managing all the cocaine labs in Bolivia. But in September 1963, after the scandal subsided, Lechin was absolved by the Bolivian Congress, and returned to work.

Despite the quiet migration of Corsicans to South America, there was little demand for cocaine in America in the early 1960s, and heroin smuggling across the Mexican border was the FBN's bigger concern. But

Customs had jurisdiction in Mexico, and it wasn't until the Kennedy administration launched its Alliance for Progress – and began sending mountains of military aid to nations that were willing to accept, as part of the deal, Special Forces counterinsurgency advisors and CIA officers posing undercover as Public Safety police advisors – that the FBN was invited to open offices in Mexico. And that's when FBN agents William J. Durkin and Renaldo "Ray" Maduro arrived on the scene.

"I was transferred from New York to Los Angeles in August 1962," Maduro recalls, "and in November Charlie Siragusa called. Charlie had been my money-man in the big Vic Stadter bust we made in 1961 at the CIA pad in New York. He had confidence in me, and during the interview he said that Treasury was transferring narcotics jurisdiction in Latin America from Customs to the FBN. It was a package deal. Durkin, who'd been Belk's enforcement assistant in Chicago, was going down too, as the agent in charge. I agreed, and Giordano signed the clearance. I went on an official passport to fill a Customs space vacated by Chili Martinez, who went to Texas.[8]

"Durkin went down first," Maduro continues, "in December 1962. Bill was tall, husky, and tight with Gaffney, and he brought along a copy of the International Book. We quickly became friends, and over the next four years we made a lot of cases together. I drove down in February 1963 and reported to the head of the Federales, Colonel Hernandez Tello, whom I'd met on the Asaf y Bala case in 1959 [and whom Jim Attie described as a drug trafficking policeman who informed on his competitors]."

To promote good relations with their counterparts in the narcotics branch of the Mexican Federal Police (the MexFeds), Maduro and Durkin provided advice and materiel aid through the US Military Advisory Group and the Office of Public Safety. Their relationship with Public Safety was especially tight, even though the CIA was recruiting, through the Office of Public Safety's International Police Academy in Panama, the same policemen and military officers – like Tello – who protected and contended with the region's drug traffickers. Meanwhile, US Army Special Forces A-Teams, under the direction of the CIA, were setting up Civic Action camps in the cocaine-producing Andes. Under cover of attending to the health and security needs of the indigenous people, the "Sneaky Petes" spied on, and ran covert operations against, rebellious Indians and labor leaders, and their Cuban advisors.

In exchange for intelligence on traffickers in South and Central America, FBN agents did favors for the CIA. In 1962, for example, a former Latin American ambassador to the US was identified as a drug courier. At Siragusa's request, Tom Tripodi met with the diplomat at the University

Club in Washington. When faced with the threat of deportation, the diplomat became an informant and, though he never produced any information that generated any drugs busts, he did provide nude photographs of the wife of the nation's Marxist vice president in bed with another man. Siragusa passed the photos to the CIA, and a political threat was neutralized.[9]

Due to the fact that the CIA protected its drug dealing assets in the Mexican intelligence service, the FBN continued to have a hard time making significant cases in Mexico. But the CIA had no hold on some Customs port inspectors, with the result that Customs made two significant seizures in Texas. The first was the 7 November 1962 bust of Milton Abramson in Houston. Abramson had purchased twenty-two pounds of heroin from Paul Mondoloni and was delivering it to Gambino family member Joseph Stassi, a former co-owner of the Sans Souci casino in Havana with Meyer Lansky and Santo Trafficante. The second case occurred in October 1963 when Gambino family member Tony Farina (having been released from prison after his arrest in the 1954 Coudert case, see chapter 10) was spotted in Laredo. A week later, Farina's Canadian accomplice, Michel Caron, was busted with thirty-four kilograms of heroin.

Under questioning by FBN officials, Caron said he was working for Lucien Rivard in Montreal. Caron said that Paul Mondoloni had put the heroin in his car with the help of Fulgencio Cruz Bonet (an anti-Castro Cuban), and that Frank Coppola in Bridgeport, Connecticut, was the intended recipient. Using Pera's precursor tracking technique, tests showed that Caron's heroin was identical to the heroin seized from Abramson in 1962, from the 1958 Pepe Cotroni case, and from a 1955 case involving Marcel Francisci. It was also identical to heroin that two Canadian traffickers were planning to sell to undercover Agent Patty Biase in August 1963.[10]

Here it's important to digress for a moment, and to note that these Canadian traffickers were supplied by Roger Coudert. As we know from chapter 10, George Gaffney arrested Coudert in 1955 (Pat Ward arrested Caron's recipient, Tony Farina, in the same case), at which point Coudert revealed that he was working with Mondoloni in Mexico. According to Gaffney, that was the first time the FBN had heard of Mondoloni. Coudert spent the next three years in prison, but was released after testifying for Siragusa at the Apalachin trial. By 1963, when he was arrested in the Biase case, the incorrigible drug trafficker – who was either "the stupidest drug trafficker ever," as Gaffney calls him, or an FBN informer – was also involved with the Air France ring, and the Charles Marignani organization, which sheltered the "bigger" diplomat the FBN had been searching for since 1960.

Getting back to the Caron case: further investigation revealed what had been known since 1960, that Mondoloni was supplying the Gambino family through drug traffickers Jorge Moreno Chauvet and José Garcia Aiza, an Arab millionaire in Mexico. Luckily for the traffickers, Garcia was a friend of Ramon Luzo, Attorney General of Mexico's federal district and the drug ring's protector. One interesting facet of this investigation is that Robert Kennedy became personally involved, and sent an Assistant US Attorney to Canada on 1 November 1963 to escort Caron back to the US for debriefing.[11] Despite the deep personal loss that resulted from the tragic event that occurred three weeks later, Kennedy's interest in the Mondoloni case never faded, and may have been fueled by an anonymous letter, dated 25 November 1963, that arrived at FBN headquarters, telling how Mondoloni moved heroin in false-bottom suitcases from labs in Nice, through Panama, Uruguay, Buenos Aires, and the Yucatan, to Chauvet in Mexico City.[12]

Based on this anonymous letter, and reports written by Hank Manfredi and other CIA agents, Bobby may have believed that the plan to assassinate JFK was effected in Mexico through Mondoloni's protected drug route. A little-known fact is that Bobby went to Mexico in the fall of 1964 on business concerning the assassination.[13] It isn't clear if he was conducting an investigation, or shutting one down; like Lee Oswald's activities in Mexico, Bobby's have not been satisfactorily recorded. What is known is that Lucien Rivard was indicted in the US on 17 January 1964, based on the testimony of the defendants in the Abramson and Caron cases – but Paul Mondoloni was not.

Patty Biase's resignation from the FBN was another quiet occurrence that followed these strange events. There is nothing to report about his reasons for resigning. That last year in the FBN he divided his time between the frolics of the Gambling Squad and his closely held Coudert investigation in France. Not even the Paris agent in charge, Vic Maria, was told that Biase was operating undercover there. Biase had initiated the case on 25 May 1962, when, at his direction, his informant George Farraco called Canadian trafficker Roger Laviolette to arrange a transaction. Farraco was murdered a week later, allowing Biase to adopt the identity of Farraco's fictitious brother, Jack. The case fizzled out, but thanks to Biase's "spectacular testimony" in Paris on 29 November 1963, Laviolette was sent to trial.[14] Laviolette was sentenced to only one year in prison, but he did drop the bombshell that his source, "Old Roger" Coudert, got "his stuff from behind the Iron Curtain."[15]

In 1964, Biase reportedly purchased a Bonanza Steak House franchise. After becoming nauseous at the FBN's 1966-67 New Year's Eve party, he was taken to a nearby hospital by one of his friends in the NYPD, and was pronounced dead a few hours later, to the amazement and sorrow of his friends. He was thirty-seven years old.

THE SECOND AMBASSADOR CASE

While the Rivard case was unfolding in Canada, a related case was developing there as well. In 1961, FBN officials began to think that a Mexican diplomat in Ottawa, Salvador Pardo Bolland, was the diplomat even "bigger" than Rosal. Although Pardo suspended his activities in the wake of the 1962 French Connection case, the Court House Squad continued to gather information on him and his associates and when he finally got back into the game, the FBN was ready and waiting. In February 1964, while under FBN surveillance, Pardo traveled from the Netherlands to France using a fake passport he had issued to himself. In Cannes he met with Gilbert Coscia, operations manager of the Marignani drug ring, and Juan Carlos Arizti, an official with the Uruguayan Foreign Ministry. From Cannes he was followed to Paris, where the investigation went into high gear.[16]

"Mike Picini and I followed him on foot," Vic Maria recalls, "and Mike even talked to him at the Air France terminal in Orleans. Pardo was flagged, and when Arizti left the suitcases at the terminal, we sat on them. In case we were watching, which he didn't know for sure, Pardo flew into New York as a decoy, and the next day Arizti left with the heroin for Montreal. The French gave us permission to let it leave the country, but they insisted that two French policemen accompany it on the plane."

While Pardo flew to New York, Arizti flew to Montreal and checked the four suitcases at the local railway station. While Arizti booked himself into a local hotel, the Mounties emptied 136 pounds of heroin from his luggage and refilled the packages (except for one) with flour. None the wiser, Arizti retrieved his bags and traveled to New York, where on 21 February 1964, at the corner of Eighth Avenue and 57th Street, he was arrested with Pardo and merchant seaman Rene Bruchon, the ring's link to the Mafia since 1947!

As Morty Benjamin recalls, "When Artie Fluhr arrested Pardo Bolland, it was the first time an FBN agent had his face on the front page of the *Daily News* and hadn't done something wrong."

After his conviction, Pardo told an astonishing tale about a smuggling ring formed by five diplomats assigned to the Middle East in 1951: himself;

his Argentine colleague Enrique F. Lupiz in Turkey; his Mexican colleague Marco Aurelio Almazan Diaz in Lebanon; Uruguayan Chargé d'Affaires Jose Manzor in Beirut; and Juan Arizti in Tel Aviv until 1954, then Athens until 1961. Initially, Almazan (who admitted to making nineteen drug smuggling trips into the US) and Lupiz were hired by Sami Khoury's partner Antoine Araman to move morphine base from Syria to Beirut. Pardo went to work for Araman in 1956 and, after he was assigned to Canada in 1958, delivered heroin to Jean Jehan, mastermind of the French Connection case. In 1959, Pardo joined forces with three people Etienne Tarditi named in 1960 after his arrest in the First Ambassador case: Gilbert Coscia, Jean-Baptiste Giacobetti, and Charles Marignani. Upon completing a tour in New Delhi in June 1961, Pardo was assigned to the United Nations and began supplying one of Roger Coudert's contacts in New York, Szaja Gerecht.[17]

In early 1962, Pardo was reassigned to Bolivia, where Colonel Luis Gomez Aguilera managed the cocaine trade, apparently with CIA and SDECE protection. As Andy Tartaglino recalled, "We asked the CIA for help [locating Pardo], and it turned out he was … playing bridge on a regular basis with the ranking CIA man there."[18]

That says something memorable about that particular CIA officer's ability to sniff out crooks. (One wonders if Laughlin Campbell, the station chief in Paris, was playing tennis with Paul Mandoloni.) And in yet another bizarre and totally unexplored twist to the case, Gil Coscia said the ring's financier was an American, a Mr. Amato, living in Tangiers.[19]

Loose ends aside, the Second Ambassador case generated fabulous publicity for the FBN, and in a March 1964 article in *Parade* Magazine, Jack Anderson heaped praise upon Henry Giordano and his intrepid agents. The FBN had smashed a cabal of crooked diplomats that was responsible for a large percentage of the illegal narcotics that entered the US every year. But the bust itself could not have been more poorly timed, for during Pardo's trial in March, President Johnson was meeting in Palm Springs with Mexican president Adolfo Lopez Mateos to discuss the tidal wave of heroin washing over the border.

As Gaffney recalls, "Secretary of State Dean Rusk called and asked if we were trying to embarrass Johnson, and if there was any way to release Pardo. I said no to both questions, and explained that I had informed Robert Kennedy, and that we were in constant communication with the Mexican Desk at the State Department on every development."

Even great successes were turning into political defeats: as Charlie Siragusa had predicted, Giordano and Gaffney were messing it up, to the extent that they had alienated the president of the United States. But the FBN and its allies in Canada and Mexico soldiered on. Chauvet and ten of his accomplices were arrested in Mexico in March 1964, and Rivard was arrested in Montreal that June. Mondoloni, however, escaped to France and in August 1964, with Jean Francisci (Marcel's brother), met with smugglers Louis Douheret and Achille Cecchini. Since 1959, Douheret (aka Jacques the American) had been the Orsini group's liaison to American Mafiosi Benny Indiviglio and Arnold Romano (who had a virtual monopoly over wholesale distribution on the Lower East Side). As a crime lord, Orsini was not involved in the production of heroin in clandestine labs in France, but he did finance smuggling ventures, and thus had an abiding interest in the sale of the merchandise. Orsini, according to Douheret, entrusted his narcotics ventures to Jean Nebbia, who bought significant amounts of heroin produced in France through his supplier, Achille Cecchini. Nebbia then arranged for Michel Victor Mertz and his assistant, Jean Bousquet, a wealthy Parisian contractor, to move the heroin to Douheret, his man in America.[20]

In August 1964, Mondoloni and Francisci presented Cecchini and Douheret with a proposition. According to Douheret, he occasionally had trouble obtaining narcotics and other times was overstocked, so Mondoloni and Francisci graciously offered to manage those aspects of their operation. Douheret felt they were trying to squeeze him out of the Orsini operation, and he turned them down flat, saying such an arrangement would mean "total subjugation to a competition group."[21]

He would also have lost a lot of money. Since 1959, Nebbia and Douheret, under the auspices of Orsini, had been moving ninety kilograms of heroin a month to Indiviglio and Romano, who operated under the auspices of Santo Trafficante. But Mondoloni's return to France would bring about a major change and, as we shall see in a subsequent chapter, the FBN would uncover the Nebbia–Douheret facet of the Orsini operation in December 1965. Perhaps coincidentally, this would clear the way for Mondoloni, who would survive for a few years longer, as would SAC member Cecchini. SDECE Agent Mertz, as noted in the previous chapter, would continue to move narcotics to America until 1969!

Obviously, international drug smuggling would not abate with the demise of Rivard and the Ambassador ring. Other smugglers were eagerly waiting to pick up the slack, and within a year, fugitive Tom Buscetta would visit Mexico and Montreal as an emissary of Carlo Gambino and the Badalamenti clan in Sicily and begin setting up replacement drug routes to the Mafia in New York. Buscetta would also begin to finance Ricord's

Group France in South America in what amounted to the total reorganization of international drug smuggling that followed on the heels of the Rivard and Second Ambassador cases.[22]

THE CIA'S SOUTHEAST ASIAN CONNECTION

Paul Mondoloni, Michel Mertz, Tom Buscetta, and Maurice Castellani would evade their pursuers for years. But other traffickers were not so fortunate, and on 8 October 1964, FBN Agent Albert Garofalo and a contingent of French policemen under Commissaire Michel Hugues raided Jo Cesari's lab at Clos St. Antoine and seized sixty-four kilograms of morphine base. Not only was it the first heroin conversion lab found in Marseilles in over ten years – as well as a testament to Picini's policy of working with, rather than against, the French authorities – but by exposing Cesari's Armenian cousin, Edouard Toudayan, the raid also highlighted the importance of Turkey as a major source of supply in the French connection. Shutting down Turkey's underground opium economy would be one of the highest priorities of federal drug law enforcement from the mid-1960s through the early 1970s.[23]

Another important incident occurred a month later, when a hundred pounds of heroin was stolen from one of Mertz's America-bound Citroens. Orsini blamed Jean Bousquet, although the culprit may have been Mondoloni. Having lost huge investments in the Abramson and Caron seizures, Mondoloni was anxious to grab a larger share of the French market and, in August 1964, he had vainly offered to facilitate Douheret's operations. Faced with a recalcitrant rival, Mondoloni may have hijacked Bousquet's heroin as a way of recouping his losses and establishing himself as the dominant force in France. Or, the drug smuggling world being what it is, Bousquet may have stolen the load for Mondoloni, and gone into business with him and Mertz. In any event, Orsini abandoned Bousquet and began working through Jean Nebbia with a retired US Army major, paving the way for the FBN's next great case. Made in America by Frank Selvaggi and Frank Waters, the Nebbia case would track back to Paul Mondoloni and the Southeast Asian connection – the inevitable missing link in the CIA's elusive international narcotics conspiracy.

The FBN's intrusion upon this most important CIA drug smuggling operation began in February 1963, when agent Bowman Taylor was assigned to Bangkok on a permanent basis. Hired in 1951 in Dallas, Taylor had served continually in Texas. But his career had stalled and, though an overseas assignment did not suit his parochial personality, he accepted the post in search of advancement. "There was no preparation," Taylor notes. "I just packed my bags and went."

Finding friends in Thailand was not easy, for no one at the Embassy wanted to jeopardize his career by being sullied by the mess a federal narcotic agent would surely make in the Kingdom of Opium. Shunned by his colleagues, Taylor forged relations with the Thai narcotics bureau and with a colonel in the Thai Army's CID. Three months after his arrival, Taylor received additional help when Agent Charles Casey arrived. A midwesterner with as little understanding of the Far East as Taylor, Casey teamed up with a Chinese-American FBN agent from San Francisco to make a case on Kuomintang drug smugglers in the Shan States of Burma. For CIA-related reasons, with which the reader is well acquainted by now, the case collapsed after several months.

At Taylor's direction, Casey next made a case on two Thai lieutenants serving with the CIA-advised border police. But they were the CIA's "best" lieutenants, according to Taylor, and after their arrest the Agency simply sent them to manage a drug network in Laos. In another instance, a CIA pilot left a suitcase full of opium at the Air America ticket counter in Bangkok. Taylor and a Thai police officer tailed the pilot to an American air base outside Tokyo; but the pilot was whisked away to the Philippines and put under protective custody by CIA security officers.

Joining Taylor and Casey in 1965 was Agent Al Habib. Fluent in Arabic and French, Habib, as we know from chapter 15, had a very interesting background. After leaving Tunisia and arriving in San Diego in 1955, he had met Ike Feldman at a synagogue. Feldman recognized that Habib had all the natural attributes for undercover work, and introduced him to George White, who hired Habib five years later, immediately upon his acquisition of US citizenship.

Assigned to San Francisco, Habib assisted White in the MKULTRA project and became a member of the office's Asian intelligence group. Central to the group were Chinese-American agents Milton Woo, William Wang, and Alton Bok Wong, upon whom the other FBN agents relied for the interrogation of Asian suspects and the recruitment of Asian informants. White's enforcement assistant, Daniel Casey, and Peter Niblo, a former CIA agent who knew the Chinese telegraphic code, were also in the group. According to Habib, Feldman was scheduled to go to Bangkok, but elected to remain in New York rather than serve under Bowman Taylor. Eager to get back abroad, Habib took his place. "I went on a ninety-day TDY," he recalls, "and after the initial shock, I wound up staying two years."

The initial shock, of course, was the CIA. "Taylor had gotten in trouble in Laos," Habib recalls, "and eventually he sent me there to patch things up. I reported to the Embassy in Vientiane, where I was met by a CIA officer. He asked me what I wanted, and I told him I was there to make narcotic cases. Well, that made him nervous, so he called the marine guard. Then he told me to 'Stay here until we come to get you.' And I sat there under guard until they took me to see Ambassador William Sullivan."

Habib laughs satirically. "I'm sitting in Sullivan's office surrounded by a gang of menacing CIA officers. Sullivan introduces himself and asks if I would please explain what I'm doing in Laos. I say I'm there to work under-cover with the police, to locate morphine labs. To which he replies, 'Are you serious?' At which point a CIA officer says to me, 'You! Don't do nothing!' Meanwhile Sullivan goes to his office and composes a yard-long telegram to Secretary Rusk saying, in effect, 'Don't they know that Laos [which had withdrawn from the Single Convention in 1963] is off-limits?' Then they tell me how Taylor set up an undercover buy from a guy. He got a flash roll together and went to the meet covered by the Vientiane police. When the guy steps out of the car and opens the trunk, the police see it's the king of the Meos. The police run away, and Taylor busts General Vang Pao, alone."

"It's true," Taylor laughs. "I made a case on Vang Pao [the general just happened to be the commander of the CIA's private army of indigenous, opium-growing tribesmen in Laos] and was thrown out of the country as a result. But what you weren't told was that the prime minister gave Vang Pao back his Mercedes Benz and morphine base, and that the CIA sent him to Miami for six months to cool his heels. I wrote a report to Giordano, but when he confronted the CIA, they said the incident never happened.

"The station chiefs ran things in Southeast Asia," Taylor stresses, adding that the first secretary at the Vietnamese Embassy in Bangkok had a private airline for smuggling drugs to Saigon. "I tried to catch him, but there was no assistance. In fact, the CIA actively supported the border police, who were involved in trafficking." He shrugs. "The CIA would do anything to achieve its goals."

Habib returns to his story. "A few days after Sullivan sends his telegram, Rusk writes back and says, 'Let him at them.' So Sullivan calls me into his office and says, 'Okay. You can work. But don't forget, they're fighting a war for us.'"

In effect, Sullivan limited Habib's investigation of the regional heroin traffic to the involvement of non-CIA Americans. Sullivan referred Habib to Public Safety Advisor Paul Skuse in this regard, and Skuse said that no Americans were involved, that Air Force General Ouane Rattikone was the drug lord, but that the Laotian prime minister protected him. The local US Information Service officers likewise said no Americans were involved, as did Robert Rosselot, president of the CIA-connected Continental Air Service. One lead Habib obtained came from Air America's security officer, Luther F. Gilbert. Gilbert implicated an American mercenary named Elias L. Papp, and Habib launched an undercover operation against Papp, but without success. [24]

Next Habib met with CIA station chief Douglas Blaufarb and his deputy, James Lilley (a close friend of former president George H. W. Bush), regarding heroin factories in Luang Prabang and Houei Sai. According to Habib, the CIA officers were "very well acquainted with the opium traffic in Laos" [25] and actually had photos of the heroin factories. They allowed Habib to study the plants for five days, and as a result of his investigation, Habib identified General Rattikone, Rattikone's brother-in-law, Luang Prabang's police chief, and a Colonel Huang Hsiang-chun as the protected ringleaders of the regional drug traffic.

"Well, the Laotian officials are off-limits," Habib says, "so I spent most of the time in Houei Sai, where Corsicans were flying opium into Vietnam. I got two French informants and focused on them. The first, Gerard Lebinsky, had a plane but no money, and he made a case on François Mittard: eighty kilos of morphine base seized in Bangkok. Mittard owned the Concorde restaurant in Vientiane, where I went undercover and tried to make a case on [Bonaventure "Rock"] Francisci, who owned an air force [Air Laos Commerciale]. But there was no money to pay the informants, and a case is only as good as the informant." [26]

"My other good informant," Habib continues, "was introduced to me by an Army major in the Vietnamese Embassy in Bangkok. He knew the Vietcong were buying opium and taking it to Saigon, and through him I was introduced to a VC agent in a park in Bangkok. The VC were using small boats to transport small amounts to the Chinese in Saigon, and using the profits to buy guns. They wanted someone with a plane, so I agreed to play the part of the pilot.

"The ambassador gave his approval, and I went to Saigon, where I met with the deputy ambassador and an air force major. Well, the major gets excited and says, 'We gotta bring in the CIA.' Next thing I know, three CIA officers are in the room. One of them tells the major that we, the FBN, can't run the operation. We have to introduce our informant to Vietnamese Customs. I told them to screw off. Later it turns out that Vietnamese Customs had a warehouse full of confiscated opium which they were selling out the back door."

Evidently, it wasn't profitable enough to simply protect its warlords and so, as Sal Vizzini noted in chapter 18, the CIA was actually flying opium to them. This was proven to be true on 30 August 1964, when Major Stanley C. Hobbs, allegedly a member of MACV Advisory Team 95, was caught smuggling fifty-seven pounds of opium from Bangkok to a clique of South Vietnamese officers. He had flown into Saigon on Air America. His general court martial in November 1964 at Ryukyu Island was conducted in secret for "security" reasons, and the defense witnesses were all US Army and South Vietnamese counterintelligence officers. The records of the trial have been lost, and though convicted, Hobbs was merely fined $3,000 and suspended from promotion for five years. As a protected drug courier, he served no time.[27]

FBN Commissioner Henry Giordano was well aware of the case and wrote a letter to Frank A. Bartimo, assistant general counsel (Manpower), at the office of the assistant secretary of defense, complaining about the sentence Hobbs received. After Andy Tartaglino asked for a record of the trial, which was not provided, Giordano sent a letter to Senator Thomas J. Dodd asking for help obtaining information. But Dodd was stonewalled too. Which only goes to show that in the mid-1960s, the espionage Establishment was, as it still is today, powerful enough to subvert federal drug law enforcement at the legislative level.

SUMMATION

By 1964, the FBN had more agents stationed overseas than ever before. Bill Durkin and Ray Maduro were in Mexico, and Jim Daniels (real name Snockhaus) was in Peru. Mike Picini was the supervisor in Rome, Hank Manfredi was his deputy, and Joseph Dino his administrative assistant. Vic Maria was in Paris, and Al Garofalo in Marseilles. Joseph Arpaio was the agent in charge in Turkey, and Dennis Dayle was raising hell in Beirut. Bowman Taylor and Charles Casey were in Bangkok, and gregarious, reckless Peter B. Niblo was in Hong Kong working closely with customs service Agent Stu Adams. Niblo had served in the CIA's Audio Surveillance Division from 1951 until 1955, when he first joined the FBN, and had worked for Public Safety in Vietnam from 1960 until 1962, when he rejoined the FBN. He was well acquainted with the Far East and was the first American to work with Hong Kong's police narcotics unit and its British advisor, John Browett. When he reported to Hong Kong in December 1963, the specific instruction Niblo received from Browett was

"No undercover work, period!" Hong Kong had delicate relations with China at that point, which it did not want Niblo to disrupt, so as in every other place the FBN worked overseas, unilateral operations were strictly forbidden – though they were periodically conducted by TDY agents on special assignments.

Like his fellow agents abroad – who never numbered more than seventeen while the FBN was in existence – Niblo was a member of one of America's most unique and extraordinary fraternities. It was a wolf pack not unlike the Gambling Squad, but scattered far and wide. As Dennis Dayle says, "We'd meet periodically in Rome, where Joe Dino had arrived as Picini's administrative assistant to take the burden off Hank Manfredi. Joe was my old street partner from Chicago. Joe Arpaio in Turkey had been in Chicago too, so we were all old friends, and we stuck together."

Alas, by 1965 even the FBN's overseas wolf pack was already being targeted for extermination by the CIA.

22

THE EVE OF DESTRUCTION

"The only way you can make cases is if your informant sells dope."
Agent Lenny Schrier

Sal Vizzini remembers when it all started coming apart. "There was a clique of case-making agents the Bureau relied upon, but got rid of starting around 1964," he says, "after which their cases went sour because 'the good guys' screwed them up.

"My own problems began in August 1964," he continues. "Giordano calls me up to Washington. Gaffney's there too. They say they're going to demote me from a grade twelve to an eleven because I gave a Lambretta to a Thai police captain in Bangkok – and for a few other things. I've got thirty days to appeal.

"'Don't make waves,' Gaffney tells me. 'Don't resign. In a year you'll be back.' So against my better judgment I take the demotion and go under-cover into Puerto Rico for Gaffney and Justice Department Attorney Robert Peloquin, who said that drugs were passing through Puerto Rican casinos on their way to New York. They gave me a refresher course in dealing cards, then I went in with my informers, Joey Rosa and Chester Gray. And through the narcotics chief down there, José Barber, I got a job as a croupier and made nineteen buys at the Ali Baba club. Nineteen cases! I think I'm going to work my way back in, but then three guys jump me in an alley. My back gets screwed up and I go on disability leave. That's May 1965. By then Gene Marshall had been bagged, and within a week the whole shooting match goes to hell."

Rick Dunagan, the rough-and-tumble agent introduced in chapter 19, was a witness to the emotionally charged events that led to the arrest and conviction on bribery charges of Gene Marshall, the high profile FBN agent in charge in Miami.

"It was early 1965," Dunagan says, "and Nick Navarro was the new deputy sheriff assigned to the office [after his predecessor, Anthony DeLeon, became a fugitive]. Ray Cantu was there too. Ray was an older man who'd made cases along the lower Rio Grande and then gone with Public Safety in Panama. After that, he came back to the Bureau in Miami. Vizzini was claiming disability and wasn't around much, and I was working undercover cases with Gene Marshall. Gene would play 'Johnny Manila,' and I'd pretend to be a diamond thief, and that's how we made cases.

"Marty Saez had come down from Detroit. Marty was straight, and together we began making a case on the biggest Black trafficker in Miami at the time, Holton Newbolt. My informant, Sinbad, knew a junky named Old Willie who bought dope from Newbolt's number two man, Slimy Smith. Sinbad put us with Old Willie and through Old Willie we made three buys off Slimy Smith."

When Dunagan and Saez arrested Slimy, he had $3,000 in cash and a .25 automatic. But when Gene Marshall wrote up the report, he said that Slimy only had $300 and no gun. Dunagan complained, and the gun was returned to the office safe the next day. The money, however, went missing, and at his pre-trial hearing, Slimy made allegations against the FBN agents. Before he disappeared, Slimy also wrote a fifteen-page document about corruption in the Miami FBN office. Keeping in mind that drug defendants often give perjured testimony, his most serious charge, according to Dunagan, was that he had sold five ounces of heroin to an agent in an elevator in the federal building, in the presence of an Assistant US Attorney. Meanwhile, Holton Newbolt flipped and presented evidence to IRS Inspections about his financial relationship with Gene Marshall. Working with FBN headquarters, IRS Inspections tapped Marshall's office phone and wired one of his informants, and on 20 April 1965 he was arrested at the home of the informant while taking a bribe.

"Gene Marshall was my idol," Dunagan says emotionally, "and I got to know him well. His real name was Jacob Rosenthal. He was born in Germany and came to America before the war. I thought he was so cool. It wasn't until afterwards that I started to see his flaws."

Agent Gene Marshall, a handsome ladies' man and one of Anslinger's favorite agents, was thirty-eight when he was arrested and charged, with two Miami detectives, for taking bribes averaging $2,000 a month. The new enforcement assistant at FBN headquarters in Washington, John Enright, and the district supervisor in Atlanta, Daniel P. Casey (formerly George White's enforcement assistant in San Francisco), participated in the arrest. "They were at the stool's house," Dunagan recalls, "when this new kid comes up and arrests Gene Marshall. Gene Marshall, who was 'Mr. Narcotics' in Miami, arrested by a rookie agent! It was just too much for the man, and during the trial he went goofy and pled insanity.

"It was Ray Cantu who finally had the guts to tell Casey about Marshall's wheeling and dealing," Dunagan says with grudging respect. "I remember wanting to punch Ray out at the time. I just couldn't believe that Marshall was wrong. I was so mad I wanted to resign. But the secretary in Atlanta, Alice Lee Ginn, talked me out of it. 'Rick,' she said, 'you've got seven kids already.'"

THE DETERIORATING SITUATION IN NEW YORK

In New York, the case-making agents were feeling the heat too. Charles J. Leya, Jr., a Pace College graduate and former Marine Corps lieutenant, joined the FBN in 1960 after a stint with the Nassau County Police Department. "My first job with the Bureau was keeping track of addicts as part of a survey for Congress," Leya says. "Then I went into Group Two, and for the next three years I worked closely with three detectives from the NYPD's Special Investigative Unit in the Bronx. This was at a time when most of the city detectives were deeply suspicious of the federal agents.

"There were about ninety agents in the New York office by then," Leya continues, "and most of the integrity cases were isolated events, and were handled by the enforcement assistant or the district supervisor. But with the Joe Hermo incident, headquarters started getting involved again, like it had under Lee Speer.

"Hermo was in Group Four, and by the time I got there in 1964, Art Mendelsohn was in charge, and some of the agents in the group were pretending to be city cops when they kicked in doors. They'd hit an apartment, flash a detective's shield, then make a deal with the occupant [not to arrest the person if he agreed to pay a bribe]. That's what Hermo and a new guy named Danny McLinden did. The next day Hermo sends McLinden back to collect the money. But the occupant had complained to the police, and when McLinden arrived, inspectors from the NYPD's Office of Internal Affairs were there waiting to bust what they thought were 'bent' city cops. Instead what they got was a federal agent. So they locked McLinden up, and he folded right away. Then they went after Hermo. They both lost their jobs, and the case opened up other investigations."

While the Hermo case put the New York agents back under the microscope, sweeping social changes were heightening the racial tensions in the office. The 1964 Civil Rights Act established the Equal Employment Opportunity Commission and allowed minorities to qualify for management positions. Then the Johnson administration, which was already growing to dislike the FBN, enacted privacy laws that prevented cops from kicking in doors on suspicion. This measure was taken, in part, after six FBN agents forcefully entered a man's apartment in November 1965 and arrested him for alleged narcotics violations. The agents cuffed Mr. Bivens in front of his wife and children, and threatened to arrest his entire family if he resisted arrest. Although no drugs were found, they took him to the federal courthouse in Brooklyn, where he was interrogated, booked, and subjected to a strip search. Bivens was so enraged he sued the agents – none of whom the author was able to identify – and won his case in court.[1]

Wiretaps on crooks that accidentally uncovered political corruption were also becoming an issue, so the Johnson administration imposed greater restrictions on electronic surveillance. And in 1966, the Miranda Law would prohibit compulsory self-incrimination and guarantee legal counsel to persons under arrest. The result of all these new "liberal" laws was fewer cases, and that meant fewer promotions for White agents, prompting some to complain that minority agents were being held to a lower standard at the expense of their Caucasian colleagues. "John Coursey got his grade eleven after only four years on the job," one agent gripes.

On the flip side, as addiction spread in America's increasingly angry and volatile ghettos, Black and Hispanic agents were asked to do more and more of the dangerous undercover work. They resented the fact that Norey Durham, as head of the Radio Shack, was still the only agent of color in New York at a grade twelve, and in a supervisory position, and eventually a group of Black agents filed suit with the Equal Employment Opportunity Commission.

When asked about racism in the FBN, Black undercover agent John T. Coursey bridles. "If everyone had been making cases, there wouldn't have been a problem. But management was unable to guide people to that end. They were hung up on the formality of conducting investigations, of following 'proper procedures,' and making the process technological so they wouldn't have to deal with people. Eventually it got to the point where there was no place left to put the people. But the policy-makers weren't on the street. They never got a gun stuck in their ear. So it became a different problem to everyone, and from my perspective, the only significant White agent was Lenny Schrier. Lenny understood. The others were all on the fringe. Among the Black agents, Jack Peterson was the most significant. He and I caused the last panic in 1962–1963."

Hired in 1959 and known as "the Egyptian," sensible John Coursey knew how to make cases while not making waves. But some Black agents were politically outspoken, and they paid a price. John Kreppein, for example, had a reputation as one of the bravest agents in the office. "Kreppein would walk into the middle of a riot in Harlem and arrest someone," a fellow agent says with awe. "But he was an admirer of [the US Representative from Harlem] Adam Clayton Powell, so a lot of White agents didn't like him."

One reason for Congressman Powell's unpopularity among FBN agents was that, on 18 February 1965, he charged on the floor of Congress that cops were protecting drug dealers in Harlem at the going rate of $3,000 a month. On 4 March 1965, he named seven protected drug dealers in his district, including Leon Aikens and Frank Johnson. His accusations, along with his denunciation of the *New York Times* for its biased reporting, caused a furor and focused public attention on the fact that without police protection, there would not be so many addicts. Other Black leaders like Malcolm X went further and claimed that law enforcement allowed the Mafia to sell dope in ghettos as a form of political repression. Muslims thought to be working for the CIA or FBI assassinated Malcolm X on 21 February 1965. Powell also paid for his righteous attacks against the Establishment with an IRS investigation and, eventually, compulsory self-exile.[2]

By the mid-1960s, the racist, reactionary foundations of America's drug problem, and the related issues of official corruption and the subversion of drug law enforcement by the espionage Establishment, could no longer be ignored. Columnist Carl Rowan noted that Major Stanley Hobbs, though convicted of smuggling fifty-seven pounds of opium into Vietnam (as noted in chapter 21), received only a fine and a stipulation that he wouldn't be promoted for five years. "A kid in the slums who steals a loaf of bread will draw stiffer punishment than that," Rowan quoted a "disgusted" official – Missouri Senator Stuart Symington – as saying.[3]

But outrage and disgust were minor irritants to an Establishment bent on expanding its empire and privileges, and America's drug and race problems would only worsen as official corruption flourished under the protection of the national security state.

UNFORTUNATE INFORMANTS

In early 1964, after he had finished filing his reports on the Gambling Squad, Lenny Schrier was finally, after five years of waiting, made a group leader. First he was put in charge of Group One, replacing Art Fluhr, who became George Belk's executive assistant. Six months later Schrier took over Group Two, again for about six months, and while he was there, his group made a big case on Ramon Marquez, a Puerto Rican club-owner and drug dealer connected to members of the Genovese family. At the time of his arrest in December 1964, Marquez was credited with moving $25 million in cocaine from Corsican suppliers in Chile and Argentina, through anti-Castro Cubans operating in Honduras and Mexico, to other anti-Castro Cubans in Miami, as well as to the Angelet brothers in New York. The case was connected to the one Sal Vizzini was working on in Puerto Rico, and was representative of the new face of international drug trafficking. It was also an early sign that the Mafia was losing its monopoly over drug distribution in America.[4]

Finally, in early 1965, in recognition of his status as New York's premier case-making agent, Lenny Schrier was made the leader of the reactivated International Group. FBN headquarters revived the International Group, after a four and a half year hiatus, to coordinate the organization's expanding overseas operations with those in the United States. The revival of the International Group was also a tacit admission that headquarters officials, group leaders, and case-making agents were damaging the organization by running secret operations that undermined other agents' cases. Alas, this attempt at reform came too late.

"I finally became a group leader in 1964," Schrier jokes, "even though my case-making days were just about over, because I didn't have many informants anymore." He pauses, and then adds solemnly, "Because most of them were dead."

Dead is one way of putting it; murdered is another. This was no small matter, and the issue of murdered FBN informants (over two dozen by 1968) was a major reason why the Treasury Department's assistant secretary for law enforcement, David Acheson, would approve a secret integrity investigation of the FBN's New York office in 1965. The rivalry between Schrier and the Ward–Dolce–Biase clique was at the center of this issue, and according to Schrier, the problem dated back to 1959, when Deputy Commissioner Henry Giordano decided to make his protégé, Mike Picini, the district supervisor in Boston. "But Mike needed management training first," Schrier explains, "so Giordano formed a fifth group in New York.

He did this by taking a few guys from each of the other four groups and giving them to Mike." Schrier rolls his eyes. "And I got to go over to Mike's new group from Group One."

Picini's group made two cases, and Schrier was behind both. The first was on a cocaine dealer on the Upper West Side, and the second was made through Ernie Lamantia, the highest-ranking Mafia informer Schrier ever had. How he acquired Lamantia is worth noting. Fred Dick, then an agent in Group One under Ben Fitzgerald, had made a buy from an unknown Italian, who covered himself by driving a car with fake plates that led to a fake address. Frustrated because he couldn't identify the man, Dick asked Frankie Waters for help. Waters started hanging around the neighborhood and one day he saw the Italian's car, with a parking ticket stuck under a windshield wiper. Through an employee he knew at the Department of Motor Vehicles, Waters found over forty parking violations for this car on a specific street in New York's Little Italy. He told Fred Dick, and Dick loitered on the street until the car showed up, and then he grabbed the Italian: Ernie Lamantia.

"Lamantia was a rarity," Schrier stresses, "an Italian informant. The Italians had the code of silence, but now we can make cases on Italians.

"I was in Picini's group when Lee Speer asked me to do a submarine job on old Ed Murphy [the FBN agent] in Connecticut. I turned it down, but Fred Dick accepted it – which is how Fred got into Internal Affairs. And while Fred's slithering around Connecticut, he turned Lamantia over to his group leader, Ben Fitzgerald. When Picini left for Boston, I went back to Group One, and that's when Fitz gave Lamantia to me.

"Meanwhile Hunt and Mendelsohn located Frank Russo. Out of the twenty-seven defendants indicted in the Orlandino case, Russo was the only one to flip. He had a screwdriver in his pocket when we arrested him, and when we searched his apartment I saw that some screws had been loosened on the door panel to his refrigerator. We opened it up with his screwdriver and found fifteen ounces of junk inside. So now I had Russo in my stable of informants, which included Ernie Lamantia.

"That's around 1962, and that's when the troubles started. There was a guy from East Harlem, Georgie Farraco, selling to Blacks. Artie Fluhr was on night duty, and he gets an anonymous call about a load going to Farraco's apartment. It sounded good so we decided to hit him. I remember that night very well. Artie called me up and said, 'Bring your Kaopectate and your gun.' So we arrested Georgie, and when we arrested him, he said, 'You'll hear from somebody.' And sure enough the next day Patty Biase's waiting in the hall. He points to Farraco and says, 'He's with me.' Well, a few weeks later they find Georgie's car double-parked. It'd been there twenty-four hours. Seems somebody told on him.

"The next incident occurred about a year later, and involved Frank Russo. Russo's a good informant, but to be a good informant, he has to sell narcotics. The only way you can make cases is if your informant sells dope. But you have to protect him. You can't let him sell dope to another agent's informant, and you can't introduce him to an undercover agent. So I met him alone, and only my group leader, Ben Fitzgerald, and the enforcement assistant, Pat Ward, knew that Russo was mine.

"John Dolce ran Group Three, then became the enforcement assistant. Dolce was a good agent," Schrier says with respect. "He was my only competition. But he was 'in' with Ward and Gaffney, and he had adopted Patty Biase. So Ward tells Dolce, and Dolce tells Biase, and that's how Biase found out that Russo was my snitch. This was in 1963 during the Gambling Squad, but I'm still making cases with Russo. And Biase didn't warn Russo off when he had the chance, so Frank got killed. He was stomped to death in an alley outside a pool hall on 108th Street. When they found his body, rigor mortis had already set in. His face was contorted and he was lying on his back with his arms and legs up in the air."

Schrier takes a sip of Dewars. "Russo was my first informant to get killed, and Ernie Lamantia knew who did it. Ernie told me the names of the four guys who killed Frank Russo. I told a narcotics cop, Al Villafono, and he told Homicide. But there was a pay-off and nothing was done. I asked Sonny Grosso how that could be, and he said it was like anything else: the cop on the beat takes a sandwich; narcs make money off dope; homicide detectives make money off what's available to them: murder cases.

"Ernie Lamantia was living with three different women," Schrier continues. "He had kids by all of them and lots of expenses. He wasn't a big dope dealer, but he was connected, and he was giving good information. He was talking about the Five Families long before Valachi. He was friends with Fat Artie Repola, who'd gotten a big name because he was busted with Waxy Gordon [in 1951] and did eight years. Fat Artie supplied Ernie, and Ernie let me take a free look. I saw it happen a few times and I could have made Artie easy, but Ernie didn't want me to. The deal was just to follow Artie and see who he sold to. Ernie and Artie would meet in the Bronx, get into Artie's car, and I'd follow them.

"Then one Sunday night I get a call. Ernie's in a bar in the Bronx. He tells me that he's going to buy a kilo from Artie, and that Artie wants to borrow his car. 'A kilo's too much,' I said. 'Don't do it.' Then I hear Ernie say, 'Here comes Artie now. I gotta go.' Half an hour later they find Ernie with a bullet in his head and his car motor running. The next morning Biase makes a comment. He knew about that too."

Steam is coming out of Schrier's ears. "Now I've got two informants dead," Schrier continues, "and I'm infuriated. I felt sorry for Ernie's families, and for a year I had the same dream every night: I'm standing in a hallway with my gun on Artie Repola, who's on the lam.

"Then a couple of smart cops arrested Artie at his mother's gravesite on the anniversary of her death. They couldn't arrest him for Russo's murder, but they had him on a parole violation, so they turned him over to me, and I tried to flip him.

"Meanwhile Belk goes to the War College and I'm made acting district supervisor, during which time I get a call from Fitz. Fitz is now head of the Court House Squad, and they grabbed an Air France steward with a couple of keys up in Canada. At the same time Fat Artie's up there to cop from Carmine Paladino. Turns out Artie's a stool for Fitz, but he never told me!

"Now I'm in a blind rage. I told everyone that Fitz stole my stool and well, I must have told the wrong person, because in no time Artie's dead. He was shot four times. That's June 1965. Artie was shot in the liver and it took him nine days to die. But he never said who did it."

Unknown to Schrier, Fat Artie Repola was an informant for Ben Fitzgerald at the Court House Squad, and was gathering information about people involved in the Air France case. That's why Fitzgerald, and presumably District Supervisor Belk and George Gaffney, the enforcement assistant at headquarters, didn't tell Schrier – even though he was running the International Group. The need to protect Repola also explains why they and the RCMP agreed not to arrest Carmine Paladino on 24 March 1965, when Paladino received six kilograms of heroin from his Canadian contact in Montreal. Paladino was the Mafia's courier to the Air France ring, and the RCMP agreed not to arrest him for two reasons. First, because "federal agents took advantage of the courier's brief absence to seize the merchandise." And secondly, because the FBN needed to keep Repola "intact" in order to make cases on the people, like Ernie Lamantia, he was supplying in New York.[5]

Apparently, Fitzgerald, Belk, and Gaffney didn't care that Repola had murdered Schrier's best informant; they were content to sacrifice the smaller cases Schrier and Lamantia were making in New York, so they could make a splashier case in Canada. And it was a very important case, leading to seizure of thirty-seven pounds of heroin and the arrest of Georges Henrypierre, an associate of Simone Christmann from the 1961 OAS case.

It also exposed Henri La Porterie, "the man in charge of the ring and a close associate of Paul Mondoloni."[6]

But in another respect, the obsession with secrecy backfired, for by enraging Schrier, Artie Repola got murdered – and, as a result, his FBN case agents lost the chance to make cases on a group of Mafia narcotics traffickers, including Joseph Bendenelli, Vincent Pacelli, and Gennardo Zanfardino, then operating in New York.

THE RESIGNATION OF JOHN DOLCE

In 1964, FBN headquarters had finally, to its credit, recognized that there was an urgent need to end the factional infighting and secret operations that resulted in busted cases and murdered informants. One faltering step in that direction was the revival of the International Group under Lenny Schrier. Another was John Dolce's resignation, on 9 July 1965, to become chief of Public Safety in Westchester County, a job he would hold for the next thirty years.

Why Dolce resigned is unclear. He would not speak with the author. But three explanations – ranging from the popular, to the plausible, to the controversial – have been offered. The most popular, although speculative, explanation is that the IRS had concluded that Dolce's lifestyle was lavish beyond his means, even though his lovely wife Lola was an heiress. Most New York agents agree that John Dolce left the FBN simply to avoid a hassle with the IRS.

Miami agent Rick Dunagan offers a more plausible account. "Right after Marshall was busted," he says, "Johnny Dolce came down to Miami to straighten out the office. Dolce was sharp, and within a week he had us on the sheriff's frequency. He'd have been a good boss, but he didn't last long. One day I walked into his office. Nick Navarro, who'd been a barber in Cuba, was cutting his hair. Dolce was on the phone with Gaffney, and he was very upset. 'I told you that under no circumstances will I take this job on a permanent basis,' he said. And sure enough, at the end of thirty days, Dolce told Gaffney, 'I'm going home. Book me out.' And he was gone."

Dunagan's explanation is hard to refute. But the FBN was steeped in underworld intrigues and office infighting, so naturally there is a more complex and controversial explanation for Dolce's sudden departure. It makes sense of the unexpected, rapid transfer of New York's enforcement assistant to Miami. It's also related to the unresolved French Connection case of January 1962, and the on going investigation of Angie Tuminaro's younger brother Frank. This part of the story requires a little catching up.

Having made an undisclosed deal with the authorities, Angie Tuminaro, at the age of fifty-two, surrendered in Miami in the early summer of 1962. But his brother Frank continued to deal narcotics in New York with Alexander "Tootie" Schoenfeld, owner of the garage where courier Jacques Angelvin parked the car that may have contained the French Connection case heroin. In May 1963, naive Jacques Angelvin was convicted and sentenced to six years in prison (he got out in four). Unrepentant François Scaglia received a stiffer sentence and was incarcerated in Attica Prison without revealing anything about his French accomplices. Neither Jean Jehan, who had slipped away to France with the money, nor his mysterious accomplice J. Mouren, could be located, so the French Connection case heroin was kept in the NYPD's property clerk's office as evidence, should the French fugitives ever be brought to trial in New York.

Meanwhile, Sonny Grosso, Eddie Egan, and Frankie Waters commenced a leisurely pursuit of Frank Tuminaro. And finally, after three years of obser-vation (during which time Egan earned the nickname "Popeye" from the effects of pep pills and from watching everyone through binoculars for so long), Tuminaro was arrested on 3 February 1965 with thirteen accomplices, including Schoenfeld and William Paradise. Tuminaro immediately jumped bail and stayed on the lam until he was murdered in 1968.

With this background, and that from the French Connection case chapter in mind, Lenny Schrier and Frankie Waters provide the contro-versial explanation for why John Dolce resigned. Schrier says that Waters, while under his supervision in early 1965 as a member of the International Group, followed Tuminaro's delivery man to Dolce. "The guy could have been his informant," Schrier muses, giving his archrival the benefit of the doubt. In addition, Waters and Sonny Grosso allegedly tape-recorded a conversation Tuminaro had with Dolce. This in itself does not imply complicity, for again, like his deliveryman, Tuminaro may have been Dolce's informant – and as we will learn in the next portion of this chapter, string-ing informants along was part of the narcotics game. In any event, this information was allegedly passed to District Supervisor George Belk at a secret meeting held at the CIA's 13th Street pad; and as a result, Belk and Henry Giordano – despite Gaffney's best efforts to prevent it from happening – gave Dolce an ultimatum: take the job in Miami or quit. As Schrier dryly observes, "Dolce resigned not long after that."

Whether his decision was voluntary or forced upon him, Dolce's resignation marked the end of an era in FBN history. In 1964, Pat Ward left New York to become the district supervisor in Chicago, and Patty Biase moved into private enterprise and an early death, either from a heart attack or a cerebral hemorrhage; or, by Tom Tripodi's account, from poison administered by a retired NYPD detective at a 1966–67 New Year's Eve party. In any event, by the summer of 1965, the ruling Ward–Dolce–Biase clique was gone and in its absence, Lenny Schrier, Frank Waters, and Frank Selvaggi emerged as New York's dominant case-making triumvirate.

ANDY TARTAGLINO'S MYTHIC TRANSFORMATION

As a result of the Marshall and Hermo affairs, IRS inspectors were already probing the financial affairs of every New York FBN agent when an ex-con and small-time drug dealer named Joseph Kadlub killed a policeman on 31 July 1965. "Kadlub was sitting in a Bay Shore bar waving a gun and busting the waitress's chops," an agent recalls, "so an off-duty cop named Maitlan Mercer, who just happened to be there, takes him outside. Kadlub turns around and shoots Mercer dead. Mercer's partner rushes outside and shoots Kadlub dead. And that's how that problem began."

The problem was that Kadlub was FBN Agent Frank Farrell's informer. An agent for less than two years, Farrell was using Kadlub to make a case on Carmine "Junior" Persico, an up-and-coming soldier in the Colombo family. Kadlub, alas, was playing a double game and, while working for the FBN, he was helping crime reporter Dom Frasca investigate FBN corruption. Using wiretap equipment provided by the FBI, Frasca – perhaps at the FBI's instigation – recorded a phone call from Kadlub to Farrell, in which Farrell said he was shaking down Persico for two grand a month on a phony narcotics charge. Immediately after Kadlub's death, Frasca charged the FBN with systematic corruption in a series of articles in the tabloid *New York Journal-American*. In his articles, he made sure to emphasize that District Supervisor George Belk had monitored Farrell's incriminating chat with Kadlub. Henry Giordano, however, steadfastly refused to investigate the allegations, and Farrell was exonerated when Belk explained to the press that tricking informants was part of the narcotics game, and that they were merely stringing Kadlub along.[7]

Belk may have been telling the truth, but fallout from the Kadlub affair further riled the White House, and Lyndon Johnson's pain was felt at Main Treasury, where, by a portentous twist of fate, Andy Tartaglino had arrived with a preconceived plan on how to purge the FBN of all its sinners. But other matters would come first. "Fred Douglas [the Treasury Department's aging liaison to Interpol and the CIA] had had a heart attack," Tartaglino explains, "and had fallen behind on his correspondence. So Gaffney, who wanted me out of his hair anyway, sent me to Main Treasury to replace Douglas and to work with Arnold Sagalyn, the new law enforcement coordinator."

Tartaglino resolved the correspondence problems with Interpol and took over Douglas's contacts with the CIA. "It took about six months to straighten things out," he recalls, "and just about then David Acheson arrived as [Treasury Secretary C. Douglas Dillon's] assistant for law enforcement. Acheson's first job was to reorganize the Secret Service in the wake of the JFK assassination, and he was very busy doing that. I had just finished the Interpol assignment and he needed help, so he asked me to stay at Main Treasury as his assistant, to help resolve a problem between Henry Giordano and Customs Commissioner Lester Johnson."

Giordano had complained to Acheson that Customs was subsidizing drug dealers in Mexico and, through its misuse of convoys, losing loads of heroin. Customs denied the charges and, in retaliation, stopped communicating with the FBN. This had serious consequences, and in one instance an FBN informant actually bought heroin from a Customs informant, and neither of their case agents realized it until after the exchange had taken place. Agents from the rival organizations were subverting each other's investigations, and finally shots were exchanged in a border town. "There was so much anger between Johnson and Giordano," Tartaglino says, "that a compromise could not be reached.

"Luckily," he adds, "Johnson had been the Customs Attaché in Rome when I was there in the late 1950s. We'd formed a rapport, and when Johnson saw me at Main Treasury, he asked Acheson if I could replace Giordano as the FBN's representative to Customs. Giordano and Acheson agreed, and I did a six-month border study. The final report set guidelines for convoys and the use of informants inside Mexico, and paved the way for a compromise that was never followed."

More problems lay ahead. "After the Customs dispute was settled," Tartaglino says, "Gene Marshall was arrested in Miami and Kadlub was killed in New York – right after he'd gone to the *Journal-American* – and Acheson, to say the least, was concerned. He was supposed to be reorganizing the Secret Service, but he'd complain at staff meetings that he was spending all of his time on Narcotic Bureau problems. He needed help, so he brought on Bob Jordan to handle the Secret Service, and Tony Lapham to handle the FBN. Lapham was a young Washington lawyer from an old San Francisco banking family, well connected in the Democratic Party.

And if not for Tony [whom Tartaglino says was a CIA officer and who, in 1976, became the CIA's General Counsel under DCI George H. W. Bush], I wouldn't have been able to form the anti-corruption group. Lapham saw so much corruption he said, 'You have to do something.'"

Choosing his words carefully, Tartaglino says: "I told Lapham, 'I want to help, but I can't serve two masters.' So Lapham and Acheson went to Giordano, and Henry agreed that I should be autonomous. I was assigned to Main Treasury full-time, as Acheson's executive assistant, and Acheson asked me to devise a plan."

Tartaglino, as noted, had been contemplating an integrity investigation for years, and already had a course of action in mind. He told Acheson there was wrongdoing in New York, "up to the district supervisor," and that the investigation had to begin where Lee Speer had left off, by reviewing what Fred Dick and Bill Durkin had done in 1961. He also asked that IRS Inspections be directed to examine the tax returns of every FBN agent who had served in New York from 1950 through 1965. Acheson agreed to both approaches. While Tartaglino and Henry Petersen at the Justice Department began a review of the Speer investigation, Acheson approached Vernon "Iron Mike" Acree, the chief of IRS Inspections. Already in the business of routinely checking the tax returns of some freewheeling FBN agents, Acree assembled a team of top-notch criminal investigators and auditors and began a clandestine investigation of all current and past FBN employees. Acree reported directly to Acheson in this regard, and for the moment, Tartaglino was not involved.

The irony, obviously, is that Gaffney had exiled Tartaglino to Main Treasury, thinking that would get him out of his hair. But the plan backfired, and through the formation of an independent anti-corruption unit, Tartaglino would exact revenge on the people he felt had hounded Charlie Siragusa out of the Bureau, and who, out of pure spite, were continuing to chip away at his legacy. Orlando Portale is a case in point.

"Orlando was a deported mobster who told Charlie how the mob was organized in several US cities," Tartaglino says. "For years Orlando was not believed, but he was vindicated by Apalachin, and when the people arrested at Apalachin were charged with consorting to conspire, Charlie offered Orlando's services to [prosecuting attorney] Milton Wessel. But there were threats on his life, so when it came time to testify, Charlie brought Orlando into the country clandestinely. The paperwork was fudged, and Orlando testified under the alias Roger Kent. After the case ended, he stayed in America. But his protection ran out when Charlie retired, at which point Gaffney tried to have him deported back to Italy."

Tartaglino braces himself: "Orlando called me while I was at Main Treasury, working on the special projects. I went to INS, and they put the deportation on indefinite hold, and Orlando was allowed to remain in the country."

Gaffney, as ever, begs to differ. "Siragusa had convinced the prosecutors that this man could make a major contribution to their probe. But I cannot recall anything of any value ever attributed to Roger Kent." He takes a deep breath. "As for Andy, he was a good agent before he came to Washington. When he was in Europe he came up with good information, but he never could find the labs. Speer asked me to get rid of him because of that, but I refused. I asked Speer, 'How many labs did you find?' So I'm the one who prevented Andy from being fired, and I'm the one who suggested that he come to Washington. But then he developed an unbridled ambition, and I was personally very disappointed."

THE EMERGENCE OF THE CIA'S CUBAN CONNECTION

As the FBN expanded its overseas operations, displacing Customs in the Far East and Mexico, the CIA grew ever more interested in its affairs, especially in drug-infested Miami, where former FBN Agent Tom Tripodi arrived in 1965 as the CIA's security chief. According to Tripodi, "The break in the Marshall investigation came through my predecessor, Bill Finch, the CIA's liaison to the FBN in Miami. Bill would take Marshall out for sumptuous lunches, and Marshall would keep the receipts and then claim he'd paid for them. Marshall was also claiming payments to an informant [a CIA double agent masquerading as an FBN informant], but never reported that he was reimbursed for those payments by Finch."

Finch told Ray Cantu about Marshall's indiscretions, and Cantu told District Supervisor Dan Casey in Atlanta. (Finch went to Cantu because the CIA had employed Cantu while he was teaching foreign policemen how to conduct drug investigations at the International Police Academy in Panama.) Once Casey had been informed, he had no choice but to tell headquarters, and that's when the corruption investigation of Gene Marshall began. The CIA, through Tony Lapham, would use this same process – gathering evidence of an FBN agent's wayward activities, and then using it to have him arrested or forced to resign – with great success, throughout the entire organization, in the months to come. The FBI, as demonstrated in the Kadlub affair, was already employing this same modus operandi, and would continue to do so, too.

Marshall's removal, notably, paved the way for the CIA's reorganization of drug law enforcement in Miami, in line with its pseudo-national security need to protect its irregular army of cocaine-crazed, anti-Castro terrorists. The problem with the uncontrollable Cubans had climaxed in September 1964, when Manuel Artime and his goon squad – composed of Ralph Quintero, Felix Rodriguez, and Ricardo Chavez – sank a Spanish ship off the coast of Cuba. Working out of a ranch in Costa Rica owned by Nicaraguan dictator Anastasio Somoza, Artime's team regularly mounted torpedo boat attacks on Cuban vessels. But in a fatal case of poor spelling, they hit the Sierra Aranzazo instead of the Sierra Maestre. The ship's captain was killed, and the US government had to pay $1 million in damages and admit its error publicly.[8]

Not long after the Sierra Maestre flap, Artime's camp on Somoza's ranch in Costa Rica was identified as a transit point for Colombian cocaine. Subsequently, Artime went to work as Somoza's business agent in Miami, and his lieutenants – Quintero, Rodriguez, and Chavez – were sent to the Congo to fight rebels receiving assistance from the legendary Argentine revolutionary, Ernesto "Che" Guevara, and some one hundred Cuban advisors. And here, with Guevara, the CIA's counterinsurgency, counter-intelligence, and narcotics operations merged with surprising results.[9]

According to Tom Tripodi, Che left Africa in March 1965 and, on behalf of the Communist Chinese, built a series of cocaine labs in Chile, Peru, and Bolivia. If this is true, Guevara's narcotics were probably reaching his sworn enemies in Miami's exile community. Incredible as it may seem, Tripodi says that Castro would turn off his radar at certain times to allow the double agent smugglers in his employ to slip into Cuba with badly needed embargoed items. Through electronic monitoring posts its infiltration teams had concealed in Cuba, the CIA knew when the radar was down, and would insert its agents at those times. Tripodi would like us to believe that only Castro's double agents were coming back with cocaine, not the good guys in the CIA's employ. The truth is that they were all smuggling dope, and the CIA didn't give a damn. As Tripodi explains, "The CIA was happy, because the smuggling gave a sense of purpose and a means of funding to a group it had trained for a counter-revolution that every day seemed less likely to occur."[10]

As the CIA's security chief in Miami, Tripodi's job was to identify double agents within the CIA's mercenary army and political infrastructure. His concern was that an infiltration team, managed by CIA contract agent Greyson Lynch, had been penetrated by Castro's drug-smuggling agents. Helping him to identify these double agents were Miami policemen Joe

Fernandez – later to join the CIA and be disgraced in the Iran Contra scandal – and FBN Agent Nick Navarro, later to become sheriff of Broward County. Through his security function, Tripodi discovered that the CIA's anti-Castro Cuban drug smugglers were unloading cocaine at secret bases in the Florida Keys, and selling it on the streets of Miami. Within Miami's exile community, the smugglers were using cocaine profits to fund a shadow war between rival political factions. But they were also serving a valuable counterintelligence function, and as they expanded their drug trafficking operations into Europe, Latin America, and the Far East, the Cubans were able to keep tabs, Tripodi said, on "thirty to forty French traffickers with intelligence connections."

In yet another strange twist to the CIA's convoluted Cuban connection, CIA officer E. Howard Hunt inherited Tripodi's assets. Hunt would use some of these same Cubans to burglarize Daniel Ellsberg's psychiatrist's office and bug Democratic Party headquarters in Washington in 1971, thus provoking the Watergate scandal. By then, the CIA's private army of Cuban drug smugglers would rival such well-established narcotics organizations as those of the Mafia, the Kuomintang, and the Corsicans.

THE MIAMI SHUFFLE

Tom Tripodi arrived in Miami with a new contingent of CIA officers led by JM/WAVE's new station chief, John Demer. The previous station chief, Ted Shackley, was reassigned as station chief in Laos, the Agency's primary source of narcotics. Having met General Vang Pao during his "cooling off" period in Miami (after he'd been caught selling fifty kilograms of morphine base to FBN Agent Bowman Taylor), Shackley was well prepared for the job that awaited him; as was the loyal clique of CIA officers he brought with him. Meanwhile, Robert Nickoloff arrived from San Francisco to replace Gene Marshall as the FBN agent in charge in Miami. Nickoloff had served as George White's administrative assistant since 1963. But when White retired in July 1965, Henry Giordano appointed Fred Dick as San Francisco's new district supervisor, and Dick replaced Nickoloff with his own ally from Los Angeles, John Windham. As part of the shuffle, veteran San Francisco Agent Dan Casey became the FBN's district supervisor in Atlanta, and gladly accepted his old friend Bob Nickoloff (in accordance with CIA and FBI wishes) as the ineffectual agent in charge in Miami.

As Rick Dunagan explains, "After White retired, Nickoloff needed a place to go. Well, 'Smiling Dan' Casey was Nickoloff's rabbi, so Nickoloff gets Miami – and drug law enforcement comes to a standstill. The first thing Nickoloff did was undo everything Dolce had done. He took us off the sheriff's frequency, and then he hired Nick Navarro and sent him undercover to New York, where Nick got in a load of trouble.

"There were still only five agents in Miami when Nickoloff arrived: me, Marty Saez, Vizzini on disability, Jack Greene, and Ray Cantu, the acting agent in charge. But because we had all worked for Marshall, Casey and Nickoloff decided to scatter us to the four winds. I don't know where Cantu and Greene ended up, but Marty went to Texas, and I," Dunagan sighs, "was sent to Fred Dick in California.

"Miami was not what it is today," Dunagan says. "There were no big conspiracies. That wouldn't happen for another year, when the Cubans took over. Trafficante, in Tampa, was being watched, but the intelligence came out of New York's International Group. Then BDAC [the Bureau of Drug Abuse Control] comes around and clouds the picture. The entire drug world was changing. We were seeing less heroin and more pharmaceuticals, and more minor dealers were popping up. It was becoming a free for all, but it stayed the same for the agents, whose ability to make cases still depended on their ability to turn drug dealers into informers, and to choose cases that could go somewhere. There were still the same old money problems too; you ran out of money in April and had to dip into your own pocket until July. And there were still the same old punishments if you kicked down the wrong door. Mistakes were always the critical factor."

THE MAFIA SHUFFLE

In the wake of the Kennedy assassination and the transfer of political power from the northeast to the Johnson administration in the southwest, the underworld underwent important changes. In December 1963, Profaci family boss Joe Magliocco died MK-BORGIA style, from a poison pill allegedly administered by assassins working for his friend, Joe Bonanno. According to one source, Joe "was noted for it."[11]

Bonanno had been plotting with Magliocco against the Gambino and Lucchese families, and reportedly murdered Magliocco to assure his silence in the matter. Bonanno also skipped to Canada and applied for citizenship, prompting the Mafia Commission to make two important decisions. At the urging of Stefano Magaddino, it named Joe Colombo as head of the venerable Profaci family. A good money-maker, Colombo was an expert at using stolen stocks and bonds as collateral for loans to foreign investors in Europe and Africa – and his loan sharks were famous for stealing back the paper and reselling it to other suckers. Magaddino also interpreted Bonanno's foray into Canada as an attempt to intrude on his holdings, and so, at his request, the Commission named Gasper Di Gregorio as Joe Bonanno's successor. This decision prompted the famous Banana Split, with Bonanno, his son Billy, and their loyal followers fighting Di Gregorio and those Bonanno family members who had defected to his side.[12]

Picking up where Bobby Kennedy had left off, US Attorney Robert Morgenthau continued to wage war on crime by convening three grand juries: one on the Five Families; one on Joe Bonanno; and one on Tom Lucchese. As a result, Bonanno was expelled from Canada in early 1964, and in August was summoned before Morgenthau's grand jury. He took the Fifth and in October was either kidnapped by Magaddino and sent to Haiti to avoid the grand jury, or was hired by the CIA and sent to Sicily then Tunisia to oversee the Mediterranean facet of international drug trafficking. In either case he vanished and was not seen again until May 1966. His reticence at this particular time is understandable, considering his reputation as an FBN and FBI informant, and his work for the CIA in various assassination attempts against foreign leaders in countries where he and the CIA had pecuniary interests.[13]

In the summer of 1965, Morgenthau granted immunity to aging Tom Lucchese; Lucien Rivard was extradited to Texas to stand trial in the Caron case; Jorge Moreno Chauvet was convicted and imprisoned, briefly, in Mexico; and Sam Giancana was slammed in a Chicago jail for contempt of court. Million-dollar man Joe Bonanno continued to elude the law, and the new boss of bosses, Carlo Gambino, summoned Tom Buscetta to New York, set him up in the pizza business as a cover, and had him launch a new international narcotics trafficking syndicate with Gaspar Di Gregorio and their mutual contacts in Italy, including Michele Sindona, the Vatican banker with a hell of a lot of penance to pay.

By 1964, Sindona had formed a new Mafia money-laundering mechanism, Moneyrex. Composed of over 800 client banks, Moneyrex invested for Italy's ultra Masonic order P2, the Vatican, and the Mafia through Christian Democrat Senator Graziano Verzotto. Employed as manager of Sicily's State Mining Corporation, Verzotto wrote kickback checks to Buscetta's Mafia allies. Buscetta's protectors, the Badalamenti clan, used at least some of the money to combat their new rivals, the LaBarberas.[14]

In September 1964, Hank Manfredi received the Treasury Department's coveted Exceptional Service Award and began searching for Joe Bonanno in Sicily. On 4 October 1965, Pope Paul VI made history by becoming the first pontiff to visit the US. After meeting with President Lyndon Johnson, the pope – who had worked with the OSS while managing the Vatican's intelligence operations, and later paved the way for Sindona to manage the Vatican's investments – made an impassioned appeal for world peace at the United Nations. Notably, his bodyguard and interpreter throughout his visit was Hank Manfredi's close friend, Paul Marcinkus. Marcinkus would soon become a bishop and, as manager of the Vatican Bank, start working with Sindona. As one Bureau agent notes, the FBN had "an old secret file [undoubtedly compiled by Siragusa and Manfredi] down at Playhouse 90 [a reference to FBN headquarters on 90 Church Street in New York], detailing the pontiff's "unsavory pals who had connections to the mobs." There was even a rumor that the mob was blackmailing the man. But that consecrated aspect of international drug trafficking's intelligence angle was too unholy for anyone to handle.

23

THE NEW
FRENCH CONNECTION

"During the time men live without a common power to keep them in awe,
they are in that condition which is called war; and such a war as is
of every man against every man."

Thomas Hobbes, *Leviathan*

Francis E. Waters joined the FBN in September 1956 following a three-
year stint in the Coast Guard and a summer as a lifeguard at Jones Beach
on Long Island. Thomas M. Dugan (Tommy Ogg to the lads in the Irish
clique, Young Tom to everyone else) broke him in on the Anthony
Carminati conspiracy case, which included Joe Valachi's associates, Robert
"Fat Sonny" Guippone and Michael Galgano. As Waters likes to boast,
"Robert De Niro later made a movie about these guys called *A Bronx Tale*."

Agents James Hunt and Arthur Mendelsohn were his next partners.
Waters refers to them by their nickname, Death and Destruction, and
describes them as "wounded war veterans who hated the criminal element.
'Where were you, you guinea bastard, when I was slugging through
Normandy?' they'd say. That's how they got psyched up to go out and do
the things we did."

After about a year on the job, Waters was sent to Treasury's Law
Enforcement School. "The thing I remember most about that," he says
cheerfully, "was the Secret Service agent who taught the class. He said you
could always tell where the FBN agent lived in town, because all the junkies
would be sitting on his back porch in the morning, waiting for their fix.
'That's how narcs keep their informants,' he said. Which didn't shock me.

I'd seen what was going on." Waters cites as an example an NYPD detective who gave his favorite informant a bag of dope every day to wash his car. "That's how it worked. But you didn't tell anyone, especially not the bosses or the US Attorneys, who had to know how a case developed from the first five minutes. If you started to say the wrong thing to one of them, you'd get your leg kicked under the table by one of the older agents.

"There were over sixty agents in the New York office back then, and out of them maybe ten were making cases. The only time the other fifty agents saw heroin was when it was being weighed. These other agents came from places outside of the city, and were expected to go into Chinatown, or Little Italy, or Harlem, and bring back heroin and a defendant. They had a gun and a badge and the street – and the only thing that made it possible was that somebody else was actually doing it. Somebody else was leading the way.

"The other thing that made it possible was the competition between the case-making agents in Group One, which was mostly Irish, and the case-making agents in Group Three, which was mostly Italians. But the competition bred a subversive tone among the agents who couldn't make cases. They'd point at us behind our backs and say, 'The only reason they make cases is because they bend the rules.' And sometimes what we did was outside the law," Waters admits. "But if a guy's a criminal and he's got a gun, we figured he was planning on using it against us. So he got his lights kicked out and the gun stuck up his ass.

"I'm not putting these other agents down," Waters adds. "They weren't wrong. They came to work in car pools, worked regular hours, and led normal family lives. But you can't work regular hours and have a normal family life and still make buys. Some of these agents were so afraid they wouldn't even get out of the car. So there were these two factions: the afraid faction, which had its sense of integrity; and the case-makers, who had theirs, which is summed up in the poem, *The Law Of The Jungle*: 'The strength of the Pack is in the Wolf, and the strength of the Wolf is in the Pack.'"

A CASE-MAKER'S CONFESSION

"In making cases," Waters says, "good informants are the most desirable thing. But I never had informants. I had *instincts*, and I could read between the lines. But I wasn't like Lenny Schrier. Lenny was like a chess player with informants. He'd say, 'There's a guy coming around that corner in ten minutes. He'll be wearing a blue windbreaker and a Yankee baseball cap, and he'll have 100 ounces of heroin.' Which the guy had just bought from Lenny's informant.

"Basically I was a bull in a china closet. But I had my talents, and no one ever questioned my balls." Waters laughs. "They might question my methods, but never my balls. For twelve years I did things thinking I was invincible, and only the grace of God got me through.

"I'm what's called a self-expansive personality," he explains. "As a child I had to learn how to defend myself from anxiety. My father was an abusive alcoholic, and I developed a fear that I wouldn't be accepted, so I did things the guys would talk about in bars. In psychology they call it grandiosity. Most of my life I worked on creating the legend of Frankie Black. Sometimes I'd drink too much to relieve the stress. And I had a death wish. So I became a window man. I'd crawl into an airshaft that went into someone's apartment, or I'd climb off the top of tenement roofs onto fire escapes so we could get inside. I wouldn't let anyone else come along because they'd only slow me down. Half an hour later my hands would be shaking.

"Another one of my talents was testifying in court. It was a situation that terrified me at first, but then I did it a few times and realized I liked it, because it fueled all the grandiose ideas I had about myself. And I was good at it. I could testify about a case made in Chicago!" Waters smiles exuberantly. "They called us pinch hitters. Eddie Egan was so comfortable he'd walk into the courtroom and yell, 'Everybody rise!' And they would. Then he'd walk to his seat and do a little Irish jig before he sat down, while everybody just stood there in awe."

It didn't matter that some agents couldn't testify well, he adds, especially in big cases where as many as twenty of them might be involved. "Say Agent Joe Blow seizes the most crucial piece of evidence – a note that's essential for the jury to understand the case. Joe's a great agent, but he freezes if he has to speak in front of a crowd. A block away is his articulate partner. I'm the case agent, to whom they both submit their memos. So when I write up the final report, guess who seized the note?

"There's a bigger picture you've got to see," Waters stresses. "There's a war between good and evil, and we were losing it, and it seemed to many of us that when justice triumphed, it was by accident. So let me tell you about integrity. On the one hand you had the critics, who couldn't make cases for moral reasons, or because they were inept. On the other hand were the case-makers, who knew we had to be the superior force, because the only thing that kept the criminals from overrunning us was the knowledge that our goon squad would wipe out their neighborhood if they tried. Like the time an agent got ripped off at gunpoint and roughed up by some young wiseguy Italians from Brooklyn. Lenny was the agent's group leader and he said, 'We've got to teach these guys what their fathers knew – don't ever hurt an agent.'

"We knew who to talk to. We got Selvaggi, Hunt, and Mendelsohn, and we went to the social club where these guys hung out. Lenny waited outside." Waters is smiling. "One of them tried to get out through the window, so I grabbed him by the ankle and started pulling him in. I had his ankle in one hand, and I was whacking him in the ass with a pool cue I had in my other hand. Meanwhile Lenny's outside and he's got the guy by the collar. Lenny's trying to pull him out with one hand, while he's slugging him with the other. We had this tug of war going on, but neither of us knew it. We'd just hear the guy hollering whenever one of us hit him."

Owing to what George Gaffney called his "unorthodox methods," Waters was nicknamed Frankie Black. And because of his grandiosity, he got involved in some of the FBN's most famous cases, including the 1962 French Connection case, in which Angie Tuminaro received heroin from Les Trois Canards member François Scaglia, Jean Jehan in Canada, and a mystery man using the alias J. Mouren. After Angie surrendered in May 1962, his younger brother Frank took over the family narcotics business, and Waters, being responsible for the case, pursued Frank Tuminaro for the next three years. Thanks largely to Waters's efforts, Tuminaro was arrested on 3 February 1965 with thirteen accomplices, including Toots Schoenfeld and William Paradise.

Approximately six months later, Waters – a member of the Schrier clique that ousted the Ward–Dolce–Biase clique – was promoted and made leader of Group Four, over the strenuous objections of Deputy Commissioner George Gaffney.

THE CASTELLANI CASE

Six weeks after the arrest of Frank Tuminaro, the French connection took another bizarre turn. On 16 March 1965, Frankie Waters reported that French drug smuggler Maurice Castellani had been bringing "substantial amounts of money" to his fellow Canard François Scaglia at Attica Prison in upstate New York, near the Canadian border, since May 1964.[1] If the reader will recall, Scaglia's conviction in the 1962 French Connection case was based on flakes of heroin found in the car Jacques Angelvin drove off an ocean liner into New York – flakes that matched the heroin found in Tony Fuca's basement in the Bronx, and may have originated there.

New York District Supervisor George Belk assigned the Castellani investigation to Lenny Schrier's International Group, and when prison officials alerted the FBN that Castellani had visited Scaglia again on 25 September, Schrier assigned the case to his close friend and former partner, Morty Benjamin. Schrier asked Benjamin to respond to a request made by Hank Manfredi in Rome for reports written in 1962 by Jack Cusack, George Gaffney, and Andy Tartaglino, describing Castellani's relationship with labor leader Irving Brown. As recounted earlier, the CIA had subverted the FBN's 1962 investigation of Brown; and, as Benjamin would soon discover, the freewheeling labor leader still enjoyed protection.

On 11 October 1965, Benjamin reported that Brown and Castellani had arrived together in New York on Air France Flight 025. But Brown had not filled out the I-94 form required by the Immigration and Naturalization Service, and three I-94 forms were mysteriously missing for the flight. Benjamin also reported that Brown had "port privileges" at JFK Airport in New York and was routinely ushered through Customs without having to open his bags.[2] Benjamin gave photos of Brown and Castellani to Customs Agent Julius Zamosky, and asked if Customs would please alert the FBN the next time the drug smuggling suspects arrived in New York.

FBN agents in France were also keeping tabs on Castellani and Brown, and on 23 November 1965, they reported to Jack Cusack, now the agent in charge of international operations at FBN headquarters in Washington, that Castellani and Brown had departed for New York. Cusack notified Schrier of their imminent arrival, and he in turn instructed Benjamin and wiretap expert Norey Durham to follow Castellani to Attica Prison and to record his conversation with Scaglia. No attempt was made to follow Brown.[3]

Castellani was scheduled to visit Scaglia on the Friday after Thanksgiving, and on Thursday night, with the permission of prison warden Vincent Mancuso, Durham wired the visiting room at Attica Prison. But there were so many visitors making so much noise on Friday that he was unable to record the conversation between the drug traffickers. Benjamin, however, did overhear what was said. "Scaglia was giving Castellani directions about how to handle the business in Marseilles," he recalls. In a report dated 30 November 1965, Benjamin also stated that Castellani had traveled to and from Attica in a taxicab with Canadian and American plates (the taxicab company was owned by a local associate of the regional Mafia boss, Stefano Magaddino) and, amazingly, that American Airlines had no record of Castellani ever having boarded his flights to and from Buffalo.

Back in New York, on 27 November 1965, Castellani threw a belated birthday party for Brown at the Beaux Arts Hotel. Afterwards he met with several unknown persons, then vanished and was presumed to have returned to France. The FBN dropped its investigation, and "Le Petit" Maurice Castellani continued to traffic in narcotics for the next seven years, without ever getting caught; a fact for which there is only one reasonable explanation: the CIA wanted him to stay in business. Only they had the clout to arrange for his I-94 form and airline records to go missing, and only they could prevent the FBN from conducting a follow-up investigation in France. His immunity was certainly related to his association with Brown, for whom the CIA – most likely James Angleton – arranged port privileges and provided an open invitation to smuggle. But Castellani had protection on other fronts as well. "When I got back to headquarters," Benjamin says, "I read a report indicating that Castellani was a confidant to the Pope." According to Tom Tripodi, Castellani had connections with SDECE front groups as well.

The significance of Castellani's escape from New York in November 1965, and his return to drug smuggling with the support of the CIA and SDECE (and perhaps the Vatican), cannot be overstated. INS records indicate that he visited America in 1968 and 1970, and DEA records show that during that period he was associated with Jean Claude Kella, the French supplier of one of New York's biggest drug traffickers, Louis Cirillo. DEA records prove that Castellani was involved in a major heroin smuggling ring with SDECE Agent Andre Labay (a former advisor to Moshe Tshombe in the Congo), and Interpol in 1970 reported that he was "in relation with" Paul Pasqualini, co-owner of a bar in Madrid where emissaries of Ricord's South American Group France met their European contacts.[4]

Pasqualini's source (and thus Castellani's) in 1966 was SDECE Agent Ange Simonpierri, one of two Corsicans then known to be obtaining narcotics in Indochina.[5] From his castle in France, Simonpierri had been sending heroin couriers to the US since 1955, when he was the source of supply for Harry Stromberg.[6] His protector and neighbor, Pierre Lemarchand, had commanded the anti-OAS forces with which Simonpierri had fought in Algeria, and had managed a special anti-OAS terror squad in Paris for General de Gaulle.[7] Last but not least, the French CNO would report in 1972 that Castellani was involved with French trafficker Joseph Signoli and was still running Les Trois Canards.[8]

While SDECE Agent Maurice Castellani and CIA Agent Irving Brown were slipping away, two major French connection cases were brewing in late 1965, both of which, like Castellani, would return to haunt the FBN and drug law enforcement in the United States.

THE NEBBIA CASE

The Nebbia case began on 14 December 1965, when French authorities, based on SDECE wiretaps, told FBN Agent Vic Maria in Paris that Louis Jacques Douheret in Sao Paulo, Brazil, had closed a deal with Joe Orsini in Madrid for "a maximum delivery" of narcotics.[9] The French knew that Douheret (as mentioned in chapter 21) worked for Joe Orsini's narcotics manager, Jean Nebbia, as Nebbia's contact to American drug traffickers, and that Nebbia obtained heroin, produced in clandestine labs in France, from Achille Cecchini. Douheret, Nebbia, and Cecchini were not on the International List, however, and for some reason the French sat on the information for a month before telling Maria – so everything that happened next, came as a sudden surprise for the man in charge of the case, Lenny Schrier, head of New York's International Group.

As the French knew, Douheret had arrived in New York on 8 December, and Nebbia arrived three days later. After being informed of these developments on 14 December, International Group member Tony Mangiaracina checked the INS I-94 files and found out that Nebbia was staying at the plush Waldorf Astoria Hotel. Within hours his phone was tapped, and Nebbia's chats with his mistress, Suzanne Couergou, led FBN agents straight to Douheret and his assistant, Joseph Nonce Luccarotti.

The next day, FBN agents tailed Douheret to a meeting with Frank Dioguardia, the powerful Miami-based Teamster and Mafioso. The Corsican and the American had only known each other for a week, but during that time Dioguardia had purchased the Nebbia facet of the French connection from his close associate, Santo Trafficante, after its previous owner, Arnold Romano, went on the lam after being implicated in the Air France case in Canada. Dioguardia returned to Miami on 17 December, and the next day Morty Benjamin followed Nebbia and Douheret to La Guardia Airport. Sensing something was amiss, he radioed the office and told trouble-shooter Frankie Waters what was happening. Waters raced to the airport and, as the passengers were boarding the plane, he flashed his badge and climbed aboard. He was armed and wearing his favorite sloppy sweatshirt and dungarees.

"As soon as we arrived in Columbus, Georgia," Waters recalls. "I called Lenny Schrier in New York, then alerted the local police. Lenny sent down Tom Dugan, Norman Matouzzi [Belk's new enforcement assistant], Frank Selvaggi, and a new agent, Jack Kiere. Kiere spoke French and had sat on the bug at the Waldorf. We still didn't know where the heroin was at, and our job was to find it.

"To make a long story short, we end up in a big car chase. Selvaggi and I are riding with the Georgia State police and we follow the Frenchmen [Nebbia and Douheret] to the Black Angus Motel off Veterans Highway. They know they're being followed, so they drive right through and out onto the highway again. Everyone else is watching the Frenchies, but as we drive by the motel, I see a guy standing in the shadows on the second-floor balcony, and I get one of my telegrams from God." Waters arches his eyebrows. "I tell the trooper to stop the car, grab Selvaggi by the collar, drag him out of the car, and we check into the place. Then we lay low.

"After a while we ask the motel manager about the guy I saw. His name is Sam Desist and he's a retired Army major. The manager lets us check his room when he's not there, then we arrange to get a rental car so we can follow him. The next day we follow the major to Gaylord's department store and watch while he meets a young guy with a crew cut. I'm in my sweatshirt. Selvaggi's in his black overcoat, looking like Count Dracula. We're hiding behind the racks in this redneck department store, as conspicuous as raisins in rice pudding, but Desist and Conder don't notice us." Waters laughs. "But we see them buy four suitcases, and right away we know they're dirty. We see them put the suitcases in the young guy's van, and we follow them across town to a trailer park near Fort Benning, where the young guy, Warrant Officer Herman Conder, lives with his wife.

"We take turns watching the trailer, and pretty soon we see Conder take the suitcases to a shed out back. There's a freezer in the shed, and it looks like Conder's going to take the dope out of the freezer and put it in the suitcases, so I rush over to a gas station across the street and call Matouzzi in Atlanta. I tell him we're about to nail the bad guy. Then I go up to the trailer with Selvaggi. We make the arrest, and then we make Conder take us over to the shed, where we find 190 half-kilogram bags of heroin in the suitcases. Eventually Matouzzi arrives with everyone else, and we take the junk back to our room, call New York, and tell Lenny, 'We got it! Arrest everybody!'"

A few hours later, FBN agents arrested Dioguardia in Miami, and Nebbia, Douheret, and Luccarotti in New York. On 22 December, Vic Maria and Emil Angles, deputy director of the Central Narcotics Office in Paris, arrested Sam Desist at his home in Orleans, France. Desist had a relative in the Mafia, and as Maria recalls, "From Desist we got information about military personnel who were transporting heroin to bases in America, at which point the Pentagon launched its own investigation."

Because the military took over the investigation, the FBN was prevented from pursuing leads arising out of the Nebbia case, and would not discover

– until Douheret opened up in August 1968 – that Orsini had first sent Douheret to America in 1959 to contact Benny Indiviglio, the Gambino man operating in New York and Texas under the aegis of Santo Trafficante. The FBN never knew that between 1959 and 1964, Douheret delivered ninety kilograms of heroin a month to Indiviglio and Arnold Romano in New York. They knew Romano had a French connection, but they didn't know it was Nebbia until December 1965; and the FBN never learned, not even after the case was made, that Douheret had received deliveries from Jean Bousquet and SDECE Agent Michel Victor Mertz, while Mertz was wearing his French Army uniform! Douheret's arrangement with deliverymen Mertz and Bousquet had lasted from 1960 until September 1964, when Orsini broke with Paul Mondoloni's representative, Bousquet, and turned to Desist. In 1968, Douheret would reveal that Mondoloni was the receiver for the Francisci clan, but more importantly, in 1966, Douheret and Nebbia would name Paul Mondoloni, Michel Mertz, Achille Cecchini and Marcel Francisci "as responsible for the traffic." [10]

Despite the military's obstructionism, the Nebbia case produced another significant piece of information as well. A search of Nebbia's belongings led to Albert Dion, president of a Corsican association in New York, and to Blaise Gherardi, a restaurateur and friend of Philippe de Vosjoli, SDECE's liaison officer to James Angleton until 1963.[11] De Vosjoli and James Angleton had often dined together at Gherardi's Rive Gauche restaurant in Washington![12]

In addition, FBN agents found the number of Nebbia's Swiss bank account and traced it to Sami Khoury's financial manager, Hersh Gross. Tough Joseph Luccarotti remained silent, but the investigation exposed his contacts in Sao Paulo and Jamaica. Assigned to an engineer battalion at Fort Benning when he was busted, Herman Conder became the government's chief witness and received a mere suspended sentence. Sam Desist and Frank Dioguardia were convicted in July 1966. Dioguardia's links to Frank Dasti in Montreal were revealed, as were his receivers in New York – Armand Casoria and Joseph Mangano.[13]

Further investigation revealed that Casoria supplied Gennardo Zanfardino, as well as Frank and Joseph Malizia (aka the Pontiac brothers). Zanfardino would soon become an object of Frankie Waters's attention, and, according to Tom Tripodi, so would the Malizias.

As noted, the intelligence angle of the Nebbia case would return to haunt the FBN. Achille Cecchini was arrested in the case but released, and resumed his position as heroin supplier to the Mertz SDECE operation, which continued to smuggle an estimated quarter ton of heroin annually to

America through 1968. When Mertz was finally arrested in November 1969, he served only six months in jail and, as reported by the *Newsday* staff in *The Heroin Trail*, then retired to his 1,400-acre estate in Loiret, France, under the protection of his patron, SDECE Colonel Nicholas Fourcaud.[14]

The CIA had known about Mertz all along, but chose to look away. This fact became evident in October 1972, when *Newsday* reporters asked Paul Knight for information about Mertz. Then a CIA agent, as well as the federal narcotic agent in charge of European operations, Knight, who'd been in the business for twenty years by then, said he never heard of him.

THE BEN BARKA AFFAIR

Two months prior to the Nebbia case, another political espionage-charged French Connection case had climaxed in October 1965 with the murder of the exiled Moroccan leader Mehdi Ben Barka. As nothing is what it appears to be in this affair, a little background is helpful in understanding why Barka became a drug trafficking suspect, and how the FBN played a central role in his murder.

Several years before Barka's exile in July 1963, the CIA struck a deal with Morocco's King Hassan II and the top managers of his security forces. It was agreed that Hassan would allow the CIA to use Morocco's Kenitra Air Base to launch covert operations in Africa and the Middle East, and in exchange the CIA would provide technical assistance in identifying and eliminating his domestic opponents, including Ben Barka. But Hassan was considering a pardon for Barka in the summer of 1965 and, having agreed to chair the January 1966 Tri-Continental Congress in Havana, Barka's real enemy was the CIA, which considered his visits to Moscow and his potential return to Moroccan politics as direct threats to US security interests in the region.[15] Barka, who was a socialist and not a communist, may also have known about CIA and SDECE involvement in the hash traffic between Morocco and France – very likely out of the aforementioned Kenitra Air Base – and that dirty little secret may have been the real reason both parties wanted him dead.[16]

Moroccan intelligence officers and French gangsters killed Ben Barka, but the CIA and FBN paved the way. Members of de Gaulle's administration were afraid that Barka would return to Morocco and reform its government and were thus susceptible to manipulation. Knowing this, the CIA, through its chief asset in the Moroccan security service, General Mohammed Oufkir, had Barka's name entered into the Paris vice squad's narcotics watch list, as a pretext for arresting him while he was in Paris. The French swallowed the CIA plan hook, line and sinker, thus providing the CIA with a patsy, as well as a plausibly deniable means of eliminating Barka, while achieving its goal of weakening Charles de Gaulle and strengthening his chief rival, Prime Minister Georges Pompidou. The CIA wanted to see Pompidou succeed de Gaulle, and the former was apparently aware of the CIA's plan to frame Ben Barka on the phony narcotics charge, and then murder him.

During this period, FBN Agent Vic Maria was working closely with Paris narcotic agents Roger Voitot and Louis Souchon. "We copied their reports," Maria notes, "and Cusack made regular trips to Paris to check their index files."

Sadly for Barka, his name was entered into a report linking him to narcotics smuggling. Maria copied the report and sent it to Cusack, and from Cusack it went to the CIA. But, Maria stresses, "Barka was not a criminal. He was investigated simply to satisfy those who were controlling the budget. It was to their advantage to make the problem bigger, as their accomplishment would grow in stature as a result."

Barka, meanwhile, was lured from his residence in Geneva to Paris by the prospect of starring in a propaganda film. He fell into the trap, and on 29 October 1965, Paris stupes Souchon and Voitot, at the direction of SDECE Agent Antoine Lopez, arrested Barka outside the world-famous Brasserie Lipp on suspicion of drug trafficking. Lopez at the time was working for the CIA-infiltrated SDECE faction loyal to Pompidou. According to investigative reporter Henrik Kruger, Pompidou personally arranged for Lopez's assignment as Air France security chief at Orly airport (where he bugged the VIP waiting room), as a cover for his narcotics-related activities as a double agent.

Following the arrest, Lopez and the Paris stupes took Barka to a villa owned by Georges Boucheseiche, a lieutenant in the Jo Attia Gang who operated a string of brothels in Morocco. From Boucheseiche's villa Barka was taken to the Château d'Aunoy and put under guard by the Bande de la Tour, a shadowy organization (the remnants, perhaps, of a unit formed by General Boyer de La Tour to provide security for Morocco's prison system during French Protectorate days), described by Vic Maria's informant, Dick Jepson, as "Southern people from the Compagnies Republicans de Sécurité." As Jepson explains, "The château had a moat and high walls and was surrounded by barbed wire. It was a secluded place where political people could be held. Algeria's first president, Ben Bella was locked up there too, along with seven or eight others."

According to Jepson, the Moroccans slowly tortured Barka to death at the Château d'Aunoy. However, a 10 January 1966 article in *L'Express* alleged that General Oufkir had killed Barka at another location. The article, which was delivered to the magazine by Lyon Gang member Joseph Zurita, and which was undoubtedly CIA disinformation, was widely believed and cast blame where it did not belong. That in itself is very interesting, but what is important for the subject of this book is that, immediately after delivering the article, Joseph Zurita applied for a US visa. Zurita listed his address as 10 rue de Dobropol. When arrested, Jean Nebbia had the same address among his papers, which directly ties their drug rings together. Upon arriving in New York, Zurita met daily with Maurice Castellani from 20 to 26 April 1966, thus bringing him as well into direct association with Nebbia, Mertz, Mondoloni and Francisci.[17]

These impressive facts confirm that the CIA, through Castellani and other drug traffickers, manipulated political developments in France to its advantage. And decent FBN agents felt the sickening effects. As Vic Maria ruefully recalls, "I had a Corsican informer in the Attia Gang who said that Attia was definitely not into drugs. But the CIA said to pursue it, even if he wasn't. That's how they operated. They'd front you, then tell you to fade the heat, which in this case meant that cooperation with the French authorities ended for quite some time after the Barka affair."

On the other hand, the successful elimination of Ben Barka helped certain FBN agents grow in the CIA's esteem, and it widened the gap between SDECE's warring factions, which were still reeling from Angleton's allegations that they were penetrated by the Russians. Convinced that the CIA had arranged Barka's murder through double agents within SDECE, de Gaulle fired SDECE chief Paul Jacquier. What he didn't know was that the CIA plot "went beyond certain French Intelligence units to ... the men closest to de Gaulle."[18] In this way the Ben Barka affair assured de Gaulle's demise, and Pompidou's ascent, thanks in part to the CIA's successful exploitation of a self-serving faction in the FBN.

One other important development began with the Ben Barka affair. Joseph Zurita, the man who fed the phony CIA article to *L'Express*, established narcotics connections in New York in April 1966 through Maurice Castellani. He did this on behalf of the emerging Lyon Gang, which was chiefly involved in armed robbery, but in 1965 switched to the more profitable and less dangerous activity of narcotics smuggling. Within a few years, as the new French connection, it would rival the Corsican gangs for supremacy in this arena.[19]

THE NEW FACE OF THE FRENCH CONNECTION

The changing face of French politics was reflected in the movement of Corsican smugglers to Latin America and the emergence of the Lyon Gang in Paris. Composed primarily of French nationals, the gang's involvement in drug trafficking was uncovered by François Le Mouel and the Paris Brigade of Intelligence and Intervention. Formed in 1964 to disrupt an armed robbery ring, Le Mouel's Brigade learned in 1965 that Lyon Gang members were smuggling heroin on biweekly flights to New York. When the Brigade learned that seven false passports had been obtained in Belgium, surveillance of the seven suspects was initiated at Orly Airport. The first arrests were made within ten days, in late November 1965, and the Lyon Gang's contacts were identified in New York, Montevideo, Spain, and Montreal. New York buyer Oswaldo Alfonso was identified, and leads were initiated into parallel rings managed by Domingo Orsini and Jack Grosby. What the Brigade had uncovered, without the aid of the FBN, was an entirely new French narcotics network. It also represented a new determination on the part of certain French officials to combat narcotics trafficking in France.[20]

After Pompidou's election as president of France, François Le Mouel would assume national responsibility for narcotics investigations and, between 1972 and 1974, with the assistance of Paul Knight, would smash, once and for all, the criminal element of the French connection, without implicating either country's intelligence services. But that development was years away, and in the mid-1960s, the French connection was still flourishing, primarily as a function of unconventional political warfare waged by SDECE and the CIA.

In the Ben Barka case, the CIA used Vic Maria and Jack Cusack to frame and murder a political enemy. Having undermined the FBN's investigation of Maurice Castellani and Irving Brown, the CIA also enabled Joseph Zurita to meet with Castellani and establish contacts for this new French connection on behalf of the Lyon Gang. For its part, SDECE had protected Michel Mertz since March 1961, when he first delivered 100 kilograms of heroin, concealed in a Citroen, to New York. Mertz made another delivery in October 1961, which, ironically, may have been the source in the 1962 French Connection case.[21] This makes it likely that either Mertz, his courier Jean Mounet, or Maurice Castellani was mystery man J. Mouren.

Consider also that SDECE had wiretaps on its own agent, Achille Cecchini, and these generated the Nebbia case. This action was taken in

November 1965, on the heels of the assassination of the Ben Barka scandal; and that sequence of events raises the distinct possibility that Mertz and the pro-de Gaulle faction within SDECE sacrificed Nebbia as a way of focusing public attention on the role of the CIA and US Army – which had already been exposed by the arrest of Major Hobbs in Saigon – in Southeast Asia's narcotics trade. This tit-for-tat explanation is not mere speculation. As Frank Selvaggi says, "The French let a hundred shipments go through, then they give us Conder. But we weren't supposed to make that case, and a lot of people were mad as a result."

A temporary end to good relations with the French was not the only price US drug law enforcement paid for its role in the Barka affair: Customs officer Jacques Changeux, an undercover CIA agent, was forced out of his position, and his replacement refused to cooperate with Vic Maria. Maria was further isolated when George White's partner in the Luciano Project, John Hanly, arrived in Paris as the new Secret Service officer. Hanly, probably at the insistence of the CIA, refused to allow Dick Jepson to assist the FBN, forcing Maria to look for a new informant. Fortunately he found one. A Greek photojournalist living in Belgium, Constantine Fondoukian was fluent in seven languages. And through Fondoukian's courage and initiative – and the assistance of SDECE Agent Lopez – Maria would develop significant leads into the Lyon Gang and Ricord's Group France in South America.

Meanwhile, the king of Corsican drug traffickers, soft-spoken Paul Mondoloni, would continue to represent Marcel Francisci in their mutual dealings with the Orsini–Spirito organization. Of all the Corsican clans, the Franciscis alone maintained protection in France after 1965. Most of the drug smuggling Corsicans were betrayed by de Gaulle, and in 1964, former SAC veteran Armand Charpentier – a member of Ricord's Group France – tried to assassinate the French president in Argentina.[22]

Knowing that the shadow war against the CIA, along with his former Corsican allies, had spread to South America, de Gaulle in 1965 assigned Dominic Ponchardier (the former chief of his private security corps) as ambassador to Bolivia, and he posted Colonel Roger Barberot (former chief of the Corsican-staffed, anti-OAS Black Commandos in Algeria) as ambassador in Uruguay.[23] The CIA, then cuddling up with every dictator in South America, did not welcome the intrusion. On 12 July 1966, a cocaine lab in Montevideo exploded, killing Ricord's chief chemist, Luis Gomez Aguilera.[24] The explosion signaled a new *sale guerre* in South America, and after June 1966, every Corsican with SDECE or SAC credentials seemed to arrive at the Club Ex Combatants in Buenos Aires, ready to rumble. The most prominent of the new arrivals was Christian David. A former SAC agent, David had killed Robert Blemant's assassin in the fall of 1965, at the same time that Blemant's successor as head of Les Trois Canards, Maurice Castellani, was under FBN surveillance at Attica Prison. Once thought to be a member of the Guérini gang, David was actually a double agent working against Guérini on behalf of the Francisci clan, with the approbation of de Gaulle's closest advisor on such dubious affairs of state, Pierre Lemarchand.[25]

Then in a development that ties Blemant's assassination to the CIA sponsored assassination of Mehdi Ben Barka, David shot and killed police inspector Maurice Galibert on 2 February 1966. The circumstances are revealing. While investigating the murder of Ben Barka, Galibert was told that a suspect could be found at the Saint Clair restaurant in Paris. When Galibert arrived, he found David playing cards with Belkacem Mechere, "the deputy prefect of the interior ministry police." According to Henrik Kruger, "When Galibert invited David to police headquarters for questioning, Mechere protested. David flashed his SAC ID card, but Galibert stood his ground."[26] At which point David shot and killed the policeman and fled to Uruguay where, on behalf of Barberot, he infiltrated the Tupimaros revolutionary group, while engaging in extensive extortion and drug smuggling ventures with Ricord's Group France.

The CIA was ready and waiting for the influx of exiled Corsican murderers and drug smugglers. Its station chief in Uruguay, John Horton, had served in Hong Kong for the previous three years, and understood the central role that self-financing drug smugglers played in the *sale guerre*. Within weeks of Horton's arrival in Uruguay, the CIA-advised Uruguayan secret police force was also working diligently to suppress the Tupimaros and its foreign links, and had chased the Continental Congress for Solidarity with Cuba to Chile, where Che Guevara was rumored to be setting up cocaine labs for the Communist Chinese.[27]

THE MONEY TRAIL

None of the politically related drug trafficking incidents and developments described above would have been possible without underworld financing. The US Treasury Department was aware of the shift in drug money to South America, and that in July 1966, Meyer Lansky's broker, John Pullman, was in Bogotá, Colombia, negotiating a lucrative mine deal. Lansky's Bolivian venture was, according to Professor Alan Block, "one part of an elaborate organized crime network of businesses" that "permitted organized crime enormous flexibility in moving and laundering funds as subsidiaries were placed in the United States, Europe, and the Caribbean."[28]

Following the Mafia's drug money trail was essential to smashing the French connection, and the money trail inevitably led to Meyer Lansky, the Mafia's banker since the 1930s. It was known that he invested $10 million in Italian real estate through the Banque de Crédit International (BCI) in Geneva. The problem was that Tibor Rosenbaum, a Mossad agent, owned the bank. Rosenbaum was close to the Italian royal family and James Angleton, and his institution laundered money for the Latin American clients of Investors Overseas Services (IOS).[29] Founded by flamboyant Bernard Cornfeld, and very likely a CIA front company, IOS was an international mutual fund for anonymous investors in, among other things, Vietnamese and Israeli bonds. IOS employees funded the company through a clever "equity participation" scheme that freed them from Security and Exchange Commission oversight. Cornfeld's chief advisor was Rosenbaum, "one of organized crime's Swiss bankers."[30]

Rosenbaum's activities and connections underscore the Mossad's involvement in international narcotics trafficking, and its apparent subsidizing of Lansky's ventures in Acapulco, where former Mexican president (1946–52) Miguel Aleman had developed a chain of hotels and casinos. Aleman worked with a cousin of Italy's Princess Beatrice (the introduction was certainly made by Rosenbaum), and deposited his money in the Banco Mercantil de Mexico, "the correspondent bank to Bank Leumi," the "Israeli banking giant" that served "as a major laundering vehicle for the revenues of international dope traffic." As reported in *Dope, Inc.*, Leumi's president sat on BCI's board of directors in Geneva, and owned a company that moved diamonds between Israel and Hong Kong – a perfect channel for smuggling drugs.[31]

James Angleton alone possessed the coveted Israeli account; and through his relationships with Italian royalty, Rosenbaum, Charlie Siragusa, Hank Manfredi, and Mario Brod, he was certainly aware of Lansky's central role as the Mafia's banker in the Caribbean – where Lansky's mob associate from Las Vegas, Moe Dalitz, opened an account at Castle Bank[32] – as well as in Mexico, where Angleton's friend, Winston M. Scott, was station chief, and certainly kept tabs on Lansky's associate, former Mexican president Miguel Aleman. As ever, Angleton and Lansky were the dark stars of the intelligence and financial aspects of international drug smuggling.

Federal law enforcement officers knew all this, and that the prestigious Mary Carter Paint Company had decided to build a resort hotel on Paradise

Island in the Bahamas in 1965. This was perfectly legal, but when the company teamed up with Wallace Groves to open a casino, US Attorney Robert Peloquin, having just conducted a narcotics investigation in Puerto Rico with the FBN, was sent to investigate. In his report, Peloquin cited a situation that was "ripe" for a Lansky skim.[33] But the venture went forward anyway, because the CIA had hired Groves and Mike McLaney, manager of Lansky's Miami Beach dinner club, to suborn the Bahamian government. Indeed, the venture not only went ahead, but Peloquin and former Justice official William Hundley would leave government service and join in the profiteering by forming a private firm to provide security for Resorts International, the company that owned the Paradise Island hotel and casino.[34]

With the CIA running interference, the Mafia washed its drug and gambling money in the Bahamas, Las Vegas, and Mexico; then brought the cash back to Miami where Lansky divided the proceeds among his investors. The bagmen included Benny Sigelbaum (a partner of LBJ's erstwhile personal secretary, Bobby Baker), and Sylvain Ferdman, a close associate of John Pullman and Tibor Rosenbaum, who functioned as the link between Lansky and IOS.[35]

Lansky was the financial nexus, and for decades the FBN kept him under surveillance, hoping in vain to tie him to a narcotics conspiracy case. In November 1965 – in the midst of the Castellani, Nebbia, and Barka affairs and the emergence of the Lyon Gang – Al Garofalo wrote a report on Lansky's French connection associates in Nice. Based on this document, FBN headquarters concluded that Lansky's front men were traveling the world to purchase drugs and make arrangements for their boss's smuggling operations.[36] But the mingling of Mossad, CIA, and Mafia funds in offshore banks provided the crime lord with an invisible protective shield. When it came to Meyer Lansky, the FBN, as ever, was stymied. It could only do what had been done for years; and that was to make cases on individual drug smugglers.

AN AGENT'S VIEW OF MARSEILLES

Replacing Al Garofalo in Marseilles in 1965 was Bob DeFauw. Hired into the FBN in 1960, DeFauw was a talented agent and, in 1962, he attended Fort Holabird's wiretap and surreptitious entry school. "Thereafter I did all the Mission Impossible jobs in Chicago," he says with a smile.

"Pat Ward was the boss," DeFauw says, "and one day I got a call to see him, which usually meant you were in trouble. But this time he told me to call John Enright, the enforcement assistant in Washington. Enright said, 'You have a French name. Do you speak French?' I said I'd had some French in college, and he said that was good enough, that I'd be going to Marseilles to replace Al Garofalo. He said that I should probably sign up for a refresher course at Berlitz, which I did. The FBN paid half. Afterwards I went out to dinner with Tony Pohl, and we spoke French, and I passed the test. I'd just bought a new T-Bird; Cusack said sell it. When I asked about my personal belongings, he said, 'You're single. Get rid of them.' They expected me there in sixty days. And those were the circumstances of my assignment to Marseilles.

"I got there in July 1965 and quickly got oriented and went to work. My job was to identify and work around local corruption, gather intelligence needed to set up deliveries and allow them to arrive in areas under FBN control, then seize the drugs and arrest the traffickers. Or to allow the narcotics to go through for the purpose of gathering additional information and setting up the bust of a bigger trafficker down the road. I was also there to penetrate the Corsican underworld, which was the hardest thing to do. Remember, in those days de Gaulle was funding his political action teams through the drug trade. Many of the traffickers were heroes of the Resistance who worked closely with SDECE in countries where their drug trafficking took them, and as mercenaries in places where it was unwise for SDECE officials to move. SDECE acted as a conduit for drug trafficking Corsicans abroad, and de Gaulle protected them all. As a result, the lines between undercover narcotics work and intelligence work were blurred.

"The last thing de Gaulle would permit was CIA agents spying on his domestic political operations, so whenever I came across SDECE, including any of the traffickers in its employ, I had to back off or risk being accused of being a spy. It was touch and go. SDECE had an assassination squad that de Gaulle used to silence his enemies, and every morning I had to check under my car for bombs. But I had to maintain relations too, because the French telephone service was owned by the government, and when I needed a wiretap, SDECE did it. They could tap every room in a 200-room hotel if they wanted.

"In Marseilles I was aligned with two of the Police Judiciare who were assigned as narcotic detectives: Claude Chaminadas and Antoine Barbazza. They were trusted like Americans [one of them mistakenly], but it was difficult because their boss, Commissaire Hugues, had forbidden his men from working with us. So we had to meet out of town in unheard of places where they wouldn't be recognized. Then we'd work up our cases; they'd give me information, and in return I'd give them items I'd gotten through American channels, like toilet paper from the PX, or ammunition off aircraft carriers at the Naval base, and even .38 caliber revolvers.[37]

"The other problem was indifference. France didn't have drug addicts, so it wasn't their concern. Their problem was lack of the bare necessities. They lived in tiny apartments like tenements in New York, and were ashamed to invite us over. Everyone was in the black market trying to make ends meet, and in early 1967 we actually mounted an operation against a French Customs official, Thomas Magozzi. We took pictures of him loading a little truck with eighty-six pounds of morphine base that came off a Turkish ship, the Karadeniz. He was arrested, but he was a friend of Marseilles Mayor Gaston Defferre, so his punishment was a transfer two piers down, where he continued to move morphine. Arrested with him was Edouard Toudayan, the key to the Turkish end of the business.

"It was hard to get informants in France too, so we relied heavily on Dick Salmi in Istanbul, and Dennis Dayle in Beirut, to develop the intelligence we needed. We focused a lot on three Turkish ships – the Askindrini, Karadeniz, and Akdeniz – that moved hundreds of kilos of morphine base. And we paid cash to informants in the Bekka Valley in Lebanon, in exchange for license plate numbers. We made big cases working like that, including the Watermelon case, in which Hasan Saheen traveled from Istanbul through Bulgaria into Italy at Trieste.

"The Watermelon case began in April 1966, when we learned from Salmi that Hasan was leaving Istanbul. But we didn't know what his schedule was, and there was no way of tracking him while he was in the East Block countries. So we put the border on alert, and Hank Manfredi in Trieste alerted us when Hasan's truck crossed into Italy in September, at which point Chaminadas and I went to Italy. We followed Hasan through Switzerland and intercepted him at St. Julien as he crossed into France.

"Hasan's truck was loaded with watermelons, and it's an awful long haul from Turkey to France just for that," DeFauw observes. "We felt sure there was morphine in the truck, so we took it apart. It took two days, but we finally found a false wall in the back. Inside the compartment were 525 kilograms of opium and fifty-four kilos of morphine base packed in five-gallon Shell Oil cans. The seizure led us to a major French lab owner, George Calmet, who was arrested in 1969. It was a huge success, except that Commissaire Hugues was furious that Salmi had gotten the plate number. He felt if anyone got credit, it had to be him.

"If we hadn't seized the truck, and the delivery had been made, the truck would have returned to Turkey with Belgique weapons which the Turks would have sold to the Kurds in Iran. This link to the black market arms trade is an important feature of the international drug trade. All our best informants were arms merchants, often quite wealthy and very influential, and dealing in gold and diamonds as well. Some were bankers too. They had tremendous political clout, and this is why narcotic agents were so valuable to the CIA: our sources were often their principal means of evaluating and corroborating information. Like the CIA, narcotic agents mount covert operations. We pose as members of the narcotics trade. The big difference is, we're in these foreign countries legally! And not only were we operational, we were accepted by police agencies throughout the world, particularly in source countries. Through our police and intelligence sources, we could check out just about anyone or anything [or plant fabricated incriminating evidence as in the Ben Barka case]. So the CIA jumped in our stirrups.

"When I got to Marseilles, Picini was the boss in Rome. At one time the route went through Rome, but by 1966 it went right to Marseilles. Hank Manfredi was Picini's deputy but because he was CIA, Hank would always be the number two. We all worked closely with the CIA, but Hank and Paul Knight were actually with them. Hank in particular was a fabulous man," DeFauw says with respect. "He was my mentor when I first arrived. He called two or three times a week to see if I was okay, and when he returned to the States in 1967, he asked me to go along as his assistant at the foreign branch. Knowing I'd be working with him made it a tempting offer, but I'm a field man and I decided to stay."

Despite the shift in drug smuggling routes, the Italian–Corsican link was still the axis, and not long after DeFauw arrived in Marseilles, Bill Durkin in Mexico sent him Joe Catalanotto, a venerable trafficker turned informant. Born in Sicily, Catalanotto had matured with the major Mafia drug dealers in Detroit. Convicted on drug charges in 1952, he was deported to Italy in 1957, but fled from there to Cuba. He spent a few years in Cuba but, at Charlie Siragusa's request, was deported to Italy again in 1959. Next he fled to Mexico, where he approached Durkin seeking work as an informer. "Durkin told the old man that he couldn't use him in Mexico, but that if he made cases in Marseilles, the Bureau would try to get him back into the States," DeFauw recalls. Catalanotto agreed, and began providing valuable information about the Sicilian and American Mafia, their Corsican connections, and even Meyer Lansky's involvement in hiding and investing narcotics money.

"Old Joe was special and I treated him that way. I remember Thanksgiving 1966; we cooked a turkey in my apartment and shared it alone. He talked about his family and how lonesome he was for his daughter, who was stricken with polio and living with his family in Michigan." DeFauw pauses. "I remember how he cried when I returned one day from Madrid with medals of the Black Madonna, which we sent to his daughter and family."

With Old Joe's assistance, DeFauw would spend three years in Marseilles making a string of big cases, despite interference from veteran Marseilles narcotic detective Robert Pasquier, who, according to DeFauw, "sold us out." Another problem was that "no one in headquarters was watching." As DeFauw explains, "Ours is a cut-throat business in which the guys who make the most cases get promoted. You work alone, and it can ruin you. It's a Hobbes' War that creates the Schriers and Waters: the guys who short-circuit because they're getting cut out and not getting promoted."

These same guys were also about to become the focus of Andy Tartaglino's cataclysmic integrity investigation.

24

THE NEW BARBARIANS

"The new barbarian is no uncouth desert-dweller; he does not emerge
from fir forests: factories bred him; corporate companies, college towns
mothered his mind, and many journals backed his beliefs."

W. H. Auden, "The Age of Anxiety"

In the post-Anslinger era, America's drug habits were changing as rapidly as its demographics. Heroin addiction was on the rise, yes, but it was confined mostly to the ghettos, while a wide range of unregulated manufactured drugs – like Black Beauties, a potent amphetamine made in Mexico – were available cheap and were becoming the most abused drugs in America. So, from the mainstream point of view, the pressing concern was the proliferation of amphetamines, barbiturates, pot, and LSD – any of which might incite an impressionable suburban youth to irrational acts of rebellion in the Civil Rights, Free Speech, or Anti-War movements.

The old guard at the FBN viewed the counterculture with a cold eye: uppers and downers were a regulatory problem; pot was a "kiddie" drug; LSD an aberration. What else could they say? As veteran FBN Agent Matt Seifer recalls, "Congress offered Anslinger jurisdiction over speed and barbiturates, but he turned them down flat. He said, 'If you include them, you'll never have enough jails, even if you bring in the Army and the Navy.'"

Keeping faith with Anslinger's orthodoxy, the FBN was unwilling to adapt to the sweeping social changes that were rendering it obsolete; a dismantling process that began in January 1963, when the Kennedy administration formed the Prettyman Commission to study the growing problem of dangerous drugs. Unlike studies that had been done under

Anslinger's watch, the Prettyman Commission accepted input from a variety of sources, including foreign governments and Anslinger's critics. Thus, in a report issued on 5 April 1963, the Commission suggested seven ways of reforming federal drug law enforcement, including one recommendation that the Department of Health Education and Welfare assume responsibility for tighter control of non-narcotic drugs. It also proposed better training for FBN agents, closer cooperation between the Bureau and the Justice Department, and reduced prison terms for marijuana users.[1]

In January 1964, eighteen additional recommendations were added to the original seven, including a controversial proposal (acted upon four years later) that the FBN be moved from the Treasury Department to the Justice Department – a suggestion that prompted George Gaffney to dub the Prettyman Commission "a group of misfits."[2]

THE BUREAU OF DRUG ABUSE CONTROL

Although the FBN's conservative hierarchy ridiculed the liberal mood swing in middle-class America, its bureaucratic rivals smelled blood, and on 26 November 1964, Food and Drug Administration (FDA) Commissioner George P. Larrick announced at a press conference that organized crime was taking over pep pill distribution "in a very substantial way."[3] Larrick's charge was a direct challenge to the FBN to accept responsibility for the burgeoning problem of manufactured drugs. But Commissioner Henry Giordano kept the fundamentalist faith and refused to dilute the FBN's mission. At which point LBJ asked Congress to find a solution.

From the FBN's perspective, the timing of the president's request could not have been worse, for it came while the Interstate Commerce Committee was monitoring a major pep pill case the FDA was making in Virginia. Lawrence "Jerry" Strickler, the FDA undercover agent on the case, had purchased 250,000 uppers from a dozen dealers in three East Coast organizations. The dealers were stationed at truck stops and were purchasing the pills from a crooked doctor who bought his huge mail-order supply from a range of wholesale houses.

Strickler's case underscored the immensity of the new pharmaceutical drug problem, and contributed to the passage of the Drug Abuse Control Amendments, which gave the FDA the authority to regulate the manufacturers and wholesalers of pills that affected the central nervous system. Unregulated distribution of these drugs was deemed illegal, and in February 1966, the Bureau of Drug Abuse Control (BDAC) was created as the FDA's buffed-up enforcement arm. BDAC agents were empowered to carry guns and make arrests. Their job was to locate clandestine labs and interstate traffickers, monitor the records and facilities of drug manufacturers and distributors, and investigate drug stores and doctors suspected of diverting drugs onto the black market.

John Finlator, the chief administrator of the General Services Administration, was hired as BDAC's director, on the recommendation of Mike Acree, chief of IRS Inspections. (Acree, if the reader will recall, was Andy Tartaglino's partner in the Treasury Department's ongoing integrity investigation of the FBN.) Finlator had no drug law enforcement experience, and his approach was to emphasize modern management techniques, training, research, and public education, as well as standard criminal investigations. In keeping with this methodology, Finlator filled BDAC's senior staff positions with professional managers from such unlikely places as the Department of Transportation, the Department of Labor, and the National Institute of Mental Health. He hired several senior FBI agents to help in managing criminal investigations, and in a move that satisfied the CIA, he hired FDA chemist Dr. Frederick Garfield as his deputy for science and technology. Garfield's CIA connections assured that the spy agency would continue to have control over experimental drug policy.[4]

JUMPERS AND CHICKEN PLUCKERS

For thirty-six years, the FDA had complemented, not challenged, the FBN. The reason for this is quite simple: there were only two-dozen agents in the FDA's Central Investigative Unit, and they had to call in FBN agents, US Marshals, or state or local cops just to make arrests. But a simple stroke of the president's pen gave BDAC as many agents and as big a budget as the FBN. BDAC wasn't handicapped by an outdated orthodoxy or a legacy of bureaucratic rivalries either. As part of his progressive philosophy, Finlator encouraged cooperation with other law enforcement agencies, and he actively forged close ties with charter members of Anslinger's Army in the Pharmaceutical and Wholesale Drug Associations. He even persuaded the American Medical Association to submit to BDAC oversight, and he formed a good working relationship with Customs Commissioner Lester Johnson.[5]

Finlator's style was effective, and in 1966, to the horror of FBN agents and executives, long-haired BDAC undercover agents – dressed in bell bottoms and wearing love beads – started making splashy busts across the nation. They even started arresting marijuana users, sparking a contentious jurisdictional battle between Giordano and Finlator. Worst of all, dozens of FBN agents jumped to Finlator's shiny new ship. Many were agents whose careers had stalled; others were under investigation by Tartaglino and the IRS; all were enticed by the instant promotions that were part of the deal. Giordano complained to David Acheson in a futile attempt to stop the mass migration, but the Civil Service Commission ruled that the transfers and promotions were legal. And, adding insult to injury, it prohibited Tartaglino from telling BDAC's managers about the jumpers he suspected of wrongdoing. They all got a clean bill of health and a fresh start in life.

About seventy FBN agents transferred to BDAC, including Dennis Dayle (who became its chief of special investigations), Jack Brady, Peter Niblo, and Charlie McDonnell. Summing up the sentiments of his fellow jumpers, Tony "Grapes" Mangiaracina said, "After the government legalized gambling, which pushed the mob deeper into drugs, I'd finally had enough. So I joined BDAC in Baltimore. It wasn't the popular thing to do, but I didn't take it to heart."

Taking it very much to heart, loyal FBN agents branded the jumpers as treacherous opportunists who couldn't have gotten promoted otherwise. And because some FDA personnel had degrees in animal husbandry, or had served as poultry inspectors prior to joining BDAC, all BDAC agents were mockingly referred to as "chicken pluckers." Cooler heads found comfort in the notion that BDAC was freeing the FBN to concentrate on international heroin conspiracy cases. But BDAC's mere existence was a painful reminder that the FBN was moribund, and that a new breed of professional, progressive managers was changing the tenor of drug law enforcement – a game whose stakes were growing higher as the children of narcotic agents began to experiment with pot, uppers, and downers, and the CIA's bastard brainchild, LSD.

THE NEW *BÊTE NOIRE*

After the Drug Abuse Control Amendments were enacted in 1966, there was no more licit production of LSD. Senator Thomas Dodd railed against the drug at congressional hearings, and in March 1966, *Life Magazine* published an article claiming that it drove people insane. There were even rumors that it caused chromosome damage and mutant babies. The bad (though totally inaccurate) publicity prompted the world's largest producer of LSD, Sandoz in Switzerland, to voluntarily recall all of the acid it had distributed to research scientists. From then on, only the National Institute of Mental Health (NIMH) was permitted to toy with LSD.[6] Ironically, two CIA specialists were assigned to the joint FDA/NIMH Psychotomimetic Advisory Committee that processed research applications: Dr. Harris Isbell, who'd kept seven heroin addicts addled on acid for seventy-seven days straight at the Lexington Farm, and Dr. Carl Pfeiffer, who'd tested LSD on unwitting convicts at the Atlanta Penitentiary. Under their dubious direction, all independent scholastic and scientific research involving LSD ground to a halt, leaving the CIA alone in possession of the psychedelic's sacred secrets – secrets it had gleaned over fifteen years of experimentation, much of which had been conducted in FBN safehouses. And the government began pursuing terrible Tim Leary, America's most vocal promoter of acid for the masses.[7]

A flagrant self-promoter with a self-destructive Messiah complex, Leary, in one respect, was a victim of government propaganda. By any measure, his methods were more humane than those of Isbell or Pfeiffer, for Leary's subjects were all willing volunteers. But he vociferously advocated the use of what had become an illegal substance, and he'd made the unforgivable mistake of giving LSD to Mary Pinchot Meyer, the ex-wife of CIA officer Cord Meyer, Jr. Mary's murder on 12 October 1964 remains unsolved, and may have been related to the fact that she had given LSD to members of the Washington Establishment, including, perhaps, her lover, President Kennedy. Mary Meyer and Leary had struck up a friendship in the early 1960s, and she had kept him apprised of the Establishment scions to whom she gave LSD.[8] There was an espionage angle as well. Her sister was married to *Washington Post* editor Ben Bradlee, a CIA asset, and Mary had attended Vassar with James Angleton's wife, Cicely d'Autremont. Angleton became the custodian of Mary's children, and for reasons that undoubtedly concerned the CIA's relationship with Leary and LSD, he absconded with her diary within days of her death.[9]

If not directly involved in the CIA's intrigues, Leary was at least aware of its central role in sprinkling LSD at the upper levels of society and academia, from whence, with his assistance, it trickled down to the hoi polloi. But he was neither a physician nor a protected CIA specialist. On the contrary, he advocated LSD as an antidote to authority, and after being fired from Harvard for distributing acid without a medical license, he became the resident LSD guru on the New York estate of William M. Hitchcock. A nephew of Andrew Mellon, Hitchcock had financial ties to Bernie Cornfeld's shady international mutual fund, Investors Overseas Services. Leary also teamed up with the grand wizard of acid, Augustus

Owsley Stanley, the inventor of a floating lab technique for making top-notch LSD. Hitchcock, Leary, and Owsley (the grandson of a Kentucky Senator) joined forces with the Brotherhood of Eternal Love – the official church of LSD, formed in 1966 by motorcycle gang leader John Griggs in Laguna Beach, California – and thus became the object of every decent American mother's disapproval.[10]

After his dismissal from Harvard, Leary relocated to Mexico and on 23 December 1965, while returning to the United States, was arrested in Laredo, Texas, for possession of three ounces of pot. The charge carried with it a potential thirty-year prison sentence. The process of public vilification accelerated in April 1966, when a demented county prosecutor, G. Gordon Liddy, led an old fashioned swoop raid on Hitchcock's Millburg utopia. Tim Leary was acquitted of all charges, because dimwitted Liddy hadn't read him his rights, but the blundering former FBI agent gained the admiration of law and order advocates everywhere, and the spectacular arrest catapulted Leary into a *bête noire* status formerly reserved for Lucky Luciano.[11]

With all the publicity generated by Leary, the focus of federal drug law enforcement came to encompass LSD and pharmaceuticals, as well as heroin. But the CIA was still immune from scrutiny and continued to subsidize LSD specialists like Dr. Louis West. Famous within his circle for having administered a lethal dose of LSD to an elephant, West had also examined Jack Ruby prior to Ruby's cryptic 1964 interview with Warren Commission chief, Earl Warren.[12] Through cutouts like West, the CIA established second-generation MKULTRA substations around the country. The Center for the Study and Reduction of Violence at UCLA, for example, programmed "pre-delinquent" urban Black males at the California Medical Facility at Vacaville State Prison. The ulterior motive was to create a covert army of push-button agent provocateurs, in anticipation of a general uprising by society's new barbarians. As part of this secret police program, George White's friend from the OSS days, Dr. James Hamilton, conducted LSD experiments on an estimated 1,000 inmates at Vacaville, starting in 1967.[13]

THE NEW DRUG LORDS

Ever eager to expand its arsenal of biochemical weapons, the CIA, through its Special Operations Division, searched the world for wonder-drugs. In this endeavor it hired retired CIA officer J. C. King (former head of the Western Hemisphere Division and initiator of assassination plots against

Fidel Castro) to form the Amazon Natural Drug Company in 1966 in Peru. A CIA proprietary company, ANDCO's stated purpose was to "explore the commercial uses of natural plants and chemical derivatives thereof."[14] Helping King were CIA officers familiar with the local folklore and trained to identify the region's various lethal and hallucinogenic drugs, including yage, a potent psychedelic called "the final fix" by William Burroughs.[15]

Curiously, a CIA officer named Garland "Dee" Williams arrived in Peru in 1967 as ANDCO's director of operations. This is intriguing, first because Garland H. Williams is such an important figure in FBN history, and because he retired from government service in May 1964, which left him available for a secret assignment in South America. Our Garland Williams was a career narcotic agent, and Garland "Dee" Williams "knew the way of drug smugglers."[16] Our Garland was a professional soldier and dedicated anti-communist, and "Dee" Williams and J. C. King used ANDCO as a cover to advise Peru's special forces in jungle warfare operations, so they could combat the indigenous people and their Cuban advisors. Furthermore, our Garland had a background in chemical warfare, and may have helped George White set up the MKULTRA pad in San Francisco, while Garland "Dee" Williams was involved in MKULTRA research. To this end he hired exotic animal exporter Mike Tsalickis as his guide. Tsalickis based his operation in Leticia on the Amazon River, where Peru and Colombia rub shoulders. While serving as the government's consular officer in the region, Tsalickis helped Williams and King obtain plant specimens for use in post-MKULTRA projects.

Arrested for smuggling over a ton of cocaine into Florida in 1988, Tsalickis was still in prison in 1996 when the author sent him a photo of former FBN agent Garland H. Williams and asked if the man in the photo was Dee Williams from ANDCO. Tsalickis said he was not. Garland Williams's family insists that after leaving Africa in 1963 and retiring in 1964, he married and settled down near Memphis, Tennessee.

Despite this curious case of the name "Garland Williams" appearing in regard to an espionage affair with a drug angle – for there was also the "Colonel Williams" who funded the Pawley–Cooke public relations blitz in Taiwan in 1950 – it seems more than mere coincidence that the CIA was present at the hub of world cocaine production in 1966, just as Ricord's Group France, with Mafia financing through Tom Buscetta, was organizing the business into a global industry. One member of Group France, Corsican Paul Chastagnier, had been an associate of Paul Mondoloni since 1954 and was based in Guayaquil, Ecuador, which is described by researcher Gerard Colby as "home of a bevy of cocaine processing plants thriving under a

CIA-backed military dictatorship." [17] The implication is that Chastagnier's operation, which would become a target of the FBN's largest international investigation, was known to the CIA, if not actually protected by it until 1967, when the CIA decided to reorganize the region's drug trade.

In the same way that big-city vice squads across America managed the Mafia's drug distribution operations, the CIA oversaw the international narcotics trade on behalf of the Establishment. In South America, as elsewhere, it invariably did so in concert with right-wing dictatorships. CIA counterinsurgency advisors (like Dee Williams) in Colombia, Peru, and Ecuador "greatly enhanced the power of drug-smuggling uniformed warlords and Nazi refugees." [18] The purpose in bolstering these mercenaries was to facilitate the anti-communist crusade, and in April 1967, CIA officer Felix Rodriguez, a former subordinate of anti-Castro terrorist and drug smuggler Manuel Artime, traveled to Bolivia to assassinate Che Guevara. Notably, the cocaine trade "was already so widespread in the guerrilla's area of operations that Guevara's training camp was first discovered by police looking for a cocaine-processing plant, not for revolutionaries." [19]

CIA officer Felix Rodriguez led the team of Bolivian soldiers that captured, killed, and dismembered Che Guevara. But Guevara's whereabouts were discovered by a Bolivian narcotics unit and, in this respect, his assassination illustrates how the CIA selectively exploits drug law enforcement for political purposes. As FBN/CIA Agent Tom Tripodi explained, the Communist Chinese, through Guevara, were believed to have set up a network of cocaine labs in Chile among the Chinese population. The network soon spread to Peru and Bolivia. "It was a classic case of a covert intelligence operation utilizing drug trafficking as a double-barreled weapon," Tripodi said. [20]

It was classic in the sense that all the major intelligence agencies, be they American, French, Bulgarian, or Chinese, use the illicit drug trade to advance their national security interests.

COMPROMISING POSITIONS

Back in the states, the FBN continued to cover the CIA's MKULTRA political and sexual blackmail schemes at its various safehouses. As Art Fluhr recalls, "After Gaffney was sent to headquarters as part of the general house cleaning, Belk stepped in as district supervisor in New York and was given a CIA contract. How it happened I don't know. George said that he never actually met anyone from the CIA, but that Siragusa told him to cooperate if and when he was contacted. Later the CIA did call. They told Belk, 'You'll have this checking account, but don't write any checks other than for rent and the maintenance of the [13th Street] apartment.'"

According to Fluhr, the CIA used Belk's account as a slush fund for foreign officials on its payroll. "Sometimes we were told to babysit people for the CIA while they were in town. One time it was a group of Burmese generals. They came to New York for a couple of days and when they weren't at the UN, they used the money in Belk's account to go on a shopping spree. They went down to the electronics shops on Canal Street and filled suitcases full of stuff."

Like Irving Brown, the close friend of Corsican drug smuggler Maurice Castellani, the Burmese generals had been ushered through Customs without inspection, and one can imagine what they brought into America in those same suitcases!

Fluhr frowns. "One day Belk comes up to me and says, 'It's the strangest thing: some days the account's got a million dollars in it; the next day it's empty and I can't pay the rent!'"

While the CIA was busy suborning the FBN, it was also conspiring with Customs, and using Customs positions to cover its agents, at a time when Customs and the FBN were fighting for hegemony in Latin America and the Far East. Leading the charge on behalf of Customs was Dave Ellis, protégé of Al Scharff and a member of a secret, ruling clique within Customs. Having distinguished himself in the Holy War against the FBN, which started with the George White scandals of 1954, Ellis was rewarded with a transfer to Washington headquarters in 1959, where he reorganized the customs service's Investigations Branch. In 1961, he became the point of contact for domestic CIA operations. The Agency was responsible for these special investigations, but Customs units handled the bugging and wiretapping, and whatever else was needed. Ellis organized one special CIA unit in Houston, which had a covert budget of $25 million and operated out of Miami into Cuba. His prestige grew and, in 1965, Ellis became chief of operations at Customs. Meanwhile, Ernie Gentry had landed in Washington as Giordano's administrative assistant, and he and Ellis, old rivals from Texas, squared off at the highest echelons of their respective organizations. This was no easy task for Gentry, as Ellis believed the FBN was riddled with corruption.

By 1966, the FBN had been pushed to the brink of extinction through its bureaucratic wars with Customs, BDAC, and the FBI; by Andy Tartaglino's integrity investigation; and by the usual CIA shenanigans. But it was George Gaffney who inadvertently provided President Johnson with a pretext for pushing the teetering Bureau into oblivion. The catalyst was Assistant US Attorney William Bittman's investigation of freewheeling Bobby Baker, LBJ's personal secretary in the Senate for eight years. Baker was being investigated for influence peddling and fraud, and LBJ was concerned that the inquiry might reveal, as some cynics believed, that he had made substantial profits from Baker's operations, including a sizable kickback for securing a $7 billion defense contract for the General Dynamics plant in Ft. Worth, Texas. Baker had gambling syndicate connections in Las Vegas, Chicago, Louisiana, and the Caribbean, and was even thought to have directed a prostitution and political blackmail ring that catered to the Washington elite. The investigation, obviously, was fraught with political perils, but Bittman managed to flip Baker's business associate, Wayne Bromley, and Bromley agreed to lure Baker into an incriminating conversation about his shady business deals.

As Gaffney recalls, "Bittman had gone to the FBI for assistance, but Hoover had declined to investigate Baker [so as not to antagonize LBJ]. So Main Justice came to us. Giordano was out of town, and I was acting Commissioner and I had no choice: the Treasury secretary had issued a letter directing that we cooperate with Justice. So I assigned Agent Johnny Thompson to do the job."

An FBN agent since 1955, Thompson had spent his entire career in the Washington field office, doubling as the FBN's top technician and as an instructor at Treasury's technical aides school. As Thompson recalls, "When I was called into Gaffney's office, Bittman was already there with Bromley, and we wired him on the spot. I told Bromley not to turn the microphone on while he was in the airplane, then I caught another plane to Los Angeles myself."

Then assigned to the LA office, Agent Richard E. Salmi says, "Late one afternoon Fred Dick came out of his office, pointed to five guys in the room and said, 'All of you, help Johnny Thompson.' So the five of us went to the airport where we met Thompson, who gets off the plane with four KAL kits. A KAL kit is an attaché case with a tape recorder and earphones. It receives messages from a hidden microphone. Thompson didn't say who we're going to bug, only that someone was meeting someone in a hotel at eight o'clock, and that the guy was wired.

"Thompson broke us up into two-man teams and scattered us around the hotel, so we'd have the meeting covered. I went with Thompson and we checked in to a room; we set up our equipment near a window overlooking the lobby, and we waited, and after a while the machine activated and automatically turned on the tape. While I'm listening, I start scribbling notes on a yellow legal pad. As I recall, Baker and Bromley were mapping out a business deal that had something to do with grain silos in Texas. It was about a twenty-minute conversation, and I took about six pages of notes, which turned out to be lucky, because as we found out at the trial, none of the KAL sets had worked, and my notes were the only admissible evidence."

"This was all happening very fast," Thompson says. "Baker and Bromley were supposed to be in the hotel lounge, but they went into the hallway instead. So we were set up in the wrong places. But we did have Salmi's notes, which enabled the Justice Department to prosecute."

As a result of the FBN surveillance, Baker was indicted in 1966 for tax evasion and the misuse of campaign funds. Stunned, the Johnson administration drafted a bill restricting wiretaps on anyone but political subversives. Next, Senator Edward Long (D-MS) decided to hold hearings on illegal FBI wiretaps, and through his inquiry he came to learn of the FBN's safe-house activities on behalf of the CIA. Long asked Treasury under secretary Joseph Barr for an explanation, but Barr had no idea of what was going on behind his back. So, on 22 January 1967, Barr summoned the CIA's assistant deputy director of plans, Desmond Fitzgerald; MKULTRA boss Sid Gottlieb; the Treasury Department's General Counsel, Frederick Smith; the acting assistant secretary for law enforcement, True Davis; and Andy Tartaglino's boss at Main Treasury, undercover CIA officer Tony Lapham.[21]

Barr commenced the meeting by asking if the CIA was using the FBN as a cover for illegal domestic operations. Playing coy, the Agency men said the only activities they knew about were old ones, in which audio equipment had been loaned to the FBN for tests and then returned. They noted that Pete Niblo had been transferred to the San Francisco office in 1955, but they neglected to add that George White was setting up his little MKULTRA shop of horrors at the time. Though unaware of the MKULTRA Program, Barr confronted the CIA with the fact that audio equipment had been purchased by the FBN, "for CIA purposes" – at which point the disingenuous CIA officers checked their watches and said they had to go. A meeting to discuss that delicate issue was scheduled for the following day.[22]

At the 23 January meeting the CIA officers met alone with Treasury General Counsel Smith and admitted that they had given the FBN $20,000 worth of receivers and microphones. There was no indication that these were the KAL sets used in the Baker surveillance, nor was there any mention of Marty Pera's dalliance with Devenco in New York. Smith, however, did ask if the equipment was used by the FBN so the CIA could get around "jurisdictional troubles" with the FBI. He also inquired if it was true that the FBN maintained "a lab" for the CIA on the West Coast. A deafening silence ensued, and a third meeting was hastily scheduled.

On 24 January, at the direction of Richard Helms (acting director of central intelligence since June 1966), Gottlieb met alone with Henry Giordano. According to Gottlieb, Giordano said that if the CIA wanted to avoid a flap, it ought to "turn the Long Committee off." The meeting ended on a sour note, and the CIA decided to help LBJ and the FBI pull the plug on the FBN.

At a final meeting on 25 January, Gottlieb told Smith that the CIA had, in fact, given money to the FBN for a "pad" (not a lab), but that it was used only for FBN operations. Gottlieb admitted that the CIA had shared in the intelligence take and had "obtained information from the FBN on informant behavior … which was of obvious interest to us in connection with our own investigative work." But, he added, the arrangement had been terminated in 1965.

Gottlieb's explanation satisfied Barr, Smith, and Senator Long, and by Tartaglino's account, Tony Lapham ordered him to shut down the New York MKULTRA pad shortly thereafter. As Art Fluhr recalls, "We gave the furniture to the Salvation Army, and took the drapes off the windows and put them up in our office." And Tartaglino opened a more luxurious CIA safehouse on Sutton Place.

Like any CIA cover story, the one given to the Treasury officials and Senator Long was plausible enough, and the implications frightening enough, to subvert their investigations. The truth, however, is that the CIA was deeply involved in the drug business, at home and abroad. Guarding this dirty little secret was its motive for wanting to eradicate the FBN, which was rapidly expanding overseas and trespassing on the CIA's covert operations. But first the CIA had to protect its FBN assets, including incorrigible Sal Vizzini.

CIA DAMAGE CONTROL

"When I got to Bangkok in 1963, it was the same thing as Turkey," Vizzini explains. "I had to grease the foreign cops to send out crews, and when they were ready to make the case, I'd step in to supervise and take photos. So I put down in a report that I was in Chiang Mai when a seizure was made, even though I got there four hours later. You're not supposed to do that, but Siragusa had sent me to Thailand specifically to steal cases from Customs, so we could justify setting up an office in Bangkok. Then Charlie found out about the CIA hit gun I'd found in his car in Italy, and that's when he forgot that he sent me to Thailand to sink Customs. Next thing I know I'm down from a twelve to an eleven. He also accused me of profiteering on the black market in Turkey, which was totally untrue. Hal Fiedler, the CIA officer in Istanbul, had asked me to buy, and later sell, some office equipment as a way of bringing certain police officials into his camp. None of the money went into my own pocket. But the last straw came when I stood up for Gene Marshall. I testified at his trial that I thought he'd been set up."

Gaffney wanted Vizzini to stay in the FBN and accept a transfer to San Francisco, but the CIA told Vizzini to fade the heat. They said they'd take care of him, and when he resigned in June 1966, they helped him to get a job as police chief in South Miami. Vizzini was protected, as were other FBN agents, like Ike Feldman. But by 1967, the FBN's overseas contingent was stumbling onto more and more CIA drug deals, so the spooks decided to commandeer overseas drug law enforcement altogether. The decision was shared with the protected few, but everyone felt the impact, and not everyone liked the feeling.

FBN Agent John G. Evans, for example, was not happy with the way things were unfolding. A case-maker and a man of rock-solid integrity, Evans joined the FBN in 1955 and served continually in his hometown of Detroit until his transfer to Washington in 1966, where he became an assistant to enforcement chief John Enright. At this point in time, according to Evans, Giordano and Gaffney had argued over personnel assignments and were no longer on speaking terms.

"Headquarters was still very small," Evans recalls. "There was a chief counsel, two lawyers, two inspectors, and Andy as liaison to Treasury. And there was a planning and research office under Ernie Gentry and Walter Panich, which kept watch over Customs and the BDAC deal.

"Enright had about 260 agents worldwide, but Cusack alone handled intelligence. Cusack had the foreign desk and worked with Schrier's International Group and the agents overseas. I had domestic enforcement, and my big problem was James V. Bennett, the director of the federal prison system. Bennett was complaining to federal judges that the prison system was overflowing with small-time drug violators, and that there were disciplinary problems as a result, all because of the Daniel Act. So the law was rewritten and Main Justice told the US Attorneys that, henceforth, they needed permission to proceed under the mandatory sentencing rule.

"My other problem was the CIA. Giordano sent Cusack to Australia, where the Mafia was moving in through the vegetable business, and while he was gone I covered foreign operations; and that's when I got to see what the CIA was doing. I saw a report on the Kuomintang saying they were the biggest drug dealers in the world, and that the CIA was underwriting them. Air America was transporting tons of Kuomintang opium." Evans glares angrily and says, "I took the report to Enright. He said, 'Leave it here. Forget about it.'

"Other things came to my attention," Evans adds, "that proved that the CIA contributed to drug use in this country. We were in constant conflict with the CIA because it was hiding its budget in ours, and because CIA people were smuggling drugs into the US. But Cusack allowed them to do it, and we weren't allowed to tell. And that fostered corruption in the Bureau."

According to FBN enforcement assistant John Enright, "The deepest, darkest secret of the FBN was its relationship with the CIA. It was a legacy of Anslinger, who wanted to be a spy. That's why he accepted Andy Tartaglino like he did Charlie Siragusa. Siragusa was crude and unsophisticated, but was held in awe by Anslinger because of his CIA contacts. George White too."

Enright sighs. "Vietnam was the worst. We called Air America 'Air Opium.' Our office in Bangkok made a case on an Army major [Hobbs] who was caught with opium. But the major just disappeared, because the CIA was behind it."

For his part, George Gaffney claims to have met with the CIA on only two occasions: when he signed nondisclosure statements in New York and Washington. He does acknowledge that the CIA was involved in the Cotroni and Pardo Bolland cases, but he won't say how. "I only sent one piece of information to them about an associate of a dope pusher we seized," Gaffney claims. "I never went to CIA headquarters, and the CIA passed along only useless information to me."

CIA officer Jim Ludlum begs to differ. After transferring to the CIA from the FBI in 1955, Ludlum served as a desk officer, then joined head-master Angleton's counterintelligence staff as a planner, working with the Pentagon, FBI, State Department, and White House to plan operations around the world. In 1962, he became Angleton's deputy chief of liaison, handling the CIA's relations with domestic law enforcement agencies. "Jane Roman was the boss," Ludlum recalls. "She personally handled liaison with the FBI through Sam Papich, and I had everything else, including the FBN. About once a month I met with Giordano or Gaffney just to keep it alive, though there wasn't much to report. I also worked with Larry Fleischmann at Customs. In any case, there was no narcotic coordination before I got the job."

"Listen," Gaffney says, changing the subject when confronted with Ludlum's statements. "It got so bad after Valachi that I applied for the San Francisco job. White was getting ready to retire, and I asked Henry to be transferred there as district supervisor. Henry said the job was Fred Dick's." Gaffney grimaces. "Then Belk said I was leaning on him, so Henry banned me from New York. From 1966 until 1968, I was a fifth wheel. I had no authority, except over import-export documents, and I couldn't make any personnel appointments. But Andy Tartaglino did."

Gaffney was not the FBN's only fading light, and Tartaglino was not its only rising star. "Fred Dick was a Giordano man," Enright explains, "and on a trip to Los Angeles to investigate an illegal wiretap that Fred had authorized, I met with George White and his wife Albertine in San Francisco. White was a fire marshal then, and very ill; he had gone down from about 225 pounds to about 175. Somehow White knew about the wiretap and was glad to talk about it, because he hated Fred Dick. He actually threw his badge on the floor in front of Fred on the day Fred took over the office. White said in disgust: 'Here! You've always been after this.'"

Ironically, soon after White retired, the specter of MKULTRA threatened to surface publicly for the first time when New Orleans prosecutor Jim Garrison decided to investigate the Kennedy assassination. According to an FBI teletype, Garrison's inspiration was David Copeland, an attorney from Waco, Texas.[23] As stated in a book he wrote on the JFK assassination, Copeland's source of information was a report written jointly by an FBN agent and a Customs agent tracking Kennedy's assassins to a group of Texas ultras.[24]

Knowing that the investigation might lead to MKULTRA assassination plots, the CIA galvanized its forces, and in its 1967 IG Report, there is even a section titled, "Should we try to silence those who are talking or might later."[25] After Garrison arrested Clay Shaw and charged him with the murder of JFK in March 1967, the Agency began to discredit Garrison by linking him to Carlos Marcello in an 8 September 1967 *Life Magazine* article titled "Brazen Empire of Crime." Texas Governor John Connally helped as well by preventing Sergio Arcacha Smith's extradition to New Orleans as a witness in Clay Shaw's trial. If the reader will recall, Smith was identified as having traveled to Dallas with Rose Cheramie, who was murdered on 4 September 1965.[26]

Seeking protection, John Roselli dutifully fed Washington attorney Ed Morgan a tall tale, fabricated by James Angleton, which Morgan in turn passed to columnist Jack Anderson. Printed in the *Washington Post* in March 1967, the story claimed that three Cubans, captured in a raid on Cuba in 1963, were turned by Castro and sent back to kill Kennedy out of revenge.[27]

This concerted effort to deceive the public tracks back to the FBN's involvement in the MKULTRA Program, and the CIA's overarching need to keep that a secret. It also concerns Andy Tartaglino's integrity investigation, which in 1967 included Ike Feldman and some strange things that were happening at his CIA-funded safehouse at 212 East 18th Street. Unlike the other FBN agents Tartaglino targeted, Ike Feldman, then leader of Group One, had an ace up his sleeve, and he allegedly threatened to expose the FBN's involvement in the CIA's assassination and sexual blackmail plots, unless Tartaglino backed off. Such an admission would lead the inquisitive to the CIA's use of the MKULTRA safehouses to move drugs on behalf of its Kuomintang and Burmese clients. Just to prove his point, Feldman, according to George Gaffney, leaked some tantalizing tidbits about MKULTRA to certain congressmen and to Walter Sheridan, a former FBI agent serving as a consultant to NBC on the Garrison disinformation case. Having got his message across, Feldman accepted a transfer to Boston, and two years later he retired.

Roselli was spared for the time being, as was Robert Maheu, whose boss, Howard Hughes, had sold his shares in TWA for a cool $546 million and had bought the Desert Inn in Las Vegas from a group that included Meyer Lansky's close associate Moe Dalitz. Hughes terminated Maheu's services and replaced him with the CIA-backed Robert Mullen security firm. Hughes's move on Las Vegas, and his hiring of the Mullen firm, reflected the CIA's realignment with organized crime on behalf of an evolving Establishment. A major player in this southwestern element of the espionage Establishment, Hughes had been working with the CIA since 1953, when his Houston-based aircraft manufacturing company started making spy planes and satellites for the Air Force. From 1960 to 1963, he let the CIA use his Caribbean island to launch raids against Castro. In return for these and other services, Hughes's helicopter business would make millions off the Vietnam War.[28]

At this critical juncture, the CIA dispensed with another liability. After spending a year in jail for refusing to testify to a grand jury, Sam Giancana was released in late May 1966 and fled to Cuernavaca, Mexico. According to his son, in the book *Double Cross*, Giancana managed the CIA's narcotics operations through Santo Trafficante in Asia, Carlos Marcello in Latin America, and Carlo Gambino in Europe.[29] This seems an outrageous claim; and yet, upon his return to America in June 1975, Giancana was shot in the head, CIA execution-style, while eating a bowl of sausage and peppers, just a few short weeks before he was due to testify to Congress about the Kennedy assassination. One month later, Jimmy Hoffa disappeared. A year after that, following a meeting with Santo Trafficante in August 1976, John Roselli was murdered, dismembered, stuffed in a 55-gallon drum, and dumped in the Miami River.

In 1967, the protectors were working overtime. After Senator Long proposed a bill to limit electronic surveillance, he was accused by *Life Magazine* of having taken a $160,000 bribe from Jimmy Hoffa. Though exonerated, Long was soundly defeated in his next election.[30]

Plugging the last hole in the national security safety net, LBJ signed the FBN's death warrant. The process began in January 1967, when Johnny Thompson testified at Bobby Baker's trial. In an effort to get Thompson out of the line of fire, Giordano had transferred him in 1966 to Albuquerque, New Mexico. But that wasn't far enough away.

As Thompson recalls, "I was visiting with an informant in Gallop, and I called the office just to let them know I was there. Well, a few minutes later the phone rings. Gaffney's on the line. 'Don't get excited,' he says, 'but we're going to have a conference call. Where will you be?' I asked him to call me back at my motel. The moment I get there the phone rings; it's General Counsel Smith at Treasury, and he wants to know what happened with Bobby Baker. I tell the truth and forget about it. A few days later, I'm called back to DC to meet a Justice Department attorney, who says he's going to put me on the stand for the Baker trial.

"Well, the reports from the wiretaps were never written up, and I'm worried. But it didn't get that far. The first question the defense asked me was, 'When did you join the FBI?' Not the FBN, the FBI. They thought I was an FBI agent! At which point the truth about the FBN came tumbling out."

Thompson shrugs. "A few years later, when I was acting chief inspector at the Bureau of Narcotics and Dangerous Drugs, the chief counsel, Don Miller, took me aside and said, 'You know, LBJ tried to fire you over the Bobby Baker thing.'"

"Thompson testified in the afternoon," George Gaffney recalls, "and within an hour, two White House aides had come over to Bureau head-quarters and picked up my and Thompson's personnel files. It was late afternoon, and I had to go to Secretary Barr to explain. He was livid, and wanted to know why I got the FBN involved in a non-narcotic case. Hoover had turned it down. So why did I do it?"

Gaffney stiffens. "I told him, 'I'm not J. Edgar Hoover. I don't have the weight to say "No" to the Attorney General.' Then I referred him to the letter issued by Bobby Kennedy directing that all Treasury heads cooperate with Justice. When Barr said he'd never seen the letter, I suggested that he have his secretary dig it out of the files. Then I got up and walked out."

With immense sadness, Gaffney says, "After our role in the Baker affair came to light, we incurred the wrath of LBJ and the Bureau was abolished out of revenge."

25

THE LAW OF THE JUNGLE

"And the Wolf that shall keep it may prosper,
but the Wolf that shall break it must die."

Rudyard Kipling, "The Law of the Jungle"

John Enright had been around the block: as a street agent in New York in the early 1950s; spearheading the Genovese case at the Court House Squad in 1958; as district supervisor in Atlanta; as acting district supervisor in New York prior to George Belk's arrival; as a consultant to the McClellan Committee; and, after attending the Industrial War College, as the FBN's assistant for enforcement, the number three position in the organization.

"By the mid-1960s," Enright recalls, "the big problem was drugs other than heroin. But Anslinger had refused to accept responsibility for them, so Congress created BDAC, which led to bitter jurisdictional fights. We were also fighting with Customs, and we were mad as hell at the FBI. Within the organization there was an incredible amount of tension between Giordano and Gaffney, and I was right in the middle of that too. As you know, George was my close friend, and my first wife came from his home town. But none of his friends were getting the big jobs, and there was all this tension. So finally Henry calls me in one day and asks, 'Where does your loyalty lie?'

"I told him: 'With the Bureau of Narcotics.'"

Enright chuckles. "The Vietnam War was another big concern. The military was afraid that drugs would break down discipline among the troops, so I worked with the Pentagon on that. But my primary focus was on domestic cases, which meant lots of inter-district work. I knew all the documented informants and if a case was important, I might get personally involved in it. When it came to overseas cases, Jack Cusack ran the show: no one else knew what was going on in that respect. He read all the teletypes and functioned as a one-man intelligence squad. Then Giordano sent Cusack to Australia, where the Mafia was making inroads through the produce business, and John Evans stepped in until Hank Manfredi, who'd had a heart attack, came back to headquarters to take over foreign operations in 1967."[1]

FBN headquarters was not closely monitoring foreign operations in 1966 and 1967. By default, much of the oversight passed to Lenny Schrier's International Group in New York. Apart from that, the individual overseas agent was responsible for managing his affairs, which in every case presented unique and often enormous challenges.

MOUNTING OPERATIONS IN MEXICO

Having been swept up in the corruption scandal surrounding Gene Marshall in Miami, Rick Dunagan found himself, in the fall of 1965, faced with an interesting choice: he'd been officially transferred to Los Angeles; but, being fluent in Spanish and eager for adventure, he'd also been selected to become the FBN's third agent in Mexico. As Dunagan recalls, "Before I went to Mexico, I was sent to teach technical investigative techniques at the Public Safety School in Caracas, Venezuela. It was a test to see how well the Latinos would receive me. I was there for two weeks and everything went okay, then Cusack sent me back to Venezuela to pick up a Cuban fugitive from Miami. That was another test, which I also passed, and a few weeks later I was sent to Los Angeles, where the agent in charge, Ben Theisen, told me to call District Supervisor Fred Dick in San Francisco. Dick said I had an hour to make my decision about the transfer to Mexico. I called my wife in Miami, described the smog in LA, and we decided to go."

Dunagan shrugs. "I spent the next five months flying back and forth to Miami, cleaning up old cases and testifying at Marshall's trial, which was excruciating. Gene acted crazy and claimed he was innocent, but wound up doing two years. Then in February 1966, I drove down to Mexico City with my wife and seven kids, and when I got there, Bill Durkin told me, 'Make a case, get a grade.' And I believed him. But I quickly learned that Durkin didn't need me around. He relied totally on Ray Maduro. They did things together, while I did everything alone."

Being ignored by his boss was not the only thing that contributed to Dunagan's sense of isolation. "Our office was in the Embassy basement," he explains, "where the lower echelon State Department people *might* hang out with us, if they weren't afraid of being shunned by their senior colleagues. The FBI had an agent there as its chief of foreign counter-intelligence, and the CIA had a huge contingent of case officers with loads of cash. The CIA would provide us with flash rolls, but they never shared informers. And Durkin never pushed them. Customs still considered Mexico its turf, and Customs Attaché Mario Padilla was Durkin's arch-enemy – which didn't help. Mario's primary job was as liaison to a group that was in charge of security for the major Mexican banks. IRS was working with Customs, and the Secret Service was investigating counterfeiting and gold trafficking by the number two man in the Mexican Federal Police."

Having been left on his own, Dunagan initiated his first narcotics case in typical case-maker style: Marty Saez, his former partner in Miami, had given him the telephone number of a suspected drug trafficker, so Dunagan called the suspect "cold," without an introduction. The suspect agreed to meet and Dunagan flew to Guadalajara. He made the first two buys alone, but for the third buy and arrest he brought along Ray Maduro and a team of MexFeds as backup. "We found the lab," Dunagan recalls, "and the guy admitted that he'd been dealing to Canada for twenty-five years. I'm in seventh heaven, but when I get back to Mexico City, Durkin's in a rage. Without consulting with him, I'd asked the comptroller to pay to send my youngest daughter to school. Headquarters was upset that I'd done that and Durkin, who was 'The Company Man,' told me to drop the suit.

"'No,' I said. 'I'm allowed.' And eventually I won. They called it 'the Lisa Decision' after my daughter. But Durkin never forgave me. He dummied up my promotion, and it just sat on his desk with no signature."

Dunagan sighs. "Things get worse. Durkin sends me to Bogotá with an unproven informant, a Peruvian they'd caught in New York with five kilos of cocaine. I get there and we're set up by the deputy chief of police. Punches get thrown, knives come out, I pull my gun. It's a standoff, and nobody's made, because they're all cops! I return to Mexico City with a bleeding ulcer and dysentery, and what does Durkin do? He sends me to Guadalajara with Hymie Wallberg, a top MexFed who was later busted in a stolen car ring.

"Hymie and I go to the mountains to get a sample of opium. The farmers have it stashed in fifteen-gallon cans, but the MexFeds won't go in. The Army won't go in either, so I go in alone. But it's a premature bust and the bad guys put a carbine to my head. Finally Wallberg shows up, but too late." After a pause, Dunagan says very softly, "Maduro was there as my back-up. Well, that was the last time I worked with Ray, who quit shortly thereafter."

Maduro, notably, quit the FBN to take a job as assistant director of security for the Swiss-based mutual fund Investors Overseas Services, the "fast-money laundry for organized crime, corrupt Third World dictators, wealthy expatriates, and freelance swindlers."[2] Beginning in June 1967, Maduro developed a commercial intelligence network for IOS throughout South America. "I'd been a grade twelve for four years," he explains, "and I wanted out of Mexico. My dream was to open an FBN office in Madrid, but that never happened. Then I met a Naval officer who'd run boat operations in Vietnam. He was working for IOS and he offered me a job. After Durkin got the okay from Gaffney, we took a trip to Geneva to see Bernie Cornfeld. There was a chance to make lots of money, so I joined."

Maduro joined IOS despite the fact that the IRS was investigating its links to the Meyer Lansky gambling excursion scam on Paradise Island in the Bahamas. The IRS had also linked IOS with Billy Hitchcock, alleged financier of the Brotherhood of Love, which was manufacturing LSD and smuggling marijuana from Mexico and hashish from Afghanistan, and distributing its products through the infamous Hell's Angels motorcycle gang. Hitchcock reportedly had a secret account at a Bahamian bank that lent several million dollars to the operators of the Paradise Island casino, including Lansky associates Lou Chesler, CIA Agent Wallace Groves, and Eddie Cellini.[3]

IOS was known to be moving money from South American investors to the Banque de Crédit International (BCI) in Geneva. As mentioned in chapter 23, BCI was owned by Tibor Rosenbaum, a likely Mossad agent and business associate of Meyer Lansky. The IOS operation was featured in an 8 September 1967 *Life Magazine* article, "The Brazen Empire of Crime," in which Lansky boasted that organized crime was "bigger than US Steel." Genovese family member "Fat Tony" Salerno from East Harlem and Florida was invested in IOS, as was Carlos Marcello. But CIA clients were mingling their money in IOS too, so the IRS investigation fizzled out, and equity participant Ray Maduro eventually moved into the Nixon administration.

Back in Mexico, Rick Dunagan was experiencing the usual unusual. "I'd been down near Guatemala for a week, just before Christmas 1966, waiting to do a deal that never happened. As I look back, I realize I was sent there to get me out of the way. So I come back for Christmas and as we're landing, the plane quits." Dunagan describes climbing out of the wreckage, commandeering a taxicab, arriving at his home, tired and shaken, just glad to be alive. "On Christmas Day," he recalls with emotion, "Durkin calls and says, 'I'm sending you to Lima tomorrow.'

"Jim Daniels had been sent to open a one-man office in Lima, but he couldn't make a case. So Durkin sent me down with an informant who owned an Oldsmobile dealership and was close to the Peruvian president. I'm there undercover, and Daniels cuts me into an Italian. The Italian cuts me into a Japanese chemist, and I arrange to buy five kilos of coke. But when it comes time for delivery, the Peruvian cops won't get out of their cars, and I have to make the seizure myself – at which point the cops descend, steal the cocaine, and turn the informer into a smuggler!"

Dunagan shakes his head in disbelief. "Then Durkin leaves and George Emrich arrives from Chicago as the new agent in charge. I'm working on Paul Mondoloni's partner, Jorge Moreno Chauvet. Moreno had been sent to jail in 1965, but in 1967 he's living six blocks from my house! I persuaded my wife to go along. She pretended to be my girlfriend. We knock on his door and I ask for Chauvet by name. They say that Chauvet's in bed, and they ask who's calling, and I give the name of a guy we'd busted in Detroit. They bring me inside and when I look around, I see two MexFeds I know in the living room.[4]

"Everything down there was so bizarre," Dunagan says in disgust. "Basically, I hated it. I have five daughters and two sons, and people were trying to entice them. One of those people was the son of the minister of the Mexican Navy. He was paid off the first time, but after it happened the second time, I'd finally had enough."

TURNING TO TURKEY

The culture shock that upset Rick Dunagan's family, and the official corruption that disrupted his professional investigations in Mexico, were also present in Turkey, where the FBN's influence, thanks to Agent Dick Salmi, had been growing since he, Hank Manfredi in Italy, and Bob DeFauw in France had joined forces to make the seminal Watermelon case of 1966. Medium-built, blond, and brave, Salmi was born in Santa Monica, California. While attending the University of Perugia in Italy in 1958, he read about Andy Tartaglino's work on the Nick Gentile case and decided to become a federal narcotic agent. After a stint in the Santa Monica Police Department, and a two year hitch with the Office of Naval Investigations, Salmi's dream came true, and in April 1962 he was inducted into the wolf pack.

"Charlie Siragusa came out to Los Angeles," Salmi recalls, "and I told him I wanted to work overseas. He said okay, but that I had to prove myself undercover first, so I started doing a lot of work in Mexico and Southern California. I did well, and I was sent to Las Vegas with a prostitute who had volunteered to take an undercover agent around the hotels. I pretended to be her pimp from Hollywood, and through her I started making buys from Italians. Then came the Bobby Baker surveillance, after which I got my reward. When I was sent to Istanbul in 1966," Salmi says with unabashed pride, "I was only the seventeenth FBN agent overseas.

"It was incredible. I had no language training, and the conditions we lived in were primitive; when my wife gave birth to our first child in an Istanbul hospital, the baby nearly died of a staph infection. I can remember the bloody bandages on the floor. There was a lot of anti-Americanism too, and FBN agents were the low men on the Embassy totem pole. We were given the worst space available in a room over the Embassy garage. But unlike what happened to Rick Dunagan in Mexico, we had a tight community.

"The agent in charge, Nick Panella, returned to New York about six months after I arrived, and Charlie Casey, who'd spent the previous two years in Bangkok posing as a down-on-his-luck seaman, replaced Nick as agent in charge. Charlie was close to the military, and they provided us with a lot of support. But I did all the undercover work.

"There were three defining issues in 1967," Salmi asserts; "the Arab–Israeli Six Day War, Vietnam, and opium coming out of Turkey. And once we had established that Turkish opium was a major source of French connection heroin, the Istanbul office became the FBN's center of overseas activity, encompassing a network of informants and operations throughout the Middle East. The problem was that the Turkish farmers would grow one hectare of opium for the government, and another for themselves. So we tried to seize the raw opium going to the bad guys, and interdict the morphine base at the labs, or on its way out of the country."

According to Salmi, Turkey's underworld was comprised of ten families, whose biggest criminal enterprise was smuggling opium and morphine base out of the country, and arms back in. The arms were sold to the Kurds, a disenfranchised minority group in Eastern Turkey, fighting insurgent wars in Iran and Iraq. Narcotics going out of the country were often hidden in the trucks and cargo of Turkish workers going to Germany. One group of smugglers set up the Overland Company specifically to move morphine base to Europe and return with weapons. "It was an Overland truck that was carrying the drugs in the Watermelon case," Salmi says, "but we didn't learn about the guns until a few weeks later, when another Overland truck, packed with weapons, was seized in Austria on its way back to Turkey. So by 1967 there was a proven correlation between arms and drug smuggling. We knew which Turks were involved, how the payoffs were made, and the routes they used through Bulgaria and Hungary."[5]

The involvement of East Europeans in the drug trade and the movement of guns to the Kurds were issues of tremendous interest to the CIA station in Turkey. As a way of exploiting the situation for its own purposes, the CIA convinced the FBN that a surge in terrorism in Turkey was not the result of internal political unrest, but of the KGB's control of the Bulgarian drug trade. The FBN was glad to assist the CIA by providing the spy agency with Interpol reports identifying drug traffic transit points in Bulgaria. The CIA also professed to share an interest with the FBN in making a case on the Kulecki and Cil clans, the dominant alliance in the guns-for-drugs trade between Turkey and Bulgaria. But both families were very well protected. Mehmet Kulecki, owner of the Kennedy Hotel in Istanbul, was arrested in 1965 for possession of 147 kilograms of opium, but before the case got to court, the opium was exchanged for river mud and Kulecki was set free. Huseyin Cil, the owner of several hotels on the Syrian border, was so well protected that he actually got away with murder. But daring Dick Salmi decided to go after them anyway.[6]

The case against the Turkish crime lords began in February 1967, when an American soldier of fortune, Tom Garrity, was arrested for conspiring to smuggle 48,000 bullets to Kulecki. Garrity, between 1964 and 1967, had smuggled over 15,000 guns into Turkey; he knew the smuggling business from top to bottom, and his decision – made with the consent of Turkey's CIA-advised secret police force – to work for the FBN was a major breakthrough. Agent-in-Charge Charlie Casey put Garrity with undercover Agent Salmi, and they set up a sting with the Turkish secret police, its CIA advisors, and the US Air Force Office of Special Investigations (OSI). Covering for the CIA, OSI agents helped with the surveillance of Kulecki and Cil, and provided the FBN with cars and flash rolls.

Mercenary Tom Garrity initiated the case in September 1967 when he arranged to buy fifty kilograms of morphine base from Yuksef Sedef, Cil's front man in Ankara. A few days later, Garrity introduced Salmi to Sedef. Posing as an arms smuggler, Salmi said he would smuggle the fifty kilograms of morphine base to France, sell it there, and return with weapons for Sedef. Sedef agreed, but on the condition that Salmi proved that he was a real criminal by delivering a load of semi-automatic pistols to Istanbul.

Although it was illegal, the Turks, at the urging of the CIA, agreed to let the deal go down, and that night Salmi drove with a group of arms smugglers to Istanbul. To his surprise, he ended up in a garage half a block from his house. The smugglers put a hundred pistols in his car, and Salmi drove back to Ankara, where the receivers purchased the guns. The CIA-advised Turkish security police tailed the receivers to their Kurdish contacts, as the CIA had planned all along.

Sedef, meanwhile, was in another part of Ankara, waiting to sell the first thirty kilograms of morphine base. Salmi hustled over to Sedef's house and made the buy, at which point Casey, the Turkish police, and several OSI agents descended and arrested everyone. Garrity then drove to Kilis, a town on the Syrian border, and contacted Cil's supplier, Mr. Kayican. Unaware that Sedef had been busted, Kayican agreed to sell the remaining twenty kilograms of morphine base directly to Salmi. A few days later, Huseyin Cil arrived in Gaziantep and the deal went down. As Salmi recalls, "Garrity and I inspected the base in the presence of Kayican and Cil. When I was satisfied as to the quality of the contents, I gave a prearranged signal from a window, and Casey, the Turkish police, and the OSI agents entered the hotel and assisted in the arrests." Cil, however, having bought protection, was found not guilty in the Gaziantep court.

"The big problem was corruption," Salmi reiterates. "The average Istanbul cop made about fifty dollars a month, and his rent was sixty, which meant that a lot of cases were sold out."

The illegal activities of the Turkish police force were well known at FBN headquarters. In 1962, Jack Cusack had reported that the chief of the Central Narcotics Bureau in Ankara "extorted kickbacks from informants." Istanbul's police chief considered the traffic of morphine base "a source of revenue," and the head of Istanbul's narcotics unit believed the problem was the importation of drugs by non-Turkish citizens. The only reliable cop was Turkey's Interpol representative, Halvit Elver. But Elver was on the CIA's payroll and was shunned by his colleagues, who called him disparagingly "the American tail."[7]

As in France, official complacency was related to the fact that Turkey had very few heroin addicts of its own. In addition, smoking hash was part of its culture. As a result, one of Salmi's hardest chores was persuading the Turk narcotics squad to even consider conducting drug investigations. He had little technical support, either. There were no radios, and he used the same 1957 Chevrolet that Sal Vizzini had used six years before. But he loved his work and despite the brutality of the Turkish police (as vividly depicted in the movie *Midnight Express*), Salmi made an unprecedented string of cases, as the focus in drug law enforcement shifted from war-torn Lebanon to Turkey.

THE ISRAELI CONNECTION

In 1965, Turkish smugglers were already bypassing their traditional Syrian and Lebanese middlemen and dealing directly with Italians and Corsicans. The quantity of narcotics moving to Western Europe had reached record highs, and Dennis Dayle, though stationed in Beirut, was spending more time in Turkey than in Lebanon, often on behalf of the CIA, from whom he obtained front money in return for services rendered. In one instance the station chief gave Dayle nine million Turkish liras for an undercover job. "And I didn't even have to sign a receipt," he recalls with muted awe.

But trouble lay ahead. "Paul Knight introduced me to Carlo Dondola," he explains, "and through Carlo I contracted to buy a ton of opium in Mersin, a city on the Turkish coast, not far from Syria. One of the smugglers was the brother of the regional police chief, so I went there with the police from Andana, and we seized the dopers and locked the opium up in the local jail; a ton of opium, which I field tested as positive. Then I mailed samples back to DC for verification. But when I got back to Beirut, I was notified that the Turks had determined that it was river mud."

Very coolly, Dayle says, "The sample was high grade, the seizure was mud. Which leaves only two conclusions. And fraud was the conclusion reached by Washington."

According to John Evans, then acting chief of foreign operations at FBN headquarters, "Dennis was blasted out of Beirut, and the CIA moved in."

Having been set up by the CIA, Dennis Dayle returned to Chicago for a year, and in April 1966 jumped to BDAC. In the meantime he was replaced in Beirut by Agent Arthur Doll. Described by Dick Salmi as "a midwestern hayseed," Doll, although liked by the Lebanese, had a hard time adjusting to Middle Eastern culture, and he deeply resented the fact that suave CIA Agent Paul Knight had been given official diplomatic credentials as the region's Treasury Attaché. This cover put Knight above Doll in the Embassy's hierarchy, and enabled the Knights, not the Dolls, to attend Embassy parties and make all the important contacts. Doll's persistent objections to this arrangement alienated Knight, and without his support, Doll was rendered ineffective at the same time the Arab–Israeli "Six Day War" altered forever the political climate of the region – and with it the nature of international drug trafficking.

One early casualty was the reigning Lebanese drug lord, Sami Khoury. According to Joe Salm, Khoury and his partner, ex-Lebanese Sûreté officer Mounir Alaouie, crossed the River Jordan and were never seen again after "they failed to honor an obligation" with a trafficker who happened to be the king of Jordan's uncle and the boss of the Bedouin. Knight heard that Alaouie had been "naughty in money matters." In either case, the result was the same.[8]

Another sign of the shifting scene was the collapse of Intrabank and the mysterious death in November 1966 of Youseff Beidas, its wealthy Palestinian founder. Among Intrabank's holdings were shipyards in Beirut and Marseilles, an airline, and the infamous Casino du Liban, where Alaouie and Khoury had consorted with Corsican crime lord Marcel Francisci. According to author Jim Hougan in his book *Spooks*,

> The Palestine Liberation Organization (PLO) was said to extract a percentage of the [Casino Liban's] skim to finance terrorist operations against Israel, and law enforcement authorities contended that the gaming tables and the Intra Bank itself were used to launder the proceeds from heroin transactions conducted by the casino's manager, Marcel Paul Francisci."[9]

In a provocative passage in his book, Hougan claims that French industrialist Paul Louis Weiller, after putting Intrabank Beirut out of business in 1967, joined forces with three people: Eduardo Baroudi, a notorious arms trafficker; Conrad Bouchard, a Canadian heroin smuggler associated with Pepe Cotroni; and Marcel Boucon, a Mediterranean smuggler – and thereafter emerged, under Richard Nixon's protection, as the major force in a new facet of the French connection.[10]

Be that as it may, with the forced retirement of Khoury and Alaouie, the increased security measures in Beirut that accompanied the Six Day War, and the murder of Beidas and the failure of Intrabank, Corsican crime lord Marcel Francisci had no choice but to retreat to Marseilles, where he was forced to engage the rival Guérini gang in a bloody turf war.

Increasingly isolated and ever more dependant on America, Israel was forming closer relations with the FBN too. As Bob DeFauw recalls, "Yitzak showed up at my door about two weeks after I arrived, and thereafter visited me about three or four times a year. He was a general in the Mossad and had responsibility for the same geographical areas as I. His people had the book on everything that went on in their backyard, and whatever I needed to know about the Bekka Valley in Lebanon, he got for me. In return, Yitzak liked hearing about what we had on the Lebanese heroin families, the Makkoots and the Maaloufs. He was also interested in gunrunning: 'Where are the guns coming from?'[11]

"The Israelis helped us move people around too. They'd fly a guy to Franco's people in Spain where, if there were drug charges pending, we could deal with them. We're talking serious interrogations. So these people became useful informants by virtue of the Israelis moving them to places where they'd face problems."

In June 1967 came the Six Day War and the subsequent alliance of the PLO with Syria's Ba'ath Party. Having anticipated this development, an army of CIA officers descended on Beirut, including Air America's former operations manager in Vietnam, Moe Kuthbert. With the arrival of "Air Opium" on the scene, knave spookery and drug smuggling merged in the Middle East more closely than ever before, putting greater pressure on FBN agents. "We had a Palestinian informer in France," Vic Maria explains, "who worked for the Israelis, the PLO, and the Lebanese. We see him go into the Israeli embassies in Rome and Copenhagen. Do we give this to the Lebanese police?"

The answer was an emphatic no, because the Israeli connection was one of James Angleton's most closely guarded secrets, and was protected in every instance in order to preserve the Mossad's ability to monitor political, military, and economic developments in the region. As Maria observes, "French Jews in Algeria and Morocco had the connections, which is why the traffic, which follows linguistic channels, went through South America, Florida, and Texas, to the French in America."

The FBN had known about the CIA–Israeli connection at least since 1957, when Paul Knight reported that Edmond Safra and his brother were smuggling morphine base from Beirut to Milan, and laundering the profits through Safra's bank. That investigation was quietly closed for political reasons, but in June 1966, after Safra opened the Republic National Bank in New York, the FBN launched another investigation into his affairs. Again, in September 1966, the case on Safra was closed, this time after Interpol reported that it was not in possession of any information that would confirm any implications that influential Edmund Safra was involved in drug trafficking.[12]

Before he passed away, Paul Knight acknowledged that Safra had indeed helped to launder drug money, and that his brother had smuggled morphine base. But Paul feared being sued, or labeled anti-Semitic, so he never talked publicly about what he privately knew to be true.

THE FRENCH CONNECTION ENCORE

The Six Day War brought about a change in drug routes, but the French connection was still the focus and, in 1967, with the FBN compromised at every twist and turn, it was far from being dismantled. One enduring problem was that the major traffickers were protected by top French officials. Specifically, Paul Mondoloni and Jean Jehan, mastermind of the famous 1962 French Connection case, were named in the December 1965 Nebbia case; but Jehan was never extradited to the US, and Mondoloni was released the day after he was arrested at Orly airport.[13] Although charged with moving ten tons of heroin worth $10 billion over two decades, Mondoloni would meet with the Cotronis and other "key gangsters from Canada and the US in Acapulco, Mexico in 1970."[14] He was still at large in the mid-1970s, overseeing the Mexican connection, and operated with impunity until his assassination in Marseilles on 29 July 1985.

In the mid-1960s, thanks primarily to official corruption at every point on the drug trafficking map, the narcotics business was booming as never before, and big cases were there for the making, as was demonstrated in May 1966, when Vic Maria got a tip that generated the FBN's next great success, the Oscilloscope case. Maria's informant (whom he had acquired from SDECE Agent Antoine Lopez) revealed that Paul Chastagnier in Guayaquil, Ecuador, was about to send six kilograms of heroin to an unknown New York buyer. A veteran trafficker, Chastagnier had smuggled narcotics with Paul Mondoloni, whom he referred to as his "big boss," since 1954.[15] In 1966, he co-owned an import-export firm in New York City with the wife of Georges Boucheseiche, the Attia Gang member to whom Paris stupes Louis Souchon and Roger Voitot, and SDECE Agent Lopez, had delivered Mehdi Ben Barka for torture and assassination on 29 October 1965.

Based on Maria's information, members of Lenny Schrier's International Group placed Chastagnier under surveillance upon his arrival in New York in December 1966, but they saw no evidence of illicit activity on his part. French officials, however, discovered through SDECE wiretaps that Chastagnier had developed a method of smuggling heroin in oscilloscopes, and that another shipment was being prepared for delivery on 20 March 1967. The French informed Maria that Louis Bonsigneur was to receive the heroin at Chastagnier's office on 90 West Street in New York, and then deliver it to Albert Larrain-Maestre, a Puerto Rican national soon to become the FBN's most wanted man.

On 20 March 1967, without alerting Chastagnier or any of his accomplices, Maria and Inspector Marcel Carrere seized two cartons packed with oscilloscopes at Orly airport. Each carton contained six oscilloscopes and each oscilloscope held one kilogram of heroin. Keeping one carton so the French could claim credit in the case, Carrere departed from the strict letter of French law, which does not allow narcotics to leave the country, and, in an effort to establish good relations with New York District Supervisor George Belk, allowed the others to be put on the plane. Accompanied by French detectives, the cartons were flown to New York and delivered to Chastagnier's company, where FBN agents arrested Chastagnier's sales manager as he accepted them. But Chastagnier's arrest in Paris had, by then, already been reported by the French press, and his partners in America, Louis Bonsigneur and Albert Larrain-Maestre, were able to flee.

As Morty Benjamin recalls, "We knew that Maestre's girlfriend was a passenger service manager for Trans-Caribbean Airlines. We'd seen her with one of Maestre's customers, so we rushed right over to her apartment after the arrests. When we got there, Maestre's bags were downstairs with the doorman. We ran upstairs to his room, but all we found was a drawer full of money. Maestre wasn't there. So we ran back down and when we got outside, his bags were gone! We were five minutes behind him all the way."

The manhunt for Maestre would forever undo the myth that Castro's Cuba was the major transit point of narcotics from Europe and South America. Instead it would prove that heroin from Joe Orsini in Madrid was transported to Puerto Rico through the Dominican Republic on Spanish and French ships, which picked up cocaine in Venezuela and Mexico along the way, before delivering the narcotics to receivers in New York. Another significant revelation was that Maestre, while on the run and searching for new customers and a source to replace Chastagnier, met with Norman Rothman in Miami in June 1967. A member of the drug traffickers' hall of fame, million dollar man Rothman was a close friend of Meyer Lansky and several senior CIA and FBI agents.[16]

Upon his arrest in Madrid, Spain, on 5 December 1967, Maestre would betray his accomplice in Spain, Domingo Orsini, and his customers in New York, Chicago, and Los Angeles. His testimony would lead to the indictment of Auguste Ricord in Argentina, and open a major investigation into Group France in South America. Chastagnier's sales manager would also provide numerous leads into this same far-reaching network, centered in Marseilles.

Most significantly, Maestre's association with Norman Rothman underscored the fact that Meyer Lansky was still pulling the financial strings behind the scenes. Lansky's organization, with the consent of his Mafia associates, engaged in insurance fraud and tax evasion through offshore bank accounts and ghost companies. It used stolen securities as collateral for loans and, with the help of Panama's ambassador to Great Britain, Eusebio Morales, it laundered the Vegas skim through the Panama branch of a Swiss bank. Lansky, notably, had been introduced to Morales by Tibor Rosenbaum, the likely Mossad agent and owner of the drug money-laundering bank, BCI. And for that reason, Lansky, the dark star of organized crime, remained above the law.

THE LAW

Faced with the harsh reality of its limitations, the FBN's small overseas contingent was learning, as Marseilles Agent Bob DeFauw observes, "that there was one set of rules domestically and another internationally. To begin with, our informers weren't working off cases. They were mercenaries, but they were your partners too. Often they had police credentials, and they always carried a gun. So you learned how to work with everyone. There was a priest who ran a school in Rome and delivered morphine base to Paris. There were old Nazis too. When a hit was ordered [on some unfortunate leftist], these old Nazis were imported through the collaborator network in Europe, North Africa, and South America. Many were granted asylum in Spain where they served as anti-communist informers for the Franco regime."[17]

FBN agents were also, finally, learning to be wary of the CIA. "So much of their information was classified, you could never tell if a guy [like Rosenbaum or Safra] was material," Vic Maria explains. "As a result, lots of [potentially explosive] information wasn't acted on. Other times you ended up following a guy [like Ben Barka] who wasn't in narcotics."

Fewer ethical restraints, however, and the return of Marcel Francisci to Marseilles, meant that fomenting dissent among traffickers was easier than ever overseas. "We shot Joe Catalanotto [the veteran Mafioso drug smuggler from Detroit turned FBN informant in Mexico] into Joe Orsini," DeFauw recalls with delight. "We had him tell Orsini that Antoine Guérini was setting up his shipments and telling the police where his labs were. Antoine was killed in June 1967, and his son barely escaped with his life. When Antoine's brother Meme Guérini found out who did it, he took the guy to a cliff, broke every bone in his body, then threw him over."

Meme Guérini went to jail for that murder, and Antoine was dead, which meant that the Guérini gang had been effectively eliminated as a major link in the international drug trade. "But there was a downside to that operation." DeFauw sighs. "Old Joe did such a good job that we promised to ask the INS to allow him to return to America to visit his family. But the process was too slow for Joe, and against my wishes he went to Italy to visit his family there, using fake ID we had furnished. And that's when [Marseilles Police Inspector Robert] Pasquier gave him up. Old Joe was arrested, and for fear of creating an international incident we dropped him, and he was banished for life to Bari."

NEW MAFIA NAMES AND FACES

After taking the Fifth before a grand jury convened by US Attorney Robert Morgenthau in October 1964, and then vanishing, Joe Bonanno's whereabouts had become a *cause célèbre* by 9 February 1966, when the *New York Times* reported that he was in Tunis handling international narcotics transactions for the Sicilian Mafia, and that five federal agents from an unnamed agency had gone to Palermo to search for him. The *Times* did not name Bonanno's Sicilian contacts, but it did imply that he was a government snitch. Evidently some disgruntled Bonanno family members had reached the same conclusion, and, on 28 January 1966, renegade Frank Mari took a few shots at Bonanno's emotionally unstable son Billy and his aides, John Notaro and Frank Labruzzo. Mari and Michael Consolo had deserted the Bonanno family for a splinter faction formed, with the Mafia Commission's consent, by Gaspare Di Gregorio in 1965.[18]

Then on 17 May 1966, Bonanno magically appeared at the federal court in New York, and afterwards settled back into his routine, without legal problems and without explaining where he had been. He tried to stabilize his family, but by then the Banana Wars were spinning out of control. The New York tabloids gleefully kept score as Bonanno family loyalists and rebels murdered one another individually and in groups around the city. Competition for narcotics connections further inflamed the situation when Bonanno family rebels Frank Mari and Michael Consolo forged an alliance with Carlo Gambino's brother, Paul, on behalf of Di Gregorio. Bonanno loyalists, led by the imprisoned Carmine Galante, were infuriated at the Gambino family over this development, and Consolo was murdered as a result in March 1968. Frank Mari vanished forever that September.[19]

Meanwhile, Carlo and Paul Gambino had been joined by their Sicilian cousins Giuseppe, Rosario and John (an associate of Mafia banker Michele Sindona), in Cherry Hill, New Jersey, and were embarking on one of the most enduring drug trafficking enterprises ever, the famous Pizza Connection case.[20] At the center of the ring was Tom Buscetta, the indispensable link between the Sicilian, Canadian, and American Mafias, and the liaison to Ricord's Group France and its Italian partners in Latin America and Mexico. Gaetano Badalamenti in Sicily supplied the Gambinos through middlemen in Mexico and the Cotronis in Montreal. Critical to the new organization was an old scheme, devised before the war and perfected by Vito Genovese, in which young Sicilians were brought to America to handle distribution. Working on this project with Buscetta was Salvatore "Saca" Catalano, a top Sicilian Mafioso and fugitive from the 1963 Ciaculli massacre, then living in Brooklyn. Saca's cousin Toto arrived in 1966 and, with Mafia financing, opened one of the first pizza parlor fronts in a new national distribution network.[21]

The central player in this New World Narcotics Order, Buscetta, after fleeing Sicily in 1963 at the age of thirty-eight, traveled with his girlfriend, Vera Girotti, a beautiful Italian television star, from Milan to Mexico City, where he underwent plastic surgery. From Mexico he traveled to Toronto, where the Cotroni syndicate put him in touch with Domingo Orsini, a Corsican resident of Argentina since 1949, and an associate of Auguste Ricord, Paul Chastagnier and Albert Larrain-Maestre. In 1965, Buscetta slipped through Canada into Brooklyn and, with $10,000 provided by Carlo Gambino, opened his own pizza parlor. Having established his front, he contacted his Sicilian associate Pino Catania in Mexico City. Catania, "through a Mexican industrialist in textiles" had formed relations with a veteran drug trafficker mentioned several times before in this book, Jorge Asaf y Bala. Catania also introduced Buscetta to New York distributor Carlo Zippo, owner of the Brazitalia Company, an electronics shop near Times Square.

Many of Buscetta's movements and activities were known to the FBN. The Italian police had been searching for him since the Ciaculli massacre, and since 1964 the FBN had suspected him of importing heroin from Ontario into the US through Detroit. In February 1966, the FBN opened a confidential correspondence with Italian authorities regarding his new organization, but the investigation was dropped in June 1966 after Buscetta was detained in New York by INS agents for using the passport of a deceased Mexican labor leader. Deportation hearings were initiated, but – like Maurice Castellani before him – Buscetta mysteriously slipped away. By one account he was recruited by the CIA to spy on the Latin American politicians and Corsican spies complicit in his drug-smuggling operations.

There is circumstantial evidence to support the theory that he had been recruited by the CIA, for immediately after his interview with the INS, Buscetta began financing August Ricord's Group France and its major operators, Françoise Chiappe, Lucien Sarti, Françoise Rossi, Christian David, Michel Nicoli, and Claude Pastou, all of whom were "auxiliary agents" of French Intelligence. If the CIA wanted to monitor the activities of the Mafia and the Group France, what better way than through elegant, ubiquitous Tomasso Buscetta?

26

GOLDEN TRIANGLE
ENTERPRISES

*"It was a superstition among them that a lover who smoked
would always return, even from France."*

Graham Greene, *The Quiet American*

Robert Kennedy's vaunted war on crime was a faded memory on 22
September 1966, when thirteen major Mafiosi were arrested for "consorting with criminals" at La Stella Restaurant in Forest Hills, New York.
Among those present were Carlo Gambino, the boss of bosses; Genovese
family boss Tom Eboli and his *consigliere* Mike Miranda; Profaci family boss
Joe Colombo and his erstwhile rival Joe Gallo; Santo Trafficante, the Mafia's
narcotics manager, based in Tampa, and his close associate Carlos Marcello
from Louisiana. After their release, the audacious hoods thumbed their
collective nose at the Law, and imperiously invited the press to attend a
meeting they held the following day.

Several reasons have been given for the mini-Apalachin, including the
need to address the disruptive Banana Wars. Another reason concerned
Joey Gallo, whose crew had helped New York Mayor John Lindsay quell
race riots in Harlem that summer. "Crazy Joe" had acquired a measure of
political protection as a result, and the Mafia mini-summit was convened
to welcome him into the fold and seal a truce between him and Colombo.
But the primary reason for the meeting was the need to organize the New
World Narcotics Order through sleepers (non-Mafia members) like Carlo
Zippo, by then the biggest distributor in New York.

Though not represented at La Stella, the Lucchese family was also busy
reorganizing its narcotics activities. On 23 January 1967, emissaries from

Anthony "Tony Ducks" Corallo, the family's narcotics manager, met with Marcel Francisci in Paris. At Fouquet's restaurant, Francisci and Corallo's emissaries discussed the formation of a new narcotics syndicate, using Francisci's contacts (most likely Jean Croce and, a mere two weeks after his arrest, Paul Mondoloni) to move heroin from France, through the Dominican Republic, to the US.[1]

Unraveling this New World Narcotics Order would test the skills of FBN agents beset by IRS investigations, subversion by the FBI and CIA, and an alliance between BDAC and Customs that was starting to trespass on Bureau operations overseas. This latter problem began in June 1967, when BDAC boss John Finlator declared that the Mafia was importing and distributing LSD and other pharmaceutical drugs, and then sent Agent Ed Anderson to London and Rome to conduct a joint investigation with US Customs, Scotland Yard, and Italy's Ministry of Health. This international case focused on Mafia banker Michele Sindona and others "involved in the illicit movement of depressant, stimulant and hallucinogenic drugs between Italy, the United States and possibly other European countries."[2]

When Commissioner Henry Giordano heard that BDAC had ventured to Europe and was working with Customs, he went straight to Main Treasury and petitioned for redress. But LBJ had already signed the FBN's death warrant, and Giordano's protestations fell on deaf ears.

Making matters worse, Customs had formed a four-man narcotics unit in New York that was gathering significant French connection-related intelligence and making major seizures. The Customs narcotics unit was connecting the dots in a way the FBN wasn't, and it wasn't sharing the picture it was forming with the Bureau. But it was revealing its information to the CIA's counterintelligence staff, which had helped put the unit together. The result was a considerable increase in the number of Customs informants (who worked by default for the CIA as well) inside August Ricord's South American facet of the French connection.[3]

PANDORA'S BOX

Adding to the FBN's woes was the deluge of drug traffickers setting up shop in the Far East and exploiting America's escalating military involvement in Vietnam. Meyer Lansky's emissary, John Pullman, landed in Hong Kong in April 1965, and began buying into casinos and arranging for Filipino and Malaysian couriers to transport heroin to America through Canada, the Caribbean, Chile, and Paraguay. Other mob couriers moved morphine base from Hong Kong and Bangkok to Europe and America.[4]

Santo Trafficante was also establishing a foothold in the Far East through his emissary, Frank Furci. The son of a lieutenant in Trafficante's Florida-based family, Furci landed in South Vietnam in 1965 with the first wave of American troops. His patriotic purpose was to equip military social clubs with hamburgers, soft drinks, jukeboxes, and vending machines, while on the side he provided prostitutes and drugs to the troops. Although he was forced out of Saigon in 1967 for illegal currency transactions, Furci resurrected his enterprise in Hong Kong with a group of retired Army sergeants.[5] But this too was a typical Mafia scam that cheated the clubs and their customers out of millions of dollars, and eventually became the focus of a congressional investigation – which was subverted by the same system of graft, bribes, and kickbacks that enabled Lansky and Trafficante to grab a controlling chunk of the Far East rackets, with the blessings of military and CIA officials willing to do anything to win the war.

This enduring accommodation with the Mafia was an extension of the Luciano Project, and in 1967, Albert Anastasia's son-in-law, Anthony Scotto, then vice president of the International Longshoreman's Association, would be called upon to send one of his henchmen to protect the Port of Saigon from saboteurs and thieves who were stealing shiploads of cargo, and selling it on the black market to the Viet Cong.[6]

That was not the full extent of the CIA's Faustian pact with the Mafia in Vietnam. The CIA believed that French president, Charles de Gaulle, was obstructing America's war effort through a network of resentful French landowners and businessmen. Supposedly, de Gaulle's motive was to improve France's standing with the Soviet Union and the People's Republic of China, both of whom were aiding the Vietnamese insurgents. James Angleton wanted to penetrate this SDECE apparatus, and in 1965 he sought to establish an independent CIA counterintelligence unit in Saigon. But the military rejected his initiative, so the CIA turned to its old Mafia allies to help fight an underground war against the French and their Corsican gangster accomplices.

The CIA's major asset in this effort was Air Marshal Nguyen Cao Ky, a willing strongman it had recruited in the wake of the assassination of President Diem in November 1963. This bloody *coup d'état* was supposed to win popular support for the Americans by replacing the repressive, Catholic Ngo regime with a Buddhist general. But the military men and politicians comprising the new Government of Vietnam (GVN) were more interested in making money than making war, and within a year the insurgents had seized control of the countryside. Taking matters into its own hands, the CIA in early 1965 arranged for Ky, then commander of the First Transport Group, to be appointed as the GVN's national security chief. Trained as a pilot in France and married to a French woman, Ky then placed his right-hand man, Air Force General Nguyen Ngoc Loan (also trained in France) in control of the law enforcement, intelligence, and security branches of the GVN.

In return for having been granted such power, Ky awarded the CIA the right to establish the Revolutionary Development (RD) Program in Vung Tau – where, fifteen years earlier, SDECE had based its opium smuggling Operation X. The RD Program was designed to win back the loyalty of Vietnamese in the countryside through a mixture of civic action, propaganda, and counter-terror operations. In July, Ky appointed General Nguyen Duc Thang as RD minister, and in August 1965, Edward Lansdale, a CIA officer masquerading as an Air Force general, arrived as the CIA's liaison to General Thang and the RD Program.

Lansdale's resumé included experience in an array of political and psychological warfare operations that involved drugs. In 1953, he had viewed the vast Laotian opium fields, and in 1955, he had chased the French out of Saigon and installed the Catholic Ngo regime. The Ngo regime's own drug smuggling operation was directed by Diem's brother Nhu (an opium smoker) through his secret police chief, Dr. Tran Kim Tuyen. (Ky's First Transport Group was at Tuyen's disposal and shuttled Tuyen's drug couriers between Laos and Saigon from 1956 until 1963.) In 1960, Lansdale had investigated SDECE's involvement in drug smuggling, and in 1962 he'd employed drug smuggling Mafiosi in the CIA's shadow war against Cuba and its KGB advisors. Possessed of a wild imagination, Lansdale had even proposed the introduction of cheap marijuana as a way of undermining Cuba's economy.[7]

In mid-1965, Lansdale assembled a team of American unconventional warfare experts and Filipino mercenaries to wage, undercover of the RD Program, a secret war against French nationals supporting the insurgents. His arrival in Vietnam also occurred just as "political upheavals" forced the Corsican airlines in Laos out of business.[8] According to Professor Alfred McCoy, the first thing Lansdale did was to arrange a "truce" with the Corsican drug smugglers in Saigon.[9] Lansdale's motive was to protect himself from anyone who might still be holding a grudge from the *sale guerre* of 1955. In return for a guarantee that he would not be harmed, Lansdale gave the Corsicans free passage and thus enabled them, their Mafia associates, and a group of Vietnamese officials to control Saigon's lucrative drug market.

Assisting Lansdale was his *consigliere*, Lucien Conein. The most adept member of Lansdale's team, Conein was born in Paris and raised in Missouri. He joined the OSS in 1940 and reportedly formed guerrilla groups in Southern France using Corsican outlaws. In late 1944, he was transferred to OSS headquarters in Kunming, China, and fought alongside French Special Forces units conducting sabotage operations against the Japanese in Northern Vietnam.

After the war, Conein married a Vietnamese woman, and during this tumultuous period, he became acquainted with the Vietnamese gangsters, Kuomintang Chinese, SDECE and Sûreté officials, and Corsican policemen (perhaps even Paul Mondoloni) and seamen involved in Saigon's opium trade. He also hobnobbed with the upscale business and political crowd that gathered at the Continental Hotel, including Monsieur Franchini, its influential owner. Conein joined the CIA shortly after its formation, and in 1954 was assigned as Lansdale's deputy in Vietnam. His help was instrumental in snatching the divided nation away from the French and the nationalists led by Ho Chi Minh. In 1956, Conein joined a military intelligence unit operating in Germany and Luxembourg, and from 1960 through 1962, he trained Iranian Special Forces in the opium-rich outlands of Iran. In 1962, he returned to South Vietnam as a floating emissary. Reporting directly to the White House, Conein coached the cabal of military officers that murdered Diem and Nhu. Afterwards he helped recruit Catholic refugees from the Ngo regime into top jobs in the police, intelligence, and security agencies of the de facto parallel government established by the CIA.

Conein's knowledge and contacts were invaluable when Lansdale returned to Vietnam to manage the RD Program, and among his many functions, Conein served as the guardian angel of Lansdale's protégé, Daniel Ellsberg. Sent to Vietnam by the Defense Department to monitor the RD Program, good-looking, fast-talking, quick-witted Dan Ellsberg shared quarters with tall, swarthy Frank Scotton. A CIA officer working undercover with the US Information Service, Scotton had created the RD Program's "motivational indoctrination" component. A subtle form of brainwashing, motivational indoctrination was the key to transforming average soldiers into the programmed assassins that operated secretly inside the RD Program's civic action teams.

Ellsberg began working with Scotton's counter-terror teams and participating in operations against the insurgency's political leaders. His photographic memory and pleasing personality also qualified him as a potential spy, and soon Conein and Scotton had introduced him into

Saigon's swinging in-crowd. Ellsberg's mission was to engage Vietnam's leading political thinkers in conversation and then report what they said directly to John Hart, the CIA's station chief in Saigon.

Then Ellsberg threw a wrench into the works. At a party at the fashionable Cercle Sportif, Scotton introduced Ellsberg to a beautiful Eurasian woman named Germaine. Ellsberg found her simply irresistible, although she was engaged to Michel Seguin, a Corsican opium trafficker. Germaine, however, shared Ellsberg's passion, and they began a torrid love affair that forced Seguin to defend his honor. After slipping into Ellsberg's villa late one night, he put a pistol to Ellsberg's head, and warned him to stay away from his fiancée. According to Scotton and Conein, the only thing that saved Ellsberg's life was a promise they made to Seguin; that if anyone hurt Ellsberg, they would wage a bloody vendetta against the Corsicans.

Here the plot thickens. Lansdale claimed that he had nothing to do with the Corsicans after they reached their truce in 1965. But, by another account, the truce allowed the Corsicans (including, presumably, Seguin) to traffic in narcotics, as long as they served as contact men for the CIA. In this role, the Corsicans kept their CIA case officers posted on the price, quality, and availability of narcotics. The truce also endowed them with free passage at a time when, according to McCoy, Marseilles's heroin labs were turning from Turkish to Southeast Asian morphine base.[10]

After Professor McCoy published *The Politics of Heroin in Southeast Asia* in 1972 and exposed this truce, Conein wrote to McCoy's publisher and insisted that his meeting with the Corsicans was solely to resolve a problem caused by "Ellsberg's peccadilloes with the mistress of a Corsican."[11] Conein didn't say what the problem was, but one can infer that Ellsberg's affair with Germaine threatened to upset a very sensitive counterintelligence operation, in which the drug-smuggling Corsican contact men were serving as double agents and reporting on French nationals involved with the insurgents.

Ellsberg told this writer that Conein and Scotton never intervened on his behalf, and that their statements were CIA disinformation designed to impugn his character, because he leaked the Pentagon Papers (the military's top secret account of the official lies that led to the Vietnam War) in the summer of 1971, and thus inadvertently helped bring down the Nixon administration. He also insists that Lansdale had nothing to do with narcotics trafficking while in Vietnam.

Ellsberg's assertions may be true, but what is important is that Lansdale and Conein knew that certain Corsicans in Saigon shipped morphine base to associates in Marseilles. Although Conein, in his letter to Harper Row, denied having said so, McCoy quotes him as stating that it was impossible to completely stop the Corsicans from smuggling drugs, unless someone put the opium growers in Laos out of business. According to McCoy, that is "why Conein and Lansdale did not pass on the information they had to the US Bureau of Narcotics." [12]

CIA officers Lansdale and Conein knew that Corsican drug smuggling in Vietnam relied on the CIA-protected opium growers in the Golden Triangle, but they didn't tell the FBN; which brings us back to the overarching fact, discovered by FBN Agent Bowman Taylor in Laos in 1963, that the CIA was not only protecting the opium growers in Laos, it was facilitating the drug trade in Vietnam. As FBN Agent Al Habib explained, "Vietnam was off-limits" because, as Sal Vizzini observed, "the CIA was flying opium to its warlords." The FBN knew about the CIA's involvement in the Hobbs case in 1964, and that Air America (aka Air Opium) was smuggling opium to Vietnamese officials. As we shall see, the FBN knew that top officials like Air Marshall Ky's right-hand man, General Loan, were involved, as was Customs Director Nguyen Vinh Loc. As Habib noted in chapter 21, Vietnamese Customs had a warehouse full of confiscated opium that it sold "out the back door."

The CIA's complicity in the Southeast Asian drug trade was known to the FBN in 1965, and yet it listed only two Southeast Asian drug smugglers in its International Book: Rolf Schmoll, a Corsican later identified as SDECE Agent Ange Simonpierri (the source in the Nebbia case and, through Paul Pasqualini, to Maurice Castellani); and Michel Libert, a Corsican residing in Saigon. And by never making public its knowledge of CIA drug smuggling, the FBN itself became complicit in the great conspiracy it had been searching for since its inception. [13]

STRATEGIC INTELLIGENCE NETWORK 118A

Not only was the CIA protecting the GVN's top drug smuggling politicians and generals, their Corsican accomplices, and its private army of opium growers in Laos, it was managing the caravan that delivered raw opium to the world's biggest opium market in Houei Sai, Laos. CIA officer William Young helped to initiate this operation. The son of an American missionary in Burma, Young learned the local dialects before he mastered English. During the Second World War, his family was forced to move to Chiang Mai in northern Thailand, and afterwards, Young's father taught Ambassador William Donovan about the intricacies of the region's opium business.

Following a tour of duty with the US Army in Germany, Young was recruited into the CIA and, in 1958, was posted to Bangkok. When the CIA pretended to move its Kuomintang mercenaries out of Burma, he was reassigned to Chiang Mai, and from there led a succession of CIA case officers to the strategically placed Laotian and Burmese villages that would eventually serve as Agency bases. It was Young who introduced General Vang Pao, chief of the opium-growing Meo tribesmen, to Joe Houdichek, Pao's first official CIA case officer.

From his headquarters at Long Tieng, the CIA's major air base on the south side of the opium-rich Plain Of Jars, Vang Pao conscripted some 30,000 Meo tribesmen into a secret army to fight the Laotian communists and their Vietnamese allies. In exchange for selling his people as cannon fodder, he was allowed to make a fortune selling opium. Much of the brokering was done at the village of Houei Sai in western Laos on the Thai border, in the heart of the opium-rich Golden Triangle formed by the borders of Burma, Thailand, and Laos. Vang Pao's front man was the chieftain of the local Yao tribe, but behind the scenes Bill Young coordinated Pao with the generals and politicians running the Laotian Opium Administration, as well as with three Kuomintang generals inside Burma. These generals operated clandestine CIA radio listening posts inside Burma, and in return were allowed to move 90 percent of the opium that reached Houei Sai.[14]

It was a happy arrangement until October 1964, when the Chinese detonated an atomic bomb at Lop Nor. That seminal event signaled a need for better intelligence inside China, and resulted in the CIA directing Bill Young to set up an intelligence network at Nam Yu, a few miles north of Houei Sai. The purpose of the 118A Strategic Intelligence Network was to use a Kuomintang opium caravan to insert agents inside China. The agents placed by Young in the caravan were his childhood friends, Lahu tribesmen Moody Taw and Isaac Lee. Young equipped them with the best CIA cameras, and while in China they photographed Chinese engineers building a road toward the Thai border, as well as the soldiers massing along it. Knowing the number and location of these Chinese troops helped the CIA plot a strategy for fighting the Vietnam War.

Once the 118A Network was up and running, Young turned it over to CIA officer Lou Ojibwe, and after Ojibwe was killed in the summer of 1965, Anthony Poshepny took charge. A Marine veteran who had served with the CIA in the Philippines, Indonesia, and Tibet, "Tony Poe" was the balding, robust model for Marlon Brando's Colonel Kurtz in *Apocalypse Now!* He also served as a father figure to the junior CIA officers (including

Terry Burke, the future acting chief of the Drug Enforcement Administration) he commanded in the savage jungles of Laos.

In an interview with the author, Poe said he "hated" Vang Pao because he was selling guns to the communists. But Poe was a company man, and he remained silent and dutifully made sure that the CIA's share of opium was delivered from Nam Yu to the airfield at Houei Sai. The opium was packed in oil drums, loaded on CIA C-47s, flown by Taiwanese mercenaries to the Gulf of Siam, then dropped into the sea and picked up by accomplices in sampans waiting at specified coordinates. The people on the sampans ferried the drugs to Hong Kong, where the opium was cooked into heroin by Kuomintang chemists and then sold to Mafiosi. As described by Young and Poe, this was the CIA's private channel to its old Luciano Project partners in Hong Kong.

Albert Habib, in a Memorandum Report dated 27 January 1966, cited CIA officer Don Wittaker as confirming that opium drums were dropped from planes, originating in Laos, to boats in the Gulf of Siam. Wittaker identified the chemist in Houei Sai, and fingered the local Yao leaders as the opium suppliers.

By 1966, when Agent Doug Chandler arrived in Bangkok from New Orleans, the existence of the CIA's 118A opium caravan was also known to the FBN. As Chandler recalls, "An interpreter took me to meet a Burmese warlord in Chiang Mai. Speaking perfect English, the warlord said he was a Michigan State graduate and the grandson of the king of Burma. Then he invited me to travel with the caravan that brought opium back from Burma." Chandler pauses. "When I sent the information to the CIA, they looked away, and when I told the Embassy, they flipped out. We had agents in the caravan who knew where the Kuomintang heroin labs were located, but the Kuomintang was a uniformed army equipped with modern weapons, so the Thai government left them alone."

Meanwhile, Thai and Vietnamese officials were buying opium at Houei Sai, as were Corsicans and CIA renegades working for Air America and yet another CIA airline, Continental Air, which had a State Department contract to fly food and supplies to the Yao in Houei Sai. Also involved was Prime Minister Souvanna Phouma's son, Panya, who built a Pepsi-Cola bottling plant in Vientiane, Laos, with US State Department support. Better than the real thing, the plant served both as a cover for buying the chemical precursors necessary for converting opium into heroin and as a money laundry for Vang Pao's profits.[15]

THE VIETNAMESE CONNECTION

The FBN began documenting the CIA and Vietnamese drug smuggling conspiracy on 13 July 1966, when US Army Major Lee Waring introduced Al Habib to Tran Ngor An, a Military Security Service (MSS) agent assigned to the Vietnamese Embassy in Bangkok. Tran told Habib that one of his agents had penetrated a Viet Cong smuggling ring in Bangkok. Americans were the recipients in Saigon, and the Americans were sending the opium to Hong Kong to be refined into heroin. Tran then asked Habib to arrange for the US Air Force to ship 250 kilograms of opium to Saigon, in a controlled delivery, so the Vietnamese could bust the culprits there. Although Tran would not identify his agent, or say where the opium was stashed, or provide the names and addresses of the recipients, he did grant Habib permission to accompany the shipment to Saigon – so Habib naively went ahead with the deal. On 5 August, he obtained the approval of the CIA station chief in Bangkok, Robert Jantzen, and of Major General Joseph Stilwell, the ranking US military commander in Thailand.[16]

Then things got weird. Habib traveled to Saigon to meet General Loan's assistant for foreign affairs, Nguyen Thanh Tung. At their meeting, Tung told Habib that Tran's original plan had been changed, and that General Loan now wanted the 250 kilograms of opium to be delivered to the American receivers without an arrest being made. Tung justified this change in plan by explaining that the MSS agent in Thailand had irrefutable information that the VC were planning a second, larger shipment, consisting of two tons of opium. Tung reasoned that if the first shipment were allowed to pass freely, the MSS would be able to identify everyone in the VC's opium smuggling network in Thailand, Malaya, and Laos. They could then make a more valuable seizure and arrest all of the enemy agents, as well as the Americans.

On 11 August, Habib presented the plan to William F. Porter, the deputy US ambassador in Saigon. Porter adamantly refused to go along with it. He didn't trust Loan, and "was apprehensive of a set-up by the Vietnamese which could possibly involve blackmail."[17] Referring to the Hobbs case, Porter rhetorically asked Habib what it would be like if the Vietnamese seized 250 kilograms of opium on a US Air Force plane. On the other hand, Porter wanted to know what the Vietnamese were plotting, so he directed Habib to proceed with the plan, but to delay the operation by telling Tran that there was a problem getting the plane. Porter also instructed Habib to introduce an undercover CIA agent into the investigation – at which point the case began to unravel.

Upon arriving back in Bangkok, Habib was introduced by Tran to Le Dinh Tam, the second secretary at the Vietnamese Embassy in Bangkok. Tam handled the logistical aspect of the Vietnamese smuggling operation in Thailand, and at a meeting on 16 August, Tam threatened to cancel the 250-kilogram shipment unless Habib immediately supplied the US Air Force plane. When Habib refused, Tam flew to Saigon to confer with Tung, and when he returned on 2 September, he told Habib that the MSS had transported the shipment by boat to Saigon, delivered it to the recipients, and, with Vietnamese Customs, seized the opium and arrested two suspects. Tam then surprised Habib by revealing that he was in possession of the additional two tons of opium, which he had obtained in Houei Sai. He insisted that the Americans transport that immense shipment immediately, as a sign of good faith, or else the Vietnamese would do it themselves.

Confounded and amazed at Tam's audacity, Habib traveled to Saigon and – after checking with Vietnamese Customs and its American advisors – found no evidence of any drug seizures or arrests. Suspecting foul play, he approached the CIA and, at an 8 September meeting with someone named Lucid (perhaps Lucien?), he was told that Ambassador Henry Cabot Lodge would not allow him to continue with his investigation. Habib returned to Bangkok, and Tam proceeded to deliver the two tons of opium to waiting Americans in Saigon.

THE REAL POLITICS OF HEROIN IN VIETNAM

As a result of Habib's investigation, the CIA was forced to conduct a perfunctory investigation of Loan's activities, after which he was cleared of any wrongdoing. The reason for this was quite simple: Loan provided personal security to CIA officers in Saigon. That's right. Just as Lansdale had forged a truce with the Corsicans to protect himself, CIA officers protected the GVN's official drug ring because their lives depended on it. The situation hadn't changed since 1955, when Lansdale kicked the French out of Saigon and installed the Ngo regime. McCoy quotes Conein as saying that, after the Ngos were assassinated in November 1963, "the same professionals who organized corruption for them were still in charge of police and intelligence. Loan simply passed the word among these guys and put the old [drug smuggling] system back together again." [18]

Within this system, Nguyen Thanh Tung, alias Mai Den, was Loan's narcotics manager. Tung had learned the ropes while serving in Dr. Tuyen's secret drug smuggling secret service, and he had gone to work for Loan after the 1963 *coup d'état*. To help conceal Tung's activities, Loan appointed him chief of the Central Intelligence Office's Foreign Intelligence Branch in early 1966, right after Habib discovered the Bangkok operation. Created by the CIA in 1961, the CIO was the GVN's equivalent of the CIA, and CIO officials worked within all the political, security, and military branches of the GVN. In this way, with the support of the CIA, Tung "used his CIO agents to weave a net of drug contacts across the Golden Triangle."[19]

McCoy's assertions about Tung are qualified by Colonel Tulius Acampora, the US Army counterintelligence officer who for six years had conducted joint CIA/FBN drug smuggling cases with his friend, Hank Manfredi, in Rome. In mid-1966, Acampora was reassigned to Saigon as General Loan's CIA advisor on security matters. Acampora maintained this counterpart relationship with Loan throughout the war, and formed a close friendship with him as well. He came to know many of Loan's deepest secrets, and he says that Loan was not aware of everything that Tung did. Acampora describes Tung as "a former Binh Xuyen gangster and hatchet man for the Kuomintang who was appointed over Loan's objections."

This is not to suggest that Tung had snookered Loan. The two men had reached an unspoken accommodation. In the same way Mafiosi bring out the voters and otherwise serve politicians in America, Tung was granted free passage in order to serve his patrons. For example, it was Tung's goon squad that quelled the Buddhist riots in Hue in the mid-1960s, thus sparing the regular Army unit commanders from suffering any political backlash. Tung's thugs also tried to offset the political influence the CIA exercised through its unilateral recruitment of Ky's political enemies, including labor leaders, Buddhist monks, and private businessmen.

A sophisticated man who enjoyed his Courvoisier and Gaulloises, Loan did not ask Tung how he financed his goon squad. Nor did he presume to challenge the prerogatives of the Kuomintang Chinese, French landowners, or Corsican gangsters who provided him with similar services. For example, the owner of the Continental Hotel, Monsieur Franchini, had wired the most elegant rooms so that Loan's agents could conduct the same sort of MKULTRA sexual blackmail schemes that the CIA used to bring politicians into line in America. Only in this case, the people being blackmailed were the Americans in charge of administering the war in Vietnam.

GOING TO THE SOURCE IN LAOS

As American participation in the war escalated through 1966, Laos became the critical flanking operation. Of particular concern was the Ho Chi Minh

Trail, which wiggled through Laos into Cambodia, and enabled the North Vietnamese Army to supply the Viet Cong. Interdicting the Ho Chi Minh Trail was necessary to winning the war, but Laos was a neutral country, so the quiet Americans relied on extra-legal methods: bombing the trail to smithereens was the job of the CIA-managed 56th Air Commando Wing in Thailand, while the task of interdicting troop movement along the Trail fell to the CIA's secret army of hill tribesmen, stationed in strategic outposts along the so-called Laotian Corridor.

Chief among these outposts was Pakse, a city of 8,000 on the western edge of the Bolovens Plateau in a southern province ruled by Prince Boun Oum Champassak, an advisor to the Laotian Opium Administration. The CIA base chief at Pakse, where opium was sold openly on the streets, was David Morales. A former station chief in Havana, and a former member of Lansdale's Operation Mongoose, Morales (aka Poncho) facilitated the opium trade in Pakse for the local Laotian police and military commanders, in coordination with Air America.

According to McCoy, Pakse was the site of the biggest South Vietnamese opium-smuggling operation, managed jointly by Laotian officials working with Nguyen Cao Ky's elder sister, Mrs. Nguyen Thi Li; KMT financier Huu Tim Heng; Loan's spymaster Mai Den; and Major Pham Phung Tien, Ky's successor as commander of South Vietnam's CIA trained and equipped First Transport Group.[20]

The CIA knew all about this operation too, but it looked the other way, because the American military's ability to bomb the Ho Chi Minh Trail depended on the Laotian and South Vietnamese air forces, which were based in places like Pakse. That's why, in 1966, the CIA launched Operation Palace Dog in concert with the US Air Force. The stated purpose was to train Laotian and South Vietnamese pilots, but its secret mission was to provide security for the joint Laotian/Vietnamese drug-smuggling operation. It may also have been the conduit by which the CIA flew narcotics directly to the United States. Palace Dog aircraft were used to fly medicines from the World Medical Relief warehouse in Detroit to Vang Pao's secret army at Long Tieng. It's not hard to imagine what came back to Detroit in Palace Dog planes, and by 1967 the military and the US Customs service were conducting secret investigations of both Palace Dog and Air America.

"It was getting bad," recalls senior Customs official Dave Ellis, who was then making regular trips to Vietnam. "It was an ugly war, so the CIA looked away from Air America and Continental Airlines. But as the war started escalating, they started getting apprehensive."

As world attention focused ever more closely on America's conduct in the Vietnam War, the CIA's need to conceal its major role in the regional drug trade became a top priority. The climactic point came in June 1967, when Burmese warlord Khun Sa decided to sell sixteen tons of opium in Houei Sai. Construing this as a challenge to their precious monopoly over supply, the Kuomintang generals mobilized their forces in Burma and marched across the border into Laos. Apprised of the situation, CIA station chief Ted Shackley in Vientiane informed Pat Landry, chief of the CIA's major support base in Udorn, Thailand. Landry ordered Air Force Major Richard Secord to send a squadron of T-28s to the rescue. Within hours, the battle had ended with both Khun Sa and the Kuomintang in full retreat, and the Laotians in total control.[21]

However, the widely reported Opium War had put a dent in the CIA's armor and, in greater need than ever of a failsafe security system, it took one last drastic step and formed a special unit to provide security for its opium-smuggling operation. This unit was modeled on the CIA's infamous Phoenix Program, which targeted the civilian leaders of the Vietnamese insurgency for assassination. As a former CIA agent explains, "This was not part of the Phoenix pacification Program," which used death squads and a network of secret interrogation centers to neutralize its enemies in Vietnam. "This facet of Phoenix was strictly compartmented."

GOLDEN TRIANGLE SECURITY SYSTEMS

Oddly enough, Robin Moore, author of *The French Connection*, predicted the advent of this special drug smuggling security unit in his novel *The Country Team*. Written in 1966 and set in mythic Mituyan (a country resembling Thailand), the novel features a character called Mike Forrester. A privateer, Forrester had been chased out of Cuba in 1959, had recouped his losses, and then purchased a rubber plantation in Mituyan. As the book develops, the CIA asks Forrester to buy up the local poppy crop before the Mituyan Communists (MitComs) can get to it and sell it to American Mafiosi. Angry because his workers are being extorted by the evil MitComs, and afraid that he might be kicked out of yet another easily exploitable nation, Forrester takes the job.

The CIA tells Forrester that it will sell the opium crop to American pharmaceutical companies, and that he can have half of the profits to keep his machine "oiled."[22] The machine consists of spies who will identify and then kill the Chinese Communists and their MitCom cronies. Forrester then arranges to buy the harvest from a tribal chief who resembles the real one in Houei Sai. He brings along a CIA-supplied press to squeeze the opium into bricks, and when the deal is consummated, the vengeful MitComs, as anticipated, descend on his plantation and into the CIA's trap. Waiting for the MitComs is a Phoenix assassination team managed by a CIA officer named Scott working undercover for the US Information Service. When Scott (a character seemingly based on the aforementioned Frank Scotton) meets Forrester, he produces a deck of cards. Each card is black "with a hideous white eye in the center." As Scott explains, the US Information Service printed 20,000 such cards in South Vietnam: "When we discovered who the Communist agents in a city or village were, we assassinated them and put this eye on the body." Scott then deploys his Phoenix team on Forrester's plantation, to ambush the MitCom drug dealers.[23]

Two things are factually noteworthy about this fictional story. First, the US Information Service did produce 50,000 Eye of God playing cards in South Vietnam. As noted by Georgie-Anne Geyer in the February 1970 issue of *True Magazine*, the cards were "left on bodies after assassinations." But what is truly remarkable is that Geyer's source was none other than Dan Ellsberg's housemate, Frank Scotton, "whose movement," she explained, "evolved into something called the ... Counter-Terrorists" – which was another name for the death squad facet of Phoenix.[24]

The second notable fact is that the Phoenix drug security unit was still in place in 1971. That year, Customs officer Dave Ellis was traveling with Thailand's finance minister when they stopped to attend a party in Chiang Mai. Around midnight, the US counsel pulled Ellis aside and said there were two men upstairs who wanted to talk to him. One was an Army major on loan to the CIA, working with Vang Pao's troops on the Plain of Jars. The major told Ellis they were trying to win the war, and asked him to please stay away. Then Ellis went across the hall to another room. The man in the room said to him, "You don't remember me, but I used to work for you. You hired me for the Customs school in Houston. Then I went to another organization."

This former Customs agent, now employed by the CIA, told Ellis that five provinces in Eastern Thailand belonged to the Thais by day and the communists by night. The Thai officials in charge were furnishing the communists with weapons in exchange for drugs. It was an inside job by greedy Thai generals and, according to Ellis, federal narcotic agents on the scene were letting them get away with it, for their own purposes. The man in the room told Ellis that he had two helicopter gunships and twenty-five men. They called themselves "the Trackers," and their job was to kill the members of this communist-connected drug smuggling ring, whether they were in Laos, Thailand, or Vietnam.

Moore's *roman-à-clef* alludes to other unspeakable truths, like the fact that the CIA's management of the region's drug trade was approved by the highest members of the US government. As Forrester tells the under-secretary of state, "oriental gangsters pass on the morphine base to the Mafia, who make it into heroin."[25]

All of this brings us back to the French connection. Moore visited Fort Bragg in 1963 and, with the permission of the commander of its Special Warfare School, General William Yarborough, he was allowed to tag along with a Special Forces A-Team in South Vietnam for several months. Moore then wrote *The Green Berets*, glorifying America's elite unconventional warriors. He became enmeshed in their secret culture, which included trafficking in precious commodities, and then wrote *The Country Team*, detailing the CIA's involvement in drug trafficking. But only after being initiated into the CIA's inner circle did Moore follow the heroin trail to New York and, in 1972, publish *The French Connection*. It may not be included in Moore's book, but Frankie Waters, the FBN agent who made the French Connection case, identified a Michelin rubber-plantation executive as a potential co-conspirator in the case.[26]

Taken together, the facts are compelling: Lansdale's truce with the Corsicans; the Mafia receivers in Saigon and Hong Kong; Ky's operation in Pakse; Loan's operation in Bangkok; the 118A caravan in Houei Sai; the heroin-producing Pepsi plant in Vientiane; Vang Pao's opium business; and the complicity of numerous anti-communist Thai, Laotian and Vietnamese officials – the entire apparatus required protection, and so the assassination of rival drug smugglers, or anyone who might blow the operation, became official, albeit unstated, CIA policy. This policy was also applied to the political war in South Vietnam and in June 1967, the CIA asked vice president Ky for permission to implement its Phoenix Program in South Vietnam. But Loan was a committed patriot who feared, correctly, that the CIA planned to use the program to eliminate Ky's supporters, and he advised Ky to reject the proposal, which he did. At which point the CIA began to plot Ky and Loan's demise.

Eager to take over some of Ky's rackets in Vietnam, President Thieu agreed to support Phoenix as a way of ousting Ky. To this end, Thieu allowed CIA officers, posing as US Customs officials, to arrest Customs Director Loc's niece, a stewardess for Air Laos, at Ton Son Nhut Airport in December 1967. The niece had 200 pounds of opium in her luggage.[27]

Not long after that, Loc was forced out of office and Ky relinquished control of the Air Force. General Loan lost a leg in a firefight in May 1968, Ky's inner circle was wiped out by a missile from a Marine helicopter in June, and the New World Narcotics Order was established in South Vietnam simultaneously with Santo Trafficante's meeting in Saigon "with some prominent Corsican gangsters." [28] After this meeting with Corsicans he'd probably known since their happy days in Cuba, Trafficante began supplying sleeper Louis Cirillo through Benny Indiviglio in Montreal.

THE PHOENIX COMES HOME TO ROOST

By 1967, with its attendant erosion of respect for corrupt authority and fatally flawed traditional values, the Vietnam War was altering the American psyche and drug scene; to wit, the abundance of Southeast Asian heroin had opened the door to enterprising Afro-Americans, who realized they no longer needed the Mafia and went into business for themselves. One example is the famous Body Bag case involving Herman Jackson and his partner, Leslie Atkinson. Retired soldiers, Jackson and Atkinson opened a bar in Bangkok in 1967, and began using a network of Black enlisted men to move heroin, stuffed in the cadavers of dead soldiers, from Saigon on military transport planes to military bases in America. Heroin shipments transported in this way were seized in 1967 and 1968, and in 1969 the smugglers were put on trial. But the government's informant was murdered, and they continued to operate until 1972.

The Vietnam War altered federal drug law enforcement too, and contributed mightily to the decimation of the FBN and the formation of a new drug law enforcement organization whose overseas operations were almost totally under CIA control. A federal narcotic agent would not be assigned to Vietnam until 1969, when Fred Dick got the job. To their credit, the few federal narcotic agents in the Far East had, by 1968, accumulated a wealth of informants and intelligence on the region's drug trade, but the CIA prevented them from acting on the information. As a result, drug abuse in America steadily increased, and concerned citizens were wondering, as ever, why.

Vic Maria sums up this schizophrenic policy as follows: "We went overseas to prove that opium was grown and converted into morphine base in Turkey, then moved through Syria and Beirut to France, where it was made into heroin. We proved you could buy opium in Turkey and morphine base in Beirut. It got to the point that, when the bosses wanted to make a case in

Milan, we could send someone to Milan to set up a buy, and we could make the bust in Milan. We developed the ability to make cases anywhere, but it was all for the aggrandizement of the bosses! Then we began to imagine that all the drugs in the world concerned us, to the point of chasing down some little guy with an ounce of hashish in a bicycle pump in Calcutta."

Maria asks, "But why go to Beirut to get informants and make heroin cases? Was it there before we arrived?" It sounds as if he doesn't think so. "One day Osman Osman took me to the Bekka Valley and showed me three areas where they were growing marijuana. We looked around, and then he pulled out a press clipping from California. It said the best pot in the world was being grown in Eureka. Osman asked me, 'Why are you here? Most of our crop goes to Egypt!'

"Who developed the heroin traffic out of the Middle East?" Maria inquires rhetorically.

The answer is that it was the same crowd that developed it out of the Golden Triangle. And much of it reached New York, where conservative estimates in 1967 put the addict population at 35,000; half of what it supposedly tallied nationwide. Shaking his head in disbelief, Frank Selvaggi swears there were that many addicts in one Harlem neighborhood alone. He describes a midnight walk along tenement rooftops, amidst the surrealistic image of dozens of junkies nodding out, and the unearthly sensation of not knowing if they were alive.

Meanwhile, the Black Panthers were blaming the CIA for Harlem's heroin epidemic. Determined to squelch such outbursts, the CIA imported Phoenix to America and called it Chaos. Monitored by James Angleton and designed to connect foreign enemies with leaders in the Civil Rights and Anti-War movements, Chaos opened files on some 300,000 American citizens. In conjunction with military intelligence, the CIA pursued those it considered most dangerous, while the FBI, through its aptly named Operation Hoodwink, used fabricated documents to pit the Mafia against the Communist Party, to the Establishment's glee.[29]

As part of Chaos, the CIA, through the NYPD's Bureau of Special Services and Intelligence (BOSSI), infiltrated the Black Panthers, the Nation of Islam, and even its own creation, Alpha 66, the anti-Castro Cuban terrorist organization. Alpha 66 financed its operations through drug trafficking, and reportedly obtained its heroin from Albert Larrain-Maestre. One BOSSI member investigating Alpha 66 was Richard Nixon's future security chief, Jack Caulfield. And in this way the intelligence aspect of international drug trafficking impacted the deep politics of America long after the FBN was destroyed.

Several FBN agents got involved in the crusade to rid America of security risks. Having helped hunt down Che Guevara in Bolivia in March 1967, Tom Tripodi was transferred to James Angleton's Special Operations Division, where Chaos was headquartered. His cover was with a private security firm set up to conduct extralegal domestic covert activities. When he left the CIA to rejoin the FBN in 1968, Tripodi's functions "were transferred to a unit supervised by Howard Hunt."[30] A few years later, Hunt would bring that program, and its anti-Castro Cuban drug smugglers, into the Nixon White House, with a little help from his friend, Lucien Conein.

Hunt and Conein had served together in the OSS and, at Hunt's request, Conein became a narcotic advisor to the Nixon White House in 1971. In 1972, Conein became an employee of the FBN's successor, the Bureau of Narcotics and Dangerous Drugs. And in 1974, he would head a special operations unit in the DEA that utilized Hunt's anti-Castro Cuban assets to investigate Santo Trafficante (without success), and which was investigated by Congress for mounting assassination plots.

As demonstrated, the CIA's ability to manage political developments in America relied, to some extent, on its ability to manage international drug trafficking. By 1967, that meant abolishing the FBN, and its main weapon in that regard was Andy Tartaglino's integrity investigation in New York, which focused on case-makers Lenny Schrier, Frankie Waters, and Frank Selvaggi – all of whom had worked on the Nebbia case. Waters and Schrier had investigated the Brown–Castellani case, and Waters was still plumbing the depths of the 1962 French Connection case. All these investigations tracked back to Golden Triangle Enterprises and, to put it mildly, the CIA was afraid these most effective agents might unmask the Mafia and Corsican smugglers in its employ. So, to prepare the way for a drug enforcement agency that would exist under the CIA's control, the Establishment enabled Andy Tartaglino to destroy the FBN from within.

27

MY ONLY FRIEND

"When should you leave an FBN party?
Right after the fighting, and just before the shooting."

Assistant US Attorney John Bartels

Frank Selvaggi sits at a table in an Italian restaurant, looking forlorn. The waiter has cleared the dishes away, and we're having a glass of wine. Over dinner he explained how he made Joe Valachi, and how, out of revenge, Valachi accused him of being a made member of the Bronx mob. After that, Charlie Siragusa had seen the end in sight and had invited Frank to come with him to the Illinois Crime Commission. But Selvaggi stayed in New York. There was really no other choice. "I was thinking about your father having been a prisoner of war," he says to me. "That's the way it was in the New York office: we were trapped, and there was no place to go.

"After the Valachi Hearings," Selvaggi says, "I went back to New York and everything was okay for about a year. Then Gaffney calls. He wants me to come down to Washington to meet Jack Anderson, right away, to talk about Valachi. George is looking to make points, and Belk says, 'Okay, do it.' This is February 1965. I'm driving to the airport and I skid on the ice on the Saw Mill River Parkway. The car hits a tree and my head goes through the windshield. I end up with a hundred stitches, and miss the interview. Meanwhile Peter Maas is working on an exclusive article about Valachi, so Gaffney arranges for me to meet Anderson at the CIA pad in New York. Anderson's a nice guy, and at Gaffney's insistence, I give him a photo we'd taken of Valachi with his Jewish girlfriend at a bar on Castle Hill Avenue in the Bronx."

One result of Anderson's interview with Frank Selvaggi was a March 1965 article in *Parade Magazine*, titled "The Underworld of Killer Joe Valachi," giving the FBN the credit it deserved for making the case. The other result was that the FBI decided to rewrite history. The FBI opened up its files (including the notes Selvaggi had taken while interrogating Valachi) to its chosen author, Peter Maas, and it introduced Maas to Valachi. In 1968, the same year the FBN was abolished, Maas published his very successful book *The Valachi Papers*, which credited the FBI with making the case.

"If you read *The Valachi Papers*," one agent quips, "you wouldn't even know the FBN was involved." Another agent takes it a step further and swears that the FBI kept a file on every FBN agent. He says that Frank Selvaggi – having made Valachi and given the Anderson interview, and thus having upstaged J. Edgar Hoover – was tops on the FBI's hit list, and that, out of revenge, the FBI set him up in Florida. Selvaggi has come to agree with that conclusion, and he tells how it happened.

"For three years I'd been at the Court House Squad without acquiring any new informers. Then I was assigned to Feldman's Group and was given a new partner, Pete Scrocca, 'the blond Italian.' Scrocca came from Morris Avenue in the Bronx and had that Bronx wiseguy humor – you know, always making cracks, but you didn't know what he really meant? He said something wise to Lenny Schrier once, and Lenny set him straight. After that, Belk wanted him gone. Belk sends Fluhr to me, and Fluhr says, 'Get rid of Scrocca.'

"In those days, when the boss wanted someone out, the senior partner got the job. It was easy: you say he writes bad reports, or doesn't show up on time. But I liked Scrocca, so I protected him, and we ended up being partners for two years.

"Anyway, by the summer of 1965 I needed a break. I hadn't taken a day off since I'd started, so I decided to take my family on a vacation. The travel agent makes reservations at the Colonial in Miami Beach. We fly down in August and rent a car at the airport, but when we get to the Colonial, we find out that the reservations had failed. We end up in a fleabag motel, the last place on the strip. The kids are crying, my wife's complaining, I gotta find another place.

"The next day I'm checking out the Thunderbird Motel. I'm having a drink at the bar and I meet a guy, Emmett Costello. He owns a big truck stop and he's there with his lawyer and some Teamsters from Chicago. He's buying all the ladies drinks and cartons of cigarettes, and he invites me to sit down at his table. I recognize one of the guys sitting with him. I know the guy from New York. But I'm a federal narcotic agent, and I can't show them anything. So I sit down.

"The guy I recognize had a gorgeous Irish girlfriend, a stripper named Autumn Leaves. We were trying to get her to work for us when I was in Group Three. We went up to her apartment in Riverdale, and Patty Biase took her cabaret card. But she was tough and wouldn't fold. And while we're there she gets a call. I'm on the extension and I hear the guy say, 'Tell them to get the fuck out!' He slams the phone down and comes over. He pounds on the door, and when he comes in, he starts screaming at us." Frank is somewhat awed. "The guy's Guido Penosi. He's a made guy from the Bronx. He's a friend of Frank Dioguardia and Trafficante, and that's why he's in Florida at the same time I am, in August 1965. He's there to bid on the French connection shipment that goes to Dioguardia in the Nebbia case.[1]

"You have to understand," Selvaggi stresses, "that Guido Penosi was not my friend. His brother-in-law, Tony Castaldi, was a defendant in the Rinaldo case, and we put Penosi in the case as an unindicted co-conspirator. So there was that, along with the incident with his girlfriend. But there's no way I could refuse to face him over drinks at the table.

"At the time, my informant, Sal Rinaldo, is the main witness in a huge conspiracy case against dozens of traffickers. There's a million-dollar contract on his life, and I've got him living in my house in Valhalla, painting the rooms. I'm secretly taking him to various locations to testify against violators in Italy, upstate New York, and Canada. The prosecutors want to take some of the pressure off him, so they ask me to talk to everyone I know, to see if anyone wants to cut a deal – which is why I think it's okay to talk with Penosi, even if someone is watching. And someone is. I know, because I see them sitting in a line of cars parked bumper to bumper on Collins Avenue. They're taking pictures of everyone, so I go out and show them my badge. Then I get the plate number off Penosi's Cadillac and give it to a Miami agent.

"So what? So they know.

"When I get back from vacation, Dolce is gone. He'd quit. But there's a rumor floating around about what happened down in Miami. Then Tendy calls me and says, 'Come to the office. Somebody's got a beef on you.' They think I flew down to Florida with the mob and was picked up by the mob at the airport. There's a rumor that I used Penosi's car when I was there. They think he paid my motel bill. $690." Selvaggi shakes his head in disbelief. "I offered to go down and drag him back, but the US Attorney said, 'Don't do it.'

"Now I'm getting hot, and Lenny Schrier says, 'You need to cool down.' That's when he sends me to Georgia with Frankie Black, and we arrest the warrant officer, and make the ninety-five-kilogram case in Columbus. By the time I get back to New York, it's January 1966. Fluhr gives me a note that says, 'See Belk.' I go to his office. Greenfeld's there, and he shows me a photograph of me and Penosi. They've been checking it out for five months! The guy I gave the plate number to, an agent from California, had only been in Miami for a few days and he didn't remember." Frank scowls. "And why did Hundley at Organized Crime sit on it for six months? Did they want to see what would happen in Georgia? Things were happening so fast, I couldn't put it together at the time."

Selvaggi lights a cigarette. "Just last year I met an FBI guy in Florida. I knew him in New York during the Rinaldo case, and he'd been with the Strike Force in Miami in 1965. Belk said that 'an outside agency' had provided the photograph of me and Penosi, so this FBI guy does some checking and tells me it was 'the Whiz Kids,' meaning Wachenhut.* And I start wondering how come everyone else's reservation went through; how come Penosi just happened to be there.

"You know," Selvaggi says quietly, "I used to be Charlie's chauffeur when he came to town. One time he had me take him to the CIA pad where he met a CIA agent, an Irish guy with graying black hair, well dressed and tough-looking, like Frankie Waters, but taller. I'm listening in the other room and I hear the guy ask Charlie if he knows anybody in the mob that can kill Castro. Charlie looks at him, then turns to me and says, 'Ask him.'"

Frank suggested, "Somebody like Guido Penosi." But he qualified his suggestion by asking, "What are you going to give him in return? He's not going to do it for patriotism."

"Now it's 1966," he continues, "and guys are jumping to BDAC. It was easy to go over. Charlie Mac goes over, Russ Dower, and Jack Brady too. They wanted me to go, but I couldn't do it, because I'm finally making cases again with Richard Lawrence."

Selvaggi takes a drag on his cigarette. "Richard Lawrence is a Black guy who'd been a deserter in the Second World War. He'd killed a guy in a crap game and done ten years to the day. I got him from his parole officer, and he went to work for me bringing [undercover Agent] Jack Peterson

---

* Wachenhut is a private investigations firm formed in 1954 and staffed largely by retired FBI agents.

around. Lawrence made about twenty cases, including one that leads to Leon Aikens, the biggest dealer in Harlem at the time, up on 110th Street. Joe Bendenelli is another. Pure heroin, weight to the T.

"One day Lawrence says, 'I'll get you into Joey Beck's brother.' Joey Beck is Joe DiPalermo. His brother was short and fat and was always playing cards at the union hall. Lawrence knew him from Attica.

"So Lawrence orders a kilo from Joe Beck's brother, and Scrocca takes him down to the Lower East Side in a cab. I'm covering the meet. We've already got one buy, then a faction from the SIU starts knocking off our cases. When Scrocca and me go to arrest Beck's brother, Vinnie Albano's in the hall. That's SIU Detective Vinnie Albano, who was later killed by the mob. Well, it's a federal case, but he's 'Just nosing around.'

"Then Sal Giovino's protégé, Mike Antonelli, comes down from Buffalo and starts working with [SIU detectives] Burmudez and Watson. First they grab Lawrence, then they knock off Wilbur Johnson, another one of my informants." [2]

Selvaggi is steaming. "The one rule is, 'Never hit another agent's informer.' But Belk does nothing. Yellow sheets* are showing up on the street, five cases in a row get blown, and Belk suspects the worst.

"After Dolce left, we all rejoiced. Then the desk smellers come in, and we're audited by the IRS. Two IRS guys start picking up our informers and everyone's laying low. I get a lead to Rocco Sancinella, and he tells me about a guy who's bringing in dope from Rangoon in a boat. There were leads to Allie Romano, who had the French connection behind Dioguardia in Georgia. But we'd all stopped taking chances by then, because of Andy's Rangers.

"Meanwhile the Rinaldo case is climaxing and I've got to testify." The trial had begun in Italy in February 1967. Seven defendants were tried in Italy, several others were fugitives, and some were in jail in the United States. "When it comes time to try the people here," Selvaggi continues, "the Italians insist on trying the case on Italian soil, at the Italian Embassy in New York. I'm told that the Italian judge wants to see me first, and that the head of the Carabinieri wants to make sure I'm presentable. Tony Consoli's the interpreter, and the first thing General Oliva asks me is, 'What's your rank?'" [3]

---

* Yellow sheets are first draft, official FBN reports that contain confidential information, misinformation, or speculation that is excised in finished reports that are presented in court or otherwise distributed outside the office.

Selvaggi lowers his eyelids. "I meet the judge at the CIA pad on Sutton Place. Big deal. He's with his girlfriend.

"By May 1967, it's all coming home. The three main witnesses are Sal Rinaldo, Matteo Palmieri, and Vito Agueci. I'm the only agent who's going to testify. I've got Rinaldo at my house, and I've got Palmieri stashed in a motel nearby. Agueci's in prison. In late May, I'm called to testify. Al Krieger's the defense attorney. He asks me, 'Who was your informant in the case? Who gave you Rinaldo?'[4]

"'Shorty Holmes,' I say. Holmes was one of Valachi's customers, and Valachi turned him over to Rinaldo. Well, Holmes is dead, and he can't deny it.

"Then in early June I'm called back. Krieger asks me, 'Was there a wiretap?'

"The case hung on that point, and Krieger thought he had my ass, because if the information was the fruit of an FBN wiretap, the federal case is gone.

"Well, the truth is that there was a wiretap, but it was a police wiretap.

"So Krieger asks me, 'Why were you there that day?' I tell him that the cops overheard Palmieri telling Rinaldo that something 'big' was coming in. He gave the details about where and when the ship was coming in. The cops told us, and that gave us the right.

"Meanwhile, Andrew has me slated for the sacrificial altar." Selvaggi heaves a heavy sigh. "When Andrew was working for Charlie, he was nice to me. He was Charlie's pilot fish back then, doing all of Charlie's paperwork. Then he started calling it 'My Bureau,' and that's when the calls start coming in. An agent calls and says, 'We're choosing up sides.' Then they start asking, 'How much money did you steal when you were on the Gambling Squad?' I'm riding around with Rinaldo, whose got a million-dollar price tag on his head. The Gambino family is going to shoot me up in the Bronx. It was getting crazy," Selvaggi says in dismay, snuffing out his cigarette. "The bottle was my only friend."

He looks away for a moment. "Finally an anonymous letter comes to the office, naming twenty-seven agents who are corrupt. We didn't know it as fact, but from the language you could tell it was written by an Italian from the Bronx. Meanwhile Feldman's on the block, so I asked for a transfer to the fugitive squad. Two weeks later Belk says, 'You're being transferred to San Francisco.' But my wife was pregnant with our fourth kid, and she didn't want to go.

"At that point I didn't know what to do anymore, so in August I quit. They threw a farewell party for me at Toot Shores, and some of the Assistant

US Attorneys were there. John Bartels [who became the first head of the DEA in July 1963] was there, and Rudy Giuliani [later mayor of New York], and Tendy. But no Belk, no Fluhr, no Matouzzi – Matouzzi, my friend, who had nineteen years on the job, and whose head was on the block too.

"After I quit I took a job with the sheriff's office in Westchester. But I'm not a federal agent anymore, and I've got enemies. Patty DeLuca hated my guts. DeLuca worked for Benny DeMartino in bookmaking, not drugs, but he loaned his car to Johnny Montera, who delivered half a kilogram of heroin to an agent. When Lenny Schrier arrested Montera, he put DeLuca in the case because Montera was in his car. Later on I arrested DeLuca. And when he gets out of jail, he's seeking revenge.

"One night after work, I go to Tony Amandola's place, the Chateau Pelham, where Scrocca got married. Nick Panella's there with some other agents. DeLuca walks in and starts yelling out remarks. I'm not an agent anymore, but no one else is saying anything!" Selvaggi makes a gesture. "Well, I'm the same man, with or without the badge. So I tell him, 'You're out of order. You're throwing rocks at the jailhouse.'

"I had to retaliate," he says, "but when I leave the place, DeLuca and three other guys are in the parking lot. They shove me around. Next time I go back to the Chateau Pelham, Amandola tells me I'm not welcome anymore. This is a guy whose son I went to high school with!

"Next I lose the job at the sheriff's office. Andrew has [FBN general counsel] Don Miller call them up, and that's that. So I took a job teaching business administration at New Rochelle High School. But the phone calls are still coming in, so my wife and I decided to sell our house, and I took a job collecting money for an insurance company in Florida. Eventually we used our savings to set up a delicatessen, and I spent the next ten years slicing baloney.

"Picture that," Frank Selvaggi says sardonically. "Me, slicing baloney."

28

ANDY'S GANG

"We had 300 agents worldwide:
290 were working integrity cases on each other,
and the other ten were keeping score."

Agent Joseph A. Quarequio

If you talk to his supporters, Andy Tartaglino comes across as the FBN's high priest and exorcist. But if you talk to the agents he targeted in his integrity investigation, you hear about a "scorpion" or a "tarantula" (a play on his name, even though in Italian it means "little turtle"), a merciless grand inquisitor who used his bureaucratic powers to destroy his personal enemies.

According to one of his victims, Chuck Leya, "When Andy came back from Italy, he was unassigned and started hanging out at the Court House Squad. By all appearances he was a good guy. Then he gets into Internal Affairs and gets a taste of blood. Soon it becomes an obsession. The man becomes rabid, and before you know it, a lot of innocent people get dragged in." Leya's words are laced with venom. "He sold himself as the strong-willed enforcer of principles, but he had his own problems, and among ourselves, we questioned his motives."

"Andy was a good agent before he went to Washington," George Gaffney agrees. "Then he changed. He developed an unbridled ambition."

He'd also become very powerful. He was serving as executive assistant to David Acheson, the Treasury Department's assistant secretary for law enforcement, and since 1965, he had been the engine of an anti-corruption unit that included Acheson's personal assistant for FBN affairs, Tony Lapham (the CIA officer who told Tartaglino to shut down the MKULTRA pad on 13th Street in New York); Henry Petersen at Main Justice; and Vernon "Iron Mike" Acree, the chief of IRS Inspections. By late 1966, Acree's team had assembled enough data on the targeted agents to allow Tartaglino to begin his inquiries.[1] But there was no way to conceal the investigation, and FBN Commissioner Henry Giordano was able to insist that New York District Supervisor George Belk be kept fully informed. Belk in turn assigned Art Fluhr, his trusted executive assistant, as his liaison to the IRS, and thereafter Fluhr kept Giordano abreast of any important developments.

Tartaglino and Inspector Irwin Greenfeld moved into an office on lower Broadway and began squaring agent net-worth and tax statements. "In one case an agent deposited $60,000 in his bank account," Tartaglino recalls with a mixture of amazement and contempt. "One deposit! I checked to see what cases had happened at the time, and found that two days before the deposit, the agent had arrested a guy with $300,000." He shakes his head and asks, "How stupid can you get? They think that because they're cops, they're above the law, and that no one will challenge them."

Inevitably, Tartaglino's integrity investigation uncovered corruption within the NYPD, as well as the FBN, and he began working with the NYPD's Office of Internal Affairs. Also joining him at this time was IRS inspector Thomas P. Taylor, a hard-bitten former New York detective. Since March 1967, Taylor had been investigating the NYPD for everything, in his words, "from attempted bribery and shakedowns, to sticking up crap games, to allegations about corruption in the Special Investigations Unit and the Bureau of Special Services and Investigations.

"I'd gone to the *Journal American* reporters who'd done the Kadlub investigation," Taylor explains, "and they turned their notes over to me, including the anonymous letter naming twenty-seven FBN agents as being involved in corruption. Some of the allegations were specific, so I sent the letter to Washington where it landed on the desk of Acheson's replacement, James Hendricks. Then came the June 1967 arrest of Secret Service Agent Gene Ballard and FBN Agent Jesse Spratley. They'd raided an apartment in New York, seized half a million dollars in counterfeit bills, and kept twenty grand for themselves. So this was a cumulative thing, with more and more people getting involved as the investigation expanded.

"We had information on informants," Taylor adds, "plus allegations about agents, and agents resigning – all of which culminates with the arrest [on 12 December 1967] of Frank Dolce and Jack Gohde. Dolce and Gohde had quit the FBN in 1966 and gone to work for the Nassau County narcotics squad, and they were actually selling dope out of their office. Gerson Nagelberg and his wife, Vivienne, were their source of supply, but we couldn't show it, because the informants were deathly afraid of Gohde, who'd allegedly killed someone for the love of Viv."

THE NAGELBERGS

Gerson "Gerry" Nagelberg played a central role in Tartaglino's integrity investigation. Born in 1912 in Germany, he came to America as a young man, became a citizen and served in the Second World War. Afterwards he made enough money in bookmaking to buy several nightclubs, which he used as fronts for his drug dealing operations. As an insurance policy, he paid former NYPD narcotic detectives to manage his bars, and his bar on Amsterdam Avenue in Harlem was a favorite hangout for several FBN agents. Morty Benjamin says, "They'd go in for a drink, have dinner on the house, and then Gerson's wife Vivienne would ask a small favor: 'Will you run a plate for me?' If they did, Viv would say, 'Let me thank you.' She had a stable of gorgeous girls who provided the favors, and that was her hook. A few weeks later she'd call the agent again, wanting to know the price of an ounce of heroin on the street. She got them to violate small rules first, then once she got her hooks into them, she got them to break the big rules."

Nagelberg came to the FBN's attention in the late 1950s, and Lenny Schrier arrested him in 1961. Charlie McDonnell and John Coursey did the undercover work on the case, at the Place Pigale on Amsterdam Avenue. Nagelberg became Schrier's informant, although it's unclear how many cases, if any, he enabled Schrier to make over the next few years. What's known is that in 1965 Nagelberg traveled to Marseilles and acquired a French connection through Dimitrio Porcino, an associate of the Guérini crime family in Nice. Couriers were hired and the machinery set in motion, and all went well for Nagelberg and Porcino until 1967, when Bob DeFauw uncovered their operation.

"Schrier and Frankie Waters were always calling me," DeFauw says irritably, "asking about the Guérinis. Schrier even talked to Antoine through an interpreter. So I had Joe Catalanotto set up a delivery into Montreal." DeFauw notified Customs Inspector Frank Cornetta (a former FBN agent) about the delivery, and on 27 May 1967, two of the Nagelbergs' couriers were caught bringing six kilograms of heroin into Dorval International Airport.

"Early that day I got a call from Lenny," Morty Benjamin recalls, "saying there was a load coming into Dorval, so I hopped on a plane and flew up to Montreal to work with Fred Cornetta, the Customs inspector up there. We're looking around the airport while Canadian Customs was making the bust, and I see Viv standing off to one side! I'd met her back in 1961 when Lenny first busted Gerry. So Fred and I grab her and take her to a room, where she tells me she's working for Jack Gohde. She thinks Gohde's still with the FBN! So I immediately called Lenny to verify what she had said. Lenny says, 'I'll get right back to you,' and he calls Gohde. Gohde denies everything, so I return to New York and write a memo that includes all the allegations Viv made about drug dealers who had their hooks into agents, and vice versa." [2]

Benjamin wrote his initial report on 9 June 1967, reciting Vivienne's allegation that she had introduced Gohde to "the Fraulein" (a prostitute named Ursula working for Ike Feldman, perhaps in a MKULTRA blackmail scheme that targeted Russians and East Germans at the UN), and that Gohde had shot drug trafficker John Cangiano. She named FBN agents Frank Bishopp, Cleophus Robinson and Lenny Schrier, and Assistant US Attorney Bill Tendy, as her friends. She said that "even your district supervisor, Mr. Belk, owes me a favor too."

"Belk wouldn't front the money to make the call to Marseilles to confirm Jack Gohde's tie to Nagelberg," Benjamin frowns. "Maybe he thought I was wrong. Maybe not."

Or maybe Belk was covering himself. In 1965, he wrote a letter to federal prosecutors that got Gerson Nagelberg off his 1961 bust. Belk wrote the letter because Schrier said the Nagelbergs were his best informants. But were they? "He had to attribute the cases he was making to someone," an agent comments, "so maybe he wrote them off as being made by Nagelberg?"

TARTAGLINO'S TACTICS

By the summer of 1967, Tartaglino had indexed every New York agent's tax returns, and had started questioning them about their finances. "You're trying to get leads," he explains, "but you're also trying to sew up a case against the agent; and to get perjury, you have to know the answers to some of the questions you ask. That's how you get them to lie under oath. It was lots of work, and it was frustrating too, because we'd have a good case going, then suddenly the agent would quit and jump to BDAC."

As Art Fluhr recalls, "Treasury sent in the IRS inspectors, and the first thing they did was investigate Belk and me. They did an in-depth audit of our net worth, and we were cleared, and I was made the liaison between

Giordano and the IRS. Then Andy starts coming in with cases. In one case he says, 'You've got a guy here who never filed an income tax statement in his life.'

"I said, 'Andy, you're telling me something, but what's it got to do with the FBN? If the agent's got a job on the side, and he's not reporting it, how the hell is Belk supposed to know?' But Andy insisted, so I asked him why he hadn't filed. He says, 'I'm single, so they take it out anyway.' I tell him, 'You gotta file.' So he files and gets a refund! But like a lot of guys, he's so mad he quits. He starts a security firm for Motown Records, and soon he's making ten times more money than he ever did with the Bureau.

"When Andy came in," Fluhr snarls, "it was all corruption, and fifty good agents went down the drain for nothing."

Having backed the agents into a corner, Tartaglino began to examine their informant files. "If an agent has an informant who's going to get twenty years," Tartaglino explains, "the agent will tell him, 'Make cases for me and I'll get the sentence reduced.' And that's okay. But some of the agents weren't doing anything to get the sentences reduced. They were keeping the informants on a string. And then, in some cases, the informant would die."

Tartaglino's eyes are twinkling. "Say I've got three buys on Gotti through my informant, Pascoli, who has to testify at the trial. So I arrest Gotti, and in the car I mention where Pascoli lives. Gotti leaves a bundle of cash on the seat, and the next thing you know, Pascoli gets killed. And that's how it worked."

Knowing it was the only way to make cases on bad agents, Tartaglino decided to take over the FBN's entire stable of informants. Chuck Leya was in the office when Belk assembled all the agents and delivered the news. "As you can imagine," Leya says, "the impact was explosive: FBN operations in New York came to a screeching halt, the good agents got demoralized, and the bad agents ran to the US Attorney's office to cover their asses — and they started calling their informants too."

Tartaglino then started hiring informants, including Richard Lawrence, to set up the bad agents. The scheme worked like this: Andy would have the informant call up his case agent and say, falsely, that some other agent was selling dope. If the case agent did not report the allegation, no matter how outlandish, he could be fired. But many of the informers double-crossed Tartaglino. After promising to cooperate, they'd call up their case agent and sell updates on his progress. When he found out that this was happening, Tartaglino tried to checkmate the bad informants by asking US Attorney Robert Morgenthau not to "write off" any more cases.

"If you have an informant who'll cooperate," Chuck Leya explains, "you've got to play along with him in order to make cases. But headquarters didn't see it that way, so it was tough to begin with. Then Andy had everyone turn over his informers, and that's when it mushroomed. That's when Andy started turning the informants against the agents. Now if I'm an informer and I'm compromised, Andy's going to be my savior. It happened to me with one of my informants. He tells Andy that I used the office car for personal reasons and that my reports weren't accurate. Soon I'm heading for an administrative hearing. So I quit."

MYSTERIOUS RESIGNATIONS

Morty Benjamin vividly remembers the day, 3 November 1967, that his friend and mentor, Lenny Schrier, was called up front. "The inspectors were there," he says, "and a few hours later, Lenny comes out, white as a sheet." Morty whispers softly, "He passed right by me without saying a word, cleaned out his desk, and I never saw him again."

A few minutes later, Benjamin was called into the front office, and Artie Fluhr told him that Schrier had been asked to explain a large deposit in his bank account. Schrier said his father had been a cab driver all his life, and had saved a large sum of money in a box, which he gave to Lenny to deposit in his account. According to another source, Schrier said the money was a cash inheritance his wife had received from a former employer. But apart from the money, there was also the issue of his relationship with the Nagelbergs, and six days after Schrier resigned, two more of Nagelberg's couriers were caught at Orly Airport with five kilograms of heroin, while boarding a flight to Bermuda. As Vic Maria recalls, "When we made the bust, the [couriers] implicated Lenny Schrier. So we just naturally assumed that Morty Benjamin, who'd worked for Lenny all those years, was involved too."

As the Nagelberg investigation expanded to include Benjamin, former FBN agents Frank Dolce and Jack Gohde – then investigators for the Nassau County Sheriff's office – were arrested on 12 December 1967, based on information provided by cooperating informant Eddie Mitchell. Also arrested that day were FBN Agent Cleophus A. Robinson, and NYPD Special Investigations Unit detectives Raymond Imp, Marvin Moskowitz, and Charles Kelly. Robinson was charged with selling marijuana; Kelly, Imp and Moskowitz were charged with selling cocaine; and Dolce and Gohde were charged with selling heroin.

"That's when the case breaks wide open," Tom Taylor says excitedly. "We had wired Jack Gohde's informant, and he'd met with Dolce and Gohde at various places. Then we make a heroin buy from them right in the Nassau County Sheriff's office! The arrests weren't pleasant, but they didn't resist. Then the Nassau DA put out a press release saying he had done all the work." Taylor laughs. "He hadn't. He just had the balls to say he had."

Around this time, the Paris office (which had set up the bust of Nagelberg's couriers at Orly Airport and in Montreal), gave Tartaglino the ammunition he needed to oust a corrupt group leader, whose name Tartaglino would not reveal for ethical reasons. "The group leaders in New York were talking on a regular basis with Vic Maria in Paris," Tartaglino explains, "exchanging information so as not to get into hassles with the French over unilateral operations and wiretaps. Then an informant in Paris calls us up and says he can buy anything out of the New York office. He says a group leader would call Customs to let him through, and Customs would do it. The informant didn't say he was carrying drugs on these trips, but if he is, it's a big problem.

"I didn't tell Belk," Tartaglino continues, "but we planted a false set of facts in the office through Interpol, and the day before the informant was going to buy the information, I asked Belk to call a group leaders' meeting for the next day. All of them showed up except one, who was on the phone with the informant." Tartaglino adds with a level look, "The Assistant US Attorney said that one buy was not enough to indict, and the person quit two days later."

THE DAY OF INFAMY

"New York was like an agency unto itself," Art Fluhr says, "and Andy was after anyone who'd been there during 'the corrupt days.' But most of all he wanted Frankie Waters.

"Waters was the reason I was demoted the first time," Fluhr adds laconically, "by which I mean the shooting incident in Paramus, New Jersey, on October 21, 1967 – what I call, 'The Day of Infamy.' At the time, Waters was teaching a course in investigative techniques to some local cops in Ramsey, New Jersey. The course had ended, and we were having a graduation party at a local gin mill. Belk's there with most of the group leaders, and he makes a wisecrack about some guy's wife. The guy makes a move on Belk, and Waters flattens him with a barstool. A fight breaks out between the cops and the agents, so we hustle Belk the hell out of there, and take him to another saloon up the line, where the police chief of Paramus is having a party. It's two in the morning. The place is closed. We're inside and we hear shots. We go outside and see Frankie Black on the hood of my Buick Riviera. He'd put a bullet through the windshield!

"Next morning I get a call. All the wives are talking. So I go back to Paramus, knock out the windshield and drive the car across the George Washington Bridge to a repair shop. Later that day Pat O'Carroll calls. Pat was the training chief down in Washington, and he'd been up for the festivities. Pat tells me the police chief is upset: some innocent bystander has a broken arm and the chief's going to have a line-up of FBN agents to try to identify who did it."

Fluhr takes a sip of his bourbon. "Belk was supposed to go to the graduation ceremony that day. Now he can't. Then a sergeant comes by with a reporter and Nick Panella's Hunter College ring, which is the only evidence they have. I smooth things out, get the ring back, and nothing's said for two months, until Waters gets drunk one night and tells Chan Wysor, who tells Gaffney, who calls me down to Washington. Gaffney's looking to nail Belk, so I covered his ass. I said it was all my fault, and that's how I got demoted the first time."

"Oh, no!" Frankie Waters bellows. "It didn't happen like that! Fluhr was Belk's assistant, and he decided who got to use the seized cars. I'm a group leader, and he promises me a nice new Oldsmobile that's sitting in the garage. I wait three months for the thing, then he goes and takes it for himself!"

Frankie Waters smiles his demonic smile. "At the time I was teaching a class at the police academy in Bergen County. I'm teaching rookie cops how to be a lawman within the Bill of Rights. Miranda-type stuff. I'm teaching this course because I can articulate the rules," he laughs, "not because I followed them.

"Anyway, after the course is over the students throw a party for the instructors. Everyone gets drunk and Belk says something totally out of character to a woman. That's the way it is with episodic drunks. Anyway, her date gets up to smack Belk, so I hit him with a barstool. He was a big guy, and I was glad he stayed down. Then we fled the scene. We drive up to this place where Fluhr has that nice new Olds parked outside. Seeing it there was too much for me to bear, so I put a round through the window."

Rather than take a transfer to Dallas, Frankie Waters resigned "for service reasons" on 1 December 1967. And thus, by the end of 1967, Frank Selvaggi, Lenny Schrier, and Frankie Waters had resigned, bringing the era of freewheeling case-making agents to a close.[3]

THE TASK FORCE

"By late 1967," Tartaglino says, "about 140 people are being investigated, but it's hard to make cases because resources are scarce. It was time to do something more substantial, so I suggested to James Hendricks that we create a Task Force, which would use the same techniques to investigate agents that agents used to investigate dope dealers. Hendricks sent me to Giordano for approval, and Henry said, 'Do you know what you're doing to me?'

"I asked him, 'What do you want me to do?'

"Hendricks was generous," Andy continues, "and okayed four people for the Task Force. I wanted a cross-section, from conservative to liberal, but all with solid integrity, and each a district supervisor with status. Frank Pappas from Baltimore was strictly by the book. John Evans from Atlanta and Bowman Taylor from Boston were in the middle, and John Windham from Kansas City was our conscience. They were all very conscientious. We'd have meetings and manage by consensus, thumbs up or thumbs down. I'm also a strong believer in documentation – that whenever someone tells you something you write it down, and afterwards decide whether it's worth saving. Down the pike, this is very important."

John Evans is a medium-built man, forthright, tough as nails, and hard to impress. He compares the New York agents who protected drug dealers to the FBN executives who protected the CIA drug dealers. "Conscience starts where digestion stops," he says.

Evans is a sentimentalist too. He dedicated his life to the FBN and has the scars from three open-heart operations to show for it. Raised in a tough section of Detroit, he pulled himself out of a street gang, graduated from Michigan State, and, after a stint in the military, joined the FBN in his hometown as a member of District Supervisor Ross Ellis's infamous 'Purple Gang' (which, of course, is a play on the name of a gang of criminals that dominated Detroit in the 1920s and 1930s).

"The legend of the Purple Gang," Evans explains, "is that George Belk and Phil Smith, who came out of Detroit, had control of the Bureau. But the legend grew because Ellis promoted his agents faster than the other district supervisors. In some regions you sat at grade seven for three years, but Ross promoted guys to grade nine after one. That fostered a spirit of cooperation, and we stuck together. We also worked with the Detroit cops and the Michigan State Police. Friendships formed, and that's how it got to be known as the Purple Gang."

After making a big case on a Lebanese trafficker, Evans in 1962 replaced Walt Panich as Ross Ellis's enforcement assistant. He advanced again in

1965, becoming the domestic enforcement chief in Washington under Ray Enright, and in 1966 he was made district supervisor in Atlanta.

"I was in Atlanta," he recalls, "when Andy called from New York and said, 'Come up right away. It's secret.' I arrived the day after New Year's and started working with Bo Taylor and Ike Wurms. John Windham worked with Pappas, while Andy went on his own track regarding the suicide of Crofton Hayes, and some other areas that were of personal interest to him.

"New York," Evans emphasizes, "was not a place I liked. The agents were bitter and salty and, according to them, no one but them ever got anything he deserved. Ross Ellis had been an agent in New York after the war, and he told me stories of agents shooting up in the men's room on the sixth floor at 90 Church Street. Another time we sent four agents from Detroit to New York. Three went bad, and the fourth came back and said, 'The moment you step on the street, you're into felony shit.' So I had some idea of what to expect. But God knows I came away wizened: agents were committing murder one, selling kilos of dope, and running all sorts of scams.

"There was one guy," Evans says, "who produced a lot of cases working with the SIU. But they were shaking guys down. He'd give the cops a hundred dollars for each case they came up with in state court, then they'd work together on paper to meet his case initiation quota. He'd make out his daily reports once a week. Then he'd go to Belk and say, 'This informant can make Vito, so let's not run him through the process.' Then he'd go to the US Attorney and say, 'I'm using the guy, keep him cool.' Belk and the US Attorney would agree, so now his informant reports are covered, too.

"Then comes the payoff. The cops arrest Vito and tell him, 'It costs two grand a week to stay out of jail.' Vito asks, 'What have I got to do to fix it once and for all.' They tell him, 'Forty grand.' The case is going to federal court, where they need the informant to identify Vito – and that's when the informant gets iced."

Belk, according to Evans, was an honest cop who inherited the corruption and the CIA shenanigans, and got caught in the middle of Gaffney's power struggle with Giordano. "Belk was close to Giordano," he explains, "but not Gaffney, and when Giordano sent Belk into New York, Gaffney was worried about what he'd find. So Belk and Giordano shut Gaffney out. Then Andy went over Giordano's head to Hendricks, which is why Art Fluhr couldn't cover Belk's ass. And which is why, when push came to shove, Giordano backed off and let Belk fade the heat.

"The mandate from Hendricks was to get people off the job," Evans says, "and our main targets were the higher-ups – group leaders and above.

We also tried to solve the murder of an informant, which no doubt happened, although no one was ever caught. But the partners who were involved were removed on other charges. That's how it worked. When we couldn't nail them for criminal violations, we'd get them on administrative. So there was lots of broom-sweeping."

Among the Task Force's main targets were Gaffney, John Dolce, Pat Ward, and former members of Group Three and the Gambling Squad. As Evans recalls, "Dolce owned a beautiful house and wore expensive clothes, all of which he explained by saying that his wife was an heiress. But he was a friend of Pat Intreri [who resigned in 1972, formed a private investigation firm, and became a bodyguard for drug trafficker Vincent Papa] at the SIU, and with Deputy Chief Inspector Ira Bluth, who ran the NYPD's Narcotic Bureau until we came along. Dolce was also close to Pat Ward, who Andy believed was 'the Grand Architect' of corruption in New York. But Dolce resigned in 1965, and Ward got out of New York just in time and went to Chicago."[4]

Tom Tripodi offers a hypothetical reason for why Pat Ward was considered "the Grand Architect" of corruption in New York. "An agent makes a buy off an Italian," Tripodi explains, "and the enforcement assistant knows. He says, 'Go back and make a second buy.' But the day after we make the first buy, someone goes to the Italian and says, 'For two big ones you won't go to jail.' On the day before the second buy, the Italian flees. The enforcement assistant knows the guy's in Miami, then Canada, then he says, 'Well, he's gone. Close that case out.'"

Tartaglino had another, personal reason for targeting Ward. They had worked together in New York in the early 1950s, and he never forgot how Ward would cup one hand behind his back and joke in Italian about "the cripple." The image was of a man taking a bribe, and Tartaglino hated the ethnic slur, as well as the implication that taking bribes was humorous.

Discussing Tartaglino's pursuit of Ward is not an easy thing for George Gaffney to do. "Pat was appointed district supervisor in Chicago and served there until 1968, when they gave him orders to go to Detroit. He'd just bought a house, so he applied for the job of chief investigator for Ed Hanratty, the Cook County DA. He was about to take the job when [FBN General Counsel] Don Miller calls up Hanratty and says, 'We will not work with you if you hire him.' When Hanratty asked why, Miller simply repeated the ultimatum."

Gaffney pauses to compose himself, then says, "Pat Ward was never charged with anything, but he was hounded until he was forced to quit."

Gaffney tells how it felt to be isolated and targeted himself: "At one point I received orders in writing from the assistant secretary of Treasury, saying I could no longer exercise any control in New York. Not even to visit the office! I was so far out of the loop, Lenny Schrier was off the job three months before I knew about it." With an icy glare, Gaffney says, "Eventually I was called to Main Treasury and asked to resign. I told them: 'It'll be a cold day in hell before I do that. And don't try to force me out either, unless you're ready to have an explosion.'

"In the old days," Gaffney says philosophically, "agents exercised initiative and ingenuity. We didn't call headquarters for permission, which is why we were successful. We weren't micro-managed. We had 300 agents with a $3 million budget, which was less than 4 percent of the budget for federal law enforcement, and yet we accounted for 15 to 20 percent of all the inmates in federal prisons. We put away more Mafia than everyone else combined. Then they accuse us of corruption." Gaffney shakes his head in disgust.

Art Fluhr agrees that there was no proof that Pat Ward was the Grand Architect of corruption in New York. "Andy made a lot of accusations and caused a lot of turmoil, but the agents who went to jail went because of local offenses, not through anything Andy found. Andy's Gang was all petty bullshit. He'd come into my office and say, 'You got a guy here who took the tires off a surplus car and put them on a government car.' And I'd say, 'For Christ's sake, Andy, we get $250 dollars a month to repair seven cars!'

"The focus of Speer's investigation was Group Three," Fluhr says bitterly, "but Andy's investigation hit everyone, whether they were right or wrong!"

John Evans agrees. "Andy got affected. He was too close, too long."

HOW THE TASK FORCE WORKED A CASE

Tartaglino's investigation soon spread from New York to St. Louis, Chicago, Baltimore, and New Orleans, where agent Luis Gonzalez found his head on the chopping block in the spring of 1968. A Puerto Rican-American from the wiseguy section of South Brooklyn, Luis loved being an FBN agent. Working for public sanitation, or becoming a cop, were the two avenues of escape from his neighborhood, and he felt like he had become "a corporate executive" when he was hired by John Dolce in 1960. He served for the honor of serving.

Among his colleagues, Luis earned a reputation as one of the best undercover agents ever. From Lenny Schrier he learned how to develop informers, and from John Coursey he learned how to stay in control of the situation. "They taught undercover work at the Law Enforcement

School," Luis says matter-of-factly, "and you can pick up stuff there – but it's not like the action."

In the course of his career, Gonzalez worked on the French Connection case, and testified against Ambassador Pardo Bolland. He was the first Puerto Rican to get inside the Mafia, and he made the case against a famous Mafioso, Gianotti Salzano. "The conviction was based on my word against his," he says with pride. But more often than not, Gonzalez worked on major Hispanic violators, and he made cases on Patsy Vellez, Carlos Ortiz, Willie Angelet (who was half Italian, half Puerto Rican), "One-Eyed" Benny Rodriguez, and Enrique Carbonelle. A drug trafficker who had been in Batista's Army in Cuba, Carbonelle became an informer and took Gonzalez and John Coursey to "El Cubiche." Better known as Felix Martinez, El Cubiche was a major drug trafficker with a French connection through Argentina.

Gonzalez's problems with Andy's Gang began shortly after his transfer in 1967 to Miami, where the resident, non-Hispanic agents had been unable to develop any major cases, and where he found himself entangled in CIA intrigues. "Tripodi was there with the CIA," Gonzalez says, "and through him I was introduced to a few of the CIA Cubans who were messing around with guns and drugs. One of them, cab driver Rudy Garcia, introduced me to a Mexican who wanted to sell dope. I told the Mexican I wanted to buy, but I wanted to meet his man first.

"The Mexican was prepared to take me to his source," Gonzalez says, "but the agent in charge in Miami, Bob Nickoloff said there wasn't enough money in the budget.

"To make a long story short, Nickoloff and I didn't get along after that, so they send me to New Orleans in early 1968. I'm there a few weeks," Gonzalez says with a shudder of emotion, "and I get a phone call at the office. There's no one else in the office, and the guy asks for me, specifically. He says he's been making trips to South America. He's a co-pilot, and he's going again soon with the pilot to pick up several kilograms of cocaine.

"'Why are you telling this to me?' I ask him.

"'I don't want to get in trouble,' he says. 'If you don't believe me, I'll give you a sample.' He tells me where the hotel is, and then he says, 'But you'd better come over right now, because we're leaving soon.'

"So I go to the hotel, which is near the airport. The rule is to always take someone along, but no one else is there, so I go alone." Gonzalez struggles to maintain his composure. "The guy's in a pilot's uniform. He takes half an ounce of coke out his flight bag. When he shows it to me, I see a small vial inside the bag. I tell him, 'Take that out, too.'

"'It's for the pilot's personal use,' he says. 'If I give it to you, he'll know.'

"'Okay,' I say. It's five in the afternoon. I wait around outside. I see a guy in a pilot's uniform enter the room, and I see them leave. They get in a car and I follow them. But I lose them, so I head back to the office and turn the half-ounce over to the agent in charge, Jim Bland, and we open the case. But when I report to work the next day, Bland comes in and says, 'Frank Pappas and John Windham are here and they want to see you. Bring your dailies.'

"I ask him, 'What's this about?'

"'You'll see,' he says."

Gonzalez is stone-faced. "Pappas was the pilot, Windham was the co-pilot. They cite me for leaving the office without an escort, and for letting dope leave the country. Then they come at me from leftfield; they mention Gohde and Dolce. They try to flip me, and that's when I blew up."

A case-making agent who kept the faith, Luis Gonzalez smiles bravely. "So I agreed to leave for falsification of documents and frequency of transfer, which was bad for the health of my kids. But I was never told I could have legal advice, and they got me to resign in the heat of the moment. It was a total set-up."

REQUIEM

"Andy's Rangers were supposedly after the group leaders and the supervisors," Frank Selvaggi says solemnly, "but who gets hurt? Luis Gonzalez, an undercover agent."

Selvaggi grimaces. "There was never any reason for it. They say that Nixon got $5 million from the mob. Milliken steals billions. There's heroin disappearing from the NYPD Property Clerk. Siragusa says the Pope has a mistress and the mob is shaking him down. I meet Guido Penosi in Miami: I lose my wife, my kids, my pension, my career."

"I think it's significant," Frankie Waters says about the December 1965 Nebbia case, "that out of the multitude of cops and agents – not just from the FBN, but from Customs and the CID too – that descended on Columbus from all over Georgia, Florida, and North Carolina, that it was two New York City street agents who did the crucial surveillance, uncovered the cache, and made the pivotal arrest. That's me and Frank Selvaggi, and we did it alone.

"We – whose methods were so awful, and who were later vilified – brought down the beast. And while the others gathered to feast on it, and survive on its entrails for years to come, the street agents moved out to seek and bring down another beast."

No statement better captures the fate of the wolf pack. Its methods were often unlawful, so the Establishment it had faithfully served turned on it and hunted it down. Having gone the way of the Latin Mass, the greatest federal law enforcement agency ever faded from America's collective consciousness without fanfare, amidst the turmoil of the Tet Offensive, the assassination of Martin Luther King, and a rapidly unraveling, drug-addled society.

EPILOGUE

"Bureaus die when the structure of the state collapses."

William Burroughs, *Junky*

By 1967, studies and statistics showed that drug related arrests (most involving kids under twenty-one) were rising faster than those in any other category of crime, and that drug abuse was a factor in the civil rights and anti-war demonstrations that were dividing the nation. Seizing upon this issue, the opportunistic Republicans blamed the problem on the liberalizing effects of LBJ's Great Society, and they made "Law and Order" in general, and drug law enforcement in particular, a central theme in the forthcoming presidential campaign.

Enter Joseph Califano, the point man in the Johnson administration's war on drugs. A Brooklyn-born Harvard graduate, Califano had been inspired by JFK's call to public service, and had left a lucrative job with a powerful law firm to join Defense Secretary Robert McNamara's staff as a specialist on Latin American affairs. Recognized as one of the "best and brightest," he was hired by the White House in 1965 to prepare legislation and public relations campaigns to help quell the domestic political unrest that was causing the Johnson administration so much grief. After meeting with a number of criminologists in 1967, Califano concluded that one of the things that would help was a state-of-the-art drug law enforcement organization, situated for maximum effectiveness in the Justice Department.

Having determined that the FBN was obsolete, Califano in late 1967 sent emissaries to BDAC director John Finlator and Assistant Treasury Secretary James Hendricks with a proposal to combine BDAC and the

FBN. Both bureaucrats recoiled in horror. But irresistible forces were at work. Treasury Secretary Henry Fowler was pressing for spending cuts and Representative Wilbur Mills, Chairman of the Ways and Means Committee, wanted to trim social programs. So on 7 February 1968, the Johnson administration introduced Reorganization Plan No. 1, in which it proposed to combine the FBN and BDAC into the Bureau of Narcotics and Dangerous Drugs (BNDD) in the Justice Department. The stated reasons were: to end fragmentation by consolidating authority; to pave the way for closer relations with state and local governments; to improve worldwide operations by working more closely with other nations; and to conduct a nationwide public education program on drug abuse "and its tragic effects." [1] The unstated reasons were LBJ's wrath over the FBN's involvement in the Bobby Baker snooping incident, and the CIA's need to manage drug law enforcement without interference, especially in Southeast Asia.

After the initial shock – enforcement assistant John Enright likened it to "a drunken sailor marrying an old maid" – FBN executives scrambled to get with the program. Training chief Pat O'Carroll, for example, stepped out of character and, employing the techno-jargon of the era, said the merger presented an opportunity for "a rebirth, like a phoenix arising from the ashes ... using the instrumentalities of imagination, intellect, research and experience to establish an ecological, holistic point of view." It's hard to imagine an FBN agent buying that sales pitch, but there was more. According to O'Carroll, the rebirth was to be based on "a systems approach, rigorous comprehensiveness, and manipulation of models to achieve a dynamic creative equilibrium." [2]

While dazed FBN agents wondered what the hell a "creative equilibrium" was, a Task Force was formed in the office of the Deputy Attorney General to effect the reorganization. The principal representatives were BDAC's executive officer, Nelson Coon, and Ernie Gentry from the FBN. Subcommittees were formed to manage the transition and, according to O'Carroll in his thesis, the Task Force was the epitome of effective management, relying on Herbert Simon's theory of "systematic scanning of the environment, and sensitivity to problems and challenges."

Sensitivity, smensitivity. According to Walter Panich, a member of the FBN's Plans and Policy staff, the mood at headquarters was alternately frantic and bitter. "Giordano came back from a meeting with the Treasury secretary," he recalls, "and we had one meeting to prepare for this merger with BDAC. Gentry and I did most of the negotiations with Hugh Nugent, the Task Force chief at Main Justice, and with Assistant Secretary of Administration, Art Weatherby, at Main Treasury. And that was all the support we had."

In March, the Government Operations Committee held hearings on Reorganization Plan No. 1, and accepted the idea with the proviso that the National Institute of Mental Health be included, at which point the CIA quietly seized control of BNDD's Office of Science and Education. Having control of this aspect of drug law enforcement was crucial to the CIA, which fully intended to continue testing and employing "behavioral agents," even after October 1968, when it became a felony to manufacture, sell, and distribute LSD and other dangerous drugs.

A resolution to stop Reorganization Plan No. 1 was submitted by legislators concerned that BNDD's placement in the Justice Department would put too much emphasis on law enforcement, and not enough on research and prevention. They raised the specter of a Gestapo–style national police force. Worried that stiffer controls would reduce profits, the pharmaceutical industry also raised objections, but was persuaded that consolidation would lower costs. There were even mild protests from within the FBN itself. But, as George Gaffney recalls, "When Reorganization Plan No. 1 was being considered by the Senate, orders came to us from Treasury that we were not to lobby against it. It passed by five votes."

The resolution was rejected and in April 1968, Reorganization Plan No. 1 was signed into law by Deputy Attorney General Warren Christopher. The BNDD was officially in business. A few days later, Henry Giordano and John Finlator were appointed acting associate directors, with the understanding that a director would be chosen by June. Composed of 483 people from the FBN, 466 from BDAC, 12 from Main Treasury, and 60 from the Department of Health Education and Welfare, the new organization was to be phased in at 91 field offices under the direction of a joint Review Board. A timetable for implementation was set up, targeting October for complete "integration."[3] Letterhead paper was ordered and, in May, a corresponding Narcotics and Dangerous Drug Section was formed in the Justice Department under US Attorney William Ryan. Through this office, BNDD would obtain indictments and wiretap authorizations under Title III, and participate in Justice Department Strike Forces nationwide.

ENTER JOHN INGERSOLL

Joseph Califano, meanwhile, was meeting separately with Finlator and Giordano, telling each one not to worry. And on the day of reckoning, the eager executives arrived in the Attorney General's office wearing their best blue suits, each one fully expecting to be chosen as BNDD's director. Instead they were introduced to John E. Ingersoll.

"I was there afterwards," Andy Tartaglino recalls, "when Giordano went to Hendricks to complain. Hendricks asked him, 'What exactly did Califano say?' 'He said he'd take care of me,' Henry replied. 'But did he promise you the job?' To which Henry hung his head and said, 'No.'"

On 12 July 1968, Attorney General Ramsey Clark announced John Ingersoll's appointment as BNDD's director, knocking many a proud FBN agent to his knees. Not only had they been forced into a shotgun wedding with the chicken pluckers, but their new leader had never made an undercover buy or bust. To make matters worse, Ingersoll projected nothing but disdain for the FBN's legacy, along with a fierce desire to put as much distance as possible between himself and the growling wolf pack he had inherited. It was not an auspicious beginning.

Ingersoll's qualifications for the job were strictly managerial. He had a degree in criminology and public administration, and as a policeman in Oakland in the 1950s, he had come under the tutelage of law enforcement guru Orlando Wilson, and was chosen by Wilson to head a showcase research unit in the Oakland PD. On Wilson's recommendation, Ingersoll in 1961 was appointed director of Field Services for the International Association of Chiefs of Police (IACP) and began his ascent to national prominence. Ingersoll was appointed to Kennedy's Blue Ribbon panel, where he (gasp) expressed his opposition to mandatory sentencing – the backbone of drug law enforcement – and advocated the transfer of the FBN from Treasury to Justice.

"He was trying to grapple with the problem on an intellectual level," a supportive colleague explains.[4]

Ingersoll's intellectualism may not have been appreciated by the FBN, but it did enable him to achieve results. As director of IACP's Field Services he conducted a study of the Charlotte, North Carolina, Police Department. The study resulted in his appointment as Charlotte's police chief in July 1966, and by applying his progressive ideas, he defused the department's racial tensions and curbed corruption in its narcotics squad. Ingersoll's program became a model for big cities around the nation, and he became the IACP's poster boy. Knowing it would increase his benefactors' clout in Congress, he allowed himself to be promoted as a clean-cut family man, above moral reproach, who could unite federal, state, and local agencies in an enlightened, systematic approach to drug law enforcement.

In preparation for his job as director of the BNDD, Ingersoll was briefly assigned as an assistant director at the pork barrel Law Enforcement

Assistance Administration (LEAA), which allotted federal dollars to politically correct state and local police departments. While there he tracked the reorganization and met with staff officers and field supervisors from BDAC and the FBN. Preceded by their cynical reputations, the FBN agents were received less warmly than their earnest BDAC rivals, who quickly adopted Ingersoll's policies in hopes of obtaining key positions.

At Ingersoll's direction, BNDD was divided into divisions for Enforcement, and Regulatory and Scientific programs. Giordano became associate director for Enforcement, and George Belk became his special assistant. Enforcement had three offices: Domestic Investigations under John Enright; Foreign Operations and Intelligence under former BDAC executive Ed Anderson; and Investigative Services under Walt Panich. John Finlator, as associate director for Regulatory and Scientific Programs, oversaw the Office of Training under Pat O'Carroll, the Office of Compliance under BDAC Supervisor Patrick W. Fuller, and the Office of Science and Education under Fred Garfield.

To protect himself from the wolf pack, Ingersoll circled himself with friends. Chief among the patronage appointees were Perry Rivkind (a wealthy Illinois Republican politico), as his executive assistant, and Michael Sonnenreich, who, as deputy to chief counsel Donald Miller, served as Ingersoll's *consigliere*. Ingersoll's top staff officers were Nelson "Bill" Coon, chief of the Office of Administration, and Andy Tartaglino, as chief of Office of Inspections. Like Ingersoll himself, this inner circle (except for Tartaglino) was regarded by FBN veterans as pudgy, arrogant, and naive.

Despite his awkward entrance, Ingersoll made a good impression on a few FBN agents, including George Gaffney. "He came in while I was on leave," Gaffney recalls, "and when I got back, all the top posts were filled. But Ingersoll was a gentleman, and he gave me a good assignment as his special assistant running a cooperative program with the Mexican government. The job was largely out of the office, working with the State Department and using AID money to provide the Mexicans with equipment and technical assistance – mostly small planes and helicopters – in an effort to eradicate marijuana and opium." Gaffney also represented Ingersoll at Interpol sessions, and served as Ingersoll's liaison to a Drug Abuse Committee at the Pentagon. The military's problem, of course, was escalating drug addiction on military bases and among soldiers in Vietnam.

PLAYING FOR POSITIONS

In breaching the walls of the BNDD, Ingersoll's most important personnel decision, made secretly, was awarding Andy Tartaglino the job of chief inspector. "I'd met with Ingersoll in April," Tartaglino says, "and had asked to be transferred from Main Treasury into BNDD, with status." In view of his own concerns about lingering corruption, Ingersoll agreed and, with Tartaglino as his filter, began the critical task of selecting eighteen regional directors. As Tartaglino recalls, "Ingersoll made every decision himself, in consultation with Giordano and Finlator." But he also privately asked Tartaglino about each candidate's "lifestyle" before the interview.

When the process was over, former FBN district supervisors held most of the regional director jobs in the BNDD, positions that were equivalent to their old ones. William Durkin acquired the prized New York regional director (RD) post, and George White's protégé, Dan Casey, won the equally desirable Los Angeles RD post. Not surprisingly, the four members of Tartaglino's anti-corruption Task Force all landed on their feet: Frank Pappas became the RD in Baltimore; John Windham got the RD job in Kansas City; Bowman Taylor became deputy RD in the newly created Miami region; and John Evans became chief of General Investigations under John Enright at the Office of Criminal Investigations. Giordano loyalist Fred Dick was sent to the National War College.

Some BDAC veterans did get RD posts – Otto Heinecke in Chicago, William Logan in Miami, and Richard A. Callahan in Boston – but generally speaking, BDAC veterans and outsiders fared better than FBN veterans in securing administrative positions. Top headquarters positions went to Edward Anderson as chief of Intelligence and Foreign Operations, and Edward Mullin as his deputy in charge of Intelligence. Mullin had served in the FBI, and reportedly spent a few years in the CIA's clandestine services. Accustomed to the latest technological advances, he was shocked to find that the FBN had no intelligence files or register of informants. Also a former FBI agent, Anderson quickly earned a reputation as a nitpicker who made stupid demands and kept his staff bogged down in unnecessary paperwork. At one point Hank Manfredi, the deputy in charge of Foreign Operations, went to John Evans at General Investigations and said about Anderson, "This guy's gonna drive me nuts!"

As one overseas FBN agent recalls, "The FBI was unbelievably jealous after Apalachin, and the sorehead attitude lasted until they had enough clout to put in Mullin and Anderson at BNDD. But they didn't have a clue. They were elegant window dressing, and when those two were there, we didn't know who was in charge."

Hank Manfredi's presence as chief of Foreign Operations provided some operational continuity, but he was suffering from heart disease, and wanted a sinecure post at the United Nations. Making matters worse, he had to wait while the books were cooked to square the differential between his FBN and CIA salaries; and while he waited, the UN job went to Pat O'Carroll. A promotion in July 1968 helped ease the pain, but by the end of the year the Nixon regime had seized control of the BNDD and had begun using it for nefarious political purposes. Instead of coasting to retirement, Manfredi found himself knee deep in Nixonian dirty tricks, powerless to protect himself.

A similar dilemma confronted CIA officer Paul Knight after he was ostensibly hired into the BNDD and made a staff assistant to Henry Giordano. According to Knight, his job was to prepare policies and procedures for the BNDD's rapidly expanding stable of overseas agents. In doing that, Knight stressed the need for a knowledge of foreign languages and laws: he taught incoming agents how to work with foreign cops and the diplomatic corps; how to acquire and handle the freewheeling soldiers of fortune who worked as informers overseas; and how to differentiate between "fascinating, accurate, and useless intelligence." No one, however, remembers seeing Knight at headquarters.

The selection process produced as many losers as winners, and caused considerable resentment. Several cases loom large. Ernie Gentry was so upset he retired. Pat Ward, who had just bought a house in Chicago, quit after being forced to take a transfer to Detroit. An agent since 1940, and the founding father of the Purple Gang, Detroit District Supervisor Ross Ellis was sent to Seattle, where he became despondent and took a demotion in order to return to Detroit as a group supervisor. Both Ward and Ellis had been long-time foes of Charlie Siragusa and, of course, Andy Tartaglino.

The indignities heaped upon Ward and Ellis did not sit well with many FBN agents. They blamed Ingersoll, Finlator, and Tartaglino, but the transition period had rendered them temporarily powerless. So they bided their time, barely concealing their resentment, and to the hundreds of new agents hired into the BNDD, the Purple Gang, under the leadership of Bill Durkin, George Belk, and Phil Smith (Belk's liaison to Justice Department's Strike Forces), came to include all former FBN agents – a fierce faction awaiting the day when they could crush pretentious John Ingersoll and his BDAC sycophants, exact revenge on Andy Tartaglino, and regain control of what was rightfully their organization.

CLEANSING THE SYSTEM

In his effort to modernize drug law enforcement, John Ingersoll appointed professional administrators to head the offices of Management Analysis, Personnel, and Finance, and he assigned accountants and financial experts as staff officers to the regional directors. And to help headquarters exert greater control over operations, a new breed of agent was cultivated. The ideal recruit was a Marine captain with Vietnam War experience and a college degree. More women and minorities were hired, and accelerated promotions and incentive payments became standard procedure. The training school was expanded to include a course for foreign policemen. Recruits were trained for six weeks rather than two in an expanded curriculum that included courses in how to work with the public, as well as with local and foreign law enforcement agencies.

One of Ingersoll's top priorities was internal security. Certain that many corrupt FBN agents had evaded justice by slipping over to BDAC, he asked Andy Tartaglino to pick up where the Task Force had left off in April 1968. Tartaglino leaped into action and began organizing his inspections staff at his office at 633 Indiana Avenue. The original members were Irwin Greenfield, Robert Goe, and – having ostensibly transferred back from the CIA – Tom Tripodi. The focus of Tartaglino's attention was still New York, where he worked closely with inspectors Tom Taylor (who had joined the BNDD) and Ike Wurms.

Not everyone was happy with this arrangement, and when John Finlator learned that Tartaglino had been appointed chief of inspections, he immediately contacted Criminal Division chief Henry Petersen at Justice, and complained that Tartaglino "operated alone," was "obsessed," and should not be left unsupervised. "To resolve the problem of fairness," Tartaglino recalls, "an assistant chief of the Criminal Division, Robert Rostall, was assigned to oversee the establishment of the inspections staff. To satisfy Finlator, Dick Callahan in Boston monitored the process. Callahan was a Finlator confidant whom I briefed before the merger."

With Callahan watching from the wings, Rostall reviewed the performance of Andy's Gang and declared it a success. He then traveled with Andy to make cases on agents in California, St. Louis, and elsewhere. Tartaglino and Rostall generated an average of two indictments per month, but Tartaglino's greatest triumph was a case he made on Charlie McDonnell, the sharp undercover agent from Group Three who had worked for Dan Casey in San Francisco before jumping to BDAC. Described as "affable" and "a gentleman," McDonnell was always dressed in a jacket and tie, and never let a partner buy turkey. As titular head of Black agents in New York, he had once slapped Bill Newkirk for coming to work drunk.

Alas, Charlie Mac was as wrong as a three-dollar bill.

The case on McDonnell began in New Orleans in 1967, when FBN Agent Jack Compton busted drug trafficker Marvin Sutton with a quarter-kilo of junk. Sutton flipped and named Joe Miles as his source. A former heavyweight boxer from Baltimore, Miles sold junk in New Orleans, where he owned a house of ill repute, and in New York, where he had worked for years as an informant for several agents. In 1967, he was secretly sharing an apartment, out of which they dealt narcotics, with Charlie McDonnell, BDAC's deputy director in Baltimore. Despite the fact that Agent Jack Peterson had blackballed Miles, he was utilized by McDonnell and Russ Dower, a former member of Group Three and the Gambling Squad in the FBN, who had followed Charlie Mac into BDAC. [5]

"We were developing a conspiracy case against Miles," Compton said in a statement given to US Attorney John E. Clark in Texas on 20 August 1975. [6] "Then Tartaglino and Company started leaning on me hard to get an arrest warrant for him. But we weren't ready to pull the plug, and the US attorney agreed that we should not prosecute at that time. But the inspectors wouldn't accept that, and Miles was arrested in New Orleans in March [1968]. It was a flimflam deal in which we loaned him a lot of money to come down. On hand for the bust were Tartaglino and my boss at the time, Frank Pappas.

"We're talking to Miles," Compton said in his affidavit, "and he starts making allegations about narcotic agents – that they'd been hijacking loads in New York. Out and out armed robberies. That they were taking ten-pound seizures of narcotics and giving them to Miles, who'd break off half and cut it back, to make what he was supposed to have. They'd turn in the weaker seizure, and Miles would sell the rest. They were actually peddling narcotics," Compton said incredulously, "but it wasn't coming fast enough, so the New York agents bought their own Italian connection. They were buying dope, just like any other dope peddler. [7]

"Miles said he was actually handling narcotics for these agents," Compton continued, "and he agreed to set up buys. So I recorded his conversations, with his permission, and we started making buys. But there was an ulterior motive," Compton added, "and that was to embarrass BDAC. We were making the buys on FBN agents who'd gone over to BDAC. And the first guy we bought off was the deputy director of BDAC in Baltimore, Charlie McDonnell. In the meantime the inspectors come down and took control of Miles. So my active participation with Miles ended, except I'd run into him every now and then on the street, and he'd tell me what they were doing – how they were buying off all these agents."

To help corral McDonnell in Baltimore, Andy recruited Tom Tripodi, Hank Manfredi, and Joseph "Nickel Bag Joe" Arpaio, head of the Washington field office. Tripodi knew the history, having investigated McDonnell once before in 1962, at Charlie Siragusa's request, regarding a suspicious deposit McDonnell had made in a Washington bank. Manfredi, meanwhile, was interviewing Joe Valachi at La Tuna Prison in Texas, about suspected New York agents.

By early 1968, the groundwork had been laid, and in April, Tartaglino and Arpaio watched while Miles bought two kilograms of heroin from McDonnell on a golf course in Maryland. The second buy was made in the Baltimore apartment that Miles and Charlie Mac shared. McDonnell (who had resigned from BDAC in May) was indicted in June and was arrested on a hot afternoon in July. David R. Wiser, having transferred from the CIA to the BNDD only a month before, was on the scene. "Charlie was at the dry cleaners where he was working," Wiser recalls. "I was outside with another new agent, Gary Warden, and some old-timers. When it came time to make the arrest, Arpaio sent Charlie Vopat into the store. Charlie was in the back, running the pants press machine. Vopat saw him there, came out, and gave us the signal that it was time to take him off."

When he was arrested, McDonnell was no longer an agent, but he quickly cut a deal with US Attorney Steve Saxe. The thing that helped McDonnell the most was that he said he had bought his heroin from Frankie Waters. He also had critical information in some 200 pending drug cases. In addition, Saxe knew that if the arrest were made public, he would not be able to make cases on McDonnell's accomplices. So he agreed to keep it quiet. But even then McDonnell was not fully forthcoming. In order to get anything at all, Saxe and Tartaglino had to resort to "a little code system." If McDonnell said a guy was "an agent's agent," it meant he was wrong.

The evidence was flimsy, but it was enough to start files on more than two-dozen agents, including Russ Dower and Frankie Waters. Intending to build his strongest case on Waters, Tartaglino hired Joe Miles as an agent provocateur, and obtained an arrest warrant for Dower, who was then serving as a BNDD agent in Connecticut. But Tartaglino wanted to use the warrant as leverage to get Dower to testify against Waters, and, mistakenly, he didn't execute it right away. "I asked if I could put it in my back pocket," Tartaglino says regretfully, "and Saxe gave his permission."

Next, Tartaglino had Miles call Dower to arrange a meeting, but Dower refused to talk on the phone. Although Miles's arrest record had been sealed, McDonnell had managed to sound the alert, and Dower was aware that he was being set up. So Tartaglino instructed Dower's boss in Boston, Dick Callahan, to order Dower to meet Miles in Washington, and to wear a wire. It was an order Dower could not refuse without projecting consciousness of guilt, so he went. But he went very cautiously, and when Miles started talking about McDonnell's allegations about Waters, Dower turned the wire off. Not easily outflanked, Tartaglino had wired Miles on another frequency and caught the subsequent conversation anyway.

"We arrested Dower in DC," Tartaglino says. "We showed him the warrant and the tape, and he talked for about three hours. He admitted some things, and laid other things out. But then he went and hired attorney Ed Rosnor, who told him to retract everything. Which he did. And when the case went to court, the judge said the tapes were inadmissible, because we had not advised him of his rights."

With Dower's flawed arrest, making a case on Frankie Waters became harder than ever. But Tartaglino forged ahead. Wasting no time, he ordered McDonnell to call Waters and arrange a meeting at the Eastern Airline lounge at La Guardia Airport. Tripodi wired Charlie Mac, and two agents secretly accompanied him on the plane. Other agents set up surveillance in the airport lounge, while Ike Wurms and Tom Taylor sat in a van in the parking lot, hoping to tape the conversation between Waters and McDonnell over the airport static.

"We saw a Lincoln Continental with DC plates pull up," Taylor says excitedly. "The driver's a tough-looking Black man. Frankie gets out of the Lincoln and goes inside the terminal. Frankie's a badass, and when we tell Charlie Mac that he's coming, we could feel the tension over the wire. Frankie sat down at the bar, and the first thing Charlie said to him was, 'I'm going back on the next flight, so we only have a few minutes.'

"Waters could tell by McDonnell's demeanor that something was wrong. 'Wait a minute,' Frankie says, 'I gotta talk to you.' At which point Charlie mumbles, 'They got one of your prints.'

"'We better lay low,' Frankie whispers back. Then Charlie says out loud, 'I need a quarter-key.' At which point Frankie invites him for a ride. Then the reception breaks apart. Frankie fades into the night, and Charlie Mac goes back to DC."

When told of Taylor's account, Frankie Waters gets visibly upset. "It's totally untrue that I went to meet Charlie in someone else's car. I went from my house in Hempstead in my Buick and returned the same way. I didn't want to talk to Charlie, and I never would have said, 'Hey, I gotta talk to you.' And he never said to me anything about my prints. Pure fiction."

When asked why he met with McDonnell, Waters says, "When Charlie was the BDAC boss in Baltimore, he made a lot of calls to me about cases. Even after I quit we talked a lot. But when we met at La Guardia, he was acting weird. So I excused myself and went to the men's room, and when I got there, Bob Williams [a National List narcotic violator and the man who was driving the Lincoln] was standing at the urinal. We go to have a drink, and he tells me funny stories." [8]

Some of the funny stories probably concerned the allegations made by McDonnell and Miles. And it must be stressed that, based on those allegations, Waters was tried and acquitted of selling heroin to McDonnell. In addition, McDonnell served a mere eleven months in prison for selling several pounds of heroin to Miles. "Don't you think it's significant that Charlie Mac was let out of jail after eleven months?" Waters asks rhetorically. "It's because he testified against me!"

Similarly, drug trafficker Joe Miles served no time, in exchange for his work in Tartaglino's investigation of agent corruption. As Jack Compton recalled in his affidavit, "My informants were telling me that Miles was selling narcotics, so I called Tartaglino and Company and told them. But they said, 'Leave him alone.' They came down on one occasion and busted his pad, with him in it." Compton added that Miles somehow got away, apparently with a kilogram of heroin that "never surfaced anywhere. He did it twice" – Compton told the prosecutors – "and my informants were starting to get the message. They started thinking that I was taking payoffs from Miles, because they could make him, and they wanted to make him. But [the inspectors] wouldn't touch him."

Compton concluded this portion of his affidavit by noting that shortly after Frankie Waters was charged, "Miles got seriously dead in New Orleans, and I don't think anybody has ever bothered to look very damned far in that case."

The Charlie McDonnell integrity case had repercussions that lasted for the next six years, during which time Andy Tartaglino would earn a reputation as a zealot whose purge destroyed the good, along with the bad and the ugly. And the tactics he used set a dangerous precedent. Years before, he had told David Acheson that in order to make a case on a bad agent, an inspector must use the same tactics an agent used to set up drug dealers. By 1968, those tactics included the same sin for which suspected agents were being investigated – enabling an informer to sell drugs with impunity.

THE SYSTEMS APPROACH

Providing informants with free passage had long been standard practice for the CIA, whose drug trafficking assets ranged far and wide around the world. Indeed, the CIA's involvement in international drug trafficking was so pervasive that eventually the spy agency decided to use Tartaglino's integrity investigation as a pretext to infiltrate the BNDD's inspections, intelligence, and special operations staffs, and seize control of most of its foreign operations. The CIA's infiltration of the BNDD was a development that fit neatly with the Agency's ever-expanding counter-terror operations worldwide, the political war it was waging in Washington on behalf of the Establishment, and with John Ingersoll's defective innovation, the "systems approach" to waging war on drugs.

Ingersoll's grand idea was to dispense with the old "two buys and a bust" approach. Agents would no longer pursue individuals; instead, the entire organization would be directed against several major drug trafficking systems. To effect this new strategy, the extant bits and pieces of information that existed in BDAC and FBN files were gathered, analyzed, and assembled by a think tank that featured George Belk on enforcement matters and Hank Manfredi on intelligence. Information about ongoing investigations was factored into the emerging systems and, after a year of preparation, the experts established nine general drug trafficking systems to investigate – nine being a number large enough to engage the entire organization, but small enough to be managed by desk officers at headquarters.

What emerged was an extrapolation of the biggest cases already being investigated, the most important being the French connection, which was held responsible for the majority of heroin entering America. Also targeted were systems encompassing anti-Castro Cubans, the world's biggest purveyors of cocaine; the Mexican marijuana cartels; criminals trafficking in non-narcotic drugs like LSD; and five others, including one for the Mafia. A desk officer monitored the system he was assigned to, provided money to the regional directors investigating the system, and worked with individual field agents to select targets of opportunity within the system. The incubation period lasted until December 1969, by which time the BNDD totaled 900 agents. Meanwhile, Ingersoll hired consultants from IBM to computerize the BNDD's administrative and operations offices.

Theoretically, the systems approach would allow for better allocation of resources, and enable managers to better coordinate domestic investigations with the BNDD's rapidly expanding foreign operations. Like the imperialists in Congress who had given Harry Anslinger his overseas mandate in 1930, Ingersoll in 1970 determined that "going to the source" was the only way to solve America's drug problem. That is where he concentrated the organization's resources, and that is what the FBN's overseas agents, at first only minimally affected by the massive reorganization at home, were already doing with substantial results.

In 1968, for example, federal narcotic agents seized over 5,000 kilograms of opium and 800 kilograms of morphine base in Turkey. Based on this statistic, and arguments presented by Jack Cusack (Ingersoll's advisor on Turkish affairs), the Nixon administration decided that Turkey was the source of 80 percent of the morphine base that was fueling the French connection in Marseilles. And by 1970, the State Department had adopted an extraordinary plan, developed by Cusack, to purchase Turkey's surplus opium crop.

The French connection was Ingersoll's major preoccupation, and in this regard he would break with traditions set by Anslinger and Giordano. With Tony Pohl as his interpreter and guide, Ingersoll would directly approach French officials and, in January 1970, would forge the landmark Franco-American Accord, in which the French agreed to talk to the Turks, and focus their enforcement efforts on Marseilles.

Ingersoll vastly expanded BNDD operations into Latin America, where Auguste Ricord's Group France was trafficking in tons of narcotics. Many permanent posts were established throughout the region, and scores of BNDD agents were sent on intelligence-gathering missions. In many areas their passage was made easier by CIA officer Byron Engle, chief of AID's Public Safety Program. AID, for example, provided the funds and aircraft for George Gaffney's marijuana eradication program in Mexico. There was, of course, a quid pro quo. Wherever Castro's agents were inciting revolution, the CIA was mounting counter-operations through its covert army of drug-smuggling anti-Castro Cubans. In exchange for providing the BNDD with covert financial and operational assistance, the BNDD granted drug-smuggling anti-Castro Cubans free passage; which, as one narcotic agent notes, "caused us problems, particularly in Bolivia and Mexico."

With the systems approach, BNDD agents began forming closer ties with the CIA in Turkey too. For example, the Bulgarian Secret Service was thought to be facilitating the smuggling activities of the Turkish Mafia, so in June 1968, Dick Salmi began working with CIA officer Duane Clarridge to chart the Bulgarian arms and drug connection to France, as well as arms and drug-smuggling routes through Afghanistan, Iran, and Iraq.

But as BNDD agents soon found out, the CIA was doing the same thing as its enemies. As part of its covert war against terrorism, the CIA hired arms traffickers to smuggle guns to counterinsurgents in dozens of foreign nations, and in exchange the gun smugglers were allowed to move drugs out. One CIA officer insists that the drug traffic was unintentional, the result of unscrupulous assets who exploited their free passage. "Just because they're dealing," he says, "it doesn't necessarily mean they're dealing for their respective secret services. Right?"

In response, another CIA officer notes that, "It is nice to have plausible deniability."

The problems of free passage and its stepsister, the controlled delivery, were the fatal flaws of the systems approach, as it was cast worldwide under the guidance and with the expertise of the CIA. To map out an entire system, BNDD agents had to stand back and watch the dope flow from one end to the other. They might have to repeat the process several times, and they might even have to provide security to keep the system intact. In other words, Ingersoll's foolproof systems approach was merely an extrapolation of Lenny Schrier's modest dictum that in order to make cases, an agent's informer has to deal narcotics. The systems approach was that practice, on a grand scale, and for that reason it undermined the BNDD's integrity and fueled America's drug epidemic of the 1970s and 1980s.

As Bowman Taylor caustically observes, "I used to think we were fighting the drug business. But after they formed the BNDD, I realized we were feeding it."

CODA

By November 1968, the Nixon administration was rattling the White House doors, and in an attempt to preempt the Republican invaders, Attorney General Ramsey Clark held a farewell news conference to proclaim the Johnson administration's success in killing off the Wolf Pack. "32 Narcotics Agents Resign in Corruption Investigation Here," read the headline in the 14 December 1968 *New York Times*. Clark noted that five of them – Russ Dower, Jack Gohde, Frank Dolce, Charlie McDonnell, and Cleophus Robinson – had been indicted, and that additional prosecutions and resignations would soon be forthcoming.

"After Clark made his announcement," Andy Tartaglino says dejectedly, "our informers were no good anymore. The integrity investigation was called off, but the job was only half-done."

However, with the help of the CIA, Tartaglino's corruption probe would soon be revived, only this time it would target some of the BNDD's highest executives, and in 1974 it would nearly kill the BNDD's successor organization, the Drug Enforcement Administration, in its cradle. But that calamity was yet to come. With the corruption purge swept under the carpet for the time being, the fledgling BNDD turned its attention to Richard Nixon's escalating and, as ever, deeply political war on drugs.

APPENDIX

PAGES FROM THE FBN INTERNATIONAL LIST BOOK

RESTRICTED - FOR OFFICIAL USE ONLY

NAME

Santo TRAFFICANTE Jr.

INTERNATIONAL LIST NO.

· 234

ALIASES

Samuel Balto

SIGNATURE FACSIMILE

DESCRIPTION

Born in Tampa, Florida on November 15, 1914; white; male; height 5'10½"; weight 175 lbs.; build medium; eyes blue; hair brown, balding; gun shot wound scar on upper left arm; small pit scar on forehead; wears glasses; uses contact lenses.

LOCALITIES FREQUENTED

Maintains home at 523 N.E. 71St., Tampa, Florida but resides at 2505 Bristol Avenue, Tampa, Florida. Frequents Italian restaurants in Tampa area and the better hotels in Miami Beach, Florida; visits major cities on the Eastern Seaboard of United States.

CRIMINAL ASSOCIATES

Antonio and Frank Diecidue of Tampa, Florida; Martin Fox; Frank Dioguardi and Michael Coppola of Miami Beach, Florida; Cuban racketeers in Miami, Florida involved in bolita operations.

(See Reverse)

CRIMINAL HISTORY

Record dates back to 1946 and includes arrests for general investigation; vagrancy; bribery; conspiracy to violate Federal Wagering Act. Arrested on 5-20-54 by Sheriff's Office, Clearwater, Florida for bribery; sentenced on 9-27-54 to 5 years in Florida State Prison; conviction reversed on 1-23-57 by Florida State Supreme Court. Picked up for inquiry on 1-3-58 by Department of Investigation, Cuban National Police.

MODUS OPERANDI

Knows most of the major sources of supply of narcotics in Central and South America. Suspected of smuggling narcotics into the United States. Involved in bolita operations in all of Florida. A powerful Mafia figure in Tampa, Florida. Attended the underworld meeting at Apalachin, New York on November 14, 1957.

AGENCIES FAMILIAR WITH INDIVIDUAL

Bureau of Narcotics, Bureau of Customs, Secret Service and Internal Revenue Service of the U.S. Treasury Department; Tampa, Clearwater, Miami and Orlando, Florida, Police Departments; NYC P.D.; New York State Police; F.B.I.

CRIMINAL IDENTIFICATIONS *(Agency & No.)*

Florida P.D. # A 37991.

F.B.I. # 482531B; Miami Beach,

FINGERPRINT CLASSIFICATION

19 0	14	U	000	0
I	22	R	00M	I

RESTRICTED - FOR OFFICIAL USE ONLY

NAME	INTERNATIONAL LIST NO.
Meyer LANSKY	129

ALIASES	SIGNATURE FACSIMILE
Meyer the Lug; Bugs Meyer; Little Meyer.	

DESCRIPTION
Born in Grodno, Poland on July 4, 1902; Jewish extraction; Naturalized in New York City on September 27, 1928; white; male; 5'6"; weight 136 lbs.; build medium; eyes brown; hair brown; complexion sallow; 2 brown marks on right side of face; suffers from stomach ailment.

LOCALITIES FREQUENTED
Resides at Box 546 Hallendale, Florida. Allegedly part owner of the Carlsbad Spa, Hallendale, Florida. Part owner of the La Boheme and Green Acres gambling clubs in Hollywood, Florida.

CRIMINAL ASSOCIATES
Joseph Sadlow; Vincent Alo; Joseph Stracher; Joseph Pollard; Hymie Abrams; Harold Gaines; Hymie Siegal; Babe Mann; Joseph Flax; Philip Kovolick; Morris Rosen; Santo Trafficante Jr.; Michael Coppola; Harry Stromberg.

(See Reverse)

CRIMINAL HISTORY
Dates back to 1918 and includes arrests for felonious assault; disorderly conduct, homicide, violation of 1930 Tariff Act and National Prohibition Act, vagrancy and common gambler; violation of the Federal Narcotic Laws.

MODUS OPERANDI
Important underworld leader closely associated in illegal gambling activities and the narcotic traffic with high echelon Mafiosi in New York City and Florida. Smuggles narcotics and diamonds across the Mexican border into the United States at Laredo, Texas.

AGENCIES FAMILIAR WITH INDIVIDUAL Bureau of Narcotics and Customs Agency of the U.S. Treasury Department; Federal Bureau of Investigation and Immigration and Naturalization Service of the U.S. Department of Justice; New York City Police Department; Miami Police Department; New York State Police.

CRIMINAL IDENTIFICATIONS (Agency & No.)	FINGERPRINT CLASSIFICATION
F.B.I. # 791783; New York City P.D. B# 70258; Sheriff's Office Balliston Spa, New York #5337.	18 L 32 W I00 I 16 W 0II

NAME

Paul MONDOLONI

INTERNATIONAL LIST NO.

162

ALIASES

Paul Begin; Jacques Desmarais;
Jean Kreaber; Roland Samuel.

SIGNATURE FACSIMILE

DESCRIPTION

Born in Sartene, Corsica, France on
September 27, 1916; French national; white; male; height 5'6";
weight 140 lbs.; eyes blue-gray; hair brown.

LOCALITIES FREQUENTED

Resides at Rue Villeneuve, Marseille,
France. Patronizes Bar Artistic, Cours Joseph Thierry and Bar
Le Gondolier, Quai du Viex Port, Marseille, France. Travels to
Paris, France.

CRIMINAL ASSOCIATES

Albert Bistoni; Jean Baptiste Croce; Jerome
Leca; Antoine Galiano; Antoine D'Agostino; Roger Coudert;
Joseph Patrizi; Joseph Orsini; Nathan Behrman; Giuseppe Cotroni.

(See Reverse)

CRIMINAL HISTORY

Arrested by the French Police in 1953 and 1957 for
armed robbery. Served 2 year sentence on these charges.

MODUS OPERANDI

Maintains close ties with narcotic traffickers in
Mexico, Canada and the United States and supplies them with heroin obtained by him
and his associates in France. Originally became notorious as an international
jewel thief.

AGENCIES FAMILIAR WITH INDIVIDUAL

Bureau of Narcotics of the U.S. Treasury Department;
Federal Bureau of Investigation of the U.S. Department of Justice; French Surete
Nationale.

CRIMINAL IDENTIFICATIONS *(Agency & No.)*

F.B.I. # 564009B; French
Surete Nationale ID # 156802.

FINGERPRINT CLASSIFICATION

19	L	10	T	00
	M	5	U	000

RESTRICTED - FOR OFFICIAL USE ONLY ~~DEAD~~

NAME	INTERNATIONAL LIST NO.
Vito GENOVESE	105

ALIASES
Vitone; Don Vitone; Airto
Genoses; The Old Man.

SIGNATURE FACSIMILE

DESCRIPTION
Born in Risigliano, Italy on November 21, 1897; Naturalized citizen of the United States; white; male; height 5'7"; weight 160 lbs.; medium build; eyes brown; hair black, balding; complexion sallow.

LOCALITIES FREQUENTED
Last known residence, 68 Highland Avenue, Atlantic Highlands, New Jersey. Frequented Lower East Side area of New York City.

CRIMINAL ASSOCIATES
Frank Costello; Thomas Eboli; Gerardo Catena; Richard Boiardi; Michele Miranda; Anthony Strollo; Thomas Lucchese; Carlo Gambino; Joseph Biondo; John Ormento; Vincent Gigante; Meyer Lansky; most of the important racketeers in the United States.

F.D.H. NEW YORK, N.Y.
H 10496
V. GENOVESE

(See Reverse)

CRIMINAL HISTORY
Record dates back to 1917 and includes arrests for possession of a gun; carrying a concealed weapon; felonious assault; homicide with a gun; larceny and murder. Sentenced on December 28, 1961 to 15 years in Federal Prison for violation of the Federal Narcotic Laws.

MODUS OPERANDI
Head of the largest of the 5 Mafia organizations in New York City. This syndicate engages in smuggling large quantities of heroin from France, Italy and Mexico into the U.S.A. for distribution in local and interstate traffic. Other illicit activities of this mob include extortion; illegal alcohol and shylocking; prostitution; labor racketeering and control of union funds and activities. This organization also possesses clandestine ownership of restaurants, bars, and real estate.

AGENCIES FAMILIAR WITH INDIVIDUAL
Bureau of Narcotics and Bureau of Customs of the U.S. Treasury Department; Federal Bureau of Investigation and Immigration and Naturalization Service of the U.S. Department of Justice; New York City Police Department.

CRIMINAL IDENTIFICATIONS *(Agency & No.)*
F.B.I. # 861267; New York City
Police Department B# 59993.

FINGERPRINT CLASSIFICATION
19 L 17 W 100
M 1 R 001 8

RESTRICTED - FOR OFFICIAL USE ONLY

NAME	INTERNATIONAL LIST NO.
Samil KHOURY	127

ALIASES
Samil Khoury; Salim Khoury; Salim Alameddine; Samil El Houris; Samil El Khoury ; Sami Salim Khoury.

SIGNATURE FACSIMILE

DESCRIPTION
Born in Zahle, Lebanon on May 7, 1927; Lebanese national; Lebanese; white; male; height 5'8"; weight 140 lbs.; eyes brown; hair black, wavy; complexion dark.

(See Reverse)

LOCALITIES FREQUENTED
Resides at Rue Badero, Beirut, Lebanon. Frequents Casino du Liban; Cave du Roi, Beirut, Lebanon. Travels to Egypt; Spain; Switzerland; Germany; Libya and Morocco.

CRIMINAL ASSOCIATES
Henri Abdil Jalil; Mounir Alaouie; Antoine Araman; Joseph Skaff; Richard Haddad; Omar Makrouk; Antoine Harrouk; Haj Abou Selim; Naguib; Camille Choueri; Naguib Nahas of Frankfort, Germany; In France: Albert Ansan Bistoni; Jean Baptiste Croce. In Canada: Giuseppe Cotroni.

CRIMINAL HISTORY
Has been arrested several times for drug trafficking and released for lack of evidence. Convicted in Egypt for hashish smuggling. In France for possession of counterfeit United States dollars; in Lebanon in 1959 for bribing a narcotic law enforcement official, sentenced to 4 months in prison;in Lebanon for smuggling cigarettes and in Germany for possession of cocaine.

MODUS OPERANDI
Employs couriers to smuggle narcotics via ships or secret compartments in cars. Travels frequently in Asia and to Europe and Africa. Acts as spokesman for his criminal associates and arranges for the smuggling of narcotics, tobacco and arms in exchange for money or merchandise.

AGENCIES FAMILIAR WITH INDIVIDUAL
Bureau of Narcotics of the U.S. Treasury Department; Police of Lebanon, Egypt, France, Germany and Switzerland; ICPO-Interpol.

CRIMINAL IDENTIFICATIONS *(Agency & No.)*
Frankfort, Germany Criminal Police #62/1684; ICPO-Interpol booklet of Near and Middle East Narcotic Drugs Traffickers DRMO 5-61; Interpol #675/55.

FINGERPRINT CLASSIFICATION

RESTRICTED - FOR OFFICIAL USE ONLY

NAME		INTERNATIONAL LIST NO.
Marcel FRANCISCI		098

ALIASES	SIGNATURE FACSIMILE
Marcel.	

DESCRIPTION

Born in Giamammacce, Corsica, France on November 30, 1919; son of Francois and Angele nee Santucci; French citizen; white; male; height 6'1"; weight 200 lbs.; build heavy; eyes brown; complexion olive.

LOCALITIES FREQUENTED

Resides at 108 Rue Suchet, Páris, France and at 8 Rue Rochefort, Paris, France. Frequents Bar Artistic, Cours Joseph Thierry, Marseille, France and the Restaurant Fouquets, Avenue Des Champs Elysees, Paris, France.

CRIMINAL ASSOCIATES

Jean and Xavier Francisci (brothers); Dominique Venturi; Paul Mondoloni; Charles Henry Faccia; Gabriel Carcassonne; Dominique Reissent.

(See Reverse)

CRIMINAL HISTORY

Well known by reputation to the French Surete Nationale and French Customs authorities. No criminal record available.

MODUS OPERANDI

He and his brothers organize the smuggling of large quantities of morphine base into France from the Middle East. This morphine base is then converted into heroin in clandestine laboratories in France for shipment to the United States.

AGENCIES FAMILIAR WITH INDIVIDUAL

Bureau of Narcotics of the U. S. Treasury Department; French Customs; French Surete Nationale.

CRIMINAL IDENTIFICATIONS *(Agency & No.)*	FINGERPRINT CLASSIFICATION
French Surete Nationale # DI 149511.	29 W MO 16 20 W 00

RESTRICTED - FOR OFFICIAL USE ONLY

NAME
John ORMENTO

INTERNATIONAL LIST NO.
170

ALIASES
Big John; Governor; Giovanni Ormando; John Armando; John Forte.

SIGNATURE FACSIMILE
DEAD

DESCRIPTION
Born in New York City on August 1, 1912; Italian extraction; height 5'10"; weight 240 lbs.; eyes brown; hair black-gray; complexion dark.

LOCALITIES FREQUENTED
Prior to present incarceration resided at 18 Audrey Drive, Lido Beach, L.I., New York. Frequented E. 107th St. area of East Harlem, New York City; Copacabana night club, 10 E. 6oth St., New York City; Garment District, New York City; Miami Beach, Florida; Canada.

CRIMINAL ASSOCIATES
Vito Genovese; Joseph Di Palermo; Salvatore Santora; Rocco Mazzie; Natale Evola; Carmine Galante; Andimo Pappadio; Benjamin Levine; Carmine Polizzano; Daniel Lessa; Joseph Vento; Raffaele Quasarano; Frank Garofolo; Rocco Pellegrino; In Canada: Giuseppe Cotroni; Frank Cotroni; Vincent Cotroni; Rene Robert; Peter Stepanoff.

(See Reverse)

CRIMINAL HISTORY
Record dates back to 1937 and includes several arrests for bookmaking and for violations for State and Federal Narcotic Laws. New York State narcotic case dismissed on March 18, 1955. Sentenced on July 10, 1962 to 40 years in Federal Prison for conspiracy to violate the Federal Narcotic Laws.

MODUS OPERANDI
A member of the Thomas Lucchese organization which imports large quantities of heroin from France, Italy and Canada into the United States for distribution in local and interstate narcotic traffic. Attended the Apalachin Meeting on November 14, 1957. In the past, associated with setting up and supervising operations of clandestine laboratories in New York City metropolitan area for conversion of opium into heroin.

AGENCIES FAMILIAR WITH INDIVIDUAL
Bureau of Narcotics and Customs Agency Service of the U.S. Treasury Department; New York City Police Department; Federal Bureau of Investigation of the U. S. Department of Justice.

CRIMINAL IDENTIFICATIONS *(Agency & No.)*
City P.D. B# 158044.

F.B.I. # 1321383: New York

FINGERPRINT CLASSIFICATION
21 W M
4 W I 14

NOTES

I THE BIRTH OF A BUREAU

1 Leo Katcher, *The Big Bankroll: The Life and Times of Arnold Rothstein* (New York: Harper, 1959).

2 *New York Times*, 27 November 1928, 1. The Society of St. Tammany was organized in 1778 in New York City by enlisted men of the Revolutionary War to offset the Society of the Cincinnati formed by Alexander Hamilton and the Army's officers. The Democrats stem from the former, the Republicans from the latter.

3 *New York Times*, 11 December 1928, 26:2.

4 William O. Walker III, *Opium and Foreign Policy: The Anglo-American Search for Order in Asia, 1912–1954* (Chapel Hill: University of North Carolina Press, 1991), 233. The League of Nations created the Opium Advisory Committee in 1921. It was dominated by colonial nations with opium monopolies in the Far East.

5 *New York Times*, 27 November 1928, 1.

6 Terry Parssinen, unpublished manuscript, chapter 10: "America and the World Narcotics Market, 1920–1954," 36.

7 Ibid., chapter 10, 2.

8 Jonathan Marshall, "Opium and the Politics of Gangsterism in Nationalist China, 1927–1945," *Bulletin of Concerned Asian Scholars*, July–September 1976, 29.

9 Parssinen, chapter 10, 30.

10 The Editors of Executive Intelligence Review, *Dope, Inc.: The Book That Drove Kissinger Crazy* (Washington, DC: Executive Intelligence Review, 1992), 431.

11 *New York Times*, 8 August 1921, 1:4.

12 Ibid., 5 May 1927, 6:2.

13 Ibid., 8 May 1927, 20:1.

14 Marshall, "Gangsterism," 32.

15 Ibid., 33.

16 Melvin L. Hanks, *NARC: The Adventures of a Federal Agent* (New York: Hastings House, 1973), 162–6.

17 *New York Times*, 9 July 1929, 18:2; 12 July, 2:14; 13 July, 32:2; 14 July, 16:5; 23 July, 17:3; 24 July, 23:3; and 7 September, 17:2.

18 Ibid., 29 December 1929, 1; 30 December 10:5; 31 December, 2:5.

19 Ibid., 15 January 1930, 1.

20 Ibid., 21 February 1930, 1.

21 Douglas Kinder, "Bureaucratic Cold Warrior: Harry J. Anslinger and Illicit Narcotics Traffic," Pacific Coast Branch, American Historical Association, *Pacific Historical Review*, 1981, 172–3.

22 On 15 January 1930, the same night Roland Nutt declared his innocence, Treasury Secretary Mellon threw a dinner party in honor of President Hoover. Among the honored guests were Mrs. and Mr. David K. E. Bruce, daughter and son-in-law of the host; the Chinese minister, Mr. Wu and his wife; and Mr. and Mrs. William Jardine. In *The Traffic in Narcotics,* with William F. Tompkins (New York: Funk & Wagnall Co., 1953) 97, Anslinger referred to Mr. Jardine's namesake forebear as "the greatest and most influential of the opium smugglers."

2 THE COMMISSIONER AND HIS CLIQUE

1 *The American Heritage Dictionary*, New College Edition (Boston: Houghton Mifflin Company, 1969).

2 Harry J. Anslinger, *The Protectors: The Heroic Story of The Narcotics Agents, Citizens, and Officials in Their Unending, Unsung Battles Against Organized Crime in America and Abroad* (New York: Farrar, Strauss, 1964), 39–50.

3 Charles B. Dyar, Official Personnel Folders, US Office of Personnel Management, St. Louis, Missouri. Anslinger, *The Protectors*, 6–24.

4 Garland Roarke, *The Coin of Contraband: The True Story of United States Customs Investigator Al Scharff* (Garden City: Doubleday & Company, Inc., 1964), 330–8.

5 Ibid., 336–7.

6 Ibid., 338, 347.

7 Parssinen, chapter 10, 34.

8 Harry J. Anslinger, with Will Oursler, *The Murderers: The Story of the Narcotic Gangs* (New York: Strauss and Cudahy, 1961), 70.

9 Dyar, Official Personnel Folders, 27 July 1940, letter from Scharff to Mr. H. S. Creighton.

10 Ralph H. Oyler, Official Personnel Folders, US Office of Personnel Management, St. Louis, Missouri, provided by John C. McWilliams.

11 Ralph H. Oyler, "America's Lone War Against Dope," draft article submitted to Colonel L. G. Nutt, Internal Revenue Bureau, US Treasury Department, New York, 30 March 1926, provided by Paul D. Newey.

12 *New York Times*, 10 September 1921, 1.

13 Benedict Pocoroba report, "The Mafia," 21 April 1947, provided by Paul D. Newey.

14 Al Ostrow, "Violent Action for Dope Sleuth," *Saint Louis Post Dispatch*, 25 December 1949, provided by Paul D. Newey.

15 Garland Williams, Official Personnel Folders, US Office of Personnel Management, St. Louis, Missouri, provided by John C. McWilliams. Anslinger, *The Protectors*, 15.

16 Jill Jonnes, *Hep Cats, Narcs, and Pipe Dreams* (New York: Scribner, 1996), 105.

17 Fred J. Cook, *The Secret Rulers; The Criminal Syndicates and How They Control the US Underworld* (New York: Duell, Sloan & Pearce, 1966), 122–5.

18 Cook, *The Secret Rulers*, 122.

19 Ibid., 148.

20 George Wolf, with Joseph DiMona, *Frank Costello: Prime Minister of the Underworld* (New York: William Morrow & Company, Inc., 1974), 123.

21 Robert Lacey, *Little Man: Meyer Lansky and the Gangster Life* (New York: Little Brown & Company, 1991), 59.

22 Sid Feder and Joachim Joesten, *The Luciano Story* (New York: David McKay Company, 1954), 58, 70–1. Leonard Katz, *Uncle Frank: The Biography of Frank Costello* (New York: Drake Publishers, Inc., 1973), 89.

23 Anslinger, *The Murderers*, 88.

3 ANSLINGER'S ANGST

1 Maurice Helbrant, *Narcotic Agent* (New York: The Vanguard Press, 1941), 273–81.

2 Ibid., 275.

3 William O. Walker III, *Drug Control in the Americas* (Albuquerque: University of New Mexico Press, 1981), 143.

4 Douglas Clark Kinder and William O. Walker III, "Stable Force in a Storm: Harry J. Anslinger and United States Narcotic Policy, 1930–1962," *The Journal of American History*, vol. 72, no. 4, March 1986, 919 n. 33.

5 Peter Dale Scott, *Deep Politics and the Death of JFK* (Berkeley: University of California Press, 1993), 103.

6 Walker, *Drug Control*, 147–50.

7 Marshall, "Gangsterism," 28.

8 Kinder and Walker, "Stable Force," 916.

9 Parssinen, chapter 10, 4.

10 Marshall, "Gangsterism," 29.

11 Walker, *Opium and Foreign Policy*, 78.

12 Marshall, "Gangsterism," 28.

13 Ibid., 28.

14 Jonnes, *Hep Cats*, 95.

15 John C. McWilliams and Alan A. Block, "All the Commissioner's Men: The Federal Bureau of Narcotics and the Dewey–Luciano Affair, 1947–1954," *Intelligence and National Security* (London: Frank Cass, 1990), 174–84.

16 John H. Davis, *Mafia Kingfish: Carlos Marcello and the Assassination of John F. Kennedy* (New York: McGraw-Hill Publishing Company, 1989), 45.

17 Anslinger, *The Protectors*, 119.

18 Melvin L. Hanks, *NARC: The Adventures of a Federal Agent* (New York: Hastings House, 1973), 125–44.

19 Rodney Campbell, *The Luciano Project; The Secret Wartime Collaboration of the Mafia and the US Navy* (New York: McGraw Hill, 1977), 173–81.

20 Ibid., 139–40.

21 Richard Harris Smith, *OSS: The Secret History Of America's First Central Intelligence Agency* (Berkeley, University of California Press, 1981), 105.

22 Scamporino report, Palermo, Sicily, from: Exp. Det. G-3, Sicily, to: Exp. Det. G-3, Algiers, 13 August 1943. Scamporino documents provided by his son.

23 Alfred W. McCoy, *The Politics of Heroin: CIA Complicity in the Global Drug Trade* (Chicago: Lawrence Hill Books, 1991), 35.

24 Smith, *OSS*, 85.

25 Ibid., 86.

26 Ostrow, "Violent Action."

27 Serge Peter Karlow, *The War Report, Office of Strategic Services* (Washington, GPO, July 1949), 195.

28 Smith, *OSS*, 124.

29 Portions of George White's diary were provided by Alan Block, other portions were obtained from the CIA through three Freedom of Information Act requests (F-1993-02381, F-1998-01108, and F-1998-01939) filed by the author: all will hereafter be collectively referred to as White's Diary.

30 Martin A. Lee and Bruce Shlain, *Acid Dreams: The Complete Social History of LSD, the Sixties, and Beyond* (New York: Grove Press, 1992), 3–4. Alan W. Scheflin and Edward M. Opton Jr., *The Mind Manipulators* (New York and London: Paddington Press Ltd, 1978), 135.

31 Alain Jaubert, *Dossier D … comme Drogue* (Paris: Editions Alain Moreau, 1973), 37–40.

32 John Marks, *The Search for the Manchurian Candidate* (New York: Times Books, 1979), 7.

33 Interview with Howard Chappell.

34 William Peers and Dean Brellis, *Behind the Burma Road* (Boston: Little Brown, 1963), 64.

35 Milton Miles, *A Different Kind of War* (New York: Doubleday, 1967), 194.

36 Martin A. Gosch and Richard Hammer, *The Last Testament of Lucky Luciano* (New York: Little, Brown and Company, 1974), 272–4.

37 Charlie Siragusa with Robert Wiedrich, *On the Trail of the Poppy: Behind the Mask of the Mafia* (New Jersey: Prentice Hall Inc., 1966), 58.

38 Alan Block, "European Drug Trafficking & Traffickers Between the Wars: The Policy of Suppression and Its Consequences," *Journal of Social History*, vol. 23, no. 2 (winter 1989), 151–60.

39 Ibid., 159.

4 INSIDE THE FBN

1 Anslinger, *The Protectors*, 75.

2 Kinder and Walker, "Stable Force," 920.

3   Ibid., 921.

4   Gon Sam Mue with W. J. Slocum, "They Haven't Killed Me Yet," *Saturday Evening Post*, 23 August 1952, 118.

5   *Washington Times Herald*, 3 November 1945, 1; 5 November, 1.

6   Alan A. Block, "Fascism and Organized Crime," *Space, Time & Organized Crime*, (New Jersey: Transaction Publishers, 1994), 147–56.

7   After leaving the Justice Department, Cohn would defend Carmine Galante in a narcotics case and later go into business with Joe Bonanno.

8   Block, *Space, Time and Organized Crime*, 150.

9   Jim Hogshire, *Grossed-Out Surgeon Vomits inside Patient: An Insider's Look at Supermarket Tabloids* (Venice, California: Feral House, 1977), 95–107.

10 White's Diary.

11 Ed Reid, *Mafia* (New York: Signet Books, 1954), 96.

12 Ostrow, "Violent Action."

13 Reid, *Mafia*, 89.

14 Douglas Clark Kinder, "Bureaucratic Cold Warrior: Harry J. Anslinger and Illicit Narcotics Traffic," *Pacific Historical Review*, 1981, American Historical Association, 179–80.

15 Reid, *Mafia*, 41.

16 Cook, *The Secret Rulers*, 160–79, 233.

17 Helbrant, *Narcotic Agent*, 310.

18 Anslinger, *The Protectors*, 85.

19 Ibid., 22.

20 Among the notable Black agents who preceded Davis were Wade McCree, Johnny Boxill, Josh Taylor, Jimmy Fletcher, and Bill Jackson, who was poisoned in South Carolina. Notable Black agents who followed Davis included Malcolm P., Richards, Marshall Latta, Charles McDonnell, Norris "Norey" Durham, William H. Turnbou, Earl Graves, Robert Brown, and William Newkirk.

21 Kinder, "Bureaucratic Cold Warrior," 176.

5 GOD'S WORK

1   Williams report to Anslinger, "Charles Luciano @ Lucky International List # 198," 28 March 1947.

2   Olivera report to Williams, "Salvatore (Lucky) Luciano et al.," 21 March 1947.

3   Oyler's undated report to Anslinger, "China Theater Mission."

4   Oyler's undated report to Anslinger, "Highlights and Sky Lights."

5   John C. McWilliams, "Seeing Red: Harry J. Anslinger and the Politics of Drugs in the China Question, 1949–1971," unpublished paper, 33 n. 6.

6   Walker, *Opium and Foreign Policy*, 17, 85.

7   Ibid., 79.

8   Ross Y. Koen, *The China Lobby in American Politics* (New York: The MacMillan Company, 1960), 228.

9   Smith, *OSS*, 277–8.

10   Burton Hersh, *The Old Boys: The American Elite and the Origins of the CIA* (New York: Charles Scribner's Sons, 1992), 444. Jack Lait and Lee Mortimer in *Washington Confidential* (New York: Crown Publishers, 1951), 29, say it was "politic" for the FBN to deny "leakage" from diplomats.

11   Anslinger, *The Murderers*, 54.

12   Ed Reid, *The Mistress and the Mafia: The Virginia Hill Story* (New York: Bantam Books, 1972), 42.

13   Ibid., 90.

14   Ibid., 90.

15   Ibid., 123.

16   Richard Mahoney, *Sons & Brothers: The Days of Jack and Bobby Kennedy* (New York: Arcade Publishing, 1999), 269.

17   Reid, *Mistress*, 129.

18   Scott, *Deep Politics*, 8.

19   Kinder and Walker, "Stable Force," 923.

20   Terry A. Talent's report to Anslinger, November 1946.

21   DeLagrave report cited in White's Diary.

22   Reid, *Mistress*, 74.

23   Scott, *Deep Politics*, 142.

24   Ray Richards, "Lucky Luciano Heads Mafia's World Gang," *Detroit Times*, 25 February 1947, 1.

25   Scheflin and Opton, *The Mind Manipulators*, 497 n. 145.

26   Scott, *Deep Politics*, 175.

27   Davis, *Mafia Kingfish*, 32.

28   Scott, *Deep Politics*, 99.

29   Hersh, *The Old Boys*, 229.

30   Scott, *Deep Politics*, 174.

31   Gaia Servadio, *Mafiosa: A History of the Mafia from its Origins to the Present Day* (London: Secker & Warburg, 1976), 70.

32   Michael Stern, *No Innocents Abroad* (New York: Random House, Inc., 1953), 101–5.

33 Evan Thomas, *The Very Best Men* (New York: Simon & Schuster, 1995), 47.

34 Ibid., 49.

35 Hersh, *Old Boys*, 300.

36 Bruce Cumings, *The Origins of the Korean War* (Princeton: Princeton University Press, 1981, 1990), 133.

37 Ibid., 361.

38 Ibid., 512.

39 Williams reports, 10 June 1948, 21 January and 1 February 1949, Box 6 File 4, Anslinger Papers at Labor Archives and Historical Collections, Pattee Library, Penn State University.

40 Michael Straight, "Corruption and Chiang Kai-shek," *The New Republic,* 8 October 1951, 10.

41 Marshall, "Gangsterism," 22.

42 Lait and Mortimer, *Washington Confidential*, 108.

43 Carl Baldwin, book review of *The Murderers*, *St. Louis Post Dispatch*, 7 January 1963, provided by Paul D. Newey.

44 Lait, *Washington Confidential*, 107–8.

45 Ibid., 110.

46 Straight, "Corruption and Chiang Kai-shek," 12.

6 CREATING A CRIME

1 William Burroughs, *Junky* (New York: Penguin Books USA, Inc., 1977), 56–7.

2 Cook, *The Secret Rulers*, 160.

3 Jack Lait and Lee Mortimer, *USA Confidential* (New York: Crown Publishers, 1952), 29.

4 Ed Reid, *The Shame of New York* (New York: Random House, 1953), 51, 63–78.

5 Ibid., 195.

6 William Howard Moore, *The Kefauver Committee and the Politics of Crime, 1950–1952* (Columbia: University of Missouri Press, 1974).

7 Moore, *Kefauver*, 115.

8 Ibid., 125, 132–3, 182.

9 Ibid., 124.

10 Lait and Mortimer, *USA Confidential*, 323.

11 Moore, *Kefauver*, 152.

12 Reid, *Mafia*, 32.

13   Moore, *Kefauver*, 105.

14   Ibid., 101.

15   Lait and Mortimer, *USA Confidential*, 82–3.

16   Moore, *Kefauver*, 125.

17   Ibid., 195–9.

18   Ibid., 188.

19   *New York Times*, 2 May 1951, 17:1.

20   *New York Times*, 28 September, 22:3.

21   Lait and Mortimer, *USA Confidential*, 215.

22   Cook, *Secret Rulers*, 275. Ryan hired Anslinger's private investigator, Ulius Amoss, to investigate Moretti's murder.

23   Alexander Cockburn and Jeffrey St. Clair, *Whiteout: The CIA, Drugs and the Press* (New York: Verso, 1998), 152–4.

24   Eleanora W. Schoenebaum, editor, Oral History Review of Oscar Ewing, *Political Profiles: The Truman Years* (Harry S. Truman Library, New York: Facts on File, Inc., 1978).

25   Jonnes, *Hep Cats*, 146–7.

7 CONTINENTAL CAPERS

1   Richards, "Lucky Luciano."

2   Ian Sayer and Douglas Botting, *Nazi Gold: The Biggest Robbery In History – A Real Life Thriller about the Theft of a Fabulous Treasure* (New York: Grove Press, Inc., 1984), 333–9.

3   Ibid., 455–6.

4   Ibid., 434.

5   Charles B. Dyar, Narcotics Officer, Confidential Report to Branch Chief, Narcotics Situation in Garmisch-Partenkirchen, 3 April 1948, provided by Ian Sayer.

6   Guenther Reinhardt, *Crime without Punishment* (New York: Signet Book, 1953), 124–5.

7   Walker, *Opium and Foreign Policy*, 207.

8   Ibid., 177.

9   *New York Times*, 5 June 1948, 4:7.

10   Ostrow, "Violent Action."

11   Department of State incoming telegram from Marseilles to Secretary of State, No: 128, "For Commissioner of Narcotics Anslinger From White," Control 7858, Rec'd June 22, 1948, 6:05 p.m.

12   Henry Manfredi, Official Personnel Folders, US Office of Personnel

Management, St. Louis, Missouri. Anslinger letter commending Manfredi, 24 November 1948.

13 White's Diary.

14 Ostrow, "Violent Action."

15 Stern, *No Innocents Abroad*, 52.

16 Ostrow, "Violent Action."

17 Jonnes, *Hep Cats*, 149.

18 Williams reports, 10 June 1948, 21 January 1949 and 1 February 1949, Box 6 File 4, Anslinger Papers at Labor Archives and Historical Collections, Pattee Library, Penn State University.

19 Hersh, *The Old Boys*, 330. According to Arnold Taylor in *American Diplomacy and the Narcotic Traffic 1900–1936* (Durham: Duke University Press, 1969), page 312, future CIA director Allen W. Dulles, as a foreign service officer in Constantinople in 1923, reported on Persia's refusal to abide by The Hague Convention. In December 1925 he met with Mrs. Elizabeth Wright (widow of Hamilton Wright, father of the Harrison Narcotic Act), Congressman Porter, and Frederic A. Delano (a member of the Federal Reserve Board) to discuss Persia's involvement in narcotics smuggling. Dulles certainly knew, as Taylor said in *American Diplomacy*, page 308, that "The wealthiest class in Persia [including the Shah] and many of the most influential clergy were opium producers and merchants."

20 Robert Daley, *An American Saga: Juan Trippe and his Pan Am Empire* (New York: Random House, 1980), 309, 338–56, 385, 392, 416, 426.

21 Siragusa, *On the Trail*, 58–60.

22 *New York Times*, 21 October 1948, 54:1.

23 Lacey, *Little Man*, 174.

24 Siragusa, *On the Trail*, 108.

25 Interviews with Alan Block and Colonel Tulius Acampora.

26 Siragusa, *On the Trail*, 130–42.

27 *Project Pilot, Part III*, the product of an interagency study group comprised of representatives from the Drug Enforcement Administration, the Bureau of Customs, and the Central Intelligence Agency, as a worldwide reference guide to international narcotics trafficking, with an emphasis on the French connection, circa 1974, 10–21.

28 Lafitte later revealed that Maurice Thabet, Lebanon's representative to the UN, was involved in the 1952 Orsini case and that Thabet's opium came from Macao. Edward Ranzal, *New York Times*, 7 February 1958.

29 Anslinger, *Traffic in Narcotics*, 77.

30 *New York Times*, 2 April, 1952, 8:4.

31   Scott, *Deep Politics*, 176.
32   Jaubert, *Dossier D*, 46 n. 20.

8 THE BEIRUT OFFICE

1   Siragusa to Anslinger, Progress Report No. 4A, 3 May 1951.
2   More than two dozen FBN documents, specifically about the Pahlevi and Griffel cases, were provided by the Knight family.
3   Charles Siragusa in Rome to James C. Ryan in New York, 4 August 1953.
4   Siragusa in Paris to Anslinger, dated 22 February 1954.
5   Siragusa in Paris to Anslinger, dated 22 February 1954.
6   Jean-Pierre Charbonneau, *The Canadian Connection* (Montreal: Optimum Publishing Company Limited, 1976), 98–9.
7   *New York Times*, 28 November 1948, 5:3.
8   *New York Times*, 2 July 1951, 5:1.
9   Undated Italian document, signed "Il Colonnello Comandante Del Nucleo (Gaetano Polizzi)," provided by Paul E. Knight.
10   Siragusa in Rome to Anslinger, 19 July 1954.
11   Siragusa, *On the Trail*, 6.
12   Ibid., 3–32.
13   Robert Wiedrich, *Chicago Tribune Magazine*, 30 May 1965, 8.
14   "Senators Told of US Fight against Dope," *San Francisco Chronicle*, 3 June 1955.

9 THE SECRET POLICEMAN

1   Memorandum from Commanding Officer, Naval Medical Research Institute, to Commissioner of Narcotics, "Procurement of Certain Drugs," 9 February 1951.
2   Scheflin and Opton, *The Mind Manipulators*, 132.
3   Michael McClintock, *Instruments of Statecraft* (New York: Pantheon Books, 1992), 111.
4   Marks, *Manchurian Candidate*, 87–104.
5   Scheflin and Opton, *The Mind Manipulators*, 137.
6   Interview with and documents provided by Clarice Stein Smithline.
7   Reinhardt, *Crime without Punishment*, 116–7.
8   Anslinger, *The Murderers*, 233.

9   Marks, *Manchurian Candidate*, 56–7.

10 James Alexander Hamilton, letter to Gary Stern, 21 February 1995.

11 Bradley Smith, *The Shadow Warriors: The OSS and the Origins of the CIA* (New York: Basic Books, 1983), 389.

12 Walker, *Opium and Foreign Policy*, 210.

13 Ibid.

14 Anslinger, *Traffic in Narcotics*, 84.

15 Walker, *Opium and Foreign Policy*, 168.

16 McCoy, *Politics of Heroin*, 133–45.

17 John Earman, "Report of Inspection of MKULTRA/TSD," 14 August 1963, (hereafter known as Earman Report), 13.

18 Jack Kelly with Richard Mathison, *On the Street: The Autobiography of the Toughest US Narcotics Agent* (Chicago: Henry Regnery Company, 1974), 47–8, 70.

19 The author obtained ninety-six numbered documents about MKULTRA from the CIA through a Freedom of Information Act request. They shall be referred to by the number the CIA assigned them, as in this case: MKULTRA Document 85, "Undated Memo For The Record."

20 Ed Reid, in *The Shame of New York*, page 54, said, "A mob fixer once boasted in underworld circles that he knew someone who could fix Williams, but he failed to come through."

21 Marks, *Manchurian Candidate*, 73–82.

22 Kelly, *On the Street*, 69–75. According to Richard L. G. Deverall in *Red China's Dirty Dope War: The Story of the Opium, Heroin, Morphine and Philopon Traffic* (New York: Free Trade Union Committee, American Federation of Labor, 1954), 55, Gelb got his heroin from "Red China."

23 Anslinger, *The Murderers*, 98, 233.

24 McWilliams and Block, "All the Commissioner's Men," 176–85.

25 Ibid., 177.

26 Cockburn and St. Clair, *Whiteout*, 132.

27 McWilliams and Block, "All the Commissioner's Men," 177–8.

28 White's Diary.

29 McWilliams and Block, "All The Commissioner's Men," 186–7.

30 Reid, *Mafia*, 54.

31 1964 Senate Hearings, 989, 1047.

32 *New York Times*, 24 December 1954, 28:8. According to Charles Faddem of the Seafarers' Union, many Seafarers' Union members were smugglers and junkies and worked on Jardine Matheson ships going to and coming back from the Far East.

33 1964 Senate Hearings, 1074–5.

34 Interview with Gregory Poulos.

35 Marks, *Manchurian Candidate*, 101.

10 TRUE DETECTIVES

1 The authors of *Pilot Project III* (19), said "There is strong evidence that D'Agostino was receiving heroin from the Far East." This is not surprising, knowing that Paul Damien Mondoloni had been police chief in Saigon and that his partner, Jean-Baptiste Croce, had been a seaman in the Far East. According to Charbonneau in *The Canadian Connection* (76), Croce had supplied narcotics to François Spirito prior to World War II in league with Mafioso Francesco Pirico in Milan. Pirico was connected to Lucky Luciano and the Caneba brothers, a major source in Sicily.

2 Roarke, *Coin of Contraband*, 392.

3 Kelly, *On the Street*, 123.

4 MKULTRA Document 76, Memorandum for the Record, "Telephone Interview with George Gaffney." Gaffney disliked White immensely. He told the author, "Tom Dugan and I found him one morning sitting on a curb in the Village. He was incoherent. We tried to get him home, but he cursed us and pushed us away. White was like that: a falling-down drunk who bragged about the Japs he'd killed during interrogation, and made insulting cracks, even when he was trying to be nice."

5 Roarke, *Coin of Contraband*, 393–5.

6 Marks, *Manchurian Candidate*, 94. Interview with Ira Feldman.

7 McWilliams, "Seeing Red," 6.

8 Tom Mangold, *Cold Warrior* (New York: Simon & Schuster, 1991), 105.

9 Dr. Harry Berger and Dr. Andrew A. Eggston, "Should We Legalize Narcotics?" *Coronet*, June 1955, 34.

10 McWilliams, "Seeing Red," 17.

11 *New York Times*, 1 August 1955, 3:8.

12 Alfred R. Lindesmith, "The Traffic in Dope," *The Nation*, 25 April 1956, 228.

13 Darrell Berrigan, "They Smuggle Dope by the Ton," *Saturday Evening Post*, 5 May 1956, 42, 156–8.

14 John O'Kearney, "Opium Trade: Is China Responsible?" *The Nation*, 5 October, 1955, 320–322.

15 Berrigan, "They Smuggle Dope."

16 Smith, *The OSS*, 356.

17 Scott, *Deep Politics*, 165–6. Alan Block, *Masters of Paradise: Organized Crime and the Internal Revenue Service in The Bahamas* (New Jersey: Transaction Publishers, 1991), 161–73.

11 ST. MICHAEL'S SERGEANT AT ARMS

1 Ethan A. Nadelman, *Cops Across Borders: The Internationalization of US Criminal Law Enforcement* (University Park: The Pennsylvania State University Press, 1993), 134–5.

2 Interview with Myles Ambrose. Nadelman in *Cops Across Borders* (135), quotes Ambrose as saying that "agents from the Bureau of Narcotics abroad could claim and did claim to be Interpol agents to give their work a veneer of legitimacy."

3 Jack Kelly in *On the Street* (48) said that Crofton Hayes had "cleaned out the vault in Newark of all the seized narcotics under his control." He didn't mention him by name, but Kelly also referred to Leo Palier as "an attorney who had graduated first in his class at Harvard," and then "took up with prostitutes and had them working for him to support his habit before the Bureau forced him to retire." A bachelor, Palier was known for rushing home at noon to feed his beloved cats.

4 DiLucia joined the FBN in 1935, then served with the OSS in Madrid, posing as the Treasury representative. He may have been an undercover CIA agent in Italy.

5 Toni Howard, "Dope Is His Business," *Saturday Evening Post*, 27 April 1957, 38.

6 Letter from Tartaglino to Siragusa, "Last night Frias and Salm knocked off El Etir and Omar Makkouk," 19 June 1957.

7 Manfredi, Official Personnel Folders.

8 Luigi DiFonzo, *St. Peter's Banker* (New York: Watts, 1983), 25. Claire Sterling, *Octopus: The Long Reach of the International Sicilian Mafia*, (New York: W.W. Norton & Company, Inc., 1990), 190–202.

9 Sterling, *Octopus*, 100.

10 Williams, Official Personnel Folders.

11 Millspaugh, *Americans in Persia* (Washington, DC: The Brookings Institute, 1946) 69.

12 Ibid., 133.

13 Kim Roosevelt, *Counter-Coup: The Struggle for Control of Iran* (New

York: McGraw Hill Book Company, 1979), 44–6, 128–9.

14   Interview with George Gaffney.

15   Seymour M. Hersh, *The Dark Side Of Camelot* (Boston: Little Brown, 1997), 194.

16   Mark Fritz, Associated Press, "Ex-CIA Official James Critchfield Dies," 23 April 2003.

17   Alan A. Block and John C. McWilliams, "On The Origins of American Counterintelligence: Building a Clandestine Network," Journal of Policy History, vol. 1, no. 4, 1989, Pennsylvania State University Press, University Park and London, 367.

12 GANGBUSTERS

1   Scott, *Deep Politics*, 157.

2   1964 Senate Hearings, 1010.

3   Dan Moldea, *The Hoffa Wars: The Rise and Fall of Jimmy Hoffa* (New York: SPI Books, 1978), 69–70.

4   Ibid., 74–7, 90–1.

5   *New York Times*, 14 November 1957, 1:1.

6   *New York Times*, 10 January 1958, 1:3.

7   Tom Tripodi with Joseph P. DeSario, *Crusade: Undercover against the Mafia and KGB* (Washington: Brassey's, 1993), 60.

8   Charbonneau, *Canadian Connection*, 122–3.

9   Memorandum report by Thomas J. Dugan, 5 February 1960. Thomas M. Dugan, also assigned to the New York office, was affectionately known to the Irish clique as "Tommy Ogg," meaning "Young Tom" in Irish.

10   Charbonneau, *Canadian Connection*, 79–82, 101–4.

11   At this point a top NYPD narcotic detective reportedly made one of the most often quoted statements in FBN folklore: "Take it out back, lads, and give it a whack for me!"

12   Memorandum to Mr. Mollo from Mr. Tendy, 27 April 1960.

13   Charbonneau, *Canadian Connection*, 148–51

14   *Project Pilot III,* 60. Charbonneau in *The Canadian Connection* (103) says "Mondoloni was associated with Santos Trafficante, Jr. who ran a rich Havana casino called the Sans Souci for … Meyer Lansky."

15   Charbonneau, *Canadian Connection*, 112.

16   John T. Cusack, memo to H. J. Anslinger, 24 November 1958.

17   Roarke, *Coin of Contraband*, 421–2.

18 Charbonneau, *Canadian Connection*, 143 n. 19.

19 Scott, *Deep Politics*, 201.

13 ANGLOPHILES AND FRANCOPHOBES

1 Among the documents in White's Diary is a letter OSI officer Arthur Giuliani wrote to George White, dated 3 March 1958, saying that Siragusa "had worn out welcome with the Italians" and that the "local CIA boy" didn't know if Manfredi or Knight would take over. The CIA "boy" was looking for recruits and, while Manfredi had more contacts, Knight had more finesse – so Giuliani recommended Knight to the CIA.

2 Sal Vizzini with Oscar Fraley and Marshall Smith, *Vizzini: The Secret Lives of America's Most Successful Undercover Agent* (New York: Arbor House, 1972).

3 The secretaries were Mary Lapore, Ruth Bridentath, Monica Atwall, and Yolanda Palucci.

4 Interview with Colonel Tulius Acampora.

5 Anslinger, *The Murderers*, 223. Siragusa, *On the Trail*, 185–200.

6 Block, *Masters of Paradise*, 30–8, 45–57, 68–72.

7 Jonnes, *Hep Cats*, 172.

8 Williams's report, "The Narcotics Situation in South Asia and the Far East," 25 July 1959, 19–23. The link dated back to 1943, when Vincent Scamporino and the OSS contacted Bonaventure "Roch" Francisci, a Corsican gangster who operated a charter airline, Air Laos Commerciale, between Saigon and points in Laos and the Golden Triangle.

9 McCoy, *Politics of Heroin*, 176. *New York Times*, 20 May 1959, 3:4.

10 Anslinger, *The Murderers*, 230.

11 1964 Senate Report, 1131.

12 Scott, *Deep Politics*, 167.

13 Williams report, "The Narcotic Situation," 25–6.

14 McCoy, *Politics of Heroin*, 297–8.

15 Peter Dale Scott, *The War Conspiracy: The Secret Road To The Second Indochina War* (New York: The Bobbs-Merrill Company, Inc., 1972), 207, n. 65.

16 Tripodi, *Crusade*, 185.

17 Scott, *War Conspiracy*, 15–20.

18 US House of Representatives, The Committee on Foreign Affairs, *The*

World Heroin Problem, Report of Special Study Mission (Washington, DC, GPO, 27 May 1971), 45.

19 Memo from Knight in Beirut to Cusack in Rome, 4 December 1959.

20 Jonnes, *Hep Cats*, 178. Interview with Paul Sakwa.

21 *Project Pilot III*, 21, 65–7.

22 Charbonneau, *Canadian Connection*, 155–6. Anslinger, *The Protectors*, 68–9.

23 Herbert Brean, "Crooked, Cruel Traffic In Drugs," *Life Magazine*, 25 January 1960, 94.

24 Memorandum (in confidence) to White and Gentry from Deputy Commissioner Giordano, 23 May 1961.

25   As identified in *Project Pilot III* (45–51), the four groups were: the Charles Marignani Organization; the Spirito–Orsini Group, including Marcel Francisci and "the Great Boss" in Rome; the Joseph Patrizzi Organization, including Mondoloni in Mexico; and the Aranci Brothers. The labs were run by Dom Albertini, who was said to be an informer for an investigating judge at Marseilles; Rene Gaston, a close friend of a police commissaire in Interpol; and someone unknown.

26 Jonnes, *Hep Cats*, 185.

27 Ibid., 184.

28 *Project Pilot III*, 42–3.

29 According to Gaffney, the case began in New Orleans when a woman with CIA connections offered information to agent Arthur Doll.

30 *Project Pilot III*, 8, 367–372, 629; Colonel Manuel Dominguez Suarez was a major narcotics trafficker and in 1967 his source in East Berlin was Simon Goldenberg, known to the French as a communist agent. Arrested in May 1970, Suarez committed suicide at La Tuna Prison in Texas in August 1971. The Suarez case was said to have all the "earmarks of an intelligence rather than a heroin trafficking operation."

31 Chappell says the CIA gave him sanctuary afterwards, but he would not discuss the details.

32 Agents from the FBN's San Antonio office made regular forays into Mexico. Agent Jim Bland made about two dozen himself into border towns.

14 A SHOOFLY IN THE OINTMENT

1 *New York Times*, 21 February 1930, 1.

2 Tripodi, *Crusade*, 21: "You kick in the door. If you make the case,

fine. If not, you're Detective Andrews from Homicide."

3 Memorandum to Mr. John E. Ingersoll, Director, Bureau of Narcotics and Dangerous Drugs, from Andrew C. Tartaglino, Chief Inspector, 21 November 1968, Subject: Integrity Investigation – New York Office History, Recommendations and Conclusions. The author obtained this document, portions of which were redacted, through a Freedom of Information Act request from the DEA. It is cited in the Interim Report of the Committee of Government Operations, US Senate, Permanent Subcommittee on Investigations, 94th Congress, 26th Session, Federal Narcotics Enforcement (Washington, DC: GPO, 1976), 65–9.

4 Tripodi, *Crusade*, 25.

5 Interim Report of the Committee of Government Operations, US Senate, Permanent Subcommittee on Investigations, 94th Congress, 26th Session, Federal Narcotics Enforcement (Washington, GPO, 1976), 65–6.

6 Ibid., 68–9.

7 Benjamin DeMott, "The Great Narcotics Muddle," *Harper's Magazine*, March 1962, 50–1. According to DeMott, Anslinger wanted a Seventh Day Adventist, Dr. Edward R. Bloomquist, to succeed him.

8 Ibid., 48.

15 THE MAGIC BUTTON

1 Marks, *Manchurian Candidate*, 99.

2 Siragusa interview by CIA officer Michie, 24 March 1977 (hereafter known as Michie Memo), document provided by Richard E. Salmi.

3 Hearings before the Subcommittee on Health and Scientific Research of the Committee on Human Resources, Human Drug Testing By The CIA, US Senate, 95th Congress, 1st Session (Washington, DC: GPO, 20 and 21 September, 1977), 117 (hereafter referred to as Human Drug Testing).

4 CIA Memorandum for the Record, Subject: Report on Plots to Assassinate Fidel Castro, 23 May 1967 (hereafter known as 1967 IG Report), 14–55, 70.

5 Scott, *Deep Politics*, 90–1.

6 Gus Russo, *Live by the Sword* (Baltimore: Bancroft Press, 1998), 246, citing 21 July 1961 FBN memo.

7 Interim Report of the Select Committee to Study Government Operations with Respect to Intelligence Activities, Alleged Assassination

Plots Involving Foreign Leaders, United States Senate, 94th Congress, 1st Session, Report No. 94–465 (Washington, GPO, 20 November 1975), 58–60 (hereafter known as Church Report).

8　1967 IG Report, 38–9.

9　Hersh, *The Old Boys*, 187–8. David E. Murphy, *Battle Ground Berlin, CIA vs KGB in the Cold War* (New Haven: Yale University Press, 1977), 217.

10　"Notes in Draft re. ZR/RIFLE Project," provided by the National Archives Assassination Records Review Board as part of the CIA Historical Review Program (hereafter known as Harvey's Notes), 10.

11　Dispatch from Chief of Station (deleted) to William Harvey, 11 October 1960.

12　Harvey's Notes, 8.

13　Moldea, *The Hoffa Wars*, 127.

14　Michie Memo.

15　Scott, *Deep Politics*, 352 n. 35.

16　Memorandum to David W. Belin from Mason Cargill, Subject: Search of Files for Materials Relevant to Assassination Plans, 1 May 1975, (hereafter known as Cargill Memo), photocopy from the Gerald R. Ford Library, document provided by Gus Russo.

17　Richard Mahoney, *Sons And Brothers: The Days of Jack and Bobby Kennedy* (New York: Arcade Publishing, 1999), 91–2. Drug trafficker Robert Blemant (object of Paul Knight's sting operation in 1959 and the founder of Les Trois Canards) is proposed as possibly QJ/WIN by Steve Rivele in "Death of a Double Man," Washington, *The National Reporter*, Spring 1987, 48–50.

18　"QJ/WIN," 1977 HSCA Staff Report, provided by the National Archives Assassination Records Review Board as part of CIA Historical Review Program, 1994, 2.

19　Harvey's Notes, 4.

20　*New York Times*, 18 July 1958, 8:2; 25 July 1958, 3:8.

21　QJ/WIN's 201 File (201-236504), provided by the National Archives through the 1994 CIA Historical Review Program, (hereafter known as QJ/WIN Dossier), Dispatch from Chief, WE, to (illegible), 17 July 1959.

22　QJ/WIN Dossier, Classified Message from Director to Chief, WE, Luxembourg Narcotics Lead, 29 April 1959.

23　QJ/WIN Dossier, Message to Commissioner of Narcotics from Deputy Director, Plans, Subject: Chinese Communist Narcotic Activity in Europe, 5 May 1959.

24 Harvey's Notes, 4.

25 Church Report, 45.

26 Siragusa, *On the Trail*, 199.

27 *New York Times*, 30 March 1962, 68:1; 31 March 1962, 2:5.

28 Dispatch from Chief of Station (deleted) to William Harvey, 11 October 1960.

29 Letter from Cusack in Rome to Anslinger in Washington, 29 July 1960, 2.

30 Cusack, letter to Anslinger, 29 July 1960, 11.

31 *Project Pilot III*, 142.

32 Henrik Kruger, *The Great Heroin Coup: Drugs, Intelligence, & International Fascism* (Boston: South End Press, 1980), 41–3.

33 Garland Williams, Official Personnel Folders.

34 Richard Stratton, "Altered States of America," *Spin Magazine*, vol. 9, No. 12, March 1994, 87.

35 Michie Memo. MKULTRA Document 87, Richard Salmi and Frank Laubinger, interview with Feldman.

36 Stratton, "Altered States," 97.

37 Frias's monthly report, 1 November 1958.

38 Jonnes, *Hep Cats*, 197.

16 MAKING THE MAFIA

1 Selvaggi's account of this incident makes it likely that he was the seaman who gave the FBN the tip-off it needed in the Frank Scalici case of 1957 (see chapter 12), information which subsequently led to Scalici's assassination.

2 Eboli reportedly was a liaison between the Mafia and the CIA.

3 Though not charged in the Rinaldo–Palmieri case, Mogavero was sentenced to fifteen years in the 1964 Frank Borelli case, which Selvaggi initiated, and which stemmed from the Rinaldo–Palmieri case. Mogavero's sentence, however, was reversed.

4 Charbonneau, *The Canadian Connection*, 156 n. 2.

5 In 1963, Selvaggi would see Simack (perhaps an alias for Szaja Gerecht) with Mexican Ambassador Salvador Pardo Bolland. A few months later he got a description of Simack's plant-man, whom he randomly spotted one night and followed to an apartment in Riverdale. He broke into the apartment and found six empty traps. When he went back in 1964, after Pardo was busted in the Second Ambassador case, the traps were gone.

6   Gosch and Hammer, *The Last Testament of Lucky Luciano*, 442–3.
7   Charbonneau, *Canadian Connection*, 168.

17 AGGRAVATING EDGAR: BOBBY KENNEDY AND THE FBN

1   Anthony Summers, *Official and Confidential: The Secret Life of J. Edgar Hoover* (New York: Pocket Star Books, 1994), 67.
2   Ibid., 155–6.
3   Ibid., 175–6.
4   Ibid., 220.
5   DeMott, "The Great Narcotics Muddle," 48.
6   Summers, *Official and Confidential*, 272–82.
7   Ibid., 267–8.
8   Anslinger, *The Protectors*, 209.
9   Tripodi, *Crusade*, 60.
10 Davis, *Mafia Kingfish*, 139.
11 Moldea, *The Hoffa Wars*, 138.
12 Davis, *Mafia Kingfish*, 99–100.
13 Hersh, *The Dark Side*, 192.
14 Scott, *Deep Politics*, 179.
15 Sandy Smith, William Lambert, and Russell Sackett, "The Congressman and the Hoodlum," *Life Magazine*, 9 August 1968, 20–26.
16 Interview with Tom Tripodi.
17 Mahoney, *Sons and Brothers*, 46–9.
18 1967 IG Report, 57–62.
19 Mark Riebling, *Wedge: The Secret War Between The FBI and CIA* (New York: A. A. Knopf, 1994), 163–4.
20 Moldea, *The Hoffa Wars*, 128–9.
21 1967 IG Report, 63.
22 Mahoney, *Sons and Brothers*, 46.
23 Summers, *Official and Confidential*, 334.
24 Russo, *Live by the Sword*, 66–7.
25 Hersh, *The Dark Side*, 286–7.
26 Mahoney, *Sons & Brothers*, 133, citing DOD Task #69, 3 August 1962.
27 Church Report, 336.
28 Block, *Masters of Paradise*, 161–73.
29 Smith, *The OSS*, 307, n 1.
30 Anslinger, *The Protectors*, 204, 75.
31 Block, *Masters of Paradise*, 34–45.

32   Scott, *War Conspiracy*, 210–12. Lee, *Acid Dreams*, 245–6.

33   Warren Hinkle and William Turner, *The Fish Is Red: The Story Of The Secret War Against Castro* (New York: Harper & Row, 1981), 297.

34   Block, *Masters of Paradise*, 72–3.

35   Ibid., 51.

36   Jim Hougan, *Spooks: The Haunting of America* (New York: Morrow, 1978), 212–14

37   Block, *Masters of Paradise*, 49.

38   Scott, *War Conspiracy*, 208.

39   Scott, *Deep Politics*, 34.

40   JFK planned to replace Air America with Seaboard World Services, whose director, John Davidson, died in a mysterious plane crash in March 1964.

18 THE FRENCH CONNECTION

1   Robin Moore, *The French Connection: The World's Most Crucial Narcotics Investigation* (Boston: Little, Brown and Company, 1969), 9–15.

2   Robin Moore with Barbara Fuca, *Mafia Wife* (New York: Macmillan Publishing Co., Inc., 1977), 121.

3   Gregory Wallance, *Papa's Game* (New York: Rawson, Wade Publishers, Inc., 1981), 20–2, 27.

4   Moore, *French Connection*, 95.

5   Tripodi, *Crusade*, 206.

6   Moore and Fuca, *Mafia Wife*, 134.

7   *New York Times*, 2 May 1962, 17:6.

8   Andrew Tully, *CIA: The Inside Story* (New York: William Morrow, 1962), 45–53.

9   Interview with Paul Sakwa. Also Sakwa's unpublished manuscript, "The Lovestone Connection." Philipsborn replaced Sakwa as Irving Brown's CIA case officer.

10   Memorandum report by Mortimer L. Benjamin, 11 October 1965.

11   Mangold, *Cold Warrior*, 315.

12   Thomas, *The Very Best Men*, 310–11.

13   Sakwa, "The Lovestone Connection."

14   Rivele, in "Death of a Double Man" (44–50), says that Blemant served with French Intelligence in North Africa during the war, was fired from the Sûreté in Marseilles in 1947, formed Les Trois Canards, and then began helping the Guérinis set up nightclubs around the Mediterranean.

By 1954, he was in Tangiers working with Luciano's reputed narcotics connection, Jo Renucci. When Renucci died in 1958, Blemant took over the Tangiers rackets with Marcel Francisci in Lebanon. Blemant's narcotics were distributed in the US by Santo Trafficante.

15   Hersh, *The Old Boys*, 42–3, 266, 226.

16   Ibid., 444–5.

17   Williams, "The Narcotics Situation," 21–6.

18   Tully, *CIA: The Inside Story*, 197.

19   Tripodi, *Crusade*, 187.

20   Charbonneau, in *The Canadian Connection* (161–9), suggests that Mouren was Marius Martin. In *Project Pilot III* (59), Mouren is identified as Jean Mounet, a French diplomat. Michel Mertz and Maurice Castellani are also likely candidates.

21   Tripodi, *Crusade*, 206.

22   Moore, *Mafia Wife*, 187. Tripodi, *Crusade*, 206, 208.

23   Group Three's secret operation was an investigation of the unfolding Air France case, which kicked off with the Christmann bust and moved to Montreal, where Mafiosi were buying heroin from Norman Rothman's associate, Lucien Rivard.

24   According to Mangold in *Cold Warrior* (121), based on information given to him by de Vosjoli, Angleton in October 1962, at a meeting at Le Rive Gauche restaurant in Georgetown, told SDECE chief General Paul Jacquier that SDECE was penetrated by the KGB. The Rive Gauche was owned by Blaise Gherardi, a figure in several FBN narcotic investigations. According to Tripodi (*Crusade*, 187), Gherardi was in communication with Albert Dion, president of a Corsican association in New York, and Vosjoli. The US Secret Service had a garage surrounding the restaurant.

25   Interview with William Harvey, dated 14 September 1975, from Frederick D. Baron to file ZR/RIFLE (12): "Siragusa was used once to go to Rome to spot assets. He was [deleted] at the time, so his participation with the CIA was an extremely sensitive matter." Put in layman's terms, being in Rome to "spot assets" meant that Siragusa was there to recruit an assassin and equip him with the .22 that Vizzini pilfered.

19 VALACHI

1   Church Report, 144

2   Summers, *Official and Confidential*, 345–50.

3   Ibid., 379.
4   Ibid.
5   Davis, *Mafia Kingfish*, 109–12.
6   Moldea, *The Hoffa Wars*, 148.
7   Ibid., 149.
8   Michie Memo.
9   *New York Times*, 27 April 1961, 24:3.
10 Ralph Blumenthal, *Last Days of the Sicilians: At War with the Mafia* (New York: Random House, 1988), 51–5.
11 Arthur K. Lenehan, "Jersey's Heroin Link," *Newark Sunday Star Ledger*, 16 November 1980.
12 Scott, *Deep Politics*, 91.
13 Interview with Gaeton Fonzi, author of *The Last Investigation* (New York: Thunder's Mouth Press, 1993).

20 THE FBN AND THE ASSASSINATION OF JFK

1   Earman Report.
2   Richard Helms, memorandum for Deputy Director of Central Intelligence, 17 December 1963, subject: "Testing of Psychochemicals and Related Materials."
3   Earman Report, 15.
4   Human Drug Testing, 119–20.
5   Mangold, *Cold Warrior*, 51.
6   Stratton, "Altered States of America," 52, 87.
7   Lee, *Acid Dreams*, 39–40.
8   Marks, *Manchurian Candidate*, 62.
9   Lee, *Acid Dreams*, 71.
10 Did someone "turn on" the world's leaders? In *Difficult Questions, Easy Answers* (Garden City: Doubleday & Co., 1973), Robert Graves says the manna the Israelis ate in the Sinai desert, which formed on tamarisk bushes like dew, was laced with ergot, the form LSD takes in nature (34). A golden pot of manna in the Ark of the Covenant was for use by priests alone, and manna, "of which I was once given a taste," said Graves, "by the late president Ben–Swi of Israel, became proverbial as a metaphor of God's enlightening mercy." This revelation has drug law enforcement significance, considering that America's first illicit LSD salesman, Bernard Roseman, purchased his LSD in Israel.

11 Todd Brendan Fahey, "The Original Captain Trips," *High Times*, November 1991, 38–40, 64–5.

12 Lee, *Acid Dreams*, 48–53.

13 Bernard Roseman, *LSD: The Age of Mind* (Hollywood, CA: Wilshire Book Company, 1966), 39.

14 Peter Dale Scott and Jonathan Marshall, *Cocaine Politics: Drugs, Armies, and the CIA in Central America* (Berkeley: University of California Press, 1991), 220 n. 38.

15 Before they were married, Hunt's wife, Dorothy, reportedly worked for the FBN after the Second World War, and served as a consultant with George White on the movie *To the Ends of the Earth*.

16 Scott, *Deep Politics*, 90. Upon arriving in Rome, Harvey befriended Hank Manfredi and, as part of his executive action responsibilities, asked him to approach Joe Adonis in Milan as a potential recruiter of assassins. "Hank knew that Adonis had worked for the military," Colonel Acampora explains, "but Adonis turned them down flat."

17 CIA Memorandum For the Record, Subject: Report on Plots to Assassinate Fidel Castro, 23 May 1967 (hereafter known as 1967 IG Report), 77–88.

18 Human Drug Testing, 118.

19 Ibid., 118

20 Mahoney, *Sons and Brothers*, 269–70.

21 1967 IG Report, 67–70.

22 Norodom Sihanouk with Wilfred Burchett, *My War with the CIA* (New York: Pantheon Books, 1972), 269.

23 1967 IG Report, 91–3.

24 Mahoney, *Sons and Brothers*, 234. Arthur Krock in a prescient article, "The Intra-Administration War in Vietnam," published in the *New York Times* on 3 October 1963 (34), quoted a high government official as saying, "If the United States ever experiences an attempt at a coup to overthrow the government it will come from the CIA and not the Pentagon. The agency represents a tremendous power and total unaccountability to anyone."

25 Mahoney, *Sons and Brothers*, 234.

26 Scott, *Deep Politics*, 151.

27 Lait and Mortimer, *USA Confidential*, 207.

28 Davis, *Mafia Kingfish*, 208.

29 Scott, *Deep Politics*, 131,138.

30 The State case is identified as Houston No. Tex-11965.

31 *Project Pilot, III*, 74.

32 The Supreme Court case is identified as Indiviglio v. US, 357 US 574, No. 753 (1956).

33 Scott, *Deep Politics*, 131.

34 Ibid., 130.

35 Ibid., 5.

36 Ibid., 133.

37 Mahoney, *Sons and Brothers*, 273.

38 Ibid., 276, 259.

39 James R. Duffy, *Conspiracy: Who Killed JFK* (New York: SPI Books, 1992), 201, citing Patricia Orr's report, "Rose Cheramie" in the Report of the Select Committee On Assassinations, US House of Representatives, 95th Congress, 2nd Session, Appendix to Hearings, vol. X (Washington, GPO, 29 March 1979), hereafter known as Orr Report.

40 Orr Report, 203.

41 Ibid., 204.

42 Ibid., 203.

43 James DiEugenio, *Destiny Betrayed: JFK, Cuba, and the Garrison Case* (New York: Sheridan Square Press, 1992), 38–40.

44 Scott, *Deep Politics*, 247.

45 DiEugenio, *Destiny*, 211.

46 Ibid., 213.

47 Dick Russell, *The Man Who Knew Too Much* (New York: Carroll & Graf/R. Gallen, 1992), 563.

48 Bernard Fensterwald, Freedom of Information Act request of the CIA, Civil Action No. 80-1056, 13 July 1982, (hereafter know as Civil Action), Document 632-796.

49 The staff and editors of *Newsday*, *The Heroin Trail* (New York: Holt, Rinehart and Winston, 1973), 112–13.

50 *Project Pilot III*, 74.

51 Mangold, *Cold Warrior*, 134–5.

52 Author Jim Marrs in *Crossfire: The Plot That Killed Kennedy* (New York: Carroll and Graf, 1989), (206–7), says that QJ/WIN obtained the release of mercenary Thomas Eli Davis III from a Moroccan prison shortly after the assassination. Davis was smuggling guns to the OAS and had in his possession a letter that referred to Oswald. Reportedly, Oswald was a member of a secret CIA defector project through Mexico into Cuba in 1963, and QJ/WIN was connected to this project, which is why QJ/WIN arranged for Davis's release.

53 Helms memo, 17 December 1963.

54 MKULTRA Document 75, Memorandum for the Record, Subject: MKULTRA Subprojects 3, 14, 16, 42, 132, 149 and MKSEARCH-4.

21 NO INNOCENTS ABROAD

1 *Project Pilot III*, 44: Arnold Romano, Andrew Alberti, and Joseph and Steve Armone and were the main members of the "Lower East Side mob" drug syndicate; Joseph and William Paradise were involved.
2 McWilliams, *The Protectors*, 164.
3 *Project Pilot III*, 50.
4 *The Heroin Trail*, 84–6.
5 Wilson fought the case for fifteen years and won. Reinstated with full pay, he retired the next day.
6 Scott, *Deep Politics*, 167.
7 *Project Pilot III*, 1, 18, 10–21, 174–5, 178, 213, 237–8. Nathan M. Adams, "The Hunt For André," *Reader's Digest*, March 1973 (reprint).
8 Maduro in March 1963 reported to the Consulate in Monterey. In June 1964, he was transferred to Mexico City and was replaced by Jim Daniels, a former Border Patrol agent in Texas who was "tight with Cusack" and opened an office in Lima, Peru in 1965. Sam Pryor was instrumental in opening the Mexico City office. "Through him," said George Gaffney, "we were able to establish a rapport with scores of representatives from around the world."
9 Tripodi, *Crusade*, 65. Through this case, Tripodi developed relations with the CIA's Security Research Services, and transferred there in September 1962.
10 Charbonneau, *Canadian Connection*, 194–7, 210, 247, 525. Fulgencio Cruz Bonet was known as Poncho, as was CIA officer David Morales, then in the Western Hemisphere Division specializing in Cuban affairs.
11 Ibid., 211.
12 *Project Pilot III*, 21, 67.
13 John Newman, *Oswald and the CIA* (New York: Carroll & Graf, 1995), 381–2.
14 Charbonneau, *Canadian Connection*, 196.
15 Ibid., 194.
16 *Project Pilot III*, 53–63.
17 Ibid., 179–82, 188, 263–4.

18 Jonnes, *Hep Cats*, 187. The station chief was most likely James E. Flannery or Thomas J. Flores.

19 *Project Pilot III*, 62.

20 Ibid., 75.

21 Ibid., 76.

22 Ibid., 189.

23 Ibid., 495.

24 Albert Habib, Memorandum Reports, 3 January 1966 and 16 January 1966.

25 Albert Habib, Memorandum Report, 3 January 1966.

26 According to Al McCoy in *Politics of Heroin* (295–8), Labinski [sic] went to work for Paul Levet's Corsican syndicate in 1954. In 1958, "Rock" Francisci, working with the Guérinis in Marseilles and Ngo Dinh Nhu in Vietnam, set up Air Laos in Vientiane. The competition between Levet and Air Laos was fierce and, in July 1963, Francisci set up Levet with the help of someone named Poncho. As noted in chapter 20, former Saigon policeman Paul Mondoloni was working in Mexico at the same time with a Cuban exile nicknamed Poncho. CIA officer David Morales was also known as Poncho.

27 *New York Times*, 27 November 1964, 45:4. Documents provided to the author in 1966, through the Freedom of Information Act Request, by the DEA, the Office of the Secretary of Defense, and US Army.

22 THE EVE OF DESTRUCTION

1 Bivens v. Six Unknown Agents of the Federal Bureau of Narcotics, 403 US 388, 29 LEd2d 619 91 Supreme Court 1999 (1971).

2 Interview with Adam Clayton Powell III.

3 Carl Rowan, "Pressure Builds for Exposing Viet Nam Graft," syndicated column cited in letter from Senator Stuart Symington to Secretary of the Army Stanley Resor, 21 November 1966.

4 *Project Pilot III*, 113–4.

5 Charbonneau, *Canadian Connection*, 245, n. 14.

6 Ibid., 246, n. 14.

7 *New York Times*, 6 October 1961, 18:4. A staunch Republican, *Journal-American* publisher Guy Richards was close to FBI Agent John Malone. According to one agent, Malone gave Frasca the wiretap equipment to embarrass the FBN. Another agent claims that presidential advisor

Dean Markham was so angry with the FBN over the Pardo Bolland affair that he encouraged the FBI to expose FBN corruption through Frasca and the *Journal-American*.

8 Interview with Thomas Clines, Artime's CIA case officer after E. Howard Hunt. Scott and Marshall, *Cocaine Politics*, 220 n. 38.

9 Tripodi, *Crusade*, 131–4.

10 Ibid., 131.

11 Gay Talese, *Honor Thy Father* (New York: World Publishing, 1971), 386.

12 Ibid., xi–xiii.

13 Ibid., 152–65. Scott, *Deep Politics*, 326 n. 16.

14 Sterling, *Octopus*, 191–2, 347 n. 6.

23 THE NEW FRENCH CONNECTION

1 Mortimer Benjamin, Memorandum Report, "Investigation into the Activities of Maurice Castellani and Joseph Irving Brown," 11 October 1965.

2 Mortimer Benjamin, Memorandum Report, 17 November 1965.

3 Mortimer Benjamin, Memorandum Report, 30 November 1965.

4 Tripodi, *Crusade*, 187.

5 *Project Pilot III*, 406, n. 14.

6 Robert J. DeFauw, "Report on Intergovernmental Committee on Narcotics," 11 December 1969, Section A, 9.

7 *The Heroin Trail*, 119–20.

8 *Project Pilot III*, 482.

9 Ibid., 68.

10 Charbonneau, *Canadian Connection*, 262.

11 Tripodi, *Crusade*, 187.

12 Mangold, *Cold Warrior*, 124.

13 *Project Pilot III*, 78–9.

14 *The Heroin Trail*, 119.

15 Kruger, *Heroin Coup*, 61–5.

16 Ali Bourequat, *In the Moroccan King's Secret Garden* (Nebraska: Morris Publishing, 1998), 60.

17 Project Pilot III, 405–6.

18 Kruger, *Heroin Coup*, 67.

19 Interview with François Le Mouel, former chief of the Paris Brigade of Intelligence and Intervention.

20 *Project Pilot III*, 393–405.

21 *The Heroin Trail*, 112–13.

22 *Project Pilot III*, 190.

23 Kruger, *Heroin Coup*, 76.

24 *Project Pilot III*, 264. CIA officer Paul Van Marx managed the Uruguayan Desk in 1964 and moved to Bogotá in 1965. Von Marx would later become integrally involved in CIA anti-narcotics operations.

25 Kruger, *Heroin Coup*, 55.

26 Ibid., 73.

27 Philip Agee, *Inside the Company: CIA Diary* (New York: Stonehill, 1975), 428–9.

28 Block, *Masters Of Paradise*, 84.

29 *Dope Inc.*, 462–8. Hougan, *Spooks*, 159. Block, *Masters of Paradise*, 82–85.

30 Block, *Masters of Paradise*, 83.

31 *Dope Inc.*, 484–5.

32 Block, *Masters of Paradise*, 161–79.

33 Ibid., 67–70, 82–4, 100.

34 Ibid., 66–70, 82–4.

35 Ibid., 82–4.

36 Ibid., 48–9.

37 Commissaire Guy Denis headed the Sûreté in Marseilles, Hugues was commissaire over narcotics.

24 THE NEW BARBARIANS

1 Anslinger, *The Protectors*, 217–18.

2 Jonnes, *Hep Cats*, 263–4.

3 *New York Times*, 27 November 1964.

4 John Finlator, *The Drugged Nation: "A Narc's" Story* (New York: Simon And Schuster, 1973), 25–7.

5 Ibid., 28–44.

6 Lee, *Acid Dreams*, 150–1.

7 Marks, *Manchurian Candidate*, 62.

8 Lee, *Acid Dreams*, 85–8.

9 Deborah Davis, *Katherine the Great: Katherine Graham and Her* Washington Post *Empire* (New York: Sheridan Square Press, 1979), 213–15.

10 Lee, *Acid Dreams*, 236–48.

11 Ibid., 117.

12   Ibid., 189–90.

13   Marks, *Manchurian Candidate*, 200–1.

14   Gerard Colby with Charlotte Dennet, *Thy Will Be Done: The Conquest of the Amazon: Nelson Rockefeller and Evangelism in the Age of Oil* (New York: HarperCollins, 1995), 497.

15   Marks, *Manchurian Candidate*, 203.

16   Colby and Dennet, *Thy Will Be Done*, 515.

17   Ibid., 521.

18   Ibid., 523.

19   Ibid., 527.

20   Tripodi, *Crusade*, 134.

21   Summers, *Official and Confidential*, 235.

22   Dr. Sidney Gottlieb, Memorandum for the Record, 30 January 1967.

23   FBI Teletype from New Orleans Agent John W. Miller to Director (62-109060) and Dallas (89–43), "Interview with Captain Roy Allemond of the New Orleans Harbor Police," 20 July 1967.

24   William Torbitt (Copeland's pen name), *Nomenclature of an Assassination Cabal* (self-published manuscript), 5.

25   Scott, *Deep Politics*, 116.

26   DiEugenio, *Destiny Betrayed*, 175.

27   Scott, *Deep Politics*, 116. 1967 IG Report, 126.

28   Charles Higham, *Howard Hughes: The Secret Life* (New York: Putnam, 1993), 207, 217–18, 221.

29   Sam Giancana and Chuck Giancana, *Double Cross: The Explosive, Inside Story of the Mobster Who Controlled America* (New York: Warner Books, 1992), 328.

30   Moldea, *Hoffa Wars*, 175.

25 THE LAW OF THE JUNGLE

1   The CIA station chief in Rome, Bill Harvey, had aligned with ultra General De Lorenzo, and the situation exploded in 1965, when two senior Carabinieri officers were exposed as having set up hit teams to murder Italian leftists. Angleton's staff blamed Harvey for the flap, and replaced the burned-out assassination expert with Seymour Russell, an old foe of Hank Manfredi's from post-war Italy days. After a confrontation with Russell in the Embassy cafeteria, Manfredi had a heart attack. Seeking refuge from Russell, he asked Tartaglino to bring him back into the FBN in the US.

2   Lee, *Acid Dreams*, 244.

3   Block, *Masters of Paradise*, 81–107.

4   Emrich died in Mexico under mysterious circumstances on 19 September 1969.

5   Richard E. Salmi, Report of Investigation, 30 November 1971.

6   Richard E. Salmi, "Operation Bruit," undated report.

7   Richard E. Salmi, Report of Investigation, 2 February 1970.

8   Charbonneau in *The Canadian Connection* (108) says Khoury and Alaouie were assassinated in 1965.

9   Hougan, *Spooks,* 213.

10 Ibid., 213–25. Jim Marrs, author of *Crossfire*, said that Robin Moore, author of *The French Connection*, confirmed that Weiller was the Air France connection.

11 "Yitzak" may have been Yitzak Shamir or Yitzak Rabin.

12 Brian Burroughs, *Vendetta: American Express and the Smearing of Edmond Safra* (New York: HarperCollins Publishers, 1992), 32–6, 158.

13 Charbonneau, *Canadian Connection*, 247.

14 *The Heroin Trail*, 173.

15 *Project Pilot III*, 87.

16 Ibid., 96.

17 Lee in *Acid Dreams* (12), says "that ex-Nazi pilots under CIA contract smuggled [heroin] out of the Golden Triangle ... during the late 1940s and early 1950s."

18 Talese, *Honor Thy Father*, 156, 240.

19 Ibid., 266–8, 275, 493.

20 Sterling, *Octopus*, 105–10.

21 Blumenthal, *Last Days*, 83–5.

26 GOLDEN TRIANGLE ENTERPRISES

1   Jaubert, *Dossier D*, 160.

2   Kruger, *Heroin Coup*, 225, citing B. Rostin, "A Chapter From 'The Godfather'?" *Village Voice*, 21 January 1980. As Kruger notes, Sindona was exonerated and in 1972 would offer $1 million to Nixon fund-raiser Maurice Stans.

3   Interviews with Edward Coyne and James Ludlum.

4   Messick, *Lansky* (New York: Putnam, 1971), 241.

5   McCoy, *Politics of Heroin*, 251–3.

6   Smith, "Brazen Empire," 102–4.

7   McCoy, *Politics of Heroin*, 203–4.

8   Ibid., 298.

9   Ibid., 249.

10 Ibid., 250.

11 Lucien Conein, letter to Harper Row, 10 October 1972.

12 McCoy, *Politics of Heroin*, 250.

13 *Pilot Project III*, 134, 495.

14 McCoy, *Politics of Heroin*, 352.

15 Ibid., 227.

16 Albert Habib, Memorandum Reports, 16 January 1966; 20 July 1966; 28 July 1966; 5 August 1966; 2 September 1966; and 16 September 1966.

17 Albert Habib, Memorandum Report, 2 September 1966.

18 McCoy, *Politics of Heroin*, 211.

19 Ibid., 228.

20 Ibid., 227–8.

21 Secord told the author, "We were never dealing opium in Laos. And if we were, it was policy."

22 Robin Moore, *The Country Team*, (New York: Crown, 1967), 114.

23 Ibid., 188–9.

24 Georgie-Anne Geyer, "The CIA's Hired Killers," *True Magazine*, February 1970.

25 Moore, *Country Team*, 266.

26 Michael C. Piper in *Final Judgment* (Washington, DC: The Wolfe Press, 1995) says, on page 275, that Moore "had solid links to the CIA."

27 McCoy, *Politics of Heroin*, 213.

28 Ibid., 253.

29 Noam Chomsky, Introduction to Cathy Perkus, ed., *COINTELPRO: The FBI's Secret War on Political Freedom* (New York: Monad Press, 1975), 14.

30 Tripodi, *Crusade*, 148.

27 MY ONLY FRIEND

1   Charbonneau in *The Canadian Connection* explains that Guido "the Bull" Penosi was a member of the Gambino family, which in 1965 was setting up the Pizza Connection with Tomasso Buscetta. By 1968 the Cotronis in Montreal were delivering French connection heroin to Penosi's receivers. Penosi would traffic in narcotics without getting

caught for several more years, a fact that supports the theory that he was one of the new breed of million-dollar men working for the FBI and CIA.

2 In 1968, Burmudez gave Lawrence to SIU Detective Bob Leuci, the infamous "Prince of the City," and the subject of a book by that title. Around that time, Lawrence went to work for Andy Tartaglino as a special employee making cases on corrupt BNDD agents.

3 In June 1967, Henry Giordano, Hank Manfredi, and George Belk received medals in the Rinaldo case. Giordano vetoed Selvaggi's award. In September 1967, Hank Manfredi received the Italian Gold Cross and a letter of recommendation in the Nebbia case. Selvaggi and Waters got no recognition at all.

4 In February 1966, Krieger got Vincent Pacelli off the Air France case with a reduced sentence. Krieger also defended Paul Helliwell's law partner, Larry Freeman, on a drug charge, as well as Joe Bonanno and John Gotti.

28 ANDY'S GANG

1 The allegations included the sale, transfer, and use of drugs by agents, sale of drugs by informants at the direction of an agent, transfer of drugs to informants by agents, planting evidence, sale of counterfeit money, leaks of information, improper handling of evidence, irregularities in informant payments, accepting gratuities, retaining confiscated guns for personal use or sale, absconding with official funds, failing to enforce the laws, and grand larceny. Over two dozen informant murders, and the deaths of several agents, were investigated as well.

2 Mortimer L. Benjamin, Memorandum Report, "Allegations made by Vivienne NAGELBERG to Agent Mortimer Benjamin at Montreal on 28 & 29 May, 1967," 30 January 1968. Vivienne and Gerson Nagelberg were arrested in April 1968, and convicted on 18 June 1970. A young Assistant US Attorney (later a Congressman), Charles Rangel, prosecuted their case. Rangel was quoted in the 15 August 1968 *New York Times* (43) as saying, "the narcotic racket could not exist in Harlem without the aid and consent of some members of the NYPD."

3 After leaving the FBN, Selvaggi opened a delicatessen. Schrier settled

with the IRS and purchased an International House of Pancakes franchise. Waters became a bartender, then a psychologist.

4 Bluth headed the NYPD's Narcotic Bureau from 2 May 1966 till February 1968. Intreri was suspected of passing the missing 1962 French Connection dope to Papa. Intreri hated Selvaggi and Waters, whom he felt had "sold out" John Dolce in the 1965 Frank Tuminaro case. Secret Service Agent Carmine Motto hired Pat Ward's son. Motto later became John Dolce's deputy in White Plains. Sal Vizzini's son Sam also went to work for the Secret Service.

EPILOGUE

1 Reorganization Plan No. 1, Prepared by the President and transmitted to the Senate and the House of Representatives in Congress assembled, 7 February 1968, pursuant to the provisions of chapter 9 of title 5 of the United States Code, "Message of the President to Congress."

2 Patrick P. O'Carroll, "Reorganization Plan No. 1: Narcotics and Drug Abuse", University of Oklahoma, undated graduate thesis, courtesy of DEA library.

3 Ibid.

4 Interview with John Warner, Ingersoll's colleague from California, and later his assistant at the BNDD.

5 Tripodi, *Crusade*, 158.

6 Jack D. Compton Statement (provided by former US Attorney Jamie Boyd), 54–6. Boyd sent Compton's statement, along with other information, to Deputy Attorney General Benjamin Civiletti on 31 May 1981. The author attempted to retrieve Boyd's letter and Compton's statement through a Freedom of Information Act request filed on 23 November 1993, but was told by the deputy director of the Department of Justice's Office of Information and Privacy that the records were not located.

7 In an interview with the author, Compton said the source's name began with the letter Z. One candidate is Gennardo Zanfardino, cited in *Project Pilot III* (78) as buying narcotics, along with the Malizia brothers, from Arman Casoria in New York, who until December 1965 copped from Frank Dioguardia.

8 Recounting what he was told by an informer, David Wiser says that Bob Williams was at La Guardia to cover Frankie Waters, which is why they met in the men's room. According to Wiser's source, after

the men's room meeting, Waters met with the Malizia brothers on a boat on Long Island Sound to discuss whether they should kill McDonnell. Waters defended McDonnell, thus saving his life. Waters denies the allegations, and denies ever having met the Malizia brothers.

INDEX